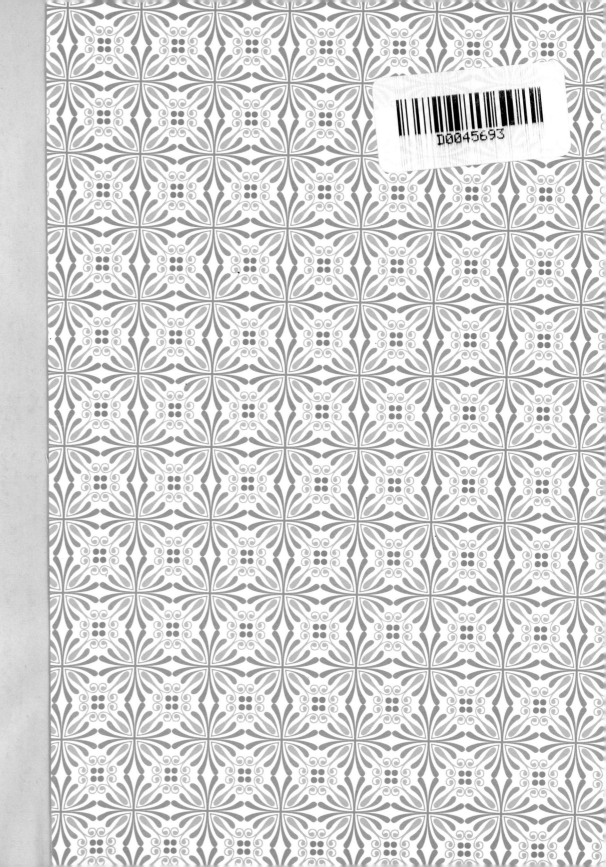

Cover Illustration: Shutterstock.com

Interior Illustrations: Hye Lim An, Art Explosion, Linda Howard Bittner, Erin Burke, Daisy De Puthod, Dan Grant, iStockphoto, Jupiterimages, Nicole H. Lee, Robert Schoolcraft, Shutterstock.com, Shavan R. Spears, Elizabeth Traynor, John Zielinski

Louis Weber, CEO
Publications International, Ltd.
8140 Lehigh Avenue
Morton Grove, IL 60053

Permission is never granted for commercial purposes.

ISBN: 978-1-4508-5395-8

Manufactured in U.S.A.

8 7 6 5 4 3 2 1

Library of Congress Control Number: 2012938148

The Book of

Extraordinary Facts

Publications International, Ltd.

Contents

✳ ✳ ✳ ✳

Expanding Your Mind
One Fact at a Time

Our modern culture is obsessed with facts. Unfortunately, some people aren't interested in anything but "just the facts," dismissing anything that smacks of wonder or curiosity. But not all truths fit into logical and sensible boxes—sometimes the facts are truly extraordinary and beyond belief.

The Book of Extraordinary Facts is chock-full of entertaining information about history, nature, celebrities, crooks, places, sports, religion, technology, and the just plain ol' weird. Inside this book, you'll also find scads of noteworthy gems, including:

* A blue whale's tongue outweighs the average adult elephant. That's a two-ton tongue!

* Competitive-eating champion Sonya Thomas set a record in 2005 when she ate 44 Maine lobsters in only 12 minutes. (Let's hope she wore comfy pants!)

* Not "digging" the traditional pine box coffin? Try a customized carrier in the shape of an egg, a shoe, a car, or—yes, really—a uterus.

* Ballet is a riot—literally! At least, it was in 1913 when three Russian artists defied all convention and premiered Igor Stravinsky's shocking ballet, *The Rite of Spring.*

* And much, much more!

Esteemed writer Mark Twain once remarked that "Truth is stranger than fiction, but it is because Fiction is obliged to stick to possibilities; Truth isn't." Dig into *The Book of Extraordinary Facts* and read about the wonderful and wacky goings-on in the world—you'll soon see that Twain was absolutely right.

Chapter One

Hooray for Hollywood

Former Jobs of 11 Celebrities

Most of us aren't born with a silver spoon in our mouths—even celebrities. Just like us, they've had to work their way up the job ladder.

✳   ✳   ✳   ✳

1. **Mick Jagger:** Before he began strutting his stuff onstage, Sir Michael Phillip "Mick" Jagger, lead singer of The Rolling Stones, worked as a porter at the Bexley Mental Hospital while he was a student at the London School of Economics. He earned a whopping 4 pounds, 10 shillings per week (about $7.80 US).

2. **Jason Lee:** Actor Jason Lee once worked at Taco Bell. Then, in the late 1980s and early 1990s, Lee became a competitive skateboarder, performing flips and other daring maneuvers. After appearing in a promotional skateboarding video shot by Spike Jonze, Lee began getting movie offers and left his skateboarding career in the dust.

3. **Paula Abdul:** During her freshman year at Cal State University, Paula Abdul tried out for the Los Angeles Lakers cheerleading squad and was selected from more than 700 applicants. Her high-energy, street-funk-inspired dance

routines were an instant hit, and it took her all of three weeks to become head choreographer. In 1984, when Abdul's routines got the attention of the Jackson family, they immediately signed her to choreograph their "Torture" video and her career went into overdrive.

4. **David Letterman:** After graduating from Indiana's Ball State University in 1969, future late-night talk-show host David Letterman landed a job at Indianapolis television station WLWI (now called WTHR) as a local anchor and weatherman. Letterman was eventually let go for his unpredictable on-air behavior, which included erasing state borders from the weather map and predicting hail stones "the size of canned hams." Those canned hams eventually became popular door prizes on *The Late Show with David Letterman*.

5. **Dennis Farina:** Italian-American actor Dennis Farina often portrays cops, detectives, or mobsters and is best known for his roles in *Law & Order, Crime Story*, and *Get Shorty*. It's no wonder that Farina is so comfortable in his roles— from 1967 to 1985, he actually was a police officer with the Chicago Police Department. Farina caught the acting bug after working with director Michael Mann as a police consultant.

6. **Clint Eastwood:** Clint Eastwood is a Hollywood icon, having gone from Westerns in the 1960s to playing a no-nonsense, rebel cop in *Dirty Harry*, to finally settling into directing in the 1980s. But before that, Eastwood earned his daily bread digging swimming pools in Beverly Hills, while at night he'd audition for bit parts. Prior to that, he put in hard time working as a lumberjack, steel mill worker, aircraft factory worker, and gas station attendant.

7. **Whoopi Goldberg:** With a long career as a stand-up comedian, actor, and TV talk-show host, Academy Award–winner Whoopi Goldberg has firmly established herself as a star. But Goldberg wasn't always living in the lap of luxury.

Growing up in the tough Chelsea projects in New York City, her first job was as a bricklayer. When that position fizzled out, she took on roles as a garbage collector and a funeral makeup artist—whatever jobs she could get to make ends meet.

8. **Ozzy Osbourne:** Growing up in England, singer Ozzy Osbourne, born John Michael Osbourne, was once a laborer in a slaughterhouse. This may have influenced some of his famous stunts, like biting off the head of a dove during a meeting with his newly signed record company and biting the head off a bat thrown onstage during a concert.

9. **Sean Connery:** Sean Connery is probably best known for portraying James Bond seven times, setting the bar very high for those who would follow. But Connery's first job was as a milkman in his native Scotland. After a stint in the Royal Navy, he took on numerous jobs, including lifeguard, ditch-digger, and artist's model. In 1953, he even competed in the Mr. Universe contest, placing third in the tall man's division.

10. **Marlon Brando:** Nearly a decade before he starred as Stanley Kowalski in *A Streetcar Named Desire*, Marlon Brando worked as a ditchdigger after he was expelled from military school for being "incorrigible." When he grew tired of manual labor, Brando became an elevator operator in New York City. His last non-acting job before his break into film was as a night watchman.

11. **Madonna:** Madonna Louise Veronica Ciccone splashed onto the music scene in the early 1980s. But the early years in New York City were tough for Madonna, and she found herself working at a number of low-paying jobs, including a stint at a Dunkin' Donuts in Times Square. But, in true Madonna fashion, she was fired for squirting jelly filling all over customers.

Behind the Films of Our Times

Apollo 13

Director Ron Howard's 1995 film told the amazing story of the unlucky and unsuccessful 1970 title spaceflight to the moon. Actors Tom Hanks, Bill Paxton, and Kevin Bacon spent weeks crammed into the 48-square-foot mock-up of the Apollo spacecraft—an area smaller than the average bathroom. Just as it had in real life, the harrowing on-screen trip came to a happy ending as the haggard astronauts exited a rescue helicopter onto the recovery ship. Hanks, playing Flight Commander James Lovell, was greeted with a handshake by the ship's captain—portrayed by the real Lovell.

Casablanca

The Oscar-winning screenplay for this Humphrey Bogart–Ingrid Bergman wartime tearjerker wasn't finished when the film started shooting. One point of contention was the ending. Bogart thought it important for his character, Rick Blaine, to get the girl, Bergman's Ilsa Lund, in the end. The producers apparently decided his concerns didn't amount to a hill of beans, and Ilsa left with her freedom-fighter husband, Victor Laszlo, played by Paul Henreid.

Annie Hall

Woody Allen's hilarious 1977 film about dating and love in New York City drew heavily from his own broken relationship with costar Diane Keaton, with whom he'd split up before filming started. When Allen was awarded the Best Director Oscar for *Annie Hall*, he was thousands of miles from the hoopla in Hollywood; the elusive winner was doing what he always did on Monday nights—playing clarinet with his New Orleans Jazz Band at Michael's Pub in New York City.

Great Movie Gimmicks

In an attempt to fill seats and boost profits, producers have introduced some mighty strange lures through the years. From mild to wild, each "grabber" was designed to enhance the movie-viewing experience as it boosted the bottom line. Sometimes, the gimmicks even worked.

✳ ✳ ✳ ✳

3-D Movies

ALTHOUGH 3-D MOVIES were being experimented with as far back as the 1890s and technical breakthroughs continue to this day, the most extensive fad in 3-D, or stereoscopic filmmaking, occurred in the 1950s. The technology's high-water mark arrived with *House of Wax* (1953), starring Vincent Price. The movie featured what has become the holy grail of 3-D scenes: a wisecracking carnival barker hitting paddleballs directly into the faces of a stunned audience. The 3-D effect was so pronounced during this memorable scene that people flinched and recoiled, doing their best to avoid being "hit" by the optical illusion. Although 3-D movies can be genuinely fun to watch, some viewers experience queasiness while wearing the goofy glasses. Today's digital technology has allowed some 3-D movies to work without the flimsy glasses, and 3-D films have staged a comeback.

Smell-O-Vision

Smell-O-Vision was the brainchild of Mike Todd Jr., son of the famed Hollywood producer best known for the epic *Around the World in Eighty Days* (1956) and for his brief marriage to Elizabeth Taylor. The idea for Smell-O-Vision was simple: After setting up a network of scent-carrying tubes beneath theater seats, a worker would manually release scent vials at crucial moments during a film. For instance, when the crack of a gun was heard, a gunpowder scent might be released. When a couple came together in a romantic embrace, the scent of flowers would waft through the air.

A small army of scents stood at the ready to mimic life and improve a film's realism, but therein lay an inherent flaw. It was soon discovered that a smorgasbord of dissimilar odors was not necessarily a pleasant thing, particularly when they intermingled in the still air of a confined movie theater. Only one film, the aptly titled *Scent of Mystery* (1960), was made using the system. Todd reportedly ended up losing his entire investment and eventually left the film business. A similar idea, Odorama, arrived with the 1981 film *Polyester*. In this incarnation, scratch-and-sniff cards were used to augment key scenes in the movie. But like Smell-O-Vision before it, the idea proved to be a genuine stinker.

Free Vomit Bags

To the uninitiated, this might sound like a genuinely bad idea, but in fact, it was pure movie genius. The bags were distributed for *Mark of the Devil* (1970), a film whose original German title translates to *Witches Tortured Till They Bleed*. The pitch, of course, was that the flick was so very shocking that it could easily produce retching. "This vomit bag and the price of one admission will enable you to see . . . the first film rated V for violence . . ." teased the blood-red writing on the side of each bag. Far from being dissuaded by such a distasteful thought, gore fans and horror aficionados rushed to buy tickets. By the standard of today's shock films, the movie might seem rather tame, but a much-hyped scene depicting a woman's tongue being severed is said to have put many a vomit bag to the test.

Sensurround

Those attending a showing of *Earthquake* (1974) got more than they bargained for, particularly if they neglected to read signs hawking "Sensurround." This special effects system developed by Universal promised to bring the sound and feel of an earthquake to viewers. To say that it succeeded would be an understatement. During the film, a low-frequency rumble was produced by a bank of strategically placed loudspeakers. This created a booming sensation that was felt as much as heard during critical portions of the movie.

For some patrons, the sensation was a genuine kick. For others, it was downright troubling, both physically and mentally. The system was used to enhance three other movies (*Midway*, 1976; *Rollercoaster*, 1977; and the theatrical print of the made-for-TV film *Battlestar Galactica*, 1978) before being retired in 1978. It was just as well. In multiplex cinemas where Sensurround had been featured, patrons attending movies in adjacent theaters often complained about carryover noise.

But that was nothing compared to what occurred at Grauman's Chinese Theatre in Hollywood. During their showing of *Earthquake*, errant pieces of plaster allegedly dropped from the ceiling, putting the safety of movie patrons in jeopardy. In a case of technology run amok, Sensurround made the movie-going experience just a bit too realistic.

Look Closer

Blow-up dolls provided much of the background crowds in *Seabiscuit*. Original plans called for 7,000 extras, which would have been too expensive for its budget—so a production assistant came up with the idea of having inflatable people fill the void. Computer effects helped them look a little livelier.

Hollywood Versus History

You may not be surprised to learn that Hollywood doesn't always get history right.

✳ ✳ ✳ ✳

Sacré bleu!
Moulin Rouge! (2001)—The Sacré-Coeur Catholic basilica seen in the Paris background wasn't completed until 1914, more than a dozen years after the time period of this story.

Does this mean their career is already over?
The Mambo Kings (1992)—When the musical group watches their appearance on *I Love Lucy*, the show opens with the later syndicated-run title sequence, not the first-run original.

And it still sounded just as awful
Air America (1990)—Although the movie is set in the late 1960s, singers in a restaurant scene perform "A Horse with No Name," which wasn't written until 1974.

You'll love his duets with his imaginary friend
The Adventures of Robin Hood (1938)—While Robin and Little John battle on the footbridge, Will Scarlett begins to strum a stringless lute.

We loved the peanut sauce
Good Morning, Vietnam (1987)—Although set in Vietnam, the film opens with a shot of the Thai Parliament Building.

We just dig cars, OK?
Quadrophenia (1979)—Rockers in this film set in 1965 wear Motorhead T-shirts a decade before that band emerged.

But he could have been in a drunk tank somewhere
The Doors (1991)—A background tableau shows a billboard advertising a film starring Nick Nolte, who was not yet in movies in 1971, when the film takes place.

Clarifications on Kong

As the most famous inhabitant of Skull Island, King Kong has long elicited both screams and sympathy from moviegoers the world over. But contrary to a popular rumor, Kong was never portrayed by a man in an ape suit.

✳   ✳   ✳   ✳

W E'VE ALL HEARD the idiom "800-pound gorilla" in reference to something considered big and bad, and in Hollywood, they don't get any bigger or badder than King Kong. Standing a whopping 50 feet tall and weighing in excess of 800 pounds, Kong has captured the imaginations of millions since his premiere in 1933.

Much has been written and said about how Kong was brought to life, and for decades many believed that in some of his scenes, Kong was simply a man in a monkey suit. But such claims are patently false. With the exception of a few scenes that featured a life-size bust or a giant mechanical hand, Kong was made real through a meticulous and time-consuming process known as stop-motion animation. Despite his towering onscreen presence, the mighty Kong was nothing more than an 18-inch articulated metal skeleton (referred to as an armature) covered with rubber and rabbit fur.

Birth of a King

When *King Kong* first hit theaters, moviegoers were awestruck. They watched in amazement as vicious dinosaurs came to life and a huge gorilla ravaged the streets of New York City until biplanes blasted him off the top of the Empire

State Building. It was unlike anything they had seen before, and the movie raked in several times the $650,000 it cost to produce.

The myth that King Kong was a man in an ape suit was started by an inaccurate article in an issue of *Modern Mechanix and Inventions*, which featured illustrations showing how a stuntman was used for the scenes in which Kong scaled the Empire State Building.

The Mighty Myth Grows

Thirty years later, a poorly researched Associated Press wire story added to the myth by reporting that King Kong had been portrayed by a Hollywood stuntman named Carmen Nigro. In the article, Nigro made a number of outrageous claims, including the "fact" that Fay Wray was an animated doll and that Nigro had worn "fur-covered ballet slippers with suction pads" to help him stay atop the skyscraper. Nigro also falsely claimed to have starred in *Mighty Joe Young* (1949) as another supersize cinematic simian created through the artistry of stop-motion animation. (Both apes were animated by the gifted Willis O'Brien, who won an Academy Award for his special-effects work on *Mighty Joe Young*.)

Although the original King Kong was only a model, he has been portrayed by a man in a suit in many other movies over the years. The Japanese monster smash *King Kong vs. Godzilla* (1962), for example, featured an embarrassingly bad gorilla suit and a storyline that had the famous ape duking it out with Japan's favorite superlizard. The movie is notable for having two endings: In the version shown in Japan, Godzilla wins. In the version seen by people in the United States, Kong is the victor.

When Stunts Become Deadly

When it comes to on-camera stunts, A-list actors depend on specially trained doubles to do the dangerous work. Sometimes, though, things go very wrong, and even the most experienced stunt professionals have no way of recovering. Here are a few examples.

✳   ✳   ✳   ✳

The Crow (1993)

IT WASN'T A stuntman who died during the making of *The Crow* but the lead actor himself. The title character, played by Brandon Lee, son of the late kung-fu star Bruce Lee, gets shot by a drug dealer lurking in his apartment. Tragically, the handgun used in the scene had a real bullet lodged in its barrel, which was propelled out by the force of the blank. Lee was hit in the abdomen and died later that day—just a few days before the movie wrapped. The filmmakers ended up finishing the movie with a combination of doubles and computer enhancement.

The Dark Knight (2008)

Heath Ledger wasn't the only person from *The Dark Knight* who died tragically. Special effects technician Conway Wickliffe died while filming a test run for a stunt. Wickliffe was on a camera truck traveling parallel to the Batmobile when the driver of the vehicle missed a turn and clipped a tree with the side of the truck that the camera and Wickliffe were on. Wickliffe was fatally injured by the impact.

Million Dollar Mystery (1987)

A stunt veteran known for flawless performances lost his life while filming this movie. Dar Robinson—who, legend has it, had never broken a single bone in nearly 20 years of stunt work—was performing a motorcycle stunt when he lost control of the bike and drove over a cliff.

Steel (1979)

A fall designed to kill a character in *Steel* ended up killing the stuntman performing it. In the scene, stuntman A. J. Bakunas falls from a construction site. In the original take, Bakunas jumped from the ninth floor and landed without trouble. But because he wanted to reclaim the record for the world's highest stunt fall, he asked to reshoot the fall, jumping from the 22nd floor. During the second attempt, the airbag Bakunas landed on broke upon impact, and he died from his injuries the next day.

Top Gun (1986)

If you think the high-flying maneuvers in *Top Gun* looked dangerous, that's because they were. In fact, stunt pilot Art Scholl died while flying one of the movie's jets over the Pacific Ocean. Scholl was engaging in a spin maneuver when he lost control of the aircraft and crashed into the water.

Twilight Zone: The Movie (1983)

Three actors died during a stunt for *Twilight Zone: The Movie*. Veteran actor Vic Morrow and child actors My-Ca Dinh Le and Renee Shin-Yi Chen were running from a helicopter during a Vietnamese battle scene. When a pyrotechnic explosion damaged the chopper's tail, it spun out of control, crashed sideways, and decapitated Morrow and My-Ca Dinh Le, then landed on top of Renee Shin-Yi Chen. Several crew members, including director John Landis and a stunt organizer, were indicted on various counts of involuntary manslaughter, but they were acquitted.

XXX (2002)

This Vin Diesel blockbuster was jam-packed with stunts, but one in particular stands out for catastrophic reasons. Stuntman Harry O'Connor was parasailing over a bridge in Prague when he hit a pillar and died. O'Connor had already completed the stunt once without incident and was doing a second take when the accident occurred.

Guess Who's Coming to Dinner

Though quaint by today's standards, Guess Who's Coming to Dinner *was a controversial shocker upon its release in 1967. Never before had the big Hollywood studios addressed the then-sensitive issue of interracial marriage in a major commercial film.*

✳ ✳ ✳ ✳

ACCORDING TO PRODUCER/DIRECTOR Stanley Kramer, the idea for the film arose from a talk between himself and screenwriter William Rose as they strolled through Beverly Hills one evening. Rose pitched the idea of a liberal, white South African man whose daughter falls in love with a black man. Kramer liked the idea of a liberal suddenly forced by circumstance to face his deepest principles and suggested setting the story in the United States, which at the time was in the midst of a fierce battle between liberal and conservative ideologies.

Perfect Casting

Kramer, whose credits included *The Defiant Ones* (1958), *Inherit the Wind* (1960), and *Judgment at Nuremburg* (1961), immediately thought of Spencer Tracy and Katharine Hepburn to play the film's liberal parents. He then contacted Sidney Poitier, who was willing to play the black man to whom their daughter becomes engaged, though the actor expressed skepticism that a major studio would touch such a sensitive topic. Poitier needn't have worried: With such a notable triumvirate of actors on board, in addition to a script by the talented William Rose, Columbia Pictures green-lighted the movie with little hesitation.

The production went off without a hitch, though concessions had to be made for Tracy, who was in ill health at the time. Kramer did his best to make things as easy as possible for his old friend, including filming only in the morning, when Tracy was at his strongest.

Hepburn jumped into the production with her usual vigor, but Poitier, though himself a seasoned professional, was nervous about working with such star performers. "I wasn't able to get it out of my head: I am here playing a scene with Tracy and Hepburn!" he wrote in his first autobiography, *This Life*. "It was all so overwhelming I couldn't remember my lines."

Critics Have Their Say

Guess Who's Coming to Dinner generated quite a bit of discussion and criticism. Poitier, in particular, came under attack by some civil rights leaders for being almost too perfect as Dr. John Prentice—nonthreatening, charismatic, and thus acceptable to white Americans. The movie's central love story was also derided for skirting the intimacy one would expect from a young couple in love. Indeed, there is very little physical contact between Prentice and his fiancée, Joey Drayton, played by Katharine Houghton, Hepburn's real-life niece. To Kramer's credit, several scenes were filmed of Poitier and Houghton kissing but were later dropped from the final version of the movie.

Despite these and other criticisms, *Guess Who's Coming to Dinner* was a huge success, grossing nearly $25 million in its initial box-office run. In addition, the film was nominated for almost every major Academy Award, including Best Picture, Best Director, and Best Actor in a Leading Role (Tracy), and received Oscars for Best Actress (Hepburn) and Best Writing (Story and Screenplay) (William Rose). And though Poitier wasn't nominated for an Academy Award, *Guess Who's Coming to Dinner* helped cement his reputation as one of the most popular (and bankable) black actors in Hollywood history, making him a bona fide movie star.

Unfortunately, there's a sad footnote to *Guess Who's Coming to Dinner*: Spencer Tracy passed away just ten days after filming wrapped and never got to see his final film on the big screen.

Behind the TV Shows of Our Times

The Twilight Zone

"You unlock this door with the key of imagination." With those opening words, TV viewers knew they had "just crossed over into The Twilight Zone." This anthology series ran for five seasons in the early 1960s, hosted—and often written—by Rod Serling. The show was a mixture of science fiction, fantasy, and drama. In all, 134 half-hour and 17 full-hour episodes were produced, featuring some of Hollywood's biggest stars. The wily Burgess Meredith appeared as four different characters in four different episodes, including the beleaguered bookworm Henry Bemis, who finds himself the last man on Earth—left alone to read all the books he wants, until the far-sighted fellow breaks his only pair of reading glasses.

Who Wants to Be a Millionaire?

At its height, this quiz show was watched across America by millions of viewers as many as three times a week. Hosted by the friendly Regis Philbin, *Who Wants to Be a Millionaire?* became an enormous hit for ABC in 1999. The game had been hugely popular in the UK, but it had been several years since a game show had been broadcast in prime time in the United States, and the show's immense success took virtually everyone—even its producers—by surprise. The first million-dollar winner was John Carpenter, an IRS agent, who made it all the way to the top with no need to use his lifelines. When the final question came up—asking which U.S. president appeared on TV's *Laugh-In*—Carpenter finally broke down and used his Phone-a-Friend lifeline. Calling his father, he calmly stated he was only phoning to tell Pop he was about to win it all, revealing the million-dollar answer was "Richard Nixon."

Double Vision

Hollywood stars often seem to have perfectly sculpted bodies, but many times those physiques are the result of a little H-town magic.

❋   ❋   ❋   ❋

IN THE 1983 HIT *Flashdance*, actress Jennifer Beals plays a welder by day and an exotic dancer by night. What most people didn't know was that much of Beals's dancing was performed by several body doubles, including French actress Marine Jahan, male dancer Richard Colón, and gymnast Sharon Shapiro, who did the famous midair dive at the end of the film.

In 1980's *Dressed to Kill*, 49-year-old actress Angie Dickinson had a 23-year-old body double stand in for her during a steamy shower scene. There is one brief wide shot of Angie, but the close-ups were the body of 1978 *Penthouse* Pet of the Year Victoria Lynn Johnson. The shots were so explicit that the film had to be edited to avoid an X rating.

Perhaps the best-known body double in Hollywood is Shelley Michelle. She has a long list of credits, but is most famous for being Barbra Streisand's legs in *Prince of Tides* and doubling for Julia Roberts in the ho-with-a-heart-of-gold flick, *Pretty Woman*.

It doesn't hurt to be related to a star to get work as a body double. Case in point: Linda Hamilton's identical twin sister, Leslie Hamilton Gearren, was her double in *Terminator 2: Judgment Day*. Linda was ripped with muscles for the movie, and so Leslie had to get in the same great shape. When she's not doubling for her sis, Leslie works as a nurse.

If you enjoy Halle Berry films, you'll enjoy her body double, Barbara Alexandre. She doubled for the Oscar-winning actress in *X-Men: The Last Stand* and *Catwoman*. Catherine Bell, however, leaped from performing as Isabella Rossellini's nude-scene body double in the 1992 film *Death Becomes Her*, to a starring role on the TV show *JAG*.

I'm Big in Japan

Hollywood celebrities have been crossing the Pacific to make commercials in Japan for decades. Check out these stars' ads!

✳ ✳ ✳ ✳

1. **Arnold Schwarzenegger**: If Ahnald is to be believed, inhaling a cup of Nissin instant noodles will provide you with enough strength to swing really heavy-looking bronze pots back and forth with ease. The bodybuilder/actor/former governor of California endorsed this and other Japanese products in commercial spots from the 1990s.

2. **Nicolas Cage**: At some point, Cage was bit by the gambling bug, so much so that he felt the need to shill for Sankyo, the manufacturer of pachinko machines. Similar to slot machines, the devices can be found in casinos across Japan. Ads from the late 1990s feature a wild-eyed Cage so obsessed by his pachinko fever that he's having trouble functioning day to day.

3. **Cameron Diaz**: There's something about Aeon English Schools that made Diaz want to sing their praises. Aeon, a private institute with more than 300 schools in Japan, has also received a boost from Celine Dion, Ewan McGregor, and Mariah Carey.

4. **Harrison Ford**: What do hiking near a volcano, dining at a sushi restaurant, sitting in a steam room, and jetting around on an airliner have in common? They all go great with Kirin beer, according to Harrison Ford, who promoted the lager in at least five different TV commercials, plus a print ad, during the mid-1990s.

5. **Anne Hathaway**: Anne Hathaway made her way into Japanese living rooms via commercials for the Lux line

of hair and beauty products. Hathaway joins a lofty list of Lux lovelies, which includes Catherine Zeta-Jones, Penelope Cruz, and Charlize Theron.

6. Jodie Foster: Jodie Foster appears to choose her movie roles carefully, opting for edgy roles that prick audience sensibilities: *The Silence of the Lambs, The Accused*, and *Panic Room*, to name a few. Her commercial résumé is a little less selective. From the mid-1990s to 2000, Foster pitched Keri beauty products, Pasona temp agency, Mt. Rainier iced coffee, and Honda, all the while smiling like she hadn't a care in the world. Clarice Starling, we hardly recognize ye.

7. Bruce Willis: In the early 1990s, the man who gave us the *Die Hard* film series pitched Maki jewelry stores, Georgia coffee drinks, Eneos gas stations, Subaru, and Post drinking water in a can.

8. Madonna: Madonna is no stranger to endorsements, having appeared in Gap, H&M, and Versace ads in the United States. In Japan, the material girl could be seen plugging Shochu rice beverages in ads that ran in 1995 and 1996. The spots show Madge slaying both a giant dragon and an evil wizard before enjoying a glass of the drink and announcing, "I'm pure." Okay…if you say so!

9. Britney Spears: Brit appeared in ads for Go-Go Tea iced tea dressed as a '60s go-go girl, complete with white patent leather boots and some killer dance moves. The ads ran until early 2003, when the singer was "not a girl, not yet a woman."

10. Ashley Judd: In this 2000 ad, Judd was thrilled to be driving a Honda Primo—so much so that she coined the phrase "Hondaful life." The actor is famous for roles in *De-Lovely* and *Kiss the Girls* and infamous for her family squabbles with sister Wynonna and mom Naomi.

Pop Quiz: Movie Taglines

Without a creative tagline, a movie might tank at the box office. See if you can match the famous movie to its tagline.

✳ ✳ ✳ ✳

1. "In space, no one can hear you scream."

2. "They're heeeere!"

3. "Just when you thought it was safe to go back in the water…"

4. "They'll never get caught. They're on a mission from God."

5. "Fear can hold you prisoner. Hope can set you free."

6. "They're here to save the world."

7. "A lot can happen in the middle of nowhere."

8. "Nothing on Earth could come between them."

9. "Why so serious?"

10. "Yule crack up!"

11. "For some, it's the last real taste of innocence, and the first real taste of life. But for everyone, it's the time that memories are made of."

12. "The adventure of a lifetime, the summer of their dreams… the dog of their nightmares."

13. "His whole life was a million-to-one shot."

14. "He was never in time for his classes… He wasn't in time for his dinner… Then one day… he wasn't in his time at all."

15. "Have the time of your life…"

16. "A 3,000-mile chase . . . That blazes a trail of TERROR to a gripping, spine-chilling climax!"

17. "Get ready for rush hour."

18. "He is afraid. He is totally alone. He is 3 million light years from home."

19. "He's good. She's good. He's just Duckie."

Answer choices:

A. *Alien* (1979)

B. *Back to the Future* (1985)

C. *The Blues Brothers* (1980)

D. *The Dark Knight* (2008)

E. *Dirty Dancing* (1987)

F. *E.T.: The Extra-Terrestrial* (1982)

G. *Fargo* (1996)

H. *Ghostbusters* (1984)

I. *Jaws 2* (1978)

J. *National Lampoon's Christmas Vacation* (1989)

K. *North by Northwest* (1959)

L. *Poltergeist* (1982)

M. *Pretty in Pink* (1986)

N. *Rocky* (1976)

O. *The Sandlot* (1993)

P. *The Shawshank Redemption* (1994)

Q. *Speed* (1994)

R. *Stand by Me* (1986)

S. *Titanic* (1997)

19. M
10. J; 11. R; 12. O; 13. N; 14. B; 15. E; 16. K; 17. Q; 18. F;
Answer Key: 1. A; 2. L; 3. I; 4. C; 5. P; 6. H; 7. G; 8. S; 9. D;

Behind the Films of Our Times

Lord of the Rings

Sean Connery turned down the role of Gandalf in the *Lord of the Rings* trilogy, which was given to Ian McKellen. Connery said he didn't want to devote the time to filming the movie in New Zealand, and he also didn't understand all the strange characters in the script.

Gone with the Wind

Bette Davis decided not to accept the lead role of Scarlett O'Hara in *Gone with the Wind*. At the time, she thought the male lead was going to be Errol Flynn, and she said she wouldn't work with him again after their experience making *The Private Lives of Elizabeth and Essex*.

Silence of the Lambs

Gene Hackman was originally set to play the part of Hannibal Lecter in *Silence of the Lambs*, but he left the project before it ever got off the ground. Michelle Pfeiffer was first approached about playing Clarice Starling but supposedly thought the movie was too dark.

The Matrix

Keanu Reeves wasn't the top choice for the star of *The Matrix*; Ewan McGregor and Will Smith were both approached first. Smith has since said he felt he wouldn't have played the part as well as Reeves did.

The Graduate

Robert Redford opted out of playing the starring role of *The Graduate* in 1967, leading to Dustin Hoffman's first big break as Ben Braddock.

Tarzan, the Ape Man

The oft-quoted words "me Tarzan, you Jane" are never actually spoken in the 1930s classic film *Tarzan, the Ape Man*. Tarzan simply speaks his name, then taps Jane and says hers.

A Sign of the Times

For more than 80 years, aspiring actors from all over the world have climbed to the top of Mount Lee in the Hollywood Hills. Their mission? To touch the famous Hollywood sign for good luck in their acting careers. Few realize that this iconic sign was originally constructed as an advertisement for a housing development.

✳   ✳   ✳   ✳

"Now *That's* a Billboard!"

IN 1923, *LOS ANGELES TIMES* publisher Harry Chandler was searching for a way to promote his new real estate development, Hollywoodland. Instead of a traditional billboard, Chandler wanted something bigger—a lot bigger—so he plunked down $21,000 for a sign placed on top of Mount Lee.

Using wood and sheet metal, the sign would spell out HOLLYWOODLAND. Each letter would be roughly 50 feet tall and 30 feet wide and would incorporate nearly 4,000 20-watt lightbulbs to illuminate the sign in sections— first *HOLLY*, then *WOOD*, and finally, *LAND*.

On July 13, 1923, the Hollywoodland sign was officially dedicated and lit for the first time. Albert Kothe was appointed the sign's caretaker.

The original plan was to remove the sign once all the plots in the development had been sold. But this coincided with the emergence of Hollywood as the epicenter of the American film industry, as well as the elevation of studio heads and major stars into America's "aristocracy" and the boom of nightclubs and restaurants on Sunset Boulevard. Thus, the sign took on meaning beyond its original intent. And years later, even after

the development was filled, the sign was deemed so enormous and awe-inspiring that it was allowed to stay.

Signs of Deterioration

By the mid-'40s, the sign had deteriorated so much that it had become an eyesore. The Los Angeles Parks Department and the Hollywood Chamber of Commerce joined forces to save the sign, but it was a massive undertaking. To cut costs, it was decided that the sign would no longer be illuminated. Also, the letters L, A, N, and D were removed so that the sign reflected the city of Hollywood rather than the subdivision.

Of course, it didn't help that the elements were taking their toll on the sign. And during the 1940s, in a bizarre twist of fate, an intoxicated man lost control of his vehicle and crashed headlong into the H, destroying it.

Over the next few decades, the sign continued to be damaged. An arsonist burned off part of the second L. In 1973, a group of pranksters, who apparently had a love for a certain green leaf, changed the sign to read HOLLYWEED. So by the end of the 1970s, there were serious discussions about demolishing the sign for good—which might have happened if help had not come from an unexpected source.

I'd Like to Buy a Vowel, Please

In 1978, *Playboy* magazine creator Hugh Hefner held a fundraiser at his Los Angeles Playboy Mansion to raise money to replace the Hollywood sign. Hef asked people to step forward and pay roughly $28,000 to "adopt" a letter. When all was said and done, the list of donors couldn't have been more diverse, including newspaper publisher Terrence Donnelly, Italian movie producer Giovanna Mazza, singer/actor Gene Autry, *Playboy* magazine creator Hugh Hefner, singer Alice Cooper, and Warner Bros. Records.

Using the money raised, nine 45-foot-high letters, ranging from 31 to 39 feet wide, were created out of steel. The new sign was unveiled on November 14, 1978. The Chamber of Commerce sold the original letters for a grand total of $10,000 to private collector Tony Wood.

The Sign Today

Today, the Hollywood Sign Trust, a nonprofit organization, handles the security, maintenance, and upkeep of the sign. In 2000, in an effort to cut down on potential vandalism, the Los Angeles Police Department installed a motion-activated security system around the sign, as well as several closed-circuit cameras, which were paid for by the Trust. The Hollywood Sign Trust relies solely on contributions from individuals and sponsorships from businesses to maintain the sign, which requires considerable upkeep. In addition to security issues, the sign is always in danger of deterioration from the elements.

The original letters were believed to have been destroyed, but in 2005, they were found inside a storage unit belonging to businessman Dan Bliss. In what was clearly a sign of the times, Bliss put the letters for sale on eBay. The winning bidder, sculptor Bill Mack, paid $450,000. Mack plans to use them as a canvas onto which he'll paint portraits of famous movie stars, many of whom were first lured to Hollywood by the sign itself.

Los Angeles residents, tourists, and movie lovers alike are all captivated by an unmistakable allure that the sign still holds after so many decades. It is a potent symbol that represents everything—both fun and tragic—that Hollywood stands for. It represents the lost dreams of those who wanted to become stars but didn't make it, as well as the future dreams of today's young hopefuls; it reminds us of the glamorous facade of the dream factory as well as the illusion and sham behind that facade. It is at once uniquely American yet it attracts tourists from all over the world. The sign beckons the dreamer in all of us because we all want to believe that the movies are still magic and that dreams of stardom still come true.

Actors Say the Darndest Things

They may make a living reading lines, but sometimes Hollywood actors are just as famous for what they say off-camera. Check out these memorable quotes.

❋ ❋ ❋ ❋

"I don't want people to know what I'm actually like. It's not good for an actor."

—Jack Nicholson

"I enjoy being a highly overpaid actor."

—Roger Moore

"I am not the archetypal leading man. This is mainly for one reason: As you may have noticed, I have no hair."

—Patrick Stewart

"Now I can wear heels."

—Nicole Kidman, following her divorce from Tom Cruise

"There are two types of actors: those who say they want to be famous and those who are liars."

—Kevin Bacon

"Just standing around looking beautiful is so boring."

—Michelle Pfeiffer

"With two movies opening this summer, I have no relaxing time at all. Whatever I have is spent in a drunken stupor."

—Hugh Grant

"I veer away from trying to understand why I act. I just know I need to do it."

—Ralph Fiennes

"I carried my Oscar to bed with me. My first and only three-way happened that night."

—Halle Berry

"Once you've been really bad in a movie, there's a certain kind of fearlessness you develop."

—Jack Nicholson

"People have been so busy relating to how I look, it's a miracle I didn't become a self-conscious blob of protoplasm."

—Robert Redford

"I'm staggered by the question of what it's like to be a multimillionaire. I always have to remind myself that I am."

—Bruce Willis

"Heartthrobs are a dime a dozen."

—Brad Pitt

"I have a love interest in every one of my films—a gun."

—Arnold Schwarzenegger

"I tell you what really turns my toes up: love scenes with 68-year-old men and actresses young enough to be their granddaughter."

—Mel Gibson

"The really frightening thing about middle age is the knowledge that you'll grow out of it."

—Doris Day

"Acting is the most minor of gifts and not a very high-class way to earn a living. After all, Shirley Temple could do it at the age of four."

—Katharine Hepburn

"Life is a tragedy when seen in close-up, but a comedy in long-shot."

—Charlie Chaplin

"I stopped believing in Santa Claus when I was six. Mother took me to see him in a department store, and he asked for my autograph."

—Shirley Temple

"When choosing between two evils, I always like to pick the one I've never tried before."

—Mae West

Hollywood Goes to War

From simple prewar patriotism to the combat films troops tagged "flag-wavers," Hollywood played a vital role in the war effort.

✳   ✳   ✳   ✳

As THE UNITED States' entry into World War II became more likely, Hollywood, largely on its own initiative, began to wean the country from its isolationist stance. Some of the films were gentle calls to patriotism, such as 1941's *Sergeant York*. This film offered a sentimental look back at one courageous American from the last war who had initially resisted the call to duty but who overcame his doubts and went on to become a hero. It couldn't have come at a more appropriate time for a reluctant nation.

Other films were more contemporary, giving audiences a glimpse of the future offered by the Nazis. Jack Warner, head of the Warner Bros. Studios, had hated the regime ever since a friend and employee of his had been beaten to death in Germany for not showing the proper respect for Hitler. As a result, he fast-tracked the 1939 production of *Confessions of a Nazi Spy*, featuring a warning that German American groups might be fronts for Fascist activity. The film was denounced by those groups, but Warner was unconcerned. The result was one of the first explicitly anti-Nazi movies to be shown in the United States.

Films of this sort may have inspired average citizens, but they drew the ire of isolationists in Congress, who in September 1941 launched investigations into the output of the movie studios, accusing them of using propaganda in an attempt to draw the country into war. Anticipating the course of events, Hollywood largely stood up to the investigations. Studio executive and film producer Darryl F. Zanuck testified that the movies were valuable not just for America but for selling the "American way of life . . . to the entire world."

He claimed that the first thing dictators did when taking control of a country was to remove Hollywood movies from the cinema, since they "wanted no part of the American way of life." The investigations didn't last long, and after Pearl Harbor, Washington and Hollywood worked in partnership for the rest of the war.

The Battle of Beverly Hills

The attack at Pearl Harbor had an immediate effect on the movie industry. Humphrey Bogart was shooting a script called *Across the Pacific* about just such a Japanese attack; the film was immediately canceled. James Cagney, who was only one day away from shooting a movie about the "damnedest patriotic man in the whole world," listened to FDR's announcement about the strike from the set of *Yankee Doodle Dandy*, and the broadcast inspired the cast and crew for the duration of filming.

The war came to Hollywood both literally and figuratively. Actor Leslie Howard (best known for his role as Ashley Wilkes in *Gone with the Wind*) was killed when the airplane in which he was traveling was shot down by the Germans. Clark Gable enlisted as a private, saying he had "no interest in acting as long as the war is going on." The army commandeered the Walt Disney studio property to set up antiaircraft guns for the defense of Los Angeles. More enduringly, all the studios were affected by the new regulatory authority given to federal agencies, such as the Office of War Information (OWI), the Bureau of Motion Pictures, and the Production Code Administration. While not always legally binding, negative comments and thematic suggestions from these groups had the practical effect of determining the content of movies throughout the war. The OWI issued a list of suggested topics they believed would benefit the American public, such as the joys of "curtailing pleasure spending in favor of war bond purchase." Other directives had longer-ranging effects. For instance, security restrictions on filming factories and other locations led to a stylistic shift in camera technique. The resulting extreme close-up shots and dim lighting paved the way for the rise of film noir.

Documentaries as "Properly Directed Hate"

Besides following the production codes, Hollywood directors and actors put their talent to use at the government's request, doing everything from shooting newsreels and victory films—short movies offering tips on how average citizens could help with the war, such as collecting scrap metal—to documentaries or just agreeing to give their normal feature films a particular spin. Many of Hollywood's elite played a part in the effort.

Particularly notable among the nonfiction films was Frank Capra's *Why We Fight* series. Initially reluctant to produce a documentary, a genre in which he had never worked before, Capra personally promised Chief of Staff George C. Marshall that he would make the "best damned documentary films ever made" for the war effort. The result was a sequence of seven pictures documenting the arguments for taking up arms against Japan and Germany, tackling topics from the philosophic differences between democracy and Fascism to the histories of individual battles. Capra was also one of the first to turn the German propaganda machine back on itself, using clips from Leni Riefenstahl's 1934 landmark *Triumph of the Will* to attack, rather than deify, the Nazi machine. By extracting sections of Riefenstahl's work, Capra was able to show audiences visions of oppressive Fascism rather than give the impression of unstoppable Teutonic supermen, as was originally intended. The technique was widely copied in other movies to great effect. The short newsreel *Hitler Assumes Command* manipulated German footage to turn goose-stepping Nazis parading in front of Hitler into a dance troupe doing a tap routine accompanied by the lighthearted British dance tune "The Lambeth Walk." The film reportedly sent Joseph Goebbels storming from his screening room in a cursing fit.

Along with giving Americans a reason to fight, Hollywood sought to portray an image of whom they were fighting against. The OWI was of the opinion that "properly directed hatred is of vital importance to the war effort." Hollywood complied and generally portrayed America's enemies in broad caricature. Germans were often played as militaristic Übermensch; Louis B. Mayer instructed William Wyler to portray the villain in *Mrs. Miniver* as a "typical Nazi son of a bitch." In Alfred Hitchcock's *Lifeboat*, the single Nazi passenger is more than a match for the other passengers individually, only being defeated when they band together and overcome him. The Japanese fared no better: They were portrayed as butchers in many films. The American public needed little encouragement to seize on the images and cheer on John Wayne in *The Fighting Seabees* when he called the Japanese enemy "Tojo's bug-eyed monkeys." America's allies naturally received better treatment, and the OWI explicitly encouraged production of films that would build sympathy for their plight. However, some of those films came back to haunt their creators: *Mission to Moscow*, *The North Star*, and *Song of Russia*, all of which attempted to portray the then-Allied Soviet Union in a positive light, were later investigated by the House Un-American Activities Committee as examples of communist propaganda.

The Big Picture

Documentaries were one thing, but Hollywood's forte was the big motion picture, and Tinseltown didn't ignore that format during the war. The conflict itself provided all the elements required for a breathtaking drama, and the studios rushed out an incredible number of explicit depictions of the war. *Wake Island* showed U.S. Marines fighting the Japanese in the South Pacific. *Thirty Seconds Over Tokyo* starred Spencer Tracy leading General Doolittle's famous bombing raid on Japan. *Sahara* depicted Bogie battling Nazi tanks in the desert, and John Wayne blasted the Japanese out of the sky in *Flying Tigers*. These semifictional portrayals of current events seemed to be natural material for wartime audiences. Those audiences included the troops overseas—the military made great efforts to get films to the troops, setting up outdoor projectors mere miles from the front or on the decks of ships.

It turned out, though, that realism was the last thing the audiences wanted to see. Veteran troops would become boisterous to the point of riot when shown a high-handed war film—they, along with the civilians, demanded lighter fare. Escapism was the order of the day. The war years yielded a surprising number of comedies—advertised as having "no message, no mission, no misfortune"—and big-budget musicals experienced a resurgence, having fallen out of favor in the prewar years.

Make 'em Laugh

Comedies were a particularly tricky subject given the innate seriousness of the war. Some attempts at humor are absolutely painful in retrospect: 1942's *Once Upon a Honeymoon* had stars Cary Grant and Ginger Rogers exclaim, upon being detained by the Nazis, "Now they think we're Jewish—this could be serious!" However, some films of the time endure as masterpieces. Charlie Chaplin put his iconic mustache to good use when he lampooned Hitler in 1940's *The Great Dictator.* The film featured Chaplin in a dual role as a simple barber who gets confused with a dictator named Adenoid Hynkel. In the most famous scene, the obsessive tyrant expresses his dreams of world domination by dancing with a large globe that eventually explodes in his face. After the war, Chaplin said that had he known about the Nazi atrocities he could never have made the film, but at the time he believed it was important that "Hitler must be laughed at."

But not all comedies were so allegorical. The Three Stooges, who all happened to be Jewish, offered a number of anti-Nazi films, including *You Natzy Spy!* and *I'll Never Heil Again,* with Moe Howard as the dictator of Moronica, in what he always remembered as his favorite role. In an incident illustrative of wartime paranoia, a still-costumed Moe rushed home from the movie set to attend his daughter's birthday party, resulting in a flood of calls to the police from concerned residents convinced they had seen Hitler running red lights in the streets of Los Angeles.

Behind the Films of Our Times

The Blair Witch Project

Made by two young filmmakers on the ridiculously small budget of $35,000, this 1999 film only brought in $1.5 million in its first week's box office. But the power of word-of-mouth and a compelling prerelease website eventually turned the largely improvised flick into a genuine blockbuster that grossed more than $140 million domestically in three months. A sequel in 2000, *Book of Shadows*, was not as successful, delivering less than 20 percent of the original's sales.

Goldfinger

The 1964 James Bond spy flick *Goldfinger* featured fast cars (including the sleek, gadget-filled Aston-Martin DB-5 and introducing the Ford Mustang to the public) and fast women. It also featured German actor Gert Frobe as master villain Auric Goldfinger—the "Man with the Midas Touch." He was also a man with a tin ear. Unable to speak English, Frobe tried to deliver his dialogue through phonetic pronunciation. The results were less than acceptable. Ultimately, the film's producers were forced to dub his entire spoken role with a voice actor named Michael Collins.

Masque of the Red Death

In the 1960s, director Roger Corman produced and directed a series of movies in the 1960s based on the stories of Edgar Allan Poe and often starring horror icon Vincent Price. While shooting *Masque of the Red Death* in 1964, Corman became friendly with starlet Jane Asher. One day, she brought a friend to watch the production, and Corman told the young lad to "stick around and have lunch," not realizing that he was Jane's steady boyfriend—Paul McCartney from The Beatles.

15 Films of Linnea Quigley

Curvy, blonde, and petite, Linnea Quigley has made more than 100 films since she moved to Hollywood in 1975. She landed her first acting gig while still in her teens, and quickly became a "scream queen"—a beauty performing mainly in R-rated horror flicks. While these films aren't necessarily highbrow, the piquant titles on Quigley's resume are totally worth it.

✳   ✳   ✳   ✳

1. ***Psycho from Texas* (1975):** A drifter is hired to kidnap and kill a Texas oil millionaire; Quigley plays a barmaid in this, her first feature film.

2. ***The Return of the Living Dead* (1985):** Flesh-eating zombies assault teens trapped in a warehouse. This was Quigley's breakthrough movie. She plays Trash, a punk rocker who performs an exotic dance atop a tombstone.

3. ***Creepozoids* (1987):** Ragged survivors of World War III straggle into an abandoned laboratory that is crawling with cannibalistic humanoids created following a botched government experiment in food research. Quigley fights monsters and takes a shower.

4. ***Nightmare Sisters* (1987):** Three geeky college girls are possessed by an evil spirit and become ravenous sex bombs. Can the boy geeks save them?

5. ***Sorority Babes in the Slimeball Bowl-O-Rama* (1988):** Skimpily attired sorority gals are trapped in a bowling alley with an evil imp who has been released from a shattered bowling trophy. Quigley battles the imp and bowls.

6. ***Hollywood Chainsaw Hookers* (1988):** A private detective runs up against prostitutes who carve up their johns in cultish blood rites. The movie's tagline: "They charge an arm and a leg!"

7. **Blood Nasty (1989):** An ordinary fellow dies and is reanimated with the soul of a serial killer. Problem: The innocent guy's mom would rather he stay dead (life insurance, you see).

8. **Robot Ninja (1990):** A lonely comic book artist transforms himself into Robot Ninja, a violent crime fighter. Besides Linnea, this one features Burt Ward, who enjoyed fame in the '60s as Robin on TV's *Batman*.

9. **Beach Babes from Beyond (1993):** Interstellar beach girls land on Earth and enter a bikini contest to help an old fella hang on to his beach house. Burt Ward makes an appearance along with Jackie Stallone (Sly's mom) and Joey Travolta (John's brother).

10. **Sick-o-Pathics (1996):** Art imitates life in this horror/comedy: Quigley plays a scream queen in a bit called "Commercial: Dr. Riker's Hair Lotion."

11. **Mari-Cookie and the Killer Tarantula (1998):** Spider queen Mari-Cookie (played by vintage cult actress Lina Romay) kidnaps men and strings them up in gigantic gooey webs.

12. **Kannibal (2001):** Quigley plays crime boss Georgina Thereshkova, who finds herself in the crosshairs of the police and a male mob chief.

13. **Corpses Are Forever (2003):** When the gates of hell open, the world is overrun with zombies. Humankind's only hope is an amnesiac spy and his odd assortment of allies.

14. **Zombiegeddon (2003):** It's a zombie apocalypse as the walking dead take over the world. At age 45, Quigley plays a school principal.

15. **Spring Break Massacre (2007):** Six sorority girls on a sleepover are stalked by an escaped serial killer. No bikini for our gal Quigley in this one—she's the deputy sheriff.

Hispanic Hollywood

Hispanic actors have been prominent in Hollywood since the silent era. In fact, some of the most successful and admired stars in Hollywood history have been of Hispanic heritage.

✳ ✳ ✳ ✳

Antonio Banderas

BANDERAS BECAME A top box-office star in Spain through his work with respected director Pedro Almodovar and made his Hollywood debut in the 1992 film *The Mambo Kings*. His striking good looks and emotional intensity made him a favorite of female moviegoers in films such as *Interview with the Vampire* (1994), *Evita* (1996), and *The Mask of Zorro* (1998).

Penélope Cruz

Like Banderas, Cruz became an international superstar through her work with Almodovar. She brought her fashion-model looks and considerable acting talent to Hollywood in films including *Vanilla Sky* (2001) and *Vicky Cristina Barcelona* (2008), for which she won an Oscar for Best Supporting Actress. Cruz is currently married to Spanish actor Javier Bardem.

Dolores Del Rio

Often cited as one of the most beautiful actresses of her era, Del Rio made her Hollywood debut in 1925. She was popular with audiences throughout the 1930s but was frustrated by the stereotypical roles she was relegated to. After returning to her native Mexico in the 1940s, she became a major star there, occasionally coming back to the States to appear in a Hollywood film.

Benicio Del Toro

Though not a top box-office draw, Del Toro cultivated a loyal audience through his distinctive portrayals of likable crooks in *The Usual Suspects* (1995) and *Snatch* (2000). He also earned the Best Supporting Actor Oscar for his sensitive performance as a conflicted Mexican cop in director Steven Soderbergh's

Traffic (2000). Soderbergh directed Del Toro again in the title role of 2008's *Che*, a two-part, four-hour biopic about famed Argentine revolutionary Che Guevara.

Andy Garcia

Garcia appeared in a number of minor film and television roles in the 1970s and '80s before getting his big break in *The Untouchables* (1987) and then *The Godfather: Part III* (1990). Ironically, in both films he portrayed an Italian American, but he would go on to celebrate his Cuban heritage in films such as *The Lost City* (2005), an homage to Havana's vibrant pre-Castro days that Garcia starred in, produced, and directed.

Rita Hayworth

Born in New York City to a Spanish father and an Irish mother, Hayworth would become one of the best-known box-office stars of Hollywood's Golden Age. Though she made more than two dozens films in the 1930s, she vaulted to prominence after assuming the image of a provocative vamp in *Blood and Sand* (1941). After that, she quickly became one of the most ogled pinup girls of the era. Her role in *Gilda* (1946) cemented her star image as a love goddess.

Salma Hayek

In the early 1990s, Salma Hayek left a successful career as a soap opera star in Mexico to take her chances in Hollywood. She received her breakthrough in a role in *Desperado* (1995), opposite Antonio Banderas. Hayek parlayed her stardom into a career behind the camera as well. In 2002, she starred in and coproduced *Frida*, a biopic about Mexican painter Frida Kahlo. In addition to coproducing films, Hayek served as executive producer on the groundbreaking TV comedy *Ugly Betty*.

Jennifer Lopez

A multitalented celebrity, Lopez has made her mark as a dancer, singer, and actress. Her film career has had its ups—*Selena* (1996), *Out of Sight* (1998), *Shall We Dance?* (2004) and downs—*The Cell* (2000), *Enough* (2002), *Gigli* (2003)—but she has always remained prominent in the public eye as a favorite subject of the supermarket tabloids.

Anthony Quinn

A charismatic man's man with a passion for life, Quinn appeared in more than 100 films in his 65-year career and won two Oscars. Born in Mexico in 1915, he was noted for his remarkable ability to convincingly portray characters of almost any ethnicity—Italian (*La Strada*, 1954), Inuit (*The Savage Innocents*, 1961), Arab (*Lawrence of Arabia*, 1962), Greek (*Zorba the Greek*, 1964), and Ukrainian (*The Shoes of the Fisherman*, 1968).

Cesar Romero

Cesar Romero was born in New York City in 1907 and began appearing on Broadway in the 1930s. Elegant, imposing, and handsome, he soon moved to film where he typically played a carefree playboy in light romances, but he also appeared in many musicals and was known for his grace as a dancer. He shifted to television roles later in his career and is well remembered for his outlandish portrayal of The Joker on the '60s series *Batman*.

Martin Sheen

Born in Dayton, Ohio, Sheen began acting in the theater in the late 1950s. His film career started in the '60s with portrayals of rebels and outsiders, culminating in his breakthrough role as a killer in *Badlands* (1973). His visceral performance as military assassin Benjamin Willard in *Apocalypse Now* (1979) remains his most memorable film role, though he is also well known for his TV work on *The West Wing*.

Lupe Velez

Velez emigrated from Mexico to the United States in the mid-1920s and by 1926 was starring opposite matinee idol Douglas Fairbanks in the silent romantic adventure *The Gaucho*. Petite, beautiful, and feisty, Velez had a natural flair for physical comedy and became best known for a formulaic series of domestic comedies in which she played "The Mexican Spitfire."

Based on a True Fake

The problem with movies that claim to be based on a true story is not the definition of "true"—it's the definition of "based on." Movies tend to take some parts of a particular story and focus on them—exaggerating their importance and relevance—while ignoring other circumstances completely. Here are a few examples.

✳ ✳ ✳ ✳

A Beautiful Mind

JOHN NASH IS a mathematician whose work in game theory earned him a 1994 Nobel Prize in Economics. He attended Princeton University and worked on his equilibrium theory. After earning a doctorate in 1950, he continued to work on his thesis, part of which became the Nash Equilibrium. In 1951, he was hired as a member of the MIT mathematics faculty. In 1957, he married Alicia Lopez-Harrison de Lardé, and shortly after that, he was admitted to a mental hospital for schizophrenia. The couple had a son in 1959 but divorced in 1963. They became friendly again in 1970, renewed their romantic relationship in 1994, and remarried in 2001.

But in the movie *A Beautiful Mind*, Nash is plagued by schizophrenia throughout his education at Princeton. He struggles to maintain relationships with his classmates but flourishes as he discovers various mathematical theories. He is also asked by the government to decode covert Soviet messages. He gets married and has a son but is slowly eaten up by his schizophrenia until he's hospitalized. Through the love of his wife and his own strength of will, however, he becomes an award-winning recluse who is happily accepted within the hallowed halls of higher education.

One catch is that Nash's true-life delusions were auditory, not visual. Also, while the movie portrayed John and Alicia's marriage as a tense one, it also portrayed it as continuous. There are at least two more important changes the movie made to Nash's life: The pen ceremony at Princeton never really happened, and

Nash didn't give a rousing yet humble speech when he received his Nobel Prize.

Catch Me If You Can

Frank Abagnale was a con artist who passed bad checks during the 1960s while impersonating a pilot, a physician, an attorney, and a teacher. Once captured, Abagnale had the dubious distinction of having 26 countries with extradition orders against him. After serving in prison for his crimes, he founded Abagnale & Associates, a legitimate company that advises businesses on fraud.

In the movie, an FBI agent chases Abagnale around the globe. In reality, there was no FBI agent, and Abagnale was never on the FBI's Ten Most Wanted list. *Catch Me If You Can* follows Abagnale's life, which already seems pretty exaggerated, and exaggerates it even more. For instance, Abagnale writes $10 million in bad checks; in reality the total was only $2.5 million.

Finding Neverland

Scottish novelist and dramatist J. M. Barrie wrote *Peter Pan*. Barrie's traumatic childhood included the death of his brother and the subsequent withdrawal of his mother. As an adult, Barrie moved to London, where he became a journalist, a novelist, and a playwright. He became friends with the Llewelyn Davies family, who provided the inspiration for *Peter Pan*.

In the movie *Finding Neverland*, we're treated to the moment when a lonely Barrie meets and befriends the Llewelyn Davies children and their mother. The movie weaves the lives of Barrie and the family together, and shows the origins of the famous tale.

The real Barrie had many literary friends, famous ones at that, and a prolific outpouring of books and plays. When the real Barrie initially met and befriended the children, their father was alive; in the movie, he's already dead. In the film, there are four children; in reality, there were five. Most importantly, Barrie suffered from psychogenic dwarfism—he was 4′10″ tall. In the film, Barrie is played by Johnny Depp, who stands 5′10″.

Play It Again . . . Ronald?

One of the most enduring Tinseltown myths is that Ronald Reagan was under serious consideration for the role of Rick Blaine in Casablanca—*a character forever associated with Humphrey Bogart.*

✳ ✳ ✳ ✳

IT TURNS OUT that the Reagan-as-Rick story was a clever publicity stunt perpetrated by Warner Bros. No actor other than Bogart was ever considered for what would become one of cinema's most iconic roles. The rumor started when the publicity department at Warner Bros. planted a false press release in the *Hollywood Reporter* on January 5, 1942, announcing that Reagan and Ann Sheridan were set to costar in *Casablanca*, which was still in the script stage at the time.

Why would a major studio intentionally plant such a falsehood? To protect its property—in this case, Reagan. Under the old studio system, production houses such as Warner Bros. worked hard to keep the names of their best talent in the public (and professional) eye. Planting false news items in the industry press and elsewhere was an easy way to accomplish this.

Interestingly, Reagan couldn't have appeared in *Casablanca* even if the role of Rick Blaine had been up for grabs. He was a second lieutenant in the Army Reserve, and Warner Bros. had been getting deferments for him for several months. But when the United States entered World War II on December 8, 1941, there was no question that the actor would be called up for active duty long before *Casablanca* began filming in April. And that's exactly what happened.

Not Coming to a Theater Near You

Given some of the duds that do make it to the screen, it may seem odd that so many promising movie ideas end up on the shelf. But Hollywood lore is full of intriguing projects that never were.

✳ ✳ ✳ ✳

Don Quixote: *Citizen Kane* director Orson Welles abandoned more movies than he actually made, including a film version of Adolf Hitler's *Mein Kampf* and the story of Jesus Christ (with Welles as Jesus). But his most infamous unfinished film was an adaptation of the 16th-century classic *Don Quixote*, about an old dreamer who imagines adventure everywhere. Welles dropped Don Quixote in 20th-century Spain and cast himself as a character making a Don Quixote movie. He started the project in 1954 and continued working on it off and on until his death in 1985, funding it out of his own pocket. In 1993, Welles associates assembled and released salvaged scratchy footage, but audiences saw it more as an epic home movie than a completed Welles film.

The Man Who Killed Don Quixote: *12 Monkeys* director Terry Gilliam has also spent years on Don Quixote. In 2000, a decade after he conceived the idea, Gilliam finally started shooting his adaptation, in which an ad executive time travels back to the 1600s. But after six days of shooting and a series of catastrophes, including a flash flood, the production ground to a halt. Insurers backed out, the movie was canceled, and Gilliam lost control of the screenplay. He's been trying to get back to the project ever since, finally regaining the script rights in 2009.

Roger Rabbit 2: After *Who Framed Roger Rabbit* raked in $325 million, a sequel was a no-brainer. Disney initially developed a prequel script that put Roger in the middle of World War II. But Steven Spielberg, who partially controls the rights to the characters, was approaching the war on a more serious note with *Schindler's List* and didn't want to cast Nazis as cartoonish villains. Eventually, Disney came up with a second script, set in the Great Depression, and produced some test footage. Disney CEO Michael Eisner liked what he saw but didn't like the projected budget, which topped $100 million. He canceled the project in 1999.

A Day at the United Nations: In 1960, *Some Like It Hot* director Billy Wilder decided to make the first new Marx Brothers film in a decade. In his film, the Marx Brothers would play jewel thieves who are mistaken for Latvian delegates to the United Nations. The Marx Brothers were interested, but when Harpo had a heart attack, Wilder decided it was too risky to proceed.

Up Against It: In 1967, avant-garde playwright Joe Orton wrote a screenplay for a third Beatles movie. In the film, John, Paul, George, and Ringo would have been revolutionaries battling an oppressive government run entirely by women. But the material was awfully dark for The Beatles (in the story, the Fab Four assassinate a female prime minister) and they opted not to do it.

Alternative Supermans: Between 1987's *Superman IV: The Quest for Peace* and 2006's *Superman Returns*, the man of steel had several failed takeoffs. In the biggest misfire, *Superman Lives*, which began development in 1994, Superman is killed but then resurrected by a cyborg. Oddly enough, producer Jon Peters dictated Superman should wear a black suit in the movie and should never be shown flying. *Clerks* writer/director Kevin Smith wrote the screenplay, Tim Burton signed on to direct, and Nicolas Cage got fitted for the cape. But after racking up millions in preproduction costs, the project fell apart. Later, the studio's attention turned to *Batman vs. Superman*, which would have featured the two heroes battling each other. Ultimately, Warner Bros. decided separate Batman and Superman movies were a better bet (more ticket sales), so the project was killed.

Inside Jokes in Animation

Moviemakers love sneaking their own inside jokes and references into films, and animation is the perfect place to pull it off. Here are some subtle examples that you might not have noticed.

✳ ✳ ✳ ✳

✳ In *Who Framed Roger Rabbit* (1988), when Eddie walks into a Toontown restroom, graffiti on a wall in the background reads: "For a good time, call Allyson Wonderland." The message originally had a phone number next to it that was rumored to have belonged to either Disney CEO Michael Eisner or then-Disney chairman Jeffrey Katzenberg. The digits were removed for the home-video release.

✳ "A113" is seen on a license plate in *Toy Story* (1995), referenced in a jail cell block number in *The Incredibles* (2004), and heard as a flight number in an airport announcement in *Toy Story 2* (1999). "A113" is the room number of the animation department at the California Institute for the Arts, where numerous Pixar animators trained.

✳ In *Aladdin* (1992), when the genie looks at his cookbook to see whether he can turn Aladdin into a prince, he briefly pulls Sebastian from *The Little Mermaid* (1989) out of the pages.

✳ Mickey Mouse makes some brief appearances in *The Little Mermaid* (1989), but you have to know where to look. First, a Mickey outline pops up in a scroll that Ursula hands to Ariel. It's hidden in the middle of some words on the page. Then, when the animals are working to break up the wedding, a woman with black hair appears on the screen. Her hair forms the shape of Mickey's head.

* When *The Lion King* was released, overzealous watchdog groups accused Disney animators of inserting a racy message into the movie. It happens in the scene in which Simba collapses on a cliff right after he talks to Timon and Pumbaa about stars. A puff of dust flies up, and if you look closely, it forms three letters. Some people thought it said "SEX," but it actually says "SFX"—the name of the special-effects team that put the scene together.

* In *Toy Story*, the Pixar people paid tribute to the company's original founder, George Lucas. The scene where Buzz is knocked out of the window features numerous references to Lucas's first *Indiana Jones* flick, *Raiders of the Lost Ark* (1981), including the film's music.

* In *Toy Story 2*, Andy has a calendar in his room that shows the characters from *A Bug's Life* (1998).

* Disney's animated feature *Tarzan* (1999) gave a subtle shout-out to a 1950s-era Disney short called *In the Bag* (1956). While Turk is tearing up the explorer's camp, two apes replicate a move called the "bump-bump step" from the film made four decades earlier.

* Pixar has an ongoing gag with a Pizza Planet truck. The fake restaurant's delivery vehicle has appeared somewhere in every Pixar movie, though it's sometimes hard to spot. In *Finding Nemo* (2003), for example, the truck zooms by the dentist's office toward the end of the film.

* Buzz Lightyear made a cameo (of sorts) in *Finding Nemo*. During the scene in the dentist's waiting room, a Buzz action figure is sitting on the floor.

* *Finding Nemo* also looked into the future: Animators slipped in a quick shot of Mr. Incredible—from the upcoming Pixar film *The Incredibles*—during the same dentist office scene. The muscular fellow is shown on a comic book that a patient is reading.

Chapter Two

Sports and Pastimes

Olympic Disasters

After years of training, even Olympic-caliber athletes are vulnerable to last-minute injuries that dash their hopes.

✳   ✳   ✳   ✳

✳ The U.S. track-and-field team for the 1900 Paris games was weakened because the French unexpectedly held events on the Sabbath. Several universities forbade their collegiate athletes to compete.

✳ Runner Harvey Cohn was almost swept overboard, and six athletes required medical treatment, when the SS *Barbarossa* was hit by a large wave en route to Athens in 1906. Several favored U.S. athletes did poorly or dropped out because of their "ocean adventure."

✳ Francisco Lazaro of Portugal collapsed during the 1912 marathon and died the next day from sunstroke.

✳ After losing his opening round at the Berlin 1936 Olympics, Thomas Hamilton-Brown, a lightweight boxer from South Africa, drowned his sorrows with food. But the competitors' scores had accidentally been switched. Sadly, the damage was done—a five-pound weight gain kept Hamilton-Brown from the final round.

* Shortly after arriving in London for the 1948 Olympics, Czech gymnast Eliska Misakova was hospitalized. She died of polio the day her team competed and won the gold. At the award ceremony, the Czech flag was bordered in black.

* During the 1960 cycling road race in Rome, Dane Knut Jensen suffered sunstroke, fractured his skull in a fall, and died.

* In 1960, the South African country of Suriname sent their sole athlete, Wim Esajas, to compete in the 800-meter race. Unfortunately, he misunderstood the schedule and missed the heats.

* Mexico City's high altitude of 7,347 feet slowed the times of endurance events in the 1968 games. Three men running the 10,000-meter were unable to finish while others fell unconscious at the finish line.

* The Munich Massacre of 1972 resulted in the deaths of eleven Israeli athletes, five Palestinian terrorists, and one German policeman after the kidnapping of the athletes.

* Sixteen-year-old swimmer Rick DeMont took two Marex pills for an asthma attack the day before his 400-meter freestyle race. His gold medal was revoked when he failed the drug test. The 1972 team physicians never checked to see whether his prescription contained banned substances. The same thing happened to Romanian gymnast Andreea Raducan in 2000. She was stripped of her gold medal for the all-around competition when she tested positive for the banned substance pseudoephedrine—an ingredient in the cold medicine provided by team doctors.

* In 1996, two people were killed and 111 were injured when American Eric Robert Rudolph detonated a bomb at the Atlanta Olympics.

Raising the Stakes

Think you're a card shark? Read on for more about the ins and outs of gambling.

Q: How would someone mark cards?

A: You need two things: very sharp eyes and a deck with a repeating pattern on the back—Bicycles, Bees, and Aviators are great, but corporate logo decks are terrible. Ideally, use cards with backs printed in a color matching a fine-tip permanent marker. Then decide what mark will encode each suit and rank, and very carefully mark the cards. Since cards can be upside-down, and since most people fan them so as to view the upper left corners, mark both the upper left and lower right of each card. Wear prescription sunglasses so people can't see you staring at the backs of the cards they're holding.

Q: Does card counting really work in blackjack?

A: Depends how many decks there are, first of all. The more decks are used at once, the less fruit card counting can bear. There are two types of card counting: in your head and mechanically assisted. The casino can't stop you from counting cards in your head; it can only make it more difficult for you. Some states have laws against mechanical assistance, and if you're caught using it, expect a quick blackball from every casino in the region.

Q: Is anyone getting away with counting cards?

A: Have no doubt of that. You'll never hear of them, because they will never be caught. Pigs get fat; hogs get slaughtered, as tax accountants say. They make reasonable money, they go to different places, they lose sometimes, they act like your everyday gambling addict or hobbyist. They don't give the game away by placing suspicious bets; they know how to behave, be friendly, flirt with employees. They stay under the radar. When the numbers are in their favor, they bet more; when numbers aren't good, they bet less, but they don't overdo it.

Q: How do casinos battle card counters?

A: First of all, from the pit boss to the security office, people are watching. When gambling you should consider yourself under surveillance from head to toe. I wouldn't put it past casinos to have night-vision cameras underneath the tables. They have a lot of experience and know what to look for. Free drinks are another tool, because hardly anyone's counting skills improve with alcohol intake. If the boss thinks you're counting, he or she may "flat bet" you—ask you to make the same wager on every hand, which is the opposite of what a counter is trying to do. What they're looking for is your reaction to that request. If you don't follow it, they'll ask you to leave.

Q: What are the best and worst games in terms of payout?

A: Casino poker, blackjack card counting, and video poker generally pay best. Slot machines are terrible, as are live keno and Wheel of Fortune. House payouts tend to range from 85 to 95 percent overall, so on the whole, the game favors the casino. Do you think all those pyramids, sphinxes, complimentary buffets, and neon lights come from the money people have won?

The World's First Rodeo

Although different towns in several states make the claim, most historians believe the world's first rodeo was held in the West Texas town of Pecos.

✳ ✳ ✳ ✳

IN THE DAYS of the Old West, Pecos was little more than a dusty cowboy town, an outpost on the cattle-driving trails linking Abilene to Montana, then a stop on the Texas and Pacific Railway. In the 1880s, it became known as a violent frontier town where arguments frequently ended in a hail of bullets and a body being dumped quietly into the Pecos River. However, when a group of cowboys at Red Newell's saloon began arguing about whether Trav Windham or Morg Livingston was the best at riding and roping, they kept their guns holstered and decided instead to hold a roping and bronco-busting competition.

Windham was a well-known figure in the area, first as a cattle driver then as a ranch foreman. Livingston, on the other hand, had a reputation as an accomplished roper. The two men chose to compete on the flat land on the west side of the river, roughly where the city's courthouse stands today. The year was 1883, and they chose the date of July 4, as it was a public holiday, which enabled more ranchers, cowboys, and townsfolk to attend.

The Stakes Are Raised

Once word of the contest spread, other cowboys clamored to take part. Cowpunchers such as Jim Mannin, John Chalk, and Brawley Oates traveled from ranches with names such as the Hashknife, the Lazy Y, and NA descended upon Pecos to compete. They were joined by spectators who arrived from every direction in wagons and buggies, on horseback, or simply on foot. Local ranchers put up a $40 purse while a young girl donated blue ribbons from the hem of her dress as prizes.

The first contest in the competition was won by Trav Windham when he roped and tied a steer in a time of 22 seconds. Morg Livingston then beat his rival in the matched roping contest. Other winners included Pete Beard of the Hashknife and Jeff Chism. According to reports, the youngest entrant, Henry Slack, didn't fare quite as well. When he attempted to rope a steer, his lasso broke, which sent him crashing from his saddle. The young man was knocked unconscious, thus missing out on the prize money, the bragging rights, and a possible blue ribbon.

The First or Not the First?

Much of the controversy surrounding Pecos's claims to holding the world's first rodeo stems from the fact that the contest didn't become an annual event in the town until 1929. But Pecos has not maintained that it holds the *longest-running* rodeo on record. Concerning its actual claim of the world's oldest, the *Encyclopedia Britannica* examined signed affidavits from many who either took part in or attended the 1883 event and concluded that Pecos had indeed held the "world's first public cowboy contest wherein prizes were awarded to the winners of bronc riding and steer roping."

In 1936, the West of the Pecos Rodeo Committee built the Buck Jackson Memorial Arena as the permanent home for the annual West of the Pecos Rodeo. Today, the event is the largest outdoor

rodeo in Texas. Spectators no longer arrive by wagons or in horse-drawn buggies, but the spirit of the rodeo remains much as it was in 1883. Instead of settling their arguments in a hail of bullets, cowboys compete to decide who is the best at roping and riding. And while the defeated may miss out on the prize money and bragging rights, they never end up face-down in the Pecos River.

Hockey's Hat Trick

One might logically assume that NHL great Gordie Howe invented the "Gordie Howe Hat Trick." Then again, when you assume . . .

✳ ✳ ✳ ✳

GORDIE HOWE DID not invent the three-pronged feat that bears his name. In fact, the term—used to describe the art of recording a goal, an assist, and a fight in a single hockey match—didn't enter the sport's lexicon until 1991. That's a full ten years after the game's longest-serving veteran hung up his blades.

Honoring a Hockey Great

Make no mistake: Howe was more than capable of achieving all three elements necessary to complete the celebrated triple play. He was a wizard at putting the biscuit in the basket, a magician at deftly slipping a pass through myriad sticks and skates and putting the disc on the tape of a teammate's stick, and he wasn't opposed to delivering a knuckle sandwich to a deserving adversary. However, the tattered pages of the NHL record books show that he recorded only one Howe Hat Trick in his 32-year career in the NHL and the World Hockey Association. On December 22, 1955, in a game against the Boston Bruins, Howe (playing for the Detroit Red Wings) scored the tying goal, set up the winning 3–2 tally, and bested Beantown left winger Lionel Heinrich in a spirited tussle.

The Record Holder

The Gordie Howe Hat Trick isn't an official statistic—in fact, the San Jose Sharks is the only franchise that lists the achievement in its media guide—but it is a widely acknowledged measurement of a skater's ability to play the game with both physical skill and artistic grace. The New York Rangers' Brendan Shanahan is the NHL's all-time leader in "Howe Hats." According to *The Hockey News*, Shanny scored a goal, recorded an assist, and had a fight nine times in the same game.

Fast Facts

✳ On May 30, 1946, Bama Rowell was the first player to smash the Bulova clock at Ebbets Field, which some have said was the inspiration for the scoreboard scene in the movie *The Natural.*

✳ In Paris, France, there are more dogs than people.

✳ It is believed that humans wore jewelry before they wore clothes.

✳ The first high jumper to use the method of jumping headfirst to clear the bar was American Dick Fosbury. His innovative maneuver was dubbed the Fosbury Flop.

✳ John D. Rockefeller's ambitions were to make $100,000 and live to be 100. He died 26 months shy of the century mark, but he left an estate worth $1.4 billion.

✳ During excavation for the building of Oriole Park at Camden Yards, the remains of a saloon were discovered. It turned out that Babe Ruth's father had owned the place.

✳ Most elephants weigh less than the tongue of a blue whale.

✳ Prior to about the 1920s, underarm hair on women was generally no big deal. The invention of the safety razor and the acceptance of scantier clothing changed all that.

✳ On Christopher Columbus's fourth voyage to the new world, he saved the lives of his crew by convincing Jamaican natives that he made the moon disappear during a lunar eclipse in 1504.

✳ Snakes have no eyelids, and their eyes turn a milky white just before they shed their skin.

✳ Dwight D. Eisenhower was the first president to use a helicopter that took off and landed on the White House lawn.

✳ California boasts the oldest known living tree—a Bristlecone Pine nicknamed "Methuselah," which is estimated to be 4,767 years old.

Jeu de Paume, Anyone?

Ever watch people playing handball and wonder, "Ow! Isn't that hell on their hands?" Well, it can be. That's why some players decided to take a different approach to handball, and used a racket instead. Here's more on the origins of tennis.

✳   ✳   ✳   ✳

Tennis: Sport of Monks

INTERESTINGLY, NO ONE is quite sure exactly when tennis was invented. Some folks believe it's an ancient sport, but there's no credible evidence that tennis existed before A.D. 1000. Whenever the time period, most people can agree that tennis descends from handball.

The first reliable accounts of tennis come from tales of 11th-century French monks who needed to add a little entertainment to their days spent praying, repenting, and working. They played a game called *jeu de paume* ("palm game," that is, handball) off the walls or over a stretched rope. The main item separating tennis from handball—a racket—evolved within these French monasteries. (The first rackets were actually used in ancient Greece, in a game called *sphairistike* and then in *tchigan*, played in Persia.) The monks had the time and means to develop these early forms of the tennis racquet: Initially, webbed gloves were used for hand protection, then paddles, and finally a paddle with webbing. The first balls were made from leather or cloth stuffed with hair, wool, or cork.

Banned by the Pope

Once outside the cloister, the game's popularity spread across the country with the speed of an Amélie Mauresmo backhand. According to some sources, by the 13th century, France had more than 1,800 tennis courts. Most of the enthusiasts were from the upper classes. In fact, the sport became such a craze that some leaders, including kings and the pope, tried to discourage or ban the game as too distracting. Not to be torn from their beloved game, the people played on.

It didn't take long for tennis to reach merry olde England. There the game developed a similar following, counting kings Henry VII and Henry VIII among its fans. Even The Bard, William Shakespeare, refers to the game in his play *Henry V.* At England's Hampton Court Palace, research suggests that the first tennis court was built there between 1526 and 1529. Later, another court was built, The Royal Tennis Court, which was last refurbished in 1628 and is still in use.

15-Love!

Those who believe that tennis originated in ancient Egypt argue that the word "tennis" derives from the Egyptian town of Tinnis. It is also possible that the term comes from the French cry of *"Tenez!"* which in this context could mean, "take this!" or "here it comes!" using the formal address. A similar version would be *"Tiens!"* As with any living language, French pronunciation has evolved, so it's difficult to know precisely whether the word came from French monastery trash-talk—but it's quite plausible.

Ever wonder what's up with tennis's weird scoring system? What does any of it mean, anyway? Here are a few pointers.

∗ The term "Love," meaning a score of zero, may descend from *"L'Oeuf!"* which means "the egg"—much like "goose egg" means zero in American sports slang.

∗ Evidently, the scoring once went by 15s (0, 15, 30, 45, and Game). But for some reason, it was decided that the numbers should have the same number of syllables. Hence, the "5" got dropped from the French word *quarante-cinq* (45), leaving just *quarante* (40), which is in use today.

∗ The term "Deuce" (when the game ties 40–40 and is reset to 30–30) likely comes from *"À Deux!"* which loosely translates as "two to win!" This is because in tennis, one must win by two.

Strongest Sluggers

Baseball's musclemen: They didn't just hit the ball, they hurt it.

✳   ✳   ✳   ✳

Jimmie Foxx

Foxx earned his nickname, "The Beast." His rippling muscles terrified American League pitchers for years. When he slugged 58 homers in 1932, he became only the third player ever to top 50. Foxx was second in lifetime homers until Willie Mays surpassed him. Jimmie's pokes were often the longest balls ever hit in (or out of) the park.

Babe Ruth

Ruth's prowess as a hitter for distance so far surpassed anyone ever seen before that they had to invent a new word for it: "Ruthian." In his first spring training game in the minor leagues in 1914, Babe cracked the longest ball fans of that town (Fayetteville, North Carolina) had ever seen. His last homer was the longest ball ever hit out of Forbes Field; it cleared the double-deck right-field grandstands.

Josh Gibson

Called the "black Babe Ruth," power-hitting Gibson slammed a number of homers that exceeded 500 feet. The color line kept him  from the majors, but Gibson set slugging-distance records that have become legendary. In his Negro League career (1930–46), he was the home run king nine times.

Ryan Howard

In his first 266 games through 2006, Howard, playing for the Philadelphia Phillies, had belted 82 home runs. At the age of 26, he won the Home Run Derby at the

All-Star Game and then finished the season with 58 homers. It's said he once hit a 430-foot homer when he was only 12 years old.

Harmon Killebrew

When Killebrew slugged long home runs, they didn't just go far—they sometimes caused damage. A long ball he hit in 1967 in Minneapolis's Metropolitan Stadium went more than 530 feet and shattered two seats in the process. Eight times he hit more than 40 home runs on his way to a lifetime total of 573, eighth best all time.

Mickey Mantle

No one ever walloped home runs from both sides of the plate like Mantle. He often played in pain, with injuries ranging from lingering osteomyelitis to a knee torn apart in the 1951 World Series. Mantle is given credit for the longest ball ever hit in Yankee Stadium.

Willie McCovey

Only four men ever hit more homers in the National League than McCovey's 521. Not a homer hitter when his career began, he hit full stride from 1963 through 1970, when he hit (in order) 44, 18, 39, 36, 31, 36, 45, and 39.

Mark McGwire

He was called one of the "Bash Brothers" when he played with Jose Canseco for the Oakland A's, but McGwire didn't rewrite the record books until he was traded to St. Louis, where he broke Roger Maris's single-season home run record in 1998 and ended up with 70. He also had four consecutive 50-homer seasons, making him both a strong and consistent slugger.

Willie Stargell

The way Willie Stargell flipped around his bat, it seemed to weigh less than an ounce. That strength and that bat came together to hit homers completely out of Dodger Stadium; he's the only person to do it twice, in 1969 and '73. Stargell also smashed more out of Forbes and Three Rivers than anybody else.

Hoop Dreams

No sport combines athletic grace, physical dexterity, and visibly stunning displays of prowess and power quite like the game of basketball. Here are a few films that properly portray basketball as the stuff of dreams.

✳ ✳ ✳ ✳

Hoosiers (1986)

INSPIRED BY THE Cinderella story of Milan High School—a school that, despite having only 73 male students, won the Indiana State Championship in 1954—this film accurately captures the spirit and substance of small-town dreams and big-time success. Buoyed by realistic dialogue and attention to detail, this endearing drama, starring Gene Hackman, Dennis Hopper, and Barbara Hershey, is considered one of the best basketball movies ever made.

White Men Can't Jump (1992)

This refreshing comedic exercise uses basketball to tear down racial and cultural stereotypes while building up the importance of friendship, tough choices, and the ability to hit nothing but net from way downtown. Wesley Snipes and Woody Harrelson star as ball-toting hustlers who learn hard lessons on the hard pavement of the inner-city courts.

Hoop Dreams (1994)

This unflinching and carefully focused documentary follows the lives and dreams of William Gates and Arthur Agee, two high school stars with NBA aspirations. Uncompromising in its portrayal and outlook, the film is a harsh criticism of American social systems that can't adequately deal with poverty or fairly treat its victims. But the underlying message is that failure can be its own reward and that making an effort is as important as achieving a goal.

Space Jam (1996)

A loving tribute to the majestic magnificence of Michael Jordan and the wacky weirdness of cartoon characters such as Bugs Bunny and Daffy Duck, this animated family film is pure entertainment. The plot follows Jordan, who is sucked into Looney Tune Land to help the classic Warner Bros. characters in a space-age basketball game against alien invaders. Other sports legends, such as Charles Barkley, Larry Bird, and Patrick Ewing, make cameo appearances.

He Got Game (1998)

Basketball serves as a metaphor for examining the tenuous one-on-one relationship between an imprisoned father (Denzel Washington) and his son (NBA All-Star Ray Allen). Director Spike Lee carefully crafts a well-paced story and extracts a believable, often brilliant, performance out of Allen, who handles the complexities of the role with the same dexterity that he often flashes on the hard court.

Love & Basketball (2000)

The title says it all. This engaging and emotional tale tells the story of a pair of star-crossed lovers (Omar Epps and Sanaa Lathan) whose bittersweet romance is complicated by daunting dreams, hopeful aspirations, and hard choices. Throw in some brilliant basketball, and you have a winning recipe that cooks courtside.

O (2001)

Call it "The Bard Under the Boards." This compelling, intricate overhaul of Shakespeare's *Othello* examines the relationship between an African American basketball star—the only black student in an all-white prep school—and his girlfriend, who is also the dean's daughter. As in the classic play, this updated tale is fraught with jealousy, doubt, and revenge, all of which collide in a chilling climax.

10 Classic Amusement Park Rides

Roller coasters get all the attention. But what about the tamer rides with shorter lines and more relaxed height restrictions? Read on to learn about the favorites among the lesser-known rides. Some are unique, some have been copied for decades, but all of them are vital to the atmosphere of the midway.

✳   ✳   ✳   ✳

1. **Tilt-A-Whirl:** In 1926, Herbert Sellner finished his design for the Tilt-A-Whirl and began building one in his backyard. Sellner's ride involved seven cars attached at various fixed pivot points on a rotating platform that raised and lowered itself. The cars themselves were free spinning, but when you added the centrifugal force and the platform's gravitational pull on the cars, they would wildly spin in countless directions at variable speeds. Calculated chaos ensued. Since then, Sellner Manufacturing Company has built more than 1,000 Tilt-A-Whirls and inspired hundreds of knockoffs. Those who look a little green or lose their lunch of hot dogs, cotton candy, and soda pop are probably just coming off a Tilt-A-Whirl.

2. **Ferris Wheel:** Ah, the mighty Ferris wheel—provider of a million romantic moments and breathtaking views. For the World's Columbian Exposition of 1893 in Chicago, engineer George Ferris presented fair organizers with his idea of a giant rotating wheel that would carry passengers in cars attached around the outer edge. He convinced organizers to allow him to build the structure, which would rival France's Eiffel Tower. Indeed, Ferris's wheel, which cost $380,000 and stood 264 feet tall with a wheel diameter of 250 feet, was a huge success. Each car held 60 people, and, at 50 cents a ride, the wheel was

one of the most popular attractions at the World's Fair. The Ferris wheel is a must-have for any carnival, and thousands of replications continue to delight passengers of all ages.

3. **Insanity:** Built in 2005 at the top of the Stratosphere Hotel Tower in Las Vegas, this ride isn't kidding around. The second-highest thrill ride in the world at 906 feet above terra firma (second to its nearby Stratosphere brother, "Big Shot"), the Insanity arm extends 64 feet over the edge of the hotel tower, spinning passengers at top speeds. If that's not insane enough for you, hang on. Soon, the spinning gets even faster, and riders are propelled upward at a 70-degree angle. Insanity creators claim that "riders will experience the thrill of being flung over the edge of the tower" as they look down for a couple of breathless seconds at a glittering Las Vegas far below.

4. **Scrambler:** There are many names for this ride and its variations, but Americans usually call it the Scrambler. Whatever name is emblazoned on its side, this ride is fast—really fast. Picture this: the ride has three arms. On the ends of each of those arms are clusters of individual cars, each on a smaller arm of its own. When the Scrambler starts, the main arm and the little arms all rotate. The outermost arms are slowed and the inner arms are accelerated, creating an illusion of frighteningly close collisions between the cars and their passengers. The Scrambler proves that you don't have to go on a roller coaster to lose your lunch or have the wits scared out of you.

5. **Bumper Cars:** If you've ever wanted to recreate the excitement and thrill of a fender bender, this is your ride! Bumper cars (or "dodgem cars"), which were introduced in the 1920s, feature a large ring or pen with a graphite floor designed to decrease friction. Riders climb into miniature electric cars that draw power from an overhead grid and proceed to slam into the other cars in the pen. Wide rubber

bumpers keep things safe—as safe as you can get with no brakes! Still, bumper cars are so popular you'll find them in just about every theme park, county fair, or carnival you visit—just follow the crashing noises and laughter.

6. **"It's a Small World"**: The theme song to "It's a Small World" is woven into American (and international) pop culture—even if you've never been to a Disney theme park, you probably know the chorus. In 1964, the World's Fair came to New York, and Walt Disney and team created animatronic children of the world that featured anthems from various countries around the globe. In order to streamline the ride, which takes guests on boats through the animated panoramas, composers Robert and Richard Sherman came up with the now famous tune. Many find the "small world" experience to be a little naive and simplistic, but that's what they were going for—people everywhere getting along so well they sing songs and hold hands. All day. For hours.

7. **Log Rides:** If you were a lumberjack in America in the late 1800s, a "log ride" wasn't something you'd line up to do. Log flumes were handmade channels created by loggers to transport felled trees to the sawmill.

Stories of lumberjacks riding logs down the flume inspired the many versions of the log rides we know today. The first one, called El Aserradero ("the sawmill" in Spanish), was located at Six Flags Over Texas back in 1963. Passengers boarded a hollowed out "log" and rushed down the flume, getting soaked in the process. The ride was so popular that the park added another log ride a few years later. Famous log rides include Disney's Splash Mountain and Perilous Plunge at Knott's Berry Farm in California, the tallest and steepest log ride with a 115-foot drop.

8. **The Haunted Mansion:** The "Happiest Place on Earth" gets a bit scary with the Haunted Mansion, another juggernaut of an amusement park attraction created by the

fine folks at Disney. The ride opened in August 1969 in Disneyland and featured ghosts, murderous brides, blood-spilling families, and a host of other specters designed to scare park-goers silly as they ride through in a "doom buggy." The Haunted Mansion is among the most popular Disney rides in history, and it even inspired a movie— *The Haunted Mansion*, starring Eddie Murphy, was released in 2003.

9. **The Rotor:** Quick! Get up and twirl around as fast as you can for three straight minutes, then jump as high as you can into the air! Feel that free-falling, vertigo sensation? If not, why not go on a rotor ride? Designed in the 1940s by engineer Ernst Hoffmeister, the Rotor has many versions in theme parks all over the world. The premise is pretty much a simple lesson in centrifugal force: Take a large barrel and revolve the walls of said barrel really fast. When it's going super fast, drop the bottom out of the barrel, and watch as all the people inside stick to the walls. Other names for this simple but popular ride include Gravitron and Vortex.

10. **Carousel:** The most elegant of all amusement park rides, the carousel dates back to around A.D. 500. Drawings from this time period show riders in baskets circling a post. The carousel, or merry-go-round, remains a carnival staple worldwide. The ride consists of a rotating platform with seats that move up and down. The seats are the really special part, made of wood, fiberglass, or plastic and shaped to look like decorated animals, such as deer, cats, fish, rabbits, giraffes, and, of course, horses. Old carousels and carousel pieces can be worth lots of money these days depending on the level of artistry that went into their manufacture. Fun for young and old alike, even when the Triple-Threat-Xtreme-Screamer roller coaster is phased out, the carousel will still be turning round.

The House of David

They were barnstorming religious proselytizers—and snazzy ballplayers, too.

✳ ✳ ✳ ✳

I N BENTON HARBOR, Michigan, around the turn of the 20th century, a religious community called the Israelite House of David was looking for ways to earn money. As a fundraiser in 1907, the House of David folks opened an ice cream parlor, which was so successful it rapidly expanded into a full-scale amusement park with a zoo, miniature car races, bowling alleys, miniature train rides, and a dance hall. Another feature of the amusement park was a ball field, complete with a two-tiered grandstand.

Unusual Barnstormers

By 1913, ball games were part of the regular weekend activities. Thanks to some genuine baseball talent, the House of David was soon playing games around the region against local nines, and by 1920 they were a full-time barnstorming team, traveling throughout the Midwest with great success. One reason they stood out was because of the way they looked: They became famous for their long hair and beards, which were highly unusual in the United States at the beginning of the 20th century. Another reason was their skill: These players were good at what they did. And in the fifth inning of every game, they really turned on the charm, pausing to do a little Globetrotter-style performance—the legendary "pepper game," in which three members of the team did impressively energetic, nearly magical, tricks with the ball as they tossed it around. The original pepper stars, Jesse "Doc" Tally, John Tucker, and George Anderson, would throw the ball back and forth, gradually increasing the speed and using sleight-of-hand tricks that made the ball seem to disappear, delighting the crowds.

The team held its own in barnstorming games against major-leaguers and often traveled with the Negro League Kansas City Monarchs. And when the prime club was on the road, various "house" teams were established—including a girls' team and a junior boys' team.

Bringing Down the House

Over the first ten years or so of their existence, the House of David teams won about 75 percent of their games. "Membership" requirements were loosened to attract star players to the traveling team. Grover Cleveland Alexander played with the team for a time. So did female players Babe Didrikson and Jackie Mitchell. In 1934, the team won the prestigious Denver Post semipro championship, with the great Satchel Paige and his personal catcher, Cy Perkins, joining up for a time to give them a little boost. And yep, these visitors were made to don false beards to fit in with the rest of the team. (The ladies, however, were exempt.)

At one time there were as many as three teams with legitimate claims to the House of David name, but there were also totally bogus "H of D" teams. These groups, who had no connection to the official religious group, understood the promotional value of the name and donned fake beards for the purpose. At one time there was even a team of African Americans calling themselves the "Black House of David."

The House of David was easily the most recognizable of the white barnstorming teams during their 40 years of existence. As members of the community aged, the league died out, but teams with the "H of D" moniker and facial hair played in weekend semipro leagues and barnstormed as late as 1955, and the religious organization exists to this day.

Seventy-plus-point Scrabble Words

Word and Definition	Points
highjack: same as hijack, to seize a vehicle while in transit	78
quartzy: same as quartzose, resembling quartz or taking on the qualities of it	78
bezique: a card game	77
caziques: native chiefs of West Indian aborigines	77
jukebox: an automated phonograph that is usually coin-operated	77
mezquit: same as mesquite, which is a spiny tree or shrub	77
oxazepam: a tranquilizing drug	77
quixotry: quixotic (extremely idealist) action or thought	77
quickly: with speed, rapidly, very soon	76
squeezer: one who squeezes or presses forcibly together	76
whizbang: slang term for a highly explosive shell or firecracker	76
zinkify: to zincify, which is to coat with zinc	76
zombify: to turn into a zombie	76
asphyxy: the condition that results from interruption of respiration	75
muzhiks: a Russian peasant in czarist times	75
packwax: same as paxwax, a strong ligament that supports the back of the head	75
quetzal: a bird with brilliant plumage	75
quizzers: those who quiz	75

Eye of the Tiger(-ess)

Think you're so tough? Read on to learn what it takes to be an amateur female boxer.

Q: What inspired you to take up boxing?

A: My grandpa was an amateur boxer in the '40s, so I have always been a fan. They sanctioned women's boxing in 1994, and I took it up in 1998. I never knew I would get that addicted.

Q: What's so addictive?

A: You never stop learning, and it's a personal challenge. It's really not about winning or losing against the opponent—it's about continually challenging yourself. A lot of people don't know that. They see a street fight and think that's what it is, and actually, it's a game of points. And there are different strategies you use in different moments, so it's not about just punching.

Q: How do you prepare for a fight?

A: Practice, practice, and more practice! Each opponent has a different style—you never know what you're gonna face. So the only way to get around that is to train for all of those situations.

Q: What's the feeling in the ring?

A: Everyone's a little nervous. There's never a fear of being injured—it's very safe. However, there's a fear of losing, there's a fear of not doing your best. You're also exposed; it's you versus another person. And if they win, it means they're better than you.

Q: What stereotypes have you run into?

A: For female boxers, it's very unexpected that women can box, period. It's a very traditional, old-school sport and even people within the game don't always support the women, because they view it as a man's sport. I also think people are surprised that you can be a professional, you can be feminine outside of the ring, and then also be a national champion.

Odd Amusements in Old Atlantic City

Long before it was the home of glittering gambling dens, the Atlantic City Boardwalk was home to some of the oddest and most outrageous amusements ever to grace a coast. Here's a look at the boardwalk during its heyday, from about 1890 to 1940.

✳ ✳ ✳ ✳

THE FIRST BOARDWALK was built in Atlantic City, but not as an entertainment center—it was made for people to scrape the sand off their shoes before they entered the city's hotels. However, it didn't take American capitalists long to realize that there was gold in them there boards. From the 1890s onward, the boardwalk became a bustling bastion of business. As Atlantic City grew in popularity, it became America's playground—with an emphasis on *play*.

Around & Around

Before the Ferris wheel was invented in 1893, Atlantic City had the Epicycloidal Diversion in the 1870s. It consisted of four wheels, each about 30 feet in diameter, that rested on a 10-foot-high revolving platform. Each wheel had cars for 16 people. Not only did the wheels revolve up and down, but they also turned sideways in a circle. The effect was that of a Ferris wheel on top of a merry-go-round.

Another popular attraction was the Haunted Swing, which appeared in the 1890s. Folks piled in the middle of what looked like a room in a normal house. In the middle of the room hung a large swing, where people sat down. The swing would then move back and forth at tremendous speed, until finally it flipped completely over as the objects in the room, including a chair, bureau, and rug, remained totally stationary. Only later did the riders realize that it was the room that was spinning around, while they stayed completely still in the swing.

Walk (and Dive) with the Animals

The Atlantic City Boardwalk was the place to see talented animals strut their stuff. For a price, you could see a chicken hit a home run (or possibly a *fowl* ball), watch the fur fly as two cats slugged it out in a tiny boxing ring, or observe a man dancing with a tiger.

However, the most famous and longest-running animal act was the High Diving Horse, an act in which horses dove from a tower into a pool of water dozens of times daily. Some horses would stand at the top of the platform for minutes, building up unbearable suspense in the waiting crowd below. Others, however, would just climb to the top and immediately jump down. "You can lead a horse to water, but you can't teach him showmanship," said one of the trainers. Two attempts to revive the tradition (one in 1993, and, most recently, 2012) were thwarted by animal rights activists.

Oddities Abound

One popular spectacle was the giant, 14-ton Underwood typewriter. Built for $100,000 by the Underwood Corporation, the machine was 1,728 times the size of a regular typewriter and had a mile-long ribbon. Operated by using a normal-sized typewriter, the giant machine typed on an equally enormous piece of paper.

The curious could also visit the Wild Man of Borneo, who wore animal skins and chewed raw bones, and "America's Luckiest Fool," Alvin "Shipwreck" Kelly, who sat for 49 days on a Steel Pier flagpole. (That's right: Flagpole sitting was a fad in the 1920s.)

Then there were the daredevils, who dived, dropped, and jumped from all manner of things into the Atlantic Ocean nearby. This became quite the rage until a sudden shift in the winds one day concluded the performance of one poor soul in shocking fashion by sending him into electrical power lines instead of the ocean.

Ah, the Atlantic City of old—a place where the Protestant work ethic took a good beating. As *The New York Times* noted, "... in New York, play is unfortunately adulterated with work. But in Atlantic City, work is not even a grim spectre in the background."

The Thrill of the Joust

The medieval competition that became known as jousting brought together horsemanship, battle-honed knights, and the brutal competitiveness of feudal Europe.

✳ ✳ ✳ ✳

Spurred into Action

YOU SPUR YOUR horse, and in an instant you're charging forward. The track is 80 yards long. There is a marker at 20 yards, and when you reach it you had better be in full gallop. You sit high in the saddle, slightly tippy with the weight of your armor and the 15-pound heft of your lance. Your fighting hand is cosseted by a heavy gauntlet, and the bell-like vamplate just forward of your grip gives some additional protection. You need it because another rider, very much like you, urged his own mount onward at the moment you spurred yours, and now he's coming at you, ceremonial plumes pushed horizontal by the power of his charge, clods of earth leaping from the impacts of his horse's hooves. You present virtually the same picture to him. Each of you grips the lance in your right hand, which means that the weapon must be angled across the crest of your horse's neck, toward your opponent. When it comes, the impact will not be as powerful as if struck dead-on, but angled lance or not, the force generated by the weight of the speeding horses will be crushing.

The 80 yards have disappeared in what seems like a heartbeat. Lances lowered, now, you and the man you face are mirror images. In another instant, you'll feel the shock of impact, and half an instant after that you'll still be in your saddle—or on your back in the dirt, the wind pushed from your lungs, defeated.

Joust Another Day for a Knight

This is jousting (sometimes called "tilting"), a practice that originated with the gladiators of ancient Rome but has more recognizable roots in Europe of the tenth century. It was then that mounted knights emerged as a potent and much-feared fighting force. The joust began as a way for these warriors to hone their horsemanship and refine their use of the lance, the weapon favored by armored aggressors during the Middle Ages.

In 1066—the year William the Conqueror invaded England and introduced the "feudal" system of land division— a French knight named Godfrey de Preuilly combined the necessity of practice with the art of formal competition. A mounted knight sized up his opponent "between the limbs," the area protected by armor. The winning knight was the one who unseated or severely stunned the other.

Today, dozens of jousting clubs operate in the United States and Canada. The Jousting Hall of Fame in Mount Solon, Virginia, has hosted an annual tournament since 1821. And in 1962, jousting became the official sport of the State of Maryland.

"A true knight is fuller of bravery in the midst, than in the beginning of danger."

—Sir Philip Sidney

Defining Moments in Sports Terminology

Fore: This term is likely borrowed from the military. When artillery shells were fired from cannons situated behind friendly troops, a warning cry of "beware before" was often used to give warning. The term was shortened to *fore* and used to warn linkside duffers that wayward golf balls were headed their way.

Slam Dunk, Air Ball, Charity Stripe, Finger Roll: Although the term *dunk* was commonly used to describe the action of propelling a basketball through the hoop from above the rim, the phrase *slam dunk* was coined by the late Los Angeles Lakers announcer Francis "Chick" Hearn. The colorful commentator also originated the terms *air ball* (ball that misses the entire backboard), *charity stripe* (foul line), and *finger roll* (rolling the ball off the fingertips).

Gridiron: The playing field for football is marked with a series of parallel lines that form a grid. In the early years of the game, an astute—and presumably sober—football fan noticed that the pattern of lines resembled a gridiron, a grate used to grill or broil foods. The name stuck.

Baltimore Chop: When he was playing for the Baltimore Orioles in the 1890s, baseball pioneer John McGraw would often slap or chop down on the ball, causing the stitched orb to bounce high in the air off the hardened area of dirt around home plate. The technique often allowed the speedy tactician to reach first base safely and became a useful offensive strategy.

Can of Corn: The phrase, which describes a pop fly that is easy to catch, comes from the era of the old-time grocery store. To reach an object on a high shelf, the grocer would use a pole or a stick to knock the item—such as a can of corn—off its perch and catch it in the fold of his apron, which he fanned out like a net firefighters might use.

Birdie, Eagle, Albatross: The terms *birdie* and *eagle* originated in the United States in 1899. When a duffer struck the dimpled orb particularly well or knocked the pill close to the pin, he was said to have hit "a bird of a shot." Soon, making a score under par on a hole was dubbed a *birdie*. In keeping with the feathery phonetics, a score two shots better than par was called an *eagle*. A double eagle, a hole played three strokes under par, is also known as an *albatross*, the rarest of birds.

Sudden Death: The origin of the term in sports comes from the wild, wild West but not from the gunslingers of the era. Gamblers used the phrase *sudden death* to describe any outcome that was decided by a single or final toss of the dice or flip of a coin. Mark Twain is often credited with originating the expression when he used it in an article he wrote describing "rot gut whiskey."

Underdog: The origin of the term is debatable, but its meaning is clear. The favorite to win—be it best in show or first in the race—is the top dog. All others are bottom—or under—dogs. The first known use of the phrase comes from a poem printed in various American newspapers in 1859 called "The Under Dog of the Fight." The key passage reads: "I shall always go for the weaker dog,/For the under dog in the fight."

Red Sox Nation: The blame for the name "Red Sox Nation" can be laid on the desk of *Boston Globe* feature writer Nathan Cobb. The fanatical fraternity was first mentioned on October 20, 1986, in an article Cobb wrote about how baseball fans in Connecticut were divided in their devotion to the Boston Red Sox and New York Mets during the 1986 World Series.

Biggest Soccer Riots of All Time

Despite its lack of popularity in the United States, soccer is by far the most popular sport worldwide. Only slightly less popular, though, is the less skilled sport of "soccer rioting"—also known as hooliganism. Here are some of the biggest riots in soccer history.

✳   ✳   ✳   ✳

Lima, Peru: May 24, 1964—This one was a doozy. During an Olympic qualifying match between Peru and Argentina, frenzied Peruvian fans grew irate when referees disallowed a goal for the home team. The resulting riot left 300 people dead and 500 injured.

Calcutta, India: August 16, 1980—Tensions were already high in post-partition India when an official's call sparked rioting during a soccer match in Calcutta. The result: 16 dead, 100 injured.

Brussels, Belgium: May 29, 1985—Nobody does soccer riots like the British, who are so good they can cause riots in other countries. Take the case of the "Heysel Disaster"—a match in Brussels between British team Liverpool and Italian club Juventus. The game hadn't even begun when a crowd of drunk Liverpool supporters charged toward a group of Juventus fans. The stampede caused a stadium wall to collapse, resulting in 39 deaths and a five-year ban on all British soccer teams in Europe.

Zagreb, Croatia: May 13, 1990—In a grim harbinger of the ethnic violence that would ensnare the region over the next few years, Serbs and Croats fought each other before, during, and after a match between the Dinamo Zagreb and the Red Star Belgrade soccer teams, leaving hundreds wounded and throwing the city into a state of chaos.

Orkney, South Africa: January 13, 1991—Fights broke out in the grandstand during a game between the Kaizer Chiefs and Orlando Pirates after a disputed goal. In the ensuing rush of panicked fans trying to flee the fights, more than 40 people were killed and another 50 were injured. Ironically, most of the deaths were a result of being crushed against riot-control fencing. Fans of these two teams would combine for another riot in 2001, in which 43 people were killed.

Accra, Ghana: May 9, 2001—Unruly fans throwing bottles and chairs onto the field during a Ghanaian soccer match were bad enough, but to make it worse, police responded by firing tear gas into the jammed grandstands. More than 100 people were killed in the resulting panic.

Moscow, Russia: June 9, 2002—When Russia lost to Japan in the 2002 World Cup, Russian fans decided to express their disappointment by setting fire to Moscow. The ensuing riots left one dead and more than two dozen injured, including a group of Japanese tourists.

Basel, Switzerland: May 13, 2006—The Swiss might be neutral when it comes to wars, but they certainly are passionate about their football. Never was this more apparent than when FC Basel lost their chance to win the Swiss League title when FC Zurich scored a late goal in their match. The resulting riot—which included fans storming the field and attacking FC Zurich's players—resulted in more than 100 injuries and became known as the "Disgrace of Basel."

Manchester, England: May 2008—Observers knew there was going to be trouble when hooligans began fighting the day *before* the 2008 UEFA Cup Final. But the rioters kicked it up a notch on game day, attacking police officers and lighting things on fire in a sad display that became known as the "Battle of Piccadilly." The impetus? The failure of a large television screen erected to give fans without tickets a view of the game.

Fast Facts

✳ Franklin Delano Roosevelt was an avid poker player, once rushing from a game directly to the microphone to give one of his signature Fireside Chats. As he delivered the address, he absentmindedly shuffled some poker chips, rendering portions of his speech inaudible.

✳ In 1979, the cable sports network ESPN launched its first broadcast in the United States.

✳ The Bible contains 32 references to dogs, but none to cats.

✳ A mouse only takes 35 days to reach its adult sexual maturity.

✳ In 1843, the first commercial Christmas card was printed in England, using illustrations by John Calcott Horsley, a noted London artist of the time. The press run was 1,000 cards. Today, in the United States alone, two billion cards are sent every Christmas—something of a hallmark.

✳ The average snail lives six years.

✳ Every single U.S. president has worn glasses at least some of the time.

✳ Before Popeye, Olive Oyl's boyfriend was named Ham Gravy.

✳ Prior to his presidential career, Gerald Ford spent some time as a male model.

✳ The most commonly used letter in the English language is "e." The most common consonant is "t," and the most common second letter in a word is "h." (No surprise—the most popular word in the English language is "the"!)

✳ There are pink dolphins in the Amazon River.

✳ The world's largest bagel weighed 868 pounds and was a full six feet in diameter. It was made at Bruegger's Bagels in Syracuse, New York.

✳ The smallest will in history was written on the back of a postage stamp—complete with witness signatures.

✳ The lit end of a cigarette reaches approximately 1,292° F when the smoker inhales.

Which Came First, the Chicken or the Crazy Crab?

Mascot alert! The unforgettable and the regrettable.

✳ ✳ ✳ ✳

BASEBALL TEAMS HAVE employed mascots as good luck charms and used illustrated characters to promote themselves for as long as the game has been played. But the furry and feathery variety dancing atop dugout roofs today can trace their heritage to a San Diego radio station promotion in 1974. It was then that KGB-FM radio convinced college student Ted Giannoulas to dress up as a chicken and distribute eggs to children at the San Diego Zoo. Encouraged by the success of the stunt, Giannoulas began appearing in costume at Padres games that year and in short stead became the biggest baseball star hatched in San Diego since Ted Williams. By the end of the 1970s, the Chicken's success had prompted other teams, including the Pittsburgh Pirates (the Pirate Parrot), Philadelphia Phillies (the Phillie Phanatic), St. Louis Cardinals (Fredbird), and Montreal Expos (Youppi), to introduce their own characters. In the 1990s, a second wave of mascots arrived as part of an effort to market the game to children: In 2006, every team except the Dodgers, Cubs, and Yankees employed at least one mascot.

The San Diego Chicken: Despite never having been an "official" Padres character—the Swinging Friar has served that role since the team's founding in 1969—the Chicken has become a traveling attraction. It is famed for physical comedy routines that include presenting an eye chart to umpires in a mock challenge to calls that don't go in the Padres' favor and, with the help of a participating catcher, re-creating the Pete Rose–Ray Fosse All-Star Game collision, complete with slow-motion replay.

The Phillie Phanatic: Phillies team owner Bill Giles introduced this wide-bodied, long-snouted creature in 1978. It won cheers in a city otherwise famous for its hair-trigger boo reflex. Originally embodied by Dave Raymond, a Phillies mailroom clerk, the Phanatic was at his best when making a straight man of whichever Phillie opponent least wanted to be part of the act. Dodgers manager Tommy Lasorda, with his low tolerance for on-field antics, was a favorite foil.

Mr. Met: The original live-action costumed mascot, the baseball-domed Mr. Met first appeared on the cover of a 1963 yearbook and debuted live with the opening of Shea Stadium in 1964. His cheery gait and smiling eyes delight children but hide a mischievous nature, perhaps suggesting that the disappearance of his one-time companion, Lady Met, is a mystery best left unsolved. Though well into middle age, Mr. Met is still one of the most visible and active Mets. His schedule of party and event appearances, merchandise tie-ins, and TV commercial spots rivals the team's most marketable stars.

Youppi: The fluffy orange giant, whose name means "Hooray" in French and whose uniform number was !, became the first two-sport anthropomorphized character. He served the Montreal Expos from 1979 until they carelessly left him behind when they moved to Washington, D.C., in 2005. Their loss was the Montreal Canadiens' gain: Youppi bolted to the NHL, signing a reported six-figure deal with the Canadiens.

The Pirate Parrot: Kevin Koch, the actor behind the green mask of the Pittsburgh Pirates' mascot for its first six years, went undercover in more ways than one: He made a drug deal while wearing a hidden transmitter to help the FBI secure evidence in its investigation of drug use among ballplayers. The dealer, whom Koch reportedly introduced to some Pirates players, later pleaded guilty to 20 counts of selling cocaine during the 1985 Pittsburgh drug trials.

Dandy: A pin-striped bird with a mustache resembling relief pitcher Sparky Lyle's, Dandy was the official mascot of the Yankees from 1982 to 1985—a fact the team's own stuffed shirts, including owner George Steinbrenner, professed not to recall. Ultimately, a cuddly mascot had difficulty finding a home within the Yankees' stodgy corporate image. Dandy rarely made an appearance beyond the upper reaches of Yankee Stadium.

Crazy Crab: Intentionally hideous, Crazy Crab was unveiled as a subversive "anti-mascot" in 1984 by the San Francisco Giants, who encouraged fans to boo the bug-eyed, belligerent crustacean and whose scoreboard admonitions—PLEASE DO NOT THROW THINGS AT THE CRAZY CRAB—practically begged fans to do just that. After a season of fan abuse, both physical (bottles and garbage hurled from the stands) and verbal (booing, hissing, and epithets), the Crazy Crab was retired. In 2006, sparked in part by a fan petition, Crazy Crab appeared during an '80s throwback promotion. The Crab, true to his sullen nature, attacked Stomper, the mascot of the visiting Oakland A's.

Mettle: Ignoring the fact that they had a perfectly acceptable mascot in Mr. Met, in 1979 the New York Mets unveiled a live mule as their new mascot. Mettle, like the team that year, often left a mess on the field, and he was quietly sent out to pasture after a single season, the worst at the gate in Met history.

✳ Ancient Egypt had its own version of the Olympics, featuring gymnastics, javelin, running, swimming, and other events.

✳ The modern marathon owes its name to the story of an ancient Greek messenger who ran nearly 26 miles from the battlefield of Marathon to Athens to proclaim the Greek victory. The story is almost certainly untrue, but the name stuck.

✳ Until 1975, rules required that all major-league baseballs be covered in horsehide. As horsehide became more expensive, it became acceptable for balls to be covered in cowhide.

Pinball Wizardry!

Fun facts about America's favorite table game.

✳ ✳ ✳ ✳

BEFORE THE ADVENT of video games, pinball was the activity of choice for people with a few minutes to kill and some change in their pocket. For many aficionados, the caroming steel ball, flashing lights, and dizzying sounds had an almost hypnotic effect as players competed for high score.

Genuine pinball games are increasingly difficult to find in arcades and bars, but it didn't used to be that way. In fact, from the 1930s through the '80s, pinball was ubiquitous.

In the Beginning

The basic concept of pinball dates back to the 1700s and a popular French table game called Bagatelle, which featured a ball, fixed pins, and holes for the ball to fall into. The game produced numerous variations and improvements over the years; in the 1930s, the first coin-operated "marble games" or "pin games" were introduced, which became pinball as we know it today. The first truly popular pinball game was Baffle Ball, introduced in 1931 by David Gottlieb. For a penny, players got to try their luck with five to seven balls—a real bargain during the Great Depression, when inexpensive fun was at a premium.

Pinball and the Law

As pinball became more popular, it didn't take long for the law to ruin everyone's fun. Some cities considered pinball a game of chance and either regulated the machines or banned them outright. New York City instituted a pinball ban in the early 1940s. For game buffs, a day that will truly live in infamy is January 21, 1942, when the city conducted a sweep and confiscated an estimated 3,525 pinball machines. Within weeks, hundreds more were located and destroyed, their wooden legs used to make police nightsticks, and their metal components—nearly five tons of the stuff, including 3,000 pounds of steel balls—were donated to the war effort. It wasn't until 1976 that pinball was officially declared legal again in New York City.

Play Ball!

As a game, pinball is both very simple and quite complicated. It must be fun and easy enough that beginning players don't become frustrated, but not so easy that it ceases to be challenging to hardcore players. According to manufacturers, the average game should last between two and three minutes, and the player should receive a free game for every four games he or she plays.

The "tilt" function, which penalizes players for trying to finesse the ball by physically moving the machine, was first instituted in 1932. Interestingly, its inventor, Harry Williams, originally called the function "The Stool Pigeon." One day while watching players with the first prototypes, Williams overheard one unlucky guy exclaim, "Damn, I tilted it!" The rest, as they say, is history.

The cost of pinball, and the number of balls allotted per game, has greatly evolved over the years. In 1931, players received seven balls for a penny. Then it was ten balls for a nickel. In 1933, when steel balls replaced glass marbles, players received between five and seven balls for a nickel. By the late '60s, players got three five-ball games for a quarter. A decade later, it was two five-ball games for a quarter.

Pinball and Popular Culture

Pinball quickly ingratiated itself into American popular culture. Writer William Saroyan featured the games in two of his works, including the 1939 stage play *The Time of Your Life*.

Pinball has also been featured in Hollywood. The rock opera *Tommy* by The Who is about a messiahlike figure who is a pinball savant despite being deaf, mute, and blind (the movie version features a bedazzled Elton John singing "Pinball Wizard."). And in the 1978 movie *Tilt*, Brooke Shields played a young pinball champion who enters a tournament to help her musician boyfriend.

9 Ridiculous "Fans on the Field" Incidents

For these misguided fans, "Take Me out to the Ball Game" could just as easily have turned into "Jailhouse Rock."

✳ ✳ ✳ ✳

1. **Ten-Cent Beer Night**—In the planning stages, selling beer for a dime probably seemed like a good promotion back in 1974. But things got a little dicey after approximately 60,000 brews were sold. Fans at Cleveland Municipal Stadium stormed the field as the Indians played the Texas Rangers. Punches were thrown, chairs were used as weapons, and the Rangers were awarded the game.

2. **Hank Aaron Breaks Babe Ruth's Record**—Considering that Hank Aaron had received numerous death threats as he closed in on Babe Ruth's all-time home run record in 1974, it may have been ill-advised for fans to take to the field and run toward the future Hall of Famer—even if they only wanted to give him a congratulatory pat on the back.

3. **Morganna**—One baseball constant during the 1970s and 1980s was Morganna the Kissing Bandit. The top-heavy blonde became famous for running onto various ball fields to steal a kiss from a player. Among those puckered: George Brett, Pete Rose, and Nolan Ryan (the Ryan kiss resulted in her arrest).

4. **Flag-Burning Rescue**—Chicago Cubs center fielder Rick Monday wasn't amused when a pair of fans ran onto the field at Dodger Stadium on April 25, 1976. He was even less amused when the spectators prepared to set an American flag on fire. Monday swooped in and snatched the flag while police arrested the scofflaws. The stadium gave Monday a standing ovation.

5. **Disco Demolition Night**—A simple promotion—blowing up disco records—featuring popular Chicago radio disc jockey Steve Dahl turned into a mob scene on July 12, 1979, at Comiskey Park. Between games of a Chicago White Sox–Detroit Tigers doubleheader, Dahl exploded a collection of records. Within minutes, thousands of fans descended upon the field, forcing the ChiSox to forfeit Game 2.

6. **A Pitcher's Duel**—Fans are accustomed to booing pitchers when they give up key runs. One fan took it to the next level in 1995 after Cubs reliever Randy Myers gave up a home run to give the Houston Astros the lead. The man rushed the pitcher's mound, perhaps to give Myers some advice on what to throw next. Instead, Myers floored him with his forearm.

7. **Attacking Fans**—Houston right fielder Bill Spiers was on the receiving end of such an attack in 1999 as the team was playing the Milwaukee Brewers. He ended up with a welt under his left eye, a bloody nose, and whiplash. The fan ended up with a beating from pitcher Mike Hampton.

8. **Attacking Fans—a Different Approach**—Chad Kreuter and several members of the Los Angeles Dodgers put a little twist on this category when they chased a fan into the Wrigley Field seats after the man grabbed Kreuter's cap.

9. **Royals Coach Attacked**—Being an MLB coach is supposed to involve strategy and a fair amount of arm-waving. Defending yourself from blows by idiotic fans is not in the job description. Tell that to the shirtless White Sox fan who, along with his son, ran onto the field at U.S. Cellular in 2002 and began beating Kansas City Royals first-base coach Tom Gamboa.

The Sad Saga of Sonny Liston

Climbing up from utter poverty, this world heavyweight champ found controversial success inside the boxing ring but couldn't maintain his balance on the outside.

✳ ✳ ✳ ✳

CHARLES "SONNY" LISTON was born the son of an impoverished sharecropper in rural Arkansas, probably on May 8, but the year of his birth is unknown. Though many who knew him said he was born in 1927, Liston himself claimed he was born in 1932, and contemporary documents seem to back him up. Emotionally and physically abused, young Liston was not unhappy when his parents split up and his mother moved to St. Louis—in fact, he followed her there as soon as he could.

Hard Time

Liston was only in his early teens when he made his way north, and like everyone else in his family, he was illiterate. He had his imposing build going for him, however, and this led local organized crime to recruit him as a debt collector. As long as Liston stuck to breaking kneecaps, he was to some degree under the mob's protection from law enforcement. But when he struck out on his own, robbing two gas stations and a restaurant with other youths in 1950, the police caught up to him, and he was busted. Liston pleaded guilty to two counts of robbery and two counts of larceny.

In the penitentiary, a priest noticed Liston's remarkable physique and urged him to take up boxing. Liston followed that advice, and after serving only two years, he was paroled to a team of "handlers" who worked for St. Louis mobster John Vitale. Vitale controlled Liston's contract for six years before selling it to Frankie Carbo and Blinky Palermo, underworld figures on the East Coast. Eventually, Liston's criminal ties would lead him all the way to the U.S. Senate, where in 1960 he testified before a subcommittee investigating organized crime's control of boxing.

The Big Time

Liston's first professional fight lasted 33 seconds—he took out Don Smith with only one punch. Just five fights later, in a nationally televised bout in Detroit, he won an eight-round decision against John Summerlin. The odds had been long, so the fight garnered the young upstart a lot of attention. He suffered his first professional defeat—and a broken jaw—from his next opponent, Marty Marshall. Nevertheless, Liston moved steadily up the ranks, and finally, at Chicago's Comiskey Park in 1962, he became the heavyweight champion of the world by knocking out Floyd Patterson in the first round.

Fighting success did not keep him out of trouble with the law, however. A total of 19 arrests and a second jail sentence made Liston an unpopular figure on the American sports scene. Many of his fights were thought to be fixed. Unfortunately for him, Liston's most famous moment was one of defeat: his knockout by Muhammad Ali on May 25, 1965. In one of the most famous sports photos ever taken, *Sports Illustrated* photographer Neil Leifer shot Liston sprawled on the mat with a screaming Ali towering over him. Some claim that Ali's punch was a "phantom punch" that never connected and that Liston had taken a dive because he feared Ali's ties to the Nation of Islam.

Strange Death

On January 5, 1971, Liston was found dead in his Las Vegas home by his wife, Geraldine. Though the coroner ruled that he had died from heart failure and lung congestion, his body was in a state of decomposition, and there was much speculation that Liston had been murdered by unsavory associates. The man who came into the world so anonymously left it in fame, but with just as many unanswered questions.

The Sin Bin: Hockey's House of Humility

This is the time-out seat of professional sports, where hotheaded hockey players go "to feel shame." It is the penalty box, an off-ice office of purgatory for on-ice transgressors.

✳ ✳ ✳ ✳

FOR THE FIRST 50 years of the National Hockey League's existence, every league arena had only one penalty box, which meant that players who engaged in a lively tussle on the ice served their penance together, with only an obviously nervous league official sitting between them to act as a buffer. Quite often, the combatants would continue their fisted arguments off the ice and inside their temporary, cramped quarters.

Dill Gets Pickled

On one occasion, this led to the infamous "pickling" of New York Rangers' forward Bob Dill. On December 17, 1944, Dill and Montreal Canadiens fireball Maurice "The Rocket" Richard engaged in a raucous set-to that banished them both to the shower stall of shame. Inside the box, the obviously dazed and confused Dill attacked The Rocket again and received another sound thumping for his lack of common sense.

It wasn't until midway through the 1963–64 season that the league introduced a rule requiring every rink to have separate penalty benches. A particularly vicious confrontation between Toronto Maple Leaf Bob Pulford and Montreal Canadien Terry Harper on October 30, 1963, precipitated by Harper's questioning of Pulford's sexual preference, spearheaded the NHL's decision to arrive at a sensible solution.

Penalty Box VIPs

The undisputed king of the sin bin was Dave "Tiger" Williams, who logged nearly 4,000 minutes sitting on his punitive throne during his 15-year career in the NHL. Having spent his formative years with the Toronto Maple Leafs, Williams had a personal affinity for the Maple Leaf Gardens' penalty box, which he described as "a gross place to go. The guys in there are bleeding... and no one's cleaned the place since 1938."

Williams may hold the career mark for sin bin occupancy, but the rap sheet for a single-season sentence belongs to Dave "The Hammer" Schultz. During the 1974–75 campaign, the Philadelphia Flyers enforcer cooled his carcass in the hotel of humility for 472 minutes, nearly eight full games. He was so at home in the house, he actually recorded a single titled "The Penalty Box," which became something of a cult hit in and around the City of Brotherly Love.

Philadelphia's post of punition was also the scene of one of hockey's most hilarious highlights. During a game between the Flyers and Maple Leafs in 2001, Toronto tough guy Tie Domi was sent to the box. Upon his arrival in the cage, he was verbally accosted by a leather-lunged Philly fan named Chris Falcone, who wisely used the glass partition to shield himself from Domi. Known as "The Albanian Assassin," Domi responded to the goading by spraying his heckler with water. The broad-shouldered Falcone lunged toward Domi, fell over the glass, and landed in a heap at Domi's feet, which resulted in a comic wrestling match between lug head and lunatic.

Marathons: By the Numbers

* The first Olympic Marathon took place in 1896 and was 40,000 meters (24.85 miles) in length. Greek postal worker Spiridon Louis completed the course in 2 hours, 58 minutes, 50 seconds. His average pace was 7.11 minutes per mile.

* The Olympic Marathon length was changed to 26 miles, 385 yards at the 1908 Olympic Games in London. The length encompassed the distance between Windsor Castle and White City Stadium (26 miles). The 385 additional yards were added to this number to facilitate a finish point in front of King Edward VII's royal box.

* The distance of 26.2 miles was officially established at the 1924 Olympics in Paris. It remains the standard to this day.

* The first New York City Marathon was held in 1970. It featured only 127 competitors. In 2011, 47,323 runners completed the NYC Marathon.

* The first Boston Marathon was held on April 19, 1897. The race's length of 24.5 miles (a distance linking Metcalf's Mill in Ashland to the Irvington Oval in Boston) would be lengthened to 26.2 miles in 1927 to conform to Olympic standards.

* Marathon deaths are rare. A 1996 study performed by the USA Track and Field Road Running Information Center estimates roughly 1 death for every 50,000 runners.

* Statistics for the annual NYC Marathon are staggering. At the starting line, volunteers will dispense more than 90,000 bottles of water, 45,000 cups of coffee, and 42,000 PowerBars. As the race progresses, 62,370 gallons of water and 32,040 gallons of Gatorade will be consumed. Thirty-eight medical aid stations outfitted with 13,475 adhesive bandages, 5 tons of ice, and 390 tubs of Vaseline will be at the standby—just in case.

Chapter Three

Health and the Body

That Sweet 'Stache

From its ancient beginnings to its 1970s heyday, folks have continued to "split hairs" over the merits of the mighty mustache.

✳ ✳ ✳ ✳

A 'Stache Is Born

THE ANCIENT EGYPTIANS drew pictures of dudes with pencil-thin lip hair as early as 2650 B.C., while Confucius and his pals were sporting mustaches in the mid-sixth century B.C. But the 'stache's popularity didn't really start growing until the eighth century A.D., when King Charlemagne epitomized French chic by proudly bearing a mustache, while other Middle Agers were still grooming their beards.

Forbidden 'Stache

But 'stache growth was cut short in 1447, when English parliament officially banned the broom. A century later, King Henry VIII introduced a tax on facial hair of any kind (even though he personally sported both a beard and mustache).

When the Protestant Reformation began in the 16th century, their priests grew facial hair as a sign of protest against Catholic priests, who kept clean-shaven because it was thought that whiskers would trap or otherwise damage pieces of the holy sacrament. Still, while Queen Elizabeth I probably appreciated the sentiment, she wasn't a fan of the lip fuzz—maybe because the 'stache was a style worn by England's French enemy. So she reinstituted the facial hair tax.

In 1838, the King of Prussia nixed nose neighbors among his troops for fear it would compromise them in hand-to-hand battle (mustache yanking = pain).

Stylin' 'Stache

Nevertheless, by 1850, 'staches were back in a big way, both in Europe and in America, where New York dandies grew 'em slim and styled above the lip, thanks to special pomades, waxes, and dyes.

The Civil War saw the rise of handlebar- and walrus-style soup strainers, which led to the rugged "Wild West" whiskers popularized by gold rushers and outlaws of the 1870s. New products such as mustache combs and cups (which featured a special ledge to keep lip hair dry while drinking) catered to the mainstream mustache. Hirsute Hollywood heroes furthered the fuzz fad from the 1920s through the '40s with Charlie Chaplin's "toothbrush," Groucho Marx's thick broom and brows, and Clark Gable's debonair duster.

Armed and 'Stached

By the time World War I broke out in 1914, the military mustache was protocol for Americans and British alike. American GIs kept their 'staches small and sleek (so gas masks could seal tightly against their faces), while British troops favored the handlebar and toothbrush. In general, mustache style was a symbol of rank among British troops: Officers wore 'em waxed and pointy, while infantrymen's 'staches were bushy and droopy.

Post–World War II, the American facial-hair fad seemed to fade—likely a result of Hitler's hairy lip—even while the push-broom boom continued across Europe, with Salvador Dali and Albert Einstein among the many to sport serious 'stache.

Super 'Stache

The hippie movement of the '60s brought the mustache back to America's upper lips with its rebellion against clean-shaven culture. A decade later, the '70s 'stache took on a "tough guy" image thanks to Hollywood hunks such as Burt Reynolds and Robert Redford. By the end of the era, many a man bore broom. But as disco dwindled, so did the mustache, and by the time Tom Selleck's *Magnum P.I.* went off the air in 1988, the 'stache was being shaved.

Back in 'Stache?

But crumb catchers could be making a comeback: More and more celebrities are sporting them onscreen, and though most seem to be for comedic effect, the seed has been planted—perhaps the 'stache will make a triumphant return.

＊ While playing on Australia's national cricket team from 1985 to 1994, Merv Hughes took out an estimated $370,000 insurance policy on his trademark walrus mustache, which, combined with his 6' 4" physique and outstanding playing ability, made him one of the most recognized cricketers in the world.

＊ Self-made millionaire Charlie Finley bought the Kansas City A's in 1960. Although he became known for his series of wacky promotions to increase attendance at games, Finley was also well known—and infamously disliked—for micromanaging the team and the management. He often demanded that players change their style of play, and he fired any manager who publicly disagreed with him. He even paid bonuses to players who grew mustaches; pitcher Rollie Fingers' handlebar mustache was the most famous result of this.

14 Unusual Facts About the Human Body

1. Don't stick out your tongue if you want to hide your identity. Like fingerprints, every tongue print is unique!

2. Your pet isn't the only one in the house with a shedding problem. Humans shed about 600,000 particles of skin every hour. That works out to about 1.5 pounds each year, so the average person will lose around 105 pounds of skin by age 70.

3. An adult has fewer bones than a baby. We start off life with 350 bones, but because certain bones fuse together during growth, we end up with only 206 as adults.

4. Did you know that you get a new stomach lining every three to four days? Without this renewal, the strong acids your stomach uses to digest food would also digest your stomach.

5. Your nose is not as sensitive as a dog's, but it can remember 50,000 different scents.

6. The small intestine is about four times as long as the average adult is tall. If it weren't looped back and forth upon itself, its length of 18 to 23 feet wouldn't fit into the abdominal cavity, making things rather messy.

7. This will really make your skin crawl: Every square inch of skin on the human body has approximately 32 million bacteria on it, but fortunately, the vast majority of them are harmless.

8. The source of smelly feet, like smelly armpits, is sweat. And people sweat buckets from their feet. A pair of feet have 500,000 sweat glands and can produce more than a pint of sweat per day.

9. The air from a human sneeze can travel at speeds of 100 miles per hour or more.

10. Blood has a long road to travel: Laid end to end, there are about 60,000 miles of blood vessels in the human body. And the hard-working heart pumps the equivalent of 2,000 gallons of blood through those vessels every day.

11. You may not want to swim in your spit, but if you saved it all up, you could. In a lifetime, the average person produces about 25,000 quarts of saliva—enough to fill two swimming pools!

12. By 60 years of age, 60 percent of men and 40 percent of women will snore. But the sound of a snore can seem deafening. While snores average around 60 decibels (the noise level of normal speech), they can reach more than 80 decibels. Eighty decibels is as loud as the sound of a pneumatic drill breaking up concrete. Noise levels over 85 decibels are considered hazardous to the human ear.

13. Blondes may or may not have more fun, but they definitely have more hair. Hair color helps determine how dense the hair on your head is, and blondes (only natural ones, of course) top the list. The average human head has 100,000 hair follicles, each of which is capable of producing 20 individual hairs during a person's lifetime. Blondes average 146,000 follicles. People with black hair tend to have about 110,000 follicles, while those with brown hair are right on target with 100,000 follicles. Redheads have the least dense hair, averaging about 86,000 follicles.

14. If you're clipping your fingernails more often than your toenails, that's only natural. The nails that get the most exposure and are used most frequently grow the fastest. Fingernails grow fastest on the hand that you write with and on the longest fingers. On average, nails grow about one-tenth of an inch each month.

Need a Lift?

If you're not happy with the body you see in the mirror, you're not alone. According to the American Society of Plastic Surgeons, nearly 1.6 million cosmetic surgeries were performed in the United States in 2011. Here are the top 14 most common cosmetic surgeries and the average surgeon fee (in 2010) for each.

✳ ✳ ✳ ✳

1. **Breast augmentation:** Breast augmentation, or augmentation mammaplasty, is the enlarging of a woman's breasts using saline- or silicone-filled implants. There were 307,180 breast augmentation procedures performed in 2011, making this the top cosmetic surgery procedure. Physician's fees averaged $3,650.

2. **Rhinoplasty:** Commonly called a nose job, rhinoplasty is the reshaping of the nose. Rhinoplasty is popular— 243,772 rhinoplasty procedures were done in 2011. Rhinoplasty will run about $4,300.

3. **Liposuction:** Liposuction is the removal of fat deposits using a tube inserted beneath the skin; fat is then sucked out using a vacuum-like device. The procedure is often performed on the abdomen, buttocks, hips, thighs, and upper arms. Approximately 204,702 liposuctions were performed in 2011. This procedure will suck about $2,900 out of your wallet.

4. **Eyelid surgery:** In eyelid surgery, or blepharoplasty, drooping upper eyelids and bags below the eyes are corrected by removing extra fat, muscle, and skin. In 2011, 196,286 blepharoplasty procedures were performed. Although the procedure doesn't improve your sight, your eyes will look better as you write the $2,900 check for physician's fees.

5. **Face-lift:** Is anything actually being raised? Not really, but excess fat is removed and muscles are tightened before the

skin is redraped. Besides, face-lift is easier to say than rhytidectomy, the medical name of the procedure. No matter what you call it, a face-lift results in tighter skin on the face and neck. In 2011, 119,026 men and women had their faces lifted. Your face will be tighter, but you won't smile when you see the average bill of $6,600 for physician's fees.

6. **Tummy tuck:** In an abdominoplasty, extra fat and skin are removed and abdominal muscles are tightened in order to flatten the stomach. In 2011, plastic surgeons performed 115,902 tummy tucks at about $5,300 each.

7. **Breast lift:** A breast lift, or mastopexy, is performed in order to raise and reshape sagging breasts. The procedure removes extra skin and repositions the remaining tissue and nipples. In 2011, surgeons performed 90,679 breast lifts; the procedure's average cost was $4,400.

8. **Dermabrasion:** Although it sounds like a medieval torture tactic, 73,433 people received dermabrasion in 2011. With dermabrasion, wrinkles and facial blemishes are literally rubbed out as a surgeon uses a high-speed, rotating tool to scrape away the top layers of skin, leaving softer, newer layers. The actual procedure will leave you a little red in the face, but the cost won't—physician's fees averaged $875.

9. **Forehead lift:** This procedure straightens out lines and droops by removing tissue and tightening the forehead skin. Americans received 46,391 forehead lifts in 2011. The average fee was $3,200.

10. **Ear surgery:** Large ears or ears that prominently stick out from the head can cause a lot of grief, especially for children. That's why kids make up most of the patients who undergo ear surgery (otoplasty), where ear skin or cartilage is removed or bent back to bring each ear closer to the head. Some 26,433 otoplasty procedures were performed in 2011. Physician's fees ran about $3,000.

11. **Lip augmentation:** If your puckers aren't as prominent as you'd like, you can pump them up with lip augmentation, where a surgeon hollows out a portion of each lip and inserts an implant to give it more body. Overall, 25,477 lip augmentation procedures were performed in 2011. How many smackers did this surgery set patients back? Physician's fees averaged about $2,000.

12. **Chin augmentation:** Those who feel their face lacks a certain amount of proportion may have their chin altered to enhance their profile. Chin augmentation, or mentoplasty, usually involves either inserting an implant into the chin or changing the shape of the bone. In 2011, 20,680 chin augmentation surgeries were performed by surgeons. Physician's fees averaged $2,200.

13. **Breast reduction (men):** A condition called gynecomastia causes some men to develop womanly breasts. There are many possible causes of gynecomastia, including hormonal changes during puberty, drug use, tumors, genetic disorders, liver disease, and some medications. The larger breasts are often due to excess fat or glandular tissue; in a breast reduction surgery, this extra matter is removed. In 2011, 19,766 breast reduction surgeries were performed on men at an average cost of $3,400.

14. **Hair transplantation:** If things are a little too bare, a surgeon can reduce the amount of scalp you have or insert clusters of hair (plugs) right into the scalp. Depending on the technique used, several visits to the surgeon over 18 months may be required. Men and women alike were the recipients of 15,754 hair transplants in 2011, shelling out $4,750 in physician's fees.

Son of a Gun

In November 1874, an article in The American Medical Weekly told a fantastic tale. What follows is an odd "how they met" story indeed.

✳ ✳ ✳ ✳

ACCORDING TO DR. LeGrand G. Capers, the article's author, a bullet struck a Confederate soldier at the Battle of Raymond in Mississippi, ricocheted, then struck a young woman at a nearby farmhouse. Both survived. Capers noted that the "Minnie ball" (a soft lead bullet) first passed through the soldier's scrotum before it ricocheted, striking the unlucky woman in her abdominal cavity. Nine months later, she gave birth to an eight-pound son. With social dictates of the period acting as a driving force, Capers was called upon to explain how the virginal girl could have become impregnated.

Three weeks later the doctor was again summoned, this time by the young woman's grandmother, who asked the physician to examine the newborn's scrotum, which had become dangerously enlarged. The doctor immediately saw that something was wrong and decided to operate. To his utter amazement, Capers found a Minnie ball embedded in the child. He reasoned that the bullet had passed through the soldier's scrotum and collected sperm cells while on its way into the woman's reproductive system, thereby impregnating her. It then worked its way into the flesh of the fetus where it now lay.

According to Capers, the soldier was notified of the bizarre occurrence and he and the young woman met, eventually married, and produced two more children by the conventional method.

Though the story was published by *The American Medical Weekly* and reprinted elsewhere, it was found to be completely false. Dr. Capers had concocted the tale as a way to lampoon fictitious Civil War stories then making the rounds.

12 Odd Beauty Products Throughout History

Before there were department store beauty counters and drugstores, there were homemade cosmetics that often had some pretty funky ingredients. Even today, you might be surprised to learn what's in the items you throw into your makeup kit. But be forewarned—what we do for beauty can get pretty ugly...and dangerous.

✻ ✻ ✻ ✻

1. **Ambergris:** Ambergris—a highly flammable, waxy substance with a sweet, earthy odor—comes from the intestines of whales and is used in perfume manufacturing. Prior to the 18th century, men and women molded ambergris into beads that were worn as an aromatic necklace. Although whales excrete the substance naturally (it's jokingly called whale barf), synthetic ambergris is now made to prevent the slaughter of whales for this highly sought-after product.

2. **Wax:** Wax is a common ingredient in many hair products and facial cosmetics today, but the men and women of ancient Egypt used wax more creatively. They would stick a cone of pomade, or scented ointment, on the top of their head, and over time, their body heat would melt the wax and give off a pleasant aroma.

3. **Kohl:** Often made from soot, kohl was used for black eyeliner in ancient Egypt, North Africa, the Middle East, and Greece. Although kohl served to protect the eyes against the harsh sun and certain eye infections, some forms of the pigment contain lead—not exactly a safe ingredient. Lead poisoning can induce insanity and death.

4. **Carmine:** The cochineal bug is a bright red insect that hangs out mostly on cacti in places such as Peru, Chile,

Mexico, and the Canary Islands. For centuries, these bugs have been crushed for the carminic acid they produce, which is used to make a bright red dye called carmine. A common ingredient in lipsticks, rouges, and eye shadow, the dye is also synthetically produced today.

5. **Guanine:** Crystals of guanine, a compound made from fish scales and guano (the excrement of bats and sea birds), refract light in a lovely, pearly way. Guanine gives beauty products, such as shampoo, nail polish, and shimmering lotions, their shiny, glittery appearance.

6. **Boar Bristles:** All hairbrushes are not created equal, at least, according to fans of the boar bristle hairbrush. Boar bristle is scaly in texture, making it effective for cleaning the hair shaft, follicle, and scalp and distributing oil along the hair shaft. Boars  needn't be harmed for their bristles, just sheared like sheep. Boar bristle brushes can be found in fine salons and online for around $35.

7. **Chitosan:** Chitosan oligosaccharide is made from chitin, a starch found in the skeletons of shrimp, crabs, and other shellfish, and helps maintain moisture in facial cleansers and creams. Not only does it keep the stuff in the tube damp, this substance keeps skin moisturized, too.

8. **Hooves and Feathers:** Gelatin and keratin are animal by-products derived from the hair, hooves, horns, skin, bones, and feathers of animals such as cows, chickens, and horses. These ingredients have long been included as binding agents in shampoos and conditioners.

9. **Propolis:** Also called "bee glue," propolis is a brownish resin collected by bees from tree buds and bark to fill crevices and varnish the hive. Due to its antiseptic,

anti-inflammatory, and anesthetic properties, bee glue can be found in many "all natural" lip balms, cosmetics, lotions, shampoos, conditioners, and toothpastes. But be careful—just because a product is "all natural" doesn't mean it's safe for everyone. Allergic reactions to propolis are fairly common.

10. **Silk:** For centuries, women in Japan have been utilizing silk in clothing and cosmetics. There are 18 amino acids in silk, making it a natural moisturizer readily absorbed by the skin. Silkworms produce silk naturally, and it's only the real stuff that provides any benefits to skin—synthetic silk has none of those properties.

11. **Civet:** The civet, which looks like a cat but is more closely related to the mongoose, has sacs near its anus that create secretions harvested for perfume. The process of obtaining the secretions is painful for civets, so animal rights activists have succeeded in reducing this practice. Fortunately, synthetic materials provide the same stuff without harming the animals.

12. **Londinium Powder:** Japanese women of the Heian era (around A.D. 800–1200) mixed water with londinium, a lead-based powder, to create a thin paste that they applied to their faces. As with lead-based eyeliners in other parts of the world, this stuff was not very good for those who used it. Lead is easily absorbed by the body and can quickly cause many health problems and even death.

"The art of procreation and the members employed therein are so repulsive, that if it were not for the beauty of the faces and the adornments of the actors and the pent-up impulse, nature would lose the human species."

—LEONARDO DA VINCI

All of Your Gray Matter Matters

If you think about it—using your whole brain, of course—the theory that humans use only 10 percent of their brains is 100 percent wrong.

✳   ✳   ✳   ✳

THE PERSISTENT AND widespread misconception that we use only 10 percent of our brains falls apart when logic is applied. As it turns out, we need all of our gray matter—and here's why.

✳ The brain is not made of muscle, though many people think it is. But if it were, and we used only 10 percent of it, it would quickly degenerate. The adage "Use it or lose it" applies to muscle. The unused 90 percent of the brain would shrink to nothingness, giving new meaning to the term "airhead."

✳ What about brain cancer and gunshot wounds to the head? Victims would have a 90 percent chance that the tumor or bullet would lodge in the useless part of the brain. If only that were true.

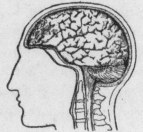

✳ An organ that requires so much energy to maintain would not have evolved if it were mostly useless. The brain consumes 20 percent of the body's oxygen and glucose. The time and energy required to develop the brain is responsible for the vulnerability of human infants and the remarkable length and difficulty of human pregnancy and childbirth.

✳ If seeing is believing, look no further than PET, CAT, or MRI scans of the brain. All reveal there is activity throughout the brain, even during sleep.

Formulating a Falsehood

The 10 percent myth began with some confusing information exchanged among scientists, and it gained traction with the false claims of advertisers, psychics, and questionable "healers."

Throughout the 1800s, it was understood that different parts of the brain were responsible for different functions. Scientists just weren't sure which part matched which function—and that's still partially true today. The idea that different parts perform discrete activities makes the idea of a "functionless" brain area inconceivable.

In the early 1900s, scientists used electricity to zap small parts of the brain to observe what it made people do (e.g., scream, blink, or lift an arm). The subjects appeared to do nothing when certain areas of the brain were zapped. These parts, called the "silent cortex," were considered by some to be functionless. They are now known to be responsible for language and abstract thought.

Others pointed to the rare cases of lobotomy patients who appeared to act normally. Of course, no one had anywhere near 90 percent of their brain lobotomized, and lobotomy patients who functioned "normally" were usually those who had been operated on as children. Young brains, we now know, are able to rewire neural pathways to compensate for damage.

Perpetuating the Same Falsehood

In the first half of the 20th century, scientists made vague claims about unused parts of the brain. This was taken up by psychics, mystics, cultists, and various religious leaders as evidence that their particular creed was the conduit to the brain's untapped powers. The 10 percent claim became popular somewhere around mid-century in advertisements for healing centers and self-help lectures. The myth is still popular in promotional ads for everything from airline companies to TV series.

15 Everyday Activities and the Calories They Burn

The simple truth of weight loss, no matter what the latest trendy diet says, is that you have to use more calories than you consume. Check out the following activities and the number of calories they burn.*

* * * *

1. **Shop 'til you drop:** Pushing a cart up and down the supermarket aisles for an hour will burn 243 calories and get you acquainted with all kinds of nutritious, healthful foods. Bag your own groceries, take them out to the car yourself, and return the cart to the corral to burn even more.

2. **Count calories instead of sheep:** Even when you're sleeping you're burning calories. Eight hours of good shut-eye will erase 360 calories.

3. **Make it shine:** Do your tables, shelves, and knickknacks fail the white-glove test? Burn 80 calories by dusting the surfaces in your home for 30 minutes.

4. **Pucker power:** It may not burn as many calories as dusting, but 30 minutes of kissing is a lot more fun, and you'll burn 36 calories.

5. **Wrinkle-free weight loss:** Burn 76.5 calories with 30 minutes of ironing; just be careful that you don't burn the clothes.

6. **Paint thinner:** You know you need to paint the house, but you're lacking the motivation. Does it help to know that three hours of house painting will burn 1,026 calories? And by putting on that second coat, you might drop a whole pants size.

7. **Sock it to me:** You can now look forward to laundry day because 30 minutes of folding clothes will burn 72 calories. Fold enough clothes and you may soon be putting away smaller sizes.

8. **Pick up trash and drop pounds:** Pick up some waste and reduce your waist by spending an afternoon cleaning up the neighborhood. In four hard-worked hours, you'll burn 1,800 calories and improve your community.

9. **Swab the deck:** Don't cry over spilled milk or anything else, especially when 30 minutes of mopping the floor will burn 153 calories.

10. **How about Texas Lose 'Em:** Three hours of playing cards burns 351 calories. Ante up and go all in, but don't load up on high-calorie chips and dip.

11. **Fire the lawn boy:** One hour of pushing the lawn mower around the yard burns 324 calories. Sorry, sitting on a riding mower doesn't count. Lose the bag attachment and spend another 30 minutes raking up the clippings and you'll burn another 171 calories.

12. **Dig the benefits:** Two hours of gardening will burn 648 calories, and you'll grow some nice healthful veggies at the same time.

13. **Get moving:** Offer to help your pals move. What's in it for you? Every hour of moving furniture burns 504 calories.

14. **Flake out:** Those of you who live in warm climates have no idea what a great workout you're missing. Thirty minutes of shoveling snow burns 202.5 calories.

15. **A lean sweep:** Moving a broom back and forth for ten minutes will burn 28 calories and you'll have a prop that can be anything from a microphone stand to a dance partner.

Based on a 150-pound person. (A heavier person will burn more calories performing the same activity.)

Fast Facts

❋ Nicotine takes around eight days to leave the bloodstream completely.

❋ Of the beheading device he proposed in 1789, Paris physician Joseph Guillotin stated, "My machine will take off a head in a twinkling and the victim will feel nothing but a refreshing coolness."

❋ An accident on the north end of Boston on January 15, 1919, flooded the area with two-and-a-half million gallons of molasses in a wave as much as 15 feet tall. Twenty-one people were killed, and 150 more were injured.

❋ The shortest reign of a Portuguese king was 20 minutes. When the royal family was ambushed in February 1908, the king died immediately and his heir, Luis Filipe, died 20 minutes later.

❋ National Bathroom Reading Week is the second week in June.

❋ In about 200 B.C., the Carthaginian ruler, Hannibal, defeated an enemy's navy by stuffing poisonous snakes into earthen jugs and catapulting them onto the decks of his opponent's ships.

❋ Maine is the only U.S. state whose name has just one syllable.

❋ Construction on the Great Wall of China began around 700 B.C. The wall was extended and enlarged to more than 4,000 miles over a period of 2,300 years.

❋ The coldest temperature ever recorded in the United States was in Prospect Creek Camp, Alaska, when the thermometer dived down to a teeth-chattering -79.8°F on January 23, 1971.

❋ Commercial deodorant became available in 1888. Roll-on deodorant was invented in the 1950s, using technology from standard ballpoint pens.

❋ Thanksgiving is celebrated on the fourth Thursday in November, by decree of President Franklin Roosevelt. Thus, the earliest date that Thanksgiving can fall is November 22.

The Origin of the *Vitruvian Man*

Leonardo da Vinci's study in symmetry resulted in one of the most commonly recognized portraits of the male figure and symbols of the workings of the universe.

✳ ✳ ✳ ✳

Who's That Man?

N EVER HAS THE name of such a famous work of art remained as unknown as Leonardo da Vinci's masterpiece, *Vitruvian Man* (circa 1490). You may not know him by name, but *Vitruvian Man* is that drawing of a naked man, his arms and legs spread wide, standing inside both a circle and a square. His image is surrounded by what looks like scrawled gibberish but is actually Leonardo's penned explanation of the strange image, written backwards.

Proportionally Perfect

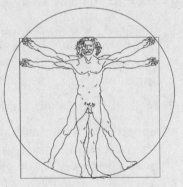

The drawing looks more like a page torn from a medieval medical textbook than a work of art, and that is just the point. Leonardo was inspired by the mathematical musings of Roman architect Vitruvius, who believed that the proportions of mankind's buildings should be based on the allegedly perfect proportions of man himself (the Romans weren't at all concerned with women). Here is the essence of Vitruvius' idea: The center of the human body is the navel. Stand a man with his arms and legs outstretched and draw a circle around him with the navel as the center. If you then draw a navel-centered square inside the circle, the tips of the fingers and toes will fit into the corners of the square while simultaneously touching the circumference of the circle.

Vitruvius made additional observations about man's proportions that have lived on forever in the form of playground bets: A palm is the width of four fingers, the length of a man's outspread arms is equal to his height, the length of the ear is one-third the length of the face—the list goes on. Vitruvius' claims don't measure up to reality, and one can only guess that he was referring to average measurements that are never realized in the body of a single person. Indeed, Leonardo's drawing reveals *Vitruvian Man*'s imperfections— in his drawing, the square and circle do not have the same center.

Stick with Symmetry, Leo

But Leonardo was less concerned with the accuracy of Vitruvius' mathematics than with the idea that there is an essential symmetry to the "human" (aka male) body. Leonardo did some measurements and calculations of his own before drawing his *Vitruvian Man*. The drawing is considered the perfect marriage of science and art. It is believed that Leonardo saw the square as a symbol for material existence and the circle as a symbol for spirituality. For Leonardo, the human body was an analogy for the workings of the universe.

✳ Leonardo da Vinci is actually credited with giving the world the first plans for human flight. In the 1480s, he began a serious study of the subject, amassing more than 100 drawings that represented the relationship between birds and mechanical flight.

✳ Gabriele Fallopio, a 16th-century Italian anatomist, was the first to discover the tubes that connect the ovaries to the uterus and was also the first to develop an effective condom, which he fashioned from pig intestines.

Dreamland

 * In an average lifetime, people spend approximately 2,100 days (almost 6 years) dreaming. Everyone dreams every night, though some of us can't remember our dreams.

 * Blind people dream. If they became blind after having sight, visual images appear in their dreams. If they were born blind, their dreams, like their lives, are made up of feelings, smells, movements, and sounds.

 * Developmental psychologists say that toddlers never dream about themselves. Children are not believed to appear in their own dreams until a developmental stage that occurs when they are three or four years old and realize they are separate from other people.

 * Rapid eye movement (REM) sleep is the stage during which we have our most vivid dreams, characterized by bizarre plots involving unlikely people or things. In contrast, non-REM dreams are more like waking thoughts. They have less imagery and tend to repeat a thought obsessively (for example, "I've lost my keys!").

 * It was once believed that dreams occurred only during REM sleep. Improved technology has allowed researchers to discover that dreams are less frequent in non-REM sleep phases but still exist. In fact, it is likely that we dream during every single moment of sleep.

 * Color in dreams is a constant source of speculation. Some monochrome dreams can have a single image that's in color, such as a bright pink poodle. Other dreams seem to speak a language of colors (e.g., red or blue lights) and shapes (repeated circles or squares). Sometimes, natural colors pervade the dream, as in waking life.

 * In the late 1950s, scientists proved that external stimuli can be incorporated into dreams. When researchers sprinkled

water on sleeping volunteers and woke them up seconds later, 14 out of 33 subjects said they had dreamed of water.

* It is believed that we rarely feel pain in dreams. When we do, though, our bodies perceive it as a signal that something is wrong, and we react by waking up.

* Studies conducted by Harvard University reveal that dreams exhibit five strange features. They have the qualities of hallucinations (seeing things that don't exist), delusions (believing something imaginary), emotional intensity (extreme feelings about a situation), amnesia (forgetting our lives and even who we are in those lives), and cognitive abnormalities (having thoughts that differ from the waking norm).

* What is the purpose of dreaming? Some experts speculate that the primitive part of the brain is overloaded during the day and cannot process all of our experiences. Dreaming gives us a way to sort through our memories and eliminate the ones that aren't useful for our growth.

Common Dream Themes

* being partially clothed or naked in public
* being chased by threatening people or things
* suddenly losing teeth or hair
* flying or falling
* failing to attend class until exam day
* forgetting addresses, phone numbers, or locker combinations
* inability to see clearly, especially when driving

19 Strange Illnesses and Disorders that Almost Nobody Gets

1. **Progeria:** It might seem like you're getting old fast, but for people who suffer from progeria—a disease for which there were only 80 certified cases worldwide as of 2011—premature aging is a reality. This condition, which speeds up the aging process, causes people to grow old and die within just a few years.

2. **Foreign Accent Syndrome:** People afflicted with FAS wake up one day suddenly speaking with a completely different accent—often from countries they've never even been to. Doctors think the odd disorder is caused by brain injury, though they aren't sure exactly what kind.

3. **Harlequin Ichthyosis:** Children with this extremely rare disorder are born with thick, scaly patches of skin covering their face, like a suit of armor. Unfortunately, the armor harms more than protects, and most afflicted with harlequin ichthyosis die in childhood.

4. **Kuru:** Kuru is a rare neuromuscular disease, but you probably don't need to worry about catching it—unless you're a cannibal. That's because the disease is only transmitted by eating infected human brain tissue. The only known cases of Kuru occurred among the Fore tribes—people of New Guinea who practiced cannibalistic funeral rites until the 1950s.

5. **Pantothenate Kinase-Associated Neurodegeneration:** PKAN is a rare degenerative brain disease that causes spasms, tremors, loss of speech, and blindness. It commonly strikes children before the age of 10, making it both terrifying and heartbreaking. Doctors estimate that only one in a million individuals are affected.

6. **Sleeping Beauty Syndrome:** For people suffering from this disorder—more officially known as Kleine-Levin

syndrome—it's no fairy tale. Sufferers of this rare hyper-somniac condition go through long stretches of their life sleeping. Worse, when they're awake they're spaced out and nonfunctional.

7. **Mermaid Syndrome:** Officially known as sirenomelia, this condition is a birth defect in which an infant is born with its legs fused together. The syndrome only strikes about 1 in 100,000 births, and to date only one child born with the disease has been known to survive longer than ten years.

8. **Cold Urticaria:** Nobody likes cold weather, but imagine being allergic to it. People suffering from cold urticaria develop rashes and hives when exposed to cold weather.

9. **Hyperthymesic Syndrome:** People with hyperthymesic syndrome never forget what day their anniversary falls on—or anything else, for that matter. People suffering from this extremely rare disorder (only three cases have been identified worldwide) remember every detail of every day for most of their lives.

10. **Reduplicative Paramnesia:** People with this unusual and rare mental disorder believe that they are in a place different from where they actually are. For example, mental patients with this disorder often believe the room they are in is their house or that the hospital is in another part of the country.

11. **Capgras Syndrome:** This rare psychological disorder makes sufferers suspicious of their loved ones or even their own reflections.

12. **Fregoli Delusion:** People with Fregoli delusion believe they're being followed by someone and that everybody they see is that person dressed up in disguise.

13. **Fields Condition:** This degenerative neuromuscular condition is so rare that there are only two known cases in the history of recorded medical science—identical twins Catherine and Kirstie Fields. The symptoms, such as difficulty moving, are being recorded as the girls age.

14. **Cotard Delusion:** People suffering from the little-seen mental disorder known as the Cotard delusion take low self-esteem to its limits. At the extreme, patients believe they do not exist. Others believe that organs are putrefying, limbs have vanished, or blood is disappearing from the body.

15. **Landau Kleffner Syndrome:** In this rare childhood neurological disorder, children suddenly lose the ability to comprehend and express language. Even more strangely, sufferers of this condition sometimes completely regain speech within a few years.

16. **Craniopagus Parasiticus:** One of the rarest of all conditions, craniopagus parasiticus describes a birth defect in which a "parasitic" twin head is attached to a newborn's head. Only ten cases of this condition have been reported in the history of medical literature.

17. **Subjective-Double Syndrome:** Don't tell someone suffering from subjective-double syndrome that you saw a person who looked like him or her on the street. He or she already believes that they have one or more doppelgängers.

18. **Dancing Eyes–Dancing Feet Syndrome:** Dancing eyes–dancing feet syndrome isn't nearly as fun as it sounds. Symptoms of this obscure condition include irregular, rapidly twitching eyes and random muscle spasms that make sitting and standing nearly impossible.

19. **Alien Hand Syndrome:** This unusual condition is pretty much what it sounds like—the sensation that a force completely beyond your control is manipulating your hands.

Nitroglycerin and Other Unlikely Medicines

Alfred Nobel quite literally rocked the scientific world in 1866 when he combined nitroglycerin with diatomaceous earth and sodium carbonate to invent dynamite. Only slightly less explosive was the discovery decades later that nitroglycerin could be used for medicinal purposes. Here are some other odd ingredients being used in contemporary medical research.

✳   ✳   ✳   ✳

Snake Venom: While snake oil was once the unlikeliest—and most fraudulent—of medicines, snake venom is drawing increased attention in the medical community as a possible cancer fighter. According to scientists, natural compounds in snake venom may prevent the growth of cancerous tumors by acting as a targeted tissue killer, as opposed to current cancer treatments such as chemotherapy, which attack cells indiscriminately.

Blue M&M'S: Millions of people around the world are fully aware that M&M'S provide a soothing emotional balm. But doctors recently made the surprising discovery that the blue dye used in blue M&M'S (and Gatorade, incidentally) could help cure patients with spinal cord injuries. Researchers at the University of Rochester Medical Center found that an injection of the dye Brilliant Blue G halted the chemical reaction that destroyed spinal tissue after an injury. Better yet, when the dye was injected into rats paralyzed from spinal cord injuries, they were able to walk again. The only side effect? They temporarily turned blue.

Nicotine: Believe it or not, some studies have shown that nicotine may have neuro-protective traits that guard smokers against developing brain diseases such as Alzheimer's and Parkinson's in their golden years. But that doesn't mean you should go light up—cigarette smokers still have a far shorter life span than nonsmokers.

Don't Get Hysterical!

In Victorian times, female hysteria was a widespread, catchall diagnosis—and a weird one at that.

✳ ✳ ✳ ✳

O F ALL THE strange medical diagnoses of yore, hysteria might be one of the strangest. Used frequently in the Victorian era (1830s–1900), it eventually became one of the most common diagnoses in the history of Western medicine.

Hysteria, particularly female hysteria, was a catchall for any kind of "woman problems" ladies might experience, which included a long list of symptoms: fainting, anxiety, insomnia, muscle spasm, mood swings, loss of appetite, heaviness in abdomen, shortness of breath, retention of fluids, disinterest in sex, etc. In other words, if you were a woman who felt at all ill or were thought to be "acting up," you were probably just hysterical and needed to get a grip!

Ancient Origins and Initial "Cures"

The word *hysteria* comes from the Greek word *hysterikos,* meaning "suffering of the womb." In fact, during ancient times, the uterus was thought to move through the body, wreaking all kinds of havoc (e.g., strangling the woman and causing disease). This phenomenon, first suggested by Aretaeus of Cappodocia, was known as the "wandering womb." According to the *Encyclopedia of Gender and Society,* wombs continued to wander throughout the classical, medieval, and renaissance periods.

The ancient Greeks believed that women were actually "incomplete" males; thus, the uterus was not cooperative and rebelled against the female body. So the cure for hysteria was to resituate the uterus or "lure it back" via rocking in a chair, riding a horse, or receiving a "pelvic massage" (which basically brought about an orgasm). It was recommended that married women have sexual intercourse with their husbands, while single women were encouraged to get married—pronto!

Victorian-Era Hysteria

In Victorian times, sex as a form of pleasure, rather than strictly a form of reproduction, was particularly taboo. Society upheld the notion of the "sexless woman." Therefore, almost any woman who deviated from this ideal or experienced sexual frustration or emotional turmoil was deemed hysterical. In fact, by the mid-19th century, physicians diagnosed a quarter of all women as hysterical. Meanwhile, the number of symptoms for this "disease" kept growing. One physician catalogued 75 pages of possible symptoms— a list he described as incomplete.

Good-bye, Leech Cures!

How to treat the hysterical masses? Doctors prescribed bed rest, seclusion, sensory deprivation, tasteless food, and pelvic massages. The latter were to be performed by a skilled physician or midwife and were often accompanied by a steady flow of water, otherwise known as a hydrotherapy treatment. The massage treatment eventually gave rise to the first electromechanical vibrator. Doctors also recommended that hysterical women stay away from any tasks that were too mentally strenuous, such as reading and writing. Of course, this sort of deprivation just created more problems. In the short story *The Yellow Wallpaper*, written by Charlotte Perkins Gilman in 1899, a woman is driven mad after being prescribed a "rest cure" for hysteria. For Gilman, this turn of events hit close to home: She, too, was prescribed such a cure.

Some alternative remedies for female hysteria included prescribing cod liver oil or applying leeches to the cervix. In the early 20th century, the studies of psychiatrist Sigmund Freud supported the idea of a female sexual drive, so society eventually retreated from the idea of the "sexless woman." By mid-century, there was a noticeable decline in the number of diagnoses, and eventually, the American Psychiatric Association omitted hysteria from the list of official medical conditions. Doctors favored more specific and accurate diagnoses, reclassifying patients as having postpartum depression, anxiety disorders, schizophrenia, or other forms of mental illness.

15 Cures for the Hiccups

When you have the hiccups, something has triggered involuntary contractions in your diaphragm. Try these tips to get rid of 'em!

✳ ✳ ✳ ✳

1. **The Drinking Cure:** Swallowing water interrupts the hiccupping cycle, which can quiet the nerves. Gargling with water may also have the same effect, but swallowing is probably the fastest way to cure hiccups.

2. **The Pineapple Juice Cure:** Some say that the acid in pineapple juice obliterates hiccups, but it's probably just the swallowing action that comes from drinking.

3. **The Gulp Cure:** Whatever you want to gulp down, go for it. Just like drinking water, swallowing any food or drink is a good way to dispel the dreaded hiccups.

4. **The Little Brother Cure:** If you stick out your tongue, you'll stimulate your glottis, the opening of the airway to your lungs. Since a closed glottis is what causes hiccups in the first place, this usually works pretty well.

5. **The Drink Upside Down Cure:** If gulping down water is good, drinking it upside down must be, too. As with many home remedies, this one is a bit unusual, but it's not totally illogical. In addition to swallowing the water, it's pretty hard to figure out how to drink upside down. The concentration needed might equalize the breathing and cure the hiccups.

6. **The Cotton Swab Cure:** This cure works just like the Little Brother Cure. Take a cotton swab and tickle the roof of your mouth. People will wonder what you're doing, but it's better than drinking upside down, isn't it?

7. **The Scaredy-Cat Cure:** The effectiveness of this cure is dubious at best, since once you ask someone to scare you, you're not going to be really, truly surprised. However, if

you have a friend with ESP, he or she might be able to help. Losing your breath or gasping might just reset your glottis automatically. Boo!

8. **The Sugar Cure:** A lump of sugar not only tickles the glottis, it gets the hiccupping person swallowing—a double threat to the hiccups.

9. **The Squeeze Cure:** Can't stop hiccupping? Squeeze those suckers outta there! Sit in a chair and compress your chest by pulling your knees up to your chin. Lean forward and feel those hiccups magically disappear.

10. **The Sleeper Cure:** Give your glottis, throat, and diaphragm a break—lie down on your back. This is a gentler way to get rid of those obnoxious hiccups.

11. **The Hear No Evil Cure:** This cure was reported in the medical journal *Lancet,* so it has to work, right? The article claims that if you plug your ears, you will, in effect, short-circuit your vagus nerve, which controls hiccups.

12. **The Brown Bag Cure:** It might be that breathing into a brown paper bag cures hiccups because the hiccupping person is taking in more carbon dioxide when inhaling. Or, it might be that the person is concentrating more on breathing, slowing it down and smoothing it out.

13. **The Hold Your Breath Cure:** This is one of the oldest hiccup remedies, and it usually works pretty well, as it forces a little more control over your breathing.

14. **The Headstand Cure:** Not everyone can stand on their head, but if you can, you might have a good hiccup cure. By standing on your head, you're probably using a fair amount of concentration and messing with your breathing. This should lead to a cessation of the hiccups.

15. **The Run for It Cure:** Run. Fast. For ten minutes. See?

Strange Eating Habits of the Rich and Famous

Ah, to be a celebrity. Massive paychecks, VIP treatment, magazine covers, and the right to demand a truly weird meal. Some of the people on this list, however, were weird eaters long before anyone paid attention.

❋　❋　❋　❋

H. P. Lovecraft

THE INFLUENTIAL "COSMIC-HORROR" writer reportedly grew up on candy and other sweets given to him by doting aunts in the late 1890s. Lovecraft might be a cult figure now, but he was relatively unknown while he lived and spent most of his life in poverty, eating whatever was most economical. His usual dinner consisted of baked beans and ice cream. In the end, his poor diet may have contributed to his death from intestinal cancer.

Beyoncé Knowles

To whittle her bootylicious figure down to a more slender silhouette for the movie *Dreamgirls*, singer-actress Beyoncé drank a mixture of lemon juice, honey, and cayenne pepper for weeks at a time and watched the pounds melt away. But she made it clear in interviews that such a diet was strictly for movie actresses who need to drop weight fast for a role—not for the general public. Of course, that certainly didn't stop the Master Cleanse from becoming the diet du jour.

Marcel Proust

French author, critic, and hero to highbrow conversationalists everywhere, Marcel Proust lived off barbiturates and café au lait during the last years of his life. In 1922, he apparently suffered a negative reaction to the drug Adrenalin, which caused internal burns to his throat and stomach. He survived on ice cream and cold beer for the next month.

Mariah Carey

If it's purple, this pop diva will eat it. If it isn't, take it away. Eating foods purple in color is just one of the ways Carey has approached her diet in recent years. Apparently, Carey believes that mauveish-colored foods (e.g., eggplant, radishes, blueberries, plums) help reduce inflammation and wrinkles, things that a public personality like Carey just can't have.

Victoria Beckham

Spice Girl, wife to soccer legend David Beckham, and media darling Victoria Beckham is seriously skinny. Rumors abound when any famous women's collarbones jut out—could it be an eating disorder? Drug use? One report claims that Vicks eats three things and three things only: lettuce, edamame (steamed soy beans), and strawberries.

Howard Hughes

This super-wealthy producer could have afforded anything he wanted to eat, but as Hughes aged and became more and more eccentric, he limited his diet to medium-rare steak, salad, peas, vanilla ice cream, and cookies. Not a bad meal, unless you eat it every day to the exclusion of everything else. And Hughes did just that—he wouldn't even venture outside the box for a different flavor of ice cream.

"I am not a vegetarian because I love animals; I'm a vegetarian because I hate plants."

—A. WHITNEY BROWN

"I feel sorry for people who don't drink. They wake up in the morning and that's the best they are going to feel all day."

—FRANK SINATRA

You Are Getting Sleepy...

From mesmerism to mind machines, we have the facts on hypnotism.

✳   ✳   ✳   ✳

✳ Before he introduced hypnotism (aka "mesmerism") in 1775, Franz Mesmer tried to heal patients by having them swallow a drink with tiny grains of iron and then moving magnets over their bodies to sway the magnetic currents. As soon as he realized that people were actually reacting to his dramatic performance and "animal magnetism," he stopped using magnets and relied on the effect of his own voice.

✳ The first recorded use of hypnosis as an anesthesia took place in the 19th century. Dr. James Esdaile, a Scottish surgeon working in India, used hypnosis successfully in hundreds of limb amputations.

✳ People with the best imaginations are the easiest to hypnotize. Researcher Theodore Sarbin calls hypnosis "believed-in imaginings." Those who are imaginative and creatively talented can easily visualize a hypnotist's suggestions and call to mind experiences that are colorful and compelling.

✳ About 10 to 15 percent of people react with either complete acceptance or outright rejection of hypnosis.

✳ Between 70 and 80 percent of people respond to certain hypnotic suggestions but not others. For example, they may scratch their head when a buzzer goes off if the hypnotist has told them to, but they won't go so far as to pour a bucket of water over their heads.

✳ King Louis XVI and Marie Antoinette believed so strongly in Mesmer's technique that they created the Magnetic Institute in France. At first, Mesmer had patients put their feet in buckets of magnetized water, with cables attached to magnetized trees. The French medical community—and visiting diplomat Benjamin Franklin—denounced him as a fraud.

* Falling under the power of a hypnotist was a legal defense in France in the 19th century. It was believed that a hypnotist could make someone "a toy in his hands" and that the person "could not reject the ideas of the beguiler." People who committed crimes under such influence could not be held legally or morally responsible for their acts.

* Today, hypnotists sometimes use a "mind machine" (aka "psycho-walkman") to alter brainwave frequencies with light and sound. It is said to create altered states of consciousness, like meditation and shamanic rituals.

* Posthypnotic suggestions can, for instance, make people forget how to read or perceive colors where there are none or believe themselves to be capable of unusual things. Dr. Stephen M. Kosslyn, a Harvard neuroscientist, explains that this is possible because all of these experiences exist inside the brain, not in the world around us. They have always been completely in our minds.

* Stage hypnotists can make participants believe they are historical figures or celebrities. In one study in the 1960s, art students were hypnotized to believe they were Leonardo da Vinci, then asked to paint. They didn't paint like da Vinci, but, believing they were great, they painted better than they had ever done in the past.

"A ruffled mind makes a restless pillow."

—CHARLOTTE BRONTË

Fast Facts

✳ The average person forgets 80 percent of what he or she learns in a day.

✳ Lightning can strike up to 20 miles away from the originating storm. These bolts, called "Positive Giants," seem to randomly come from a clear sky. They are usually much more destructive than ordinary lightning.

✳ A typical lightning bolt is hotter than the surface of the Sun.

✳ The most active hurricane season on record was in 2005. So many storms formed that year that the National Hurricane Center ran out of names on its list and had to use Greek letters for the last six storms. What's more, there were a record-breaking four category-five monsters, including the devastating Katrina.

✳ Low barometric pressure generally indicates stormy weather, and high pressure signals calm, sunny skies. The lowest pressure ever recorded was 25.69 inches during Typhoon Tip in 1979. The highest pressure, 32.01 inches, was measured in 1968 on a cold New Year's Eve in northern Siberia.

✳ To get a rough estimate of the temperature, count the number of times a cricket chirps in 15 seconds and add 40.

✳ Despite the popular saying, nowhere on Earth does it actually get hot enough to fry an egg on the sidewalk. The pavement would need to hit at least 158° F for the egg to cook, and even blacktop has been found to heat up to only 145° F.

✳ Ever had your favorite shirt lose its color from too much time in the sun? It happens when ultraviolet light breaks down the chemical bonds in the dyes and causes a bleaching effect.

✳ The coldest temperature ever recorded on Earth was a bone-chilling -128.6° F on July 21, 1983, at Vostok Station, Antarctica. The hottest was in El Azizia, Libya, on September 13, 1922, when the mercury hit 136° F.

11 People with Extra Body Parts

Doctors call them supernumerary body parts, but here are a few people who always had a spare hand (or finger, or head...).

✳ ✳ ✳ ✳

1. Anne Boleyn, second wife to Henry VIII of England, is rumored to have had 11 fingers and possibly a third breast. Historians believe that she did have an extra finger or at least some sort of growth on her hand that resembled an extra finger, but it is unlikely that she had an extra breast. This rumor may have been started by her enemies because in Tudor times an extra breast was believed to be the sign of a witch.

2. Major league baseball pitcher Antonio Alfonseca has six fingers on each hand, but he claims the extra fingers do not affect his pitching, as they do not usually touch the ball. In most cases of polydactylism (extra fingers or toes), the extra digit has only limited mobility, or cannot be moved at all.

3. Actor Mark Wahlberg has a third nipple on the left side of his chest. Early in his career, he considered having it removed, but he later came to accept it. Around 2 percent of women and slightly fewer men have a supernumerary nipple, although they are often mistaken for moles. They can be found anywhere between the armpit and groin, and range from a tiny lump (like Wahlberg's) to a small extra breast, sometimes even capable of lactation.

4. In 2006, a 24-year-old man from India checked himself into a New Delhi hospital and asked doctors to remove his extra penis so that he could marry and lead a normal sex life. The condition, known as diphallia or penile duplication, is extremely rare, with only around 100 cases ever documented.

5. Craniopagus parasiticus is a medical condition in which a baby is born with a parasitic twin head. The extra head does not have a functioning brain, which is what differentiates this condition from that of conjoined twins. In effect, the baby is born with the head of its dead twin attached to its body. There have only ever been eight documented cases, and, of these, only three have survived birth. One of these was Rebeca Martinez, born in the Dominican Republic in December 2003, the first baby to undergo an operation to remove the second head. She died on February 7, 2004, after an 11-hour operation.

6. A similar condition is polycephaly, the condition of having more than one functioning head. There are many documented occurrences of this in the animal kingdom, although in most human cases we refer to the condition as conjoined twins. One recent case was that of Syafitri, born in Indonesia in 2006. These conjoined twins were given just one name by their parents who insisted that they were, in fact, one baby girl since they had only one heart and shared a body. Syafitri died of unknown causes just two weeks after she was born.

7. Hermaphroditism—the condition of being born with both male and female reproductive organs—is more common than you might think, existing in some degree in around 1 percent of the population. In 1843, when Levi Suydam, a 23-year-old resident of Salisbury, Connecticut, wanted to vote for the Whig candidate in a local election, the opposition party objected, saying Suydam was really a woman and therefore did not have the right to vote. A doctor examined Suydam and declared that he had a penis and was therefore a man. He voted and the Whig candidate won by a single vote.

8. It might seem unusual for a woman to have two uteruses, but the condition known as uterine didelphys occurs in

about one in 1,000 women. In fact, Hannah Kersey, her mother, and her sister all have two wombs. But Hannah made history in 2006 when she gave birth to triplets—a set of identical twin girls from one womb and a third, fraternal sister from the other womb.

9. Francesco Lentini was born in Sicily in 1889 with three legs, two sets of genitals, and an extra foot growing from the knee of his third leg—the remains of a conjoined twin that had died in the womb. Rejected by his parents, he was raised by an aunt, then in a home for disabled children before moving to America when he was eight. He became "The Great Lentini" and toured with major circus and sideshow acts. He married, raised four children, and lived longer than any other three-legged person, dying in Florida in 1966 at age 78.

10. Josephene Myrtle Corbin, born in 1868, could see Lentini his three legs and raise him one. She was a dipygus, meaning that she had two separate pelvises and four legs. As with Lentini, these were the residual parts of a conjoined twin. She could move all of the legs, but they were too weak to walk on. She too was a great success in sideshows, and eventually she married a doctor with whom she had five children. Legend has it that three of her children were born from one pelvis, and two from the other.

11. Born in 1932 to a poor farming family in Georgia, Betty Lou Williams was the youngest of 12 children. Doctors claimed she was a healthy child... except for the two extra arms and legs emerging from the side of her body. From the age of two, Williams worked for Ripley's Believe It Or Not and earned quite a living on the sideshow circuit—she put her siblings through college and bought her parents a large farm.

What's Eating *You?*

There are more than 130 parasites that can inhabit the human body. While it might be a bit creepy to think of all those critters wriggling inside you, just think of it this way: At least you'll never be lonely! Here are some freaky (and intensely gross) facts about human parasites. Warning: Don't eat while reading this list.

✳ ✳ ✳ ✳

✳ Researchers suspect that instances of Crohn's disease, a once-rare inflammatory intestinal disorder, may be on the rise because of the lack of intestinal parasites in much of the first-world population.

✳ Demodex mites are also called "face mites," because they live on human hair follicles, eyelashes, and nose hairs.

✳ As they're only 0.0118 inch long, as many as 25 Demodex mites can live on a single hair follicle.

✳ There are more than 3,000 species of lice in the world.

✳ Although head lice only live for a month in your hair, each one can lay up to 100 eggs during that time.

✳ Leeches can suck ten times their body weight in blood.

✳ Tapeworms can grow to more than 60 feet long in human intestines.

✳ The tapeworm's segmented tail contains eggs. This is so that when the segments break off and are expelled from the host's body, the eggs can move on to another animal.

✳ Instead of a head, the tapeworm has a hooked knob that it uses to cling to the intestinal walls as it sucks nutrients off the surface.

✳ Tapeworms can only reproduce in humans. When the eggs are eaten by another animal, they reside in the animal's muscle tissue until that flesh is consumed by a human as under-cooked meat.

✳ Upon attaching to a human host, a chigger (also called a red bug or harvest mite) uses an enzyme to dissolve the flesh at the bite, and then it consumes the liquefied tissue.

✳ Mosquitoes help transmit botfly eggs to humans, where they hatch and burrow into the skin. To remove them, lay a slice of raw meat on the skin. The maggots will leave the body and enter the meat instead.

✳ When bathing in the Amazon, men and women always cover their genitals with one hand to prevent the parasitic candiru fish from swimming into their urethra.

✳ Roundworms grow to 15 inches long and lay as many as 200,000 eggs daily.

✳ Roundworms are the most common form of intestinal parasite, with an estimated one billion hosts worldwide.

✳ Rather than feeding on the material found in human intestines, hookworms attach themselves to feed on the blood and intestinal tissue.

✳ Occasionally, a whipworm infection is discovered when a worm crawls out of the anus or up through the throat and out through the nose or mouth.

✳ Whipworms can cause the loss of approximately one teaspoon of blood per day.

✳ After entering the human body in larval form, the two-foot-long adult Guinea worm exits by creating a hole in the flesh of the leg.

✳ Giardiasis is caused by a one-celled parasite found in dirty water; noticeable symptoms include sulfurous belches and flatulence.

Head Like a Hole

There aren't many medical procedures more than 7,000 years old that are still practiced today. Trepanation, or the practice of drilling a hole in the skull, is one of the few.

✳ ✳ ✳ ✳

An Ancient Practice

HAS ANYONE EVER angrily accused you of having a hole in your head? Well, it's not necessarily an exaggeration. *Trepanation* (also known as "trephination") is the practice of boring into the skull and removing a piece of bone, thereby leaving a hole. It is derived from the Greek word *trypanon*, meaning "to bore." This practice was performed by the ancient Greeks, Romans, and Egyptians, among others.

Hippocrates, considered the father of medicine, indicated that the Greeks might have used trepanation to treat head injuries. However, evidence of trepanning without accompanying head trauma has been found in less advanced civilizations; speculation abounds as to its exact purpose. Since the head was considered a barometer for a person's behavior, one theory is that trepanation was used as a way to treat headaches, depression, and other conditions that had no outward trauma signs. Think of it like a pressure release valve: The hole gave evil spirits inside the skull a way out of the body. When the spirits were gone, it was hoped, the symptoms would disappear.

How to Trepan

In trepanning, the Greeks used an instrument called a *terebra*, an extremely sharp piece of wood with another piece of wood mounted crossways on it as a handle and attached by a thong. The handle was twisted until the thong was extremely tight. When released, the thong unwound, which spun the sharp piece of wood around and drove it into the skull like a drill. Although it's possible that the terebra was used for a single hole, it is more likely that it was used to make a circular pattern of multiple small holes, thereby making it easier to remove a large piece of bone. Since formal anesthesia had not yet been invented, it is unknown whether any kind of numbing agent was used before trepanation was performed.

The Incas were also adept at trepanation. The procedure was performed using a ceremonial tumi knife made of flint or copper. The surgeon held the patient's head between his knees and rubbed the tumi blade back and forth along the surface of the skull to create four incisions in a crisscross pattern. When the incisions were sufficiently deep, the square-shaped piece of bone in the center was pulled out. Come to think of it, perhaps the procedure hurt more than the symptom.

Trepanation Today

Interestingly, doctors still use this procedure, only now it's called a craniotomy. The underlying methodology is similar, and the bone is replaced when the procedure is done. If it is not replaced, the operation is called a craniectomy. That procedure is used in many different circumstances, such as for treating a tumor or infection.

However, trepanation still has its supporters. One in particular is Bart Hughes, who believes that trepanning can elevate one to a higher state of consciousness. According to Hughes, once man started to walk upright, the brain lost blood because the heart had to frantically pump it throughout the body in a struggle against gravity. Thus, the brain had to shut down certain areas that were not critically needed to assure proper blood flow to vital regions.

Increased blood flow to the brain can elevate a person's consciousness, Hughes reasoned, and he advocated ventilating the skull as a means of making it easier for the heart to send blood to the brain. Some of his followers have actually performed trepanation on themselves. For better or gross, a few have even filmed the process.

Chapter Four

Food and Drink

Obscure Brands of Soda Pop

Americans drink 13 billion gallons of soft drinks every year. But until the latter half of the 1800s, selection was limited. The usual suspects for soda flavors were cola, orange, grape, root beer, strawberry, and lemon-lime. Oh, how times have changed! Some of the beverages listed below are still being produced, while others are now only available in the big soda fountain in the sky.

※   ※   ※   ※

1. **DraCola:** This was a cola product made for "Halloween fans of all ages" by Transylvania Imports. Yes, you can still find it and, no, it isn't blood-flavored. DraCola is an ordinary cola-flavored beverage.

2. **Aphrodite:** Cherry-red with a fruit punch flavor, this discontinued soda featured a different quote from a famous screen siren (such as Mae West) on every bottle. In addition, Aphrodite's suggestive slogan was "Get Some Tonight." This soda came onto the scene in 2002 and lasted only a few years.

3. **OK Soda:** This soda had a forgettable taste but a legendary marketing campaign. Aimed at too-cool Generation X in the early 1990s, OK Soda purposely employed minimalist art and negative advertising to sell the drink. The Gen

Xers didn't buy into the hype or the soda—which was a pretty run-of-the-mill, cola-flavored beverage—and OK was soon a thing of the past.

4. **Celo Polka Cola:** Created by the Sauk City, Wisconsin, Celo Bottling Company, Celo Polka Cola was presented to the world in 1991 to promote polka music and dancing. The jury's still out as to whether or not that worked, but you can order this cola-flavored beverage online and decide for yourself.

5. **Whooppee Soda:** "The Bottled Joy," a ginger ale–flavored soda, featured the innovative "Tilt-Top Cap." The best thing about this early 20th century soda was a contest offered by the company. Up to $500 in prizes were awarded to the 24 best letters in which consumers described their "saddest, most injurious or embarrassing experience in taking off the...bottle crown cap."

6. **Dr. Enuf:** Since 1949, the Tri-City Beverage Corporation has been bottling this "vitamin-enriched lemon-lime soft drink" invented by Charles Gordon. Back in the day, Dr. Enuf was said to relieve people's "untold misery" from aches and pains, stomach disturbances, and general malaise. Dr. Enuf is still available from the manufacturer but doesn't appear on most supermarket shelves.

7. **Leninade:** With slogans like, "A taste worth standing in line for," and "A drink for the masses!" you can guess that there's some humor behind this "Simple Soviet Style Soda." Produced by the Lenin Company, the fruity taste pleased communists and non-communists alike—so much so that you can still find it online.

8. **Hemp Soda:** Ah, the mid-1990s, when alternative music actually meant something and everyone was discovering hemp-based products. This "herbal" soda was produced in 1996 and featured a large hemp leaf on the can. The beverage can still be ordered online from the manufacturer "Designer Food."

9. **Nesbitt's Orange Soda:** The Nesbitt Orange Soda Company was founded in 1938 in Los Angeles and produced its famous beverage for 40 years. Real orange zest settles to the bottom of this classic orange soda that is still available online and in some stores.

10. **Brain Wash Blue:** If you have trouble placing the flavor of this soda, don't feel too bad. Jalapeño oil doesn't go into many mainstream beverages, which is perhaps why this small batch soda, courtesy of Skeleteens, hasn't hit it big. If you dare give it a try, it's available online.

11. **Tab Clear:** If you blinked in 1993, you missed Tab Clear. The Coca-Cola Company tried to hop on the clear-cola bandwagon (remember Crystal Pepsi?), but less than a year after its introduction, Tab Clear was pulled. Original Tab is still going strong.

12. **Flathead Lake Monster:** The North American Beverage Company developed this line of boutique sodas and named them for a monster said to live in Flathead Lake, Montana. Flavors include Huckleberry and Wild White Grape, among others. Limited distribution has kept these sodas obscure, though the beverages have a solid fan base.

13. **Gay Energy Cola Drink:** In the never-ending quest to zero in on and exhaust the consumer habits of a particular demographic, POWER Drinks, S.L. produced this energy drink several years ago. If you find a can of this beverage, you should keep it as a collector's item—they don't make it anymore.

14. **Pickle Juice "Sport":** This soda, conceived by Golden Beverages, Inc., isn't just the same color as pickle juice—it actually tastes like pickle juice, too. Carbonated pickle juice that is. Neither the Original Flavor nor the Sport flavor has sold well and, therefore, Pickle Juice is not easy to find in stores, but it is available online.

15. **Orbitz:** The folks at Clearly Canadian were so successful with their flavored sparkling water that they decided to take a risk. Possibly inspired by bubble teas found in Japan, Orbitz drinks featured gelatin balls floating in semi-colloidal, fruit-flavored water. Orbitz resembled a lava lamp and tasted like something you immediately never wanted to taste again.

16. **Nuky Rose Soda:** This light pink soda from the Florida-based Nuky Corporation smells and tastes like perfume. After all, it's made from rose petals.

17. **Abali "Yogurt Original Flavor" Soda:** Carbonated dairy products might be obscure to the Western world, but yogurt sodas are very popular in the Middle East, especially in Iran and Afghanistan. Most yogurt sodas are naturally carbonated, due to the magic of fermentation.

Sit 'n Sip

Soda fountains were patented in 1819. The first soda fountains were installed in drugstores, which were sterile storefronts originally intended only to dispense medicines. To attract more business, pharmacists started to sell a variety of goods, including soda drinks and light lunch fare. That way, customers could come in to shop, take time out for some refreshment, and possibly do extra shopping before they left. Soda fountains were wildly popular before fizzling out in the 1950s.

One Big, Happy, Gourmet World

Cow's tongue, escargot, chitterlings, and frog's legs: North Americans aren't strangers to strange foods. But take a quick look at these "delicacies" from around the globe for a real taste of the exotic.

✳ ✳ ✳ ✳

Puffer Fish (aka Blowfish)—This Japanese luxury with skin and internal organs that are highly toxic to humans can be delicious—if prepared correctly. If not, side effects range from lightheadedness and rapid heartbeat to coma and death.

Putrefied Shark—Though Iceland serves up a good svie (boiled sheep's head), why not go for the über-traditional hakarl (rotted shark meat)? The recipe is easy: Wash and gut a shark, bury it in gravel for six to eight weeks, then allow it to cure in the open air for another two months. Cut off the thick, brown crust, and enjoy it with the Icelandic liquor Brennivin's, or "Black Death."

Cobra Hearts—The Vietnamese get a lot of press for serving tourists still-beating cobra hearts washed down with a slug of cobra blood. Variations of the dish include cobra hearts dropped in a glass of rice wine. Pair with a few strips of roasted dog meat, and bon appétit!

Monkey Brains—Despite urban legends about certain cultures eating brains from a live, wriggling monkey locked in place, it's cooked monkey brains that many South Asian, African, and Chinese people embrace. This reputably easily digestible tissue can be made into stew and is considered a delicacy. It is also thought to cure impotence.

Spiders—Spider-eating is practiced in many countries, but Cambodia draws the most attention with its meaty, hand-size tarantulas known as a-ping. For about ten cents per arachnid, they are served fried with salt, pepper, and a bit of garlic.

Winging It

Psst: *Buffalo wings aren't made from buffalo. But they did* come *from Buffalo.*

✳ ✳ ✳ ✳

WING AFICIONADOS, BE sure to mark your calendars for July 29. The city of Buffalo, New York, has dubbed this date "Buffalo Wings Day" in a celebration that dates to 1977. Buffalo wings are deep-fried chicken wings that are covered in sauce. Butter and a vinegar-based hot pepper sauce are key ingredients. While the level of spiciness varies, most wing connoisseurs do agree that the savory appetizers taste best when paired with celery and blue cheese or ranch dressing.

But this wildly popular fare is not without controversy. Spicy debates rage over who can take credit for this culinary dynamo. Some folks claim that buffalo wings originated with a man named John Young, who started the wing-fling with a special "mambo sauce" at his Buffalo, New York, restaurant in the mid-1960s. Young went so far as to name his restaurant after the dish, calling it John Young's Wings 'n Things (he even registered said name with the county!). However, another legend credits Anchor Bar on Main Street (also in Buffalo, New York) for the fiery dish. According to one story, Teressa Bellissimo, who owned the bar with her husband, Frank, came up with the idea of broiling chicken wings (deep-frying came later) and adding a cayenne hot sauce in 1964. But Frank told a different story, insisting that when he received chicken wings instead of his usual supply order of chicken backs and necks—for use in his spaghetti sauce—he asked Teressa to do something with them. She did, and a gastronomic tradition was born.

Of course, recipes have changed over time, with every person coming up with their own special sauces and preparation methods. But one thing remains constant: Wings are hot stuff!

Setting Sake Straight

Most Americans consider sake a Japanese rice wine, but it is actually more akin to beer. Furthermore, a look back in time suggests that sake may have originated in China, not Japan.

✳   ✳   ✳   ✳

What Is Sake?

THE JAPANESE WORD for sake, *nihonshu*, literally means "Japanese alcoholic beverage" and does not necessarily refer to the specific rice-based beverage that foreigners exclusively call sake. What differentiates sake from other alcoholic beverages is its unique fermentation process. Although all wines are the result of a single-step fermentation of plant juices, sake requires a multiple-step fermentation process, as does beer. The ingredients are rice, water, yeast, and an additional substance that will convert the starch in the rice to sugar. People have always found ways to make alcohol with whatever ingredients are available, so it is likely that beverages similar to sake emerged soon after rice cultivation began. The most popular theory holds that the brewing of rice into alcohol began around 4000 B.C. along the Yangtze River in China, and the process was later exported to Japan.

The Many Ways to Ferment Rice

The sake of yore was different from the sake that's popular today. At one time it was fermented with human saliva, which reliably converts starch to sugar. Early sake devotees chewed a combination of rice, chestnuts, millet, and acorns, then spit the mixture into a container to ferment. This "chew and spit" approach to alcohol production has been seen the world over in tribal societies. Subsequent discoveries and technological developments allowed for more innovative approaches to fermentation. Sometime in the early centuries A.D., a type of mold called *koji-kin* was discovered to be efficient in fermenting rice. In the 1300s, mass sake production began in Japan, and it soon became the most popular national beverage.

Feeding Hitler

Have you ever seen a photograph of Hitler enjoying a Bavarian sausage? The answer is likely no, but it's not because he was a vegetarian.

✳ ✳ ✳ ✳

ADOLF HITLER WANTED the world to believe he was a vegetarian. This was propaganda—part of his image as a superhuman "aesthetic." He would publicly abstain from alcohol, tobacco, and womanizing so as to seem above all weaknesses. He often brought up his vegetarian diet in conversations and speeches, touting its virtues and predicting that Germany would eventually be a meat-free society. But Hitler was never a strict vegetarian.

Hitler drank alcohol (he used it to fall asleep), and he kept a mistress (Eva Braun). He also relished sausages and ham, and he had a weakness for caviar. When he began to suffer from an array of digestive problems, he was advised to take breaks from eating meat. Many of his doctors were actually quacks who prescribed a strange assortment of vitamin injections and fasting regimens. This was most likely the real reason for his occasional vegetarian diet.

But the myth of Hitler's vegetarianism has persisted. Tired of that name being included in their ranks, vegetarian activists have done much to unearth actual instances of Hitler eating meat. One of these is an excerpt from a 1960s German cookbook in which the author writes that "roast squab" was Hitler's favorite dish at a hotel where she'd worked. Apparently, he couldn't get enough of it. Leberknödel (liver dumplings) were another of his favorites.

✳ A clear demonstration of Hitler's hypocrisy was the fact that he banned vegetarian societies in Germany. Those who met openly to discuss the philosophy of vegetarianism risked imprisonment or worse.

Fast Facts

✳ The restaurant Denny's was originally named Danny's.

✳ Airlines in America buy 20 million barf bags a year.

✳ More car crashes happen on Saturday than on any other day.

✳ Lettuce is named for milk. The word is derived from the Latin word *lactuca,* which means milk. It's believed the term was used because of a white liquid that can come out of a lettuce stalk when it's snapped in two.

✳ The same person who came up with the comic book character Wonder Woman also came up with the polygraph.

✳ "Heroin" was once trademarked as a brand name. Bayer bought the rights to the word in 1898.

✳ Draft dodging between the United States and Canada has a long tradition. So many U.S. draft dodgers came to Canada during the Civil War that locals began to worry about competition for jobs. During the Vietnam War, Canada was still the draft dodger's destination of choice when as many as 80,000 men crossed the border northward. But the practice was no one-way street. Canadian draft dodgers often headed south to escape entering World War I; that is, until the United States entered the conflict in 1917.

✳ There are 21 moons orbiting Uranus.

✳ Traces of peanuts can be found in dynamite.

✳ JELL-O once tried to market a celery flavor. It also tried coffee and cola with equally poor success.

✳ The number of calories burned while eating celery surpasses the number of calories actually contained in celery.

✳ The Civil War was the first U.S. conflict in which soldiers were issued canned rations. Troops were given milk, beef, and vegetables. Union soldiers nicknamed canned beef from the Chicago meat-packing plants "embalmed beef." They made a concoction they called "milk toast" by combining hardtack with condensed milk.

The Land of Misfit Cereals

Beginning in the 1970s, nothing said "Saturday morning" like a TV blaring cartoons and a big, brimming bowl of sugary cereal. Well, that and fighting your siblings for the prize hidden at the bottom of the box. During the '80s, cereal makers started cross-promoting their products. Suddenly, bizarre cereals hawked by unlikely stars (and creatures) started popping up on grocery store shelves. Grab a spoon and dig into these misfit cereals.

✳ ✳ ✳ ✳

Nerds

IN 1983, NERDS candy was released. Fueled by the overwhelming response to the sugary nuggets, Ralston released Nerds Cereal in 1985. Like the candy, Nerds Cereal had two flavors, each in its own separate package, allowing the eater to decide which to enjoy first. The gimmick didn't translate to cereal, though, and while Nerds Candy continued to be successful, the cereal didn't fare as well and production stopped altogether.

Urkel-Os

Today, you'd be hard-pressed to get folks to admit they were fans of Steve Urkel, the ultra-nerd on *Family Matters*. But that didn't stop a cereal company from releasing Urkel-Os in 1991. While other novelty cereals used special shapes or colors to tie in the character on the box, Urkel-Os didn't even bother. Instead it simply featured banana- and strawberry-flavored "O" shapes.

Bill & Ted's Excellent Cereal

It was a hit movie and a somewhat successful cartoon, so in 1990, it seemed only natural that Bill & Ted's Excellent Cereal would work, right? Dude, totally wrong! Despite cinnamon oat squares, marshmallow musical notes, and the promise of "A most excellent breakfast adventure," the cereal was an enormous flop. Some blamed it on poor marketing while others pointed out that the cereal resembled a certain popular dry dog food. Whatever the reason, the cereal was deemed "bogus" and vanished from shelves in 1991.

Ghostbusters

Who ya gonna crunch? Originally unleashed in the mid-'80s as a tie-in to the *Ghostbusters* movie, the cereal, which featured marshmallow ghosts and fruit-flavored "no" symbols, managed to hang around for a few years. The draw seemed to be in part because the cereal company, Ralston-Purina, continually updated the box's design. When it appeared as though kids were finally tired of the cereal, Ralston-Purina tried a last-ditch selling point, marketing it as "the first cereal box that glows in the dark."

WWF Superstars

Pro wrestling is known for big, sweaty guys. Now, why anyone would think that turning said feature into a cereal was a good idea is beyond us. No wonder this 1991 cereal was gone in less than a year! Conspiracy theorists also claim that the WWF Superstars cereal was nothing more than repackaged leftover GI Joe Action Stars cereal.

Monopoly

Finally, game pieces that kids *can* put in their mouths! In 2003, General Mills teamed up with Hasbro to create Monopoly cereal, complete with marshmallows color-coded to match the corresponding property cards from the board game. Lest there be any confusion, every cereal box was clearly marked "Monopoly: Cereal Edition."

Green Slime

In 2003, General Mills unleashed their Green Slime cereal on unsuspecting breakfast aisles. The cereal featured green "slime-shaped corn puffs," which actually resembled green Xs, as well as strange orange marshmallow things that were supposed to resemble the Nickelodeon blimp logo. One can only imagine what color the milk was afterward.

Nintendo Cereal System

When the original Nintendo game system took off in 1985, Nintendo brass got together and came up with a plan to further expand their growing empire. Their hot new item was none other than the Nintendo Cereal System. The packaging for the cereal was unique: while most cereals came in brightly colored boxes, the Nintendo Cereal System box was primarily black. Also, the box was divided in half, one side filled with Super Mario Brothers cereal and the other with Zelda Adventure Series cereal. But the only difference between the two was the kind of marshmallows each featured—Mario had such objects as mushrooms and Zelda had boomerangs and other weapons.

While the cereal was only around for less than a year, it has taken on a life of its own with nostalgia buffs. Unopened boxes of the cereal have been selling for more than $100 on eBay.

C-3PO's

George Lucas was a marketing genius when he kept the "garbage rights" to his little film *Star Wars* and immediately started slapping the film's name and characters on everything from action figures to bed sheets. Still, more than a few people thought Lucas had gone to the Dark Side when he teamed up with Kellogg's in the mid-'80s and released C-3PO's, "A new force at breakfast." No one could figure out what the cereal was supposed to be shaped like, even though commercials plainly stated it was "twin rings fused together, for two crunches in every double O." Uh, tasty!

Mr. T Cereal

No, the A-Team didn't endorse it. And it wasn't anything more than corn-flavored "T" shapes, albeit with "a touch of brown sugar." Still, the commercials let us know that by eating Mr. T cereal, we were becoming part of a team "that knows how cool breakfast can be." But here's a little bit of trivia: In 1985's *Pee-Wee's Big Adventure*, Mr. T cereal was the breakfast of choice for Pee-Wee Herman.

Taste of New York

Some say it's better than an ice cream soda. Some say it's the ultimate New York City treat. (And some say it's better in Brooklyn.) But nobody says an egg cream has either egg or cream in it.

✳   ✳   ✳   ✳

So what is an egg cream, then? Traditionally, it's a careful mixture of milk, seltzer water, and chocolate syrup. As if anything about New York food was actually that simple.

First, it must be served in a small, curvy Coke glass. Second, the chocolate syrup, purists insist, must be Fox's U-bet syrup. A proper egg cream must contain seltzer, not soda water or mineral water, since those contain salt. The order in which the ingredients are added and the method by which they are then mixed is precise—though not everyone agrees on exactly how.

Lore has it that the egg cream was the early 20th-century creation of Louis Auster, who ran a neighborhood candy store in Manhattan. Why call it an "egg cream" if no eggs are involved? One theory is that "egg" in the name derives from the Yiddish word *echt*, which means "true."

Egg creams are such a part of life in New York that Lou Reed even wrote a tune about them called, well, "Egg Cream." He recalled that drinking the concoction made it easier to deal with the knife fights in his neighborhood.

Want to make one of your own? Here's the recipe: Pour an inch or so of chocolate syrup in the glass, then add an inch or so of milk (but not skim). Put in six to eight ounces of seltzer, allowing a head to form. Alternatively, add seltzer to the milk first, stir vigorously, and then gently pour the chocolate syrup down the side of the glass.

However you decide to make it, all agree you must drink your egg cream quickly before the foamy top dissipates.

Becoming an Ace of Cakes

Who wouldn't love monkeying around with frosting all day? It turns out that being a cake decorator isn't as easy as it seems.

Q: Cake decorators have been around forever, but shows such as *Ace of Cakes* seem to have brought new attention to the industry.

A: I think that people have become more educated in what they can ask for because they've seen it on TV. Although they're sometimes overeducated, because they think that's always feasible and practical.

Q: Any notable mishaps?

A: There have been times when the cakes have turned out less than geometrically correct, and there's some creative propping up. When I used to do more children's cakes, there was a lot of miscommunication between the people who took the orders and the kitchen in the back. Once, the cake form was from this woman for her daughter's birthday, and it said she wanted a "frog wearing a purple clown on its head." So we did it; then she was mad, because it was supposed to be a *crown*, not a clown.

Q: What would people be surprised to learn about cake decorating?

A: How much food touching is involved—it's very hands-on. When I was first learning, I was surprised at how aggressive you can be with cake. You can really throw it around and do a lot of moving and pushing and poking. It's a much more full-contact sport than people might imagine.

Q: In your expert opinion, what's the best accompaniment to cake: coffee, milk, or champagne?

A: Champagne. That's a no-brainer.

The Great Cheese Chase

Would you risk life and limb for a piece of cheese? For competitors in the annual Cooper's Hill Cheese-Rolling and Wake, the answer is a resounding yes, indeed.

✳   ✳   ✳   ✳

IT'S JUST BEFORE noon on the last Monday in May in western England's Brockworth, Gloucestershire, and the hills are alive with the sound of voices chanting, "Roll the cheese!"

Welcome to Cooper's Hill, which is actually more like a cliff: a 215-yard-long, almost completely vertical incline averaging a 1:2 and sometimes even 1:1 ratio in some places— a 70-degree angle nearly perpendicular to the sky. It's so steep that it's impossible to run down and maintain balance. And yet 100 people show up every year to race, tumble, and/or fall down the hill while chasing after an eight-pound wheel of double Gloucestershire cheese the size of a dinner plate.

Welcome to the annual Cooper's Hill Cheese-Rolling and Wake. No one is quite sure when the tradition began, but the earliest written record of the event is from 1826—and even then it was considered an old favorite.

Going Downhill Fast

Runners come from all over the globe to compete in one of five races, held at 20-minute intervals. After an arduous climb to the top, the runners—around 20 per race—sit in a line and wait for the Master of Ceremonies to escort the guest cheese-roller to his or her position. After the emcee gives the starting command, the runners scramble after the cheese, encased in corrugated paper and decorated with blue and red ribbons, which can reach speeds up to 70 mph. In rainy years, the hill is a muddy mess but easier for competitors to slide down; in dry years, the ground is a hard, unforgiving course ripe for scraping skin. To win, a runner must finish in about 12 seconds.

The grand prize, of course, is the cheese. Second and third place winners receive a small cash prize of ten and five pounds (about $15 and $7 respectively).

Extreme Cheese

There are an average of 30 injuries each year—mostly bumps and bruises, though the occasional broken bone and concussion are not unheard of. Spectators are also at risk: Those leaning too close to the edge may fall over. Others may get hit by a runner, or by the rampant cheese.

To minimize injuries, bales of hay are perched at the bottom of the hill to catch the runners, as is a local rugby team. Also onsite is a cave rescue team, ready to climb up after fallen contestants and carry them to nearby ambulances.

Big Wheel Keep on Turning

Nothing has ever stood in the way of Gloucestershire and its cheese roll. Even when rationing during both World Wars limited the nation's cheese supply, a wooden wheel was constructed instead, with a token nugget of cheese tucked inside for authenticity.

Recent events have canceled the public festivities a few times. In 1997, there was a record-breaking number of injuries (33), which led to the cancellation of the event in 1998 due to safety concerns. The roll has also been canceled because of the foot-and-mouth disease outbreak of 2001, and the unavailability of the local search-and-rescue team in 2003. But even so, the Gloucestershire cheese-rolling committee gathered together to roll a single cheese down the hill. After all, the cheese must go on.

7 Banned Foods

The following is a list of some foods and beverages that have been banned either because the particular species is endangered or because, if ingested, they can seriously threaten the health, safety, and well-being of the consumer.

✳ ✳ ✳ ✳

1. **Japanese Puffer Fish:** Also known as blowfish, these creatures are so named for their ability to inflate themselves to several times their normal size by swallowing water or air when threatened. Although the eyes and internal organs of most puffer fish are highly toxic, the meat is considered a delicacy in Japan and Korea. Still, nearly 60 percent of humans who ingest this fish die from tetrodotoxin, a powerful neurotoxin that damages or destroys nerve tissue. Humans need only ingest a few milligrams of this toxin for a fatal reaction to occur. Most puffer fish poisoning is the result of accidental consumption of other foods that are tainted with the puffer fish toxin rather than from the ingestion of puffer fish itself. Symptoms include rapid numbness and tingling of lips and mouth, which are generally resolved within hours to days if treated promptly.

2. **Absinthe:** The exact origin of absinthe is unknown, but this strong alcoholic liqueur was probably first commercially produced around 1797. It takes its name from one of its ingredients, *Artemisia absinthium*, which is the botanical name for the bitter herb known as wormwood. Green in color due to the presence of chlorophyll, it became an immensely popular drink in France by the 1850s. Said to induce creativity, produce hallucinations, and act as an aphrodisiac, the bohemian lifestyle quickly embraced it, and absinthe soon became known as *la fée verte* (the green fairy). But in July 1912, the Department of Agriculture

banned absinthe in America for its "harmful neurological effects," and France followed in 1915.

3. **Foie Gras:** Foie gras, which literally means "fatty liver," is what actor Roger Moore calls a "delicacy of despair." When Moore discovered how geese were tortured to create the hors d'oeuvre, he was so appalled that he teamed up with PETA (People for the Ethical Treatment of Animals) and APRL (Animal Protection and Rescue League) to educate the public. In order to create foie gras, ducks and geese are painfully force-fed up to four pounds of food a day by cramming it down their throats through metal pipes until, according to Moore, "they develop a disease that causes their livers to  enlarge up to ten times their normal size!" Investigations into foie gras farms have revealed such horrible, unabashed cruelty to animals that the dish has been banned in many countries and many parts of the United States.

4. **Casu Marzu Maggot Cheese:** *Casu marzu*, which means "rotting cheese" in Sardinian, is not just an aged and very smelly cheese, it is an illegal commodity in many places. Casu marzu is a runny white cheese made by injecting Pecorino Sardo cheese with cheese-eating larvae that measure about one-half inch long. Tradition calls for this cheese to be eaten with the maggots running through it. Sardinians claim these critters make the cheese creamier and that it's absolutely delicious. This cheese is widely, but not openly, eaten in Sardinia, even though the ban on it is only enforced sporadically.

5. **Sassafras:** Now recognized by the U.S. Department of Agriculture as a potential carcinogen, sassafras is the dried root bark of the sassafras tree native to eastern North America. Throughout history, sassafras has been used for

making tea, as a fragrance for soap, a painkiller, an insect repellent, and a seasoning and thickener for many Creole soups and stews. But the best-known use of sassafras lies in the creation of root beer, which owes its characteristic flavor to sassafras extract. In 1960, the FDA banned the ingredient saffrole—found in sassafras oil—for use as an additive because in several experiments massive doses of sassafras oil were found to induce liver cancer in rats. It should come as no surprise that chemicals and artificial flavors are used to flavor root beer today.

6. **Blackened Redfish:** In 1980, New Orleans chef Paul Prudhomme publicized his recipe for blackened redfish, which is still very popular today. The recipe was so popular that it sparked a blackened redfish craze in the 1980s, which so severely threatened the redfish stock that the Commerce Department had to step in and close down fisheries in July 1986. In Florida, strict conservation measures were enforced for two years. To this day, the state requires that anglers keep only one redfish per day and release any that do not fall into the 18–27 inch limit, handling their catch as little as possible to ensure that the fish survive upon release.

7. **Ortolan:** In the same cruel fashion as foie gras, this tiny bird has little to sing about, as historically it was horribly tortured before being eaten as a gastronomic treat by the aristocracy of France. Its fate was often to be captured, have its eyes poked out, and be put in a small cage, then force-fed until it grew to four times its normal size. Next the poor bird would be drowned in brandy, roasted, and eaten whole. Now considered a protected species in France, the ortolan is also in decline in several other European countries. Nevertheless, hunters still kill about 50,000 birds per year even though it is illegal to sell them.

Butter Sculpting

Dairy sculpting gets more and more ambitious.

✳ ✳ ✳ ✳

IF TOURISTS WANTED to see likenesses of the four greatest U.S. presidents sculpted on the side of a mountain, they would travel to Mount Rushmore in the Black Hills of South Dakota. If they wanted to see renderings of the eight presidents from the state of Ohio sculpted in 2,480 pounds of unsalted butter, they would have had to travel to the Dairy Products Building at the State Fair in Columbus during the summer of 2008.

Butter sculpting began centuries ago in Asia, with a group of Buddhists who covered altars and shrines with religious images carved from this dairy product. The art was brought to America in the 19th century and has since become a staple at state and county fairs. While cows have been the most popular subjects of the art since then, sculpted figures of such notables as Neil Armstrong, Jack Nicklaus, John Glenn, Dave Thomas, and Darth Vader have also been displayed. Tributes to the Cincinnati Bengals and Cleveland Browns were even exhibited in 2006, but the art was taken to a new level by sculptors Bob Kling, Alex Balz, Jan LaGory, and Paul Brooke in 2008.

They started their piece by building a steel and wooden frame to hold the one and a half ton "Mount Buckeye." Working in a 45-degree cooler, they began cutting from 55-pound blocks of butter and took 370 hours to finish their masterpiece. All eight Ohio presidents—William Henry Harrison, Ulysses Grant, Rutherford B. Hayes, James Garfield, Benjamin Harrison, William McKinley, William Taft, and Warren Harding—were depicted on the massive slab of butter. Close to half a million visitors viewed the group's work during the fair.

9 Winners of Extreme Eating Contests

Despite the obesity epidemic in America today, extreme eating contests are more popular than ever. Check out the world-record appetites of these extreme eaters.

※ ※ ※ ※

1. In 2006, ESPN2 televised the third annual Krystal Square Off hamburger eating contest in Chattanooga, Tennessee. The winner was Takeru "The Tsunami" Kobayashi, a 160-pound competitive eating champion from Nagano, Japan, who downed 97 square Krystal burgers in just 8 minutes. One of the top competitive eaters in the world, Kobayashi held the world record for hot dog eating until 2007, and he won the Nathan's Famous Hot Dog Eating Contest on Coney Island six years in a row (2001–2006).

2. In 2005, Sonya "The Black Widow" Thomas, from Alexandria, Virginia, became the lobster-eating champion, downing 44 Maine lobsters totaling 11.3 pounds of meat in 12 minutes, at the second annual World Lobster-Eating Championship in Kennebunkport, Maine. A mere 105 pounds, Thomas garnered her nickname for outeating male competitors many times her weight. Thomas has held more than 40 world titles, including one for eating 11 pounds of cheesecake in 9 minutes in 2004, and the 2011 Nathan's Famous Female Hot Dog Eating Championship Belt for chowing down 40 hot dogs and buns.

3. Some like it hot, and Rich "The Locust" LeFevre is no exception. In 2005, the 132-pound retired CPA from Henderson, Nevada, set the world record for scarfing 30 Tex-Mex rolls in 12 minutes; and 7.75 pounds of

huevos rancheros—a spicy Mexican breakfast dish—in 10 minutes in 2006. He also has the world record for eating 6 pounds of SPAM from the can in 12 minutes at the 2004 SPAMARAMA.

4. Wings are the thing for Joey Chestnut, a 230-pound extreme eater from San Jose, California. He's the world champion chicken wings eater, downing 182 of them in 30 minutes in 2007, at Wing Bowl 15, an annual event held in Philadelphia before the Super Bowl. In July 2007, he defeated six-time champion Kobayashi by eating 66 hot dogs and buns in 12 minutes at the annual Nathan's Famous Hot Dog Eating Contest. He beat his own record in 2009 by downing 68 hot dogs and buns in 10 minutes.

5. Shoofly pie is a rich Pennsylvania Dutch sponge cake with molasses filling. Patrick Bertoletti, a 190-pounder from Chicago, holds the shoofly pie–eating record, scarfing down 11.1 pounds (37 slices) of pie in 8 minutes in June 2007. Since he emerged on the competitive-eating circuit in 2006, Bertoletti has numerous victories under his belt, including a world record 275 pickled jalapeno pepper in 8 minutes at the 2011 La Costena "Feel the Heat" Jalapeno Eating Championship.

6. New York City window washer Bill "Crazy Legs" Conti is the world record pancake eater. In his rookie year as a competitive eater, Conti ate a 3.5 pound stack of pancakes (and bacon) in 12 minutes at the 2002 Hibernation Cup in Anchorage, Alaska. A documentary was produced about his life called *Crazy Legs Conti: Zen and the Art of Competitive Eating.*

7. Dale Boone, a 303-pounder from Atlanta, Georgia, holds the world record for eating reindeer sausages, downing 28 of Santa's helpers in 10 minutes in 2002 in Anchorage.

8. Oy, vey! Twenty-one matzo balls is a lot of dough for most people, but not for Eric Booker, a 400-pound heavyweight from Copaigue, New York. In January 2004, he ate 21 baseball-sized matzo balls in 5 minutes, 25 seconds, at Ben's deli in Manhattan to set the world record. Booker is also known in hip-hop circles as a rapper with two albums and numerous appearances on *Last Call with Carson Daly*, where he serves as announcer and "Eater in Residence."

9. Erik "The Red" Denmark, a 208-pounder from Seattle, ate a world record 4 pounds, 15 ounces of spot shrimp in 12 minutes in September 2006. He also holds the record for Native American fry bread, eating 9.75 fry breads in 8 minutes in October 2006.

✳ Bread was so important to the European diet for many centuries that a rise or fall in its price served as an indicator of economic well-being, and a baker who attempted to sell an underweight loaf could be hanged.

✳ Taste buds need 24 hours to regain full sensitivity after being exposed to cigarette smoke, spicy foods, or alcohol.

✳ A single coffee tree produces only about one to three pounds of beans per year.

✳ That early morning jolt of caffeine can be costly in Moscow. The price of an average cup of coffee is $10.19 US, the highest in the world.

✳ The human body contains approximately four ounces of salt.

Vodka: The Water of Life

Wet your whistle with some of these vodka facts.

❋ ❋ ❋ ❋

❋ This colorless alcohol hails from Russia, where its original name, *zhiznennaia voda*, means "water of life."

❋ To make vodka, vegetables (such as potatoes or beets) or grains (barley, wheat, rye, or corn) are put through a process of fermentation, distillation, and filtration. Grain vodkas are considered to be of the highest quality.

❋ The most expensive vodka in the world is Diaka, which comes in a crystal bottle that also contains crystals (much like the worm in some tequilas). The makers of Diaka attribute the vodka's exclusivity to its unique filtration process: through 100 diamonds up to a carat in size.

❋ In 1540, Ivan the Terrible stopped fighting long enough to establish the country's first vodka monopoly, and in the late 17th century, Peter the Great explored improved methods of distillation and means of export.

❋ During the reign of Peter the Great, it was customary that foreign ambassadors visiting the court consume a liter and a half of vodka. Lightweight ambassadors began to enlist stand-ins to drink so that the official could discuss important matters with a clear head.

❋ The Russian phrase *na pososhok* is a toast to the last drink given to a departing guest. It derives from the tradition that visitors traveling from afar would often facilitate their trip with a walking stick called a *pososh*, which had a hollowed-out hole on top. At the end of the visit, a glass of vodka was placed in the hole, and if the visitor could drink the vodka without touching the glass, he was likely able to get home on his own.

The Fast Food Graveyard

Some fast food restaurants seem to believe that we'll eat just about anything. But as this list of discontinued items attests, not everything passes mustard, er, muster.

✳ ✳ ✳ ✳

McDonald's McDLT

DESPITE MCDONALD'S ATTEMPT to get all acronym-y on us, the sandwich's full name was the McDonald's Lettuce and Tomato sandwich. Served inside two separate Styrofoam containers designed to keep "the hot side hot and the cool side cool," customers put their own sandwich together. Eventually people caught on that putting lettuce and tomato on top of a burger patty was something they could do in the privacy of their own homes. The McDLT went to hamburger heaven in 1990.

Burger King's Veal Parmigiana Sandwich

When most people think Burger King, they probably don't think of veal. Yet in 1988, Burger King added a veal parmigiana sandwich to their menu. Actually, it was a reintroduction, since the sandwich was originally introduced in the 1970s. Of course, after they covered it in cheese and poured tomato sauce over it, it was kind of hard to tell just what you were eating. Maybe that's what did it in—the fact that a fast food place was selling *veal!*

McDonald's HulaBurger

This was an odd concoction created by McDonald's founder, Ray Kroc, in 1963. Originally intended as a meat-free option for Catholics during Lent, the HulaBurger featured a giant pineapple slice in place of a hamburger patty. It would eventually be replaced with the Filet-O-Fish.

Taco Bell's Seafood Salad

Let's face it—nothing hits the spot after a party like a late-night trip to Taco Bell. That is, except for a brief period of time in the late '80s, when a peek at the Bell's menu would reveal an item guaranteed to induce a gag reflex: the Taco Bell Seafood Salad. The salad involved filling a tortilla shell bowl with lettuce, tomatoes, baby shrimp, and imitation crab meat. It was then topped with a variety of sauces and olive slices. It didn't last long.

Burger King Chicken Bundles

In what could best be described as chicken sliders, Burger King's Chicken Bundles were mini-sandwiches that were sold in packs of three. They were part of a 1987 marketing theme that included Burger Bundles. Neither really caught on, though, even after the burgers were renamed "Burger Buddies."

McDonald's McLean Deluxe

In 1991, McDonald's decided to add a healthy alternative to their menu. Enter the McLean Deluxe, which boasted a 91 percent fat-free patty. People were willing to put up with the sandwich's bland taste in favor of eating healthy, until it was discovered that carrageen, or seaweed extracts, was added to the meat. After that, sales plummeted; the McLean Deluxe was a thing of the past by 1994.

Burger King Yumbo

Back in the 1970s, Burger King wasn't content to merely be the home of the Whopper. Enter the Yumbo, a tasty treat with a rather unfortunate name. The Yumbo was created using ham instead of beef, a couple of slices of American cheese, and a sesame seed bun. Once all those ingredients were assembled, the whole thing was melted together into one gooey mess.

McDonald's Arch Deluxe

In one of the greatest fast-food marketing ploys, in 1996 McDonald's decided to tout their new Arch Deluxe as "the burger with the grown-up taste." While initial response to the sandwich was huge, reality soon set in: Despite the "special" mustard-and-mayonnaise sauce, the Arch Deluxe was really just a plain ol' hamburger. It was quickly removed from menus, and to this day, it is considered one of the biggest fast-food flops ever.

7 Disgusting Things Found in Food Products

You've probably heard about the woman who claimed she found a human finger in a bowl of Wendy's chili. It turned out to be a hoax, but many such claims turn out to be true. The following is a sampling of some of the most disgusting items found in food products. Bon appétit!

❋ ❋ ❋ ❋

1. In 2002, a woman was enjoying a bowl of clam chowder at McCormick & Schmick's Seafood in Irvine, California, when she bit down on something rubbery. Assuming it was calamari, she spit it into her napkin, only to find that it was actually a condom. The woman won an undisclosed amount in a lawsuit, but the restaurant unsuccessfully sued a supplier.

2. In Baltimore, Maryland, in 2003, a man was eating a three-piece combo meal at Popeyes Chicken & Biscuits when he bit down and found a little surprise wedged between the skin and the meat of his chicken—a deep-fried mouse! In fact, the restaurant had previous rodent infestation citations on its record.

3. During the summer of 2004, David Scheiding was enjoying an Arby's chicken sandwich, but it came with an unexpected topping—sliced human flesh. Turns out that the store manager sliced his thumb while shredding lettuce. Of course, he thoroughly sanitized the area, but the lettuce was still used! Scheiding refused to accept a settlement from Arby's and filed a lawsuit in 2005.

4. It's not a body part or a rodent, but *E. coli*—the nasty bacteria that thrive in the lower intestines of mammals and are excreted through feces—definitely qualifies as

disgusting. In 1993, more than 600 hungry Jack in the Box customers, mostly children, became very ill from ingesting the little buggers. Sadly, four customers died. Several multimillion-dollar lawsuits later, it was determined that the problem was with the meat supplier.

5. Imagine the surprise of five-year-old Jordan Willett of the UK when he poured a bowl of Golden Puffs breakfast cereal one morning in 2005, and out popped a snake! The two-foot long, nonvenomous corn snake was not inside the sealed cereal bag, so investigators are unsure how it got inside the cereal box.

6. In 2000, a two-year-old boy in the UK got the surprise of his life—and a stomachache—after munching on Burger King french fries that included a special treat—a fried lizard! The boy's family dutifully handed over the crispy lizard to the restaurant for further examination, and no lawsuit was filed.

7. In 2005, Clarence Stowers of North Carolina was savoring a pint of Kohl's frozen custard. Thinking that a chunk at the bottom of the dessert was candy, he decided to save it for last. How disappointed he must have been to discover that it wasn't candy, but was actually part of Kohl's Frozen Custard employee Brandon Fizer's index finger. "I thought it was candy because they put candy in your ice cream, to make it a treat," Stowers told a local news program. He refused to return the finger at first, having decided to keep it as evidence for his lawsuit.

How It All Began

Fry Daddy

Credit for America's French-fry fondness goes to President Thomas Jefferson, who sampled the thinly sliced, fried potatoes as an ambassador to France. He brought the delicacy home, serving "potatoes, fried in the French manner" at an 1801 or 1802 White House dinner.

But the food didn't become standard American fare—or even known as "French fries"—until World War I, when U.S. soldiers stationed in France developed a taste for the salty spuds. But whether or not the French fry actually originated in France is a subject of much debate. They may actually have developed in the river communities of Belgium as early as the 17th century, when folks replaced their standard fried fish with potatoes during the winter months as the river iced over.

This Spud's for You

History credits chef George Crum with inventing potato chips in Saratoga Springs, New York, in 1853, but some say it actually may have been his sister Katie. In any case, the recipe was never patented. According to lore, Crum was not only talented but also temperamental, and if an unhappy patron sent food back to the kitchen, Crum returned the dish inedible. And that's what he intended to do with the fried potatoes that were sent back for being too thick and soft.

He sliced the potatoes extremely thin, fried them to a crisp, and coated them with salt. The patron (who, according to some sources, was Cornelius Vanderbilt) loved Crum's potatoes; almost overnight, baskets of the newly dubbed "Saratoga chips" began appearing in restaurants all over the coast.

Tourists applied the recipe idea in their own kitchens. In 1895, William Tappenden took the chips from stovetop to store, delivering batches to retailers in his native Cleveland, Ohio. By 1921, potato chips were an American standard.

Funky Flavors of Jones Soda

For Seattle-based Jones Soda Co., if it's not innovative, it's not worth drinking. At least, that's how it seems when you take a gander at some of the flavors they've created over the years. Sure, they also make ho-hum ordinary flavors, like root beer, cherry, and cream soda, but how often are you going to get a chance to swig some roadkill-flavored soda?

* Antacid
* Bacon
* Bananaberry
* Black cat licorice
* Broccoli casserole
* Brussels sprout with prosciutto
* Bug juice
* Candy corn
* Christmas ham
* Christmas tree
* Dinner roll
* Dirt
* Fruit cake
* Fun
* Green bean casserole
* Happy
* Invisible
* Jelly doughnut
* Latke
* Lemon meringue pie
* Mashed potatoes and butter
* Natural field turf
* Pecan pie
* Perspiration (from the Seattle Seahawks Collector Pack)
* Pumpkin pie
* Roadkill
* Salmon pâté
* Sugar plum
* Turkey and gravy
* Wild herb stuffing

Fallacies & Facts About Food

Fallacy: Baking soda eliminates odors in the refrigerator.

Fact: Chemically speaking, the alkaline composition of baking soda may absorb and neutralize a bit of an acidic odor. But the humidity in a fridge can cause the baking soda to develop a hard crust, further reducing its already weak ability to tame tough odors. Replace the baking soda with an open canister of charcoal, which will do a much better job of soaking up smells.

Fallacy: Lobsters scream in pain when dropped into boiling water.

Fact: First, lobsters have no vocal cords. Second, lobsters, crabs, and other invertebrates have ultrasimple nervous systems that lack the receptors to feel what humans call "pain." Here's the explanation for the sound you hear: Air that is trapped under the lobster's shell expands rapidly in boiling water and escapes through small openings. So in the same way that teapots don't actually whistle, lobsters don't really scream.

Fallacy: Thanksgiving turkey makes you sleepy.

Fact: Although many people believe that the culpable compound in turkey is the natural sedative known as tryptophan, plenty of other foods (including beef, pork, and cheese) contain similar or higher amounts of the amino acid. Most likely, the other things you consume at your holiday table, including the alcoholic beverages and carbohydrates that accompany Mom's turkey, can slow your metabolism. This, along with a heavy meal that forces your diaphragm to work harder (it pulls the lungs down and hinders breathing), can leave you snoring on the couch after dinner.

Fallacy: Raw eggs carry salmonella.

Fact: According to the U.S. Department of Agriculture, 1 in 3,600 eggs is contaminated with salmonella. That's 300 dozen— if your family eats a carton every week, you may get one bad egg every six years. In many cases, the contamination is on the shell rather than in the egg itself (chickens aren't the cleanest creatures in the barnyard). The process of pasteurization, which many commercial egg plants employ, uses hot water baths to kill bacteria while keeping the egg inside the shell uncooked. When in doubt, always cook eggs completely, and be sure to purchase in-shell eggs from a dependable vendor. Also, while you're checking the carton for cracked eggs before you buy them, check the expiration date!

Fallacy: Food that falls on the floor is okay if picked up within five seconds.

Fact: Granted, the longer the contact time, the greater the amount of contamination, but food products that come into contact with any unsanitary surface can pick up pathogens in as little as two seconds. A quick retrieval may mean fewer harmful germs, but it's no assurance of safety. Bacteria can thrive on surfaces for as long as a month, so cleaning floors and countertops with a disinfectant can go a long way toward keeping your meals down—for good.

Fallacy: Dishes made with mayonnaise spoil quickly if not refrigerated.

Fact: Your family picnic may have made you queasy, but don't be too quick to blame Uncle Leo's potato salad. The commercial mayonnaise used by many home cooks contains vinegar, which inhibits the growth of the bacteria that cause food poisoning. Chances are that if you got sick from a dish made with mayo, it was because of another ingredient, such as contaminated chicken.

Champagne and the Widow Clicquot

Raise a glass of bubbly to the woman who defied odds to become the grande dame of champagne. Santé!

✻ ✻ ✻ ✻

Wining Widow

NO ONE WOULD have blamed Barbe-Nicole Ponsardin Clicquot if she'd decided to quit the wine business. She was, after all, only 27 years old and newly widowed with a toddler. The wine business her husband had left behind was failing miserably, and it was 1804—the well-heeled women of France were not expected to be seen outside of the nursery or the drawing room, much less run a business. Clicquot convinced her father-in-law to keep the wine business going. He agreed as long as she worked with a partner of his choosing: Alexandre Jérôme Fourneaux. Together they launched the company Veuve Clicquot Fourneaux (*veuve* is French for "widow").

Though the business started to make a name for itself among a small roster of Russian clients, Clicquot couldn't seem to outdo her competition, Jean-Rémy Moët, whose champagne had the distinction of being General Napoleon Bonaparte's personal favorite as well as a popular choice among Russia's royals. Not that this last point mattered for long: In 1806, Napoleon restricted trade with Russia and other foreign markets, making it difficult for Clicquot to get a foothold overseas.

In 1810, Fourneaux walked away from the struggling company, leaving Clicquot on her own. The business experienced another blow in 1812: France invaded Russia, who, quite naturally, began boycotting French champagne. Still, Clicquot refused to give up.

Race to Russia

The following year proved pivotal for the widow. The harvest of 1811 had been a good one, and her bottled champagne was coming of age just as the war between France and Russia was resolving.

The end of the war meant the end of the embargo was on its way—and Clicquot knew whoever arrived first on the Russian shore with a boatload of French champagne would have a major advantage. To beat the competition, she secretly commissioned a ship to leave before the ban was officially lifted; by the time Moët and others shipped their first load, Clicquot had a strong head start. The demand for her champagne was so great, her salesman in Russia sold out before he even left his hotel room.

La Grand Dame

The widow's second boost came in 1815 with her invention of *remuage sur pupitre*, or "moving by desk," as a better way to remove the debris from the fermenting champagne bottles. The previous process involved laying a bottle on its side and waiting for the sediment to collect, which took several months—a long time spent not making sales.

While her competitors, including Moët, searched for a more efficient process, Clicquot moved her desk into the wine cellar and asked for it to be riddled with slanted holes so the bottles could be stored upside down. Her vision cut the time down to six weeks; a mechanized version of this same process is still used today.

The widow Clicquot continued to build and expand her business, renamed Veuve Cliquot Ponsardin, until her death in 1866. It wouldn't be until 1996, however, that another woman would serve at the company's helm.

Exotic Fruit Explosion

As U.S. consumers grow increasingly fond of "superfruits," the time is ripe for some exotic new flavors.

✳   ✳   ✳   ✳

PRIOR TO ABOUT 2005, few U.S. consumers had heard of "superfruit." Coined by marketers to describe fruit that is nutrient- and antioxidant-rich (as well as somewhat of a novelty), the term quickly gained widespread usage. Some of the first fruits marketed as ultra-healthy superfruits included blueberry, mango, and pomegranate, followed by açaí, mangosteen, and goji berry.

So what other flavors are likely to achieve superfruit status? Some of the following exotic fruits have already been showing up in energy drinks, beauty products, and fancy fortified water.

Camu-camu: This fun-to-say fruit is native to Peru and is very acidic in taste. Organically prepared camu-camu is said to contain more vitamin C than any other fruit on the planet.

Cherimoya: This heart-shaped fruit from South America tastes like a tropical blend of pineapple, banana, and strawberry. Its healthy properties include vitamin C, calcium, and fiber, and it is particularly used in beverages, smoothies, or ice cream.

Lulo: Also known as "naranjilla," or "little orange," this is a small, tangy fruit hailing from Columbia, Ecuador, and Peru. Some say the green juice of lulo tastes like a combination of lime and rhubarb. The fruit contains vitamins B and C, calcium, and iron, and is popular in beverages and purees.

Rambutan: This distinctive-looking fruit comes from Southeast Asia. *Rambutan* translates to "hairy" in some Asian languages, and indeed, the fruit has a hairy exterior. Often used in desserts, the rambutan's sweet taste is similar to that of a litchi, and the fruit is a reliable source of vitamin C and calcium.

Let's Go Out Tonight...
for Canadian!

You'd be hard-pressed to find a Canadian restaurant in the United States (except for the nearly 900 Tim Hortons franchises... but we'll get to that), but Canada's cultural and geographic diversity has produced quite a few foods that can boast Canadian heritage.

✳ ✳ ✳ ✳

Arctic char: This is the northernmost freshwater fish in North America, caught commercially since the 1940s. Char is a little like salmon in color and texture, but its unique flavor elevates it to a delicacy.

Back bacon: Also called Canadian bacon in the United States, this cut has less fat than other kinds of bacon. It has a taste and texture similar to ham. Peameal bacon is cured back bacon that's coated with ground yellow peas.

Bakeapples: These are also referred to as baked-apple berries, chicoute, and cloudberries. Found mostly in the maritime provinces of Nova Scotia and Newfoundland, they taste—surprise—like a baked apple. These can be eaten raw or used in pies and jams.

Bangbelly: To ward off some of the wettest, windiest, nastiest cold on the continent, Newfoundlanders have long boiled up a pudding of flour, rice, raisins, pork, spices, molasses, and sometimes seal fat. The result is comparable to bread pudding and is commonly served at Christmastime.

Beavertails: No aquatic rodents are harmed in the making of this snack. These fried, flat pastries, shaped like a beaver's tail, are similar to that carnival staple called elephant ears. They can be topped with sugar, cinnamon, fruit, even cream cheese and salmon. An Ottawa specialty.

Bloody Caesar: Similar to the Bloody Mary, this cocktail is popular all over Canada. It's made of vodka, tomato-clam juice, Worcestershire sauce, and hot sauce, served on the rocks in a glass rimmed with celery salt.

Butter tart: Along with so many other aspects of their culture, the Scots brought these to Canada. These are little pecan pies without the pecans, perhaps with chocolate chips, raisins, or nuts. You haven't had Canadian cuisine until you've had a butter tart.

Cipaille: This layered, spiced-meat-and-potato pie is most popular in Quebec. Look for it on menus as "sea pie" in Ontario, not for any aquatic additives but because that's exactly how the French word is pronounced in English.

Cretons: Break your morning butter-and-jam routine and have some cretons instead! This Quebecois tradition is a seasoned pork-and-onion pâté often spread on toast.

Dulse: This tasty, nutritious, protein-packed seaweed washes up on the shores of Atlantic Canada and is used in cooking much the same ways one uses onions: chopped, sautéed, and added to everything from omelets to bread dough.

Malpeques: Many consider these Prince Edward Island delicacies the world's tastiest oysters, harvested with great care by workers who rake them out of the mud by hand. If you can find them, the "pride of P.E.I." will cost you dearly.

Maple Syrup: Close to 90 percent of Canada's maple syrup comes from Quebec, and Canada is the world's largest producer of this sweet, sticky pancake topping.

Nanaimo bar: New York also claims this confection, but the thoughtful Manhattanite doesn't utter that on Vancouver Island. It's a chocolate bar layered with nuts, buttercream, and sometimes peanut butter or coconut.

Perogi: Canada's large waves of Slavic immigration have brought these Polish–Ukrainian delights to the True North. They're small dumplings with a variety of fillings, including cheese, meat, potatoes, mushrooms, cabbage, and more. Top with sour cream and onions.

Ployes: Acadia, the Cajuns' ancestral homeland, loves its buckwheat pancakes. But these greenish-yellow griddle cakes contain no milk or eggs, so they're not actually pancakes. Eat them with berries, whipped cream, cretons, or maple syrup.

Poutine: Dump gravy and cheese curds on french fries: Voilà la poutine! Quebec is the homeland of poutine, but you can get it all over the nation. Ignore your cardiologist's entreaties for greater enjoyment.

Rye: This is the Canadian name for Canadian whiskey, though it's actually made with a blend of rye, corn, and barley. Prohibition in the United States created a boom for Canadian distillers, and this unique style became part of the national identity. Rye is generally sweeter than bourbon and retains a worldwide following among liquor connoisseurs.

Tim Hortons: Horton was a solid National Hockey League defenseman of long service to the Toronto Maple Leafs, but he's best known for founding a ubiquitous chain of donut shops. Though Tim Hortons sells coffee, breakfast foods, and sandwiches, the donuts are the most popular. With more than 2,700 franchises, you have to go pretty far into the Canadian bush to be deprived of your Tim's fix.

What a Gas!

So you want to be a banana gasser. Well, someone's gotta do it!

✳ ✳ ✳ ✳

Q: You gas bananas?

A: That's the short version. Have you ever wondered how bananas can make it from other continents to your grocery store in edible shape, and yet they turn black and disgusting after three days on your kitchen counter?

Q: But they're refrigerated while being shipped, right?

A: Banana pickers harvest them when they're green, and they're shipped in chilled containers. That's where I come in. New shipments are placed in hermetically sealed chambers, where I spray the fruit with gas to catalyze ripening.

Q: What type of gas do you use?

A: Ethylene, C_2H_4, which basically is what remains of the alcohol in liquor if you take out the water. Plants naturally produce ethylene, and it causes fruit to ripen. I'm in charge of manipulating the gas vents so the fruit ripens when we want it to ripen. The gas itself doesn't harm the fruit, nor does it harm people.

Q: Not to sound critical, but how hard is it to open a gas vent?

A: There's more to it than that. Here's the reality: First I have to evaluate where the bananas came from and how long they have been traveling. They go immediately into the chamber, and I have to decide how much gas to give them, what temperature to keep them at, and for how long. A given chamber's bananas need to have the same general characteristics, because one batch of fast-ripeners could cause the whole chamber of bananas to ripen too early.

Favorite Pizza Toppings from 10 Countries

Around the world, pizza toppings vary greatly, reflecting regional tastes, local foods, and cultural preferences. Take a look at some of the toppings that stack pizzas around the world.

✳ ✳ ✳ ✳

1. **India**—pickled ginger, minced mutton, and paneer (a form of cottage cheese)

2. **Russia**—mockba (a combination of sardines, tuna, mackerel, salmon, and onions), red herring

3. **Brazil**—green peas

4. **Japan**—eel, squid, and Mayo Jaga (mayonnaise, potato, bacon)

5. **France**—flambé (bacon, onion, fresh cream)

6. **Pakistan**—curry

7. **Australia**—shrimp, pineapple, barbecue sauce

8. **Costa Rica**—coconut

9. **Netherlands**—"Double Dutch"—double meat, double cheese, double onion

10. **United States**—pepperoni, mushrooms, sausage, green pepper, onion, and extra cheese

The Big Cheese

* Archaeological surveys show that cheese was being made from the milk of cows and goats in Mesopotamia before 6000 B.C.

* Travelers from Asia are thought to have brought the art of cheese making to Europe, where the process was adapted and improved in European monasteries.

* The Pilgrims included cheese in their supplies onboard the *Mayflower* in 1620.

* The world's largest consumers of cheese include Greece (63 pounds per person each year), France (54 pounds), Iceland (53 pounds), Germany (48 pounds), Italy (44 pounds), the Netherlands (40 pounds), the United States (31 pounds), Australia (27 pounds), and Canada (26 pounds).

* The United States produces more than 25 percent of the world's supply of cheese, approximately 9 billion pounds per year.

* The only cheeses native to the United States are American, jack, brick, and colby. All other types are modeled after cheeses brought to the country by European settlers.

* The top five cheese producers in the United States are Wisconsin (more than 2.4 billion pounds annually), California (2.1 billion pounds), Idaho (770.6 million pounds), New York (666.8 million pounds), and Minnesota (629.3 million pounds). These states account for 72 percent of the country's cheese production.

* Processed American cheese was developed in 1915 by J. L. Kraft (founder of Kraft Foods) as an alternative to the traditional cheeses that had a short shelf life.

* Pizza Hut uses about 300 million pounds of cheese per year.

* Someone who sells cheese professionally at a cheese shop or specialty food store is called a cheese monger.

* In 1886, the University of Wisconsin introduced one of the country's first cheese-making education programs. Today, you can take cheese-making courses through a variety of university agricultural programs, dairy farms, and cheese factories.

* Because of their ability to produce large volumes of milk, butterfat, and protein, black-and-white (or sometimes red-and-white) Holsteins are the most popular dairy cows in the United States, making up 90 percent of the total herd.

* June is National Dairy Month, and the last week in June is National Cheese Week.

* The Cheese Days celebration in Monroe, Wisconsin, has been held every other year since 1914. Highlights include a 400-pound wheel of Swiss cheese and the world's largest cheese fondue.

* Founded in 1882, the Crowley Cheese Factory in Healdville, Vermont, is the nation's oldest cheese maker still in operation.

* The Chalet Cheese Co-op in Monroe, Wisconsin, is the only cheese factory in the country that still makes the famously stinky Limburger cheese.

* Maytag Dairy Farms, maker of the award-winning Maytag Blue cheese, was founded by the same Iowa family that manufactures the popular home appliances.

* The Sargento Cheese Company in Plymouth, Wisconsin, introduced packaged shredded cheese in 1958. In 1986, the company went even further to ensure the "spread of the shred" by introducing the resealable bag.

Are You Going to Eat That?

In recent years, Hollywood has learned that people like watching others chow down on calf pancreas and camel spiders. Even so, one person's offal is another person's delicacy. Here are interesting foods enjoyed around the world.

✳ ✳ ✳ ✳

Poi (Hawaii): Taro root is boiled to remove the calcium oxalate poison, then mashed to a muddy purple paste. To most non-Hawaiians, it also tastes like muddy purple paste.

Muktuk (Alaska, Canada): Enjoy a hunk of whale blubber, which looks and feels in the mouth like densely packed cotton soaked in oil. It's attached to a thick piece of whale skin with the look and feel of worn tire tread. You cut off chunks of blubber and chew them—for a long time.

Black pudding (Britain, Ireland): Try some congealed pig blood that's been cooked with oatmeal and formed into a small disk. It doesn't taste like blood; more like a thick, rich, beef pound cake.

Chorizo (Iberia, Latin America): This is what remains after all the respectable pig offal has been made into normal sausage. By now we're down to the lips, lymph nodes, and salivary glands. It's spicy and tasty, provided you don't mind dining on an immune system.

Menudo (Mexico): Basically, it's cow-stomach soup. If you can tolerate the slimy, rubbery tripe chunks, the soup itself tastes fine. It's often served for breakfast to cure a hangover.

Scrapple (Pennsylvania): The Amish and Mennonites don't waste much, and pig butchers chop up leftover guts, cook them with cornmeal, then pour it all into bricklike molds to solidify.

Casu marzu (Sardinia): It's illegal in Italy to sell wormy cheese, so pragmatic citizens make their own by sticking a perfectly good round in the cupboard for a couple of months so flies can lay eggs on it. The larvae produce enzymes that break down the cheese into a tangy goo, which Sardinians dive into and enjoy, larvae and all.

Balut (Philippines): Ever get a hankering for soft-boiled duck or chicken embryos? Some Filipinos think there's nothing finer, even though one must sometimes pick miniature feathers out of the teeth.

Surströmming (Sweden): Primarily a seasonal dish in northern Sweden, this rotten fermented herring could knock out a wolverine. Even the Swedes rarely open a can of it indoors.

Fugu (Japan): Despite precise preparation by specially qualified chefs, this toxic puffer fish delicacy kills about 300 people per year. The emperor of Japan isn't allowed to eat fugu lest it be his last meal. For all that work and risk, it still tastes like fish, but you have to respect the chefs: To prove their skills, they must prepare and eat their own fugu.

Jellied eels (England): If you find yourself hungry as you hustle through London, grab a jellied eel from a street vendor. It tastes like pickled herring with a note of vinegar, salt, and pimiento, all packed in gelatin. Next time you're asked to bring something congealed to a potluck, interpret the request loosely and watch the fun.

Haggis (Scotland): Drink enough Scotch, and you'll eventually get so hungry you'll eat sheep innards mixed with oatmeal and boiled in the sheep's stomach. Safety-minded haggis chefs suggest poking holes in the stomach so it doesn't explode when the oatmeal expands.

Pombe (East/Central Africa): History shows that people will make alcohol from any ingredients available. That includes bananas, mashed with one's bare feet and buried in a cask. The result is pombe, an east African form of beer.

Durian (Southeast Asia): This football-sized fruit with spines poses one of the weirdest contrasts in the culinary world. It smells like unwashed socks but tastes sweet. Imagine eating vanilla pudding while trying not to inhale.

Vegemite (Australia): "Yeast extract" is a brewery by-product that looks like chocolate spread, smells like B vitamins, and tastes overwhelmingly salty. Australians love it on sandwiches or baked in meatloaf, and it goes well with cheese.

Lutefisk (Sweden): It's simply fish boiled in lye. The lye gelatinizes the fish, but if it's soaked too long, the mixture starts turning into soap. The taste is actually fairly mild; the smell depends on the fish used (reportedly, cod isn't the best choice).

Kimchee (Korea): A cultural staple, this spicy dish of cabbage fermented with salt and pepper smells like garbage to many. Most people have less trouble with the taste than the aroma, but we do taste partly with our noses.

Stinkheads (Alaska): If you travel to Alaska's Bering Sea coast someday, stop at a Yup'ik village and ask the natives about their culture. They have great fun introducing visitors to salmon heads that have spent the summer buried in the ground.

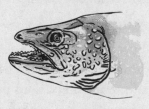

Sago beetle grubs (Papua New Guinea): Some tribespeople consider these bugs delicious. Then again, many of the same folks eat a lot of sago pulp (the inside of a palm tree). After months of eating tree innards, perhaps one would relish a roasted bug.

Qat (Horn of Africa): From Yemen to East Africa, people chew this leaf to get a little buzz. One doesn't so much chew it as pack it between his or her cheek and gum to get the full qat pleasure. Bear in mind that it is illegal in the United States.

Chapter Five

Love Is in the Air

In the Mood

Check out this list of aphrodisiacs. Some of them might even work!

✳　✳　✳　✳

Chocolate: Studies have found that chocolate and sex stimulate the same pleasure sites in the brain.

Oysters: They may be visually unappealing, but raw oysters are rich in zinc and other compounds necessary for sperm production and a strong libido.

Exercise: Getting in shape can actually make you better in bed. According to physiologists, regular exercise reduces your risk of sex-killing conditions such as obesity and diabetes. Exercise also improves heart function, which will better your endurance.

Ginseng: Long considered an aphrodisiac because of its phallic shape, ginseng contains compounds known to improve circulation.

Coffee: Caffeine is a stimulant, so it makes sense that a cup o' joe would get the heart racing and heighten one's sense of awareness.

Chili Peppers: The chemicals that make chilis spicy have long been considered an aphrodisiac, but whether they'll actually put you in the mood for love is questionable.

Yohimbe: This herb, made from the bark of a West African tree, may cause erections in men who suffer from impotency.

Offbeat Wedding Customs

Around the world, different cultures celebrate the bride and groom in some pretty unusual ways.

✳   ✳   ✳   ✳

Tying

"Handfasting" is a tying ritual practiced in one way or another throughout the world. In some African tribes, it involves tying together the wrists of the bride and groom with cloth or braided grass during the wedding ceremony. For Hindus, a string is used, and for the ancient Celts, handfasting *was* the complete wedding ceremony: A year and a day after the tying ritual, the couple was legally married.

Among the *fellahin* in northern Egypt, the priest ties a silk cord over the groom's right shoulder and under his left arm; then he says a prayer and unties him. Next, the priest ties the wedding rings together with the same cord, and after questioning the bride and groom about their intentions, he unties the rings and places them on the couple's fingers.

Though they don't call it "handfasting," Thai couples link their hands together for the wedding ceremony with a chain of flowers In a traditional Scottish wedding, the bride and groom tie strips of their wedding tartans together to symbolize the union of their two clans.

Breaking

Shattering crockery for good luck is a "smash hit" in a number of cultures. Russians throw their champagne glasses on the ground. The Greeks also throw their glasses, along with their plates. Jewish weddings end with the breaking of a wine glass to symbolize one of three things: the destruction of the ancient Temple of Jerusalem, the end of the bride and groom's lives as single people, or that the couple will share as many years as there are shards of glass.

Italian couples also count the shards from a broken glass or vase to see how many years they'll be happily married. Gypsy fathers-in-law count to see how many grandchildren they can expect, and Czechoslovakians just say the more pieces of the plate on the floor, the better the marriage.

Ukrainians follow a tradition called *Vatana*, breaking dishes with silver dollars to symbolize future prosperity, while the German custom is to host a pre-wedding dish-smashing party, called the *Polterabend*, during which family and friends shatter china (because glass is considered bad luck) for the engaged couple to clean up—the first of many messes they'll have to deal with as husband and wife. Bulgarian brides raise the stakes by filling the dish with food—wheat, corn, and raw egg—before tossing it over their heads; an English bride might drop a plate of wedding cake from her roof.

Other cultures skip the dish and just break the food. Hungarian brides smash eggs to ensure the health of their future children, and Sudanese ceremonies are marked by the breaking of an egg outside the couple's new home to symbolize the groom's role as master of the house. Many Middle Eastern cultures observe a pre-wedding "grinding" ritual in which the unmarried girls drape a cloth over the heads of the bride and groom and one of the girls—the "grinding girl"—grinds two lumps of sugar over them to repel evil spirits. The Iranian twist on this ceremony involves shaving crumbs from two decorated sugar cones over the heads of the newlyweds for good luck.

Circling

This custom may seem a little "loopy," but it's practiced the world over. Hindu couples finalize their union by taking seven steps around a ceremonial fire. Seven is also the magic number for Jewish couples. Traditionally, after stepping under the *chuppah*, or wedding canopy, the bride circles the groom seven times to represent the seven wedding blessings and seven days of Creation—and also to demonstrate her subservience to the groom. (In modern ceremonies, the bride and groom will often circle each other to show equality.)

For other cultures, three is the lucky number for circles. In the Eastern Orthodox tradition, a priest leads the couple in their first steps as husband and wife three times around the altar—to signify the dance around the Ark of the Covenant—while the choir sings three ceremonial hymns. Croatian wedding guests circle a well three times in honor of the holy Trinity and toss apples into it to ensure the couple's fertility. Moroccan brides circle their new home three times before entering it and officially assuming the role of wife.

Kidnapping

Likely a holdover from days of yore when women were stolen by rival tribesmen and forced into marriage, kidnapping is today a lighthearted custom practiced around the world. In a number of small German villages, the couple's friends kidnap the bride days before the wedding and hide her somewhere for the groom to find. The groom typically begins his search in a local pub, where he buys drinks for his friends to persuade them to help. In Latvia, the bride is often kidnapped by the groomsmen during the wedding reception, and the groom must pay a ransom (like buying drinks or singing a song) to get her back.

In some cultures, the bride and groom voluntarily leave. Danish grooms disappear during part of the reception so single men can kiss the bride; then the bride leaves so single girls can have a go at the groom. In the African nation of Burkina Faso, Fulani brides and grooms take turns hiding from each other—the bride before the wedding, the groom after. In both cases, it's up to the groom's friends to lead the search.

In Scotland, the groom isn't so much kidnapped by his friends as he is embarrassed. On "stag night," his buddies dress him up in drag, parade him to local pubs, and occasionally at the end of the night, strip him of his clothes and tie him to a tree in front of his house.

Star Power

Although he had every right to, Hugh Hefner wasn't bragging about his sexual prowess on the cover of Playboy *magazine.*

✳ ✳ ✳ ✳

IN ADDITION TO being founder and publisher of the world's largest-circulating men's magazine, Hefner also rightly holds claim to the title of "Playboy of the Western World." It's a reputation he has carefully cultivated from the moment he conceived the magazine that would make him rich and famous.

Hef's Secret Code?

Hef has made no secret of the fact that he has slept with hundreds of beautiful women over the years, so it seemed logical to many *Playboy* readers during the 1960s and '70s that the number of tiny stars that appeared on the cover each month was actually a sort of rating system for how good that issue's centerfold was in bed. In a variation on the story, the stars indicated the number of times Hef had slept with the Playmate. It was also rumored that when the stars appeared outside the "P" in "Playboy," Hef had been unsuccessful in seducing that month's centerfold.

These rumors ran rampant, and until recently the magazine's editors didn't exactly go out of their way to confirm or deny them. After all, such tales played up Hef's image as the ultimate ladies' man and *Playboy* as the lifestyle manual for the wealthy, sophisticated male. However, the truth is far less salacious than the myth: The stars merely indicated the domestic or international advertising region for that particular edition of the magazine.

"Picasso had his pink period and his blue period. I am in my blonde period right now."

—HUGH HEFNER

Putting Out the Welcome Mat: The Everleigh Club

The Everleigh sisters cashed in on the sins of the Second City.

✳ ✳ ✳ ✳

A T THE TURN of the 20th century, life was changing for American women, who enjoyed the freedom of working outside the home. Never before had more young women been out on the street—and some were *really* out on the street. Prostitution was a legal option in some areas, and many shrewd women realized that they could make enough money to live on by selling their most precious asset: themselves. In 1910, there were more than 600 brothels in Chicago.

Meanwhile, in Omaha, sisters Ada and Minna Lester—who later changed their name to "Everleigh" after their grandmother's "Everly Yours" letter sign-off—ran a successful brothel. When their Omaha establishment looked as if it had come to a climax, the sisters looked to Chicago—a juicier, more lucrative market.

In a business often linked with desperation and debauchery, the Everleigh sisters had a unique and oddly effective hook: class. The sisters claimed they had gone to finishing school; their supposed well-groomed background gave them an air of dignity.

Perfumed Fountains and Mirrored Ceilings

Ada and Minna found a place they liked at 2131–2133 South Dearborn in the Levee district. The finest linens, furnishings, and lighting were installed to make the new club stand out. Perfumed fountains were installed in every room, and a $15,000 gold-leafed piano was wheeled into the music room for some auditory stimulation. The dining room was modeled after a Pullman train car. A few mirrored ceilings and lush oriental rugs later, the Everleigh Club was ready to open. For a house of ill repute, the sisters certainly garnered a reputation for offering the most luxurious "amenities."

The doors of that house wouldn't open for just anyone, however. As the sisters would say, the club was "not for the rough element, the clerk on a holiday, or a man without a check book." No kidding—simply to enter the club cost $10, and any kind of hunger—carnal or otherwise—came at a stiff price. Dinner included caviar and was $50. A bottle of champagne would run you $12. If you wanted to spend private time with one of Ada and Minna's girls, that would take another $50. Considering the average wage for a typical worker of the time was about $6 a week, not just anyone was walking through the doors of the Everleigh.

Girls, Girls, Girls

There were also standards for the girls who worked inside the club. The sisters would say that to be given a job at the club, "a girl must have a pretty face and figure, must be in perfect health, and must look well in evening clothes." Though prostitution was rampant at the time, it wasn't glamorous; the Everleigh Club was an exception. The Everleigh girls were also exceptional for the era: They were well fed, their health was monitored, and they were paid well for less work.

And as for the kind of work they were doing, well, let's just say that Minna and Ada had a clear business plan: sell, sell, sell—and not just sex. The booze and food tabs were just as important as the tabs for "other" services. Said the sisters, "Contemplation of devilment was more satisfactory than the act itself."

The End of an Era

In 1911, Mayor Carter Harrison Jr. ordered the club to close. The Everleigh sisters went to Europe, then settled in New York. They changed their names back to Lester and spent the rest of their lives socializing and going to the theater. As for the club itself, it was razed in 1933. Today, the Hilliard Towers Apartments stand on the ever-so-sinful Everleigh grounds.

A Rose by Any Other Name...

Floriography, or the language of flowers, stems from the coded messages of the Victorian era that facilitated the exchange of feelings among the simply unpoetic or those who were forbidden to verbally communicate their passions.

✳ ✳ ✳ ✳

Traditionally, different flowers have represented particular sentiments. These are some of a wide variety of interpretations.

✳ Jonquil = Your affections are returned.

✳ Carnation = You're fascinating. I love you.

✳ Peony = I'm shy, but I like you a lot.

✳ Ivy = Marriage and fidelity are recognized.

✳ Sweet pea = You give me lasting pleasure.

✳ Red rose = I love you.

✳ Iris = Thank you, or Sending sympathy.

✳ Lily = You're a good friend.

✳ Sunflower = Congratulations, or Thank you for everything.

✳ Gerbera daisy = Cheer up, or Thank you.

✳ Tulip = Happy housewarming, or You're a great host.

✳ Floriography has roots in Persia and Turkey. In the 1600s, Turks used a simple "language" in which flowers replaced words. Floral arrangements were used to convey a variety of messages.

✳ Lilies have been a significant floral symbol for centuries, appearing as a spiritual and philosophical metaphor in mythology and folklore from Egypt to Greece. These days, the stargazer lily is considered one of the most versatile and popular flowers, and the meanings behind its exchange range from purity to prosperity.

* Roses are probably the flower most imbued with meaning—and that meaning is, of course, love. Cleopatra's first romantic encounter with Antony took place atop a one-inch carpet of roses. In ancient Greece, altars were adorned with roses and offered to the gods. In the name of a good party, the Romans sprinkled dinner guests with rose water, rubbed their bodies with rose oil, and covered floors with rose petals.

* The Greeks were among the first to use flowers in weddings, representing a gift from nature to the bride, groom, and their families. Bridesmaids were in charge of the flower bouquets and garlands and often made poesies (small nosegays) for each guest as a symbol of thanks.

* While living in Paris in 1818, Charlotte de la Tour wrote the first flower dictionary, *Le Language des Fleurs*. Inspired by this popular tome, Miss Corruthers of Inverness later wrote the book *The Language of Flowers*, and the subject blossomed. Many other reference books were written, which sometimes caused more confusion than guidance. Depending on the writers' interpretations, the meanings behind certain flowers could vary considerably. The hydrangea, for example, could refer to either the recipient's insensitivity or an appreciation for their forgiveness, so it was important that everyone was on the same page!

* Mistletoe plays a prominent role in Norse mythology. One legend involves the death of Baldur, son of Odin and Frigga, at the hands of the wicked Loki, who used a bow made of mistletoe. When Baldur is restored to life, Frigga is so grateful that she reconsiders the offending plant, making it a symbol of love and promising to bestow a kiss upon anyone who passed under it.

Fast Facts

❉ The "bones" in whalebone corsets were actually baleen—plates of "combs" in the jawbones of whales used to strain plankton from the water.

❉ A typical child laughs 26.67 times more per day than a typical adult.

❉ Ever hear someone say she wears her heart on her sleeve? Of course, that's just an expression. For a shrimp, though, it'd be literal and accurate to say it wears its heart on its head—the shrimp's blood-pumping organ is actually located there.

❉ The average lifespan of a goldfish living in the wild is 25 years.

❉ Male lions are able to mate 50 or more times in a single day. Tell your husband.

❉ A baby hippo weighs around 100 pounds.

❉ The first step on the moon by astronaut Neil Armstrong was with his left foot.

❉ Sportscaster Foster Hewitt is credited with being the first person to say, "He shoots! He scores!" It happened at a hockey game between 1931 and 1935.

❉ It is against pro table tennis regulations for a player to wear a white shirt while playing with white balls. The visibility is considered too difficult.

❉ Legend has it the striped barber pole has a bloody past. Barbers were evidently also surgeons in the old days, and tales say that they would hang up blood-soaked towels to dry on poles outside their shops, thereby creating the red-and-white stripe design still replicated today.

❉ A 100-pound woman in high heels exerts more pressure per square inch (psi) when walking than a 6,000-pound elephant. The elephant clocks in at around 75 psi, but the woman can apply approximately 1,500 psi to the heel point of her shoe.

Birds Do It

Mate for life, that is. And so do these monogamous breeds.

✳ ✳ ✳ ✳

Prairie Voles: The male of this rodent breed prefers to stay with the female he loses his virginity to, and will even attack other females.

Bald Eagles: Like all raptors, including the golden eagle, hawk, and condor, bald eagles remain faithful until their mate dies.

Wolves: Wolves and penguins practice serial monogamy. This means they have several mates throughout their lives but only one at a time. Penguins usually switch it up each mating season.

Anglerfish: Like a parasite, the male bites into the female, fusing his mouth to her skin. Their bloodstreams merge together, and the male hangs there, slowly degenerating until he becomes nothing more than a source of sperm for the female. (Sound like any bad marriages you know?)

Black Vultures: Gossip gets around—just ask a vulture. If one of them gets caught mating with a bird that's not its partner, it gets harassed not only by its "spouse" but also by all the other vultures in the area.

Gibbon Apes: These monkeys make a close-knit family unit, with mom, dad, and babies even traveling together as a group.

Red-Backed Salamanders: Males of these species are the jealous type, physically and sexually harassing their female mates if they suspect infidelity or even see them associating with another male. Yikes.

Termites: Termites can mate for life (that's about five years) and raise a family together—but they often leave each other within the first two hours of mating if something better comes along.

Brazen Bigamists

Some people really like the institution of marriage. In fact, some like it so much they get married again and again. Most of them get divorced between weddings— but a few are just brazen bigamists.

✳   ✳   ✳   ✳

Making (Serial) Marriages Work

Bigamy is a felony in 37 states, carrying a sentence of up to ten years in prison. The problem? Prosecutions are not that common, and many times, offenders come away with a slap on the wrist.

Anthony Glenn Owens was a man of God, pious and devoted to his church. At least that's what one Texas woman thought when he proposed to her in 2002. He even traveled all the way to Mississippi to ask her father for permission for her hand. Maybe her dad would have said no if he'd known what the new bride discovered. Owens was already married—to seven other women. Apparently he didn't believe in divorce.

After the couple established a new life and a church in Georgia, a female pastor told the woman that she'd seen Owens with seven other women over the years. She said he had cheated on them and stolen from them. The new Mrs. Owens began to investigate her husband's past, and she found several marriages and no divorces. So she took her findings to the police. Four of the wives came forward, claiming that Owens had used them and left them broke.

Owens was sentenced to two years in prison and four more years of probation. His defense? He never meant to hurt any-one, and as a man of God, he was misled by teachings of the Mormon faith (although he was not Mormon himself). He was released in 2005 but was back in jail by 2007 for parole viola-tions. What did he do with his free time in those 18 months of freedom? He proposed to four more women.

When You Love Love Too Much

Ed Hicks is another man who just can't get enough of a good thing. In fact, his profile on an Internet dating site claimed he was "in love with love." When the law caught up to him in 2005, he was married to two women and had been married to at least five others. In three cases, he didn't bother with divorce between the ceremonies. Unlike the devious Owens, who stole from his many wives before moving on, Hicks appears to be a sweet-talking romantic who is handy around the house. In short, the wives liked the guy.

What was once a problem for the women turned into a problem for Hicks when the ladies began to find out, and the dominoes began to fall. The last three wives have even formed an unofficial support group—and are committed to warning future wives about his secret past. Even after his arrest, Hicks began online relationships with at least four other women. The wives must know his type by now, because three of those "pen pals" were fictional women created by wife number six to see if he'd take the bait. He did.

Equality of the Sexes

Lest you get the idea that women are constant victims, and only men can cheat in the name of love, consider the case of Kyle McConnell (a woman) from Roseville, Michigan. She was charged with felony bigamy and sentenced to 22 months to ten years in prison.

The popular McConnell had a talent for finding lonely men, marrying them, and stealing their money, according to sheriff's Detective Tim Donnellon. Apparently, her pattern was to drain their bank accounts and move on to the next guy by the time the current husband found out.

It worked pretty well, too. All in all, she managed to marry about 15 men. Isn't love grand?

Wedding Chatter

✳ ✳ ✳ ✳

"Love is friendship plus sex and minus reason."

—MASON COOLEY

"I'm so in love, every time I look at you my soul gets dizzy."

—JESSE TYLER

"In Hollywood, brides keep the bouquets and throw away the groom."

—GROUCHO MARX

"Marriage is not just spiritual communion, it is also remembering to take out the trash."

—DR. JOYCE BROTHERS

"Better to have loved a short man than never to have loved a tall."

—DAVID CHAMBLESS

"Love is a game that two can play and both win."

—EVA GABOR

"Sometimes it's a form of love just to talk to somebody that you have nothing in common with and still be fascinated by their presence."

—DAVID BYRNE

"Grief can take care of itself, but to get the full value out of joy, you must have someone to divide it with."

—MARK TWAIN

"Heaven will be no heaven to me if I do not meet my wife there."

—ANDREW JACKSON

"We are all a little weird and life's a little weird, and when we find someone whose weirdness is compatible with ours, we join up with them and fall in mutual weirdness and call it love."

—AUTHOR UNKNOWN

"Never feel remorse for what you have thought about your wife; she has thought much worse things about you."

—JEAN ROSTAND

Sex on TV

It may seem like there's too much sex being shown on TV these days, but in fact, for most of television history, sex didn't appear to exist at all.

✳   ✳   ✳   ✳

First couple depicted in bed together: *Mary Kay and Johnny,* 1947. Anybody familiar with the golden age of television knows that men and women, even married ones, were never depicted in bed together. Preposterously, scenes shot in the bedroom—when there were any—showed two twin beds sitting primly beside one another. Surprisingly, though, the first couple shown in bed together on television predates the inane twin-bed scenario. According to Snopes.com, the 1940s-era sitcom *Mary Kay and Johnny,* a sort of precursor to *I Love Lucy,* often depicted the title characters sharing the same bed.

First interracial couple: *Star Trek,* 1968. The United States was undergoing some major civil rights tension at the time, so the passionate kiss between the white Captain Kirk and African-American Lieutenant Uhura definitely rocked the boat. Television stations throughout the South refused to air the episode.

First same-sex kiss, primetime: *Relativity,* 1997. Though same-sex kisses had occurred before on TV, the first depiction of homosexual smooching occurred on the short-lived series *Relativity,* which also has the honor of featuring the first recurring lesbian character in the cast of a television show.

First gay sex scene, primetime: *Thirtysomething,* 1989. Nowadays, the depiction of gay sex during this infamous episode of the hit drama *Thirtysomething* seems a little tame. In fact, there really wasn't a depiction at all—all it showed was a scene in which two gay male characters did little more than lay in bed after a presumed bout of lovemaking. Still, it was revolutionary for the 1980s. To this day, the episode has never been shown in reruns.

Getting Lassoed

What do lassos, coins, and donkeys have in common? You might encounter one or more at a Mexican or South American wedding.

✳ ✳ ✳ ✳

And Now a Word from our Sponsors

Conventionally, engaged Hispanic couples rely on the guidance of two carefully selected mentors. These "sponsors" are friends or family members, typically a male and female, who stand in as godfather and godmother. The sponsors are tasked with everything from spiritual guidance to financial assistance along the road to the altar.

Lucky 13

A traditional Mexican wedding ceremony may include the 13 coins ritual. The priest blesses the coins, and the groom bestows them upon his bride. This symbolizes the groom entrusting his new wife with his possessions, as well as his promise to support her. The bride's acceptance of the coins infers that she will honor his unconditional trust with dedication and prudence.

Bondage: El Lazo

Yee-haw! There are a couple variations to the Mexican lasso tradition, which symbolizes eternal unity. After vows are exchanged, a long, circular string of rosary beads or lasso chord is wrapped around the couple's necks, shoulders, or wrists in a figure eight. The "lasso" may first be blessed three times with holy water in tribute to the Holy Trinity. Often times, the couple will wear their lasso for the remainder of the ceremony.

Heart-Shaped Box

During the reception, guests may hold hands and surround the bride and groom in the shape of a heart during the first dance.

Ouch!

You've heard of tossing rice or confetti at newly married couples. One Mexican custom has guests pelt the bride and groom with red beads, a wish of good luck. It's not as bad as some European countries that go hardcore by throwing eggs at the happy couple!

Now You See Them...

...Soon you won't! In Venezuela, the bride and groom may play a disappearing act on their guests and vanish at some point during the celebration. It is believed to be good luck for a newly married couple to sneak out of their own party. It also eliminates the time-consuming practice of saying good-byes to everyone!

Breaking the Rules

A traditional Argentinean wedding excludes some common wedding customs. They nix the groomsmen and bridesmaids from the wedding party. Only the groom's mother and bride's father are permitted to escort the couple down the aisle. Also, the bride and groom are forbidden from exchanging rings during the vows and, instead, trade rings at the time of the engagement. Why wait?

Donkey Kong

Brazilian weddings are among the most festive and grand in the world. Vivacious receptions are marked by the *Caipirinha* (a cocktail of rum, sugar, and lime), *Casadinhos* (Brazilian "marry well" cookies), and *Pagoda* (a Samba-like dance). The bride is expected to arrive at least ten minutes late, and the groom had better be there first! For weeks prior to the ceremony, the bride may refrain from "eating directly from the pot," which is believed to ensure good weather on the big day. And how about this for a patriotic fashion statement: Instead of wearing floral boutonnieres, groomsmen may hold Brazilian flags. Perhaps the most intriguing aspect of Brazilian tradition, practiced only in certain parts of the country, is the *Bumba-Meu-Boi*. In this test of brawniness, the groom must tame an unbridled donkey to prove his worthiness.

8 Basic Rules of Nudist Camps

What really goes on at a nudist camp? A lot of non-nudists assume it's nothing but sex, ogling, and more sex. The truth is, nudist camps have very well-defined rules about appropriate behavior. And most nudists are really just there to sun, swim, backpack, canoe—even skydive—in their glorious birthday suits. So toss your misconceptions and clothes aside and remember these rules.

✳ ✳ ✳ ✳

1. **Take it off:** The most general rule is: "Clothed when practical, nude when appropriate." That means nudity may be optional while dining or at a dance, but it may be "required" in certain designated areas, including the pool.

2. **Tote a towel:** Make that two. Proper nudist etiquette deems you carry one towel to sit or lounge on and a second towel for drying off at the pool. It's all about being polite—and sanitary. And while we're at it, remember to pack that sunscreen!

3. **Don't gawk or stalk:** This is not the place to peep, pry, pick up, or be a paparazzo. Staring is considered a form of aggression.

4. **No photos, please:** Along those same lines, be sure to check the resort or facility's photography guidelines before trotting out your camera. Most nudists are rather camera-shy, and it is considered rude to take photos without asking first. After all, no one wants their boss to see photos from their nudist vacation on the Internet!

5. **Keep your hands to yourself:** In other words, ixnay the PDA. Any overt sexual behavior that causes others to feel embarrassed, offended, or uncomfortable could get you kicked out.

6. Stick with first names: Many nudists prefer to keep things on a first-name basis for privacy's sake.

7. Contain your excitement: Guys, erections are regarded as perfectly normal, but they're not exactly proper in public. If a case of overexcitement overtakes you, turn over, take a quick dip in a cold pool, or bury it in the sand.

8. No swinging allowed: Don't attend a nudist camp expecting a sexy time. Generally, nudist camps are adamant that they are not sex clubs, and anyone acting inappropriately will be kicked out. In fact, there are some camps that won't accept a married person unless their spouse also joins.

The Bare Facts

* Eager to experience the nudist lifestyle? In North America, you'll find more than 250 clubs and resorts where nude vacations are a possibility.

* One in four Americans (about 70 million people) have skinny-dipped or sunbathed in the nude.

* Nude recreation isn't just for aging hippies: 23 percent of EchoBoomers (born since 1979) and 18 percent of Xers (born 1965–1978) are looking for a nude recreation experience.

* A 2006 survey of telecommuters revealed that 12 percent of males and 7 percent of females work from home in the nude.

Fast Facts

✳ In 499 B.C., Histiaeus, tyrant of Miletus, sent a secret military dispatch by tattooing it on the head of his most trusted slave. The recipient would then shave the slave's head to read the message.

✳ George Washington's final military promotion, to general of the armies of the United States, didn't occur until 1976– 177 years after his death.

✳ The diary of King George III of England carried this entry on July 4, 1776: "Nothing of importance happened today."

✳ Before the outbreak of World War II, Winston Churchill was informed that the Italians intended to fight on the side of Germany. After consideration, Churchill responded: "That's fair; we had them last time."

✳ In 1830, Louis XIX became king of France when his father abdicated the throne. He held the title for a full 20 minutes before he abdicated as well.

✳ When the practice of smoking tobacco was first introduced to Europe, King James I of England foreshadowed attitudes 400 years later by describing it as "lothsome to the eye, hatefull to the Nose, harmefull to the braine, [and] dangerous to the Lungs."

✳ Pope Formosus died in 896, but that didn't stop him from standing trial for perjury in 897. His corpse was disinterred, dressed in papal robes, tried, found guilty, and thrown in the Tiber river.

✳ As he was being burned at the stake for heresy in 1314, Jacques de Molay reportedly demanded that Pope Clement V and King Philippe le Bel of France meet him before God to answer for their accusations. Both died within the year.

✳ After losing a congressional election in 1835, Davy Crockett told his constituents: "You may all go to hell, and I will go to Texas."

How the Birds and the Bees *Really* Do It

Humans can get pretty kinky in the bedroom, but we don't hold a candle to some of the other critters on this planet.

✳ ✳ ✳ ✳

✳ It's no fun being a male honeybee. Those "lucky" enough to engage in a mating flight with a virgin queen usually die after their genitalia snap off inside her.

✳ Flatworms are hermaphrodites, which means they have both male and female sex organs. During mating, two worms will "fence" with their penises until one is pierced and impregnated.

✳ Size matters—at least it does if you're a frigate bird. During mating season, males inflate their throat sacs while engaging in a wild dance. The females usually hook up with the males possessing the largest, brightest sacs.

✳ Size is also a consideration among Galapagos giant tortoises. When it comes time to mate, males rise on their legs and extend their necks; the male with the longest neck gets the girl.

✳ Orgies are all the rage among red-sided garter snakes. When a female awakens from hibernation, she releases a scent that attracts every male in the area. The result: a huge, writhing "mating ball."

✳ Male giraffes will not mate until they know a female is in estrus. To find out, they nudge a prospective mate's rump until she urinates—then taste her urine. If estrus is guaranteed, the male will follow the female around until she finally gives in to his advances.

✳ Male dolphins have very strong libidos. In fact, they enjoy sex so much that they've been known to mate with inanimate objects and even with other sea creatures, such as turtles.

The Lady Wore...

Before 1840, brides in the Western world were married in many colors.

❋ ❋ ❋ ❋

Why the White?

Yes, sometimes brides were married in white, but just as often, they chose other hues—even black. Their gowns might be dresses they'd worn before and would usually wear again. After 1840, however, white became the color almost every woman wanted to be married in and many demanded a "special" dress that would be worn on their wedding day and that day only.

So what happened in 1840 to change wedding style so dramatically? Young Queen Victoria of England. At just 20 years old, she married her cousin, Albert of Saxe-Coburg and Gotha, a handsome German prince. And she wore a white wedding dress. Unlike many royal engagements, this marriage was not all about power or politics, though it would certainly be advantageous in those areas. Victoria and Albert were truly in love, and their love would change not only how brides dressed but people's attitudes toward courtship and marriage.

When we think of "the Victorian age" now, we imagine a time of prudery and repression, led by an old widow in black. But when Victoria ascended the throne at age 18, she was fresh, youthful, and full of energy, if not beautiful. Her marriage to Albert was a good example of a larger trend that was taking place in the 19th century. Men didn't want to marry any ol' woman who could give them children, and women wanted to be seen as more than just housekeepers and breeding partners. Suitable companionship was no longer enough; people wanted to marry for love. And Victoria and Albert became the perfect role models. It was obvious to all that the queen had made a happy marriage that was, ahem, very active. Though Victoria loathed pregnancy and childbirth, the nine children she had with Albert make it pretty obvious that she was unable to keep her hands off her husband!

Less Purity, More Fashion

When Victoria chose white for her wedding dress, it had nothing to do with morality, purity, or virginity. It was simply a fashion statement: She wanted to use a white lace called "Honiton lace" on the dress, but she couldn't find a suitable color to pair with it. Finally, she just decided to do white on white, and the Honiton lace was sewn onto a white silk dress. Of course, once brides began imitating the queen—which they did immediately—the color white came to represent the virginity a bride was "giving" to her new husband. Purity wasn't the only perceived characteristic of a white wedding dress, however. A white dress worn for one day only was also a sign of social status. Many people simply could not afford such luxury, so those who could enjoyed showing it off and even flaunting it in the faces of those less fortunate.

Throughout the Victorian era, of course, wedding dresses were long, but starting in the Edwardian era (around the turn of the century) dresses were cut in whatever styles were popular at the time. Everything old is new again, though, and this trend reversed itself in the 1930s. Since that time, the vast majority of wedding dresses, especially those for first-time brides, have been long and white. While it is highly doubtful that Queen Victoria would appreciate, say, a strapless, mermaid-style wedding dress, she might be pleased to know that she still has at least some influence on wedding style 170 years later.

When Someone Else Knows Best

If you think arranged marriages are a thing of the past, or that they don't happen in the United States, think again.

❋ ❋ ❋ ❋

Modern Arrangements

While arranged marriage traditions are certainly controversial, and while abuse can definitely occur, they all can't simply be lumped together into one category. They are practiced by many different kinds of people and for many different reasons. For some, an arranged marriage may be for religious reasons; for others, the motive is purely cultural. Most arranged marriages are encouraged or even insisted upon by one or both sets of parents, but in others, the bride and groom themselves decide to take that route and have the freedom to give the final "yes" or "no."

Matchmaker, Matchmaker

In American Orthodox Jewish circles, many, if not most, young couples meet through the *shidduch*, a matchmaking process facilitated by parents, close relatives, or friends. They may even be paired through a professional matchmaker (known as a *shadchan*). These facilitators "check out" the prospective bride or groom as a way of shielding a loved one (or client) from emotional pain. If the prospective spouse passes muster, a meeting, called a *bashow*, is set up for the couple and both sets of parents. The parents break the ice with small talk, and then retreat to another room so that their children can speak privately. Some Orthodox Jews may even have many bashows before finding their *bashert* (soulmate), but the more conservative members of the Jewish community frown upon "dating around." A Hassidic rabbi's daughter, for example, would be expected to have very few bashows—and ideally, just one. If a bashow is considered successful, a relatively short engagement of anywhere from a few weeks to a few months is entered into.

Marriages Made to Last

Many Muslims in the United States also rely on family and friends to help them when it comes to finding an appropriate mate. This is necessary since very devout Muslims do not socialize with the opposite sex the way most young Americans do. For them, it is a way of keeping chaste and maintaining a modest demeanor. Though there can be pressure from parents to marry and have children, most Muslims deny that they would ever force a marriage on their child, citing a story in the Koran in which Muhammad spares a young woman from marrying a man she does not admire. Still, there are rare instances of adult children going through with marriages they do not really want for the sake of their parents.

Shared Expectations

Young Indian Americans also feel parental pressure to marry others from their culture and background. Of all the immigrant groups in America, their matchmaking process seems the most high tech, with websites, such as Indianmarriages.com, popping up on the Internet every day. Though their parents and immediate family play large supporting roles in their quest to find a mate, Indian American spouse-seekers may be a bit more independent and picky than those in other ethnic groups, and their techno-savvy backgrounds afford them some liberty and freedom of choice.

Bringing Back Betrothal

While most arranged marriages in the United States take place within immigrant communities, there is also a growing movement among homegrown, ultra-conservative Christians to revive "the courtship and betrothal process," and it's gaining converts rapidly. There are those who may be wary of this anti-dating crusade, in which young people are warned to "guard their hearts," but it will be decades before the fruit of its tenets can be judged.

The Curious Friendship of Cary Grant and Randolph Scott

Today, gay characters are commonplace on TV and in the movies, and stars are more likely to openly acknowledge their sexual orientation. But during the Golden Age of Hollywood, public perceptions regarding gay lifestyles could be quite biased. Usually a celeb remained in the closet for fear that it would ruin his or her career. Nevertheless, whispers and rumors persisted.

✳ ✳ ✳ ✳

The Gossip Mill

DURING THE GOLDEN AGE of Hollywood, when the major movie studios kept actors under contract, both on- and off-screen personas were constructed for their stars. The studios were adamant that nothing be done to ruin or damage those carefully groomed personas. They even had publicity departments with press agents who fed stories and photographs to fan magazines, which propagated the (glowing) images of the stars. Any aspects of their lives that did not fit their image were hidden behind the studios' carefully orchestrated propaganda.

Occasionally, an arrest, messy divorce, or scandal slipped through the gears of the star-making machine, but sometimes even those problems were covered up. The wild cards in this system were gossip columnists and nosy reporters, and it was this faction of the Hollywood dream machine that circulated veiled rumors about Cary Grant and Randolph Scott.

Closer than Close

The two actors met on the set of *Hot Saturday* (1932) and formed a quick friendship. A short time later they acquired a Malibu beach house and moved in together—supposedly to save money. Dubbing the beach house "Bachelor Hall," the pair threw lavish parties and, according to witnesses, generally reveled in each other's company. They lived in this fashion, off and on, for several years, and during that time, suspicious tongues took to wagging. Had the two really paired up to save on expenses, as had been put forth, or was something more salacious occurring? The idea of the two living together to split expenses wasn't as far-fetched as it might have seemed. Stars under contract to studios did not make the millions they do now. They made weekly salaries that went up only at the discretion of the studio. It wasn't unheard-of for up-and-coming actors to move in together.

Gossip columnist Jimmie Fiddler began to make veiled remarks about Grant and Scott's roommate status, and studio press agents only aggravated the situation when they tried to present the pair as the town's most eligible bachelors. Much later, gossip queen Hedda Hopper tried to "out" Grant in her column, but various people within the industry rallied around him, and Hopper backed off. The curious part was that neither man seemed much disturbed by the whisperings going on behind his back. In fact, each seemed indifferent to the potential backlash that might arise from their living arrangement.

So, were Grant and Scott gay? It depends on whom you choose to believe. Many friends and colleagues thought so. Director George Cukor supposedly revealed in interviews that the two were more than friends, and that Scott was willing to admit to it.

Perhaps They Were

In William Mann's book *Behind the Screen: How Gays and Lesbians Shaped Hollywood, 1910–1969*, photographer Jerome Zerbe tells of "three gay months" spent in Hollywood taking photos of the pair, in which he implies that the two were gay or bisexual, based upon his lengthy observations. Fashion critic Richard Blackwell went Zerbe one better, claiming to have slept with both actors.

But Then Again...

On the "perhaps not" side, Grant more than once declared that he "had nothing against gays, I'm just not one myself." A book entitled *Whatever Happened to Randolph Scott?*, penned by Scott's adopted son Christopher, puts forth similar, albeit somewhat predictable, denials about the famous duo's relationship. And director Budd Boetticher, who worked with Scott during the 1950s in some of the actor's most memorable Westerns, emphatically denied any rumors of the alleged romance. Further confusing the matter, Grant walked down the aisle a total of five times, and Scott took the plunge twice.

For their part, the actors let the insinuations slide past them the way a veteran actor sidesteps a bad review. If the two were gay or bisexual, they seemed rather comfortable with it. If they weren't, well, that too appeared to be okay. The most puzzling thing, however, was the fact that the Hollywood gossip machine couldn't or wouldn't bring them down. Did the actors' prodigious charm and drop-dead good looks neutralize writings about their offscreen romance? Had their studios suppressed information that proved conclusively that the two were gay? Were the actors just incredibly lucky?

More important are the films the two actors left behind and the ideals their screen personas represented. Grant's sophisticated, articulate, and well-mannered gentleman was the perfect comic foil for boisterous costars, providing audiences with classic films known for their snappy dialogue and sharp wit, including *The Philadelphia Story* (1940), *His Girl Friday* (1941), and *The Bishop's Wife* (1947). Scott's image as the stoic Western hero who always retains his integrity was used to great effect by Boetticher in *Ride Lonesome* (1959) and Sam Peckinpah in Scott's last film, *Ride the High Country* (1962). Each represented an ideal of masculinity that overshadowed their personal sexual preferences, whatever they were.

Behind the Sonnet

"How do I love thee? Let me count the ways." If this sounds familiar, it's because it is the opening line to Sonnet #43, one of the most famous love sonnets in the English language, written by Elizabeth Barrett Browning. Here is the inspiration for that enduring poem.

✳   ✳   ✳   ✳

Browning was born to a wealthy English family in 1806. She was a precocious child who published her first poem when she was 14. Her brothers received their education at boarding schools, but Elizabeth was mostly left on her own to learn what she could. Even so, she was well-versed in both classical and modern literature. Elizabeth lived with her father until she eloped to Italy at the age of 40 with the love of her life, fellow poet Robert Browning.

Robert had read a book of Elizabeth's poems and was so affected by her work that he wrote her a letter proclaiming his admiration for her. A mutual acquaintance arranged for the two to meet, and they immediately fell in love. Elizabeth wrote the love sonnet that became Sonnet #43 during the early years of their courtship.

The couple lived in Italy for the remainder of Elizabeth's life. In 1849, they had a son they nicknamed Pen, and they both continued to write poetry, acting as mutual sources of guidance and inspiration. Elizabeth published *Sonnets from the Portuguese* in 1850; the title comes from Robert's endearment for her, his "little Portuguese."

Elizabeth was successful during her lifetime, and today she is considered one of the foremost English poets. She also wrote a verse-novel and a series of political poems focused on the prominent social issues of the day. Although her love sonnets were immediately popular upon publication, they grew in fame after their connection to Elizabeth's real-life fairy-tale love was fully appreciated. Elizabeth died in Robert's arms in 1861.

Say "Yes!" to the World's Most Romantic Places to Propose

When it comes to popping the question, atmosphere is key. Below are some of the best spots the world has to offer.

✳ ✳ ✳ ✳

The Pont Neuf (Paris, France): *Ay, me. Say amour.* Paris, France: the city of lights, the city of love, and most importantly the city of *ahhh*mazing proposals. Paris is the epicenter for idyllic romance, so there is no surprise that its iconic structures follow suit. Pont Neuf, ironically meaning "new bridge," has now become the oldest bridge in France, making it a magical composition of old world charm and new age love. Available at all hours and completely void of any expense to roam, this distinctive destination overlooks the Seine River and is most striking at sunset when the city takes on an amber glow.

Overlooking the Pitons (St. Lucia): Every guy wants his proposal to be perfect. After all, it will be the story his bride will retell over and over again to anyone who will listen—at least until it is topped by the actual big day. So if the future groom wants to give his girl a ga-ga gorgeous proposal, he needn't look any further than the ga-ga gorgeous Gros and Petit Pitons in St. Lucia. Creating a picturesque backdrop of serenity, these volcanic wonders skyrocket over 3,000 feet from the admirably saturated blue waters below. Definitely a more costly alternative, this proposal spot can feature everything from a helicopter ride to a dip in the therapeutic Sulphur Springs.

Hot-Air Balloon Ride over the Masai Mara (Kenya, Africa): Hands down, one of the most well-known, well-loved adventures to experience, the calming nature of a hot-air balloon ride is undeniable, and when it's combined with the unmatched tranquility surrounding Africa's Masai Mara, there is no question of its magic. Sure, this kind of proposal can be rather expensive to accomplish, but when the outcome is a priceless result, it's impossible to compare.

A Sunset Sail in Bora Bora (Tahiti): Her timbers will surely shiver when you set sail at sunset in beautiful Bora Bora. The Le Meridien Bora Bora specializes in such proposals and can easily help any lovesick pup create a perfect memory. The epitome of Polynesian perfection, these sunset sails have all the ingredients for one outrageously quixotic "Will you marry me?" session: crystal clear waters, tropical breezes, sparkling champagne, and lovers at sunset. Bora Bora truly does offer more-a more-a!

Central Park (New York, New York): Central Park has been the mecca for romantic comedies the world over. From Carrie and Big (*Sex and the City*) to Ross and Rachel (*Friends*), film and TV watchers really connect with New York-based love affairs, making Central Park a no-brainer for proposal settings. Unlike most seemingly romantic spots, Central Park doesn't have to be warm to be beautiful. It is just as magnificent—if not more so—when it's cold...just one more perk to this already incredible park. And for a true man with a plan (and a little extra dough), the Per Se restaurant in NYC is ideal. Overlooking the entire park, the splurge-worthy dinner for two needs to be booked at least two months in advance but provides a nine-course menu, as well as personal service, to create a one-of-a-kind environment.

Vertigo Restaurant (Bangkok, Thailand): One of Thailand's most appetizing treasures, the Vertigo Restaurant—part of the Banyan Tree Hotel—provides the utmost in exotic atmosphere, but its striking appeal is only the beginning. Where this killer of cuisine really dazzles is in its efforts to keep every proposal personal. The concierge will work with every Prince Charming to provide sentimental touches, such as her favorite flowers or top-choice wine. Set 61 floors above the bustling city of Bangkok, this delectable dining experience makes a statement all on its own, but once it is accompanied by a beau down on one knee, the results are nothing short of electric.

Challenging the Times

It's never easy to buck social mores. This publisher found out the hard way that some lines are better left uncrossed.

✳ ✳ ✳ ✳

EVERY GENERATION THINKS that it's the first to discover taboo—and therefore tempting—delights. They forget that iconoclasts since the dawn of civilization have been questioning values and standards accepted by the social mainstream.

The radicals of the 1960s were no exception. And though they may not have been preaching anything new, a new generation was listening. Building on the ideas spread in the 1950s by the Beat Generation, '60s radicals confronted social issues that had long been ignored. And they dared to talk about sex.

Uncovering Taboos

One of the high priests of the era's new religion was Ralph Ginzburg, author, editor, photojournalist, and publisher. He was a controversial figure whose publications about art and erotica were ruled to violate federal obscenity laws. Who was this daring man who wanted to explore topics state and federal officials considered unacceptable?

On the surface, Ginzburg was no different than many of his generation. Born on October 28, 1929, he studied journalism, and following his 1949 graduation, he worked at the *New York Daily Compass* until he was drafted into the army in 1951. He was assigned to Fort Myer, Virginia, where he served as editor of the post newspaper.

Throwing Down the Gauntlet

After he was discharged from the service, Ginzburg returned to the world he knew so well. An independent thinker who spurned religious ties, he was determined to leave his mark on America's conscience. In 1958, Ginzburg published *An Unhurried View of Erotica*. In that book, he claimed that most English literature from the year 1070 through the 1950s contained bawdy or vulgar undertones. This scholarly publication was Ginzburg's first venture into exploring an "obscene" topic.

Government standards for evaluating pornography were changing at the time, and it was likely Ginzburg's work might have escaped notice—except for one mistake he made. In 1962, he sent out a mass mailing as part of an advertising campaign for *Eros*, a new magazine he had developed. Some of these fliers, however, were addressed to people who were not all that open-minded about sex. "*Eros* is a child of its times," one circular read. "It is the magazine of sexual candor." Unfortunately for Ginzburg, not everyone was clamoring for candor.

Going Too Far

A quarterly magazine, *Eros* contained articles and pictures about love and sex. But it also served as a means for Ginzburg to challenge establishment views on obscenity. While the second issue pictured a young couple kissing passionately on the cover, inside, Ginzburg included an essay on John F. Kennedy's sex appeal. By the time the fourth—and final—issue was published, Ginzburg had become a target of the U.S. Attorney General's office, headed by Robert Kennedy—JFK's younger brother.

Whether it was public pressure over the advertising campaign or retaliation for his inclusion of the president, Ginzburg was indicted in 1963 under federal obscenity laws. But a new movement had been set in motion. At roughly the same time, American "flower children" began glorifying the concept of "free love," and the country's value system was never the same again.

Although his conviction generated public sympathy and vocal support from some quarters, Ginzburg's judicial appeals fell on deaf ears. After serving eight months of a five-year term in Lewisburg Penitentiary, he returned to writing. Throughout his career, he published dozens of books and magazines, including the sexually explicit *Liaison* and erotic *Avant Garde*, before he died on July 6, 2006.

Wedding Chatter

❋ ❋ ❋ ❋

"My wife and I were happy for 20 years. Then we met."

—RODNEY DANGERFIELD

"Marriage is the triumph of imagination over intelligence."

—OSCAR WILDE

"I think men who have a pierced ear are better prepared for marriage. They've experienced pain and bought jewelry."

—RITA RUDNER

"One good husband is worth two good wives; for the scarcer things are, the more they are valued."

—BENJAMIN FRANKLIN

"Never get married in the morning, because you never know who you'll meet that night."

—PAUL HORNUNG

"Marriage is a great institution, but I'm not ready for an institution yet."

—MAE WEST

"'I am' is reportedly the shortest sentence in the English language. Could it be that 'I do' is the longest sentence?"

—GEORGE CARLIN

"My husband and I didn't sign a prenuptial agreement. We signed a mutual suicide pact."

—ROSEANNE BARR

"Saw a wedding at the church. It was strange to see what delight we married people have to see these poor fools decoyed into our condition, every man and wife gazing and smiling at them."

—SAMUEL PEPYS

"Love is life. And if you miss love, you miss life."

—LEO BUSCAGLIA

Alternative Marriage

Regardless of your position on same-sex marriage, it's probably safe to say that few would consider the following marriages anything but alternative.

✳   ✳   ✳   ✳

Erika La Tour Eiffel: In June 2008, a San Francisco woman legally changed her name to establish a bond with the famous tower after friends conducted a wedding between them. The bride complained, "The issue of intimacy—or rather lack of it—is forever present."

Eija-Riitta Berliner-Mauer: This Swedish woman took the German name for the Berlin Wall after "marrying" it in June 1979. Says Mauer: "In Eastern cultures people routinely believe objects have souls."

Sharon Tendler: In 2005, British-born Tendler married a male dolphin named Cindy. The monogamous type, Tendler calls herself a "one dolphin" woman.

Selva Kumar: After stoning two dogs to death, Kumar, a Hindu, made amends by marrying a female dog in 2007. He hoped that the union would lift the "curse" that followed him after his cruel act.

Mr. Tombe: A council of local elders forced a Sudanese man known as Mr. Tombe to marry a goat after he was caught having sex with the animal in 2006.

Dauveed: Mysterious Californian Dauveed popped the question to a mannequin named Clara in June 2009. While her response was presumably wooden, Clara apparently complied, and the two have made the Hollywood scene ever since.

Emily Mabou: Ms. Mabou decided to marry a dog in 2009 after being mistreated by men.

Groomzilla: The Very Married Signor Vigliotto

"Love 'em and leave 'em" could not have been a more appropriate motto for serial bigamist Giovanni Vigliotto, who wed 105 ladies without bothering to divorce any of them.

✳ ✳ ✳ ✳

VIGLIOTTO SAID "I DO" in ten different countries as he traveled the world hawking tchotchkes and furniture at flea markets. Although he was short, paunchy, and something less than Romeo-esque, the raven-haired Vigliotto had no trouble attracting ladies. Starting in 1949 at age 19, Vigliotto perfected a method that brought in a bride every time.

Something Borrowed, Something Boo-hoo'd

Vigliotto began each con by choosing an alias that seemed appropriate to whichever country or neighborhood he found himself in. (He later claimed he used too many aliases to remember them all.) After he carefully selected a woman of financial means, who also appeared lonely and vulnerable, he preyed on her sympathy by confessing that he was lonely, too. A proposal soon followed, but before the ink was dry on the marriage license, he'd find some reason to convince his new bride to sell her home and move. That left him in a position to zoom off in a moving truck laden with all his bride's possessions while she trailed behind in her car. He would then sell her purloined belongings at the next flea market.

Walter Mitty of Love

It was a profitable setup, but his luck ran out in November 1981. Earlier that year, he'd abandoned wife Sharon Clark of Indiana, leaving her in Ontario, barefoot, alone, and $49,000 lighter. With all the stubborn rage of a woman not only scorned but robbed, Clark reasoned that if she went to enough flea markets, she would eventually find her runaway groom. Sure enough, she tracked him down in Florida and caught him peddling her possessions. By that time, he was wanted in Arizona for taking Patricia Ann Gardiner, wife number 105, for $36,500 worth of goods plus another $11,474 in profits from the sale of her house. He was hauled back to Phoenix, where he stood trial in early 1983. The 53-year-old Casanova spent his time before the trial researching the history of bigamy.

Vigliotto played the wounded victim in court, asking plaintively why it was so wrong of him to open doors for women and bring them flowers, insisting that most of his wives actually proposed to him. He also painted himself as a sort of Walter Mitty of love, innocently acting out fantasies of marriage. He never did admit that it was wrong to rob the ladies after he married them.

I Do... Find You Guilty!

In less than a half hour, a jury found Vigliotto guilty on 34 counts of bigamy and fraud; the judge subsequently fined him $336,000 and slapped him with 34 years in prison, the maximum.

Vigliotto served eight years in a state prison in Arizona before dying of a brain hemorrhage in early 1991. Local papers reported various grandiose schemes hatched by Vigliotto during that time, such as a made-for-TV movie based on his life and a million-dollar deal to become the poster boy for a male virility drug, but his plans invariably fizzled, ensuring that Vigliotto's legacy will remain that of a record-setting bigamist.

✳ In 1791, Andrew Jackson married Rachel Donelson, believing that her former husband had applied for a divorce. A few years later, they were informed that no divorce had ever been sought, and the couple was being charged with adultery. Once the situation was remedied, Donelson and Jackson quietly remarried.

Tracy and Hepburn

Spencer Tracy and Katharine Hepburn are best remembered for their series of romantic comedies that rested on sharp-witted banter between the two stars. But their decades-long love affair was also one of the biggest open secrets in Hollywood.

✳ ✳ ✳ ✳

SPENCER TRACY AND Katharine Hepburn both struggled to develop their careers during a difficult first decade in the film industry in the 1930s. Hepburn had enjoyed some significant early successes, such as the 1933 films *Morning Glory* and *Little Women*, but a string of lackluster roles and her headstrong nature and independent inclinations (the woman wore *pants*, for goodness sake!) gave her the reputation of being box-office poison until she found her niche with the smash hit *The Philadelphia Story* (1940). Tracy, too, had struggled to establish himself as leading-man material throughout the early '30s and frustrated studio execs with both his ego and his bouts of drinking. He finally began to gain the respect of audiences and his colleagues after his triumphs in *Captains Courageous* (1937) and *Boys Town* (1938).

A Turning Point

When Tracy and Hepburn met for the first time while filming *Woman of the Year* (1942), both were poised to either reach the pinnacle of Hollywood stardom or slip back to the ranks of second-tier celebrities. Fortunately for them—and for movie lovers everywhere—their perfect pairing in this and the eight subsequent battle-of-the-sexes comedies they would go on to film helped solidify their star images and ensure their places in Hollywood history.

The contrast of Tracy's gruff working-class sensibility and Hepburn's haughty educated persona made them one of the big screen's most volatile couples. In films such as *Without Love* (1945), *State of the Union* (1948), *Adam's Rib* (1949), and *Pat and Mike* (1952), they exchanged brilliantly witty barbs over politics, business, and the roles of men and women in modern society as they coyly courted each other in cat-and-mouse fashion. For Hepburn, the roles softened her reputation as a brash, headstrong woman by bringing credence to her progressive viewpoints while at the same time showing that an independent woman could still find love with a traditional man. Tracy, on the other hand, expanded his stout, fatherly image to become a credible, even desirable, romantic figure.

Offscreen Passion

The pair fell deeply in love on the set of their first film and embarked on a complicated but heartfelt 25-year-long affair that did much to fuel their on-screen chemistry. Tracy had been married since 1923 and, as a devout Catholic, would not consider divorce. Though known as a philanderer long before meeting Hepburn, he was apparently wracked by guilt over his unfaithfulness and often took it out on her in public. In seeming contrast to her outspoken reputation, Hepburn put up with the abuses simply because she was in love and, as she described it, that meant putting Tracy's needs before her own. While the circumstances of their relationship were unseemly and at times even unhealthy, many of their colleagues in the industry were moved by the obvious devotion and sacrifice that characterized the couple. Tracy remained married but continued his involvement with Hepburn until his death in 1967. Theirs was a match that only could have been made in Hollywood.

The Sexual History of Corn Flakes

From the suppression of ardor comes a tasty breakfast food—
sprinkle that on your cereal in the morning.

* * * *

BY THEIR STRICTEST definitions, corn flakes and potassium nitrate (ordinary saltpeter) should have little in common. Yet at some point, these unrelated items were used to inhibit human sexual drive. Corn Flakes, the innocuous breakfast cereal known and loved by all, was devised as a sort of reverse Viagra, or *anaphrodisiac.*

John Harvey Kellogg (does the name sound familiar?) was born in 1852 in Tyrone, Michigan. His family later moved to Battle Creek, Michigan. This anonymous hamlet would eventually become world-famous as the home of breakfast cereals, but before this could happen, Kellogg would need to grow up and assume a more traditional, dignified stature.

In 1875, *Doctor* John Kellogg emerged from college and became medical superintendent for the Western Health Reform Institute. There, the devout Seventh-Day Adventist advanced his religious tenets by feeding patients a diet of bland foods. Kellogg believed that sexual abstinence promoted good health, that spicy and sweet foods stirred up passion, and that bland foods helped quell the libido. He and his brother, Will, invented many of the ardor-suppressing foods that he served to his patients.

While cooking up a batch of wheat in 1894, the brothers stumbled upon a formula that produced crispy flakes. Will wanted to add sugar to the new breakfast product and sell it outside the hospital, but John disagreed, since sugar could cause sexual arousal. Eventually, Will went on his own, changed the wheat to corn and started a company that marketed Kellogg's Corn Flakes. The cereal became one of the most successful in breakfast history. The moral: Sugar is sweet, and sex sells. Sorry, Dr. John.

Professor W. I. Thomas and the Scandal of 1918

Trumped-up charges—devised with the intent of pulverizing nonconformists—are not a modern-day concoction. Just look back to the "Scandal of 1918" and its victim to catch a glimpse of manipulative politics at its most conniving.

✳   ✳   ✳   ✳

PROFESSOR W. I. Thomas was a steadfast devotee of his two great loves: education and women. As a professor and prolific researcher, Thomas was deeply entrenched in his academic life. In his personal life, however, he was a sucker for the ladies. The combination of the two would prove to be his ruin.

An Unconventional Beginning

The son of a Methodist minister in a small Virginia farming community, William Isaac Thomas did not seem destined for academia. His ancestors stemmed from the Pennsylvania Dutch—so-called "plain people" who were more apt to drive a plow than to write a thesis. Thomas's love of learning was, at least in part, inspired by his father's insistence that he and his seven siblings be well educated. The family even moved from Virginia to Knoxville, Tennessee, the hub of the University of Tennessee, to ensure access to educational prospects.

Thomas began his voyage through academia at that university. Majoring in literature and classic languages, Thomas was awarded the University of Tennessee's first-ever doctoral degree. Upon graduation, he remained at the school and taught a wide array of classes: English, Greek, Latin, and German, just to name a few.

After studying for two years in Germany, Thomas accepted an English professorship at Oberlin College in Ohio, where he added sociology to his teaching repertoire. From there, he moved on to the University of Chicago, where he remained for nearly 25 years—until the Scandal of 1918 erupted.

Gossips Will Talk

Although Thomas was known as a womanizer, his escapades were mostly confined to episodes of overly friendly flirting rather than true acts of philandering. A frequenter of the bohemian art scene and known for his splashy presence, Thomas stood apart from his more conservative university colleagues. He and his wife, Harriet, were social activists and antiwar pacifists during World War I. The academic culture of the time was not keen on such liberal leanings, so Thomas was unsurprisingly somewhat of a professional outcast.

The real trouble began when Thomas was found in a hotel with the young wife of an army officer. Enlisting the Mann Act, local authorities were able to pinpoint a supposed illegality and file charges against Thomas. Although those charges were later dropped, the damage had been done. The scandal served to ostracize Thomas from the academic community for the rest of his life.

The Mann Act was the brainchild of James Robert Mann, a conservative lawmaker. Its purpose was to control prostitution, but it was repeatedly used in a questionable manner by authorities. One particular loophole was used to terrorize silent film star Charlie Chaplin, boxing great Jack Johnson, and legendary architect Frank Lloyd Wright. The law, designed to obstruct abductions for sexual slavery, restricted women from crossing state lines for sexual activity. Thus, the Mann Act could make a mutually acceptable drive into another state with a female pal into a criminal act of prostitution.

An Early Feminist?

Ironically, while Thomas was arrested for charges in line with the worst kind of female exploitation, his seminal work, *Sex* and *Society*, was quite feminist for its time. In it, Thomas called for a reevaluation of popular biological theories about the inferiority of women to men. Although many a modern-day woman might take offense at some of his specific language, Thomas was actually a maverick in finding more differences in intellect within the sexes than between them. Some boys are smart and others, not so much; the same holds true for girls. But, unlike the popular theory of the day, boys as a whole are not demonstrably smarter than girls. In fact, Thomas concluded that women might even hold the upper hand with their "superior cunning."

Thomas divorced his first wife, Harriet, after nearly 50 years of marriage. Soon thereafter, at age 72, he married his 36-year-old research assistant, Dorothy. It would seem that Thomas's reputation as a womanizer may not have been totally unearned after all.

Say What?

"The emotional, sexual, and psychological stereotyping of females begins when the doctor says, 'It's a girl.'"

—SHIRLEY CHISHOLM

"Never go to bed mad—stay up and fight."

—PHYLLIS DILLER

"Love is the answer, but while you are waiting for the answer, sex raises some pretty good questions."

—WOODY ALLEN

"Sex education may be a good idea in the schools, but I don't believe the kids should be given homework."

—BILL COSBY

Chapter Six

Pop Culture

Behind the Music of Our Time

✳ One of the backup singers on The Righteous Brothers' hit "You've Lost That Lovin' Feeling" was none other than a then-unknown Cher.

✳ The inspiration for Duran Duran's "Hungry Like the Wolf" came from Little Red Riding Hood.

✳ Blondie singer Deborah Harry worked as a Playboy bunny before becoming a full-fledged pop star.

✳ The Beatles' "I Want to Hold Your Hand" was the top-selling single of the 1960s.

✳ Elvis scored an unimpressive grade of C in his junior high music class.

✳ John Lennon's "(Just Like) Starting Over" is considered the best-selling posthumous hit of all time.

✳ Both pre-fame Elvis Presley and Buddy Holly didn't make the cut when they tried out for *Arthur Godfrey's Talent Scouts*, a '50s-era talent show.

20 Unforgettable Hairstyles

Some hairstyles stand the test of time while others do not. Below is a selection of hairstyles from the 1930s and beyond, for better or worse.

✳ ✳ ✳ ✳

1930s

1. **The Finger Wave:** Often hailed as the most tasteful decade, the 1930s found women styling curls and waves after Hollywood stars: Greta Garbo, Katharine Hepburn, and Carole Lombard.

1940s

2. **The Veronica Lake:** The smoky, alluring look of this 1940s screen siren was identifiable by miles of long, wavy blonde hair that covered one eye. This was the hairstyle of a star; everyday women opted for a shorter, shoulder-length version of the wavy style.

3. **The Rosie the Riveter:** Rosie was a popular icon during the war era when many women pinned back their long hair and covered it with a bandanna while working inside or outside the home.

4. **The Cary Grant:** The movies struck again, influencing the men's hairstyle of the time. This was a precise cut with a severe side part and a whole lot of styling wax to make it shine. The look was suave and debonair.

1950s

5. **The Bouffant:** When the salon-sized hair dryer was unveiled to the beauty industry, the possibilities seemed endless. Updos and blow-dried styles were literally taken to new heights as the bouffant and the beehive created big, round silhouettes.

6. **The Bardot:** The bombshell's film performances were only part of the reason women emulated Brigitte Bardot's

hairstyle—a sexy mess of long, strawberry blonde tresses. Bardot was the antithesis of the beehive and other hairstyles of the era that represented the repressed side of women at the time.

7. **The Pompadour:** This was the era when T-shirts and jeans became the uniform of young men everywhere. And the pompadour, popularized by James Dean and Elvis Presley, was the haircut that went with it.

1960s

8. **The Flip:** This spunky, youthful style was mega-popular among hordes of modern women throughout the 1960s. Shoulder-length hair was back-combed or teased slightly at the top, then the ends were curled up in a "flip" with rollers or a curling iron. Depending on the age of the woman and her willingness to push the envelope, the flip was combined with the bouffant, which meant that it got bigger and puffier. Mary Tyler Moore sported the classic flip on *The Dick Van Dyke Show*, and Jackie Kennedy had her own more conservative version, too.

9. **The Pixie:** The pinup figure went out of style when long, lean supermodel Twiggy came on the scene in the 1960s. Women everywhere tried to emulate her silhouette—and her hair. It took a reported eight hours to create the style on Twiggy the first time. The pixie was cut over the ears, with slightly longer hair on the top of the head. The defining feature was the close-cropped layers that framed the face.

10. **The Mop Top:** The influence of The Beatles on popular culture was unlike anything the world had ever seen. Girls and boys alike mimicked the boyish charm of these Liverpool lads, especially when it came to hairstyles. Longer, over the ears, shaggy, and generally floppy on all sides, the mop top was also sported by another mega-band of the time, The Rolling Stones.

1970s

11. The Farrah Fawcett: This iconic hairstyle, made famous by *Charlie's Angels* star Farrah Fawcett, came to a soft point at the top of the head, creating a triangular silhouette with long, feathered flips cascading down the sides and the back. This hairdo was revived in the 2000s as part of a retro '70s and '80s fashion trend.

12. The No-Cut Haircut: If you were a guy in the 1970s who didn't like getting a haircut, you were in luck. As the decade marched on, men simply stopped cutting their hair. Whether they were influenced by the free-loving culture of the hippies, growing antiwar sentiment, or just plain laziness, men's hair reached new lengths during this era.

1980s

13. The Mullet: No one can be totally sure when this notorious hairstyle originated, but its popularity soared in the 1980s. The mullet was achieved by cutting hair short and spiky or feathered on the top and sides of the head and keeping it shoulder-length or longer in the back.

14. The Rat-Tail: Popular with young men (and some women) of the '80s, this style was characterized by hair cut short all over except for a long strip of hair (usually ½ to 1 inch wide) growing from the nape of the neck and dangling down the back. Rat-tails were typically 4 to 12 inches in length and were often braided.

15. The Mohawk: The Mohawk had its roots in Native American culture but was popular with punk rockers in the '80s. Punk hairstyles in the United Kingdom and America reflected the attitude of these anti-establishment youngsters; hair was spiked, sprayed, shaved, and often multi-colored and sent a clear message: We're not like you.

16. The Meg Ryan: Immortalized by the romantic comedy *When Harry Met Sally*, Meg Ryan's tousled, permed locks were all the rage for women everywhere. Hairstylists reportedly did very little else for a period of several years, since women seemed to only want the spiral curls, highlights, and layered cut made famous by elite hairstylist Sally Hershberger.

1990s

17. The Rachel: Unless you lived under a rock in the mid-1990s, you knew about the group of *Friends* that hung out on the NBC sitcom for ten seasons. Jennifer Aniston's character Rachel spawned legions of hair clones. This long- to medium-length style was cut with many different layers in order to frame the face and give a woman's hair a full, healthy look.

18. The Fade: The early '90s brought hip-hop culture to the masses and the high-top fade haircut came with it. Popularized by rap duo Kid 'N Play, the fade was cut like a flattop but with the sides and back gradually fading from thickness at the top all the way to bare skin. Largely sported by African-American males, men of all ethnic backgrounds gave it a try, often with mixed results.

2000s

19. The Faux-Hawk: Want the edgy look of a Mohawk but don't want to go all the way? Consider the faux-hawk! By slicking back (or close-shaving) the sides of the hair, a fake or "faux" Mohawk can be achieved. Scores of fashionistas, both male and female, have gotten a lot of mileage out of this look in the early 21st century.

20. The Chelsea: With roots in punk rock culture, this haircut refers to the Chelsea district in London, a popular hangout for punks. But in the UK, this radical cut is called "the feather cut." In the style of many of today's haircuts, this look is one worn by both males and females. This style is achieved by shaving the entire head, except for the bangs and a little on the right and left sides of the head.

Inspiration Station

Elton's Ode to Billie Jean

The long-lasting friendship between Elton John and Billie Jean King began in 1974, when avid tennis player Sir Elton became so enthusiastic about the women's champ and her team, the Philadelphia Freedoms, that he and Bernie Taupin wrote a song about them. Elton joked that he dedicated the tune, called—what else—"Philadelphia Freedom," to King in return for a track suit she gave him, but in truth it was her passionate fight for the rights of both female tennis players and women in general that inspired him. The already wildly successful musician was nervous about playing the song for King, a feminist icon, for the first time, but she immediately loved it. "Philadelphia Freedom" was released on February 24, 1975, and quickly shot to No. 1 on the Billboard Hot 100 Chart. John and King remain close friends after all these years, working together on charity projects and, of course, playing tennis.

Postcard Inspiration

Most postcards don't cost much and are eventually tossed in the trash—pleasant to receive but nothing of lasting value. The same certainly can't be said of the postcard J.R.R. Tolkien carefully wrapped in paper and labeled "the origin of Gandalf." Gandalf, as any fan of *The Lord of the Rings* trilogy knows, is the greatest and wisest of all the wizards in Middle-earth; just one look at the painting on the postcard and it is easy to see where Tolkien got the idea for Gandalf. Painted in the late 1920s by Josef Madlener, *Der Berggeist* shows an elderly, somewhat mysterious-looking man with a long white beard and a wide-brimmed hat. Sitting on a large rock by a stream in a woodland setting, he gently pets a tame deer. While the scene is peaceful, the observer gets the sense that there is a lot going on under the surface and readily understands why this work was such nourishing fodder for Tolkien's fertile imagination.

Go Joe!

GI Joe is not a doll. No way. Here are some quick facts about this iconic action figure.

* * * *

* Joe was said to have been based on a 1963 TV show called *The Lieutenant* and named after a movie, *The Story of G.I. Joe*. The G.I. Joe action figure was created in 1964.

* Seeing the popularity of Barbie, brainstorming developers thought that a similar toy for boys would be a good idea. At the beginning, Joe had 75 different products at his disposal, all relating to the U.S. military.

* GI Joe was originally 12 inches tall, but he shrunk to 8½ inches when he became Super Joe in 1977. Shortly thereafter—partly because smaller *Star Wars* action figures became so wildly popular—Joe retired from toy stores. But Joe made a comeback, reenlisting in 1982 as a 3-inch-tall action figure and later, as a limited-time, larger "classic" collectible.

* Because the original 1964 Joe had 21 movable parts (including his waist), his twist-n-turn ability predated Barbie (who got her twist-n-turn ability in 1967).

* GI Joe had a female counterpart: GI Nurse (GI Jane to collectors), who in 1967 came with medical accoutrements for her own M*A*S*H. She only lasted a year before her enlistment was up; boys didn't want a girl doll, and girls avoided anything to do with GI Joe.

* When controversy over the Vietnam War began to hurt sales, Hasbro (makers of GI Joe) reassigned his platoon to an Adventure Team.

* Joe was never officially called a "doll." He had a brush with dolldom in 1993, though, when pranksters switched his voice with Barbie's and replaced both toys on store shelves.

Not-So-Super Heroes

Not every character in spandex can save the day. Here are five less-than-inspiring comic book heroes and villains who premiered in the 1960s.

✳ ✳ ✳ ✳

1. **Brother Power the Geek (DC Comics):** Brother Power came to life as a "puppet elemental" when lightning struck a tailor's mannequin covered with hippie clothing. He wandered California helping his fellow flower children take on "the man" but was canceled after two issues.

2. **Dracula (Dell Comics):** This second-rate batman was a descendant of the original Dracula. Hoping to clear the family name, he developed a serum out of bat blood that could heal damaged brain cells but was transformed into a bat himself when he accidentally ingested some of the elixir. However, rather than biting necks like his blood-thirsty ancestor, this Drac used his newfound powers to fight crime. The series was canceled after only three issues.

3. **Tin (DC Comics):** The Metal Men were good-guy robots made from various elements, including gold, iron, and mercury. Among the group was the irritating Tin. Weak and insecure, all he did was complain, forcing the other Metal Men to save his tin butt on a regular basis.

4. **Starro (DC Comics):** Super villains come in all shapes and sizes. Starro was. . . a giant intergalactic starfish. True, he could exert mental control over others and fire death rays from his appendages, but he was still just a starfish.

5. **Stilt-Man (Marvel Comics):** Stilt-Man, who regularly battled Spider-Man and Daredevil, had hydraulic stilts that allowed him to tower 60 feet in the air. Why his foes simply didn't knock him over and kick his keister remains one of comicdom's great mysteries.

The Golden Era of Cigarette Ads

When Sir Walter Raleigh helped popularize tobacco during the 16th century, he probably had no idea that he would be responsible for one of the largest and most profitable advertising campaigns in the history of Madison Avenue. These campaigns saw a single product go from lifestyle enhancer to pariah of the medical community within a matter of years.

✳ ✳ ✳ ✳

Give Me Your Young at Heart

BEFORE THEIR NEGATIVE association with health, cigarettes were marketed to successful young men and women as a way to relax and get more out of life. One mid-century ad for Lucky Strike cigarettes featured virile, athletic men and women prancing around tennis courts in snow-white shorts exclaiming, "WHAT A DAY…what a game…what a cigarette! Why is Lucky so much a part of moments like this?"

Like any other product that clamored for the consumer's attention, the multimillion-dollar tobacco industry embarked on a constantly evolving campaign. Advertising executives spoke to savvy young men and women about exactly how cigarettes enhanced the good life: "She swims…she rides…she's typically modern in her zest for the active life. Typically modern, too, in wanting to know the scientific facts about the cigarette she smokes," read one ad.

Showbiz Gets into the Act

Hollywood got into the action by glorifying the romance of cigarette smoking in films. A full-page advertisement in *LIFE* magazine showed a voluptuous actress draped in front of a roaring fire in her evening wear. The ad purred, "As lovely Maureen O'Hara knows, it's wise to choose a cigarette for the pleasure it gives." Even John Wayne got into the game when promoting his 1952 film, *Big Jim McClain*, boasting, "Mild and good tasting pack after pack. And I know. I've been smokin' em for twenty years."

Ironically, "The Duke" battled stomach and lung cancer, the latter of which he blamed on his six-pack-a-day habit.

About the same time, the young television industry found that Big Tobacco was only too happy to contribute millions of advertising dollars to a burgeoning industry that hadn't quite figured out how to pay for itself. One ad featuring an up-and-coming actor with political aspirations promised, "Want to be the next President? Just do what Ronald Reagan does, smoke lots and LOTS of Pall Mall Brand cigarettes! The sooner you start, the faster you'll rise to political success!"

Public Reaction

By the late 1960s, the tobacco industry became concerned with the negative association between their consumers' health and cigarette smoking. Advertisers countered these complaints with advertisements that reasoned, "Should you CUT DOWN now? Why cut down on the relief and enjoyment of extra smoking now, when you feel you need it most? Even chain-smokers find that new Julep Cigarettes banish unpleasant over-smoking symptoms. Unlike ordinary cigarettes, Juleps sparkle up your mouth, refresh your throat and keep your breath clean and inviting."

Everyone got on the bandwagon by promising that their products would minimize the unsavory side effects of inhaling hot, burning leaves: "No 'stale-tasting' mouth: Even if you chain-smoke, your mouth feels clean and sparkling all day long." Another ad ran: "No raw 'burned-out' throat: Miracle mint stays in the smoke of Juleps, and refreshes the throat. No 'dry-as-dust' rawness, even if you smoke 20–40–60 Juleps a day."

As pressure continued to rise, advertisers managed to draw the medical community into their web. Doctors (who, of course, smoked) went before television cameras and claimed, "After all, doctors are human too. Like you, they smoke for pleasure. Their taste, like yours, enjoys the pleasing flavor of costlier tobaccos. Their throats too appreciate a cool mildness." And who's going to argue with a doctor?

Fallacies & Facts: Music

Think you know your rock facts? Think again!

✳   ✳   ✳   ✳

Fallacy: The Beatles smoked marijuana in the queen's loo.

Fact: In 1965, the Fab Four went to Buckingham Palace to receive Members of the Most Excellent Order of the British Empire (MBEs) from Queen Elizabeth II. Afterward, Lennon boasted they had shared a joint in one of the palace bathrooms—though McCartney claims it was just a nerve-calming cigarette.

Fallacy: Peter, Paul and Mary's "Puff, the Magic Dragon" is about smoking pot.

Fact: The songs lyrics include references to Little Jackie Paper and the "land called Honah Lee"—thought by many to be code for rolling papers and a pot-growing Mecca in Hawaii (the village of Hanalei). Alas, the lyrics, written as a poem in 1959 by Cornell University student Lenny Lipton, are simply about the sad end to his carefree childhood. Lipton shared the poem with his friend Peter Yarrow, who made it into a song for his folk-singing trio.

Fallacy: Gene Simmons had a cow's tongue grafted to his.

Fact: Medical science can do amazing things, but surgically joining bovine and human tongues isn't one of them. The KISS vocalist and bassist does have a freakishly long lapper—and, in keeping with his shrewd marketing mind, he has gone to great lengths to exploit it.

Fallacy: Musician Marilyn Manson was a regular on *The Wonder Years.*

Fact: It's rumored that before he became the scourge of America's Bible Belt, the goth shock rocker played dweeb brainiac Paul Pfeiffer on the hit TV series. Sorry to disappoint, but that part was actually played by Josh Saviano, who went on to graduate from Yale and is now a lawyer.

Fallacy: Keith Richards underwent a full blood transfusion to kick his heroin addiction.

Fact: Rumor spread in 1973 that Richards, desperate to end his debilitating heroin habit before a Rolling Stones concert tour, checked into a clinic in Switzerland, where his smack-poisoned blood was drained and replaced with a clean supply. Actually, Richards underwent a form of hemodialysis in order to filter impurities from his blood. He later said he concocted the transfusion story to placate people who kept asking how he'd cleaned up so fast.

Fallacy: Deborah Harry was nearly kidnapped by serial killer Ted Bundy.

Fact: In 1989, the Blondie singer recalled to a newspaper reporter a night in New York City in the early 1970s when a man lured her into his car, which had no inside door handles. Freaked out, she reached through a partially rolled-down window, opened the door with the outside handle, and then ran away. She said she realized 15 years later that the creepy dude was actually Ted Bundy. Quite the tale, considering the fact that Bundy had never set foot in the Big Apple.

Fallacy: Bob Dylan didn't write "Blowin' in the Wind."

Fact: When Dylan released "Blowin' in the Wind" in May 1963, people in Millburn, New Jersey, claimed they had heard local teen Lorre Wyatt sing the tune months before. This led many to speculate that Dylan bought or even stole the song from the kid. Wyatt eventually admitted that he'd copped the tune (which Dylan wrote in April 1962) from a folk music magazine in September 1962, sang it at a band rehearsal a month later and, after wowing his audience, claimed the song as his own.

Really Stupid Hazing Incidents

Ahh, college. Institutions of higher learning, preparing the leaders of tomorrow. Oh, and along the way showing that some students can be really, really stupid—especially when it comes to hazing. Sadly, some incidents of abuse lead to death. Other times, people just look really foolish. (Not surprisingly, many of these initiations involved booze.)

✳   ✳   ✳   ✳

1. **Egg on His . . . Everything:** A University of Michigan freshman nearly froze to death in 1980 after he consumed a large amount of alcohol and then was stripped; shaved; covered with jam, eggs, and cologne; and shoved outside in near-freezing temperatures for more than an hour.

2. **No More Cold Steel on Ice:** Administrators at Kent State University in Ohio canceled the 1988 hockey season after a dozen players violated various university hazing laws. The students allegedly shaved the heads and bodies (again with the shaving!) of teammates. One student nearly died after being forced to drink alcohol.

3. **Compromising Positions:** The men's soccer team at the University of Washington was placed on probation after its members taped three rookie players to a luggage cart after posing them in . . . ahem . . . compromising positions.

4. **Tastes Like Chicken:** In 1997, a veteran baseball coach at the University of Wisconsin-Stout was suspended after senior members of the team encouraged rookie teammates to eat goldfish during a road trip.

5. **Can't Touch This:** In 1999, a state investigator confirmed a complaint of "improper sexual touching" and alcohol consumption made by members of the hockey team at the University of Vermont.

6. Shocking: Several frat boys at Stetson University in Florida were expelled from their fraternity after shocking pledges with an electrical device in 1980.

7. No More Male Bonding: The University of Vermont's 1999–2000 men's hockey season was canceled after freshmen said that they were forced to wear women's underwear and parade in a line where they were forced to hold each other's . . . manhood.

8. Deadly Turn of Events: The death of a Chico State University freshman drew national headlines in 2005 when he died of brain swelling from water intoxication after being forced to drink from a five-gallon water bottle. He was also covered in urine and feces.

9. Out of Tune: Even members of the marching band get in on the hazing freak show. Members of the Southern University marching band in Louisiana were hospitalized after partaking in an initiation. According to reports, at least one of the men was beaten more than 50 times with a two-by-four. Seven students were arrested.

10. No Comment Necessary: One website (which may or may not be serious) offers fraternities some "helpful hints" on ways to initiate pledges. Among them: paddling bare bottoms, forcing pledges to drink bodily fluids, and placing objects where objects should NOT be placed.

11. The Smoot: Not every hazing incident leads to death or pending lawsuits. Witness the case of Oliver Smoot, MIT class of 1962, whose participation in a freshman hazing stunt led to a unit of measurement being named in his honor. In October 1958, his frat buddies used the 5'7" Smoot to measure the Massachusetts Bridge. His exact height equaled one smoot (the bridge measured 364.4 smoots and one ear). For some reason, almost all MIT students know this.

Sock of Ages

Every spring, hundreds of fervent fans trek to Rockford, Illinois, home of the sock monkey, to pay homage to this all-American icon.

✳ ✳ ✳ ✳

Red Heel Is All the Rage

DOLLS MADE FROM socks aren't anything new, but there's only one "sock monkey," the iconic plush creature with giant red lips. The history of the popular monkey weaves a tale (or "yarn," if you will) dating back to 1872, when a machine was invented that guaranteed a seamless toe and heel. As with any great idea, knockoffs soon flooded the market. Though they had been making the iconic red socks since 1890, in 1932, the Rockford-based Nelson Knitting Company introduced the "De-tec-tip," a signature red heel, to help distinguish their socks as the real deal.

Sock It to Me!

During the 1940s and '50s, the company regularly sent its Red Heel socks to nuns in Wisconsin, who turned the socks into monkey dolls and then sold them to raise money. The company went ape for the idea and convinced Sears and Montgomery Ward to include a monkey pattern with each Red Heel sold. By 1953, Nelson Knitting Company had patented the design of the sock monkey, and patterns were included with every pair of socks.

The sock monkey strode through the '70s, then waned considerably until 2001, when photographer Dee Linder (known as the Sock Monkey Lady) sparked new interest with a website that showcased her photos of the primates about town. In 2005, this resurgence in monkey mania inspired Rockford to embrace its history and launch the Sock Monkey Madness Festival. Highlights of the two-day soiree include an international film festival, a sock monkey beauty pageant, monkey-making workshops, and even a "hospital" to treat old and "overly loved" monkeys.

Inspiration Station

Song for a Lost Friend

After relocating to Los Angeles in the late 1960s when he was barely out of his teens, rocker Neil Young was shocked at the rampant substance abuse in the musical community—and especially at the toll heroin use was taking amongst his friends and acquaintances. He became even more concerned after learning that many of those closest to him, members of his band and road crew, were shooting up on a regular basis.

In frustration he wrote the song, "The Needle and the Damage Done," which appeared on his 1972 album *Harvest* and is widely considered to be one of the shining gems in a career full of masterful songwriting. Sadly, his musical warning did not save his friend (and guitarist in his band Crazy Horse) Danny Whitten, who died of a heroin overdose in 1972 at age 29. Whitten was hired to play on Young's upcoming tour but was too high most of the time to make much of a contribution. Young fired him, giving him $50 for a plane ticket home. Unfortunately, Whitten spent it on the heroin that ultimately killed him. While saying he does not want to appear preachy, Young has nonetheless spoken out about the dangers of hard drugs ever since.

The Real Story of *Love Story*

Erich Segal was never a "preppy" like Oliver Barrett IV, the protagonist of his blockbuster novel, *Love Story* (that was made into an equally successful film). In fact, he grew up lower-middle-class in Brooklyn. But once he managed to get into Harvard, Segal met plenty of "Olivers"—including future vice president Al Gore, who got a lot of flack when he told *TIME* magazine that he and his wife Tipper inspired the lovers Oliver and Jenny. But Gore wasn't completely off-base: While Segal denied that Gore inspired the romantic side of Oliver, he did confirm to *The New York Times* that Oliver's difficult relationship with his father was based on the one Gore had with his dad.

10 Cool Items in the Rock and Roll Hall of Fame and Museum

Cleveland lobbied hard for the honor of hosting the Rock and Roll Hall of Fame and Museum, citing its rock 'n' roll roots—after all, disc jockey Alan Freed coined the phrase "rock 'n' roll" while working in Cleveland. Be sure to look for the following items when visiting America's best-attended hall of fame.

✳ ✳ ✳ ✳

Little Richard's 1950s black jacket with appliqués. Little Richard is a seminal architect of rock 'n' roll as we know it, having taken rhythm and blues music into the new era during the '50s. He was just as infamous for his flamboyant personal style as he was for his explosive performances.

Carl Perkins's 1956 Gibson switchmaster electric guitar. Perkins, a pioneer of rockabilly music, used this guitar while recording at Sun Studios from 1956 to 1958. Rockabilly was a core sound in the development of rock 'n' roll, and it was innovated at Sun—the self-proclaimed birthplace of rock 'n' roll—in the music of Elvis, Perkins, and Jerry Lee Lewis.

Chuck Berry's handwritten lyrics to "School Days" and "O Carol," 1957–58. Rock 'n' roll pioneer Chuck Berry scratched out the lyrics to two of his early tunes by hand. The lyrics and song directions seem simple on the surface, but they tapped into the universal experiences of teenagers.

Ringo Starr's Ludwig drumhead from The Beatles' 1964 appearances on *The Ed Sullivan Show*. Appearing on *The Ed Sullivan Show* in front of the deafening screams of the television audience escalated the popularity of The Beatles in America and spearheaded the British Invasion of the 1960s.

The Temptations' matching turquoise tuxedo jackets and The Four Tops' matching sequined jackets. Motown artists such as The Temptations, The Four Tops, and The Supremes were nearly as famous for the sartorial splendor of their stage costumes and the precision of their choreography as for their music.

Eric Clapton's hand-painted Gibson SG electric guitar, 1967. Influenced by American blues music, Clapton is a seminal figure of rock guitar playing. He has been inducted into the hall of fame as a member of the Yardbirds, Cream, and as a solo performer—the only person to be inducted three times.

Woodstock Music Festival poster, 1969. The poster's image of a white dove on a guitar embodies the spirit of Woodstock as three days of peace and music. The festival was held August 15–18, 1969, in Bethel, New York. Thirty-two of the era's most influential musical acts played for nearly half a million concertgoers.

Mick Jagger's American/Union Jack flag cape, 1981–82. Jagger's onstage costume worn while on tour included a cape made from the British flag, or the Union Jack, as well as the American flag. The costume represents both pride in being a British rocker and an irreverent attitude toward social institutions.

Run-DMC's Adidas shoes, 1986. Not since the early days of rock 'n' roll has a minority-based cultural phenomenon had such a strong hold on mainstream America as hip-hop. Part of hip-hop culture included fashion trends, such as these Adidas made famous by pioneer rap trio Run-DMC.

Madonna's gold bustier from the Blonde Ambition Tour, 1990. Like a chameleon, Madonna has continually reinvented herself throughout her career. During this time, she used her music to provoke thought about our society's prudish attitudes toward women and sex.

Warning: Disco Can Provoke Intense Anger

When most people hear disco, they want to get up and dance, right? Not everyone.

❋　❋　❋　❋

Lᴀᴛᴇ ɪɴ 1978, Chicago radio station WDAI made some changes and, in an effort to keep up with the current fads, it switched to an all-disco format. Folks everywhere were electric-boogalooing to Donna Summer, KC and the Sunshine Band, and the BeeGees. One employee, rock 'n' roll deejay Steve Dahl, got canned when the change took place.

Dahl was less than pleased with the pink slip, but he was able to snag a job at rock station WLUP, aka "The Loop." Dahl's morning radio show was soon a big hit. Still smarting from the disco fiasco—or maybe interested in drumming up publicity for his show—Dahl pitched the idea of a "Disco Demolition Night" for the July 12, 1979, Sox doubleheader against the Detroit Tigers. The price of admission would be 98 cents (for 97.9, the Loop's place on the FM dial) and a disco record. Between games, the records would be piled inside a giant box in the outfield, and the box would be ceremoniously blown up.

How It All Went Awry

Mike Veeck, the White Sox marketing director who helped organize the event, expected about 35,000 people to show up. When it came time to let people into Comiskey Park, there were 60,000 waiting for 52,000 seats. Those who couldn't get in through the gate tried to climb the fences.

In a 2009 *New York Times* interview, Tigers shortstop Alan Trammell commented, "I remember from the get-go, it wasn't a normal crowd. The outfielders were definitely scared, and Ronnie [Tigers center fielder Ron LeFlore, a former convict] wasn't usually afraid of anything."

After the first game was over, an army fatigue- and helmet-wearing Dahl, along with his entourage, drove onto the field where the huge crate full of disco records had been positioned. The DJ led the crowd in chants of "Disco sucks!" and detonated the explosives that had been rigged inside the crate. The explosion ripped a hole in the outfield grass and kept burning as the ringleaders of the spectacle drove off. As they did, people from every side of the stands rushed the field.

People burned banners, fights broke out, and many thousands wandered aimlessly, looking for a piece of the action. The Chicago police were called in after failed attempts by sportscaster Harry Caray and Sox owner Bill Veeck to get fans back in their seats. When the smoke cleared, six people were injured, 39 had been arrested for disorderly conduct, and the second game was forfeited to the Tigers, on the grounds that the Sox had failed to provide a suitable playing field.

When asked about the incident in 2009, Mike Veeck claimed that though the crowd did get out of hand, the attendees were not actually violent. He chalked this up to the fact that most of the revelers seemed to be high rather than drunk: "Had we had drunks to deal with, then we would have had some trouble."

What Did Disco Ever Do to You?

Many culture and music critics have examined what happened that night. Some say that the entire event was like a book burning, a hateful act born out of fear and rage at the minority and gay culture that had infiltrated America via disco music. Most others thought it was just a joke that got out of hand. Dahl supporters argued that they never intended to hurt anyone. They simply resented disco because it seemed to be taking over, and in their view, it was superficial and empty, while rock 'n' roll had real artistic merit.

Whatever your view, disco did start to lose its power in the coming years, but it was probably just the natural order of things.

"Crazed Publishers Forced Me to Read Their Drivel": Tabloid Sensationalism in the '60s

Looking at the cover of a 1960s-era issue of the National Enquirer *was much like slowing down to look at an auto accident—you knew you shouldn't, but you just couldn't help it.*

✳ ✳ ✳ ✳

THE NATIONAL ENQUIRER began its life in 1926 as a weekly broadsheet bankrolled by newspaper giant William Randolph Hearst, who was no stranger to sensational journalism. Yet, it was 1954 when an MIT engineering grad named Generoso Pope took over the paper and turned it into a tabloid. Realizing that magazines such as *Confidential*, with their outrageous headlines, were a huge success, Pope patterned the *National Enquirer* after them. By the 1960s, newsstands were featuring incredible cover stories:

✳ "I DRILLED A HOLE IN MY HEAD FOR KICKS!"

✳ "MOM USES SON'S FACE FOR AN ASHTRAY"

✳ "MADMAN CUT UP HIS DATE AND PUT HER BODY IN HIS FREEZER"

✳ "I CUT OUT HER HEART AND STOMPED ON IT!"

✳ "MOM BOILED HER BABY AND ATE HER!"

✳ "DIGS UP WIFE'S ROTTING CORPSE AND RIPS IT APART!"

✳ "I WATCHED A WILD HOG EAT MY BABY!"

✳ "SON MURDERS DAD FOR $8"

✳ "KILLS SON AND FEEDS CORPSE TO PIGS!"

Critical Cruelty!

When film critics speak their minds, the results can be painful!

✳   ✳   ✳   ✳

Paul Blart: Mall Cop: *"Looks like something stubbed out in an ashtray."*

—WESLEY MORRIS, *THE BOSTON GLOBE*

Miss March: *"A sex comedy that appears to have been made by people who've never actually had sex."*

—TY BURR, *THE BOSTON GLOBE*

The Women: *"It's not every movie that makes you wish Vin Diesel would run in and start blowing stuff up."*

—RENE RODRIGUEZ, *THE MIAMI HERALD*

Saw V: *"It's not a good sign when watching someone stick their hand into a table saw is easier than listening to them recite dialogue."*

—SAM ADAMS, *LOS ANGELES TIMES*

College: *"[This] film hasn't been made so much as excreted."*

—WESLEY MORRIS, *THE BOSTON GLOBE*

Disaster Movie: *"This carpet-fouling mongrel of a movie no more deserves release than do anthrax spores."*

—JIM RIDLEY, *LA WEEKLY*

Star Wars: The Clone Wars: *"A continuation of Lucas' experiments to see how much s**t his dwindling supporters will take before finally saying 'enough' and moving on to adult pursuits."*

— PETER VONDER HAAR, *FILM THREAT*

College Road Trip: *"Phi betta crappa."*

—DAVID HILTBRAND, *THE PHILADELPHIA INQUIRER*

The Love Guru: *"The most joy-draining 88 minutes I've ever spent outside a hospital waiting room."*

—DANA STEVENS, *SLATE*

Deception: *"A nonprescription alternative to Ambien."*

—LOU LUMENICK, *THE NEW YORK POST*

21 Top Toys

Times have changed since the days when an imaginative kid was happy to play with an empty cardboard box. Today, about 2.6 billion toys are sold every year, creating a $20.3 billion industry. So without further ado, here are some of the best toy fads of the 20th century.

✳   ✳   ✳   ✳

1950s

1. Silly Putty was developed in 1943 when James Wright, a General Electric researcher, was seeking a synthetic rubber substitute. His silicone-based polymer was elastic, could bounce, could be easily molded, and always held its shape. Parents liked the fact that the putty was nontoxic and nonirritating. Since its debut as a toy in 1950, more than 300 million eggs of Silly Putty have been sold.

2. In 1943, naval engineer Richard James stumbled across an invention that would become a beloved toy worldwide. Made of 87 feet of flat wire coiled into a three-inch-diameter circle, the Slinky could "walk" down stairs when one end was placed on one step and the other on the step below. The classic slinky really took off in the 1950s, and today more than 300 million of the simple-yet-clever toys have sold worldwide.

3. With his interchangeable facial features, Mr. Potato Head was patented in 1952 and was the first toy to be advertised on television. But for the first eight years, parents had to supply children with a real potato until a plastic potato body was included in 1960.

4. Intending to create a wallpaper cleaner, Joseph and Noah McVicker invented Play-Doh in 1955. Initially available in

only one color (off-white) and in a 1.5-pound can, Play-Doh now comes in a rainbow of colors. The recipe remains a secret, but more than 700 million pounds of this nontoxic goop have sold since its introduction.

5. The concept of the hula hoop had been around for centuries. Then, in the late 1950s, Wham-O, a maverick California toy company, rolled out a plastic hoop for swivel-hipped kids. The concept caught on and 25 million sold in the first six months. They cost $1.98 each, and, by 1958, 100 million of them had been sold around the world—except in Japan and the Soviet Union where they were said to represent the "emptiness of American culture." Ouch.

6. Barbie vamped onto the toy scene in 1959, the creation of Ruth Handler and her husband Elliot, who along with Harold Matson founded the Mattel toy company. Handler noticed that her daughter Barbara (Barbie) and her friends played with an adult female doll from Switzerland more than their baby dolls. So, Handler came up with her "Barbie" concept, and the rest is toy history.

7. Chatty Cathy, also released by the Mattel Corporation in 1959, was the era's second most popular doll. Yakking her way onto store shelves, Cathy could speak 11 phrases when a string in her back was pulled. "I love you" or "Please take me with you" could be disconcerting at first, but Chatty Cathy was a '50s classic.

1960s

8. Since 1963, when they were first introduced, more than 16 million Easy Bake Ovens have been sold. A lightbulb provided the heat source for baking mini-cakes in America's first working toy oven. The original color was a trendy turquoise, and the stoves also sported a carrying handle and fake range top. As children, several celebrity chefs, including Bobby Flay, owned an Easy Bake Oven, which perhaps provided inspiration for their future careers.

9. Hot Wheels screeched into the toy world in 1968, screaming out of Mattel's concept garage with 16 miniature autos. Track sets were also released in the same year so that children could simulate a real auto race. Today, more than 15 million people collect Hot Wheels cars.

1970s

10. "Weebles wobble but they don't fall down." This was the unforgettable advertising slogan for these egg-shaped playthings first released by Hasbro in 1971. Each weeble had a sticker mounted on its short, fat "body" so it resembled a human or an animal.

11. Also extremely popular in the '70s, the Big Wheel was the chosen mode of transportation for most young boys, and many girls, too. With its 16-inch front wheel and fat rear tires, this low-riding, spiffed up tricycle was even a hit with parents, who considered it safer than a standard trike.

1980s

12. Strawberry Shortcake was the sweetest-smelling doll of the 1980s. Created in 1977 by Muriel Fahrion for American Greetings, the company expanded the toy line in the 1980s to include Strawberry's friends and their pets. Each doll had a fruit- or dessert-scented theme complete with scented hair. Accessories, clothes, bedding, stickers, movies, and games followed, but by 1985 the fad had waned. The characters were revived in the 2000s with DVDs, video games, an animated TV series, and even a full-length animated film.

13. Xavier Roberts was a teenager when he launched his Babyland General Hospital during the 1970s in Cleveland, Georgia, allowing children to adopt a "baby." In 1983, the Coleco toy company started mass-producing these dolls as Cabbage Patch Kids. Each "kid" came with a unique name and a set of adoption papers, and stores couldn't keep them on the shelves, selling more than three million of the dolls in the first year.

14. Teenage Mutant Ninja Turtles were created by Kevin Eastman and Peter Laird, who had both studied art history. As such, they named their characters Leonardo, Raphael, Donatello, and Michelangelo. In 1984, with a mere $1,200, the Turtle creators launched the swashbuckling terrapins in a black-and-white comic book. More comics, as well as an animated television series, clothing, toys, and several full-length feature films followed, proving that the Green Team could earn some green, as well.

15. One of the biggest toy crazes of the 1980s was the brain-teasing Rubik's Cube. Created by Hungarian architect Erno Rubik, this perplexing puzzle was first introduced in 1977, and from 1980 to 1982 more than 100 million of the cubes sold. It sparked a trend and similar puzzles were created in various shapes, such as a pyramid and a sphere. The Rubik's Cube has seen a recent resurgence in popularity and retains a place of honor on many desktops.

1990s

16. From 1996 until around 1999, you couldn't escape the Beanie Baby. Like Cabbage Patch Kids and troll dolls of decades past, Ty Warner's Beanie Babies became a nationwide toy-collecting craze. The little plush-bodied, bean-filled animals came in dozens of different styles and colors and had special tags that included a poetic description of the character and its name.

17. Based on a Japanese toy called "Poketto Monstaa," Pokémon were tiny "pocket monsters" that battled each other when ordered by their "trainer." In 1996, Nintendo adapted the Japanese characters to promote its portable video game system, Game Boy. Pokémon trading cards and a television series were also wildly popular.

18. Undoubtedly the must-have toy of 1996, the immensely popular Tickle Me Elmo doll was based on the furry, red Sesame Street character. He'd giggle, saying, "Oh boy, that tickles," when he was tickled or squeezed. Manufacturer Tyco sold more than a million of the creatures that year, and when stores ran out of the dolls, some parents resorted to online auctions to secure one for their child.

19. Another plush gizmo, animatronic Furbies spoke their own "language" and became wildly successful in late 1998. Although they retailed for $30, they often fetched $100 or more online from desperate parents. More than 27 million Furbies sold in the first year, and a new, revamped Furby was introduced in 2005 with new features, including advanced voice recognition, so Furby can respond to questions based on its "mood."

2000s

20. The big fad toy of 2000 was the scooter, with approximately five million sold that year. These foot-propelled devices, a spin-off of the 1950s models, were made of lightweight aluminum and used tiny, low friction wheels similar to those on in-line skates. Weighing about ten pounds, they could be folded up and easily stored. Yet the scooters were relatively dangerous until operators became skilled at riding them. From January through October 2000, more than 27,000 people (mostly young males under the age of 15) were treated for scooter-related injuries.

21. Popular with kids of the new millennium (and adults, too), Heelys are a brand of sneakers with one or more wheels embedded in the soles. Somewhat similar to in-line skates, Heelys enable the wearer to roll from place to place, rather than mundanely walking. Heelys are available in a wide variety of styles and colors for the whole family. And for added convenience and safety, they also sell helmets!

Japan's Cutest Export

Wondering about that bow-clad natty catty whose image seems to grace everything these days? Check out these purrrr-fectly true things about Hello Kitty.

❉　❉　❉　❉

❋ Sanrio, the Japanese company that lays claim to Hello Kitty, was established in 1960. Fourteen years later, artist Ikuko Shimizu was asked to create a character that would appeal to children and adults. He came up with a white kitty with no mouth.

❋ In late 1974, Sanrio began distributing a vinyl coin purse with that cute cartoon cat on the side. It sold for 240 yen, or roughly 80 cents. The cartoon didn't have a name then but officially became Hello Kitty a year after its debut.

❋ According to Kitty's "biography," she lives in London with her parents and identical twin sister, Mimmy. You can tell them apart by the location of their hair bows: Kitty wears hers on her left, Mimmy on her right.

❋ Hello Kitty is in third grade and weighs the same as three apples (hence, Sanrio's charity project, Three Apples).

❋ These days, you'll find Hello Kitty in Sanriotown. She has many friends there, including a bunny, a puppy, and an owl.

❋ Hello Kitty has been licensed for nearly every cute (or *kawaii*, which basically means that the cuteness is ubiquitous in the entire culture) product you can think of. She has her own video games, an album, TV shows, and a credit card. There's even a Hello Kitty–themed hospital in Taiwan.

❋ In fact, according to Sanrio, there are 50,000 branded items available in 12,000 locations in 70 countries. You can stay at a Hello Kitty hotel, sleep on Hello Kitty sheets, work on a Hello Kitty computer, and drive a Hello Kitty car.

Behind the Songs of Our Times

"Beat It" (1983)

Michael Jackson's monster 1982 album, *Thriller*, produced seven top ten hits, including "Beat It," which was released as a single in 1983. Featuring a searing solo (reputed to have been captured in one take) from guitar virtuoso Eddie Van Halen, the song provided a unique crossover from R&B to mainstream rock radio. A popular story suggests Van Halen might have missed the gig when he didn't believe he was actually on the phone with producer Quincy Jones. Once convinced, he agreed to do the solo for free.

"You're So Vain" (1972)

The entertainment world is jam-packed with vanity. That being the case, Carly Simon's 1972 hit "You're So Vain" could be about almost anyone. Simon has never revealed who the subject of the song is, except to TV producer Dick Ebersole, who won the privilege in a charity auction and is sworn to secrecy. Many believe it could be Mick Jagger, whose backup vocals on the song stand out above the rest of the choir, or Warren Beatty, who has openly stated, "Let's be honest—the song was about me." Simon's husband at the time, James Taylor, is also a candidate. No matter who the subject is, he or she should be proud of the secret contribution.

"We're an American Band" (1973)

Hailing from Flint, Michigan, is about as American as a band can get. Grand Funk Railroad's ode to touring tells of poker games with blues artist Freddie King and meeting up with legendary groupie Connie Hamzy. Drummer and writer Don Brewer's inspiration came from a bar fight with fellow touring band Humble Pie over the merits of British bands versus U.S. groups. Brewer claimed, "Hey—we're an American band," and he wrote the rest of the song the next morning.

From the Vaults of History

Just Powdering Their Noses

Many modern Americans would be shocked to know how prevalent—and how respectable—cocaine use once was in this country. In fact, one of the most all-American products, the Coca-Cola soft drink, used cocaine in its recipe from 1886 until 1903 and even took its name from the combination of coca leaves and kola nuts. In the late 19th and early 20th centuries, there were no raised eyebrows when doctors prescribed cocaine to patients as a treatment for everything from depression to asthma. The influential psychologist Sigmund Freud made no secret of his own cocaine use, and he urged his followers to try it as well. But after a few decades, it became obvious that the drug led to addiction and psychosis; in 1914, cocaine was outlawed with the passage of the Harrison Tax Act.

You Drive Like a Girl

Ah, the Fifties. When "gals" were still "sugar and spice and everything nice," and corporations thought they could sell women anything as long as they slapped some pink paint on it. The most infamous example may have been in 1955, when Dodge designed an automobile specifically for women. Yes, you guessed it—the Dodge  La Femme was pink, though they gave the color the fancy name "heather rose." And just like a lady, the La Femme liked her accessories—she came with a kit containing matching rain hat, umbrella, purse, and cosmetics to wear while you drove the car and didn't worry your pretty little head about anything.

Dodge stopped production of the La Femme after two seasons. Arthur Liebler, the vice president of marketing and communications at Chrysler, remarked years later, "I guess we just didn't get it at the time." Now, that's an understatement!

Busted!

Breasts. Hooters. Melons. Jugs. Whatever you want to call them, they are arguably the most prominent if not alluring part of the female anatomy. Men clamor after them and women flaunt them. Meet a couple who scammed women across America with promises of bigger busts.

✳ ✳ ✳ ✳

A Man with a Plan

IN THE EARLY 1960s, Jack and Eileen Feather (doing business as the "Mark Eden Company") began marketing a simple device that was "guaranteed to add three inches to your bustline." This "Mark Eden Bust Developer" was a plastic clamshell-shaped device with a spring inside. A woman would press the two plastic sides together using her hands, and the tension of the spring would reportedly increase the size of her breasts. Sounded easy enough—the only problem was that it didn't work.

Prior to marketing the product to the public, Jack tested it on his wife and the clients of his 14 figure salons. After noticing that the Bust Developer "subtly transformed his clients as women," Jack was ready to hit the big time.

The Burgeoning Business of Breasts

Each Bust Developer purchased was accompanied with an instructional pamphlet flaunting the cleavage of actress June Wilkinson. Inside the brochure, Jack promised that after using his device, "There is an incomparable difference in the entire feminine line, shape, and grace of her whole figure. Her very presence takes on a new and subtle glow of womanliness, of sex-appeal, and yes, of glamour that is undeniable and unmistakable." Not bad for only $9.95.

After more than 18,000 Bust Developers had been sold, women began to complain that the contraption didn't live up to their expectations. At first, Jack happily refunded his customers' money. But by 1966, so many women had complained about being defrauded that the U.S. Postal Service shut down the Mark Eden operation and issued a fraud order with the federal government.

During subsequent hearings, both sides paraded a long line of experts, for and against the claims of the Mark Eden Company. The first claim to be attacked was Jack's statement that he was introducing a "scientific breakthrough" in breast enhancement. As it turned out, Jack had absolutely no scientific or medical training that would allow him to make such a statement.

Dr. Ralph Waldo Weilerstein, a noted specialist in obstetrics and gynecology, testified that there was virtually no connection between a woman's pectoral muscles and her breast tissue—a key factor in the suit. A physiologist and an orthopedic surgeon followed; they concurred that the only possible improvement that a woman might experience was her "breastline" and not the size of her breasts. Measuring a woman's breastline encompasses the muscles of the chest, back, *and* breasts. Few of the Mark Eden clients were interested in having more muscular backs.

Finally, June Wilkinson, the captivating model on the Breast Developer brochure testified that she had been well endowed long before using the Mark Eden product. She told the court that she wore a special bra for the photographs to make her bust look better.

An End to Mark Eden

The hearings continued with a wide array of witnesses and experts until it was unanimously agreed that it was impossible to develop breast tissue through exercise; hence, no "scientific breakthrough" could occur using the Mark Eden Bust Developer. The court determined that the Feathers made false representations to their clients and that the bust developers failed to live up to the claims in the advertisements. Ultimately, the Feathers were indicted on 13 counts of mail fraud, ordered to remove their products from the marketplace, and pay a $1.1 million fine.

All Dolled Up

Mattel Toys introduced the very first Barbie doll at the New York Toy Fair in 1959. Back then, Barbie was a simple, three-dimensional teenage fashion model based on the concept of paper dolls; her fabulous fashions sold separately for $1 to $5 each. As the popularity of Barbie grew, so did her closet, career options, and family tree.

✳ ✳ ✳ ✳

Pals

A DOLL'S ENTOURAGE CAN be her most popular accessory. Barbie's inner circle includes more than 8 relatives and 32 close companions.

A few of her most notable peeps (in order of introduction):

1961: Ken, on-again, off-again boyfriend

1963: Midge, Barbie's BFF (best friend forever)

1964: Skipper, beloved younger sister

1967: Francie, first African American gal pal

Pets

Over the years, Barbie has taken care of 50 different pets, including Ginger Giraffe and Zizi Zebra. No wonder she became a veterinarian in 1985, a zoologist in 2006, and a SeaWorld trainer in 2009.

Her most precious:

1985: Prince, a French poodle with beret

1988: Tahiti, the tropical bird

1994: High Stepper Horse (it really walked . . . with the help of batteries)

Places

When Barbie's not busy being an astronaut, a rock star, or a presidential candidate, it seems she just wants to kick back and be a regular girl. You can find her at the beach, the pool, the skating rink, the mall, or even the Barbie So Much to Do! Post Office.

Her favorite play scenes to be seen:

1976: The Barbie Fashion Plaza

1982: Barbie Loves McDonald's

1986: The Great Shape Barbie Workout Center

1995: The Pretty Pet Parlor

Properties

Barbie has owned more than 20 homes in various architectural designs and price ranges. Her first piece of real estate, the 1962 Dream House, was constructed entirely of cardboard.

Her other not-so-humble abodes:

1974: The Barbie Townhouse

1983: The Barbie Dream Cottage

1985: The Barbie Glamour Home

1990: The Barbie Magical Mansion

Planes, Trains, and Automobiles

Barbie's garage is filled with everything from Ten Speeder bikes and Around Town Scooters to Country Campers and too many Corvettes to count.

Barbie's passport to traveling in style:

1962: An Austin Healy sports car

1972: A United Airlines Barbie Friend Ship plane

1994: A Jaguar XJS convertible in dazzling pink

Strange Celebrity Endorsements

Need shoe polish, mail-order steak, or some dog food? If you can't trust a celebrity, who can you trust?

✳ ✳ ✳ ✳

Muhammad Ali: Wanna float like a butterfly and sting like a bee? Try the all-natural "Muhammad Ali Crisp Crunch" candy bar. Also recommended: "Muhammad Ali Shoe Polish."

NASCAR: That's right. NASCAR romance novels by Harlequin—neither written by nor featuring NASCAR stars!

Old Yeller: If you can get past the fact that the lovable Disney pooch became a rabid hound executed by his young owner, then consider giving man's best friend a bowl of "Old Yeller Dog Food." It's the only dog food served in the great beyond!

Jessica Simpson: The actress/singer has her own line of Jessica Simpson's Goldmine luggage. (Dear Reader: Please insert own "Jessica Simpson baggage" joke here.)

Sylvester Stallone: "Rocky" traded raw eggs for "Sylvester Stallone's High-Protein Pudding." "You are what you eat," he was quoted as saying. Really. He said that.

Mr. T: Pity the fool! His Snickers candy bar ad (aired only in the UK) was pulled for being homophobic. Which begs the question: Why is Mr. T. still popular in Britain?

Donald Trump: They're fired . . . on the grill! Even millionaires have to eat, so why not have them dig into a chunk of Trump Steaks—dubbed "The World's Greatest Steaks." Take that, Kobe beef!

WWF Superstars: It was the 1980s, and an ad campaign featured wrestling superstar Jimmy "Mouth-of-the-South" Hart waiting to lick Hulk Hogan (in ice cream bar form). Unnerving, even by 1980s standards.

Most Resilient Santa

Everyday life in Santa's Village can be a challenge.

✳ ✳ ✳ ✳

IN 2006, AUNTIE ANNE'S Pretzel Company conducted a survey of several hundred mall Santas. Here are its findings:

✳ 34 percent: Santas who had been peed on by a child

✳ 60 percent: Santas coughed or sneezed on more than ten times per day

✳ 45 percent: Santas who spend much of the day seeing flash spots caused by cameras

✳ 90 percent: Santas that have their beards pulled at least once per day by children

✳ 50 percent: Santas have their glasses pulled off more than ten times per day

✳ 50 percent: average percentage of Santas who said their boots are stomped on by kids at least once per day

Don't Tell Mrs. Claus

A Danbury, Connecticut, woman asked to pose with a Santa at the Danbury Fair Mall—a normal enough request. Once on his lap, the woman began fondling him inappropriately. She was charged with fourth-degree sexual assault.

And the Winner Is . . .

Perhaps the most resilient of all mall Santas was Ken Deever, a Santa from Des Moines, Iowa. In 2005, a few days before Deever's annual Santa visit to a local elementary school, a fire destroyed his family house, incinerating not only all of his personal possessions, but almost 500 wrapped gifts that were meant to be distributed to the schoolchildren. Deever spent the next two days replacing and rewrapping the gifts in time for the school visit.

The World of Voguing

When most people hear the word "vogue," they think of Madonna's hit 1990 song and music video of the same name. However, the song is actually based on a dance with a rich history and with moves far more complex than suggested by Madonna's call to "strike a pose, there's nothing to it."

✻　✻　✻　✻

The Movement Begins

THE ROOTS OF voguing may travel as far back as late 19th-century Chicago, where underground gay communities hosted elaborate drag balls. For the most part, these balls were only held on New Year's Eve and Halloween, when the participants could legitimize their drag. Other theories argue that voguing got its start in Harlem during the 1920s Harlem Renaissance, when black gays hosted costume balls.

Whatever the precise genealogy of voguing, it emerged as a distinct art form during the mid- to late-1970s, in the poor African American and Latino gay communities of Harlem. While the youths of Harlem were organizing themselves into gangs, the voguing community had a different idea. Instead of gangs, they formed voguing "houses." Each house was presided over by a "mother," and the different houses competed in voguing competitions called "balls."

Strike a Pose

The essence of voguing is that the performer flawlessly fuses together several diverse components of a dance, all while walking down a runway dressed up as a specific persona. The vogue dance varies from community to community, but it generally combines elements of jazz, gymnastics, bodybuilding, ballet, breakdancing, and karate. Complex hand and arm movements are incorporated as part of the "pose," which imitates traditional runway poses. The term voguing came as a reference to the fashion magazine *Vogue*.

Inseparable from the dance is the persona. Voguers are asked to perform in a given category, such as "businessman," "femme queen," or "school girl." Essential to the success of the performance is "realness"—the voguer must convincingly look and act like a businessman, for instance, from clothing to accessories to gesture. Voguers are rewarded with trophies and cash prizes.

Many voguers lived in poverty and made money illegally. They were often discriminated against for their sexual orientation and cast to society's edges. The different ballroom "houses" fostered a sense of community, and many voguers became skilled and devoted dancers. The underground ballroom scene had its own lingo, its own rules, and, above all else, its own dance.

The Underground Goes Overground

As the voguing movement became more popular, members of the Harlem houses would sometimes visit the midtown clubs of mainstream Manhattan. By the late 1980s, professional voguers were hired at trendy midtown hot spots, and some clubs hosted "vogue night" every week. In 1989 the ballroom scene's most famous houses staged a competitive ball at a celebrity-studded AIDS fund-raising event in Manhattan. That same year, top voguers were sent to vogue down the Paris runways. A 1989 *TIME* magazine article declared, "At the hottest clubs in Manhattan, on MTV and at Paris fashion shows, the ultra-hip are into voguing."

In 1990, filmmaker Jennie Livingston released *Paris Is Burning*, a documentary about underground ball culture that was seven years in the making. The film was critically acclaimed and spawned an avalanche of academic controversy that deserves a genre of its own.

Movie critics and academics alike were intrigued by the socially subversive nature of voguing as presented in Livingston's film.

They argued that by dressing as movie stars and fashion models, the socially marginalized voguers were actually mocking the power given these roles by society. Others vehemently disagreed with this interpretation, pointing out that the vogue competitors did not mock but rather emulated and admired these roles, thus paying homage to the very power structures that kept them down. A central part of the ballroom philosophy was that one can feel beautiful by looking beautiful; by imitating power, one can have it—at least for those few shining moments out on the runway. Voguing was thus simultaneously an act of control and escapism. Venus Xtravaganza, one of the film's stars, expressed her desire to be a "spoiled, rich white girl."

Ironic Consequences

Voguing's 15 minutes of fame did embody a puzzling irony: An underground culture that sought to imitate the mainstream was made mainstream by a documentary that sought to represent the underground. Yet, once Madonna's song hit the airwaves and Livingston's movie graced the big screen, the media's new proprietorship of voguing quickly proved that, in fact, the voguers themselves could never hope to become the spoiled, rich white girls that they dressed up to be. Madonna made millions off her song, and so did MTV. Within two years of the release of *Paris Is Burning*, all but two of the subjects featured in the film sued for a portion of the film's profits. Their case was denied. Within five years of the film's release, five of those in the film were dead. Venus Xtravaganza, a prostitute, was murdered by one of her clients.

The fear that the documentary carnivorously absorbed voguing into the mainstream is arguably the least of the concerns of the voguing community itself. Ballroom houses continue to thrive, having sprung up in Los Angeles, Chicago, and even in Indiana and Kentucky. The ballroom community is alive and well, proving once again that subcultures continue to exist, even if they aren't featured on MTV.

Smile and Wave!

Think you got what it takes to be a theme park costume character?

Q: How long do you spend in the costume each day?

A: During the winter and fall seasons, we're in them for 30 minutes at a time. In summer, if it's 90 degrees or more, we're in them for 20 minutes. [The costumes] weigh about 25 pounds. But a lot of the taller characters are a little heavier.

Q: That must take a lot of physical stamina. How do you prepare?

A: At the beginning of our shift is a warm-up that we do. Half of it or so will be aerobics and cardio, and then we'll end with stretching. It's pretty much required, because they don't want anyone getting hurt in costume. There's also a "can and can't eat" [list].

Q: Have you ever fallen down because you don't have peripheral vision, or gotten overheated?

A: Not for overheating, though some people do. It's not very common, but it has happened. Peripheral vision depends. With each costume your vision is very different. I've tripped a couple of times on something that I didn't see. I can't say I've ever fallen, though.

Q: Theme park characters seem to bring out the best and worst in people. What are some of the strongest reactions you've gotten?

A: On the negative side, I'd definitely say people that like to be physical and think it's funny to mess with your costume pieces. There's a very short amount of time where you can see the characters, like I said, and some guests will get very angry because they feel like we weren't out there long enough. On the other hand, you get to see a lot of great kids. Their eyes light up when they see the character, and they hug you and don't want to let go.

Inspiration Station

A Glamorous Homage

In the early years of MTV, music videos were often cheap and uninspired, even when used to market acts with terrific songs (the oeuvre of Hall & Oates being perhaps the most egregious example). All that changed in the late 1980s, when musicians such as Peter Gabriel and Tom Petty began using their videos to make visual, as well as musical, artistic statements.

Still, no one was prepared for Madonna's $5 million video for her hit song "Express Yourself," which made its MTV debut on May 17, 1989. Inspired by German filmmaker Fritz Lang's classic sci-fi silent movie *Metropolis* (1927), the dark and moody video set a standard for quality and creativity that is rarely met even two decades later. "Express Yourself" built on Lang's theme of holding onto one's humanity in the face of relentless, harsh industrialism by adding a distinctly feminist (or, some would argue, post-feminist) twist.

Before Britney...

Though its subject matter is controversial, Vladimir Nabokov's *Lolita* is considered by many to be the greatest novel ever written. The story of a middle-aged man who becomes obsessed with a 12-year-old girl, *Lolita* combines a taboo topic with rapturously beautiful prose. The book inspired musician Sting of the rock band The Police to write one of his biggest hits, "Don't Stand So Close to Me," which became the top-selling single in the United Kingdom in 1980. The author of *Lolita* is even namechecked in the song when Sting sings, "Just like the old man in that book by Nabokov." In the video used to promote "Don't Stand So Close to Me," Sting plays a teacher who is distracted by a young female student in his class. There are no skimpy schoolgirl uniforms, which Britney Spears would use so effectively decades later in her own *Lolita*-esque videos, but Sting does remove his shirt for no apparent reason.

Chapter Seven

Arts and Literature

All About Andy

The tomato soup cans. The portrait of Marilyn Monroe. That banana. There are some images in popular culture that are so ubiquitous, it's almost easy to forget who created them in the first place. Who's the man who put pop art on the map?

❋ ❋ ❋ ❋

ANDY WARHOL IS the guy behind some of the most recognizable art of the latter half of the 20th century. In fact, his pop art helped shape pop(ular) culture in general. Read on to discover more about the life and times (and art) of Andy Warhol.

Mama Warhola

Warhol (born Andrew Warhola in 1928) had a close relationship with his mother, who immigrated to the United States from Slovakia. She lived with him in New York City from 1952 to 1971. She sometimes created art with her son, credited as simply "Andy Warhol's Mother."

Warhol's Big Break

After attending college at Carnegie Mellon University in Pennsylvania, Warhol got work as an illustrator in New York City at magazines such as *Glamour*. Throughout the 1950s, he made a name for himself as one of the most sought-after illustrators in the industry. Warhol's extensive client list included *The New York Times*, *Harper's Bazaar*, Tiffany & Co., Fleming–Joffe leather company, Bonwit Teller department store, Columbia Records, *Vogue*, and NBC.

Those Soup Cans

Beginning in the 1960s, Warhol dedicated more time to art. He painted a series of pictures based on comics and advertisements, including the now-iconic Campbell's Tomato Soup can in 1962. The paintings were instant megahits, and Warhol's career as a pop art icon was launched.

Short Films, Long Films

Warhol wasn't just a painter—he was a publisher, writer, music producer, and film director, as well. As an auteur, Warhol created more than 600 films, many of them just under five minutes in length. His longest work was a 25-hour-long piece called *Four Stars*, which was made in 1967–68.

The Fabulous Factory

By 1964, Warhol had his "Factory" in the city, a warehouse space entirely decked out in silver. Parties for the glitterati were thrown at the Factory, where the art world at large, cross-dressers, and folks on the fringes of society were eager to attend. When it wasn't packed with guests, Warhol used it for studio space.

In 1966, Andy also opened the Gymnasium, a nightclub in New York that featured exercise equipment on the dance floor.

Avant-Garde

Warhol was the first to exhibit video footage as art, essentially creating the "multimedia" medium in 1965. Warhol also regularly taped conversations with others and dictated his ideas into a tape recorder. There are approximately 3,400 of these audiotapes.

Plastic and Velvet

For a time, Warhol tried his hand at performance art. He had a multimedia show called *The Exploding Plastic Inevitable*. Featured on the bill was the prefame (but now iconic) rock band The Velvet Underground.

I Shot Andy Warhol

In June of 1968, Valerie Solanas, a writer who had appeared in one of Andy's films, shot Warhol in the chest while in his studio. After a five-hour operation, the artist recovered. A movie about the event, *I Shot Andy Warhol*, was released in 1996.

Most Famous Quote

Even if people don't know his artwork that well, they've probably heard Warhol's most famous line: "In the future, everybody will be world-famous for 15 minutes." It's now common to hear the phrase, "15 minutes of fame."

From Sickness to Stardom

When asked what inspired his pop art, Warhol often referred to his childhood battle with the neurological disease Sydenham's chorea, commonly known as St. Vitus' Dance. A condition that causes jerking movements of the face and limbs, it kept young Warhol out of school and at home for months on end. While recovering from his sickness, he spent long hours alone in bed, with only a radio and a pile of magazines to entertain him. The colorful advertisements, whimsical illustrations, and portraits of glamorous Hollywood stars never left him, and they reemerged decades later as he reinvented the occupation of artist.

The Riots of Spring

Combine three headstrong Russians, a ballet company, and an angry audience, and what do you get? The infamous premiere of Le Sacre du Printemps, *aka* The Rite of Spring.

✳ ✳ ✳ ✳

O N A HOT night on May 29, 1913, the influential Ballets Russes premiered a work at the newly built Théâtre des Champs-Élysées in Paris. But the opening was hardly the heady event that one would expect—from the first bassoon note, the audience began to whistle and catcall. Tempers flared between those who wanted to hear the work and those who wished to shout it down. Society ladies reportedly threw vegetables, and several fistfights erupted in the aisles. The uproar originated with three Russian artists whose vision for a new understanding of ballet and theater directly challenged the old traditions. Here are the main players:

Diaghilev

In 1913, dance in Europe was seen as a transcendent art form. After centuries of marginalization to either peasant folk festivals or formal society ballrooms, dance had reemerged as a powerful form of intellectual and aesthetic expression. Leading the revival was the Ballets Russes ballet company under the direction of impresario Sergei Pavlovich Diaghilev. While he was enormously successful in his home country, a 1908 trip to Paris made him realize that the daring style of Russian dance was almost unknown to anyone but Russians. Diaghilev had long believed that true art was first and foremost a tool with the power to regenerate society: It did not teach, but inspire. It did not satisfy, but excite. Paris, he realized, was a city ripe for the taking.

Nijinsky

Dismissed from the Russian Imperial Ballet in 1911 for wearing revealing tights, Vaslav Nijinksy became an international star as a principal dancer of the Ballets Russes. Audiences thrilled to his athletic ability—he seemed to literally hang in the air during leaps—and were smitten by the brutal beauty of his performances.

But Nijinsky was not without plenty of melodrama. His choreography of Debussy's *L'Après-midi d'un faune* in 1912 shocked and disappointed audiences. They watched as the most talented dancer in the world made stiff steps that culminated in a highly eroticized series of movements with a scarf—no leaps, no athleticism. Many were convinced that Nijinsky had overstepped his role. But, in fact, Nijinsky had only just begun.

Stravinsky

By 1912, the Ballets Russes had already achieved great success with their collaborations with the Russian composer Igor Stravinsky. Shortly after the debut of his *Firebird Suite*, Stravinsky dreamed of a pagan ceremony on the Slavic steppes culminating in the sacrifice of a virgin who dances herself to death. The compelling, rhythmic music that accompanied this dream was unlike anything heard in the Western world. After he heard it, Diaghilev was convinced that this strange, primitive music needed to be let loose into the world.

Setting the Stage

On the morning of May 28, 1913, an advertisement was posted proclaiming the performance of a new work that would offer "the most surprising realization that the admirable troupe of M. Serge de Diaghilev has ever attempted . . . which will surely raise passionate discussions." No kidding. In fact, Diaghilev wanted to raise the audience's expectations to a fever pitch. Rumors had already circulated that Stravinsky and Nijinsky had fought over the work, and that many of the musicians and dancers considered the piece punishing and contrary to form.

Well, they weren't so much rumors as facts. Diaghilev, ever the plotter, knew that Stravinsky and Nijinsky would be an incendiary pairing, and he chose the distinctly modern Théâtre des Champs-Élysées, itself a work of significant artistic controversy, as the place to set his fire. The theater featured seating that allowed the straggly bohemians to sit alarmingly close to the aristocrats. Again, it was all a part of Diaghilev's master plan: To defend the work against the convention-bound dowagers and society gentlemen, he invited the wild boho set, eager to embrace anything that shocked the bourgeoisie.

The Assault

It worked. At the premiere on May 29, Stravinsky's composition was a cacophony of rhythm and dissonance, lacking standard forms or coherent thematic development. Requiring a huge orchestra dominated by percussion, it was a direct assault upon the senses. Nijinsky's choreography was equally daring, performed with toes pointed inward and elbows jutting from bodies. Wearing costumes of heavy sacks painted with squares and circles, the troupe defied every convention of ballet.

It didn't go over well. A melee ensued as the noise of public protest challenged that of the orchestra. Stravinsky, openly enraged at the audience, tried to keep Nijinsky from rushing onstage as he shouted the count to his dancers who were having trouble hearing the music. Pandemonium ruled, and a musicologist later remarked that the pagans onstage had made pagans of the audience. After a brief intermission, the performance resumed—as did the protests. Diaghilev attempted to quiet the audience but to no avail. Finally, the music—all 33 minutes of it—drew to a close, and history had been made.

Victory of the Moderns

Curiously, later performances of the work met with no resistance. It was performed to receptive (if sparse) audiences in London. Only a year later, Stravinsky was carried triumphantly from the concert hall following a performance of the work. In the weeks, months, and years that followed that tumultuous first night, many who did not attend claimed to have been there, and those who did bragged about the sheer magnitude and excitement of *The Rite of Spring* opening.

Fast Facts

❋ Shakespeare's original Globe Theatre (built in 1599) was destroyed in 1613 when a real cannon used for special effects during a production of *Henry VIII* set fire to the thatched roof, burning the building to the ground.

❋ Isaac Newton is famous for his explanation of gravity, but he also had other jobs. As Warden of the Mint, Newton disguised himself and made the rounds of London's taverns in search of counterfeiters.

❋ When King Richard the Lionhearted's (1157–1199) horse was killed under him in a battle with Saladin's forces, Saladin sent Richard a replacement horse with a note saying, "It is not right that so brave a warrior should have to fight on foot."

❋ The Spartan warrior Isadas, hearing the sounds of battle out-side his city, ran naked from his home to join the fight, killing many enemies. After the battle, he was presented with a laurel for his bravery, then fined for going into battle without his armor.

❋ During the First Crusade (1096–1099), so many horses died in the desert that the Crusaders were reduced to placing their supplies on the backs of goats and dogs.

❋ The terms "log house" and "log cabin" actually denoted two distinct types of dwellings. Log cabin timbers were left round while log houses were made from notched, square-hewn logs.

❋ Early matches were called "Lucifers" because they would burst into flame when jostled.

❋ Cupboards originated with American pioneers and were truly "cup boards"—shelves built from single boards to hold cups and dishes. It was only later that they acquired sides and fronts.

❋ Queen Anne Boleyn's head and body were wrapped in sheets and buried in an arrow chest because King Henry VIII had not ordered her a coffin.

❋ The United States uses approximately ten percent of the world's salt production each year just to salt roads.

A Match Made in Surrealist Heaven

The great surrealist artist Salvador Dalí knew how to put a brush to canvas, but after making fast friends with Harpo Marx of the Marx Brothers, Dalí was inspired to try his hand at writing comedy.

✳ ✳ ✳ ✳

Dalí the Filmmaker

SALVADOR DALÍ WAS never one to paint a dull picture. From smelting watches to roses that float in the middle of the desert, Dalí painted the world as he imagined it, not as it was. And Dalí did not limit this dreamlike vision to painting—he also designed clothing, furniture, and stage settings for Broadway productions. In effect, Dalí transferred his unique vision to whatever media would hold it. "Painting is an infinitely minute part of my personality," he said.

From a young age, Dalí had a particular interest in the surrealist potential of film. He grew up watching silent film comedic greats such as Charlie Chaplin and Buster Keaton. Slapstick acts often had a distinct surrealist slant—after all, how many pie fights can a person encounter in a day? Dalí saw the potential inherent in cinema's ability to place one image right on top of another in time, thus allowing for the juxtaposition of bizarrely disconnected images, and he described the epitome of film as "a succession of wonders."

At age 25, Dalí set to work making his imagined succession of wonders a sur-reality. He paired with friend and famed surrealist filmmaker Luis Bunuel to make a short film called *Un Chien Andalous* (1929), which is now considered a groundbreaking work in avant-garde cinema. His film career may have begun with a bang, but *Un Chien Andalous* and *Âge d'or, L'* (1930) proved to be the only Dalí films to make it into production. In 1946, he collaborated with Walt Disney on a six-minute animated film, *Destino*, that was abandoned as too strange and unmarketable.

Eventually, *Destino* was released in 2003, after Dalí's death. He also made a short dream sequence for Hitchcock's *Spellbound*, but for the most part, Dalí's film projects were nipped in the bud.

Dalí the Comedian

The inspiration behind Dalí's wackiest unmade film script was his friendship with Harpo Marx. Harpo's very persona was surreal: His character refused to speak, instead relying on the art of pantomime, whistles, and props to communicate. He wore outrageous outfits topped by his wild curly clown hair and was a self-taught virtuoso harpist.

Dalí was enthralled with Harpo. After the two met in Paris in the summer of 1936, they strummed up an appropriately peculiar friendship. Dalí sent Harpo a gift: A gilded harp with barbed-wire strings and teaspoon tuning knobs. Delighted, Harpo returned the favor by sending Dalí a photograph of himself playing the harp with cut-up, bandaged fingers.

The following year, Dalí traveled to California to see Harpo. According to the always-dramatic Dalí, upon arrival, he found Harpo lying "naked, crowned with roses, and in the center of a veritable forest of harps." During their vacation, Dalí drew sketches of Harpo at his harp, grinning with a lobster on his head. The two also began collaboration on a surrealistic Marx Brothers film called *Giraffes on Horseback Salad*. The film was to follow the misadventures of a Spanish businessman who comes to America and falls in love with a woman. The script also calls for burning giraffes wearing gas masks and Harpo catching Little People with a butterfly net. The film was never realized as MGM, the Marx Brothers' studio, refused to make it. The script does, however, still exist in a private collection—perhaps someday Dalí and Harpo's inimitable dream will come to fruition.

The Dubious Heroics of Ernest Hemingway

Legendary writer Ernest Hemingway was no stranger to war. But his exploits in World War II were atypical, to say the least.

✳ ✳ ✳ ✳

ERNEST HEMINGWAY MADE his mark writing about war and using his wartime experiences as inspiration for his compelling novels. While he had a tendency to embellish his personal involvement in the fighting, Hemingway did take part in some of the major wars of the twentieth century.

During the First World War, Hemingway was an ambulance driver in northern Italy. His experiences there gave him material for his 1929 novel *A Farewell to Arms*.

As a correspondent for the North American Newspaper Alliance in the Spanish Civil War, Hemingway wrote detailed reports about his experiences on the front lines. His epic novel *For Whom the Bell Tolls* was promoted as a literary manifestation of his real-life wartime experience in Spain. Truth was, he was seldom close to the action. However, his connections to leftist factions in Spain did attract the attention of J. Edgar Hoover's FBI, which would keep a file on Hemingway.

These "dubious battles," as Hemingway expert Kelley Dupuis has called them, helped build the Hemingway myth. The onset of World War II provided Hemingway with new opportunities to further expand the legend.

Hunting U-Boats in the Caribbean

Shortly after America's entry into the war, Hemingway volunteered to use his famed fishing boat *Pilar* to hunt for German submarines along Cuba's northern coast. The U.S. government had been using Q-ships—armed vessels disguised as civilian boats—to lure submarines and attack them with grenades and gunfire. (The plan may have had some merit, as German subs often stopped local fishing boats to confiscate their catches and provisions.) Being short of ships for the proposed operation, the government accepted Hemingway's offer to turn *Pilar* into a Q-ship.

While the U.S. government thought the plan credible, Hemingway's wife, war correspondent Martha Gellhorn, didn't. She mocked the idea as nothing more than a scheme for skirting fuel-rationing regulations so that Hemingway and his buddies could continue fishing and drinking as they pleased.

Maybe she was right. Despite regular patrols—including one of 40 days and one sighting of a U-boat—Hemingway and his crew accomplished nothing. The quixotic mission was soon ended by FBI director Hoover, partly because his agency assumed responsibility for counter-espionage in the Caribbean and stopped all Q-ship operations in October 1943, and partly because Hoover had long suspected Hemingway of being a dangerous subversive.

Storming Ashore at Omaha Beach

By June 1944, *Collier's Weekly* had hired Hemingway to work as a war correspondent and sent him to cover the D-Day landings. Hemingway rode aboard an LCVP landing craft as it approached Omaha beach. After disembarking the troops, the LCVP turned and headed back to its ship with Hemingway still aboard.

Hemingway resented that he had been kept back from the action, and with his typical embellishment, he wrote his story as if he had stormed the beach with the troops, even implying that he helped find the designated landing location. He was further insulted upon hearing that Gellhorn, by then more a rival war correspondent than a wife, scooped him by actually making it to shore the next day disguised as a nurse.

Collier's later assigned Hemingway to accompany units of General George Patton's 3rd Army as it rolled toward Paris.

Here, his fondness for showboating and military role-playing really showed. At Ville-dieu-les-Poêles, near Paris, Hemingway allegedly threw three grenades into a cellar where SS officers were hiding. He later posed as an unofficial liaison officer at Château de Rambouillet.

Things got stranger still. Hemingway soon assumed the guise of a partisan leader, making flamboyant appearances as commander of a band of irregular French Resistance fighters, and later claimed his posse was part of the first vanguard of American troops to liberate Paris. Rivals soon joked that the only thing the hard-drinking Hemingway liberated was the Ritz Hotel.

Eating Crow to Save His Bacon

As Dupuis states, by 1944, Hemingway had done such a good job of building his mythical public persona that the world routinely accepted his embellishments as the truth. Inevitably though, his ability to be so convincing got him into serious trouble.

A complaint was filed that his activities during the war violated Geneva Convention rules regarding the conduct of news correspondents in war zones. Brought before a military panel, he had to repudiate all his battlefield feats and deny having taken part in any actual fighting to avoid having his reporter's credentials revoked and being expelled from France.

For a man who spent a lifetime building and promoting his own legend, it must have been an extremely painful and humiliating moment.

＊ Hemingway's estimates of the number of Germans he personally killed varied from 26 to a gaudy 122.

＊ French civilians erroneously assumed that "Papa" was a U.S. officer—a misapprehension that Hemingway did nothing to correct. Top-quality champagne was among his largely undeserved gifts and rewards.

Women of the Beat

We mostly hear about the men of the Beat movement, but what about the women? Hey, it wasn't a boys' club after all!

✳ ✳ ✳ ✳

DIG IT: THE Beats were countercultural writers and poets who appeared during the 1940s and '50s in Greenwich Village, San Francisco, and Los Angeles. Rebelling against the postwar model of social conformity, they glorified rootlessness, creativity, and travel for travel's sake. But the male Beats were products of their generation, and many held frankly sexist views of women. Still, that didn't discourage numerous women from gravitating to the scene and developing modes of self-expression inspired by Beat thought. Here are some of them.

Joan Vollmer Adams Burroughs

Joan Adams, daughter of an affluent upstate New York family, roomed with Jack Kerouac's future wife Edie Parker at Barnard College during World War II. Joan's Upper West Side apartment became an early Beat gathering point, a place for discussion-and-substance-abuse sessions that included Parker, Adams, Kerouac, Allen Ginsberg, William Burroughs, and other seminal Beat thinkers. Adams and Burroughs became a couple in 1946. Both had drug problems so serious that they eventually moved to Mexico City to avoid charges in Louisiana. In 1951, William accidentally killed Joan at a gin-soaked party when he tried to shoot a plastic cup off her head. His family evidently bribed Mexican officials so that he avoided a probable jail sentence. He later became a world-famous writer and arts guru who often cited Joan as his greatest inspiration.

Diane Di Prima

This important Beat poet was born in 1934, making her one of the younger Beats of real importance. Di Prima dropped out of Swarthmore in 1953 and headed for Manhattan. As founder of the Poets Press and a cofounder of the New York Poets Theatre, she nurtured many young poets' creativity while making her own mark in the field. Di Prima's first poetry collection, *This Kind of Bird Flies Backward*, was published in 1958. Her early interest in alternative spirituality has invested her poetry with overtones of the paranormal and the feminine divine. Di Prima has formally written about her Beat experiences twice—first in the fact-based but fanciful 1969 book *Memoirs of a Beatnik*, and more literally in 2001 with *Recollections of My Life as a Woman: The New York Years*. She moved to California in the 1970s and was named Poet Laureate of San Francisco in 2009.

Janine Pommy Vega

Inspired at 16 by Jack Kerouac's *On the Road*, this New Jersey native began to make weekend pilgrimages to Greenwich Village in 1958 while a high school junior. She mingled with Kerouac, Gregory Corso, and other Beat luminaries and was quickly accepted as part of the scene. Pommy married Peruvian painter Fernando Vega in the early 1960s and then began a globetrot that would outlast her husband (who died in 1965) and culminate with her first collection of poetry, *Poems to Fernando*, in 1968. A subsequent hermitlike period spent along Lake Titicaca in Peru inspired two more volumes of verse. Others would follow, and Pommy Vega found additional callings as an activist, environmentalist, and prison poetry teacher.

Elise Cowen

This sensitive fixture of the NYC Beat scene was a native of suburban Long Island, the daughter of a successful but neurotic couple. But the young woman was drawn more to poetry than to her studies; she had a special fondness for Ezra Pound and other poets who expressed a dark, even cynical view of life. While attending Barnard College, Cowen dated Beat god Allen Ginsberg. Like Ginsberg, Cowen was emotionally fragile—and although she expressed herself in melancholy, highly imagistic poetry, she couldn't escape her own demons. On February 1, 1962, Cowen died after she hurled herself through her parents' living room window and fell seven stories.

Jane Bowles

A generation older than Cowen and some other Beat women, Bowles was born Jane Auer in 1917 and spent her earliest years on Long Island before moving with her mother to Manhattan when Jane was 13. Inactivity that was forced by tuberculosis encouraged the youngster's love of reading and creative expression. Her marriage to noted writer Paul Bowles was based on mutual intellectual respect but fell apart when Jane began to freely explore her lesbianism. In her life, Jane Bowles published one novel, one play, and half a dozen short stories. The play, *In the Summer House,* was produced on Broadway in 1953, and one of her short stories, "Camp Cataract," is an uncomfortably funny piece that explores blurred identity and a woman's obsessive attraction to her own sister. Tennessee Williams was convinced that she was one of the most underrated writers of her generation. She died in 1973 of complications from a stroke suffered 16 years earlier.

Hettie Jones

By the time Hettie Jones published her first book of poetry, *Drive,* in 1997, she'd been writing for more than 30 years. Born Hettie Cohen in 1934, by the mid-1950s she was living in New York, active in the literary and civil rights scenes with her husband, African American writer and activist LeRoi Jones (later known as Amiri Baraka). Kerouac, Frank O'Hara, and many other seminal Beats were published by Hettie and LeRoi's Totem Press and in *Yugen,* the couple's literary magazine. Hettie was managing editor of *The Partisan Review* from 1957 to 1961 and worked at her own poetry and other writing late at night, after putting her children to bed. Her 1990 memoir, *How I Became Hettie Jones,* is a frank look at the personal blows she absorbed because of her work, her association with the Beat scene, and her marriage. In the 1990s, Jones became deeply involved with the literary aspirations of female prisoners in New York State and assembled a collection of inmate writing in 1997.

Twain's Typewriter

Most sources will tell you that the first novel written on a typewriter was The Adventures of Tom Sawyer, *by Mark Twain. Strangely, Twain himself is the source of this persistent near-falsehood.*

✳ ✳ ✳ ✳

THE ADVENTURES OF *Tom Sawyer* wasn't the first novel written on a typewriter—but another of Mark Twain's books, *Life on the Mississippi,* most likely was. The typewriter was invented in 1868 and first sold in 1874 by the gunmakers E. Remington & Sons. The early models were clunky and difficult to work with, but Twain was enthusiastic about publishing innovations, so he bought one of the first upon their debut. Twain was working on *The Adventures of Huckleberry Finn* in 1874, but he wasn't sure which of his books was the first to be tapped out on that particular typewriter.

In a letter Twain wrote in 1904, he said, "I will now claim—until dispossessed—that I was the first person in the world to apply the type-machine to literature. That book must have been *The Adventures of Tom Sawyer.* I wrote the first half of it in 1872, the rest of it in 1874. My machinist type-copied a book for me in '74, so I concluded it was that one." Although Twain sounds fairly sure of himself in that statement, one of his biographers later investigated the claim and determined that Twain's machinist had actually typed *Life on the Mississippi,* which was submitted to publishing companies in 1883 as a typewritten manuscript.

He Said, She Said

"There is nothing worse than a sharp image of a fuzzy concept."

—ANSEL ADAMS

"When the well's dry, we know the worth of the water."

—BENJAMIN FRANKLIN

"An intellectual snob is someone who can listen to the William Tell Overture and not think of The Lone Ranger."

—DAN RATHER

"A computer once beat me at chess, but it was no match for me at kickboxing."

—EMO PHILIPS

"All of the problems we face in the United States today can be traced to an unenlightened immigration policy on the part of the American Indian."

—PAT PAULSEN

"The only true wisdom is in knowing you know nothing."

—SOCRATES

"Don't compromise yourself. You're all you've got."

—JANIS JOPLIN

"There is still no cure for the common birthday."

—JOHN GLENN

"The execs don't care what color you are. They care about how much money you make. Hollywood is not really black or white. It's green."

—WILL SMITH

"Every man has a right to a Saturday night bath."

—LYNDON B. JOHNSON

"The best way to keep one's word is not to give it."

—NAPOLEON BONAPARTE

"Start every day off with a smile and get it over with."

—W. C. FIELDS

More Than a Minor Contribution

How a Civil War surgeon-turned-madman helped shape our understanding of the English language.

✳ ✳ ✳ ✳

An Unlikely Contributor

THE OXFORD ENGLISH DICTIONARY (OED) is widely considered the definitive record of the English language. For more than a century, readers have turned to it to understand and pronounce millions of words. Less well known, however, is the fact that one of its earliest and most important contributors was William Chester Minor, a Civil War surgeon who murdered a man in England, sliced off his own penis, and wrote all his contributions to the world-renowned dictionary while locked inside the padded walls of an insane asylum.

The son of missionaries, Minor was born in Ceylon (now Sri Lanka) in 1834. At age 14, he was sent to the United States to attend medical school at Yale. After graduation, he enlisted in the U.S. Army, where he served as a physician during some of the Civil War's fiercest skirmishes.

The Definition of Madness

Though he admitted to previously having had "lascivious thoughts" in Ceylon, there is some speculation that exposure to the brutality of war hastened Minor's descent into madness. Whatever the case, he wound up in New York City shortly after the war. While there, he developed a taste for prostitutes and other assorted "pleasures" found in the city's less savory areas.

By 1868, his erratic behavior had landed him in St. Elizabeth's asylum in Washington, D.C. Soon after his release, Minor was relieved of his military commission. He eventually settled overseas in London. If the move to England was intended to halt his increasing insanity, it failed—a year after his relocation,

Minor shot and killed a man whom he suspected of breaking into his home. After a jury found Minor not guilty by reason of insanity, he was marched off to England's Broadmoor asylum in Berkshire.

A New Hobby

Because of his military pension, he was afforded comfortable quarters at Broadmoor, including two rooms, one of which he turned into a library to house his growing collection of books. Shortly after his incarceration, a public request asking for volunteers to contribute to the *OED* was released. With plenty of free time on his hands and a large collection of books at his disposal, Minor began enthusiastically contributing entries to the fledgling dictionary—a pastime that would take up most of the remainder of his life.

For the next two decades Minor pored through his library, finding quotations for thousands of words in the dictionary by keeping lists of recurring words that matched the current needs of the *OED*. Minor's lists became so prolific that the editors eventually sent Minor their lists of words they needed filled.

Minor's contributions, which are said to have numbered more than 10,000 entries, were so frequent and numerous that he eventually developed a friendship with the *OED*'s editor, Dr. James Murray, who made a trip to Broadmoor to visit the institutionalized contributor. Murray would later say that Minor's contribution to the *OED* was so enormous that it "could easily have illustrated the last four centuries [of words] from his quotations alone."

Whatever satisfaction Minor took from his meaningful work on the *OED*, it did nothing to stop his lunacy, which had grown to such a state that he amputated his own penis in 1902. Still, Murray helped guarantee Minor's release from Broadmoor, which was approved in 1910. Upon his liberation from the asylum, Minor returned to America, where he would remain until his death in 1920.

Marfa: An Unlikely Art Capital

Is it really so surprising that a small town known for ghostly lights and a literary name should sprout an artistic community?

✳ ✳ ✳ ✳

PERCHED IN THE high desert north of the Mexican border and four hours from the nearest airport, at first glance Marfa looks like many small Texas towns—dusty, hot, and underpopulated. But Marfa is anything but ordinary. For starters, it's home to the mysterious Marfa Lights, which bring thousands of visitors to town annually. And there's the iconic "Reata," the set for the movie *Giant*. Film buffs also know Marfa as the place where *No Country for Old Men* and *There Will Be Blood* were filmed.

But chief among its attractions is Marfa's thriving art scene, a cultural phenomenon that has put this sleepy town on the map. With a population of just over 2,000, it boasts more than 15 art galleries and artists' studios, several arts-oriented foundations, a growing community of working artists, and some of the most mind-boggling modern art pieces found anywhere.

Perhaps the town's literarily inspired name foreshadowed its future as an arts destination. Founded as a railroad watering stop in the mid-19th century and named for a character in a Dostoyevsky novel, by the mid-1970s Marfa was down-at-the-heels and headed nowhere—and then artist Donald Judd arrived.

The Desert Blooms

Judd, a minimalist artist from New York, was in search of an expansive setting for the oversized art he and his colleagues were creating. He found a former army post, Fort D. A. Russell, and bought up most of its 340 acres and much of the town itself. Barracks, warehouses, gymnasiums, artillery sheds, hangars, and houses were renovated and became home to dramatic art installations.

Judd was assisted in his vision by the Dia Foundation, and when it ran out of money, he formed his own Chinati Foundation. Because Judd wasn't concerned about whether the public actually came to see the art on display, Marfa's growing importance to the art world was very much on the q.t. until the Chinati Foundation started to promote Judd's legacy after his death in 1994.

Artists Begin to Colonize

By the early 1990s, more artists and art lovers had flocked to Marfa. They were drawn by the quiet, the extraordinary desert light, the serene landscape, and Judd's inspiration. Soon, bookstores, coffeehouses, and fine restaurants appeared, galleries opened, and artist studios bloomed. Newspapers, art magazines, and, of course, realtors took note.

Today, in addition to its resident community of artists, more than 10,000 people visit Marfa annually. The works of artists such as Dan Flavin, John Chamberlain, John Wesley, Ilya Kabakov, Richard Long, Claes Oldenberg, and Coosje van Bruggen—huge works in aluminum, concrete, and neon—are seen to their most dramatic advantage, set in repurposed buildings and outdoors in the wide-open spaces of the Big Bend. Judd's own installation of hundreds of large aluminum cubes set inside two enormous buildings is perhaps the most eye-catching. Also appealing is a Prada store—or what looks like one, anyway. Artists Michael Elmgreen and Ingar Dragset built a mock-up of the high-end chain store but sealed it tight, so it would always appear to be abandoned.

On a visit to Marfa in 2006, singer David Byrne found the town's vibe appealing. He blogged, "Marfa is in a dry flat area in between these outcroppings that you reach after winding through various hills and canyons. In some ways it is a typical small Texan town with a beautiful old central courthouse, a train track running through the middle, grain and cattle loading facilities . . . but that's where the ordinariness ends."

Fashion's Biggest Blunders

Fashion gives birth to red-hot ideas more quickly than most people can imagine. But these trends often depart as fast as they come, consigning racks of yesterday's brilliant inspirations to bargain-basement sale bins.

✳ ✳ ✳ ✳

Deadly Styles

The late 1800s saw men wearing highly starched necklines with pointy collars. Dubbed "the patricide," this style got its name from the tale of a man who returned home from university. Allegedly, as the student embraced his father, the sharp, pointed collar cut the father's throat and killed him.

Tightness as a Virtue

Also coming into vogue about this time was the wool bathing suit. After swimming, if the wearer lay in the sun for too long, the suit grew tighter and tighter. Because of the easy availability of wool, however, this trend lasted much longer than one might expect.

Flapper dresses were all the rage in the Roaring Twenties, but little is remembered about Paul Poiret's "hobble skirts." Heavily influenced by Asian design and color, these skirts were made to fit so tightly that it was nearly impossible for a woman to move—let alone to climb a flight of stairs or run from a fire.

Flaunting Your Features

The 1940s featured big bands and swing and ushered in the cone-shape bra. But billionaire Howard Hughes, entrepreneur and lover of cleavage, decided to take the point one step farther: To capitalize on actor Jane Russell's assets while making the movie *The Outlaw*, Hughes designed a cantilevered bra for her to wear. Subsequently, twin peaks in Alaska were named after her.

The 1950s were all about poodle skirts, saddle shoes, and pedal pushers. But the coonskin cap was one style that came and went quickly, much to the dismay of Davy Crockett fans everywhere.

Television and movies tried to influence fashion, but no fashion trend made quite as big a splash as Audrey Hepburn's classic A-style dress did in the movie *Roman Holiday*. Ryan O'Neal's "see-through" cheeks-exposing jeans in the movie *So Fine* might have showed off the garment industry's seamy side, but the public didn't buy them.

The Not-so-distant Past

The 1980s were a decade filled with fashion missteps— thankfully, paper clothes never caught fire, and green suede Robin Hood boots disappeared.

It's hard to imagine James Dean or John Wayne carrying a clutch, but the "man purse" came into style in dribs and drabs. The grunge look and Euro-trash styles were easier for celebrities to wear than for normal folks, with low-riding pants "cracking up" more than a few people.

Debacles of the 20th century have included singer Björk's much-criticized "swan dress" at the Academy Awards. In terms of hairstyles, pink wigs rocketed and then fizzled, Billy Ray Cyrus tried to revive the mullet, and pink and purple hit the racks, and then went south. Feather earrings—which first made their debut in the '70s—made a revival in the 2010s.

For lots of spare change, everyone wanted to own a few pairs of Manolo Blahniks. But in 2001, a line of razor-sharp three-inch titanium stiletto heels were pulled because they were so sharp that they cut through carpet, not to mention dancing partners' feet.

For centuries, only the well-heeled dwelled on fashion. For most people, clothes evolved from need and function, not style. But times are different, and as the saying goes, if you don't like the fashion now, just wait five minutes and it'll change.

Famous People Who Rarely Left Their Houses

Not all celebrities enjoy the spotlight. In fact, some avoid it.

✳ ✳ ✳ ✳

Howard Hughes

Perhaps the world's most famous recluse, this hermit's hermit has grown to symbolize that subgroup of people who, for various reasons, prefer to navigate life in the singular, apart and aside from others. A true Renaissance man, Hughes was an aviator, industrialist, film producer, and director; he also ranked as one of the world's wealthiest men. Hughes began to show subtle signs of mental illness in his 30s. Idiosyncrasies followed him from that point forth, but many chalked this up to the eccentricity of the well-coddled. It wasn't. On Thanksgiving Day in 1966, Hughes moved into a suite at Las Vegas's Desert Inn and dug in deep, rarely emerging from that point forward. When hotel staff finally asked him to leave, he countered by buying the hotel. Hughes would dwell reclusively in the penthouses of many more hotels until his death in 1976, remaining incognito throughout. At the time of his death, Hughes's beard, hair, toenails, and fingernails were freakishly long—a situation that suggested that personal hygiene no longer carried much weight with the billionaire.

Elizabeth Barrett Browning

The Victorian-era poet renowned for such poems as "How Do I Love Thee? Let Me Count the Ways" and "The Cry of the Children" fell into a deep depression after the drowning death of her brother in 1840. She isolated herself from the outside world and communicated, when necessary, by letter. In 1845, the poet Robert Browning sent her a telegraph: "I love your verses with all my heart, dear Miss Barrett . . . and I love you too." Love may not conquer all, but in this case, it came pretty close. The two met, fell for each other, and eloped a year later. Elizabeth Barrett

Browning lived from that day forth blessedly unencumbered by the melancholy that had once held her hostage.

Brian Wilson

The leader and chief songwriter of The Beach Boys, Wilson has fought mental illness and drug addiction for much of his life. In the early 1970s, the artist retreated to his home in an effort to dodge his problems. He would seldom leave its protective cocoon. This pattern continued for nearly three decades until Wilson emerged, returning to the studio and stage with renewed vigor. Perhaps Wilson discovered that a life lived "In My Room" isn't all that it's cracked up to be.

H. P. Lovecraft

Famed writer of horror and science-fiction novels, Lovecraft (1890–1937) was troubled from the onset by psychosomatic illnesses. When the loss of his family home pushed the budding writer over the brink, Lovecraft became depressed and reclusive. He lived the life of a hermit from the age of 18 to 23, making human contact only with his mother. When a letter to a magazine drew the attention of the president of the United Amateur Press Association, Lovecraft contributed a number of poems and essays to the organization. With his confidence now at a peak, Lovecraft was able to hold his demons at bay and rejoin the world.

J. D. Salinger

When *The Catcher in the Rye* was released in 1951, a firestorm of attention, negative and positive, drove Salinger into deep retreat. He produced books and articles only sporadically from that point on and fell completely out of the public eye. His last published work, *Hapworth 16, 1924*, appeared in *The New Yorker* in 1965. Many wonder whether Salinger's sudden reclusiveness was due to the uproar surrounding the book or if his shyness stemmed from personal fears. The jury is still out on Salinger's motives, but one thing is certain: Seldom has a writer reached this level of success only to simply walk off the stage.

The Vicious Circle

Sharp tongues and smooth martinis were standard fare in the Rose Room of Manhattan's Algonquin Hotel circa 1920, where some of the city's most prominent young literati—writers, critics, humorists, and artists—gathered daily to drink, dine, and dish.

✳ ✳ ✳ ✳

Joker's Wild

THE WHOLE THING started as a joke played on Alexander Woollcott, *The New York Times'* sharp-witted theater critic. In June 1919, publicist Murdock Pemberton organized a luncheon at the Algonquin Hotel under the guise of welcoming the caustic critic back from his overseas service as a war correspondent. In reality, Pemberton planned the event as a roast to poke fun at Woollcott and his tendency to drone on with lengthy war stories. Invitations were sent to Woollcott's friends, including well-known writers and critics such as *Vanity Fair's* Dorothy Parker and Robert Benchley. Ultimately, Woollcott had such a good time that he suggested the group meet at the hotel for lunch every day.

A Rose by Any Other Name

In addition to Woollcott, Parker, Pemberton, and Benchley, the group included a regular roster of up-and-comers on the Manhattan art scene. Novelist Edna Ferber; comedian Harpo Marx; playwrights Marc Connelly, George Kaufman, and Robert E. Sherwood; journalist Heywood Broun and his wife Ruth Hale; and *Times* columnist Franklin Pierce Adams were among the core group. Other friends and acquaintances made appearances as well, such as actress Tallulah Bankhead and playwright Noël Coward.

For more than a decade, the group lunched at the hotel six days a week (every day except Sunday). Initially they met in the Pergola Room, today known as the Oak Room. Hotel manager Frank Case served them complimentary celery, olives, and popovers and gave them their own designated waiter to ensure repeat business.

Eventually, as more guests joined the party, Case designated a large round table just for them in the Rose Room at the back of the restaurant.

At first the group called itself The Board and its lunchtime liaisons "Board Meetings." When the group got a new waiter named Luigi, they renamed themselves the Luigi Board—a play on the popular Ouija board craze of the day.

Pun-Upsmanship

Witticism was the pet pastime of the Algonquin group, who were famous for their one-liners. In one story, Benchley entered the Rose Room on a rainy day and announced, "I've got to get out of these wet clothes and into a dry martini."

In another favorite game, group members challenged one another to use obscure words in a sentence—the goal, of course, to one-up each other with clever puns, the more terrible the better. According to lore, it was during this game that Parker notably uttered, "You can lead a horticulture but you can't make her think" and "Hiawatha nice girl until I met you."

Sometimes the barbs were launched at each other. The group skewered Connelly's play *Honduras* as "the big Hondurance contest" and openly trashed Ferber's novel *Mother Knows Best*. Once, the effete playwright Noël Coward commented on the masculine cut of Ferber's suit, allegedly saying she "almost looked like a man."

"So do you," retorted Ferber.

Members of the group often collaborated; one of the most famous projects being *The New Yorker*. Editor and friend of the Round Table Harold Ross launched the magazine in 1925 with funds provided by the hotel, hiring Parker as the magazine's book reviewer and Benchley as the drama critic. (Today, guests of the Algonquin Hotel receive a complimentary copy of the magazine.)

For some visitors to the group, the constant verbal sparring proved too much, and they never came back. One guest claimed it was impossible to even ask for the salt without someone trying to make a "smartie" about it. The ruthless remarks inspired the group to call itself the Vicious Circle—although Ferber personally preferred Poison Squad. After a caricature of them appeared in the *Brooklyn Eagle* in 1920, the group publicly became cemented as the Algonquin Round Table.

The Bite Back

With so much success comes backlash, and artists outside the circle criticized the group deeply. Writer H. L. Mencken disparaged his contemporaries as "literati of the third, fourth, and fifth rate." Others complained group members were only interested in "self-promotion" and "back scratching." Still others accused the group of being too competitive and "forcing" its off-the-cuff humor, with some members even writing down one-liners in advance to casually toss out at the table.

Connelly once said that trying to remember the end of the Algonquin Round Table was like "remembering falling asleep"— it just sort of happened. But by the time the Great Depression of the 1930s hit, the Algonquin's boozy lunch bunch had all but disbanded. Some, such as Parker and Benchley, moved on to Hollywood to write for films.

Today, tourists can get a glimpse of the Algonquin Round Table's New York in a historic walking tour led by the president of the Dorothy Parker Society. Afterward, lunch is served at the hotel's restaurant, now named the Round Table after its legendary patrons.

"Being an old maid is like death by drowning, a really delightful sensation after you cease to struggle."

—EDNA FERBER

"Drawing on my fine command of the English language, I said nothing."

—ROBERT BENCHLEY

Fast Facts

✳ Dancing the tango was considered a sin in Paris during the early 1900s.

✳ It is possible for a whale to get lice.

✳ A baby elephant seal is called a "weaner."

✳ Tickets to the first Super Bowl (1967) went for $12—and that was for the most expensive seat.

✳ The exclamation point is short for the Latin word "io," which means "exclamation of joy." It used to be written with a lower-case "i" over a lowercase "o." That eventually gave way to the abbreviation (!) we use today.

✳ The dollar sign abbreviation started as a "P," to match the shorthand for the peso. It then morphed into a "P" with an "S" over it, which then gave way to the symbol ($) we use now.

✳ The idea for Wheaties cereal came from a health spa owner in Minneapolis who used bran gruel to help patients lose weight. Then one day, some of it spilled onto the stove and hardened. Voilà!—Wheaties were born.

✳ Kissing was once a crime in England. In the mid-1400s, King Henry VI declared it to be a disease-spreader.

✳ The letters "SOS" don't actually stand for "Save Our Ship." In fact, they were only selected because they translate into a simple Morse code message of three dots, three dashes, and three dots. The letters never meant anything more.

✳ The U.S. Department of Agriculture says there are likely 1,000 cockroaches in your home for every one that you see.

✳ Sea turtles absorb a lot of salt from the sea water in which they live. They excrete excess salt from their eyes, so it often looks as though they are crying.

✳ There are 318,979,564,000 different ways to play the first four moves per side in a game of chess.

One Shelluva Guy

Shel Silverstein may be most famous for his off-kilter children's poems, but his literary career ran the gamut from Playboy cartoons and country music hits to off-Broadway plays and even murder mysteries.

✳ ✳ ✳ ✳

Sketchy Existence

TRUTH IS, SHEL SILVERSTEIN disliked children's books, and he certainly never intended to write them. He was a satirist and a cartoonist, and that's how he hoped to make a living.

A native Chicagoan born at the start of the Great Depression, Silverstein got his first break while serving as a soldier in the Korean War, drawing cartoons that spoofed military life. Postwar success proved elusive, and Silverstein, a lifelong White Sox fan, split his time selling hot dogs at the stadium and pounding the pavement to peddle his cartoons. Fortunately, an upstart magazine called *Playboy* took a shine to Silverstein's work in 1956 and hired him as a freelancer—a role he filled well into the late 1970s.

Chicks to Children

Books of his *Playboy* cartoons had already sold big time when Silverstein decided to write *Uncle Shelby's ABZ Book: A Primer for Adults Only*, published in 1961 by Simon & Schuster. The book was a send-up of contemporary children's books, which he felt played down to kids with fluffy "morals to the story."

Sarcastic as it was, his friend, children's author/illustrator Tomi Ungerer, convinced him to write an honest-to-goodness children's book. Reluctantly, Silverstein agreed, but he did it in his own way—without the predictable happy ending. *Lafcadio: The Lion Who Shot Back* was published in 1963 to rave reviews. *The Giving Tree* followed (1964), as well as *Where the Sidewalk Ends* (1974), *A Light in the Attic* (1981), and *Falling Up* (1996).

Far from being the stereotypical children's author, Silverstein was a true bohemian, not content to stay with one art form, one woman (he allegedly bedded thousands but pooh-poohed marriage), or one city (he shuttled between Sausalito, Chicago, New York, Martha's Vineyard, and Key West).

Renaissance Man

While writing stories and cartoons, Silverstein also hit the music scene. Though he could only play a few chords—and reportedly had an obnoxiously screechy voice—he proved a talented songwriter across multiple genres. Popular hits include Johnny Cash's "A Boy Named Sue" and "Cover of the *Rolling Stone*" for Dr. Hook and the Medicine Show. He also wrote scores for several films, including *Postcards from the Edge,* for which he was nominated for an Academy Award in 1991.

Theater also appealed to Silverstein. He staged his first off-Broadway play, *The Lady or the Tiger Show,* in 1981 and went on to write several more, even collaborating with playwright David Mamet to write the screenplay for the 1988 film *Things Change.*

In 1996, Silverstein took up murder-mystery writing and contributed to three different anthologies, the last of which, *Murder and Obsession,* debuted in March 1999. Two months later, Silverstein died of a heart attack in his Key West home. At age 68, he had still been working on a multitude of projects, leaving behind a trove of unfinished works the world will never see.

Shel-Shocking Facts

* In Chicago, Silverstein lived at the Playboy Mansion. He preferred the Red Room.

* He suffered from extreme seasickness but loved being near water and even lived on a houseboat in Sausalito.

* Silverstein was perennially dressed in tattered secondhand clothes. At the height of his success, a bookstore clerk in Key West declined his credit card and reported that a bum had tried to pass himself off as Shel Silverstein.

The *Fasten*-ating History of Suspenders

As the saying goes, "You don't want to be caught with your pants down!" It's a sentiment with which Albert Thurston clearly agreed.

✳ ✳ ✳ ✳

BELTS ARE FINE and dandy, and they were all a man needed until the early to mid-19th century. Around that time, men's pants started to feature high waistlines. In one of the few historical instances where men bent to style conventions, British designer Albert Thurston, who was a purveyor of luxury, custom-made items for men, stepped in.

His invention, unveiled in 1822, involved two straps that buttoned onto trousers to keep them from falling down. The trend quickly caught on, and suspenders made of everything from velvet to rubber became de rigueur, even as fashion moved on and men's waistlines lowered again.

Nearly half a century later, one of America's most celebrated authors got into the game by creating a new way to adjust and fasten the suspenders using buttons and buckles and straps made of elastic. Yes, yes, Mark Twain could write. But did you know that he was also an inventor?

Still later, American firefighter George C. Hale created a set of suspenders that had a fire-retardant cord sewn loosely into the straps. When pulled, the cord would come loose, thereby allowing the wearer to lower his suspenders down from the flaming building in which he was trapped. The firefighters below could then attach a rescue rope to the suspenders. The lucky owner of the suspenders would retrieve the rescue rope, tie it to some nonflaming part of the building, and climb down to safety. Incidentally, Hale is the inventor of several other very successful fire-escaping and firefighting devices, including the water tower.

Make It Shine

Why would anyone hire someone to polish coins? We poked around to reveal the logic behind this peculiar practice.

Q: Who actually employs a professional coin polisher?

A: One place is the St. Francis, one of the older hotels in San Francisco. The St. Francis is a very luxurious hotel. When you have that kind of an image, you add little touches—such as polished coins.

Q: All right. The question is, why?

A: The practice goes back to the 1930s. Consider the type of client who could afford the St. Francis: In those days, if the patron was a woman, she might wear white gloves. You probably know how incredibly filthy money is, but also remember that coins bought more in those days, so it was more common to pay in silver and copper. Women started to complain that the hotel's coins soiled their gloves.

Q: How does one do the coin laundry?

A: It's a big operation that washes some 20,000 coins every day. The St. Francis has special machines that soak the coins; wash them with detergent and lead pellets; then rinse, dry, and sort them.

Q: I wonder why coin collectors haven't thought of that.

A: Coin collectors don't clean coins, or at least they're not supposed to. St. Francis money is kind of a San Francisco trademark. You can spot them around town in a blinding flash, because a brand-new coin from the bank is shiny but unworn. A flat-worn older quarter that shines like new is more than likely from the St. Francis.

Surprising Banned Books

Read on to find out why the following seemingly innocent tales have been banned in various locales.

✳   ✳   ✳   ✳

1. *Fahrenheit 451* **by Ray Bradbury:** Bradbury reportedly wrote this novel in the basement of the UCLA library on a pay-by-the-hour typewriter. Ironically, the story examines censorship, but unbeknownst to Bradbury, his publisher released a censored edition in 1967, nixing all profanity so the book would be safe for distribution in schools. A school in Mississippi banned the book in 1999 for the use of the very words Bradbury insisted be put back into the book when it was reprinted.

2. **The** *Where's Waldo?* **series by Martin Hanford:** Who wants to look for Waldo when there are so many more interesting things to see in the pages of these colorful, oversize children's books? Waldo-mania swept the country in the mid-1990s, but schools in Michigan and New York wiped out Waldo because "on some of the pages there are dirty things." These "dirty things" included a topless lady on the beach.

3. *The American Heritage Dictionary:* As recently as 1987, a school district in Anchorage, Alaska, went straight to the source of their problem and banned the whole darned dictionary. They didn't approve of the inclusion of certain slang usage for words like "bed" and "knockers."

4. *The Complete Fairy Tales of the Brothers Grimm* **by Jacob and Wilhelm Grimm:** Those Grimm boys sure knew how to push the envelope. Most of the fairy tales we learned as kids are watered-down versions of classic Grimm stories such as Little Red Riding Hood and Hansel and Gretel. In the original works, however, there was more blood and fewer happy endings. Concerned parents have been contesting the

literary merit—and age-appropriateness—of the Grimm Brothers' work since it was first published in the early 1800s.

5. *The Diary of a Young Girl* by Anne Frank: You're probably thinking, "I can see why this book might not be appropriate for youngsters, what with the subject matter—how do you explain anti-Semitism and the Holocaust to anyone, much less a sixth-grader?" Unfortunately, that's not why a school in Alabama banned this book. Their reasoning? They just felt it was "a real downer."

6. *The Adventures of Tom Sawyer* by Mark Twain: No one can deny that Tom Sawyer is a bit of a troublemaker, and you could say the book somewhat glorifies running away from home, but was it really bad enough to ban? Libraries in New York and Colorado banned Twain's adventurous tale soon after the book came out, claiming Tom was a protagonist of "questionable character." Twain would probably approve of the controversy.

7. *Steal This Book* by Abbie Hoffman: Sixties political activist Abbie Hoffman was cheeky as usual when naming his guide to governmental overthrow. The book was banned in Canada, and many stores in the United States refused to carry it for fear the title would prompt customers to shoplift. Had they carried the book, it would've been banned for other reasons—Hoffman describes how to make a pipe bomb, steal credit cards, and grow marijuana.

8. *Forever* by Judy Blume: Lots of authors tackle touchy topics such as divorce, racism, and death. Blume did, too, only the novels she wrote were for young adults. Blume has always felt the issues that kids deal with on a daily basis are the ones they want to read about. When she published *Forever* in 1975, parents and teachers everywhere were steaming mad about the story of a girl and her boyfriend who decide to have premarital sex. The book is still being challenged in school libraries today.

The Belle of Amherst

What caused the poet to choose a life of isolation?

✳ ✳ ✳ ✳

EMILY DICKINSON'S STRANGE, brooding, reclusive lifestyle had tongues wagging and rumors flying in her time, and her private life remains an enigma today. Though she penned 1,789 poems, only 9 were published during her lifetime; her literary fame as a founder of neo-modern American poetry came posthumously. The answer for why she chose to shut herself away from the world may lie in her poetry.

A Secret from the World

Dickinson died at her family home in Amherst, Massachusetts, on May 15, 1886, at age 56, after spending her entire adult life in almost total isolation. The cause of her death was Bright's disease, a form of kidney trouble untreatable in the 19th century. With the exception of her family and an inner circle of close correspondents and visitors, her passing went nearly unnoticed.

Seventy years passed before her immense literary contributions received the recognition they rightfully deserved. Her unconventional staggered meter, her lack of conventional punctuation, an idiosyncratic style, and the immersion of her deeply personal life into many of her poems were condemned by early literary critics—some pronounced her work "grotesque." It was not until 1955 that "The Belle of Amherst," as Dickinson was familiarly known, became recognized as an American original.

A Solitary Life

Dickinson was born in 1830 into a prominent and highly political New England family. Her father was a Massachusetts state senator who was later elected to the U.S. House of Representatives. Her mother was chronically ill for most of her life. Both Dickinson's older brother and younger sister exhibited some of the same tendencies that led Emily to be labeled a recluse. Her brother, William, married and moved next door to the family homestead where Dickinson and her sister Lavinia lived. "Vinnie," like her older sister, also lived at home and remained a spinster. Their puritanical and religious upbringing created very strong family ties—almost an unwillingness to completely cut the umbilical cord. It was Vinnie who discovered and helped assemble Dickinson's poetry for publication.

In her early years Dickinson was described as sociable, friendly, even gregarious. She attended seminary but could not bring herself to sign an oath dedicating her life to Jesus. She left the seminary after a year and never returned. Following her voluntary withdrawal from the school, Dickinson began to display the self-denying tendencies that would lead to her lifelong austerity. With the exception of brief visits to relatives, she began the reclusive lifestyle that some labeled agoraphobia. Her detractors offered darker explanations, from failed love affairs and bisexual relationships to lesbianism and an illicit relationship with her brother's wife. Only circumstantial evidence exists to give any credence to Dickinson's supposed indiscretions.

Writing from the Inside

After her stint in the seminary, Dickinson began the poetic foray that would eventually lead to the establishment of what is now known as the modern American style of poetry. At the time, her balladlike lyrics and halting meter were highly unconventional, yet they would eventually flourish and influence decades of modern poets and songwriters. The use of common meter makes her poetry adaptable to almost any type of music, from hymns to popular ballads.

Early in her poetry-writing career, Dickinson sought the advice and approbation of literary critic and *Atlantic Monthly* writer Thomas Wentworth Higginson. He recognized the potential talent in the budding poet but attempted to tutor her in employing the more orthodox style of the romantic poetry popular at the time. Dickinson rebelled at the idea and abandoned her plans to publish her poetry. Yet, the initial efforts of Higginson and editor Mabel Loomis Todd first brought Dickinson's works to the attention of the American public when three heavily edited editions of her poetry were published between 1890 and 1896. Her poetry attained some early popularity, but it did not become well known for another 60 years. In 1955, Thomas H. Johnson, America's preeminent Dickinson scholar, published a complete edition of her poetry in her original, unorthodox style.

Still Unknown Even Today

Though Dickinson's poetry grows more popular with time, the reasons behind her voluntary exile from society remain enigmatic. Her introspective personality manifested itself early in life, and as time passed Dickinson developed several eccentricities: She began dressing exclusively in white and never left her family's home, though she did entertain a few visitors.

There is evidence that Dickinson had an unrequited love affair with at least one man, known only in her letters as "Master." Although scholars have speculated on his identity, only Dickinson knew the truth. It has never been established whether or not the letters she wrote were ever sent. Dickinson and her sister-in-law, Susan, did exchange intimate letters, which gave rise to the rumors that they were having a lesbian relationship. However, this sort of passionate expression was not unusual behavior for women in the puritanical environment of the late 19th century. In fact, there is no proof that Dickinson ever consummated a physical relationship with anyone—man or woman.

The Personal in the Poetic

Many scholars are convinced that the answers to Dickinson's paradoxical and hermitic lifestyle lie in the immersion of her personal life into her poetry—poetry in which she bares her innermost thoughts. No definitive answers to the mystery have emerged, and it may keep historians guessing forever.

Haute Couture

Here are some absolutely divine facts about high fashion.

✳ ✳ ✳ ✳

✳ *Haute couture* is a French term meaning "high fashion."

✳ In the first half of the 1800s, wealthy European women paid dressmakers to copy and personalize the dresses worn by fashionable Parisians. French designers saw great possibility in custom-made garments, and haute couture was born.

✳ Though often called the father of haute couture, Charles Frederick Worth was not from France. A skilled English designer, Worth was particularly known for showing his dresses to audiences at his design firm, the House of Worth. Clients made selections at the shows and then had their garments tailor-made in Worth's workshop.

✳ The French are protective of their traditions, allowing only a few fashion houses to hold the distinction of designing haute couture. Each year, the Chambre de commerce et d'industrie de Paris creates a list of eligible designers. To be considered for couture status, a design house must (1) create custom-order items for private clients that require one or more fittings; (2) have at least one Paris-based workshop or atelier that employs at least 15 people; and (3) present a collection, twice a year, of at least 35 pieces of daywear and eveningwear.

✳ The houses that received the distinction of being haute couture in 2011 included Christian Dior, Christian Lacroix, Franck Sorbier, Jean-Paul Gautier, Adeline André, Dominique Sirop, Givenchy, Elie Saab, Valentino, and Chanel.

✳ Couture clothing is sewn by hand and uses the finest materials. A custom-made haute couture evening gown can cost from $10,000 to more than $100,000.

More Than You Ever Wanted to Know About Mimes

Mimes—you know them as the silent, white-faced, black-clad street performers who pretend to be trapped in boxes or walk against the wind. In case you want to know a little more...

✳ ✳ ✳ ✳

✳ *Pantomime* means "an imitator of nature"—derived from Pan, the Greek god of nature, and *mimos*, meaning "an imitator."

✳ The first record of pantomime performed as entertainment comes from ancient Greece, where mimes performed at religious festivals honoring Greek gods. As early as 581 B.C., Aristotle wrote of seeing mimes perform.

✳ From religious festivals, Greek mime made its way to the stage: Actors performed pantomimic scenes as "overtures" to the tragedies, depicting the moral lesson of the play to follow.

✳ The ancient Romans distinguished between pantomime and mime: Pantomimes were tragic actors who performed in complete silence, while mimes were comedic and often used speech in their acts.

✳ The sacred religious dramas of the Middle Ages were acted as "dumb shows" (no words were used), and historians believe that comedic mime was used by court jesters.

✳ Mime resurged during the Renaissance and swept through Europe as part of the Italian theater called the Commedia dell'arte, in which comedic characters performed in masks and incorporated mime, pantomime, music, and dance.

✳ British actor John Rich is credited with adapting pantomime as an acting style for the English stage in 1717. His "Italian Mimic Scenes" combined elements of both Commedia dell'arte and John Weaver's ballet.

* Meanwhile, mime flourished as a silent art in 18th-century France, when Napoleon forbade the use of dialogue in stage performance for fear something slanderous might be said.

* The classic white-faced/black-dressed mime was introduced and popularized in the 19th-century French circus by Jean-Gaspard Deburau, who was deemed too clumsy to participate in his family's aerial and acrobatics act.

* Mime started to fade in popularity at the beginning of the 1900s but was revitalized with the birth of silent films, in which stars such as Charlie Chaplin and Buster Keaton relied on elements of pantomime.

* In the mid-'50s, Etienne Decroux opened a mime school in New York City. His most famous student, Marcel Marceau, expanded modern mime's influence in the 1960s.

* The San Francisco Mime Troupe (SFMT), one of the most powerful political theaters in the United States, began as a silent mime company in 1959.

* Robert Shields, a former student of Marceau's, developed the "street mime" form in the 1970s. He performed in San Francisco's Union Square, where he occasionally received traffic citations, landed in jail, and was beaten up by people for imitating them!

* Shields and his wife, fellow mime Lorene Yarnell (they married in a mime wedding in Union Square), brought Marceau's mime technique to TV in the late 1970s with the Emmy Award–winning show *Shields and Yarnell*.

* Though the popularity of mime in the United States declined after the 1970s, it still influences aspects of current culture. Urban street dances, including break dancing, incorporate aspects of mime. Most notable is the evolution of the moonwalk, universalized by Michael Jackson, who was inspired by Marceau.

The Semi-Bookish Beginnings of National Geographic

Little has changed at National Geographic since its inception, when a bunch of trailblazing academics, adventurers, and entrepreneurs united in the simple desire to spread their love of knowledge and discovery.

✳ ✳ ✳ ✳

Hard to Classify

NATIONAL GEOGRAPHIC IS a challenge to classify: It walks like a duck, but it doesn't really quack like one. Most know it only through its monthly publication, *National Geographic* magazine. Yet the magazine is only the tip of a very large iceberg. The name is actually a blanket term for the National Geographic Society, a nonprofit organization that funds scientific research and educational programs and is involved with projects that range from educating the public about global poverty to funding scientific research that seeks to end poverty.

National Geographic is scientific, yet its magazine targets everyday readers. The magazine's articles are based on scholarship, yet they read like creative journalism. National Geographic funds research, yet it is not an academic institution. Its hodgepodge of media subdivisions, from television channels to documentaries to radio shows, has the flavor of a pop culture empire—but with philanthropic goals. In short, National Geographic is one of those rare organizations that, through its ability to resist society's typically rigid divisions, is also able to transcend them.

Knowledge for All

This combination of lowbrow and highbrow was built into National Geographic from the beginning. The society was founded mostly by academics, yet their goal was to include everybody, no matter their education level, in the pursuit of knowledge. In 1888, scientists, adventurers, teachers, lawyers, geographers, and even military officers from all over the United States met in Washington, D.C. These individuals were united by their passion to discover truths about the world, whether they be the location of the world's highest mountain peak or the customs of a different culture.

The founders wanted people to be informed of the exciting new discoveries that were taking place. They resolved that inclusion in the society should be "on as broad and liberal a basis in regard to qualifications for membership as is consistent with its own well-being and the dignity of the science it represents." The National Geographic Society was officially incorporated on January 27, 1888.

The first issue of *National Geographic Magazine* (later shortened to just *National Geographic*) was published nine months after the society was founded. Unlike academic journals, with their obscure language and esoteric references, the magazine was intended to unite people in a curiosity for the world. Gilbert Hovey Grosvenor, Alexander Graham Bell's son-in-law, was the magazine's first editor, and from the outset he established an all-encompassing criteria for geographic knowledge as "embracing nations, people, plants, animals, birds, fish. It enters into history, science, literature, and even the languages."

National Geographic's renown for publishing startlingly beautiful photographs commenced in 1905, when Grosvenor had a deadline and 11 blank pages to fill. On a whim, he published 11 pages' worth of photographs of Tibet, and from there on out made photographic journalism a focus of the publication. The first issue of *National Geographic* was sent to 165 people; today, *National Geographic* is published in more than 30 languages, with a circulation of more than 8 million. The National Geographic Channel has more than 65 million viewers, and the National Geographic Society is one of the world's largest and most influential nonprofit organizations.

Chapter Eight

History

R. L. Stevenson's Pirate Myths

Robert Louis Stevenson's novel Treasure Island *gave us a host of pirate myths that would make real pirates shiver their timbers.*

✳   ✳   ✳   ✳

Pirates had parrots perched on their shoulders. The idea that pirates and parrots go together is not entirely unfounded. A parrot made a good souvenir, bribe, or gift, and one fetched a nice price back in Europe. But other than Long John Silver, pirates didn't stomp around with parrots secured to their shoulders. A large, squawking bird would have made firing a cannon or running the rigging difficult, to say the least.

Pirates ran around yelling, "Fifteen men on the dead man's chest. Yo-ho-ho and a bottle of rum!" Almost every sailor sang sea shanties, but Stevenson made up these few lines for *Treasure Island*. Writer Young E. Allison later expanded the snippet into a six-stanza poem titled "The Derelict." In 1901, a tune was added when the poem was used in a musical version of *Treasure Island*.

Pirates marked treasure maps with an "X." It is unlikely that real pirates ever drew maps to locate their buried treasure. Not a single pirate treasure map has ever been found, and pirates would not likely have risked alerting others to their booty. Scholars doubt that pirates buried much treasure in the first place—they blew through their loot quickly because they didn't expect to live long enough to spend it in retirement.

Rome's Imperial Appetite

As they say, when in Rome, do as the Romans do—so belly up!

✳   ✳   ✳   ✳

So, What's For Dinner?

IN THE COUNTRY, Romans ate primarily what they could raise, harvest, and forage. In the cities, poor urbanites scraped by on a steady diet of subsidized grain, which they boiled into *puls* (porridge) or baked into *panis* (bread) if they had access to an oven. Many Romans of modest means took their meals at a *popina* (deli) or *taberna* (tavern), which provided food and drink as well as a place to enjoy a game of dice or a conversation away from cramped quarters. But for those who could afford them, Rome's broad conquests gave access to foods from Britain to the Black Sea. Wealthier Romans dined at home, reclining on couches with family, friends, and clients in a *triclinium* (dining room). Meals were cooked and catered by slaves. At special banquets, the courses and items could reach fabulous proportions and featured entertainment, party favors, and convivial conversation. Descriptions of over-the-top banquets, such as Petronius's satirical *Dinner with Trimalchio*, have become infamous pictures of debauched overindulgence.

The following menus come from a variety of sources and represent banquet settings for the urban poor (*Cena Proletaria*), small rural farmer (*Cena Rustica*), city dweller (*Cena Urbana*), and aristocrat (*Cena Nobilis*).

Gustatio et Promulsis
(Appetizers and Starters)

Proletaria	Rustica	Urbana	Nobilis
	Olive Medley	Cappadocian Lettuce	Bottomless Treasure Chest of Sea Urchins, Oysters, and Mussels with Carrots
	Bunch Berry and Wine Preserve	Fresh Leeks	Warbler "Trimalchio" (Whole warbler baked in a peppered egg-crème dumpling and decorated to look like peacock eggs)
	Fresh Endive and Radishes	Pickled Tuna Garnished with Sliced Eggs and Rue	
	Slow-Cooked Eggs	Slow-Cooked Eggs	Thrush Baked with Asparagus
		"Velabrum Street" Cheese	Roasted Capons and Figpeckers
			Oyster and Mussel Pasties
			Black and White Barnacles with Carrots, Sea-Smelt, and Jellyfish

Prima Mensa (Dinner and Its Courses)

Proletaria	Rustica	Urbana	Nobilis
Puls (boiled wheat cereal) or Panis (bread)	Boiled Farm Cabbage with Rafter-Smoked Bacon	Boiled Green Cabbage	Wild Boar with Turnips, Lettuce, and Radish Set in a Tangy Caraway Wine Sauce
		Sausage on a Bed of Couscous	Platter of Lamprey and Shrimp Glazed with Capanian Olive Oil, Spanish Mackerel Caviar, Wine, White Pepper, Lesbos Vinegar; Reduced in New Wine Infused with Arugula, Yellow-head, and Fresh Sea Urchins
		White Beans and Bacon	Crane Encrusted in Meal and Sea-Salt; Served with Fig-Fed Goose Foie Gras and Leg of Rabbit
			Parrot Rotisserie
			Fish and Boar Pasties

Secunda Mensa (Desserts) and Matteae (Savories)

Proletaria	Rustica	Urbana	Nobilis
Puls or Panis	Basket of Nuts, Figs, Dates, Plums, and Apples with Honeycomb Homemade Ricotta Cheesecake with Honey	Neapolitan Chestnuts Roasted with Raisins and Pears Picenum Olives Cooked Chickpeas and Lupines	Mixed Pastry and Fruit Tray Dusted in Saffron Dates "Apicius" (pitted dates stuffed with nuts and pine kernels and fried in honey) Spits of Blackbird and Squab Breasts Chicken with "Capped" Goose-Eggs

Bibenda (Drinks)

Proletaria	Rustica	Urbana	Nobilis
Posca or Cheap Wine	Posca Homemade Wine Mixed with Water and Honey or Herbs	Table Wine Mixed with Water and Honey or Herbs	Vintage Domestic and Provincial Wines, Cooled with Snow and Flavored with Honey, Herbs, or Spices

---

✳ **The Romans worshipped some very specific gods. They had a goddess for Rome's sewer system (Cloacina) and another for thresholds and door hinges (Cardea). You just can't beat a divinely protected door hinge.**

✳ **Pay up, chumpus: In Rome, if someone was behind on a debt, the creditor might hire a *convicium* (escort) to serenade the deadbeat with ridicule. As long as the song wasn't obscene, this was legal.**

Sitting on Top of the World

Many people can identify Robert E. Peary as one of the first two men to reach the North Pole, but the other explorer is not nearly as well known.

✳   ✳   ✳   ✳

MATTHEW HENSON WAS born on August 6, 1866, one year after the Civil War ended. At age 13, the young African American began working aboard a ship; it was there that he learned to read, write, and navigate. In 1887, Henson met explorer Robert Peary, who initially hired Henson as a valet, but quickly found him indispensable. "I can't get along without him," Peary said.

Henson joined Peary in 1890 to help the explorer achieve his dream of being the first man to reach the North Pole. Over the next 18 years the two men repeatedly (and unsuccessfully) tried to reach the pole. Henson's worth and value to the expeditions grew. In 1910, Peary wrote, "Matthew A. Henson, my Negro assistant. . . has shared all the physical hardships of my Arctic work. [He] can handle a sled better, and is probably a better dog driver than any other man living . . . except some Eskimo hunters."

On Top of the World

In August 1908, Peary and Henson set out once again for the North Pole. By the following April, they were closing in at last on their elusive goal. On April 6, 1909, the group—Henson, Peary, and four Inuits—set out. Henson arrived at camp 45 minutes before Peary. By dead reckoning, he figured that the Pole had been reached. When Peary arrived, Henson greeted him by saying, "I think I'm the first man to sit on top of the world."

Peary was furious and decided that the Pole was still three miles away. He left to cover the final distance on his own (without longitudinal coordinates, so knowing which direction to go was problematic) without waking the sleeping Henson. "It nearly broke my heart," Henson recalled of Peary's actions in 1910. "From the moment I declared to Commander Peary that I believed we stood upon the Pole he apparently ceased to be my friend." Upon his return, Peary was widely hailed as the first man to reach the North Pole. (Today his claim is hotly disputed.)

Was Race a Factor?

Henson's contributions were not only overlooked but also ignored, and he settled into a desk job, working as a clerk in a customs house in New York City. Peary spent the rest of his life being feted as the first man to reach the North Pole. He died in 1920, but not before controversy emerged.

In 1912, Henson wrote a book about his experiences, which enraged Peary. A debate exploded, and some people speculated that a large reason Peary had chosen Henson to join him on the expeditions was due to his race—that because Henson was African American, that he would not dare contradict Peary's claims, and if he did, people would not believe him.

In a 1939 magazine interview, Henson was stoic. "Mr. Peary was a noble man," he said. "He was always my friend. I have not expected much, and I have not been disappointed."

Gradually, because it was clear Henson's contributions had been so vital, public opinion began to turn around. In 1944, Congress awarded Henson a duplicate of the silver medal Peary had received. Presidents Truman and Eisenhower both honored him. Henson died in 1955, and in 1988, his coffin was reinterred in Arlington National Cemetery.

Finally, in 2000, the National Geographic Society posthumously awarded Henson its highest honor: the Hubbard Medal—the same award Peary had received in 1906.

From the Vaults of History

A Boho Birth

Was the 12th-century French nun and scholar Héloïse the world's first "hippie chick"? Was her son the first famous "boho baby"? The details of the love child's conception and birth seem to argue "yes" on both counts. Héloïse was known for her brilliant mind and insatiable intellectual curiosity in an era when women were rarely taught even to read. Her paramour, Pierre Abelard, was a forward-thinking philosopher and theologian. When they came together as pupil and teacher, sparks immediately flew, and sex was not far behind. When Héloïse became pregnant, Abelard offered to marry her, but she declined with a "free love" argument and proposed a no-strings-attached relationship. "The name of mistress instead of wife would be dearer and more honourable for me, only love given freely, rather than the constriction of the marriage tie, is of significance to an ideal relationship," she wrote.

Abelard persisted, and Héloïse eventually caved in, but she insisted that their marriage remain a secret, as she was seemingly embarrassed by the conventionality of it all. When their son was born in 1118, she even gave him a groovy, literally far-out name: Astrolabe.

Still Good Friends

You'd think a guy who had two of his wives beheaded wouldn't be much fun as an ex-husband, but King Henry VIII and Anne of Cleves got along much better after they split than they did when they were briefly married. They realized that there was no chemistry whatsoever, never consummated the marriage, and agreed to an amicable annulment in 1540. Anne decided to remain in England rather than return to her native Germany, and she stayed in touch with Henry's kids, even accompanying his daughter Mary on her triumphant accession parade into London in 1553. Talk about dodging a bullet—or, in this case, an ax.

Women Rule!

* Queen Elizabeth I was taught caution early in life. She learned mistrust of men from her mother Anne Boleyn's fate and was nearly executed for treason by her half-sister Mary I. Mary couldn't prove that Liz was involved in that plot, though, and transferred her from the Tower of London to house arrest in Woodstock.

* The famous Queen Cleopatra of Egypt was once booted from the throne and exiled to the desert by her co-ruler and younger brother Ptolemy XIII. When Julius Caesar came to Alexandria to mediate the sibling rivalry, she had herself smuggled into her own palace in a rug in order to meet him.

* A legendary warrior, Queen Boudicca rebelled against Roman rule in eastern Britain around A.D. 60. She raised an army and trashed several Roman cities, including Londinium (London), in retribution for crimes against herself and her daughters, and nearly caused Emperor Nero to pull his soldiers out of Britain entirely. She was later defeated, however, and like Cleopatra, she committed suicide rather than be captured.

* A master of propaganda, the female Pharaoh Hatshepsut is said to have dressed as a male king and even wore a false beard in the traditional style of pharaohs to ease common fears of a female in power. At least, that's how she was depicted in art. She ruled ancient Egypt for 20 years until her death.

* Mary I was desperate to have a child to secure the Catholic religion in England instead of her Protestant half-sister Elizabeth taking the throne. She twice thought she was pregnant, but was humiliated when both pregnancies proved false and her husband left for his native Spain.

* Princess Elizabeth was on an official trip to Kenya when her father, King George VI, died, making her the new sovereign, Queen Elizabeth II. She was at a state dinner at the

Treetops Hotel when George died, and it is often said that she "went up the tree a princess and came down a queen."

✳ Queen Anne of Britain helped her older sister, Mary II, depose their Catholic father. After Anne took the throne, she passed the Act of Unification, officially joining Scotland and England into one country—Great Britain. Though she was pregnant 18 times, none of her children survived. In order to preserve Protestant rule, Anne approved the Act of Settlement, which allowed only Protestants on the throne and cut several senior members of the royal family from the succession due to their Catholicism. This led to later uprisings by the disinherited royals.

✳ Marie Antoinette's mother, Empress Maria Theresa of Austria, was one of the dominant figures in European politics for nearly 40 years in the 18th century. A strong ruler in her own right, her influence spread greatly as she married most of her surviving children into various European royal families.

✳ Queen Victoria's reign is famous for being an era of sexual repression. However, these "Victorian" standards were instituted not by the queen but by her prudish husband, Albert.

✳ One of the great "Catholic Monarchs," Queen Isabella of Castile was a fiercely religious woman who united much of Spain when she married Ferdinand of Aragon. Together, the powerful couple drove the "heretic" Moors out of the country and began the Spanish Inquisition.

✳ Queen Joanna "the Mad" of Castile (now part of Spain) was devastated by her beloved husband's death. She insisted that his coffin travel with her wherever she went, though she didn't travel much—she was imprisoned for the rest of her life, first by her father, then by her son.

* Eleanor of Aquitaine was queen of not one, but two major European powers. As the independently wealthy sovereign duchess of Aquitaine in the 12th century, she was first married to Louis VII of France and later wed Henry II of England. A fiery and active woman, she led her own troops on a crusade with Louis, encouraged her sons in their revolt against their father, Henry, and wielded enormous power during the reigns of sons Richard I and John.

* For all her reputed beauty, men were the downfall of Mary, Queen of Scots. The former Queen of France was implicated in the murder of her philandering second husband and forced to abdicate after she married the prime suspect only three months later. After 18 years of imprisonment, Mary's connection to the Babington Plot convinced Queen Elizabeth I that Mary's continued existence was too dangerous. Mary was executed, though her actual involvement in the plot is still uncertain.

* Though not a queen in her own right, the highly intelligent Marguerite of Navarre wielded great power as a key advisor for her brother, King Francois I of France, during the 16th century. She was also a famous patroness of art and literature, and she published several works of her own.

* In nearly 2,000 years of history, Japan has had only eight empresses. The first was Empress Suiko, who held the throne from 593 to 628. Empress Go-Sakuramachi was the last; she ruled Japan from 1762 to 1771, but she eventually abdicated in favor of her nephew. Female rulers were officially outlawed in the Imperial Household Law of 1889.

Presidentially Speaking

With their riotous quips, intentional or otherwise, our chief executives have given comics a run for their money.

❋　❋　❋　❋

"I have often wanted to drown my troubles, but I can't get my wife to go swimming."

—JIMMY CARTER

"I never drink coffee at lunch. I find it keeps me awake for the afternoon."

—RONALD REAGAN

"Look, when I was a kid, I inhaled frequently. That was the point."

—BARACK OBAMA

"Too many OB-GYNs aren't able to practice their love with women all across this country."

—GEORGE W. BUSH

"Contrary to the rumors you have heard, I was not born in a manger. I was actually born on Krypton and sent here by my father Jor-El to save the Planet Earth."

—BARACK OBAMA

"For seven and a half years I've worked alongside President Reagan. We've had triumphs. Made some mistakes. We've had some sex... uh... setbacks."

—GEORGE H. W. BUSH

"Things are more like they are now than they ever were before."

—DWIGHT D. EISENHOWER

"As yesterday's positive report card shows, childrens do learn when standards are high and results are measured."

—GEORGE W. BUSH

"A conservative is a man who just sits and thinks; mostly sits."

—WOODROW WILSON

Curious Cowboys

These intriguing people gave folks something to talk about.

✳ ✳ ✳ ✳

Bass Reeves

Bass Reeves was one of the most successful U.S. marshals in the West's history, as well as the first black one. He was born a slave in Crawford County, Texas, in 1846. He escaped during the Civil War and found refuge among the Creek and Seminole tribes. After the war, Reeves eventually settled in law enforcement. He arrested more than 3,000 men and women during his 32-year career. When he retired in 1907 at age 61, he found he had too much time on his hands, so he joined the Muskogee Police in Oklahoma.

Spade Cooley

Billed as the "King of Western Swing," Spade Cooley was a protégé of Roy Rogers. Cooley even had his own immensely popular cowboy music television show, *The Hoffman Hayride*, which ran for a decade. However in 1961, when his wife informed the musician that she wanted a divorce, Cooley beat her to death in front of their 14-year-old daughter. After serving eight years in prison, he agreed to play a special sheriff's benefit. On November 23, 1969, after performing in front of 3,000 people, Cooley thanked his fans, walked backstage, and died of a heart attack.

Charley Parkhurst

Parkhurst was one of the toughest stagecoach drivers in the West—even after losing an eye after getting kicked by a horse. Once, during a torrential rainstorm, Parkhurst delivered his coach and passengers as the bridge they were crossing collapsed underneath them. But surprise, surprise: Parkhurst was really a woman. Upon her death in 1879, the doctor who performed her postmortem discovered that Charlotte Parkhurst had also conceived a child. She was technically the first woman to vote in the United States, albeit under the guise of a man.

The Bordentown Bonaparte

Not many people know that after the Battle of Waterloo in June 1815, Napoleon Bonaparte had the chance to flee to America. Though he didn't flee—at least not then—his older brother Joseph did, and wound up in . . . New Jersey.

✳ ✳ ✳ ✳

Born to Run?

As NAPOLEON'S DREAMS and ambitions crashed down around him in July 1815, the general and his brother Joseph met at Rochefort on the Atlantic coast of France. Joseph urged his brother to flee to the United States, but Napoleon was unwilling to run like a common criminal. He remained behind while Joseph set sail for America.

Joseph tried living in New York City and then Philadelphia, but found that he could not blend into the crowded city background without meeting someone who knew him. What he needed was an isolated country estate—what he found was Point Breeze in Bordentown, New Jersey.

Peace and Quiet

Situated between Crosswicks Creek and the Delaware River, Point Breeze was a 211-acre estate that gave Joseph ample opportunity to indulge his passion for landscaping, gardening, and building. Joseph closed on the property in either 1816 or 1817 (sources differ), which covered 1,000 to 1,800 acres.

Having ruled as both King of Naples and Sicily (1806–08) and King of Spain (1808–13), Joseph had developed a love of finery, and so he began building a house intended to be second only to the White House. He reveled in the peace of Point Breeze. "This country in which I live is very beautiful," he wrote. "Here one can enjoy perfect peace. . . the people's way of life is perfect."

Joseph spent hours roaming his estate and beautifying the grounds. He created artificial lakes and planted trees and a great lawn bordered with rhododendrons and magnolia bushes. He covered the grounds with miles of winding carriage lanes, placed sculptures, and built pastoral cabins. Joseph filled the house with valuable furniture, fine works of art and sculpture, and thousands of books.

Then, on January 4, 1820, the house burned to the ground.

Joseph, in New York at the time, hurried home to find that many of his treasures had been saved by the townspeople. He built an even more fabulous home with fireplaces, marble mantels, and winding staircases. He employed many locals, which endeared him to Bordentown residents. Local children played on the deer and lion statues in the park and went ice-skating on his lakes in winter.

Mystery Man

But much like Joseph, the estate was more than met the eye. He had built a network of tunnels underneath the house, ostensibly to bring supplies into the house, and for the convenience of females to move between buildings in foul weather. Later the tunnels gave rise to speculation that they were built so Joseph could escape capture by anti-Bonaparte forces.

In 1914, *The World Magazine* published a better theory: Perhaps Napoleon did not die at St. Helena in 1821, but escaped to America—and to Joseph.

"He could have been rowed from the Delaware River directly into his brother's house," postulated the writer. "And during the years that he was watching for a chance to return to power, he could have had the freedom, through a labyrinth of secret underground passages, of one of the most beautiful estates in America."

Eventually, Joseph abandoned Point Breeze and returned to Europe, where he died in 1844. Did his brother live with him in New Jersey? Unfortunately, we may never know—though the idea of Napoleon prowling the streets of tiny Bordentown late at night is too intriguing to completely dismiss.

Footnotes

Do your shoes give away your birthplace, income level, or social status? Well, they certainly did in the past.

＊　＊　＊　＊

WHEN MOSES CLIMBED Mount Sinai to chat with God, he was commanded by God to "Put off thy shoes, for the ground whereon thou standest is holy." In fact, many societies have dictated that discarding one's shoes is a demonstration of humility and piety. For the rest of us, shoes continue to speak volumes about who we are, how much money we make, and what we do for a living. Read on for some shoe-related facts!

Early Functions of Shoes

＊ Even though shoes had been around for centuries, it wasn't until the Middle Ages that simple sandals evolved into shoes that were designed for comfort as much as functionality. For the first time, shoes were made with leather uppers, mainly for warmth and protection from the elements. The *sabot* was a primitive shoe that was made in only two sizes: big and bigger. They tended to be very uncomfortable for two reasons: first, men's and women's hosiery were not always available, and second, shoes were made on a single last, so there were no "right" or "left" shoes.

＊ 1818 proved to be a big year for footwear: Shoes were finally made with unique right and left lasts. The sabot was replaced by the English clog, which had a wood sole and a fabric upper.

＊ By the 1900s, shoes were being made in part by machines, and they came in more than 150 sizes. Today, the average American woman buys more than five pairs of shoes a year, whereas men buy only two pairs.

* During the Christian Crusades, clergymen were outraged by parishioners who wore shoes whose toes were so long that they weren't able to kneel in church. As a result, it was decreed that no one wearing shoes with toes longer than two inches could attend services.

* To standardize sizing, King Edward II of England determined in 1324 that an "average" shoe measured 39 barleycorns when laid end to end. This length was rather arbitrarily decided to be a size 13. All other sizes are based on this standard.

* The largest shoe on record belongs to a Florida man who wears a size 42 (or 68 barleycorns).

Fashion Takes Over the Shoe Industry

* The Egyptians were one of the first people to wear shoes that depicted the owner's social status. Peasants tended to wear "comfortable" sandals made from woven papyrus with flat soles that were lashed to their ankles with reeds. More affluent citizens could be identified by sandals with pointed toes, particularly red or yellow in color. If you were a slave, however, chances are you went without shoes altogether.

* In the 16th century, shoes often inhibited movement instead of facilitating it. Not to be outdone by their predecessors' pumps, French women began wearing shoes with higher and higher heels. Some Venetian women wore heels that were more than 13 inches high, requiring that they be carried by servants and hoisted in and out of their gondolas. And for centuries, it was considered a status symbol for Chinese women to have "three-inch golden lotuses" for feet. This was done by a method of repeatedly breaking and binding their feet starting at age seven or so.

From the Vaults of History

Top That!

The first time that James Heatherington wore his newly invented top hat (also called the "silk hat" or "topper") in London, he caused quite a ruckus. He was immediately surrounded by a crowd of curious people. The unruly folks started pushing and shoving, dozens of women fainted on the sidewalk, and a young boy's arm was broken. The police arrested Heatherington, summoned him to court, and fined him £50 for "going about in a manner calculated to frighten timid people." Shortly after being released, Heatherington was overwhelmed with orders for the new top hat.

Another Bad Idea

Gaius Julius Caesar Augustus Germanicus (better known as "Caligula," meaning "little emperor's shoes") enjoyed a raucous and memorable reign from A.D. 37 to 41. Famous for his extravagance, cruelty, and sexual perversion, Caligula was at best a moderate ruler and a questionable general. After deciding to go to war with Poseidon, the Roman god of the sea, he ordered his men to randomly throw their spears into the water. We're guessing the outcome was a stalemate.

Morbid Moore

Anyone who has doubts about how public servants earn their money should have been present in 1971 when the Texas legislature unanimously (and astoundingly) passed a resolution to honor the Boston Strangler for his unconventional work in population control. Yes, the man who strangled 13 women to death between 1962 and 1964. Granted, the resolution was introduced by Representative Tom Moore Jr. as an "April Fools'" joke. He sought distinction for Albert de Salvo (the Boston Strangler) for his "dedication and devotion to his work that has enabled the weak and the lonely throughout our nation to achieve and maintain a new degree of concern for their future." Just to set the record straight, Moore later withdrew the resolution.

Cross-dressers Throughout History

Clothes, the saying goes, make the man. For some men, clothes also make the woman. And vice versa.

✳   ✳   ✳   ✳

A TRANSVESTITE WEARS GARMENTS of the opposite sex and sometimes assumes cross-gender identity as part of daily life. Women dress as men; men dress as women. For the record, transvestism is not a mental illness. And transvestites are not usually transsexuals (men and women who undergo hormonal and/or surgical sex change); in fact, the typical transvestite is heterosexual and comfortable with his/her gender.

Transvestite activity traces back to the earliest days of recorded civilization and recurs throughout the span of human history, across all societies and walks of life. Although ordinarily a private inclination, transvestism has occasionally been very public.

She's In Charge Here

More than 3,400 years ago, a woman named Hatshepsut ruled Egypt as a king. Her story is the first recorded instance of transvestism in history. Hatshepsut, part of the 18th royal dynasty of ancient Egypt, became pharaoh when her husband, Thutmose II, died and the heir to the throne was only nine years old. So Hatshepsut initially ruled as regent, in her capacity as both aunt and stepmother to the true royal heir. But sometime between the second and seventh years of her reign (1477–72 B.C.), Hatshepsut assumed the trappings of manhood and kinghood. She was often depicted wearing a false beard and without apparent breasts. She commanded that she be addressed as "he" and changed her name to the masculine Hatshepsu.

Like Hatshepsut, many female-to-male crossdressers throughout history have donned male garb for social, political, and even military opportunities they would never have had access to in the traditional roles of their gender. For instance, James Barry (1795–1865), a surgeon in the British Army, was a woman working as a man and was unsuspected for years. It was only at Barry's death that attending physicians were astounded to discover that their comrade was a woman—or, according to some reports, a hermaphrodite (a person born with the complete or partial genitals of both sexes).

Less open to dispute are the lives of stagecoach driver Charlie Parkhurst (d. 1879) and New York political figure Murray Hall (1831–1901)—both of whom lived entire adult lives as men, only to be discovered after their deaths to have been women. And the female jazz musician Billy Tipton (1914–1989) pursued a life and career during which everyone, including her wife, thought her to be a man.

Royal Surprises

One of history's most popular examples of a woman in men's plumage occurred in 1429, when the 17-year-old peasant Joan of Arc bravely presented herself to the court of French heir apparent Prince Charles as God's appointed ruler of the force that would overthrow occupying English forces. Her male attire, too, she said, was God's will. When Charles handed Joan command of the peasant army with which she would make history, the prince overlooked the capital crime that the Grand Inquisition, two years later, would not: "Condemn[ing herself] in being unwilling to wear the customary clothing of [the female] sex."

The French court also offers up a royal story of transvestism oriented in the other direction: King Henri III, who ruled from 1574 to 1589, was infamous for wearing gowns, makeup, earrings, and perfume. He sometimes commanded that he be referred to as "Her Majesty," and he kept a court of "mignons"—young male favorites whom the king dressed as ladies of the night.

The history of male-to-female crossdressing cuts through all social castes and sexual persuasions. The story of Henri III, who was married and evidently bisexual, splits the difference between heterosexual transvestites (such as the contemporary British comedian Eddie Izzard and the famed American B-movie director of the 1950s Ed Wood Jr.) and the campier standards of generally gay drag queens, such as pop star RuPaul.

Fun In The New World

Doomed to be outcasts according to American and European traditions, transvestites have held prominent roles in some non-Western cultures. Aboriginal nations across what is now North, Central, and South America treated cross-dressing and cross-gender role-playing as acceptable parts of society.

"Strange country this," wrote one Caucasian, circa 1850, about the Crow nation of the Yellowstone River Valley in North America, "where males assume the dress and perform the duties of females, while women turn men and mate with their own sex!"

Aboriginal women in what is today Brazil were often welcomed as male warriors and hunters—which in 1576 inspired the Portuguese explorer Pedro de Magalhaes to name the country's great river after the famous matriarchal society from Greek mythology, the Amazons.

A source of disquiet in some societies and an invitation to prestige and respect in others, transvestism will be a part of human sexuality for as long as there are gender boundaries to be crossed and explored.

Return to Sender

The Statue of Liberty is one of the world's most iconic figures. However, it wasn't always treated that way.

✳ ✳ ✳ ✳

THE STATUE OF *Liberty Enlightening the World* was the brain-child of French jurist and writer Édouard-René Lefebvre de Laboulaye in 1865, who felt the gift would commemorate the democratic bond between France and America. The informal arrangement was that France would pay for the statue, and America would foot the bill for the pedestal.

By March 1885, even as the completed statue was packed into 214 separate boxes for its trip to the United States, work on the pedestal ground to a halt for lack of funds. Cities such as Baltimore and San Francisco expressed interest in having the statue if New York could not pay for it. Frustrated, the French were uncertain if they should even send it.

Into this situation stepped newspaper magnate Joseph Pulitzer, who had bought *The New York World* and sought a popular cause to build its circulation. In print, he hammered the city's financial tycoons: "The dash of one millionaire merchant's pen ought to settle the matter."

The millionaires didn't fall for it, so when work on the pedestal stopped, Pulitzer upped the ante. He turned to the *World's* subscribers for help. "Let us not wait for the millionaires ... Let us hear from the people," he wrote.

The people responded by sending in whatever amount they could, from a few pennies to a dollar or more. Pulitzer printed every donor's name in the paper. By August 1885, an overwhelming 120,000 subscribers had donated $101,191— more than enough to complete the pedestal.

The King Is Dead … Wait, Not Yet

On January 20, 1936, England's beloved King George V—died in his sleep. Or was it actually murder? You be the judge.

✳ ✳ ✳ ✳

O N JANUARY 17, 1936, Queen Mary called the royal physician, Lord Bertrand Dawson, to attend to her 71-year-old husband, King George V, who couldn't seem to shake his bronchitis. Over the next three days, the king slipped in and out of consciousness. On the morning of January 20, the king held a ten-minute meeting with his counselors and, at some point, summoned his private secretary, Wigram, to discuss the nation's business. "How is the Empire?" he asked, with what would allegedly be his final words. Exhaustion overcame him before the conversation could continue.

That night, Dawson gave the king a shot of morphine to help him sleep and issued a brief medical bulletin to prepare the nation for the inevitable: "The King's life is moving peacefully towards its close," it said. An hour and a half later—five minutes before midnight—the king was dead.

For half a century, this is the story that the public believed. But some startling details have come to light, revealing what may in fact be a case of murder in the first degree.

Stop the Presses!

November 28, 1986, was a day that literally rewrote history. Over 50 years after the king's death and 41 after Dawson's, the physician's personal diary was published in the Windsor archives. The sordid truth about the king's demise was exposed.

According to the doctor's notes, the king simply wasn't dying quickly enough. At around 11:00 P.M. on January 20—after Dawson released the bulletin announcing the king's imminent passing—he realized it was not going to be a speedy process. "The last stage might endure for many hours," he wrote, "unknown to the patient but little comporting with the dignity and serenity which he so richly merited." What's worse, the delay would mean that the king's obituary wouldn't run in the morning edition of the London *Times*, the paper considered most appropriate for national news, but rather in some "less appropriate" evening publication. How bourgeois!

Taking matters into his own hands, Dawson called his wife and asked her to contact the *Times* to have them hold publication; there was going to be some big news coming yet that night. Then, Dawson prepared a lethal cocktail of morphine and cocaine, and he injected it into the king's jugular vein. Thirty minutes later, King George was dead—just in time to make the morning news.

In his notes, Dawson describes his actions as "a facet of euthanasia or so-called mercy killing," done to protect the reputation of the king. He also claims that both the queen and Prince Edward were in agreement that the king's life should not be prolonged if his illness was fatal. That said, his notes say nothing about efforts to consult them of his decision. Most likely, he made it on his own.

Murder or Mercy?

Euthanasia is defined as "the intentional killing of a dependent human being for his or her alleged benefit." Euthanasia by action means "intentionally causing death by performing an action such as giving a lethal injection," while nonvoluntary euthanasia is doing it without the patient's consent. Murder, on the other hand, is to "kill unlawfully and with premeditated malice."

If the question is intent, then it's hard to argue that Dawson's actions make him a murderer, even though many in England, including the medical community, believe that's just what the prominent physician was. From a legal perspective, euthanasia is and always has been unlawful in England, as it is in most places throughout the world.

In fact, Dawson himself opposed euthanasia as a legal practice. Just ten months after the king's passing, Dawson spoke against a bill that would have legalized it, arguing that it should be a choice left to the individual doctor, not the federal government. In what can now perhaps be seen as an attempt to excuse his own actions, Dawson went on to say that a doctor "should make the act of dying more gentle and more peaceful, even if it does involve the curtailment of the length of life."

Dawson died in 1945 with a glowing reputation for his years of service, but today his name is a source of anger and disgrace. As recently as 1994, the *British Medical Journal* published an article deriding him for his selfishness and "arrogance," claiming that he committed a "convenience killing" of the king in order to return to his own busy private practice in London.

And About Those Last Words. . .

It's true that King George asked Wigram, "How is the Empire?" and then drifted into sleep. But those words actually weren't the last ones spoken by the dying king. According to Dawson's notes, the king's final words were uttered just as the doctor injected him with the first dose of morphine: "God damn you."

* In 1994, Oregon passed the Death with Dignity Act, becoming the first state to legalize physician-assisted suicide, in which a patient voluntarily enlists the help of a doctor to end his or her life. (Think Dr. Jack Kevorkian.) The law didn't go into effect until 1997.

* Speaking of Dr. Kevorkian (aka "Dr. Death"), the physician was released from prison in June 2007 following an eight-year sentence for second-degree murder, of which he was convicted after administering a fatal injection to Michigan patient Thomas Youk, who suffered from Lou Gehrig's disease. Prosecutors had previously failed on four different occasions to convict Kevorkian for assisting in the suicides of terminal patients.

He Said, She Said

"The only place success comes before work is in the dictionary."

—VINCE LOMBARDI

"I think more people would be alive today if there were a death penalty."

—NANCY REAGAN

"One of the definitions of sanity is the ability to tell real from unreal. Soon we'll need a new definition."

—ALVIN TOFFLER

"Death is no more than passing from one room into another. But there's a difference for me, you know. Because in that other room I shall be able to see."

—HELEN KELLER

"There is more stupidity than hydrogen in the universe, and it has a longer shelf life."

—FRANK ZAPPA

"Nobody will ever win the Battle of the Sexes. There's just too much fraternizing with the enemy."

—HENRY KISSINGER

"I have bad reflexes. I was once run over by a car being pushed by two guys."

—WOODY ALLEN

"What's money? A man is a success if he gets up in the morning and gets to bed at night and in between does what he wants to do."

—BOB DYLAN

"Brains are an asset, if you hide them."

—MAE WEST

"Quote me as saying I was misquoted."

—GROUCHO MARX

10 Items that Went Down with the *Titanic*

When the opulent passenger liner RMS Titanic *was built in 1912, it was declared to be "practically unsinkable." But on the* Titanic's *maiden voyage from Southampton, England, to New York City, it hit an iceberg and sank in just three hours. The ship has been a source of fascination ever since, partly because of the many stories associated with its sinking, but also because of the huge wealth that went down with the ship and remains on the ocean floor to this day. Here are some of the people and cargo that were onboard that fateful day.*

✳ ✳ ✳ ✳

1. **Passengers:** The ship carried 1,316 passengers—325 in first class, 285 in second class, and 706 in third class—of which 498 survived. Around two-thirds of first-class passengers survived, compared to around one-quarter of those in third class, mainly because, at some point after the collision, the gates to the third-class quarters were locked, denying those passengers access to lifeboats. Some of the more famous first-class passengers included millionaire Benjamin Guggenheim and his manservant, who both helped women and children into lifeboats before changing into their best clothes and preparing to "die like gentlemen" (which they did). Also in first class was Lady Duff Gordon, a dress designer whose clientele included the British royal family. She and her husband survived, but they were later questioned why their lifeboat had been only half full. They were accused of bribing crew members to not allow more people into the boat. John Jacob Astor IV, the richest man in the world at the time, was also onboard. He assisted his pregnant wife, Madeleine, into a lifeboat but was not allowed to board himself because officers were applying the principle of "women and children first." Madeleine survived, but John went down with the ship.

2. **Crew:** The *Titanic* had around 900 crew members, of whom 215 survived. These staff included the deck crew (responsible for sailing the ship), the engineering department (who kept the engines running), the victualing department (responsible for passenger comfort), restaurant staff, and musicians. As the ship was sinking, its two bands came together on the deck and played to keep the spirits of the passengers up. None of the band members survived.

3. **Lifeboats:** Famously, the *Titanic* had an inadequate number of lifeboats for the number of people it carried. In fact, it had just 20, with a total capacity of 1,178 people—about half the number onboard. The ship had been designed to hold 32 lifeboats (still not enough for everyone), but the owner, White Star Line, had been concerned that too many boats would spoil its appearance.

4. **Food:** With all those people onboard, it's not surprising that the ship contained incredible quantities of food. There were 75,000 pounds of fresh meat, as well as 15,000 pounds of fish, 25,000 pounds of poultry, and 2,500 pounds of sausages. Among other items, the ship carried 40 tons of potatoes and 1,750 pounds of ice cream—that's the weight of a full-grown elephant.

5. **Drink:** Passengers needed something to wash down all that food, so the *Titanic* carried 15,000 bottles of ale and stout, 1,000 bottles of wine, and 850 bottles of spirits, plus 1,200 bottles of soft drinks and mixers, such as lemonade, tonic water, and orange juice.

6. **Tableware:** Serving all that food and drink required 57,600 items of crockery, 29,000 pieces of glassware, and 44,000 pieces of cutlery. The cutlery alone would have weighed more than 4,000 pounds.

7. **Linen:** The restaurants, cafés, kitchens, and bedrooms of the *Titanic* required so much linen that White Star Line

built a large laundry close to the docks at Southampton, so that each time the ship docked, the dirty linen could quickly be unloaded and cleaned for the next voyage. The 200,000 individual items (not including items belonging to passengers) included 18,000 bedsheets, 6,000 tablecloths, 36,000 towels, and 45,000 table napkins.

8. **Art:** Perhaps unsurprisingly, considering the wealth of many of its passengers, the *Titanic* was carrying a number of works of art, all of which were lost when the ship sank. The most spectacular of these was a jeweled copy of *The Rubáiyát*, a collection of about 1,000 poems by the 11th-century Persian mathematician and astronomer Omar Khayyám. The binding of this incredibly luxurious book contained 1,500 precious stones, each set in gold.

9. **Freight:** One important function of the *Titanic* was to carry transatlantic mail. When the ship sank, there were 3,364 bags of mail and between 700 and 800 parcels onboard, contents unknown. Other cargo claimed as lost included 50 cases of toothpaste, a cask of china headed for Tiffany's, five grand pianos, and 30 cases of golf clubs and tennis rackets for A.G. Spalding. However, contrary to popular myth, the *Titanic* was not carrying an ancient Egyptian mummy that was believed to have cursed the ship.

10. **Passenger Facilities:** The sinking of the *Titanic* also meant the loss of some of the most opulent facilities ever seen on a cruise liner. These included the first-ever onboard heated swimming pool, a Turkish bath, first- and second-class libraries, and a veranda café with real palm trees. For communication, the ship had a Marconi wireless radio station to send and receive telegrams and a 50-phone switchboard complete with operator. The *Titanic* even had its own state-of-the-art infirmary and operating room staffed by two physicians. All of this was lost when the ship sank.

Thinking Outside the Knot

Alexander the Great was a legend in his own time, a bold young king who conquered most of the civilized world.

✳ ✳ ✳ ✳

I N 333 B.C., ALEXANDER, the 23-year-old Macedonian king, was a military leader to be feared. He had already secured the Greek peninsula and announced his intention to conquer Asia, a feat no Greek had yet accomplished. His campaign eventually took him to Gordium, in the central mountains of modern-day Turkey, where he won a minor battle. Though undefeated, he still hadn't scored a decisive victory and was badly in need of an omen to show his troops that he could live up to his promise.

Conveniently, there was a famous artifact in Gordium—the Gordian Knot. Some 100 years before Alexander arrived, a poor peasant rode into the town on his oxcart and was promptly proclaimed king by the people because of a quirk of prophecy. He was so grateful, he dedicated the cart to Zeus, securing it in a temple by using a strange knot that was supposedly impossible to untie. An oracle foretold that whoever undid the knot would become the king of Asia. Alexander couldn't resist the temptation of such a potentially potent omen of future success. If he could do it, it would be a huge morale boost for his army.

Many had wrestled with the knot before, and Alexander found it no easy task. Irritated but not defeated, he decided to approach the problem from a different angle. He realized that if he took the prophecy literally, it said that the person who *undid* the knot would be king. The legend didn't specify that the knot had to be *untied,* and so he simply cut the knot in half. It may have been cheating, but it certainly solved the problem.

The prophecy was fulfilled, and Alexander used it to bolster his troops as he went on to conquer the Persian Empire and some of India, taking the title "king of kings."

High-Flying Adventurer

Whether training horses or flying solo across the Atlantic, Beryl Markham navigated new terrain.

✳ ✳ ✳ ✳

THE LIFE OF pioneering aviator Beryl Markham was marked by adventure. In her various daring pursuits, she often went where no woman had gone before.

Born in England in 1902, Beryl Markham (née Beryl Clutterbuck) moved with her parents to British East Africa (modern-day Kenya) when she was four years old. Markham grew up on the family's farm, where she lived a carefree life—one that was, in her words, "happily provincial." She hunted wild game, survived a lion attack, and speared a deadly black mamba snake. Her father began to breed and train horses, and as an adult, Markham followed suit and soon became the first licensed female horse trainer in Kenya. She also entertained a number of lovers, including the Duke of Gloucester, writer Antoine de St. Exupéry, and hunter Denys Finch Hatton.

What Markham is most remembered for, however, is her career as a pilot. She was the first woman to receive a commercial pilot's license in Kenya and spent many years transporting mail, supplies, and passengers to remote African villages. In 1936, she flew solo across the Atlantic, departing from England and crash-landing in Nova Scotia. She was not the first person to fly solo on a transatlantic east-to-west flight—though many credit her as such (Jim Mollison accomplished this record a few years prior)—but she was the first female pilot to accomplish this feat.

Her memoir, *West with the Night*, was published in 1942 after Markham's move to the United States. Ernest Hemingway called it a "bloody wonderful book," and when it was republished in 1983, its popularity soared. Markham later returned to Kenya, where she passed away in 1986 at age 84.

Potty Talk

Our bathrooms are some of the most important rooms in our homes, and they provide privacy and sanctuary—in addition to their primary function. Here are some facts about the commode.

✳ ✳ ✳ ✳

A Bathroom by Any Other Name

THERE ARE QUITE a few names for this little space—pick your favorite: restroom, powder room, crapper, loo, little boy's room, little girl's room, water closet, WC, porcelain god, lavatory, commode, latrine, the facilities, the necessary room, the john, washroom.

A Toilet Before Its Time

In 1596, an inventor named John Harrington, godson to Queen Elizabeth I, tried to create a more advanced chamber pot. The queen and her godson both used the flush model he came up with, but Harrington was ridiculed by his peers for fooling around with such a crazy idea, thus ending his career as an inventor.

Toilet Paper Beginnings

In 1857, New Yorker Joseph C. Gayetty produced the first packaged bathroom tissue in the United States. It was called "The Therapeutic Paper" and contained aloe for added comfort. The company sold the paper in packs of 500 sheets at 50 cents per pack, and Gayetty's name was printed on every sheet.

Washroom Attendants

Not so long ago, unless you were wealthy and enjoyed eating at expensive restaurants, washroom attendants were not people you'd come into much contact with. Washroom attendants are now showing up in more public bathrooms. An individual stands in the bathroom and hands out towels, dispenses soap, and usually offers gum, candy, mints, and any number of other accoutrements to patrons—for a tip, of course.

Germs, Germs, Germs

A lot of people think a public toilet seat is the filthiest place on Earth, but that may not be true. According to experts, the floor of a public bathroom is much dirtier, with around 2 million bacteria per square inch—that's 200 times higher than what's considered a sanitary surface.

Don't Go Left

In places like India and in many parts of Asia, bathrooms provide a little cup of water—but no toilet paper. When you're done doing your business, it's customary to use your left hand to wash your bum of any leftover fecal matter and then wash your hand with the cup of water. This is precisely why it's rude to shake hands with your left hand in most of Asia and the Middle East.

Protect Your Seat

What started as a fad for germophobes is now available in bathroom stalls almost everywhere—but do paper toilet seat guards work? Well, sure, but only if the seat is dry to begin with. If the seat guard is placed on a seat that's already wet or dirty, it actually sucks the bacteria and viruses up from the toilet seat onto your bare skin even more quickly.

American Restroom Association

Hey, somebody has to be a watchdog for public restrooms, right? Even though they garner more than a few snickers when they appear in the news (every year the World Toilet Summit is held in a different city), the ARA has a clear mission statement: "The American Restroom Association advocates for the availability of clean, safe, well-designed public restrooms." And no one who's ever had to use a gross public bathroom is going to snicker at that.

Tulipmania

Cabbage Patch Kids, Tickle Me Elmo, Nintendo Wii—there have definitely been some big buying fads in the past. But in the winter of 1636–37, the Netherlands went crazy for tulips.

❋   ❋   ❋   ❋

THE TULIP HAD first reached Europe from Ottoman Turkey around 1560, brought home by diplomats and merchants who admired the flowers in the gardens of Istanbul. By 1633, about 500 different varieties were being grown in the Dutch Republic alone. Fashionable varieties prized by connoisseurs for their brilliant color and unpredictable "flamed," "feathered," and striped patterns, were sold by the bulb, the price based on rarity and the weight of the bulb. The more common, single-color varieties were sold by the basket.

At first, the sale of bulbs was tied to the growing season. Bulbs were bought between June, when they were "lifted" from the ground after they had bloomed, and October, when they were planted again. But around 1634, growers began to sell tulips in the winter for future delivery, adding new instability to the unregulated tulip market. Sales contracts were written for a particular bulb from a particular location, to be delivered and paid for when the bulbs were lifted the following June. Some tulips changed hands several times before they even bloomed.

The Tulip Boom

Between 1634 and 1635, people began to go bonkers for bulbs. The plague had ravaged the Netherlands between 1633 and 1635, causing a serious labor shortage. Still, wages were high, and people could afford small luxuries. Skilled tradesmen might not be able to afford a fancy bulb, but they could easily afford a basket of common bulbs or even a single-color breeder bulb. At the same time, tulips became fashionable in France. Women wore clusters of tulips in their bosoms, and wealthy men competed to buy the most dramatic blooms. The supply of bulbs could not keep up with increased demand from both the bottom and the top of the market. Prices began to rise.

When the lifting season arrived in 1636, many varieties had already doubled in price. By December, prices were rising so quickly that the value of some bulbs doubled in little more than a week. An Admiral van der Eyck bulb was offered for 1,000 guilders—the price of a modest house. The price for common bulbs rose even more quickly than those for rare varieties, increasing 20 times over the course of a few weeks.

Bulb Bust

The tulip market reached its height at the auction of a private bulb collection in Alkmaar on February 5, 1637. Buyers bid on the bulbs. By the end of the day, the auctioneers had raised 90,000 guilders for orphaned children. (A skilled tradesman in Amsterdam earned an average of 250 guilders a year.)

A week later, the market crashed due to doubts as to whether or not prices would increase. Bulb prices dropped by the hour, and sellers began to worry they would not be paid for bulbs that already had been pre-sold. Meanwhile, buyers feared they would be forced to pay inflated prices for now worthless bulbs. The scramble was on, and conflicts over the sale of bulbs were so common that the High Court of Holland allowed tulip-related claims in the courts only if the parties could not work it out for themselves.

A Healthy Bloom

The tulip market recovered its equilibrium quickly. Connoisseurs continued to buy rare bulbs at high prices. As first the tulip and then the hyacinth became fashionable in other European countries, Dutch growers developed a thriving export trade in flower bulbs. Ironically, Dutch tulip growers shipped tens of thousands of tulip bulbs to the Ottoman court, which was rocked by its own version of tulipmania in the 1690s. Today, the Netherlands produces 60 percent of the commercially grown flowers in the world; of these flowers, tulips are still the most popular.

From the Vaults of History

A Simple Name

The all-purpose lubricant WD-40 was invented by a chemist named Norm Larsen in 1953. He worked for the Rocket Chemical Company (which has since changed its name to the WD-40 Company) in San Diego, California, and he was apparently experimenting to create a formula that could prevent corrosion and displaced water from ruining an engine. The name WD-40 comes from his laboratory notes, "Water Displacement 40th attempt."

Method Chewing

Mel Blanc, one of the best character voice actors in history, could be heard in any number of cartoons at the movies or on TV. He was arguably best known as the voice of the carrot-chomping Bugs Bunny. But Blanc didn't like raw carrots at all. In fact, recording was often stopped to allow Blanc time to spit the raw carrots he chewed for the sound effects into a wastebasket before continuing with the script. He could reportedly fill several baskets with carrot pulp during a single session.

Misunderstood

Deep down, John Dillinger, the career criminal and infamous bank robber of the 1930s, was actually a romantic. Despite his hardened exterior and chosen profession, Dillinger frequently wrote long, passionate love letters to his wife and girlfriends. His letters often gushed with promises of monogamy. He regaled the recipients with claims that he was captivated by their beauty.

A Panther of a Different Color

Born in 1925 with the name Richard Henry Sellers, Peter Sellers went on to become the embodiment of the bumbling Inspector Clouseau in the successful *Pink Panther* movies. It's a good thing that he didn't star in a movie about a purple panther. Sellers had porphyrophobia—fear of the color purple.

Peshtigo Fire Sparks Devastation

In the early evening of October 8, 1871, a fire began in Peshtigo, Wisconsin. Before it was over, it claimed more lives than any other natural fire in the history of the United States. That year was one of the driest on record, and the extreme heat and drought caused many to pray for rain. But the prayers weren't answered soon enough, so when fire struck, it was devastating. Oh, and there happened to be a big fire in Chicago on that very same night.

✳   ✳   ✳   ✳

A Forgotten Tragedy

MOST PEOPLE HAVE heard of the Great Chicago Fire, with its story about how Mrs. O'Leary's cow kicked over a lantern and started a fire that is now a part of history. Cow or no cow, that fire was the most destructive blaze ever to hit a metropolitan area, causing 250 deaths and property damage estimated as high as $200 million. Considering Chicago's urban advantages at the time, it's no wonder that this is the fire we hear about. Telegraphs, trains, and other "modern" means got word of the disaster out to the rest of the country. In contrast, Peshtigo, located in northeastern Wisconsin, had much more modest property values and very limited means to spread the word about its fire. Sadly, it also had no way to stop the terrible fire that consumed the town, forests, and surrounding farmland and left anywhere between 1,200 and 2,400 souls dead.

Boomtown Burns Out

Peshtigo, Wisconsin, was on the verge of becoming a boomtown. Situated on a railroad line and near Lake Michigan, the town was thriving thanks to the many nearby forests and the booming lumber industry. In fact, the world's largest woodenware factory was located in Peshtigo. Even with all of its economic success, the town was still no match for Mother Nature.

Weather can certainly be unpredictable, and back then, forecasting was more about feeling the heat and listening to the wind than long-range prediction. That's not to say there was no advance notice. Creeks had dried up, and small fires were commonplace. In fact, fires occurred so often that ships on Lake Michigan had to use their foghorns miles from shore because the smoke hung so thick. Perhaps people grew so accustomed to these conditions that nothing seemed out of the ordinary.

The dry conditions were, ironically, a benefit to the lumber business. Rainless days were a good time to harvest more timber, and settlers and lumberjacks alike cut trees and left in their wake piles of sawdust and tree waste, known as slash. No problem, really—until the slash caught fire. To add to the impending trouble, the drought had also caused trees to lose their leaves early, and dry leaves carpeted the forest floor—one more accelerant when the fire hit.

The Beginning of the End

At about 8:30 on that fateful night, survivors recalled hearing a loud roar. The wind had kicked up and formed firewhirls (small fire tornadoes) that spread with unprecedented speed. In fact, witnesses later called the disaster a "tornado of fire." Hurricane-force winds uprooted trees, tore the roofs off houses and barns, and sent families fleeing in panic. Flames burst high into the air, and smaller individual fires came together as one, gaining momentum. Temperatures reached as high as 2,000 degrees. The fire was so powerful that some debris that got caught in the updraft was later found as far away as Canada.

Alarming News

The lumber mills used their steam whistles as alarms to call to the tugboats out in the harbor, but the fire raged too fast to be stopped. The town's lone horse-drawn steam pump was no match for nature's fury. With no quick way to escape to safety, the residents of Peshtigo were essentially trapped in a town made of wooden buildings and sidewalks. The sawdust that covered the roads and the beautiful forests surrounding the town were suddenly horrible agents of death.

People ran from their homes and some found refuge in wells and streams, while others lay facedown on the ground. Most residents headed to the Peshtigo River or Green Bay. Sparks and debris blew onto the river, so people could only raise their heads above water for short periods. In total, the Peshtigo Fire spread over 2,400 square miles or one and a half million acres. By 10:00 that night, most of Peshtigo was gone. By daybreak, only one building—a house under construction with wood too green to burn—remained standing.

Unlike Chicago, in Peshtigo there was no cow to blame. Lightning is not thought to have been responsible, and no one really knows the exact cause of this terrible fire. It may have just been the right conditions for such an event. After all, Chicago was also alight with flame that night, along with other towns in Michigan. Dry conditions in the Midwest may have been all it took. Weather historians who study the blaze have speculated that meteor showers may have played a part. These showers are common in fall, and any sparks hitting the dry forest floor could have started numerous small fires that joined and spread in the windy conditions that night.

The next day, the blaze burned until the winds died down and the fire reached Green Bay. And the rain? It finally came. But before it did, the little town of Peshtigo, once bustling and lively, had been destroyed. A local newspaper called it a "scene of devastation and ruin that no language can paint and no tongue describe."

❋ On October 8, 1871, in addition to Peshtigo and Chicago, there were disastrous fires in three Michigan towns: Holland, Manistee, and Port Huron.

Unexpected Hobbies of U.S. Presidents

From skinny-dipping to playing saxophone, these chief executives had to do something when life in Washington, D.C., got boring.

✳ ✳ ✳ ✳

Thomas Jefferson: A noted statesman and, of course, the third U.S. president, Jefferson was also an architect. His designs included his famed home, Monticello, and the Virginia State Capitol building. Word has it he was a pretty good cook too.

John Quincy Adams: Adams liked to swim naked in the Potomac River. Apparently when you're 60-something and the sixth president, you can get away with such things. Just don't get caught. According to political legend, a reporter found Adams during a skinny-dipping jaunt and refused to let him out until the president granted him an interview.

Andrew Jackson: The former military man and seventh U.S. president enjoyed passing his free time by drinking heavily, brawling, and—according to legend—gambling and partying in the Executive Mansion.

Theodore Roosevelt: Many historians agree that the 26th president had more hobbies than any president before or since. "TR" enjoyed the outdoors and relished hunting and exploring. Roosevelt also enjoyed reading, writing, and ornithology... when he wasn't speaking softly and carrying a big stick, that is.

Calvin Coolidge: America's 30th president, "Silent Cal" lived up to his reputation as a quiet individual. His favorite pastime: napping. He purportedly justified snoozing on the job by arguing that he couldn't initiate any costly federal programs while sleeping.

Franklin Delano Roosevelt: Whenever FDR needed to take his mind off the events of the day—such as the Great

Depression or World War II—he turned to his stamp collection. The 32nd president, who took up the hobby during his childhood, was so passionate about those gum-backed pieces of paper that during his four terms in office, he helped oversee the design and promotion of about 200 stamps.

Dwight D. Eisenhower: Okay, it really isn't shocking that someone like Ike—a former U.S. Army general and the 34th U.S. president—might want to unwind with a game of golf. It's a very presidential thing to do. And Ike probably thought that rank had its privilege when he requested (in 1956) that a tree at Augusta National be removed because it was interfering with a few of his drives. Nature won out, and the so-called "Eisenhower Tree"—a pine on the 17th hole—still stands.

Lyndon Baines Johnson: Driving. Specifically, drunken driving, especially on his Texas ranch...in a specially designed convertible that had been converted for amphibious use. (Maybe to forget about the war in Vietnam for a while, the 36th chief exec would feign brake failure and plunge his magic car into the nearest body of water, taking his unsuspecting passengers with him.) Kind of brings new meaning to "All the way with LBJ!"

Bill Clinton: Since his days as a kid growing up in Hope, Arkansas, William Jefferson Clinton has always enjoyed sax. He couldn't get enough sax. Even after he became a married politician and eventually the 42nd president of the United States, he still found time for sax . . . even if it occasionally got him into trouble. He also enjoys doing crossword puzzles and contributed clues to one of *The New York Times* crossword puzzles.

Barack Obama: He may not be Michael Jordan, but this chief executive loves his basketball! Having watched tapes of Obama's high school playing career, sportswriters admitted the kid wasn't half bad—definitely deserving of the nickname "Barry O'Bomber."

By Reason of Insanity

However contentious the issues they decide, the members of the U.S. Supreme Court are usually known for sober, even-minded temperament. But that has not always been the case. At least two justices in the history of that hallowed court, including one acting chief justice, were insane for portions of their tenure.

✳ ✳ ✳ ✳

A Deranged Justice

HENRY BALDWIN, WHO served on the Court from 1830 to 1844, had an abrasive personality that angered his fellow justices and eventually morphed into lunacy. A brilliant student at Yale and a law clerk for Alexander Dallas, Baldwin established the Constitution's privileges and immunities clause, whereby a right granted by one state must be upheld by all other states. Born in 1780, the independent-minded Baldwin set a giant precedent by writing the Court's first dissenting opinions; previously the Court had issued only unanimous rulings. In the famous *Amistad* case, where the Court ruled on the side of slaves who had seized their slave ship, Baldwin—though personally opposed to slavery—argued for sending the slaves back into captivity. He also irked the other justices by criticizing the fact that they shared the same Capitol Hill boarding house, which he felt fostered groupthink.

Baldwin was burdened by terrible financial woes: He lost a small fortune in the Depression of 1820, had to rescue grown children of his who fell into debt, and saw several of his businesses go belly up. On the circuit courts of New Jersey and Pennsylvania, he tried to make money by selling copies of his judicial opinions. Like Thomas Jefferson, he sold his personal book collection to the Library of Congress to raise cash.

In 1832, Baldwin suffered a massive seizure, was hospitalized for "incurable lunacy," and missed the 1833 term. Senator Daniel Webster noted the "breaking out of Judge Baldwin's insanity." On the Court, Baldwin grew violent-tempered. In 1838, a Court officer, after talking with Baldwin's fellow judges, noted his "mind is out of order... five persons say he is crazy." In his later years, Baldwin fell victim to paralysis. At age 64, "Crazy Henry" died, impoverished but still on the Court. His family and friends paid for his funeral.

A Suicidal Judge

Few could have guessed, knowing his résumé, that Judge John Rutledge would lose his mind.

Born in 1739, Rutledge was coauthor of South Carolina's constitution and a former governor. His brother was a signer of the Declaration of Independence. During the Revolution, Rutledge helped rebuild American forces in the South after the crushing British victory at Camden, South Carolina. His efforts paid off, and a new army—under General Nathanael Greene—chased the Redcoats out of most of the state.

In his private life, Rutledge was prudent with his money. "By doing good with his money, a man, as it were, stamps the image of God upon it, and makes it pass, current for the merchandise of heaven," he wrote. In the public realm, Rutledge was by inclination a moderate. Early on, he opposed separation of the colonies from Great Britain. In the years leading to the American Revolution, he opposed separating from the motherland, instead pressing for voting rights while forbidding trade with British merchants. As a political pragmatist, however, he made an exception for the export of rice, a South Carolina staple. Once the war began, he was temperate toward the enemy: As governor, he pardoned pro-British loyalists willing to join the state's militia even though the British confiscated his considerable property—which he never got back.

Rutledge was a pivotal figure at the Constitutional Convention. He got everyone to take an oath of secrecy, placing a clamp on media-fed rumors that might have sunk an agreement. As chairman of the committee on detail, which controlled the agenda, he got almost everything he wanted. The new government assumed the states' debts, permitted slavery, and set up a system where Congress elected the president. At the same time, Rutledge was willing to compromise, stating eloquently: "Is it not better that I should sacrifice one prized opinion than that all of us should sacrifice everything we might otherwise gain?"

Things began turning for him after President Washington named him to the Supreme Court in 1789. He was very disappointed that John Jay was named chief justice instead of himself. For two years, to discharge his duties, he rode throughout the South to preside over the region's circuit courts. During this period, remarkably, the newly formed Supreme Court heard no cases. Bored, Rutledge resigned in 1791 to become chief justice of his home state's court of common pleas.

Things got much worse in 1792, when his wife, Elizabeth, died. Driven by despair, Rutledge became mentally unstable. According to Senator Ralph Izard of South Carolina, he was "frequently so much deranged . . . in a great measure deprived of his senses."

Rutledge made a critical political error in July 1795, after President Washington nominated him for chief justice to replace John Jay, the nation's first supreme Supreme. Jay had negotiated a controversial treaty with Britain to settle commercial and military disputes between the two countries. Washington's political foes, led by Thomas Jefferson, bitterly attacked the accord. Irate crowds burned Jay in effigy, crying out: "Damn every one that won't put lights in his windows and sit up all night damning John Jay!"

As an appointee of Washington and as acting chief justice, Rutledge was naturally expected to back Jay's treaty, a priority of the Washington Administration. Instead, just two weeks after his selection, he denounced

it at a public meeting in Charleston. Calling the treaty "prostitution of the dearest right of free man," Rutledge said he'd "rather the President should die than sign that puerile instrument." Rutledge added he "preferred war" with England to its adoption. Meanwhile, a reporter at the forum eagerly took down his words, which soon appeared in newspapers around the nation.

The president's Cabinet was aghast. Treasury Secretary Alexander Hamilton, under the pen name Camillus, wrote that Rutledge was an "unfit character" who had again veered into insanity. Vice President John Adams informed his wife Abigail that "C. Justices must not propagate Disunion, Division, Contention and delusion among the people." Rumors spread that the South Carolinian had taken to eating his gavel. Journals alleged he'd reneged on personal debts.

On December 15, the Senate, controlled by Washington's Federalist party and jawboned by Hamilton, rejected Rutledge's nomination by a vote of 10 to 14.

Humiliated by the torrent of criticism, Rutledge resigned from the court. He attempted to drown himself by jumping into Charleston Bay but was saved by two slaves who happened along at the right moment.

He never held another office and died in 1800.

✳ The British royal family changed its name from "Saxe-Coburg and Gotha" to "Windsor" in 1917, during World War I, because its original name sounded too German. It would have been difficult to fit onto a business card, as well. The royals are still known as the House of Windsor.

✳ In ancient China and parts of India, mouse meat was considered a great delicacy.

From the Vaults of History

A Daring Young Man

On November 12, 1859, the audience at the Cirque Napoleon in Paris was delighted and amazed to witness the world's first flying trapeze act. Jules Léotard thrilled the crowd by sailing between three trapezes and turning a somersault in midair, with only a few mattresses and carpets to protect him from a hard fall. The young daredevil's act only lasted 12 minutes, but it left a huge impression on French (and indeed all of Western) culture that lasts to this day. He called the very tight one-piece garment he wore a *maillot*, but since that time, the tights that circus performers and dancers wear have been renamed leotards. Interestingly, *maillot* now refers to a swimsuit.

A Woman Scorned

You had to be careful whom you dumped in the 12th century. King Louis VI of France wasn't too happy when his wife, Eleanor of Aquitaine, bore him only two daughters and no sons. The marriage was annulled, but Eleanor had no intention of going quietly and leading a dull, lonely life. She made sure that she retained every acre of land in southwest France that she had brought into the marriage. She also promptly married Henry II, who became king of England and made her queen. A victim of the adage, "You made your bed, now lie in it," Louis wasn't too thrilled when he realized that an English king now owned more property in France than he did.

History Quickies

* Virginia Woolf wrote all her books while standing up.

* The first American to have indoor plumbing was Henry Wadsworth Longfellow in 1840.

* Maurice Grey was the inventor of a machine that mass-produced fine textured mustard. Auguste Poupon was also an established mustard maker. In 1886, the two mustard manufacturers joined forces and Grey Poupon was born.

The Mystery of the Lost Dauphin of France

History is rife with conspiracy theories. More than 200 years later, the fate of the Lost Dauphin of France still baffles historians.

✳   ✳   ✳   ✳

Little Boy Lost

BORN IN 1785, Louis XVII, son of King Louis XVI and Queen Marie Antoinette, was the heir apparent to the throne (giving him the title of *le Dauphin*). The young boy's destiny was unfortunately timed, however, coinciding with the French Revolution's antiroyalist frenzy that swept away the monarchy. His father met his end on the guillotine in January 1793; as next in the line of succession, little eight-year-old Louis XVII was a dead boy walking.

The family was imprisoned. A few months later, on the night of July 3, 1793, guards came for Louis. Realizing that she would never see her son again, Marie Antoinette clung to Louis, and she pleaded for his life. She finally relented after the commissioners threatened to kill both her son and daughter. The boy was dragged crying and screaming from his mother.

To keep the monarchy from reestablishing, Louis was imprisoned in solitary confinement in a windowless room. Some reports state that the young boy was horribly starved and abused by his jailers. Less than two years later, on June 8, 1795, the ten-year-old Dauphin of France died. The official cause of death was tuberculosis. But instead of ending the matter, the mystery of the true fate of Louis XVII had just begun.

Pretenders to the Throne

Rumors grew like wildfire that the body of Louis XVII was actually someone else. Like any good mystery, there were plenty of stories to fuel the flames of conspiracy:

* Louis's jailers were a husband and wife. Later, the aged wife told the nuns who were nursing her that she and her husband had once smuggled out the Dauphin. "My little prince is not dead," she reportedly said.

* A doctor who had treated the Dauphin died "mysteriously" just before the boy did. The doctor's widow suggested he had refused to participate in some strange practices concerning his patient.

* The Dauphin's sister was never asked to identify his body.

* In 1814, the historian of the restored French monarchy claimed that Louis was alive.

* In 1846, the mass grave where the Dauphin had been buried was exhumed. Only one corpse, that of an older boy, showed evidence of tuberculosis.

Contenders (or Pretenders?) to the Throne

With all of these doubts about what really happened to Louis, it's amazing that only about 100 people came forward throughout the years claiming to be the lost Dauphin and rightful heir to the throne. Among them were John James Audubon, the famous naturalist. Many believed Audubon was Louis because he was adopted, was the same age that the Dauphin would have been, and spoke with a French accent. Audubon liked a good story and sometimes implied that he was indeed the Dauphin.

Another contender was Karl Wilhelm Naundorff. Perhaps the most successful of all, this German clockmaker convinced both the Dauphin's nurse and the minister of justice under Louis XVI that he was indeed the lost heir. He was even recognized as such by the government of the Netherlands. DNA tests in the 1950s disproved his claim. Finally, in 2000, DNA tests confirmed that the boy who died in prison was indeed Louis XVII. Even so, as with many conspiracy theories, many people dispute the test's finding.

Bombing the Royal Wedding

It's traditional for wedding guests to throw birdseed or rose petals to celebrate a newly married couple. But the king of Spain had something different thrown at his wedding—a bomb hidden in a bouquet of flowers.

✳ ✳ ✳ ✳

P ROCLAIMED KING OF Spain upon his birth on May 17, 1886 (his father Alfonso XII died before he was born), Alfonso XIII inherited a nation long past its imperial prime.

As a member of European royalty, Alfonso inherited status as a high-profile target for anarchist radicals, who had been terrorizing Europe since the mid-19th century. His father had survived an assassination attempt in 1878, the same year that Kaiser Wilhelm I weathered two attempts on his life. Czar Alexander II of Russia was killed in a bombing in 1881, after narrowly escaping assassination attempts in 1866 and 1879.

Royalty and heads of state were targeted by anarchists under their doctrine of "propaganda of the deed," a violent form of direct action that targeted prominent figures with the goal of gaining notoriety and support for the anarchists' cause. The turn of the 20th century saw a new spate of attacks. In 1894, French President Sadi Carnot was stabbed to death. In 1900, Umberto I of Italy was shot dead. In 1901, anarchist Leon Czolgosz killed U.S. President William McKinley. In 1902, Leopold II of Belgium survived an assassination attempt. In 1905, a bomb killed Duke Sergei Alexandrovich, fifth son of Czar Alexander II.

In Spain, Prime Minister Antonio Cánovas del Castillo had been assassinated by Italian anarchist Michele Angiolillo in 1897. Alfonso XIII's marriage to Princess Victoria Eugénie of Battenberg (a niece of King Edward VII of Britain and granddaughter of Queen Victoria) offered another tempting opportunity for propaganda by deed. After their wedding in Madrid on May 31, 1906, Alfonso and Queen Ena, as she was known, were proceeding down Calle Mayor when anarchist Mateu Morral threw a bomb concealed in a flower bouquet toward their carriage. Several bystanders and horses were killed; the royal couple escaped with only blood spatters on the queen's wedding dress. A Catalan who had quit his family's textile business to work as a librarian for anarchist educational reformer Francisco Ferrer Guardia, Morral was aided by radical journalist José Nakens. He fled the assassination attempt and committed suicide after killing a policeman as he pretended to surrender.

Unrest continued in Spain. In 1909, a general strike and five days of mob rule were followed by martial law and brutal military suppression as anarchist assassinations continued throughout Europe. In 1912, Spanish Prime Minister José Canalejas was assassinated in Madrid. Two years later, the killing of Archduke Franz Ferdinand of Austria in Sarajevo triggered the First World War. Alfonso maintained his rule and kept Spanish neutrality. WWI saw the decline of the anarchist movement, as the Russian revolution swept the communists into power and Western nations took severe measures to suppress radicalism.

Alfonso's reign would last until April 1931, when leftists won elections throughout Spain and proclaimed the Second Republic. The royal family went into voluntary exile in France in hopes of avoiding a civil war, but war broke out in 1936 between the Republicans (allied with anarchist factions) and the right-wing Nationalists. During the civil war, the Republican government of Madrid renamed Calle Mayor as Calle Mateu Morral. However, the Nationalist victory led by General Francisco Franco served as a prelude to WWII. Upon Franco's death in 1975, Alfonso XIII's grandson, Juan Carlos I, was restored to the throne.

Chapter Nine

The World Around Us

The Secret of the Stones

Though no one can definitively say who erected the massive Stonehenge monument in Wiltshire County, southern England, when and why they built it, or how they did so without the aid of modern machinery, there are no shortage of theories.

✳ ✳ ✳ ✳

Archaeologists speculate that the site took shape about 5,000 years ago, with the first stones being laid in 3000 B.C. The monument was finally completed in 1500 B.C., perhaps serving as a memorial to fallen warriors, as the burial mounds that surround the site might indicate.

Geologists claim that 80 of the 4-ton rocks at Stonehenge were quarried from the Prescelly Mountains in Wales—240 miles away—and then transported by sled and barge to their current location.

Astronomers observe that builders placed the rocks in concentric circles, thus creating a massive solar observatory through which early man could predict the arrival of eclipses and follow the passage of the seasons.

Historians think that the stones form the walls of an ancient temple—a place for people to worship the heavens. In later times, it was used by Druids to celebrate their pagan festivals.

8 Quirky Festivals in North America

Looking for somewhere wacky to have a good time? A festival-goer can celebrate animals, insects, foods, historical events, and just about any other topic under the sun. It's easy to fill your calendar with these events—just check out these examples.

✳ ✳ ✳ ✳

1. **Frozen Dead Guy Days (Nederland, Colorado):** The fun at the annual Frozen Dead Guy Days festival heats up Nederland during Colorado's typically frosty March. The fest commemorates a cryogenically-preserved Norwegian who has been kept in a shed by his grandson since 1994. Visitors are encouraged to come to a dance tagged "Grandpa's Blue Ball" dressed as a frozen or dead character. Coffin races and a parade featuring antique hearses are among the liveliest attractions, along with salmon tossing and a frozen beach volleyball tournament. The event started in 2002 and annually attracts about 7,000 visitors.

2. **Secret City Festival (Oak Ridge, Tennessee):** The annual Secret City Festival highlights the important role Oak Ridge played in World War II. In the 1940s, researchers there developed the top secret atomic bomb—hence the city's nickname—and today visitors can tour Manhattan Project sites to see where the bomb was devised. One of the country's largest World War II reenactments is also a popular draw, with roaring tanks, motorcycles, and other vintage military gear. Each June, the event draws about 20,000 people to Oak Ridge, which is nestled between the picturesque Cumberland and Great Smoky Mountains.

3. **Nanaimo Marine Festival (Nanaimo, British Columbia):** At the Nanaimo Marine Festival in mid-July, up to 200 "tubbers" compete in the Great International World

Championship Bathtub Race across a 36-mile course. Using just about every conceivable watercraft, most of which at least vaguely resemble a bathtub, contestants must make it to Vancouver's Fisherman's Cove across the Straits of Georgia. The first race was held in 1967; activities have expanded since to include a food fair, craft show, Kiddies' Karnival, and waiters' race.

4. **BugFest (Raleigh, North Carolina):** The nation's largest single-day festival featuring insects, BugFest attracts around 25,000 people to Raleigh each September. The event started in 1997 and now includes beekeeping demonstrations, a flea circus, and roach races. The festival features many exhibits about insects, from live spiders and centipedes to displays on how bugs see. At Café Insecta, attendees can sample Buggy Bean Dip with Crackers, Quivering Wax Worm Quiche, Stir-fried Cantonese Crickets over rice, and Three Bug Salad, among other aptly named goodies that actually include worms, ants, and related critters raised for cooking.

5. **Rattlesnake Roundup (Freer, Texas):** Billed as the biggest party in Texas, the Freer Rattlesnake Roundup held each May features nationally known country and Tejano artists . . . and loads of snakes. In addition to daredevil snake shows, snake-twirling displays, a carnival, arts and crafts, and fried rattlesnake to chaw, prizes are given out for the longest and smallest rattlesnakes, as well as for the most nonvenomous snakes brought to the fest by one person.

6. **Barnesville Potato Days (Barnesville, Minnesota):** Up to 14,000 visitors head to west-central Minnesota for Barnesville Potato Days in late August when this small town celebrates the lowly spud with a great menu of activities. The Potato Salad Cook-off attracts onlookers eager to compare the year's winning recipe with how Grandma used to make this popular picnic dish. Things can get messy during mashed potato wrestling, but the Miss Tator Tot

pageant is much more refined. Of course, there is plenty of food to sample, including Norwegian lefse, potato pancakes, potato sausage, potato soup, and traditional German potato dumplings. On Friday, there's even a free French Fry Feed. Tucked away in the fertile Red River Valley, Barnesville has been honoring the crop of choice of many nearby farmers with this festival since 1938.

7. **Faux Film Festival (Portland, Oregon):** For anyone who loves fake commercials or movie trailers, Portland's Faux Film Festival is the ticket to a surreal filmic never-never land. Mockumentaries and other celluloid spoofs are among the dozens of goofy entries shown in the historic 460-seat Hollywood Theatre. Past viewings have included the silly classic *It Came from the Lint Trap* and the quirky *The Lady from Sockholm*, a film noir featuring sock puppets. The fest is usually staged at the end of March, with a packed house at each screening.

8. **Contraband Days Pirate Festival (Lake Charles, Louisiana):** Legend has it that buccaneer Jean Lafitte buried an enormous treasure somewhere along Lake Charles's sandy shoreline. Since 1958, Contraband Days Pirate Festival, which attracts more than 100,000 people annually, has been honoring the legend each May. Perhaps one of the funniest sights of the festival is when the mayor is made to walk the plank after pirates take over the town. The plucky civic chief is naturally rescued quickly, then is free to enjoy the rest of the fest with its carnival, arm-wrestling competition, sailboat regatta, and bed races. With an eclectic selection of nearly 100 different events, Contraband Days is frequently chosen by the American Bus Association as a Top 100 Event in North America.

History's Little Mystery

Where's Napoleon's, uh, "little Napoleon"?

* * * *

AFTER HIS MILITARY defeat at Waterloo, French general Napoleon Bonaparte died in exile on the remote island of St. Helena in 1821. Seventeen people attended his autopsy, including Bonaparte's doctor, several of his aides, and a priest. As one version of the story goes, at some point during the autopsy, Napoleon's penis was removed and put aside to keep for posterity. There are some historians who find this implausible, yet about 30 years later, one of Napoleon's aides published a memoir in which he claims to have helped remove several of Bonaparte's body parts.

In 1924, a collector from Philadelphia named A.S.W. Rosenbach purchased a collection of Napoleon artifacts for about $2,000. Among the items he purchased was a "mummified tendon taken from Napoleon's body during the post-mortem." Upon further inspection and research, Rosenbach declared the tendon was definitely the leader's penis. Three years later, Rosenbach put the item on display in New York, and thousands of people viewed the penis under a glass case. The descriptions weren't kind; some likened the relic to "a shriveled seahorse" or "beef jerky."

Oddly, the French government was wholly uninterested in the collection. And to this day, it refuses to even acknowledge the possibility of the object's authenticity, further casting doubt on whether the object is actually Napoleon's "little general."

In the late 1970s, a urologist and professor from Columbia University purchased the penis for about $3,000 at an auction. Whether it's the genuine article is still up for debate. Until scientists get their, er, hands on it, the public will just have to speculate about this odd collectible.

Canadian Superlatives

Canada is one of the largest and most livable countries on Earth, and naturally it has a lot of biggests, firsts, and bests.

* * * *

North America's largest mall: Spread across 121 acres, the West Edmonton Mall in Alberta has more than 800 stores, an ice rink where the Edmonton Oilers practice, an indoor waterpark, miniature golf courses, hotels, and much more. There are spaces for 20,000 cars in what is considered the largest parking lot in the world.

World's largest bitumen deposits: Two-thirds of the world's bitumen reserves are in Alberta. Why, you might ask, would anyone not studying ancient Egyptian mummification care about bitumen? Because if you refine bitumen, it can fuel your automobile.

World's tallest totem pole: At 173 feet tall, the totem pole on Cormorant Island, British Columbia, represents the numerous tribes of the Kwakwaka'wakw nation. The artists carved all but five feet of the pole from a single tree.

Longest sea-fogs on Earth: The Grand Banks of Newfoundland have less than a half-mile visibility during one-third of the year.

World's biggest herd of caribou: The George River herd of northern Labrador is estimated at 750,000 head.

Largest recorded bluefin tuna catch: A 1,496-pound beast was caught in 1979 by Ken Fraser of Auld Cove, Nova Scotia. Before he finally landed it, his depth-charge launcher failed and his harpoon gun broke.

First recorded game of ice hockey: Some say it was played in 1855 in Kingston, Ontario. (The first penalty box was probably built by the end of the first period.) The first recorded public game was played in 1875 in Montreal.

World's largest skating area: On the Rideau Canal Skateway in Ottawa, Ontario, you can skate 4.8 miles if you wish (many Canadians do).

North America's northernmost national park: Situated on Ellesmere Island, Nunavut, Quttinirpaaq National Park issues quite a unique advisory: "Visitors traveling in this park must carry appropriate gear, and must be self-reliant and able to handle any medical or wildlife-related emergencies on their own. Many hazards may be encountered—from dangerous river crossings to severe cold and storms. However, the biggest hazard is the profound remoteness of Quttinirpaaq and the distance from any medical or rescue assistance. There may be few if any other visitors in the park at the same time as your visit."

World's largest winter snow removal: Montreal averages 42 million metric tons of snowblowing, shoveling, plowing, and other forms of removal per year. This is the real reason behind many residents' love of poutine (french fries covered with gravy and cheese curds)—it keeps them warm during the six months of this drudgery.

North America's first tidal-power-generation plant: Annapolis Tidal Generating Station in Nova Scotia opened in 1984. It makes sense when your tides vary by 50 feet.

World's longest undersea phone cable: This runs from Port Alberni, British Columbia, to Sydney, Australia, via Hawaii and Fiji. Measuring 9,711 miles, it's more than a third of the world's circumference.

World's largest deliberate nonnuclear explosion: This event occurred on April 5, 1958, to destroy the sharp rocks of the shipping hazard at Seymour Narrows, British Columbia. The rocks had snagged 120 ships since records were kept, averaging more than one per year.

First policewoman in North America: Rose Fortune of Annapolis Royal, Nova Scotia, took the position in 1830.

The Nazca Lines: Pictures Aimed at an Eye in the Sky?

Ancient works of art etched into a desert floor in South America have inspired wild theories about who created them and why.

✳ ✳ ✳ ✳

FLYING ABOVE THE rocky plains northwest of Nazca, Peru, in 1927, aviator Toribio Mejía Xesspe was surprised to see gigantic eyes looking up at him. Then the pilot noticed that the orbs stared out of a bulbous head upon a cartoonish line drawing of a man, etched over hundreds of square feet of the landscape below.

The huge drawing—later called "owl man" for its staring eyes—turned out to be just one of scores of huge, 2,000-year-old images scratched into the earth over almost 200 square miles of the parched Peruvian landscape.

There is a 360-foot-long monkey with a whimsically spiraled tail, along with a 150-foot-long spider and a 935-foot pelican. Other figures include a hummingbird and a killer whale. There are also geometric shapes and straight lines that stretch for miles across the stony ground. Unless the viewer knows what to look for, they're almost invisible from ground level.

The Theory of Ancient Astronauts

The drawings have been dated to a period between 200 B.C. and A.D. 600. Obviously, there were no airplanes from which to view them back then. So why were they made? And for whose benefit?

In his 1968 book *Chariots of the Gods?*, Swiss author Erich Von Däniken popularized the idea that the drawings and lines were landing signals and runways for starships that visited southern Peru long before the modern era. In his interpretation, the owl man is an astronaut in a helmet. Von Däniken's theory caught on among UFO enthusiasts. Many science-fiction novels and films make reference to this desert in Peru's Pampa Colorado region as a site with special significance to space travelers.

Coming Down to Earth

Examined up close, the drawings consist of cleared paths—areas where someone removed reddish surface rocks to expose the soft soil beneath. In the stable desert climate—averaging less than an inch of rain per year—the paths have survived through many centuries largely intact.

Scientists believe the Nazca culture—a civilization that came before the Incas—drew the lines. The style of the artwork is similar to that featured on Nazca pottery. German-born researcher Maria Reiche (1903–1998) showed how the Nazca could have laid out the figures using simple surveying tools such as ropes and posts. In the 1980s, American researcher Joe Nickell duplicated one of the drawings, a condor, showing that the Nazca could have rendered parts of the figures "freehand"—that is, without special tools or even scale models. Nickell also demonstrated that despite their great size, the figures can be identified as drawings even from ground level. No alien technology would have been required to make them.

Still Mysterious

As for why the Nazca drew giant doodles across the desert, no one is sure. Reiche noted that some of the lines have astronomical relevance. For example, one points to where the sun sets at the winter solstice. Some lines may also have pointed toward underground water sources—crucially important to desert people.

Most scholars think that the marks were part of the Nazca religion. They may have been footpaths followed during ritual processions. And although it's extremely unlikely that they were intended for extraterrestrials, many experts think it likely that the lines were oriented toward Nazca gods—perhaps a monkey god, a spider god, and so on, who could be imagined gazing down from the heavens upon likenesses of themselves.

Fast Facts

＊ Bouvet Island in the South Atlantic is the most remote island on Earth. It lies almost a thousand miles from the nearest land (Queen Maude Land, Antarctica).

＊ Leo Tolstoy, author of *War and Peace,* left all of his possessions to the stump of a tree.

＊ The top-selling tie color is blue.

＊ Honey was used to pay taxes in ancient Rome.

＊ Domino's has marketed a reindeer sausage pizza in Iceland.

＊ Apples are considered the most popular fruit in America.

＊ Blondes typically have more individual hairs on their heads than brunettes. Redheads have the fewest of the three.

＊ An average human eyebrow has 550 hairs.

＊ An average human beard has more than 15,000 hairs.

＊ The longest recorded underwater kiss was 2 minutes and 18 seconds.

＊ An average office chair moves around a total of eight miles over the course of a year.

＊ The chili and the frijole are the official vegetables of New Mexico.

＊ The square dance is the official folk dance of Utah.

＊ Princess Diana appeared on the cover of *People* magazine more than 50 times.

＊ John Lennon was the first person to be featured on the cover of *Rolling Stone* magazine.

＊ Manhattan is about half the size of Disney World.

＊ A caterpillar has five to six times as many muscles in its body as a human.

From the Vaults of History

Amiable and Unarmed

Indira Gandhi once said, "You can't shake hands with a closed fist." While that may be true, it's interesting that this gesture of friendliness has origins in armature. Most historians agree that the custom of the handshake began several hundred years ago in England as a way to not only greet someone but also to communicate that you were unarmed and empty handed. Years ago, gentlemen often concealed weapons up their left sleeves, so handshakes were performed with the left hand as a gesture of trust. As the handshake grew in popularity, it naturally shifted to the right hand as a matter of convenience.

Put 'Er There

The gesture of shaking hands is found all over the world, but in many variations. If you're a world traveler, it's a good idea to study up on a country's handshaking customs. For instance, in Japan, the handshake is often substituted with a bow. Russians frequently shake hands but always without wearing gloves. In fact, many Eastern European nations consider shaking hands while wearing gloves to be rude. The Chinese enjoy a brisk "pumping" handshake, but many Middle Eastern cultures encourage men to offer a limp wet noodle of a handshake. The French always shake each others' hands in business meetings, but when outside the conference room, it's customary to briskly buss each others' cheeks. In Kuwait, shaking hands is reserved for men—shaking hands with an unfamiliar woman is considered taboo. That also goes for folks of the Orthodox Jewish faith.

Finally, if for any reason you can't shake hands (due to arthritis, an injury, or you just sneezed in your hand), be prepared to immediately offer a polite apology. In many countries, not shaking hands is one of the easiest ways to insult a stranger.

11 Examples of Good (and Bad) Manners Around the World

Sit up straight. Say "please" and "thank you." Don't put your elbows on the table. Most of us were drilled from an early age in proper manners and etiquette. But once you leave your home country, things get a bit complicated. Here are some examples of how other cultures do things differently.

❋   ❋   ❋   ❋

1. In China and much of the Far East, belching is considered a compliment to the chef and a sign that you have eaten well and enjoyed your meal.

2. In most of the Middle and Far East, it is considered an insult to point your feet (particularly the soles) at another person, or to display them in any way—for example, by resting with your feet up.

3. In most Asian countries, a business card is seen as an extension of the person it represents; therefore, to disrespect a card—by folding it, writing on it, or shoving it into your pocket without looking at it—is to disrespect the person who gave it to you.

4. Nowadays, a bone-crushing handshake is seen as manly and admirable in the United States and UK, but in much of the East, particularly the Philippines, it is seen as a sign of aggression—just as if you gave any other part of a person's body a hard squeeze!

5. Orthodox Jews will not shake hands with someone of the opposite sex. A strict Muslim woman will not shake hands with a man; however, a Muslim man will shake hands with a non-Muslim woman. People in these cultures generally avoid touching people of the opposite sex who are not family members.

6. When dining in China, never force yourself to clear your plate out of politeness—it would be very bad manners for your host not to keep refilling it. Instead, you should leave some food on your plate at each course as an acknowledgment of your host's generosity.

7. In Japan and Korea, a tip is considered an insult rather than a compliment; for them, accepting tips is akin to begging. However, this tradition is beginning to change as more Westerners bring their customs to eastern Asia.

8. The "okay" sign (thumb and forefinger touching to make a circle) is very far from okay in much of the world. In Germany and most of South America, it is an insult, similar to giving someone the finger in the United States, while in Turkey it is a derogatory gesture used to imply that someone is homosexual.

9. Similarly, in the UK, when the two-fingered "V for victory" or "peace" salute is given with the hand turned so that the palm faces inward, it is considered extremely rude, as it has a meaning similar to raising the middle finger to someone in the United States.

10. In Greece, any signal that involves showing your open palm is extremely offensive. Such gestures include waving and making a "stop" sign. If you do wish to wave goodbye to someone in Greece, you need to do so with your palm facing in, like a beauty pageant contestant or a member of the royal family.

11. In Luxembourg, Switzerland, and France, public gum-chewing is considered vulgar, while in Singapore most types of gum have been illegal since 1992, when residents grew tired of scraping the sticky stuff off their sidewalks.

Canada's Unique Ethnic Communities

Each of these communities can lay claim to a portion of the Maple Leaf flag.

✳   ✳   ✳   ✳

French: The British kicked French authority out of Canada; then they tried without success to anglicize French Canadians, who maintained their language and traditions through great force of will. Some wish to form a République Québecoise separate from Canada, but for now, French Canadians remain Canadian—23 percent of the population.

Acadian: Acadians are Francophone Canadians who are mainly concentrated in New Brunswick and are mostly bilingual. The current Acadian population—1 percent of Canada's total— descends from the remnant that wasn't deported after 1755. Today, Acadian identity is strong.

Metis: Canadians of mixed French and First Nations heritage (mainly concentrated in the Prairies) have experienced discrimination in the past, and in the late 1800s they rebelled with armed force. Their fusion reflects cultural and spiritual aspects of both ancestries—a far cry from the outdated perception of mixed blood as a negative.

Doukhobors: Doukhobors descend from Russian immigrants who came to Canada around 1900 after being persecuted in Russia for pacifist religious beliefs. They don't do it very often today, but in the past Doukhobors have protested injustice by walking around naked. Most live in British Columbia's rugged Kootenai country, where it takes a tough person to protest naked.

Inuit: Canada's Arctic and sub-Arctic are the home of 55,000 Inuit, many of whom live in the territory of Nunavut and speak their culture's language, Inuktitut. One-fifth of the

Nunavut population lives in Iqaluit, formerly Frobisher Bay, on Baffin Island—about as far north as Nome, Alaska. Many Inuit still practice traditional subsistence methods, long proven effective in one of the world's harshest environments.

First Nations: Aboriginal Canadians who are neither Inuit nor Metis—in the United States they'd be called Native Americans—are the many First Nations bands of Canada: Haida, Salish, Blackfoot, Athabascan, Cree, Ojibwa, Iroquois, and others.

Sikhs: Some 270,000 Canadians claim Sikh heritage, mostly concentrated in cities in Ontario and British Columbia. Sikhism is not only a religion but also a cultural identity. Canada allows Sikhs to wear turbans (which are required by their faith) and possess kirpans, or daggers (which male Sikhs are supposed to carry).

Chinese Canadians: "Hongcouver" (Vancouver, British Columbia) is full of ethnic communities, but the largest is surely Chinese. More than a million Chinese Canadians have their largest concentration in this cosmopolitan city, loading it with every variety of Chinese culture one can imagine.

African Canadians: Saint John's, New Brunswick, is home to a thriving African Canadian community that dates back to black Loyalists who decided not to stick around in the rebellious Colonies. More recent waves came from former slaves after the War of 1812 and from the West Indies. African Canadians can be found all over the country—most commonly in Toronto and Montreal.

Filipinos: The Filipinos of Manitoba are among Canada's newest and most successful ethnic communities. The first generation Filipinos were mostly professionals in the medical and garment industries, but today's Manitoba Pinoy/Pinay population fits into mainstream life in true Canadian fashion: by embracing Canadian traditions and adding its own.

Who Wants to Be a Troglodyte?

Lots of creatures sleep in cozy caves or burrows—rabbits, bats, and moles, for example. Here are a few cave-based hotels and inns that are sure to make the animals green with envy.

✳   ✳   ✳   ✳

Beckham Creek Cave Haven, Parthenon, Arkansas

This combination cave and cabin was built on a 530-acre estate in the Ozark Mountains. It makes the most of its gorgeous surroundings with big windows—a facing wall, a rock waterfall, and a stalactite-studded ceiling. Below ground, guests have plenty of elbow room and can divide their time between the 2,000-square-foot great room, the spacious kitchen, the game room, and five bedrooms tucked into rocky crevices.

Les Hautes Roches, Rochecorbon, France

This hotel is comprised of an 18th-century castle and the caves that were created when stone was quarried for the Loire Valley château. Over the years, the cave was used as a refuge from war, to house monks from a nearby abbey, to grow mushrooms, and to store wine before becoming the first cave hotel in France. It now offers guests 15 rooms (12 of which are underground). A cave bar still contains the original fireplace and bread oven. Many guests use the hotel as a home base when exploring nearby mushroom caves.

Yunak Evleri, Urgup (Cappadocia), Turkey

The fairy towers and underground spaces carved out of Cappadocia's tuff (soft volcanic rock) were once used as hiding places from armies. Today, tourists use them to find seclusion. One of the many hotels built into the areas caves, the Yunak Evleri contains 30 rooms. The hotel actually consists of six fifth- and sixth-century cave houses and a 19th-century Greek mansion. Each room features whitewashed rock walls, hardwood floors, and antique Turkish rugs.

Kokopelli's Cave Bed & Breakfast, Farmington, New Mexico

This 1,650-square-foot, one-bedroom luxury cliff dwelling was not built in a natural cave. In 1980, geologist Bruce Black excavated the cave out of 40-million-year-old sandstone and turned it into an office 70 feet below the earth. During the next 15 years, Black worked to make the cave habitable. Bruce and his wife live in the cave, and since 1997, they've been welcoming paid guests. The cave entrance is located in the cliff face and is accessible via a steep path, 150 hand-hewn sandstone steps, and a short ladder. Guests are encouraged to pack light.

PJ's Underground B&B, White Cliffs, Australia

White Cliffs was home to the first commercial opal mine in Australia. Because it is self-supporting and easy to carve, the local sandstone made it easy for miners to create dugouts. In fact, most residents of White Cliffs dug their own dwellings with only a jackhammer and a wheelbarrow. Low humidity and constantly cool temperatures (70°F year-round) make the dugouts comfortable living spaces. PJ's offers guests six underground rooms, an underground cottage, homegrown vegetables, homemade bread, and help arranging visits to the opal mines.

Las Casas Cueva, Galera, Spain

In ancient times, when a woman from the Andalusia region of Spain discovered she was pregnant, her first chore was to dig the baby's bedroom out of the limestone walls of her cave. Today, a tourist complex known as Las Casas Cueva de Galera sits at the top of the hilly, prehistoric village of Galera. It is the largest cave hotel in the region. Each cave includes a fireplace, a kitchen, and a Jacuzzi.

Countdown to Doomsday

Making some long-term plans? Well, forget about them.
According to the Doomsday Clock, you don't have much time left.

✳ ✳ ✳ ✳

YOU'VE PROBABLY SEEN it before: a street corner prophet delivering a chilling warning that the end of the world is nigh. History has been full of such doomsayers, running the gamut from spiritualists, shamans, and clairvoyants to philosophers, scholars, and crackpots. Like the prophet on the corner, they were laughed at by most people. But there is one contemporary group of apocalypse prognosticators that may not be so easy to laugh off.

This would be the board of directors of the *Bulletin of the Atomic Scientists* seated at the University of Chicago. Since 1947, this learned group of scientists and academics has maintained the infamous Doomsday Clock, the figurative timepiece that appears on the cover of every issue of the *Bulletin* and serves as a constant reminder of how close humankind is to destroying itself.

What Is the Doomsday Clock?

The Doomsday Clock is a symbolic clock face that shows the hour hand positioned at midnight and the minute hand variably positioned minutes before.

The clock face and positioning of the hands symbolize humankind and its nearness to obliteration:

* The clock itself represents the human race.

* Midnight represents the cataclysmic moment marking the end of the human race—doomsday.

* The minutes before midnight represent the threat humankind poses to itself through nuclear war, environmental degradation, and emerging technologies.

* The positioning of the hands on the clock represents the degree of that threat to humankind. The closer the minute hand is to midnight, the nearer our self-destruction. The farther away it is from midnight, the smaller the threat.

* The positioning of the hands—or the time displayed—is determined by the board of directors of the *Bulletin of the Atomic Scientists*. The board periodically adjusts the minute hand forward or backward in response to the state of world affairs. The more perilous the world seems, the closer to midnight the board sets the Doomsday Clock.

The Perils Facing Humankind

According to the board, humankind has excelled in creating perils that threaten to do it in, the most prominent being nuclear weapons. The Doomsday Clock was originally conceived in response to the emergence of the nuclear age after World War II. The spectre of war between the two nuclear superpowers—the United States and the Soviet Union—and the apocalyptic doctrine of mutually assured destruction was the primary threat manifested in the minutes before midnight. The periodic settings of the clock were prompted by developments in superpower relations and specific world events that brought the two countries either closer to or further from the brink of war.

Even in the post–Cold War world, the board still considers the possibility of nuclear holocaust to be the number-one threat to humankind. It cites the thousands of nuclear weapons that the United States and Russia still have aimed at each other—ready for launch at a moment's notice. Though it's unlikely either of the two countries would unleash an attack, the sheer number of warheads in position guarantees annihilation in the event of a nuclear exchange caused by accident or error.

The nuclear danger is further compounded by the development of nuclear weapons programs by other nations in defiance of nuclear nonproliferation treaties. India and Pakistan now threaten each other with nuclear warheads, and other nations either have—

or are moving toward—nuclear capability. Added to that is the menace of nuclear terrorism as critical materials required for making nuclear weapons remain unsecured and in danger of falling into the hands of groups that seek to cause mass destruction.

The board also identifies two other perils peculiar to the modern age. One is environmental degradation, more specifically, potentially disastrous climate change due to the widespread use of fossil-fuel technologies. The other is emerging technologies such as advances in genetics, biology, and nanotechnology that— if placed in the wrong hands—could be used for destruction.

Humankind, it seems, has made its own world a dangerous place. The Doomsday Clock is intended to remind us just how dangerous it has become.

Eighteen Time Changes since 1947

The initial time setting on the Doomsday Clock in 1947 was seven minutes to midnight. Since then, the time on the clock has changed 18 times.

The gloomiest setting occurred in 1953. After the United States and the Soviet Union successfully tested thermonuclear devices within eight months of each other, the board set the clock to two minutes to midnight.

The most optimistic setting of the clock thus far occurred in 1991. The board set the clock to 17 minutes to midnight in response to the end of the Cold War and the Strategic Arms Reduction Treaty signed by the United States and Russia, which greatly reduced stores of nuclear weapons.

In January 2007, the clock was set at five minutes to midnight— its most pessimistic setting since 1984. As justification for the move, the board cited the coming of a second nuclear age as more nations moved to acquire the bomb, as well as the continued damage to the planet by global climate.

The clock is ticking.

From the Vaults of History

Glad to Be Sad

Robert Burton, a vicar of St. Thomas Church at Oxford, made a giant leap in the understanding and treatment of mental illness when in 1621 he published *The Anatomy of Melancholy*. The popular book included such pithy observations as "Who cannot give good counsel? 'Tis cheap, it costs them nothing." But perhaps Burton's most interesting comment is one that has been rephrased many times by modern-day comedians such as Jim Carrey and Robin Williams: "Aristotle said . . . melancholy men of all others are most witty."

Kilt Complex

You don't see kilts worn much these days. In fact, before 1745, Scottish aristocrats wouldn't have been caught dead in kilts. The plaid skirts were considered distinctly lower class— the uniform of tradesmen and farmers. That year, the kilt was banned by the British Parliament. Suddenly Scotsmen of all social classes decided that they just loved kilts. The fact that the kilt had actually been invented by an Englishman, Thomas Rawlinson, was conveniently ignored by everyone on both sides of the controversy.

✳ In the 1995 movie *Braveheart,* William Wallace's wardrobe had historians shaking their heads: He wears a kilt even though they weren't introduced to Scotland for another 300 years.

A National Shame

The American internment of thousands of Japanese Americans during World War II is common knowledge. But not as many people know that Canada also rounded up and imprisoned its own citizens.

✳   ✳   ✳   ✳

NATIONAL CONCENTRATION CAMPS in Canada started with World War I; key to the establishment of these concentration (later called "internment") camps was the War Measures Act, passed on August 22, 1914. This law gave the Canadian government the authority to do whatever it deemed necessary "for the security, defense, peace, order and welfare of Canada." One of the Canadian government's first orders under the War Measures Act was the registration and, in some cases, the internment of aliens of "enemy nationality." All had to register as "enemy aliens" and report regularly to local authorities.

Twenty-four internment camps were constructed throughout Canada. They were supposed to contain only individuals who ignored regulations or posed a security threat, but many Canadians were interred for reasons ranging from "acting in a very suspicious manner" to simply being poor and unemployed. Between 1914 and 1920, more than 8,500 Canadians were shipped to internment camps. Approximately 5,000 of these people were of Ukrainian descent. Of the total people in the camps, only 2,321 were actual prisoners of war; the rest were civilians. Later, during World War II, the "enemy aliens" were defined as "all persons of German or Italian racial origin who have become naturalized British subjects since September 1, 1922."

Enemy Aliens

All told, approximately 30,000 Canadians were affected by the order. And in New Brunswick, more than 700 Jews who had fled the Holocaust in Europe were interred in Canada— at the request of British Prime Minister Winston Churchill, who suspected that spies had infiltrated the group.

Living in an internment camp was a nightmare. Upon their arrest, the internees' private property, businesses, and personal possessions were taken by the government and sold. Inside the camps, the internees' correspondence was censored, and mistreatment by guards was common. Those who were able-bodied were forced to work maintaining the camps, on railway and road construction, or for private companies. This source of free labor proved so helpful and profitable for Canadian corporations that the internment program continued for two years after the war's end.

Following the bombing of Pearl Harbor on December 7, 1941, the Canadian government issued an order authorizing the removal of "enemy aliens" within a 100-mile radius of the British Columbian coast. Twenty-two thousand Japanese Canadians were given just one day to pack before being sent to internment camps. Those who complained or broke minor rules were sent to prisoner-of-war camps in Ontario. Conditions were notoriously poor. Hideo Kukubo lived in one camp for four years. "When it got cold the temperature went down to as much as 60 below. We lived in huts with no insulation," he said.

Picking Up the Pieces

At the end of the war, the government extended an Order in Council to force Japanese Canadians to either move to Japan and give up their Canadian citizenship or move to eastern Canada. In fact, it was illegal for Japanese Canadians to return to Vancouver until 1949.

It took the government nearly four decades to acknowledge those who had been imprisoned under the War Measures Act. In 1988, an official apology was extended and the government admitted that many of its actions had been provoked by racial discrimination. A redress agreement provided $21,000 each to those affected, although it hardly compensated for the gross mistreatment they experienced.

The Story of the Tasaday

A 1972 National Geographic *article announced the discovery of a gentle, pristine Stone Age people in the Philippines: the Tasaday. Skeptics say the Tasaday were a hoax perpetrated by the Marcos government—but are they right?*

✻ ✻ ✻ ✻

In 1971, strongman Ferdinand Marcos was dictator of the Philippines. His wealthy crony, Manuel Elizalde Jr., was head of Panamin, a minority-rights watchdog agency. In a nation with 7,107 islands, 12 major regional languages, and hundreds of ethnic groups, such an agency has its work cut out for it.

The Discovery

The Philippines' second-largest island, Mindanao, is bigger than Maine, with lots of jungle. According to Elizalde, a western Mindanao tribesman put him in contact with the Tasaday. The tribe numbered only a couple dozen and lived amid primitive conditions. Their language bore relation to nearby tongues but lacked words for war and violence. They seemed to be living in gentle simplicity, marveling at Elizalde as a deity and protector. For his part, Elizalde clamped the full power of the Philippine state into place to shield his newfound people. One of the few study groups permitted to examine the Tasaday was from *National Geographic*, which introduced the Tasaday to the world in 1972.

After Marcos fell from power in 1986, investigators studying the lives of the Tasaday revealed that it was all a fraud. According to reports, Elizalde had recruited the Tasaday from long-established local tribes and forced them to role-play a Stone Age lifestyle. The Tasaday eventually became the "Tasaday Hoax."

A Scam Revealed?

A couple of Tasaday told a sad story: They normally farmed nearby, living in huts rather than caves, but Elizalde made them wear loincloths and do dog-and-pony shows for paying visitors. The poorer and more primitive they looked, the more money they would get. In one instance, a group of German journalists who set out to document the Tasaday found them dressed primitively—sort of. They were wearing leaves, but they had stuck them onto their clothing, which was visible beneath the foliage. Scientific skepticism soon surfaced as well: How could they have remained that isolated for so long, even on Mindanao? Why didn't modern disease now decimate them? Why did their tools show evidence of steel-knife manufacturing?

Elizalde didn't back down easily. In an attempt to keep up the charade, he flew a few Tasaday to Manila to sue the naysayers for libel. With Marcos ousted, however, Elizalde was less able to influence investigators or control what they had access to. Eminent linguist Lawrence Reid decided that the Tasaday were indeed an offshoot of a regional tribe—but one that had been living in the area for only 150 years, not more than a thousand as was claimed. Likely as confused as everyone else at this point, previous Tasaday whistleblowers now confessed that translators had bribed them to say the whole thing was a hoax.

The Aftermath

Elizalde later fled to Costa Rica, squandered his money, and died a drug addict. If he had indeed fabricated the history of the Tasaday, what was his motivation? It could have been a public-relations ploy, because the Marcos government had a well-earned reputation for repression. A strong minority-rights stance in defense of the Tasaday could be expected to buff some tarnish off the government's image. Commerce likely played a role, for the Tasaday episode denied huge tracts of jungle to logging interests. Perhaps those interests hadn't played ball with Marcos and/or Elizalde.

Elizalde did not "discover" the Tasaday, but that doesn't mean they were total fakes. What is clear is that they were pawns in a socio-political chess game far greater than the jungle of Mindanao.

Worst Case Scenarios: The All-Time Deadliest Disasters

✳ ✳ ✳ ✳

Dino-B-Gone

The deadliest disaster in Earth's history may have struck long before humans even existed. According to leading scientific theory, the dinosaurs (and many others) checked out when a massive asteroid slammed into Earth about 65 million years ago. The resulting destruction dwarfs anything that's happened since:

* Scientists estimate the asteroid was about six miles wide—bigger than Mount Everest.

* The energy of the impact was likely equal to hundreds of millions of megatons. That's about a million times more powerful than the explosion you would get if you detonated all the nuclear bombs in the world at once.

* The asteroid hit in what is now the Gulf of Mexico, blasting massive amounts of scorching steam and molten rock into the sky and creating tsunamis that were hundreds of yards high and that moved 600 miles per hour.

* The resulting shock wave rocked the entire planet and killed everything for hundreds of miles around.

* Molten rock fell back to Earth for thousands of miles around the impact, setting much of the planet on fire.

* The kicked-up material darkened the atmosphere everywhere and generated nitric acid rain.

* All told, the asteroid wiped out as much as 75 percent of all life on the planet.

King of Plagues

The worst disaster on record in terms of human death toll was the Black Death—a pandemic thought to be bubonic plague, pneumonic plague, and septicemic plague, all caused by bacteria carried by fleas:

* The plague infected the lymphatic system, resulting in high fever, vomiting, enlarged glands, and—in the case of pneumonic plague—coughing up bloody phlegm.

* Bubonic plague was fatal in 30–75 percent of cases; pneumonic plague was fatal in 75 percent of cases; and septicemic plague was always fatal.

* Between 1347 and 1350, the plague spread across Europe and killed approximately 75 million people—nearly half the European population.

* Improvements in sanitation helped bring the Black Death to an end, but the plague still pops up now and then in isolated outbreaks.

An Extra Large Shake

The deadliest earthquake and string of aftershocks in recorded history rocked Egypt, Syria, and surrounding areas in 1201:

* Of course, nobody was measuring such things back then, but experts believe the initial quake ranked as a magnitude 9.

* As luck would have it, Egypt was already experiencing a major drought, and damage from the quake exacerbated the problem, leading to mass starvation (and a bit of cannibalism to boot).

* Historians put the total death toll at about 1.1 million.

The Storm of Several Centuries

The deadliest storm on record was the Bhola Cyclone, which hit East Pakistan (now Bangladesh) on November 13, 1970:

* The storm's winds were in excess of 120 miles per hour when it finally hit land.

* It generated an astonishing storm surge of 12 to 20 feet, which flooded densely populated coastal areas.

* Parts of the Ganges River actually turned red with blood.

* According to official records, 500,000 people died (mainly due to drowning). Some sources put the total at closer to one million.

Blast from the Past

The deadliest known volcano eruption occurred in Indonesia in 1815:

* When the 13,000-foot Mount Tambora erupted, it blew two million tons of debris 28 miles into the air and continued to burn for three months.

* The seismic energy generated massive tsunamis, leading to widespread flooding.

* Three feet of ash covered much of the surrounding area, killing all vegetation and resulting in a devastating famine.

* The debris in the atmosphere darkened skies all around the world and continued to block sunlight for years afterward.

* In 1816, parts of the United States saw snow in June and July, thanks to the persistent cold caused by the eruption on the other side of the world.

* All told, the eruption claimed more than 70,000 lives.

---

* **The Torino Impact Hazard Scale is used to categorize the chances of an asteroid or comet hitting Earth. The scale goes from zero to ten, with zero being no risk and ten being a certain collision, with global catastrophe imminent.**

Fast Facts

✳ In the 11th century, an English monk named Eilmer of Malmesbury built and launched himself in a glider, flying for about 220 feet before crashing and breaking both legs. His abbot forbade any further attempts.

✳ In 1917, the German government sent a telegram to Mexico, promising the return of Texas, New Mexico, and Arizona in exchange for Mexico entering World War I against the United States.

✳ Franz Ferdinand, whose assassination would precipitate World War I, survived the first attempt on his life. Unfortunately, later that same day, his chauffeur took a wrong turn, driving the archduke past a café where one of the failed conspirators, Gavrilo Princip, was waiting to buy a sandwich. Pricip fired two shots, killing both Ferdinand and his wife.

✳ Ants stretch when they wake up. They also appear to yawn in a very human manner before taking up the tasks of the day.

✳ Some historians believe one contributing factor to Napoleon's defeat at Waterloo was his strange failure to survey the battle from his customary seat on horseback. His reluctance was brought about by a particularly bad flare-up of his chronic hemorrhoids.

✳ Franklin Delano Roosevelt was an avid poker player, once rushing from a game directly to the microphone to give one of his signature Fireside Chats. As he delivered the address, he absentmindedly shuffled some poker chips, rendering portions of his speech inaudible.

✳ Approximately one out of a thousand baby sea turtles survives after hatching.

✳ Earth weighs approximately 5,940,000,000,000,000,000,000 metric tons.

✳ After being killed at Trafalgar in 1805, Horatio Nelson's body was preserved in a cask of French brandy that, according to legend, had been captured during the battle.

Sunken Civilizations

Researchers have discovered the tantalizing remains of what appears to be advanced Mesolithic and Neolithic civilizations hidden for millennia under water or sand. But are the ancient cities real, or is it just wishful thinking?

✳ ✳ ✳ ✳

La Marmotta: Stone Age Lakefront

WHAT IS NOW the bottom of Italy's six-mile-wide Lake Bracciano was once a lovely and fertile river floodplain. In 1989, scientists discovered a lost city, which they named La Marmotta. Dive teams have recovered artifacts ranging from ancient timbers to uneaten pots of stew, all preserved under ten feet of mud.

The site dates back to about 5700 B.C. around the late Stone Age or Neolithic era. Though not much is known about the people who lived there, scientists do know that the city's residents migrated from the Near East or Greece in 35-foot-long, wooden dugout boats with their families. They had domesticated animals, pottery, religious statues, and even two species of dogs. They laid out their village with large wooden houses. Items such as obsidian knives and greenstone ax blades show that La Marmotta was a busy Mediterranean trade center. But after 400 years of occupation, it seems the village was hastily abandoned. Why the residents fled still puzzles researchers.

Atlantis Beneath the Black Sea

Ever since the Greek writer Plato described the lost island of Atlantis in the fourth century B.C., scholars have searched for its location. One oft-suggested candidate is a grouping of underwater settlements northwest of the Black Sea. Researchers claim this advanced Neolithic population center was once situated on shore along a freshwater lake that was engulfed by seawater by 5510 B.C. Ancient landforms in the area seem to have centered around an island that roughly fits the description of Atlantis. Similarities between the lore of Atlantis and this settlement include the use of a form of early writing, the existence of elephants (from eastern trade routes), obsidian used as money, and circular observatory structures.

Japan, Gateway to Mu

According to Japanese geologist Masaaki Kimura, a legendary lost continent called Mu may have been discovered off the coast of Japan. Kimura says underwater formations that were found in 1985 at Yonaguni Island indicate that they were handmade and that they possibly once resembled a Roman city complete with a coliseum, a castle, statues, paved streets, and plazas. Although photos show sharp, step-like angles and flat surfaces, skeptics still argue these "roads" were actually created by forces such as tides or volcanoes. Nevertheless, Kimura maintains his belief that the ruins are the proof of a 5,000-year-old city.

Ancient Alpine Lake Towns

Today, most people would associate the Alps, the mountain region that borders Germany, Switzerland, and Italy, with skiing. But in the late Stone Age or Neolithic period (6000–2000 B.C.), the region's lakes dominated the action. A dry spell in the mid-1800s lowered water levels and allowed evidence of ancient villages to surface within many lakes in the region. One site at the Swiss town of Obermeilen yielded exciting finds such as wooden posts, artifacts made from antlers, Neolithic clay objects, and wooden utensils. It is now believed that the posts supported large wooden platforms that sat over the water, serving as docklike foundations for houses and other village structures.

Hamoukar: City of Commerce

Until the mid-1970s, when the ancient settlement of Hamoukar was discovered in Syria, archaeologists believed the world's oldest cities—dating back to 4000 B.C.—were in present-day Iraq. But the massive, 750-acre Hamoukar, surrounded by a 13-inch-thick wall and home to an estimated 25,000 people, was already a prosperous and advanced city by 4000 B.C.

Situated in the land between the Tigris and Euphrates rivers, Hamoukar was sophisticated enough to support commercial bakeries and large-scale beer breweries. People used clay seals as "brands" for mass-produced goods, including delicate pottery, jewelry, and stone goods. The city was also a processing area for obsidian and, later, copper. The settlement was destroyed in a fierce battle around 3500 B.C., leaving more than 1,000 slingshot bullets in the city's ruins.

The Great Danes

They sure ate a lot of shellfish—that much is known about the Mesolithic European culture that lived along the coast of what is now Denmark between 5600 and 4000 B.C. The now-underwater cities were investigated in the 1970s; the first is known as Tybrind Vig and its people are called the Ertebölle. The Ertebölle skeletons resemble those of modern Danes, but some also show Cro-Magnon facial features such as protruding jaws and prominent brow ridges. Archaeologists have found implements made of antler, bone, and stone sticking out of the Danish sea floor. They also found large piles of shellfish at the oldest sites, indicating that the inhabitants loved seafood. Preserved remains of acorns, hazelnuts, and other plants showed their diet was well rounded.

The Ertebölle made clever use of local materials. They lived in wattle or brush huts; "knitted" clothing from plant fibers; made ceramic pots decorated with impressions of grains, cord, and bones; and created art from polished bone and amber. Eventually, it is assumed, the Ertebölle hunter-gatherers either evolved into or were replaced by people with farming skills.

Mystery of the Bimini Blocks

The reason adventurers Robert Ferro and Michael Grumley traveled to the Bahamas was that they had read psychic Edgar Cayce's 1936 prediction that Atlantis would be found in the late 1960s off Bimini Island in the Bahamas. Their discovery in the late '60s of giant rows of flat, rectangular blocks resembling a road off northern Bimini was a tad controversial.

The sunken, geometrically arranged rocks stretched for an estimated 700 to 1,000 feet. Several investigators estimated the "structure" dated back to 10,000 B.C. Since then, other explorers have claimed to find additional stones that may have once formed part of an encircling wall around the entire island. Author Charles Berlitz observed that the stones resembled work by pre-Incan Peruvians.

However, geologists have noted that island shore rocks may split into regular planes due to a combination of solar exposure and shifting subsoil—formations resembling the Bimini Blocks also exist off the coast of Australia.

Global Warming and the Polar Ice Sheets

Both polar ice caps fluctuate annually, but lately they've been retreating. This process builds on itself because it changes Earth's surface reflectivity: less white ice (heat reflective) replaced by more blue ocean (heat absorbent) means we slurp up more solar energy, accelerating the melting.

A total Antarctic melt would raise the seas by more than 200 feet—enough to swamp several island nations and nearly every coastal city on Earth. Most doubt the melting will reach that extreme, however. The topic pushes hot buttons because fossil fuels are believed to accelerate global warming as their by-products trap atmospheric heat.

It is not certain how much the seas will ultimately rise. Given the potential global consequences, humanity can hardly dismiss the question out of hand.

City of Darkness: Kowloon Walled City

Today, it's a gem of a tourist attraction: a traditional Chinese garden in the heart of Hong Kong, filled with historic relics. But just 25 years ago, this lush expanse was home to what locals called Hak Nam—the City of Darkness, one of the world's most dangerous slums.

✳ ✳ ✳ ✳

Wonder Wall

LOCATED ON THE Kowloon Peninsula, the Walled City originated as a simple fort. Chinese soldiers built it after the British takeover of Hong Kong Island (right across the bay) in 1841 to protect mainland China from possible attack. Then, to further ensure China was safe from British invasion, they built a stone wall around 6.5 acres surrounding the fort, with six watchtowers and four guard gates. Behind the walls, a city began to emerge as more military men moved with their families to the area.

In 1860, the British took control of the southernmost tip of the Kowloon Peninsula, and the Walled City became an even better spot for the Chinese to observe the actions of the British. Over the next few decades, the city's population rapidly grew, with an influx of not only Chinese soldiers but also civilian business owners and their employees. In most cases, these "businesses" were opium dens, gambling houses, and brothels. With a prime location between British territory and mainland China, the Walled City became a popular stop for folks to get a quick fix before heading on their way.

Exception to the (British) Rule

The year 1898 marked the infamous signing over of Hong Kong, the Kowloon Peninsula, and all of the surrounding territories to the British under a 99-year lease—with one exception:

Kowloon Walled City would remain a Chinese territory and the Chinese military could stay there so long as its actions supported colonial efforts.

Within a year, the agreement was void: In 1899, Chinese troops helped peasants revolt against the new British rule, and, as could be expected, the colonial government changed its mind about letting the Walled City remain under Chinese jurisdiction. By the end of the year, the last of China's administrators had been kicked out of town. Still, the British couldn't get a foothold in the Walled City. On a good day, the stubborn citizens ignored the colonial laws outright; on a bad day, they rebelled violently.

Caught in a kind of limbo—*within* British territory but *without* British authority—the "city within a city" quickly spiraled into anarchy and squalor.

Boom Town

During World War II, Japanese troops tried to destroy the city by removing the wall around it—but they couldn't remove the people. In fact, just the opposite happened. The population of the now wall-less Walled City exploded after the war, with thousands of refugees flocking to the tiny area (which measured only 656 by 492 feet) in search of asylum from poverty, political persecution, and famine.

The burgeoning community was a blight on the British, who sought to demolish the Walled City in favor of a park. In 1948, the colonial government tried to take a stand by evicting 2,000 settlers from the area; local residents promptly set fire to the British consulate in protest.

The colonial government's last attempt to interfere came in 1966, when residents flew a Communist flag over the city. British officials attempted to remove the flag, but violent revolts led them to drop the issue—leaving the Walled City to fend for itself.

Vice City

Over the next 20 years, ramshackle tenements sprang up throughout the city, reaching as high as 10 to 12 stories. The buildings were packed so tightly that no four-wheeled vehicle could fit on the streets, and barely a shred of sunlight could pass through, even at high noon.

Without any official government in place, power fell to the Chinese street gangs, who ruled over the Walled City's dank, dark alleyways, which teemed with drugs, prostitution, and unlicensed medical and dental practices. (Chinese doctors and dentists who lacked the proper license to practice under British rule often set up illegal shops in the Walled City, offering services at a deep discount.)

Nevertheless, with water and electricity illegally siphoned from Hong Kong, the city had become a fully functioning town in its own right.

Garden Walk

Meanwhile, tensions continued to mount between the Chinese and British governments about what to do with this enclave of anarchy. While the British clearly wanted it gone, the Chinese resisted. Finally, in 1987, the two parties reached an agreement to raze the city and build a park on its grounds by 1997, the year Hong Kong would officially return to Chinese rule.

Between 1988 and 1992, more than 35,000 people were ousted from the Walled City's cramped slums, and by April 1994, demolition was complete. The Kowloon City Walled Park officially opened on December 22, 1995, featuring relics from the city's original stone wall and military fortress.

The Road of Death

You're packed on an old bus, fog obscuring the mountainous road. The hairpin turns and the bus fishtailing on the muddy road make you queasy. Not exactly how you imagined your summer vacation, right?

✳ ✳ ✳ ✳

EACH YEAR, HUNDREDS of people die on Bolivia's Yungas road, earning it the title of "most dangerous highway in the world." Built in the 1930s, it runs between La Paz and Coroico and is the main connection between coffee plantations in the highlands and a third of the country. It starts in La Paz, at an altitude of 11,900 feet. The road winds its way through the Andes mountains, where it reaches a peak of 16,500 feet, then drops 15,000 feet to the tropical rainforest lowlands.

The 43-mile drive takes four hours, on average; that is, if there are no heavy rains, mist, mudslides, or accidents blocking the road. With soaring cliffs on one side, steep drops on the other, blind turns, and no guardrails to speak of, this road is not for the faint of heart. For most of its length, the one-lane, two-way road is only ten feet across. Alongside the road are makeshift memorials of crosses and flowers.

In 2006, a Yungas bypass was opened. The Bolivian government and foreign investors financed this wide, paved highway for the purpose of opening up trade in the region. The $500 million, 20-year project was touted as a life-saving alternative for commercial trucks and tourist buses. However, Bolivian drivers have rejected it so far because the new route is considerably longer.

The deadly road is now one of Bolivia's most popular tourist attractions. It is especially popular with mountain bikers who enjoy the nearly 40-mile-long stretch of continuous downhill riding. Meanwhile, locals report hearing the tourists' screams as they plunge over the cliff.

10 Surefire Signs You're Living in a Dictatorship

1. Your president's face is staring back at you all the time. Is your president's face on a banner in the town square? In framed photos in the dining room? How about on your currency? Yep, it's a dictatorship.

2. Your nation's leader sports interesting facial hair. Stalin, Hitler, Hussein, Pinochet, Castro, Trujillo—all had trademark facial hair. The lesson? Vote for the clean-shaven candidate.

3. Your nation's artists and writers are in prison. One of the first things to go under a dictatorship is freedom of speech. Have more poets in prison than in literary journals? You're probably living under a dictator.

4. Your nation's leader is getting progressively stranger. Idi Amin declared himself "Conqueror of the British Empire" for no apparent reason and was rumored to have dined on his enemies. Kim Jong-Il wore oversized sunglasses and ate live lobsters with silver chopsticks. Hitler was a hypochondriac who hated moonlight and whistling. There's something about being a dictator that brings out the eccentricities in people.

5. Your president wears his army uniform in public. Nothing says "dictator" like army uniforms weighed down by several dozen medallions and ribbons. See: Idi Amin, Manuel Noriega, Rafael Trujillo, Benito Mussolini, and Saddam Hussein.

6. **The ruling party won "reelection" by an enormous margin.** By their very nature, political elections are hotly contested—unless you're a dictator rigging the polls. Never was this more obvious than in 2002, when 100 percent of nearly 12 million eligible Iraqi voters "voted" Saddam Hussein in for another seven-year term.

7. **Your government talks about "plans" and trumpets its successes.** Plans, usually of the five-year variety, have been a hallmark of dictatorships dating back to Josef Stalin. Another hallmark is trumpeting the successes of those plans—almost always fabricated—through government-run media outlets.

8. **The president is the richest man in the country.** We all know that even in free countries, politics is dominated by the wealthy, but when your leader is using the nation's coffers as his personal bank account, you've got problems. Perhaps nowhere was this more blatant than in Nigeria, where from 1993 to 1998 dictator Sani Abacha reputedly pilfered billions from the national government.

9. **Your leader was put in charge by a relative.** In democracies, rulers are voted in. In dictatorships, dictators hand the reins over to relatives, most often their children. See: Papa Doc and Baby Doc Duvalier of Haiti.

From the Vaults of History

All in the Family

The Karni Mata temple in Deshnok, India, is a place where rats are worshiped, fed sumptuous meals, and pampered in every possible way. Why would the humans in this place devote themselves to an animal that is despised in nearly every other place in the world? It all began with a woman named Karni Mata, who in the 14th century was known for her good works and devotion to the poor. When Karni Mata's son drowned, she used her powers as the incarnation of a goddess to bring him back to life. She also decreed that no other members of her family would ever die; instead, her loved ones would return in the form of rats. That is why the human descendants of Karni Mata (now called the Goddess Karni) take such good care of their rodent "relatives" at the temple.

Medical Mystery as Myth

Sudden Unexplained Nocturnal Death Syndrome (SUNDS) is a disease that seems to target young, healthy people of Japanese and Southeast Asian descent. What scientists can't figure out is why 99 percent of those people are men and 80 percent of them are between the ages of 22 and 45. SUNDS kills these men in their sleep by way of massive, sudden heart attacks, leaving the victims dead on their backs with a look of horror on their faces. This frightening way of death has been reported to affect young males in the Philippines since at least 1917, and Filipinos have even developed a myth to explain these random tragedies: They say the *bangungot* is a fat man who sneaks into bedrooms by the dark of night and sits on the heads of the unlucky ones.

The Mystery of Easter Island

On Easter Sunday in 1722, a Dutch ship landed on a small island 2,300 miles from the coast of South America. Polynesian explorers had preceded them by a thousand years or more, and the Europeans found the descendants of those early visitors still living on the island. They also found a strange collection of almost 900 enormous stone heads, or moai, standing with their backs to the sea, gazing across the island with eyes hewn out of coral. The image of those faces haunts visitors to this day.

✳ ✳ ✳ ✳

Ancestors at the End of the Land

EASTER ISLAND LEGEND tells of the great Chief Hotu Matu'a, the Great Parent, striking out from Polynesia in a canoe, taking his family on a voyage across the trackless ocean in search of a new home. He made landfall on Te-Pito-te-Henua, the End of the Land, sometime between A.D. 400 and 700. Finding the island well-suited to habitation, his descendants spread out to cover much of the island, living off the natural bounty of the land and sea. With their survival assured, they built ahu—ceremonial sites featuring a large stone mound—and on them erected moai, which were representations of notable chieftains who led the island over the centuries. The moai weren't literal depictions of their ancestors, but rather embodied their spirit, or mana, and conferred blessings and protection on the islanders.

The construction of these moai was quite a project. A hereditary class of sculptors oversaw the main quarry, located near one of the volcanic mountains on the island. Groups of people would request a moai for their local ahu, and the sculptors would go to work, their efforts supported by gifts of food and other goods. Over time, they created 887 of the stone moai, averaging just over 13 feet tall and weighing around 14 tons, but ranging from one extreme of just under 4 feet tall to a behemoth that towered 71 feet. The moai were then transported across the island by a mechanism that still remains a mystery, but that may have involved rolling them on the trunks of palm trees felled for that purpose— a technique that was to have terrible repercussions for the islanders.

When Europeans first made landfall on Easter Island in 1722, they found an island full of standing moai. Fifty-two years later, James Cook reported that many of the statues had been toppled, and by the 1830s none were left standing. What's more, the statues hadn't just been knocked over; there were boulders placed at strategic locations around many of them, clearly intended to decapitate the moai when they were pulled down. What happened?

A Culture on the Brink

It turns out the original Dutch explorers had encountered a culture on the rebound. At the time of their arrival, they found two or three thousand living on the island, but some estimates put the population as high as fifteen thousand a century before. The story of the islanders' decline is one in which many authors find a cautionary tale: The people simply consumed natural resources to the point where their land could no longer support them. For a millennium, the islanders took what they needed: They fished, collected bird eggs, and chopped down trees to pursue their obsession with building moai. By the 1600s, life had changed: The last forests on the island disappeared, and the islanders' traditional foodstuffs disappeared from the archaeological record. Local tradition tells of a time of famine and even rumored cannibalism, and it is from this time that island history reveals the appearance of the spear. Tellingly, the Polynesian words for "wood" begin to take on a connotation of wealth, a meaning found nowhere else that shares the language. Perhaps worst of all, with their forests gone, the islanders had no material to make the canoes that would have allowed them to leave their island in search of resources. They were trapped, and they turned on one another.

The Europeans found a reduced society that had just emerged from this time of terror. The respite was short-lived, however. The arrival of the foreigners seems to have come at a critical moment in the history of Easter Island. Either coincidentally or spurred on by the strangers, a warrior class seized power across the island, and different groups vied for power. Villages were burned, their resources taken by the victors, and the defeated left to starve. The warfare also led to the toppling of an enemy's moai—whether to capture their mana or simply prevent it from being used against the opposing faction. In the end, none of the moai remained standing.

Downfall and Rebound

The troubles of Easter Island weren't limited to self-inflicted chaos. The arrival of Europeans also introduced smallpox and syphilis; the islanders, with little natural immunity to the exotic diseases, fared no better than native populations elsewhere. As if that weren't enough, other ships arrived, collecting slaves for work in South America. The internal fighting and external pressure combined to reduce the number of native islanders to little more than a hundred by 1877—the last survivors of a people who once enjoyed a tropical paradise.

Easter Island, or Rapa Nui, was annexed by Chile in 1888. As of 2009, there are 7,781 people living on the island. There are projects underway to raise the fallen moai. As of today, approximately 50 have been returned to their former glory.

Chapter Ten

Conflict and Combat

Quirky and in Command

From nervous ticks to unrelenting ambition, a few Union and Confederate officers stood out among the ranks—but not always in a good way.

✳ ✳ ✳ ✳

George Armstrong Custer

Army: Union

Major Battles: Chancellorsville, Brandy Station, Gettysburg

Eccentricities: George Armstrong Custer had a love for flamboyant uniforms and possessed a blind, unrelenting ambition that often led him to take risks. After he was promoted to brigadier general, Custer took the opportunity to outfit himself in an extravagant ensemble that included a black velveteen vest, sharply polished boots (which he never let get dirty), and a crisp white shirt edged with silver trim and stars. His hair was expertly coiffed, and he often used perfumed oils and colognes to overpower the stench of the battlefield. He wanted to appear as a noble, romantic figure, and he cultivated friendships with journalists in an effort to create a positive public image. His lasting renown was ultimately achieved after the Civil War for being on the wrong side of the fighting at Little Bighorn.

James Ewell Brown "Jeb" Stuart

Army: Confederate

Major Battles: Fredericksburg, Gettysburg, The Wilderness

Eccentricities: Custer's Southern cavalry counterpart, Jeb Stuart, was no less ostentatious, also outfitting himself with a spectacularly fancy uniform that was anything but inconspicuous. Astride his horse on scouting missions, he wore a long gray cape with red lining, and his hat was adorned with a large peacock feather. In his regiment, Stuart had a personal banjo player who traveled with him to sing a song that detailed his daring victories. Like Custer, Stuart used colognes and was concerned with his public image. So focused was he on his wardrobe that when he lost his cape to Union troops in 1862, he demanded revenge. He and his troops returned to confront the forces of General John Pope, not only overrunning them with ease but also capturing Pope's entire uniform in the process.

Alfred Pleasonton

Army: Union

Major Battles: Antietam, Chancellorsville, Brandy Station

Eccentricities: Alfred Pleasonton is the man who taught Custer everything he knew about flashy uniforms and shameless self-promotion. In the 1830s, Pleasanton's father had been involved in U.S. Treasury scandals and was fired from his job, which left the family in shame. The younger Pleasonton was determined to overcome that reputation, but his antics and ambition instead alienated nearly everyone he met. He constantly exaggerated his role in battle. Wounded at Antietam, he argued that his division had turned the tide of the battle and that he should be promoted to major general. This wasn't true, but he made such a fuss that his superiors gave in and upped his rank (though not as high as he'd wanted). At Chancellorsville, he claimed to have personally stopped Stonewall Jackson's advance—again, he hadn't, but it was enough to secure his promotion to major general. When confronted with failures, Pleasonton refused to accept responsibility.

John Bell Hood

Army: Confederate

Major Battles: Seven Days Battles, Antietam, Chickamauga, Gettysburg

Eccentricities: General John Bell Hood was perhaps the most resilient soldier of the American Civil War. At Gettysburg, he was severely wounded and lost the use of his left arm for the rest of his life. He soldiered on, only to have his leg amputated at Chickamauga. Most people would have called it quits at that point, but not Hood. He returned to duty just months later, commanding troops in the Army of Tennessee. To work around his disabilities, he strapped himself into his saddle on his horse and used a specially designed French cork leg to dismount. Though his post-injury career was not very successful, he never stopped fighting and was on his way to Texas to raise another army before being apprehended on May 31, 1865. After the war was over, he returned to civilian life, married, and fathered 11 children. He died of yellow fever in 1879.

Dan Sickles

Army: Union

Major Battles: Seven Pines, Chancellorsville, Gettysburg

Eccentricities: When General Dan Sickles took a cannonball to the leg at Gettysburg, he refused to drop his composure—instead he tried to improve his troops' morale by smiling broadly and chomping on his lit cigar as the doctors amputated it. Once his mangled leg was removed, he donated it to the Army Medical Museum in Washington, D.C., where he often visited it after the war. It's still on display at the National Museum of Health and Medicine.

Fast Facts

✳ The exact number of Confederate enlisted men during the Civil War years is unknown. Authoritative estimates range from as many as 1.4 million to as few as 600,000.

✳ Almost 39 percent of the Confederacy's population were slaves.

✳ After the war, Confederate General James Longstreet became a Republican. He renewed his friendship with Ulysses S. Grant and served as Grant's minister to Turkey.

✳ Postal service was abolished between the North and South in 1861. At the time, the basic postal rate was 3 cents, with adjustments for distance. The South established a 5-cent rate for distances less than 500 miles but standardized its rate at 10 cents for all distances in 1862. The North standardized the 3-cent rate in 1863. Express service cost from 15 to 25 cents.

✳ Typical Union gear included a musket, a bayonet, a cartridge box with 40 rounds, a belt, a cap pouch, a haversack, a canteen, a knapsack, a ground blanket, a shelter half, a winter greatcoat, a tin cup and plate, and leggings.

✳ Abraham Lincoln credited his first presidential victory to two things: a speech he gave at Cooper Union in 1860 and a widely distributed portrait taken by Mathew Brady.

✳ Benjamin Harrison, the 23rd U.S. president and the grandson of 9th president William Henry Harrison, entered service as a second lieutenant of the 70th Regiment of Indiana Volunteers and rose to the rank of brigadier general by the end of the war.

✳ After the Union defeat at Bull Run, enlistment periods for Union troops were increased from three months to two years.

✳ As president of the United States, Abraham Lincoln's annual salary was $25,000.

The Story of Uncle Sam

Uncle Sam may be one of the most familiar icons to people in the United States, but no one is sure of the origins of this goateed, flag-theme-attired image. Was he an actual person or just snippets of people and images from popular culture?

✳ ✳ ✳ ✳

✳ During the War of 1812, the U.S. Army needed provisions and supplies—especially protein. Samuel Wilson, a meat-packer in Troy, New York, provided the troops with barrels of preserved meat stamped "US," likely as a stipulation of his procurement contract. In fact, this "Uncle Sam" was a clean-shaven, short, and pudgy man, and he likely did not dress up for fun.

✳ The Uncle Sam character we know today was born in the influential images of Thomas Nast, a prominent 19th-century political cartoonist who depicted several similar flag-themed figures.

✳ The most enduring Uncle Sam image—which depicts him pointing a finger and saying "I Want You"—comes from World War I recruiting posters drawn by James Montgomery Flagg, who also modeled the famous stern, craggy visage.

✳ Uncle Sam is actually a national personification: an image that sums up a national identity. Other countries' examples include John Bull of England—a stout, thick-necked, top-hatted guy—and Moder Svea (Mother Sweden), a sword-bearing woman in chain mail and a flowing skirt.

✳ It wasn't until 1961 that Congress recognized Samuel Wilson as the original Uncle Sam. This didn't do Wilson much good, as it came more than a century after his death, but it was a good deal for Troy. The city began to pitch itself as the "Home of Uncle Sam," as it does today.

Terror by Night!

Life during the Blitz was a constant struggle for millions of Britons.

✳ ✳ ✳ ✳

AFTER FRANCE, POLAND, and other nations had fallen before the German blitzkrieg at the onset of World War II, Hitler turned his attention to Great Britain. But the Nazis were unable to gain air superiority over the British during the Battle of Britain, so Hermann Göring, head of the German Luftwaffe, authorized a sustained, punishing air assault that came to be known as the Blitz.

Bombs over London

The goal of the Blitz was to terrify and demoralize the British government and its citizenry into surrendering without the need for an invasion. So rather than attack Royal Air Force bases, the bombings focused on British cities, particularly London.

The first intentional wave of bombings over London occurred on the afternoon of September 7, 1940, and continued for 57 consecutive nights. By the time the Blitz came to an end in May 1941, more than 40,000 civilians had been killed (more than half of them in London) and one million homes had been destroyed. Smaller attacks over the course of the war brought the civilian death total to over 51,500.

Surviving the Blitz

Life during the Blitz was a constant struggle for Londoners and those living in other targeted cities. Because the aerial assaults occurred primarily at night, blackout rules were strongly enforced. Families were required to cover their windows with black material to make it more difficult for German pilots to find their targets. Street lamps were extinguished, and automobiles were required to drive with their headlights off, which made road and pedestrian travel perilous. Traffic accidents were common, and several people drowned after accidentally walking off bridges.

When German bombers were spotted, air raid sirens sounded to warn the populace. Many families hunkered in their basements or in specially constructed bomb shelters on their property. Those who didn't have a home shelter sought refuge in municipal bomb shelters or underground subway stations. However, even these ready-made shelters were not entirely safe. In January 1941, a bomb fell directly above the Bank subway station, killing 111 people. The bombs fell, loud and frightening. Jack Court was a young paperboy at the time. "It was always a great shock to anyone experiencing the blitz for the first time," he recalled for the BBC. "The great, great, noise, the never before heard of sounds, the echoes that hurt the chest."

Once air raid wardens gave the "all clear," people would emerge from their shelters. Many returned to find their homes destroyed, and family members and neighbors dead or missing. A common peril was unexploded ordnance, which required special disposal. "Unexploded bomb" signs were common throughout the devastated cities as people did their best to go about their daily lives.

At the war's start, some London families sent their children to the country, where they were safer from German bombs. For many city youngsters, it was an eye-opening experience as they saw farm animals and fresh produce for the very first time.

Rationalizing Rations

During the Blitz and throughout the war, rationing was a common part of daily life for all Britons. Three major commodities were rationed throughout much of the conflict: food, clothing, and gasoline. Food, in particular, became increasingly sparse, because England was forced to import what it could not raise or grow on its own. Other nations, especially the United States and Australia, were willing to help, but German U-boats destroyed many supply ships before they could reach their destinations. As a result, food was heavily rationed and meat became a rare luxury.

Gasoline was another coveted commodity during the war. The lion's share went to power Britain's war machines—trucks, tanks, and planes. As a result, the majority of people came to rely on public transportation, such as buses and the subway, to get around.

The Blitz took a heavy toll on everyone in Britain, but it ultimately failed in its intended goal of demoralizing the British people into submission. In fact, the effect was just the opposite, instilling in all Britons a deep resolve that carried them through the war. Germany was able to conquer almost all of Europe, but it found in the British a strength and perseverance that could not be defeated.

✳ German tactician General Hans Guderian described the basic concept of Blitzkrieg warfare as "One hits somebody with his fist and not with fingers spread."

✳ The Blitz created dangerous morale problems in Britain. To galvanize the people, Churchill lied and said that a German invasion might be imminent. The fib worked, and the British rallied.

✳ Nearly 180 Londoners died during a raid on March 3, 1943— but not from bombs. A woman tripped entering an underground station; the crowd rushing for cover crushed her and many others, suffocating them.

The Quite Imaginary Sue Mundy

How an entire state was terrorized—and enthralled by—
a fictional female operative.

✳   ✳   ✳   ✳

SUE MUNDY WAS a powerful fictional product of the guerrilla war in the border state of Kentucky in 1864. Even though she never actually existed, Mundy became the most feared military operative in the state, a potent symbol of Confederate stealth and resistance.

As the Civil War stretched into its fourth year, the Confederacy's military fortunes were fading on all fronts. The Union was making efficient use of its superior numbers in both soldiers and resources, and Union commanders, using their wider range of options, began to dominate the Confederate opposition. In response, some Southern fighters resorted to guerrilla tactics.

Femme Fatale

Sue Mundy, "The Girl Guerrilla," was largely a creation of George Prentice, the pro-Union editor of the *Louisville Journal*, who intensely disliked General Stephen G. Burbridge, the Union commander in Kentucky. The ground was fertile for Prentice because guerrilla attacks were undeniable problems for Union forces in Kentucky. Many of the raids were planned and coordinated by Jerome Clarke, whose raiders caused considerable damage in northern Kentucky throughout 1864. The son of a wealthy Kentucky landowner, Clarke joined the Confederate army in 1861 at age 17 and rode with General John Hunt Morgan's raiders until Morgan's death in 1864. Clarke was a slim 20-year-old man with long hair and somewhat feminine features. His looks helped inspire the Sue Mundy character.

Prentice staged a public relations attack on Burbridge with a series of newspaper articles on the subject of recent hit-and-run attacks against Union targets. Prentice claimed in print that a

Confederate raider named Sue Mundy had masterminded the guerrilla actions. The journalist then mocked Burbridge's army for being unable to keep Kentucky safe from the actions of a "mere woman." Prentice chose the name "Sue Mundy" on purpose—it was also the name of a notorious Louisville prostitute. The insult worked, and Prentice stirred powerful opinions in Kentucky.

Under Pressure

In early 1865, Clarke linked his Kentucky raiders to the most feared of the Confederate "bushwhackers," William Quantrill's Missouri Partisan Rangers. Quantrill's guerrillas were more renegades than soldiers. They epitomized the "Terror of the Black Flag," the no-surrender, no-prisoners, no-quarter form of warfare that was contrary to all contemporary rules of engagement.

The pressure on Burbridge's Union forces to catch and neutralize Sue Mundy swelled. In response to guerrilla operations that killed both Union soldiers and civilians, Burbridge declared that in reprisal for every Union soldier killed by a raider, four Confederates would be executed.

Mundy's notoriety peaked when Clarke and Quantrill coordinated a joint attack on a railway depot at Lair Station in Kentucky, on February 3, 1865. Just over a month later, on March 12, Clarke and two of his subordinates were forced to surrender. He was later deemed by the Union to be the notorious Sue Mundy, and he was hung as a common criminal just three days later on March 15—before a military tribunal could even hear his case.

Maintaining his fiction to the end, editor Prentice wrote that Union forces had still failed to capture the real Sue Mundy.

Rebel Yell

You say you want a revolution? Well, what happens when no one shows up? Read on about some failed uprisings.

❋ ❋ ❋ ❋

Keep Your Powder Dry

THE GUNPOWDER PLOT of 1605 was certainly one of the times when the rebel script didn't work out. Planned by Guy Fawkes and a few revolutionary cronies over an ale or two in a London pub called The Duck and Drake, the plot entailed blowing up England's Houses of Parliament while the Members and Lords were in session. Fawkes assumed that before the rubble even settled, the oppressed populace would rise in arms to take over the country.

The conspirators managed to secrete 36 barrels of gunpowder in the cellar of the Parliament buildings, but Fawkes was nabbed before he could put flame to fuse. A few of his co-conspirators escaped to the countryside where they decided to make a last stand. Unfortunately, their gunpowder was wet. They put the explosive near an open fire to dry it out, which worked—but then it blew up in their faces.

As for the uprising, no one informed the populace of it happening. Even so, the citizenry declared November 5 to be Guy Fawkes Day. For years, a popular saying stated that Fawkes was "the only man ever to enter Parliament with honest intentions."

Canceling *la Revolución*

Fidel Castro made a lot of people angry after he ran General Fulgencio Batista out of Cuba in January 1959. First in line was Cuba's now-displaced gentry, whom Castro had also chased off. He'd done the same to some of the American organized crime families who ran Havana's hotels and casinos. There was tension with the U.S. government, which had helped finance his revolution. Moreover, he cozied up to the Soviet Union—not at all politic at the height of the Cold War.

But Cuban exiles weren't willing to simply mellow out and work on their tans in Miami—they wanted their turf back. They vigorously lobbied the U.S. government, arguing that an incendiary event—say, an invasion—would spark a popular uprising by the oppressed Cuban masses. The exiles were prepared to supply the troops if the United States would train them and provide equipment and air support on the big day. They thought they had a deal.

The exiles rounded up some likely rebels, including 200 veterans of Batista's defeated army, and training got underway. On April 12, 1961, President John F. Kennedy announced that the country would not militarily intervene in Cuban affairs. The ex-pats thought that was a great piece of disinformation. On April 17, 1961, the rebels landed at the Bay of Pigs. Castro's army was there to greet them—the U.S. air support, however, was not. Thereafter, Cubans learned to keep their mouth shut regarding Castro's regime. In fact, any Cubans who did rise up publicly did so to protest the invasion.

Timing Is Everything

Unlike the Gunpowder Plot, the locals had plenty of notice of an 1837 uprising in Upper Canada; after all, a "Declaration of Independence" had already been publicized. Its firebrand leader, William Lyon Mackenzie, figured that thanks to the Declaration and his advertisement posting in a local newspaper, at least 5,000 people would show up on the appointed date and location: December 7 at a local pub in York (present-day Toronto).

But word was slow to get around. Then someone changed the date to December 4. Consequently, only a few hundred farmers showed up. The weather was nasty, sleet and ice were on the roads, and the pub ran out of food. Most of the farmers returned home.

Everyone was back at the pub the next morning. The plan was to march into the town, put the run on any resistance, and hang the British-appointed governor. Rebels with muskets led the march, followed by the rank and file armed mostly with clubs and pitchforks. The local sheriff, backed by a couple dozen soldiers, confronted the rabble on the main street. They exchanged a round of musket fire. When the rebel shooters knelt to reload, the farmers following them thought they'd all been shot. Figuring their big guns gone, the farmers promptly hied it back to their respective homesteads.

The townsfolk paid the affair little attention. Top on the agenda at the next town council meeting wasn't the abortive rebellion; instead, they hotly debated a bylaw designed to prohibit citizens from letting their pigs roam freely on York's streets. The bylaw passed.

---

* When the American colonies became the young United States, a hatred of British taxation led to strict rules about how the new republic could tax itself. Soon the founding fathers realized they'd have to get creative, so they taxed whiskey. That was a hot button in a relatively drunken nation, and it led to the Whiskey Rebellion in 1791.

* In 1856, Albert Sidney Johnston led U.S. forces against the Mormons in the Utah War when the administration of President James Buchanan deemed the Mormons in rebellion against the United States. Ironically, Johnston died at Shiloh on April 6, 1862—the 32nd anniversary of the founding of the Mormon church—commanding his own force in rebellion against the United States.

Comic Book Heroes Go to War

American comic book heroes fought both on the home front and on the battlefront, doing everything from shaping public opinion to socking the Führer square on the jaw, a sentiment no doubt shared by the troops who rabidly followed their adventures.

✳   ✳   ✳   ✳

IN THE LATE 1930s, American opinion over the turmoil in Europe was split. Many citizens believed in isolationism—why should America solve a European problem? Others were horrified by Japan and Germany's sudden aggression. Popular culture mirrored this division, and comic books were no different.

In 1938, an issue of *Action Comics* featured the colorful new hero Superman uncovering a plot by a dastardly senator bent on getting America involved in a European conflict. Fortunately, Superman was able to keep the United States out of trouble by forcing the sides to overcome their differences.

Other citizens and artists had different visions, however. In a conscious effort to "take a stand," Jack Kirby and Joe Simon transformed a weakling unfit for military service into a super-soldier through a secret government experiment, and Captain America headed off to Europe to personally confront Hitler a year before the United States entered the war. The authors received threatening letters for their efforts. Kirby and Simon were far from alone in predicting the entry of the United States into the war: Leverett Gleason publications issued a *Daredevil Battles Hitler* comic in 1941, and a prescient November 1941 issue of *National Comics* depicted a fictional attack on Pearl Harbor.

"The Sentinels of Liberty Stand Alone!"

After the actual attack on Pearl Harbor took place a month later, the isolationist viewpoint all but disappeared, and comic heroes went to war with a vengeance. Captain America served in the army. Wonder Woman became a nurse. In the pages of *All-Star Squadron*, the Justice Society suspended operations so that all the heroes could join the military. By 1941, Superman himself had reversed his neutralist stance and battled domestic saboteurs or fifth columnists in every issue.

Along with the traditional characters developing patriotic streaks, the war saw the rise of some inarguably pro-American characters. *Startling Comics* introduced Fighting Yank, whose powers came by way of a Revolutionary War ancestor; *National Comics* featured a character called Uncle Sam.

Hitler served as the perfect foil for the costumed crusaders: here was a real-life figure bent on world domination, a character as evil as any writer could possibly imagine. Heroes such as Daredevil and Sub-Mariner battled the Nazis overseas, but others waged war at home. Since Superman could easily have ended the war with his powers, his creators contrived to keep him home by having Clark Kent fail his military physical. Superman contented himself with battling enemy agents in the United States, at one point even testifying before Congress that American forces were easily powerful enough to triumph without his aid.

"The Japs Started Their Treacherous Attack!"

Publishers began to realize that rather than mirroring common sentiments, their characters could help to shape wartime opinion—not to mention sell a lot of comic books. Superheroes began selling war bonds, organizing scrap metal drives, and offering lessons on how to be a proper American. Along with such positive messages, however, a fair amount of effort went into demonizing the enemy, usually in brutally graphic ways. Germans were depicted as cold, calculating, and ruthless, often sporting monocles or facial scars; Mussolini became a clown.

The Japanese were portrayed as bucktoothed ape-men with a predilection for butchering prisoners in stories with titles like "The Slant Eye of Satan" (from a Green Hornet comic book.) Very occasionally, comics admitted the possibility that enemy civilians might be decent people, albeit hopelessly misguided by their leaders, but those portrayals were relatively uncommon.

Sunset of the Golden Age

World War II proved to be a gold mine for comic book publishers. The backdrop of the war and the identification of superheroes as icons of patriotism helped circulation double from 10 to 20 million issues a month from 1941 to 1944, despite wartime paper shortages. An estimated 44 percent of the armed forces read comics regularly. Men passed the books around until they fell apart, and in 1943, military post exchanges reported that comics outsold *Reader's Digest, Life,* and *The Saturday Evening Post* combined by a 10–1 margin. Following the war, the heroes of the comic pages went on to further encourage the American way of life and fight the Red Scare in the Cold War. But in many ways the World War II era marked their zenith, and fans today remember that time as the Golden Age of Comics.

❋ Many U.S. athletes were drafted into service during the war, leading some draft rejects to fill positions on professional sports teams. The long-hapless St. Louis Browns, which included a man missing one arm, won their first and only American League pennant in 1944.

❋ Italy's first naval engagement of the war was tragicomic. After the Royal Navy sank the cruiser *Colleoni,* the British hurried to rescue the survivors, but were driven off by Italian aircraft.

❋ To explain the Lend–Lease program with Britain to Americans, President Franklin D. Roosevelt compared it to lending a garden hose to a neighbor to put out a fire. "I don't say... 'Neighbor, my garden hose cost me $15; you have to pay me for it'... I want my garden hose back after the fire is over."

At War on the Air

During World War II, Axis and Allies alike unleashed a powerful new weapon: broadcast radio. Recognizable radio personalities spread disinformation over the airwaves and attacked enemy morale.

✳ ✳ ✳ ✳

Lord Haw-Haw

WILLIAM JOYCE—NICKNAMED "Lord Haw-Haw" for his nasal drawl—broadcast propaganda for Germany. A member of the British Union of Fascists, Joyce fled to Germany in 1939; there, he offered his services to the Nazis. His weekly broadcasts began with the tagline "Germany calling" and featured inaccurate reports of British defeats and German saboteurs in Britain. At the height of the war, Joyce garnered almost as many listeners as the British BBC station. Even Mel Blanc, the voice of Bugs Bunny, parodied him in a Looney Tunes cartoon.

After his arrest in May 1945, Joyce was tried in England for treason, even though he had been born in the United States and was a naturalized German citizen. The prosecution argued that Joyce owed allegiance to Britain as long as he held a British passport, legal or not. Joyce was found guilty and hanged.

Tokyo Rose

"Tokyo Rose" was the collective name given by American servicemen in the Pacific to female announcers who played popular music and read disparaging war reports on Radio Tokyo.

After the war, Iva Toguri D'Aquino, who had broadcast under the name Orphan Ann, became the face of Tokyo Rose in America. D'Aquino was an American citizen of Japanese descent who had gone to Japan to care for an ailing aunt. Stranded in Japan after Pearl Harbor, D'Aquino was forced to broadcast propaganda to American troops. Known for her bouncy delivery, she opened with, "Greetings, everybody! This is your No. 1 enemy, your favorite playmate, Orphan Ann on Radio

Tokyo—the little sunbeam whose throat you'd like to cut." Upon her return to America, D'Aquino was tried for treason as Tokyo Rose. Found guilty in 1949, she served six years of a ten-year sentence. D'Aquino insisted she was innocent and had actually worked with American POWs who helped her write broadcasts that would sabotage the program with on-air flubs, puns, and innuendo. In the 1970s, a public inquiry established D'Aquino's innocence. President Gerald Ford pardoned D'Aquino in 1977.

Axis Sally

American actress Mildred Gillars was a familiar voice throughout Europe, the Mediterranean, and North Africa during the war. She identified herself as "Midge on the mike," but to American servicemen she was "Axis Sally." Her program on Radio Berlin, "Home Sweet Home," was a mixture of popular music, anti-Semitic diatribes, and speculation on the infidelity of the girls back home. Gillars made her most famous broadcast just before the Allied invasion of Normandy: a radio drama called "Vision of Invasion," in which an American mother dreams that her son died crossing the English Channel. Gillars was convicted of treason for that broadcast, which was played at her trial. She served 12 years of a 30-year sentence. Afterward, she entered a convent in Columbus, Ohio.

Propaganda by Accident

British writer P. G. Wodehouse, creator of the characters Bertie Wooster and the inimitable Jeeves, was living in Le Tourquet when the Germans invaded France in 1940. Wodehouse was arrested and sent to a German internment camp. After he was released, he was still stranded in Europe, so he made five broadcasts on German radio. The broadcasts were classic Wodehouse, poking fun at himself, the Germans, and his fellow internees. The Brits who laughed at Lord Haw-Haw's vitriolic attacks were incensed by Wodehouse's lighthearted description of the trials of internment, and they denounced him as a Nazi sympathizer. An investigation after the war, however, found the broadcasts were made "in all innocence and without any evil intent."

Fast Facts

✳ German-born actress Marlene Dietrich ignored a personal directive from Hitler ordering her to return to Germany in 1937. She was outspoken about her distaste for the Nazi party, and in 1939 she became a U.S. citizen.

✳ About 12,000 Allied aircraft supported the Normandy invasion.

✳ When U.S. Marines landed on Guam, they were greeted by a sign that read, "Welcome Marines." The sign had been left by U.S. Navy frogmen who had earlier scouted the area for mines.

✳ President Franklin Delano Roosevelt was elected to a fourth term in 1944 with a narrow 53 percent majority of the popular vote over Thomas Dewey. However, he received 432 electoral votes to Dewey's 99.

✳ General Douglas MacArthur had to cancel his planned victory parade through Manila in the Philippines because the city had been almost completely destroyed.

✳ In 1939, the Nazis developed a plane capable of flying from Berlin to New York in about 20 hours. Hitler had his own Focke Wulf Fw 200, Immelmann III, on standby in case he needed to escape to Japan.

✳ Roughly 1,115 German V-2 rockets were fired at England between September 1944 and March 1945, killing 2,754 people. In that same time, Antwerp, Belgium, was subjected to 1,265 attacks. An article in the March 1945 issue of *Time* referred to Antwerp as the "City of Sudden Death."

✳ In 1945, Magda Goebbels gave each of her six children drugged candy to put them to sleep before fatally poisoning them in the Fürherbunker.

✳ On May 5, 1945, 560 Japanese kamikaze attacks were launched against the U.S. fleet supporting the Okinawa invasion.

✳ Between 1943 and the end of the war, the Broadway musical *Oklahoma!* gave 43 free performances for servicemen.

The Dirty, Dirty Boer War

The last great conflict of the 19th century and the first of the 20th century was a far cry from a "Gentleman's War."

✳ ✳ ✳ ✳

The Beginning

IN THE FALL of 1899, hostilities broke out between the British Army and Dutch settlers (called Boers), who controlled the South African regions known as the Transvaal and the Orange Free State. The reasons for the conflict lay not only in the discovery of gold and diamonds in the region but in Britain's desire to consolidate its imperial holdings. Certain of British aggression, the Boers struck first and dealt the overly confident and ill-prepared British soldiers a series of swift defeats. The British quickly regained their footing, however, and within a year had captured all of the major cities in the region. Unfortunately for all involved, this was just the beginning.

A White Man's War

With the capture of the Boer capital cities in the spring of 1900, the British Army considered its job complete. It was the first time since the Crimean War (1853–56) that British soldiers had fought against white opponents, and many were proud that the indomitable spirit of the glorious British Empire had once again held sway against a worthy opponent. No doubt, more than one English soldier was already imagining the stories he would tell his grandchildren many years hence.

The only spot of difficulty was that the Boers, a proud farming people who considered the land theirs by right of seizure and dominance over the native black population, refused to surrender. With their leader, Paul Kruger, safely ensconced in Holland, the Boers began a guerrilla war that, with their keen knowledge of the terrain and superior Mauser smokeless rifles, soon began to extract a heavy toll. The Boers struck swiftly from horseback or ambushed select targets from well-concealed positions in the African veldt. They were excellent marksmen who could disappear at will into the countryside, live off the sympathetic farms, and reappear to attack elsewhere.

British commander Lord Horatio Herbert Kitchener soon realized that the only way to eliminate the Boers was to deprive them of their support. To this end, Kitchener established a policy of total war in which British troops were ordered to burn farms (more than 30,000 buildings were destroyed), kill livestock, take no prisoners, and round up the Boer wives and children. In addition, the British established a dense network of block-houses that could alert garrisons to the presence of belligerent Boers in a particular area. These tactics proved murderously successful, and after two years of bloody conflict, the Boers were forced to concede defeat.

The Women and Children's War

Before the start of the Second World War, British Prime Minister Neville Chamberlain complained to German Field Marshall Hermann Goering about the Nazis' use of concentration camps to contain political prisoners. Goering, obviously prepared for the assault, brandished an encyclopedia in which the invention of concentration camps was credited to the British. Chamberlain, apparently, had no rebuttal because it was true.

In 1900, Lord Kitchener began a policy of collecting all non-combatant Boers, mostly women and children, into "refugee" camps. This was done partly to protect them, since the British had burned their farms and killed their livestock, and partly to separate the women and children from the men fighting in the veldt. But 27,927 women and children died in the camps due to unsanitary conditions and inadequate nutrition. Moreover, the camps placed "Hands Uppers," those families that wanted to surrender, side-by-side with "Bitter Enders," those who vowed to resist the British at all costs. This often resulted in violence.

The Africans' War

Boer women and children were not the only ones to suffer in concentration camps; thousands of native Africans were similarly imprisoned. Unlike the Boers, however, the Africans were not issued a food ration but were expected to grow or earn their daily morsel. In the end, approximately 14,000 natives died in the camps, though the exact number will probably never be known.

The Boer War was significant not only as the first use of concentration camps, but because whites armed blacks against whites. Somewhere between 10,000 and 30,000 Africans were given arms by the British to suppress the Boers. What the tribal natives lacked in discipline they made up for in zeal, often using the opportunity to avenge past wrongs against the actively racist Boer settlers who had seized their land. The natives' belief that the British would prove better rulers than the Boers, however, was misguided. The Treaty of Vereeniging, which ended the Boer War, denied rights promised to the African population by the British.

The Boers, who became known as Afrikaners, eventually formed the white supremacist Union of South Africa in 1910 with European and British support.

✳ **Though the Hope Diamond is more famous, the Cullinan is the largest diamond ever found. Unearthed in South Africa in 1905, this 3,100-carat monster was cut into several stones that are still part of the British Crown Jewels.**

Molly Pitcher: Rebel Militiawoman

Historians disagree about Molly; not over whether she lived, but over her true identity. Did a cannon-cocker's wife truly step up and serve a gun under fire in the American Revolution?

✳ ✳ ✳ ✳

Was Molly Pitcher real? A couple of Revolutionary women's stories sound a lot like Molly's. Because women have "pitched in" during battle in just about every war, that's neither surprising nor a revelation. It wasn't rare in that era for wives to accompany their husbands on military duty, to say nothing of those daring few women who masqueraded as men. So who was Molly? Many historians say she was an Irish immigrant named Mary Hays (later McCauly). Some believe that Molly was Margaret Corbin, a Pennsylvania native. The most likely case is that both were real women who did pretty much as history credits them and that the legend of Molly Pitcher commingles the two.

What did Mary Hays do? The story, likely accurate, credits her first with bringing water (the "pitcher" part explained) to the artillery gunners at the Battle of Monmouth (1778). It wasn't just drinking water; a soldier had to wet-sponge a cannon after a shot in order to douse any residual embers. If he or she didn't, the person pushing in the next powder charge would suffer the consequences. Accounts describe Mary as a woman who was always ready with a choice profanity and was as brave as any man, and she is widely credited with evacuating wounded men. After her husband fell wounded, she stepped forward to help crew his gun. Mary died around 1832.

And Margaret Corbin? Her tale begins at the Battle of Fort Washington (1776) and has her first helping her husband crew a cannon, then firing it unassisted after his death in action. (That would be possible, but very slow.) Taken out of action by grapeshot—a cannon firing musket balls as a super shotgun—she was evacuated and given a military pension by the Continental government. Considering said government's notorious poverty and lousy credit, there's doubt whether poor Margaret ever collected any money in time to help her. She died in 1789, a partly disabled veteran.

How did the stories get so muddled together? One must consider the times. No one videotaped Mary or Margaret; eyewitnesses spoke or wrote of their deeds. Others retold the tales, perhaps inflating or deemphasizing them. As the war lingered on, people who had heard both stories probably assumed they were variants of the same story, and they retold it in their own words. Regardless, dozens of American women besides Mary and Margaret fought for independence; many thousands more helped the cause with all their strength. Molly Pitcher is an emblem, a Rosie the Riveter of her era.

The Quotable Nathan Hale

In 1776, Revolutionary War hero Nathan Hale was hanged by the British for espionage. Allegedly, his last words were: "I only regret that I have but one life to lose for my country." Brave words, but did he actually say them?

Those noble words are consistent with Hale's character: He was a volunteer who dared a dangerous task, conducted himself like a gentleman after capture, and went bravely to the noose. The quote sounds paraphrased from Act IV of Joseph Addison's inspirational play *Cato,* one of Hale's favorites: "What pity is it, that we can die but once to serve our country!"

Hale may have said the words, or something like them when he gave a pre-death oration, but unfortunately, there were only a few eyewitnesses. Revolutionary-era media printed several variants on the theme, and Hale soon became a valiant martyr.

You've Come a Long Way, Baby

During World War II, to make up for the lost male workforce, thousands of American women traded in their aprons for typewriters, rivet guns, and forklifts. The following excerpts are from the article, "Eleven Tips on Getting More Efficiency Out of Women Employees," taken from the July 1943 issue of Transportation Magazine, *which instructed managers and supervisors how to hire women. Today, these tips would garner loads of lawsuits.*

✳ ✳ ✳ ✳

✳ Pick young married women. They usually have more of a sense of responsibility than their unmarried sisters, they're less likely to be flirtatious, they need the work or they wouldn't be doing it, and they still have the pep and interest to work hard and to deal with the public efficiently.

✳ When you have to use older women, try to get ones who have worked outside the home at some time in their lives. Older women who have never contacted the public have a hard time adapting themselves and are inclined to be cantankerous and fussy. It's always well to impress upon older women the importance of friendliness and courtesy.

✳ General experience indicates that "husky" girls—those who are just a little on the heavy side—are more even-tempered and efficient than their underweight sisters.

✳ Give every girl an adequate number of rest periods during the day. You have to make some allowances for feminine psychology. A girl has more confidence and is more efficient if she can keep her hair tidied, apply fresh lipstick, and wash her hands several times a day.

✳ Be tactful when issuing instructions or in making criticisms. Women are often sensitive; they can't shrug off harsh words the way men do. Never ridicule a woman—it breaks her spirit and cuts off her efficiency.

Fast Facts

✳ Abner Doubleday, credited (erroneously) with the invention of baseball, is also credited with firing the first shot of the Civil War.

✳ Tennessee was the last of 11 states to secede from the Union in 1861 but the first state to be readmitted when it rejoined in July 1866.

✳ The only American Indian nations that took an active part in the Civil War were the Cherokee, Creek, Choctaw, Chickasaw, and Seminole.

✳ General Henry Heth graduated dead last in his West Point class. During the Confederate Pennsylvania Campaign, he commanded a division in General A. P. Hill's corps. General Lee had ordered Hill to avoid any sort of engagement with the enemy before he could assemble his full army, but Henry Heth made history by accidentally starting the Battle of Gettysburg. He sent two brigades ahead on reconnaissance, and they encountered and engaged Union troops.

✳ Because of heavy casualties, Civil War soldiers devised a sort of makeshift "dog tag" before going into battle. The tags were handkerchiefs or pieces of paper with the soldiers' names and addresses on them. They were pinned to the soldiers' uniforms to simplify identification if they didn't survive the battle.

✳ Prior to her rebuilding as an ironclad, the CSS *Virginia* was known as the USS *Merrimack*. The ship was named for the Merrimack River, but its name is often misspelled when people leave off the *k*.

✳ No effort was made to standardize the uniforms of Union troops until after the First Battle of Bull Run.

✳ In July 1862, David Glasgow Farragut was promoted to rear admiral, the first officer to hold that rank in the history of the U.S. Navy.

Keeping an Eye on Things

The Union relied on many spies—both male and female—to remain informed of the Confederacy's actions and strategies.

✳ ✳ ✳ ✳

The Spy Onstage

PAULINE CUSHMAN WAS born in the bayou of New Orleans in 1833. Her family eventually moved to Grand Rapids, Michigan, but that wasn't big enough for the ambitious Cushman. As a young woman, she headed to the East Coast for a successful theatrical career.

In 1863, Cushman was in Louisville, Kentucky. Although a Union town, Louisville had a fair share of Confederate supporters. One day, Cushman was dared by Southern officers to offer a toast to Jefferson Davis during a play. She agreed, tipping off the local Federals. When the toast came, so did the marshals, and audience members who cheered were arrested. Cushman's life as a Union spy had begun.

A beautiful woman, Cushman managed to fool unsuspecting Southerners by donning a false mustache and posing as a man. Later in 1863, she was sent deep into a Confederate camp near Shelbyville, Tennessee. But before she could complete her mission, Cushman was captured. A quick trial found her guilty of spying, and she was sentenced to hang. Quickly advancing Union soldiers, however, soon drove the Confederates from Shelbyville, and Cushman was saved.

Fame ended Cushman's spying days. Still, she received the honorary title of "major" and continued performing, sometimes in shows by P. T. Barnum, billing herself as "Miss Major Cushman." When she died in 1893, she was buried with full military honors.

A Light and Bright Life

In 1861, 19-year-old Spencer Kellogg Brown joined the U.S. Navy, serving on the Essex. He bravely volunteered to infiltrate the shores near Forts Henry and Donelson on the Tennessee and the Cumberland rivers to seek intelligence. Caught after several days, Brown convinced his captor to release him so he could join the Confederates. He actually did join for a brief time in Louisiana, only to escape and bring his findings personally to General Grant.

In 1862, Brown was dispatched to attack a ferry supplying Confederates at Fort Hudson in Georgia. Although the mission was successful, Brown was captured as a spy and tried in Richmond. Found guilty, he was hanged in 1863. His last words were reported to be, "Did you ever pass through a tunnel under a mountain? My passage, my death is dark, but beyond all is light and bright."

The Unassuming Spy

Not much is known about Mrs. E. H. Baker, a Chicago-based member of the Pinkerton Agency. What is known is that she single-handedly saved the Union navy that patrolled Virginia's James River.

In November 1861, Baker, posing as an apolitical woman on an extended visit, called on some old Richmond friends. She soon discovered that these friends had a young son who was a captain in the Confederate army. At a party on the shore of the James River, Baker witnessed the South's secret weapon—a submarine. The demonstration included the attachment and detonation of an explosive charge to an old scow. Union ships traveling the river would be the next targets.

Baker soon became "homesick" and departed Richmond. When she arrived in Washington, she delivered a complete account, including sketches, of the entire submarine demonstration. Thanks to her, the Confederate plot was foiled on its first attempt. For her part, Baker returned to the Pinkerton Agency and disappeared into anonymity.

The Christmas Truce

On Christmas Eve 1914, the realities of war took a backseat to the realities of being human.

✳ ✳ ✳ ✳

A Festive and Brief Affair

IN AUGUST 1914, World War I broke out in Europe in an atmosphere of almost festival-like celebration. "Bring on the enemy, and we'll make short work of 'em," was the general consensus on both sides. But four months later, hundreds of thousands of men had been killed, wounded, or gone missing. Soldiers were floundering about in fetid trenches filled with putrid water. It was painfully clear that the festival had been canceled.

Pope Benedict XV suggested a Christmas cease-fire, but the idea was rejected by both sides. The Allied High Command had a better idea to lift the morale of the soldiers rotting in the trenches: an offensive. But it failed, and as Christmas approached, No Man's Land on the Western Front became filled with bloated bodies.

Gifts from Home

Both sides received Christmas gifts from home to lighten their misery. The British received "Princess Mary boxes" containing candy, tobacco, and a picture card of Princess Mary, among other items. German troops received large meerschaum pipes from Kaiser Wilhelm II, while officers got boxes of cigars.

The two sides began to communicate with each other through the trenches. A week before Christmas, some Germans smuggled a chocolate cake into the British trenches, with a message that they wanted to have a concert that evening for their captain's birthday and invited the British to attend. That evening the concert was performed, with the British applauding. The Germans asked the English troops to join in on the chorus, but a killjoy snapped, "We'd rather die than sing German."

"It would kill us if you did," responded a German affably.

Christmas Trees

On December 24, some German troops began placing small trees adorned with candles at the top of their trenches. English soldiers crawled out of their trenches to ask the Germans about the curious sight. It was not a huge leap from there to an informal truce between both sides. "We all walked out and one of their officers came to meet us," remembered a British artilleryman. "We all saluted, shook hands, and exchanged cigarettes."

The two sides spontaneously came together at various places along the Western Front. Germans and Scots kicked a soccer ball through a muddy field where they would have been shot dead just hours earlier. "Scots and Huns were fraternizing in the most genuine possible manner. Every sort of souvenir was exchanged, addresses given and received, photos of families shown, etc.," wrote a British officer.

Other meetings were grimmer. Sometimes the two sides got together to bury their dead comrades, who had been lying neglected in No Man's Land. Even so, the occasion could turn festive, as one Englishman remembered, "We gave [the Germans] some wooden crosses . . . which completely won them over, and soon the men were on the best terms and laughing."

The British High Command, toughing out the war in a luxurious château 27 miles away from the front, were horrified to learn about the truce, since they realized how hard it would be to make killers again of men who had become friends. But because so many officers took part in the truce, in the end, very few were disciplined.

Eventually, the truce ended, and the two sides resumed shooting at each other—but perhaps with a little more reluctance.

Code Breakers Crack the Enigma

Oversights in the German code and the Allies' ability to capture working cipher machines gave decrypters at Bletchley Park the edge they needed to decipher Enigma messages.

✳ ✳ ✳ ✳

ENIGMA WAS THE code name for a portable cipher machine used by Germany to encrypt and decrypt secret messages. Invented in 1918 by a German engineer named Arthur Scherbius, the machine was initially marketed to businesses as a way of preventing corporate espionage. By 1933, the German Army, Navy, and Air Force were producing their own modified versions of the machine. With hundreds of millions of letter combinations, the German military thought the code was unbreakable.

How Did It Work?

Enigma encoded messages by performing sequential substitutions using electrical connections. The machine resembled a typewriter; it had 26 keys—one for each letter of the alphabet. When a key was depressed, an electrical impulse traveled through a plug board at the front of the machine to a rotor contact inside the machine. The surface of each rotor also contained 26 electrical contacts, again representing letters of the alphabet. Each contact was wired to a key on the keyboard as well as to a contact on the next rotor. An output device illuminated the cipher letter that the system created. The rotors were interchangeable, and extra rotors could be added. Enigma also used a device called a reflector, which redirected the electrical impulses back through the machine a second time. The code was exceedingly complex.

The Enigma was small enough to be carried into the field, but it required three men to operate: One typed the coded message into the machine, a second recorded the encrypted output one letter at a time, and a third transmitted the result in Morse Code.

Poland's Big Break

In 1932, Poland's intelligence corps received a package from its French counterparts containing Enigma guidelines that had been obtained by a German intelligence clerk named Hans-Thilo Schmidt. Schmidt was later arrested by the Nazis for the theft; he committed suicide in 1942 while in prison for treason.

Using some of Schmidt's information and a commercial version of the Enigma, in 1933, three of Poland's brightest cryptanalysts successfully recreated the Enigma code and its indicator system. Though the commercial version was much different from the machines used by the Germans, the cryptanalysts deduced the internal wiring of Enigma's rotors. They used advanced mathematics, exploiting the German error of repeating the message setting (a three-letter sequence at the beginning of the transmission). The Poles developed two electromechanical machines that functioned similarly to those the Germans were using to decipher messages.

Britain's Best and Brightest

The Germans increased the sophistication of Enigma in 1939. By July of that year, Poland felt its independence threatened. The Polish Cipher Bureau gave its French and British counterparts all of its research in the hopes their teams could crack the new German code. The British intelligence community organized its code-breaking operations north of London at an estate called Bletchley Park.

Staff at Bletchley Park consisted of chess experts, mathematicians, linguists, computer scientists, and even crossword enthusiasts. They made several important discoveries, which allowed them to break the Enigma code even when it was altered every two days. Their success was due in part to German methods of coding:

* The reflector ensured that no letter could be coded as itself.

* Because the keyboard contained only letters, all numbers had to be spelled out.

* Military ranks, military terms, and weather reports appeared often, making it easier to decode these words.

* The Germans would not repeat rotor order within a month, and the rotors changed position every two days. This greatly reduced the combinations used in the machines by the end of the month, making it easier to crack those messages.

Allies eventually captured German U-boats and surface ships with intact Enigmas and codebooks, giving code breakers the knowledge they needed to anticipate changes to the code. By 1943, most coded German communications were read routinely.

To Act, or Not to Act

Intelligence gleaned from decrypted Enigma messages fell under Ultra, the code name used by Britain, and later the United States.

The codes of the Luftwaffe were the first broken by Britain's team of cryptologists, and Britain monitored the Luftwaffe traffic to learn of planned raids during the Battle of Britain. They also alerted Prime Minister Churchill to the fact that Germany wanted air superiority before launching an invasion of Britain.

Messages intercepted between Rommel and Hitler revealed some of Rommel's planned tactics in Africa, giving the Allies an edge at Alam Halfa. Cracking the Enigma was perhaps most useful to convoys crossing the Atlantic. As codes were broken and manuals captured, the Allies were able to locate and avoid U-boat patrols.

While the breaking of the Enigma code did not win the war for the Allies, there can be no denying that the feat shortened the war, saving many lives in the process.

World War II Facts

✳ As Allied troops surged across Germany in the waning months of the war, some happily helped themselves to citizens' food, jewelry, small arms, artwork, and other personal valuables.

✳ The Italian CR-42 biplane fighter looked utterly obsolete—until one battled it. While it was slow, underarmored, and lacked radar, its maneuverability caught Spitfire pilots by surprise.

✳ Denmark was the only European country to cut back on its military after war broke out.

✳ Prickly Switzerland did not take airspace violations lightly. Swiss fighters shot down 116 intruding aircraft (mostly German) and forced down or interned more than 100 Allied heavy bombers.

✳ While dictator Francisco Franco of Spain stayed out of World War II, he contributed a division of volunteers to Germany: the highly regarded 250th Infantry "Blue" Division.

✳ U.S. riflemen often used condoms to keep mud and dirt out of the barrels of their rifles.

✳ A Soviet soldier's daily vodka ration was 100 grams, or about 3.5 ounces. For a senior lieutenant commanding mortars at Stalingrad, it wasn't nearly enough. "Ivan the Terrible" pirated his dead troops' vodka rations. When a supply clerk reported him to headquarters to cancel the ration, Ivan came unglued. He called upon his batteries, gave them coordinates, and three heavy mortar rounds landed on the supply clerk's warehouse. Headquarters was unsympathetic this time—they told the clerk to just give Ivan his vodka. After all, he had just been given the Order of the Red Star.

✳ The greatest hero of Paris might be Germany's General von Choltitz, who commanded the defense of the city. Choltitz disregarded Hitler's direct order to destroy the city prior to withdrawal.

Beyond Recognition: Coping with the Destructiveness of War

War has disfigured people since the first warring human bashed in another's cheekbone with a club, then spared his life. These days, humans have become remarkably efficient killers— yet we were less so during World War I. With the advent of battlefield medicine and popular photography, World War I let the mutilated vets live—but then forced them to face a society that might not have been ready to face them.

＊　＊　＊　＊

Blast, Fire, and Beyond

WORLD WAR I was the first war to use some of the technology of the era, such as airplanes, tanks, and wireless communication. Great adventure and glory beckoned. Each side stood convinced of righteousness in a noble, manly struggle. The soldiers looked so young and proud.

But they were headed off to squalor, mutilation, and pestilence. They were as likely to die from war-related dangers like disease as from something that sounds good in a folk song—such as a bullet piercing a proud young heart. World War I dragged on with aerial bombings, blindness from chlorine and mustard attacks, observation balloons bursting into balls of flame, brutal machine-gun mow downs, slow deaths while trying to cut barbed wire, trenches lined with a biohazardous mud-blood-urine sludge, and armored monsters belching steel, cordite, and death.

"I Can't Even Face Myself"

Those civilians who had deluded themselves with visions of war as a gallant pageant could deny the sordid reality no longer. The contrary evidence had just returned from the army hospital, and to look upon it frightened them.

By 1918, everyone was tired of war, and none were wearier than those veterans who had lost jaws, eyes, noses, or cheeks—sometimes all of the above. Modern medicine did all it could, more than ever before in history, but doctors proved better at saving lives than salvaging smiles. On Armistice Day, thousands of disfigured Allied soldiers—known as *mutilés* in France—had relatively little reason to cheer. That is, assuming they could still hear the cheers or see the revelers.

When doctors could reconstruct features, they did so, inventing and refining plastic surgery as they went. Yet all was not quite lost for the grenadier who had sacrificed himself on the war's bloody altar. What if someone could make customized masks to cover and resemble the victims' missing parts? (The alternative was to have them wear veils or hoods, hiding their ruined visages from the eyes of the public—an unfair if understandable solution.) Near-normal looks might mean near-normal lives. Children might not hide from them; adults might not stare. Here was born the new discipline of anaplastology—making artificial versions of lost or deformed body parts.

Welcome to the Tin Noses Shop

In Sidcup, England, in 1916, Francis Derwent Wood founded the Masks for Facial Disfigurement Department, or the Tin Noses Shop, as wounded soldiers facetiously called it. Wood's mission was to sculpt a small mask of copper and paint it to resemble the victim's prewar look. When possible, a mask was shaped using a detailed plaster cast of the unmarred side of the face; when impossible, a prewar photo provided the artist with a basis for painting. Glasses held the masks in place.

The vast majority of the artists were supposedly female, and they faced special creative challenges. They needed to match the flesh tone yet compensate for different types of sunlight. Often the mask was painted while being worn to best match the veteran's skin tone. The artists even had to match eyes and the looks of eyes. If the soldier had a mustache or an eyebrow that needed to be re-created, the victim's real hair was harvested and applied, or silver wire was used. The artist had to be part nurse, part sculptor, and part painter.

The most prominent artist helping French and American wounded was Anna Coleman Ladd, the wife of a Boston physician, who went to France to open a Red Cross anaplastology studio. When she heard of Wood's work with British soldiers, she did in France what the Tin Noses Shop's founder had done in Britain. Reports from the period describe her work as perhaps the finest in the field. In 1932, a grateful French Republic invested Ladd with the Legion of Honor in the Grade of Chevalière (knight).

Whither the Prostheses?

The manufacture of these masks stopped around 1920, and sadly, few survive. They wore out after a few years—enamel paint on soft, thin metal doesn't hold up well in day-to-day life. Perhaps some were repainted, but many owners were vulnerable to infection and other health problems related to their wounds, and thus didn't often survive long.

One theory as to why so few of the hundreds of masks so carefully made have survived is that they were buried with their owners. But we do have black-and-white photos to show us how the men looked wearing their metal masks. It was the best that could be done for them at the time.

"It's all a damned mess! And our two armies ain't nothing but howling mobs!"

—A CAPTURED CONFEDERATE PRIVATE, ON THE BATTLE OF THE WILDERNESS

On the Scene

A U.S. Army Special Forces medic isn't your garden variety hospital worker or battlefield medic. Here's what sets this job apart.

Q: How did you end up a Special Forces medic?

A: First I was with the 82nd Airborne; then I signed up for Special Forces, aka the Green Berets. Medic is one of the hardest specialties in Special Forces, but it's the most rewarding.

For one thing, we train for more than a year. I'm legally allowed to perform just about any medical procedure I think is necessary, short of opening up the braincase. But if enemy action opens up someone's braincase, I'll even have to do my best in there. While I am not yet a medical doctor, in field situations from sanitation to trauma to veterinary care, I do much of what an M.D. would do—and much that goes beyond what an M.D. would do.

Q: Why do Special Forces teams need medics trained to that level?

A: Our primary mission is to work with indigenous people in combat zones—to learn their language and customs, earn their trust and allegiance, help them help themselves. I could be on another continent next week, delivering babies and teaching a tribe why it's a bad idea to let the goats urinate in the water supply. From their perspective, that obviously can't be harmful because the tribe hasn't died out yet. So I may have some convincing to do.

Q: Do you carry a weapon in war zones or are you unarmed?

A: Unarmed? Not Special Forces medics. I'm cross-trained in demolition, for example. Most of our likely adversaries would just laugh if you told them that they weren't supposed to shoot at medics or ambulances. I usually carry a Swedish K submachine gun on ops.

From Light to Blight

The simple, mesmerizing elegance of the swastika lends itself to curves, serifs, and any other artistic touch one might add. If not for the Nazis, one might even call it beautiful.

✳   ✳   ✳   ✳

THE HOOKED CROSS we know as the swastika is an ancient symbol recurring throughout history in so many contexts that it's impossible to pinpoint its origin in a single era or region. The term "swastika" is derived from the Sanskrit words *su* and *asti*, meaning "it is well" or "well-being." Hindus and Buddhists have long associated the symbol with good fortune, long life, and success. When ancient Troy was rediscovered, artifacts in its ruins bore the swastika, common in Greek culture for many centuries as the *tetraskele*. Several Native American peoples have used it as well as decoration or to symbolize the four directions. The Ashanti (Africans in what became Ghana) marked golden weights with the swastika. The ancient Norse—a source of much cultural inspiration to the Nazis—carved swastikas in stone as the whirling might of will symbolized by the sun.

Most people in Europe knew the swastika as a good-luck sign. In America in the late 19th and early 20th centuries, the symbol adorned poker chips, children's books, and board games. Adolf Hitler's burgeoning Nazi Party adopted the swastika in 1920. Within 15 years it became the emblem of a cataclysmic mass movement. Why did Hitler choose it?

In 1920, a Party dentist brought Hitler a sample flag in red, white, and black depicting the swastika. Hitler made some careful modifications, and the swastika was adopted to symbolize the Nazi Party. Hitler briefly mentions what the symbol meant to him in *Mein Kampf*:

> "Not only because it incorporated those revered colours expressive of our homage to the glorious past and which once

brought so much honour to the German nation, but this symbol was also an eloquent expression of the will behind the movement. We National Socialists regarded our flag as being the embodiment of our party programme. The red expressed the social thought underlying the movement. White the national thought. And the swastika signified the mission allotted to us—the struggle for the victory of Aryan mankind and at the same time the triumph of the ideal of creative work which is in itself and always will be anti-Semitic."

The national flag that so prominently represented Germany during Word War II was adopted on September 15, 1935. Variations were adapted for government and military organizations. The Nazis tarnished the ancient symbol; it has become synonymous with hatred. But in other countries, the swastika is a religious and cultural symbol still used in festivals and ceremonies.

Swastikas on Display Today

Yuma, Arizona, United States: Americans decorated the Laguna Diversion Dam with swastikas in the early 1900s; it may have been a nod to Native American traditions, or perhaps an architect thought it looked neat. Though vandalized, the swastikas remain visible at this writing.

Dar-es-Salaam, Tanzania: Some buildings are decorated with repeated swastikas, most likely due to centuries of Hindu influence on this ancient Indian Ocean island port.

Lantau Island, Hong Kong, China: A large Buddha statue displayed here bears a swastika on its breastbone. Swastikas remain a common ornament on Buddhas throughout the world, especially in Asia.

Swastika, Ontario, Canada: Founded in 1908, this northern mining town sits near the Québec boundary. It was named for the Swastika Gold Mine at a time when the swastika was just a good-luck symbol.

Chapter Eleven

Science and Technology

Pennies from Heaven

You may have heard that a penny dropped from the top of the Empire State Building kills on impact. Not so!

✳   ✳   ✳   ✳

WHEN A PENNY falls from any great height, it gains speed due to the force of gravity, but it is also slowed by air resistance. Myth-busting amateurs have unanimously declared that by the time a penny hit a pedestrian's head, the most damage it could cause would be a small cut. The variables in determining terminal velocity, such as air density and surface area of the object, are difficult to pin down. The surface area depends on whether the penny falls flat—which would slow it down more—or turns on its edge. But regardless of the specifics of the calculation, the penny would certainly be going slower than 100 miles per hour as it approached the base of the building—probably a lot slower.

Even without the weapon of fancy math, the Empire State Building has falling-penny-prevention tricks up its sleeve. First is the 83rd floor, which juts out and "catches" pennies and other debris. Second is the unique updraft created by the building's massive structure. Wind travels up the side of the building with such power that things thrown off the top are often thrown right back up, usually landing on the 81st floor. So pedestrians can rest assured that a penny wouldn't do much damage—in fact, it would probably never reach the ground.

How It All Began

Tomcatting Made Easy

Keeping an indoor/outdoor cat can be a hassle. That's why many owners install kitty doors. Resident cats quickly learn to use them. Unfortunately, so does every stray in the neighborhood. To solve the problem, David Chamberlain invented a microchip for the door that scans a recognition microchip implanted in the resident cat.

But, what happens when the resident feline brings home a trophy mouse, mole, or bird? For these intrepid hunters, one owner came up with image recognition software hooked up to a minicam. How long, one wonders, before a pet owner-cum-inventor dreams up a meow-recognition kitty door?

The Nose Knows

In 2008, 38.4 million American households owned cats; 56 percent of them owned two or more cats. That's a lot of kitty litter—and a whole lot of smelly litter boxes.

Brad Baxter of Pontiac, Michigan, came to the rescue, possibly making himself a cat owner's best friend. In 2000, he debuted an automated, self-cleaning litter box. Built-in pressure plates alert the box when the cat climbs in, then again when it has done its business. A small electric motor rotates the box, dropping the clump of whatever  into a plastic bag, and that's about it. Once a week the owner changes bags and tops off the litter. No yuck whatsoever. Unfortunately, it only comes in two colors—but custom designer colors for finicky cats probably aren't far in the future.

Sail by the Stars, Plant by the Moon

Natural forecasting may seem like folkloric fancy to some, but often there is a kernel of truth behind the sayings.

✳ ✳ ✳ ✳

Red Sky at Morning

WHILE MANY MEANS of natural weather forecasting are relatively arbitrary, some actually have a basis in science. The oft-quoted proverb, "Red sky at morning, sailor take warning; red sky at night, sailor's delight" is actually a reasonable indicator of short-term weather trends, particularly in the middle latitudes of the Northern Hemisphere. The sinking air mass in a high-air pressure area holds air filled with particulates closer to the earth. This air tends to dispel shorter wavelengths of light and allow the longer (and redder) wavelengths, which cause a red sky at sunset. Since high-pressure systems typically herald fair weather, any sailors observing the sunset could rest easy knowing that clear weather and good sailing is on its way.

However, a red sky at sunrise indicates that the high-pressure front has already passed, as weather systems most often move from west to east in the mid-northern latitudes. A low-pressure system is likely to follow, with the likelihood of clouds and precipitation.

Other weather proverbs have some meteorological basis as well. "Mare's tails and mackerel scales make tall ships take in their sails" is a reference to two types of clouds: the cirrus and cirrocumulus. Both are harbingers of a warm front, bringing a change in wind pattern and possible precipitation.

The Farmer's Friend

Farmers also need some indication of coming weather to plan their crops. The heavenly bodies seem to be a good indicator, as both "Clear moon, frost soon," and "When the stars begin to huddle, the earth will soon become a puddle" have some basis in science. The "huddle" is in reference to groups of stars only visible through gaps in cloud cover. Some weather lore, like "A year of snow, a year of plenty," is fairly reliable, as late snow cover prevents fruit from blossoming until the time of the killing frosts has gone.

Fauna and Flora Forecasters

Sailors and farmers aren't the only ones keeping their eyes on the skies—many animals are extremely sensitive to changes in weather. So while it may seem as if an animal is "predicting" future weather, in fact, it is just responding to an existing condition. For instance, companion animals such as dogs and cats are well known for becoming restless before large-scale weather events such as tornadoes, hurricanes, or extreme electrical storms.

Low-flying swallows or low-nesting crows are both indicators of poor weather to come—a phenomenon supported by the fact that falling air pressure causes discomfort in birds' ears, so they fly low to mitigate it. These same pressure systems can cause deer and elk to seek the shelter of lower ground in anticipation of inclement weather.

As is the case with most natural forecasting, one just needs to take note of what's happening around them. For instance, farmers have noticed that cows tend to group together and lie down if a storm is approaching. Also, ants tend to increase the slope of their hills and cats tend to wash behind their ears with greater frequency just before a rain.

While observations of animal behavior are dependent upon the interpretations of the observer, watching flora is more reliable. The scales of pinecones open and stiffen in dry weather, but they return to their relaxed state in times of moisture.

Even humans are not immune to these changes in barometric pressure. Many people report suffering from headaches, and aching or pressure in their arthritic joints, recently healed fractures, or corns and bunions when the weather changes.

Have You Lost Weight?
Canada's Gravity Dips

Ah, gravity. It keeps our feet—and everything else—firmly on the ground. But due to some (literally) heavy geological history, in some parts of Canada, gravity is a matter of opinion.

✳ ✳ ✳ ✳

Ice, Ice Baby

IF YOU HAD been hanging out in North America 20,000 years ago, you would have needed to bundle up. At the time, the world was enduring the last major Ice Age, and glaciers covered a sizable chunk of the continent. In some places, the ice sheet was about two miles thick.

As you can imagine, that ice was also pretty heavy. In fact, the ice sheet was so dense that the Earth's crust sagged under its weight until the ice finally melted away approximately 14,000 years ago. After the big melt, most of the ground popped up to its original shape, but parts of Canada have yet to bounce back.

Up, Up, and Away!

The result of these still-sagging areas of the Earth is what scientists call a "gravity dip." The anomaly seems to be centered around the Hudson River region. These dips occur when parts of the ice-squashed earth get stuck in their Ice Age positions. Some people would regard the result as unfair: Most people who step on a scale in that area will weigh less than you, even if pound for pound, the two of you weigh the same. Scientists believe that in addition to the crust-sagging activity that occurred, a layer of lava in the Earth's mantle also plays a role in creating the gravity dips.

Whatever the reason, don't get too excited: A gravity dip doesn't mean that your sandwich is going to float off into space. Most of the benefits are purely scientific. As one researcher said, "We are able to show that the ghost of the ice age still hangs over North America."

Newton's Apple

Could a falling apple have triggered one of the greatest scientific discoveries of all time? Probably not—but it's a cute story.

✳   ✳   ✳   ✳

THE TALE OF the apple landing on Isaac Newton's head during an afternoon nap has been told for hundreds of years as the explanation for his discovery of the law of gravity. If only it were so simple. His understanding of gravity did not come to him as a flash of insight. Rather, it was the result of years of painstaking study.

The Plague of 1665 probably had more to do with Newton's intellectual feat than a round, red fruit. Newton was a 23-year-old student at Cambridge when the plague gripped England. As a result, the university closed and students were sent back to their homes in the countryside. Newton used this time to devote himself to his private studies, and in later years, he would refer to this period as the most productive of his life. He spent days working nonstop on computations and nights observing and measuring the skies. These calculations provided the seeds for an idea that would take years of covert and obsessive work to formulate—his Theory of Universal Gravitation.

Accounts of the apple story began appearing after Newton's death in 1727, probably written by the French philosopher Voltaire, who was famous for his wit but not his accuracy. He reported having heard the story about the apple from one of Newton's relatives, but there is no sound evidence to support that claim.

The falling apple will always be associated with Newton's great discovery. Many universities claim to own trees grown from grafts of trees from Newton's orchard, perhaps to remind overworked students that the theory of gravity was no piece of pie but, rather, the fruit of hard labor.

Correct Change Only!

From live bait to neckties, you can buy it all from the world's vending machines.

✳ ✳ ✳ ✳

VENDING MACHINES ARE ubiquitous in today's society—almost every city street corner, it seems, has at least one machine selling something or other. Most vending machines offer the kind of stuff you'd normally expect, such as soft drinks and snacks. But depending on where you live, vending machines can sell much, much more.

Get Your Holy Water Here!

Most people consider vending machines a modern convenience, but the concept is actually eons old. The very first vending machine was developed in the first century A.D. by Hero of Alexandria, a talented engineer who invented a device that dispensed holy water when a coin was inserted into it. The coin landed on a pan attached to a lever, which opened a valve and dispensed a fixed amount of water. A counterweight then pulled the lever back into position, stopping the flow.

It was a pretty ingenious device, but it didn't really catch on; centuries passed before vending machines as we know them really caught on with the general public. The first modern vending machine was installed in London in the 1880s and dispensed postcards. The first American vending machine, introduced in 1888, sold chewing gum at train stations.

Today, you can buy almost anything from a vending machine. Here's a list of some of the more bizarre items sold via vending machines in the United States and abroad:

✳ **Medical Marijuana:** That's right, you can buy dope from vending machines at certain dispensaries in California, but it's not as simple as you might think. You'll need a prescription from a physician noting your medical need, and you'll be fingerprinted by a security guard before being allowed to purchase a vacuum-sealed packet of medicinal weed.

❋ **Live Bait:** Anglers around the United States who can't wait for the bait shop to open can now buy night crawlers from converted sandwich machines. Don't worry about a mess— the night crawlers are delivered in sealed plastic bags containing oxygen tablets.

❋ **Soccer Balls:** How many times have you had to cancel your soccer game for lack of a ball? In New York City, such crises are easily averted by vending machines that sell Nike soccer balls for just $20. Game on!

❋ **Fresh-Baked Pizza:** People love pizza but hate waiting around. The solution? Wonder Pizza, a vending machine that bakes a hot, nine-inch pizza in just minutes. The downside? You get a pizza made by a vending machine.

Only in Japan...

The Japanese are absolutely passionate about their vending machines, the sales from which total more than $50 billion a year. What can you buy from a vending machine in the Land of the Rising Sun? A better question would be: What can't you buy? A recent survey found vending machines selling the following items. Buyer beware!

❋ **Men's Ties:** Appearance is everything in Japan, especially if you're a businessman on the go. But what if you spill soy sauce on your tie during lunch and have a meeting with the big boss immediately afterward? No problem. Just drop a few coins in a nearby vending machine and—voilà!—you get a brand-new tie, ready to wear.

❋ **Farm-Fresh Eggs:** For those times when you just don't feel like walking that extra block to the nearest grocery.

❋ **Ten-Kilo Bags of Rice:** To go with your vending machine eggs, maybe?

* **Umbrellas:** For rainy days and Mondays.

* **Hot Popcorn:** And from Hello Kitty, no less!

* **Hot Ramen Noodles:** Since ramen noodles are a staple among college students, one has to wonder why these machines haven't popped up on college campuses in the United States.

* **Fishing Equipment:** Includes a rod, line, and lures. Don't worry: You can get bait from that other vending machine over there.

* **Toilet Paper:** It's about time someone came up with this idea!

* **Beer:** Nothing like cutting out the middle man.

* **Pornography and Sex Toys:** As a plus, the machine allows the purchaser to sidestep the embarrassment of interacting with another human for this exchange.

* **Designer Condoms:** A nice complement to your vending machine pornography and sex toys.

* **Fresh Flowers:** We'd suggest picking up some flowers to go along with the items above. You can never go wrong with flowers!

* **Frequent Flyer Miles:** Japan Air Lines (JAL) has a machine that reads a credit card and boarding pass and issues frequent flyer miles.

* **Dry Ice:** Sold at supermarkets for keeping frozen food cold until the customer gets home.

* **Water Salad:** Don't feel bad, we don't know what this is, either. But if you want it, there's a machine that will sell it to you.

* **Rhinoceros Beetles:** In the United States, people squash weird bugs. In Japan, they keep them as pets. And apparently buy them from vending machines.

Surviving in Space

It's cold in space... or is it? Here's what it takes to survive the unforgiving conditions of vacuum.

Q: Is there anything out in space?

A: There's always something everywhere, but in space there isn't much of it. Notably, there's no air to speak of. If you somehow found yourself out of the airlock of a spacecraft, you wouldn't last long. If you were out there less than 90 seconds, you didn't hold your breath (that would rupture your lungs), and you received immediate medical care, you might survive. Linger in that environment for longer than 90 seconds, and you're a goner.

Q: Besides enabling you to stay alive, what are the functions of a space suit?

A: It supplies oxygen at a stable internal pressure, and it protects you against heat or cold by regulating temperature. Your space suit also serves as a shield against radiation and those pesky little micrometeoroids, which are things such as space pebbles, sand, and dust. They may not appear threatening, but you'll think otherwise when you realize that they're traveling at an incredibly high rate of speed.

Q: Isn't it hard to keep from freezing in space, which is pretty close to absolute zero?

A: Remember that with no air in space, things lose heat through thermal radiation (slow), not heat conduction (fast). A good contrast might be how quickly you freeze in water that's 35° Fahrenheit (no one can survive long) as opposed to air that's 35° Fahrenheit (a piece of cake for many people). Water conducts the heat right out of your body, and it does so a lot faster than air does. Thus, with solar radiation hitting astronauts in space, and a heated spacecraft, they actually need cooling. Under the suit, the astronaut wears a Liquid Cooling and Ventilation Garment with a water-cooling system.

What to Do When Your Single-Engine Plane Conks Out

1. Locate the nearest landing area. This can be anything from an airport to a cleared field or a parking lot. Roads and highways are also possibilities.

2. Maintain level flight until airspeed is reduced to optimum glide speed (the speed at which the airplane can glide the farthest). Then, begin descent. Continually adjust trim for best glide speed.

3. Check to see if the propeller is still spinning. This indicates that the engine has not seized, and a restart may be possible.

4. Perform flow pattern check and adjustment (right to left) of engine controls and instruments in an attempt to restart the engine. Necessary alterations such as enriching carburetor air-fuel mixture, engaging carburetor heat, changing throttle position, switching on backup electric fuel pump, switching magneto ignition systems, and switching fuel tanks should be performed as deemed necessary.

5. Set discrete transponder code (aka squawk code) to 7700. This shows up as an aircraft in distress on air traffic control radar.

6. Set communications radio to 121.50 MHz and broadcast "MAYDAY." The closest air traffic controller should respond.

7. Adjust flight path as necessary. Example: Perform S-turns or circles to reduce altitude, lower flaps as required, and so forth.

8. On short final approach, shut down fuel and electrics. This lessens the chance of fire upon touchdown.

9. Finally, the best priority sequence during an engine failure or other in-flight emergency is aviate/navigate/communicate—in that precise order.

Fast Facts

* The word "salary" comes from the word "salt," which ancient Roman soldiers received as part of their pay.

* The bikini swimsuit, which debuted in July 1946, was named after the American detonation of an atomic bomb at Bikini Atoll in the South Pacific on July 1. Designer Louis Réard hoped his swimsuit would make a similar explosion in the fashion world.

* Celery was once considered a trendy, high-fashion food. It was served in its own vase, which was placed in the center of the table as a centerpiece.

* New York bookseller Harry Scherman started the first book-of-the-month club in 1926 to target people who lived in remote areas or were just too busy to keep up with new releases. The first selection was *Lolly Willows, or The Loving Huntsman* by Sylvia Townsend Warner, which was sent to 5,000 readers.

* The working title of the Beatles' hit "With a Little Help from My Friends" was "Bad Finger Boogie."

* According to Hollywood lore, silent film actress Norma Talmadge started the tradition of stars putting their footprints in the cement at Grauman's Chinese Theatre when she accidentally stumbled onto the freshly laid sidewalk in front of it in 1927.

* The only active diamond mine in the United States is in Arkansas.

* Ancient Romans believed the walnut was a physical model of the brain: The hard shell was the skull, the papery partition the membrane, and the two pieces of nut were the two hemispheres of the brain.

* Crocodiles and alligators are surprisingly fast on land, but they lack agility. If you're being chased by one, run in a zigzag line.

* Isaac Newton, a notoriously distracted man, claimed that upon arising some mornings he would sit motionless for hours upon the edge of his bed as new thoughts, presumably freed by the night's sleep, occurred to him.

What Makes a Meteorologist

It's one of the most misleading job titles there is, because it has nothing to do with meteors. Here's what it's really all about.

Q: "Meteorologist" just means "weather forecaster," right?

A: That oversimplifies it a lot, because there are so many specialties that fall under the umbrella of meteorology. Most of us aren't the smiling person in the business suit on the local TV news.

Q: Describe some of the specialties—especially yours.

A: I'm an agricultural meteorologist, which incorporates a little bit of agronomy and geology. I'm concerned with temperature and precipitation and wind as they relate to wheat, corn, sorghum, pasture grasses, and whatever else companies cultivate. The Air Force has aviation meteorologists, who study weather's effect on flight. There are research meteorologists, who are currently arguing about whether global warming is going to submerge our coastal cities, or they're trying to gain a better understanding of how the global weather puzzle fits together.

Q: Why can't meteorologists predict the weather more accurately?

A: There are two answers to your question. The first is that we do predict it more accurately, and farther out, with every passing year. In tornado-alley states, any time we see a cumulonimbus (thunderstorm) cloud possibly forming, we have our eyes on it because those clouds can create cyclones. You've seen the pictures: total devastation, yet few lives are lost. That's because we get the word out, and people take cover.

Q: You said two answers, though.

A: Sure did. Weather is a naturally chaotic system, tending to defy predictability. Our work is to beat that chaos. Sometimes we expect one result and another happens—it's that simple.

Predicting weather is like predicting the result of a college football game. If a mid-major team plays the number-three-ranked team in the country, you'll probably bet on the ranked team. But the scrappy mid-major opponent might just pull off the upset. No one could or would have called that one in advance. Same with meteorology.

Q: Can you get a college degree in meteorology?

A: You can get one in atmospheric sciences or meteorology. A typical career path would be to go into the Air Force or Naval ROTC on a scholarship, like I did, and get experience in the armed forces. Of course, if Uncle Sam has too many weatherpeople at that time, there's the risk you could spend your service running a bulldozer platoon or a shore-patrol detachment.

Q: So as an agricultural meteorologist, how do you spend your days?

A: There's data gathering, and the interpretation of that data. In the old days, everything was in the farmer's head: when to plant, how to plant, cultivation tips, how to guess the weather, accounting, etc. Today's agribusinesses replace the farmer's brain with a bunch of experts who make those calls. I'm whichever lobe of the corporate brain decides how much precipitation we'll get, the likelihood of hail, when conditions will be ideal to plant the winter wheat, that kind of thing.

Q: What's the question you get asked most often?

A: "Why do the weather people get it wrong so often?" Sometimes, it's as if I'm the complaint department for all meteorology, and folks think I have the power to fix it. I answer: "The weather people always get it right. Unfortunately, nature changes its mind." In the time it takes them to consider the answer, I'm out of there.

Dynamite! The Life and Times of Alfred Nobel

It was a legacy that was hard to live down. But Alfred B. Nobel—inventor of the explosive dynamite—took what many considered to be a negative and used it to give back to humanity. Nobel's story is one of lifelong learning and perseverance, as well as isolation and loneliness.

✳ ✳ ✳ ✳

The Initial Spark

ALFRED NOBEL WAS born in Stockholm, Sweden, in 1833, the son of Immanuel and Andriette Nobel. His father was a natural inventor who received three mechanical patents at the young age of 24. Yet, due to a series of financial disasters, Nobel's family was mired in bankruptcy. Frail and sickly, he excelled in academics during a brief stint in grade school. The family moved to St. Petersburg, Russia, when Nobel was only nine years old. He showed an amazing facility with languages, eventually becoming fluent in five: Swedish, Russian, French, English, and German.

Nobel's formal education concluded with a series of tutors, including a chemistry professor named Ninin who introduced a teenage Nobel to the volatile liquid nitroglycerine. Discovered by Italian chemist Ascanio Sobrero in 1847, the oily and highly unstable fluid was extremely sensitive to shock, making it a dangerous explosive. Sobrero was convinced that the substance could never be tamed. But Nobel's father had become an expert in manufacturing armaments, such as land and sea mines, so Nobel's interest in nitro served the family business as well.

The end of the Crimean War sent the Nobel and Sons munitions company into bankruptcy. Returning to Stockholm, Nobel and his three brothers formed a new company, appropriately named Brothers Nobel, and continued working with nitroglycerine. The Swedish military showed great interest in the brothers' efforts, so a demonstration was arranged. Nobel filled an iron barrel with half gunpowder and half nitro and urged everyone to step back. The result was a bit *too* successful—a thundering explosion rocked the area, prompting the military to deem the mixture much too risky. They immediately ceased all contact with the Brothers Nobel.

Stockholm Becomes a Boomtown

Nobel became obsessed with calming the wild nitroglycerine, working nonstop for days at a time. By 1863, he succeeded in igniting a mixture of gunpowder and nitro by means of a fuse. The triumph resulted in new manufacturing plants in Sweden, Germany, and Norway, although his efforts were not without disaster.

In the fall of 1864, Nobel's younger brother Emil was mixing chemicals at the plant in Stockholm. More than 40 gallons of nitroglycerine were stored there, so when a tremendous explosion rocked the area, it literally blew its six victims, including Emil, to pieces. For safety's sake, Nobel moved his experiments to a barge in Bockholm Bay, Sweden.

A Flash of Ingenuity

In an 1889 letter, Nobel noted his greatest invention by writing, "I prepared and detonated the first dynamite charge . . . in November 1863," although most sources note the patent date of 1867. Nobel finally calmed nitro by mixing it with kieselguhr—a chalky mineral made mostly of silica. The result was a paste that could be safely handled and rolled into paper tubes. He called his new creation *dynamite*, from the Greek word for "power." Dynamite became a safe means of removing large amounts of earth for mining and tunneling, as well as construction. Establishing worldwide manufacturing and distribution of dynamite, Nobel became wealthy and successful.

But there was a problem with this new invention: When it was stored, the nitro would slowly leak from the dynamite, once again resulting in an unstable and dangerous liquid. Nobel studied the problem and came up with the solution in 1876. He mixed nitro with wood pulp and other minerals, creating a compound Nobel called blasting gelatin. When ignited with a separate detonator, it became an even better method for excavation.

The Final Blast

Nobel knew that his invention would not be used for only constructive purposes. A substance as devastating as dynamite would also be used for violence and crime. Nobel had no wish to be remembered solely as the inventor of dynamite—after all, he amassed more than 350 patents in his career, many in the field of synthetic materials. He also wrote a tragic play, *Nemesis*, late in his life.

An incorrectly placed obituary in an 1888 French newspaper prematurely told of Nobel's passing, referring to him as "the merchant of death." Such a sobriquet did not suit Nobel. In fragile and failing health, he wrote a will in November 1895; the will stipulated that his fortune be used to establish a fund for making annual awards to individuals who "shall have conferred the greatest benefit on mankind." Five prizes would be given, one each in the fields of chemistry, physics, medicine, literature, and peace—"the best work for fraternity between the nations, for the abolition or reduction of standing armies, and for the holding and promotion of peace." (A sixth prize, for economics, was established in 1969.) Nobel, satisfied that he had left the world with a sense of hope and promise, died on December 10, 1896, following a stroke. The first Nobel Prizes were given in 1901.

Past Nobel Prize Winners

Peace Prize

Teddy Roosevelt

Woodrow Wilson

Mikhail Gorbachev

Al Gore

Barack Obama

Martin Luther King Jr.

Jimmy Carter

Mother Teresa

Albert Schweitzer

Literature

Rudyard Kipling

George Bernard Shaw

Sinclair Lewis

Eugene O'Neill

Pearl S. Buck

William Faulkner

Winston Churchill

Ernest Hemingway

Boris Pasternak

John Steinbeck

Jean-Paul Sartre

Toni Morrison

Sciences and Medicine

Marie Curie (twice)

Irene Curie

Linus Pauling

Frederick Sanger (twice)

Wilhelm Roentgen

Guglielmo Marconi

Max Planck

Albert Einstein

Niels Bohr

Aage Bohr

Enrico Fermi

Ivan Pavlov

Economics

Milton Friedman

James Tobin

Also-Rans

Thomas Edison

Robert Oppenheimer

Nikola Tesla

Dmitry Mendeleyev

Mohandas Gandhi

A Fine *Finnish*

When Reuters presented a story about Russian scientists exploring the ocean under the North Pole—and provided visual evidence to back the boasts of the expedition—few people doubted the validity of the claim. But was the polar-cap caper really a Russian ruse?

✳   ✳   ✳   ✳

I N AUGUST 2007, Reuters news agency reported that a group of Russian scientists had successfully explored the bottom of the Arctic Ocean bed, a little more than two and a half miles beneath the North Pole. The story was accompanied by dramatic footage of two Finnish-built *MIR-1* and *MIR-2* submersibles in active exploration of the area. The feat was heralded around the world, and accolades poured in to the Russian Academy of Sciences for its researchers' achievements. Shortly after the story hit the airwaves, a 13-year-old Finnish film fan by the name of Waltteri Seretin noticed peculiar similarities between the footage exhibited by Reuters and some key scenes in the 1997 blockbuster movie *Titanic*.

After careful scrutiny, it was discovered that the footage Reuters used, which purported to prove that the submersibles had reached the bottom of the ocean under the polar cap, consisted of segments from *Titanic* that showed the deep-sea machines exploring the wreckage of the famed ocean liner. Amid howls of a hoax, it was eventually determined that the filmed fodder, sent by the Russian organization merely as an example of what the undersea vessels were capable of accomplishing, had been mislabeled. The usually meticulous medium assumed the footage was faithful and used it to provide a visual accent to a remarkable news item. Embarrassed by the error, Reuters later provided further evidence that the expedition had indeed taken place and that the Russian Academy deserved the praise it had received.

The Way the Future Wasn't

By the year 2000, we were all supposed to be zipping around with tubes of combustible fuel strapped to our backs. What happened?

✳ ✳ ✳ ✳

THE FIRST REAL attempt at developing a personal jet pack was made by German engineers during World War II. Called the Skystormer, it consisted of two simple jet engine tubes, or pulse tubes, attached to a vest. Fortunately—for the Allies, at least—the Skystormers never got far off the ground, probably because pulse tubes that were small enough to be worn carried too little fuel for extended flight.

After the war, the U.S. military sponsored several jet pack projects. In the early 1950s, Wendell Moore of Bell Labs came up with a "jump belt" that relied on canisters of compressed nitrogen gas for thrust. Within two years, the belt had morphed into the Aeropack, a rocket pack that was strapped to the wearer's back and propelled by hydrogen peroxide.

On April 20, 1961, engineer Harold Graham strapped on the Aeropack and became the world's first genuine rocket man by flying 112 feet in 13 seconds at a height of 20 inches above the ground. Graham made at least 64 demonstrations, including one in front of President Kennedy at Fort Bragg, North Carolina. Despite Graham's success, however, the Aeropack never became commercially viable. Expense was one major drawback. Plus, keeping yourself upright while airborne requires a lot of skill.

That doesn't mean jet packs are gone for good. Swiss pilot Yves Rossy gave personal flight enthusiasts a real lift when he flew across the English Channel from Calais, France, to Dover, England, with his winged jet pack on September 26, 2008, covering 21 miles in less than 10 minutes. Things are looking up. The future may be closer than we think.

Open Up and Say "Ugh"!

Leeches, maggots, and scum-sucking fish: All three have earned solid places in the medical community—simply by doing what comes naturally.

✳ ✳ ✳ ✳

The Flies Have It

MAGGOTS ARE NOTHING more than fly larvae—one of the most basic forms of life. For the majority of people recovering from life-threatening wounds, contusions, and limb reattachments, antibiotics provide much of the necessary follow-up care. But for a small percentage of patients who do not respond to modern medicines, maggots slither in to fill the gap.

Applied to a dressing in the form of a small "cage," maggots are attached to almost any area that does not respond well to conventional treatment. The maggot thrives on consuming dead tissue (a process called "debridement") while ignoring the healthy areas. After several days, the maggots are removed—but only after they have consumed up to ten times their own weight in dead tissue, cleaned the wound, and left an ammonialike antimicrobial enzyme behind.

While maggot therapy may not be everyone's cup of tea, it is effective in treating diseases like diabetes, where restricting circulation for any reason can often result in nerve damage and even loss of limbs.

Golden Age of Leeches

Similar to maggots, leeches are small animal organisms that have been used by physicians for over 2,500 years to treat everything from headaches and mental illnesses to—gulp—hemorrhoids. And while they might appear to be on the low end of the evolutionary scale, leeches actually have 32 brains!

Leeches are raised commercially around the world, with the majority coming from France, Hungary, Ukraine, Romania,

Egypt, Algeria, Turkey, and the United States. Used extensively until the 19th century, the "Golden Age of Leeches" was usurped by the adoption of modern concepts of pathology and microbiology. *Hirudotherapy*, or the medicinal use of leeches, has enjoyed a recent resurgence after their demonstrated ability to heal patients when other means have failed.

Leeches feed on the blood of humans and other animals by piercing the skin with a long proboscis. Oftentimes this is the most effective way to drain a postsurgical area of blood, and it can actually facilitate the healing process. When leeches attach to their host, they inject a blood-thinning anticoagulant; they continue until they have consumed up to five times their body weight in blood. The host rarely feels the bite because the leech also injects a local anesthetic before it pierces the skin.

The Doctor (Fish) Is In

Another unlikely medical ally is the doctor fish, found in bathing pools in the Turkish town of Kangal. The therapeutic pools in Kangal are popular destinations for people suffering from fractures, joint traumas, gynecological maladies, and skin diseases. While the pools themselves have a number of beneficial qualities such as the presence of selenium (a mineral that protects against free radicals and helps with wound healing), they are most famous for the doctor fish.

At only 15 to 20 centimeters in length, doctor fish are relatively small and do not physically attach themselves to their hosts like leeches or maggots. Instead, they surround a person's skin, striking and licking it. They are particularly fond of eating psoriatic plaque and other skin diseases that have been softened by the water, eating only the dead and hyper-keratinized tissue while leaving the healthy tissue behind.

While many people might be uncomfortable at the thought of being surrounded by a school of fish feasting on their skin, many actually enjoy the pleasant and relaxing sensation of getting a "micro-massage."

10 Memorable Meteor Crashes

Every day, hundreds of meteors, commonly known as shooting stars, can be seen flying across the night sky. Upon entering Earth's atmosphere, friction heats up cosmic debris, causing streaks of light that are visible to the human eye. Most burn up before they reach the ground. But if one actually survives the long fall and strikes Earth, it is called a meteorite. Here are some of the more memorable meteor strikes in history.

✳ ✳ ✳ ✳

1. The Ensisheim Meteorite, the oldest recorded meteorite, struck Earth on November 7, 1492, in the small town of Ensisheim, France. A loud explosion shook the area before a 330-pound stone dropped from the sky into a wheat field, witnessed only by a young boy. As news of the event spread, townspeople gathered around and began breaking off pieces of the stone for souvenirs. German King Maximilian even stopped by Ensisheim to see the stone on his way to battle the French army. Maximilian decided it was a gift from heaven and considered it a sign that he would emerge victorious in his upcoming battle, which he did. Today bits of the stone are located in museums around the world, but the largest portion is on display in Ensisheim's Regency Palace.

2. The Tunguska Meteorite, which exploded near Russia's Tunguska River in 1908, is still the subject of debate over 100 years later. It didn't leave an impact crater, which has led to speculation about its true nature. But most scientists believe that around 7 A.M. on June 30, a giant meteor blazed through the sky and exploded in a huge ball of fire that flattened forests, blew up houses, and scorched people and animals within 13 miles of the impact site. Scientists continue to explore the region, but neither a meteorite nor a crater have ever been found. Conspiracy theorists contend

that what actually hit Earth that day was an alien spaceship or perhaps even a black hole.

3. Michelle Knapp was idling away at her Peekskill, New York, home on October 9, 1992, when a loud crash gave her a start. When she ran outside to investigate, she found that the trunk of her red Chevy Malibu had been crushed by a football-size rock that passed through the car and dug a crater into her driveway. Michelle alerted police; they impounded the stone and eventually handed it over to the American Museum of Natural History in Manhattan. Turns out the meteor was first spotted over Kentucky, and its descent was caught on more than a dozen amateur videotapes. As for Michelle's Malibu, it was purchased by R. A. Langheinrich Meteorites, a private collectors group that has taken the car on a world tour of museums and scientific institutions.

4. In terms of casualties, a red Malibu is nothing compared to an entire population, but many scientists believe that a meteorite was responsible for the extinction of the dinosaurs. The theory holds that approximately 65 million years ago, a six-mile-wide asteroid crashed into Earth, creating a crater about 110 miles across and blowing tons of debris and dust into the atmosphere. Scientists believe the impact caused several giant tsunamis, global fires, acid rain, and dust that blocked sunlight for several weeks or months, disrupting the food chain and eventually wiping out the dinosaurs. The theory is somewhat controversial, but believers point to the Chicxulub Crater in Yucatán, Mexico, as the striking point of the asteroid. Skeptics say the crater predates the extinction of dinosaurs by 300,000 or so years. Others

believe dinosaurs may have been wiped out by several distinct asteroid strikes, rather than just the widely credited Chicxulub impact. Scientists will likely be debating this for centuries—or at least until another gigantic asteroid strikes Earth and wipes us all out.

5. As Colby Navarro sat at his computer on March 26, 2003, he had no idea that a meteorite was about to come crashing through the roof of his Park Forest, Illinois, home, strike his printer, bounce off the wall, and land near a filing cabinet. The 4-inch-wide rock was part of a meteorite shower that fell on the Chicago area, damaging at least six houses and three cars. Scientists said that before the rock broke apart, it was probably the size of a car. Thank heaven for small favors.

6. The Hoba Meteorite, found on a farm in Namibia in 1920, is the heaviest meteorite ever found. Weighing in at about 66 tons, the rock is thought to have landed more than 80,000 years ago. Despite its gargantuan size, the meteorite left no crater, which scientists credit to the fact that it entered Earth's atmosphere at a long, shallow angle. It lay undiscovered until 1920, when a farmer reportedly hit it with his plow. Over the years, erosion, vandalism, and scientific sampling have shrunk the rock to about 60 tons, but in 1955, the Namibian government designated it a national monument, and it is now a popular tourist attraction.

7. Santa had to compete for airspace on Christmas Eve 1965, when Britain's largest meteorite sent thousands of fragments showering down on Barwell, Leicestershire. Museums immediately started offering money for fragments of the rock, which caused the previously sleepy town to be inundated with meteorite hunters and other adventurers from around the world. Decades later, the phenomenon continues to captivate meteorite enthusiasts, and fragments can often be found for sale online.

8. Arizona would be short one giant hole in the ground if it wasn't for a 160-foot meteorite landing in its northern desert about 50,000 years ago, which left an impact crater about a mile wide and 570 feet deep. Known today as the Barringer Crater, or Meteor Crater, the site is now a popular tourist attraction. Scientists believe the meteorite that caused the crater was traveling about 28,600 miles per hour when it struck Earth, causing an explosion about 150 times more powerful than the Hiroshima atomic bomb. The meteorite itself probably melted in the explosion, spreading a mist of molten nickel and iron across the surrounding landscape.

9. At 186 miles wide, Vredefort Dome in South Africa is the site of the biggest impact crater on Earth. And at an estimated two billion years old, it makes the Chicxulub Crater look like a spring chicken. Today, the original crater, which was caused by a 6-mile-wide meteorite, is mostly eroded away, but what remains is a dome created when the walls of the crater slumped, pushing granite rocks from the center of the meteorite strike.

10. Second in size only to the Vredefort Dome, the Sudbury Basin is a 40-mile-long, 16-mile-wide, 9-mile-deep crater caused by a giant meteorite that struck Earth about 1.85 billion years ago. Located in Greater Sudbury, Ontario, the crater is actually home to about 162,000 people. In 1891, the Canadian Copper Company began mining copper from the basin, but it was soon discovered that the crater also contained nickel, which is much more valuable, so the miners changed course. Today, the International Nickel Company operates out of the basin and mines about 10 percent of the world's nickel supply from the site.

Sounds for Space

This gold record doesn't climb the charts—it sails through deep space.

✳ ✳ ✳ ✳

SOMEWHERE IN SPACE, two unmanned scientific probes—Voyagers 1 and 2—move through previously unexplored areas of our solar system. NASA launched the twin probes in 1977, hoping they would uncover valuable information about Jupiter, Saturn, and the outer planets. And indeed they have: The spacecraft found active volcanoes on one of Jupiter's moons and a surprising amount of structure in Saturn's rings. *Voyager 2* launched first, but *Voyager 1*, moving at a brisk 38,000 miles per hour, has probed the farthest.

Aboard each *Voyager* is a 12-inch, gold-plated copper disc called The Golden Record. This disc is a time capsule of sorts, containing a hodgepodge of sounds and images intended to convey to extraterrestrials what life on our planet is like. That's right: It's an LP for aliens—on the infinitesimally small chance that they exist and that the record will reach them in the distant future.

Astronomer Carl Sagan curated the project along with his wife, Ann Druyan, and a committee of scientists. The group selected 115 images to depict human life, as well as sounds from nature, including birdsongs, wild dogs, and wind. They also included music from various cultures, including Peruvian panpipes, an Indian raga, the song "Johnny B. Goode" by Chuck Berry, greetings in 55 languages, and printed messages from U.S. President Jimmy Carter and UN Secretary-General Kurt Waldheim.

As Sagan noted, the likelihood of an advanced civilization encountering the record is slim, yet "the launching of this 'bottle' into the cosmic 'ocean' says something very hopeful about life on this planet." In 2008, *Voyager 1* slipped out and away from our solar system—who knows who (or what) will find its cargo?

Loudest Noises

What is the loudest noise ever made? The answer is subjective, but here are a few impressive noisemakers of note.

✳   ✳   ✳   ✳

Krakatoa: When this volcano erupted on August 27, 1883, scientists estimated the volume at 180 decibels. The cataclysmic blast was so loud that it was heard nearly 3,000 miles away.

Fireworks: They can reach a deafening 150 decibels at their bursting point. But that's usually far, far away from human ears.

One-Ton Bomb: Anyone standing within 250 feet will experience 210 decibels. But that'd probably be the least of your worries.

Tunguska Event: On June 30, 1908, a comet or meteor exploded over the uninhabited Tunguska region of Russia with the force of a 1,000-megaton bomb. The blast flattened trees for miles, and scientists have estimated the noise at between 300 and 315 decibels—almost certainly the loudest single event in history.

Gunfire: Markspeople wear ear protection for a reason—gunfire can produce blasts as loud as 155 decibels.

Space Shuttle Launch: NASA protocol requires that anyone watching a shuttle launch on site be a minimum of a half-mile away. Why? Because these space-faring juggernauts unleash an overpowering 170 decibels as they race toward the heavens.

Blue Whales: The cries of these massive animals can reach more than 185 decibels and can travel for miles through the water. As a result, the blue whale is regarded as the loudest creature on earth.

Noises by the Numbers

125 dB: the volume at which people begin to experience pain

190 dB: the volume at which most people's eardrums burst

198 dB: the volume at which death can occur

Magnetic Hill Phenomenon

This worldwide phenomenon describes places where objects—including cars in neutral gear—move uphill on a slightly sloping road, seemingly defying gravity.

✳ ✳ ✳ ✳

MONCTON, IN New Brunswick, Canada, lays claim to one of the more famous magnetic hills, called, appropriately, Magnetic Hill. Over the years, it has also been called Fool's Hill and Magic Hill. Since the location made headlines in 1931, hundreds of thousands of tourists have flocked there to witness this phenomenon for themselves.

Much to the dismay of paranormal believers, people in science once assumed that a magnetic anomaly caused this event. But advanced physics has concluded that it is due "to the visual anchoring of the sloping surface to a gravity-relative eye level whose perceived direction is biased by sloping surroundings." In nonscientific jargon: It is an optical illusion.

Papers published in the journal of the Association of Psychological Science supported this conclusion based on a series of experiments with models. They found that if the horizon cannot be seen or is not level then people may be fooled by objects that they expect to be vertical but aren't. False perspective is also a culprit; think, for example, of a line of poles on the horizon that seem to get larger or smaller depending on distance.

Engineers with plumb lines, one made of iron and one made of stone, demonstrated that a slope appearing to go uphill might in reality be going downhill. A good topographical map may also be sufficient to show which way the land is really sloping.

Other notable magnetic hills can be found in Wisconsin, Pennsylvania, California, Florida, Barbados, Scotland, Italy, Australia, Greece, and South Korea.

The Jeep

As the Nazi regime scored victories in Europe, American military planners foresaw the need for a lightweight all-terrain vehicle.

✳ ✳ ✳ ✳

I N EARLY 1940, the Army Quartermaster Corps issued a call to manufacturers to produce a prototype all-terrain universal military vehicle. The military gave interested parties just 49 days to complete the task. The Army's Ordnance Technical Committee set out the following specifications for the new vehicle:

* Vehicle weight of less than 1,300 pounds. This specification was later deemed unrealistic and raised to 2,160 pounds.

* Four-wheel drive.

* A wheelbase of 80 inches or less, a tread of 47 inches or less, and a minimum of 6.25 inches of ground clearance.

* An engine that could produce 85 pound-feet of torque.

* A payload capability of 600 pounds.

Vying for the Contract

While more than 135 companies were invited to participate, the American Bantam Car Company and Willys–Overland were the only two to express interest in the project. The Ford Motor Company was courted because of its production capabilities, but initially declined the offer to participate.

Bantam was the first to respond to the government's challenge with actual blueprints. The company enlisted the help of Karl Probst, a Detroit-area freelance automotive engineer. Probst began work on a prototype on July 17, 1940, and in only two days he had finished the plans for the Bantam model.

Government officials examined Bantam's design, and after receiving the go-ahead, Bantam engineers hand-built their working model in just seven weeks. Company officials delivered the prototype to army officers at Camp Holabird, Maryland, on September 23, 1940. After being subjected to grueling tests over the course of several weeks, the Bantam vehicle, Model BRC-40, was deemed a success in virtually every category.

Despite Willys's failure to submit a prototype by the deadline and the Ford Motor Company's complete lack of interest in the project, designers and engineers from both companies were allowed access to the army's trials of the Bantam-designed vehicle, as well as to Bantam's blueprints. Willys and Ford subsequently built prototypes using many of Bantam's design features. Though both late-arriving manufacturers failed to meet the stated deadline and had problems with their designs—the Willys vehicle was too heavy, while the Ford model had insufficient engine power—army officials allowed the two latecomers to participate in the process. Both companies eventually submitted prototype vehicles for testing.

In March 1941, the military awarded contracts to all three companies to produce 1,500 vehicles each. Four months later, army officials had tested each company's model in the field. Bantam's lack of mass-production facilities and poor financial position led to the army awarding the final contract to Willys. The Willys model also won on the merits of its more powerful engine, having a silhouette lower to the ground, and having a lower production cost per vehicle.

Bantam vehicles, which had already been delivered to the army, were shipped to Britain as the new Willys model was delivered. The Willys vehicles were given to America's Russian allies through the Lend-Lease Act. After losing the contract to Willys, Bantam quit the car business and switched production to torpedo motors, various aircraft parts, and trailers.

In order to meet production requirements, Willys granted the government a nonexclusive license to their design. This move gave the government the right to let other companies manufacture the vehicle, and Ford was quickly awarded a contract to produce it based solely on its production facilities.

Why Were They Called Jeeps?

Good question. One theory is that the name came from the army designation "GP," an acronym Ford used to differentiate between vehicles it produced for government and civilian use: The letter "G" stood for government, while the letter "P" signified the size of the wheelbase, which in this case was 80 inches. Others claim the name referred to cartoonist E. C. Segar's cartoon character Eugene the Jeep, Popeye's impish animal friend.

The first public reference to the name came in a *Washington Daily News* story, when a reporter witnessed a jeep demonstration on the steps of the Capitol. Her story ran with a photo caption, "Jeep Creeps Up Capitol Steps."

Jeep Makes Its Mark

More than 600,000 jeeps were pressed into service in every theater of operation during World War II. Journalist Ernie Pyle was quoted as saying the jeep was "as faithful as a dog, as strong as a mule, and as agile as a goat." Besides their reconnaissance role, jeeps were also used as ambulances, weapons platforms, and communications and supply vehicles. The jeep was light enough to be packed into C-47 cargo planes and dropped with airborne troops behind enemy lines. The Canadians, British, and Russians also used jeeps in their armed forces.

The first civilian-use Jeep (the name became a registered trademark) was produced in 1945. The Willys-Overland CJ-2A was initially marketed as a vehicle for construction workers and farmers. Today, the Chrysler Corporation, which owns the Jeep trademark, has more than 1,000 registrations for the jeep worldwide.

Fast Facts

✳ The Chinese emperor Shen-Nung was the first person to use acupuncture as a medical treatment in 2700 B.C.

✳ Christmas wasn't declared a national holiday in the United States until 1890.

✳ When Grover Cleveland beat incumbent Benjamin Harrison in 1892, he became the first (and, so far, only) person to win nonconsecutive terms as president.

✳ Of all the people who eventually signed the Declaration of Independence, only John Hancock and Charles Thomson actually signed it on July 4. Most of the others didn't sign until August 2; the last signature was added five years later.

✳ Rivals John Adams and Thomas Jefferson died on the same day, July 4, 1826—the 50th anniversary of the signing of the Declaration of Independence.

✳ William Henry Harrison was the first U.S. president to die in office (in 1841). He also holds the record for the shortest term in office—32 days.

✳ The phrase "wear your heart on your sleeve" originated in the Middle Ages, when young men and women drew names to see who their valentines would be. They would then wear these names on their sleeves for one week.

✳ The phrase "second string," which today means "replacement" or "backup," originated in the Middle Ages, when an archer carried a second string in case the one on his bow broke.

✳ Although Ohio is officially the 17th state in the Union, Congress forgot to vote on the resolution to make it a state until August 7, 1953, which technically makes it the 47th state.

✳ James Buchanan was the only president to remain a bachelor while in office.

How It All Began

Alarmed and Dangerous

Historians say the Greeks devised an alarm clock as early as 250 B.C. that used rising water to trigger a mechanical whistle, 15th-century Germans had a large iron wall piece rigged with bronze bells, and chimes have sounded on clocks since the Middle Ages.

But the modern alarm clock we all know and love (or hate) got its start in Concord, New Hampshire, in 1787, courtesy of clockmaker Levi Hutchins. He gutted a large brass clock, placed the innards inside a pine cabinet, and inserted a gear tripped to sound at 4 A.M. (However, it couldn't be set for any other time.)

Hutchins's idea worked, but he never patented it. That credit goes to the Seth Thomas Company, which, in 1876, patented a bedside windup alarm clock that could be set for any hour. Eighty years later, General Electric–Telechron introduced the snooze alarm (thank goodness).

Wrist Assured

At the turn of the 20th century, manly men carried pocket watches. Only women wore the more-jewelry-than-timepiece "wristlet," popularized by Parisian ladies in the early 1900s.

But wartime changed this. Pocket watches were clumsy and awkward in combat, so soldiers began fitting them into leather straps to wear on their wrists. This wasn't entirely new: In the 1880s, Swiss watchmaker Girard-Perregaux "armed" the German Imperial Navy with watches on leather straps, which proved essential for synchronizing attacks. British soldiers even credited watches for their victory in the Anglo–Boer War in South Africa. American troops didn't discover the wristwatch until they joined the British in World War I. As U.S. soldiers returned home sporting souvenir watches on their wrists, the gadget quickly went from being a frou-frou fashion piece to a badge of bravery that civilians wanted, too.

Franklin Flies a Kite

As it turns out, Benjamin Franklin did not discover electricity. What's more, the kite he famously flew in 1752 while conducting an experiment was not struck by lightning. If it had been, Franklin would be remembered as a colonial publisher and assemblyman killed by his own curiosity.

✳   ✳   ✳   ✳

Before Ben

B LESSED WITH ONE of the keenest minds in history, Benjamin Franklin was a scientific genius who made groundbreaking discoveries in the basic nature and properties of electricity. Electrical science, however, dates to 1600, when Dr. William Gilbert, physician to Queen Elizabeth, published a treatise about his research on electricity and magnetism. European inventors who later expanded on Gilbert's knowledge included Otto von Guericke of Germany, Charles Francois Du Fay of France, and Stephen Gray of England.

The Science of Electricity

Franklin became fascinated with electricity after seeing a demonstration by an itinerant showman (and doctor) named Archibald Spencer in Boston in 1743. Two years later, he bought a Leyden jar—a contraption invented by a Dutch scientist that used a glass container wrapped in foil to create a crude battery. Other researchers had demonstrated the properties of the device, and Franklin set about to increase its capacity to generate electricity while testing his own scientific hypotheses. Among the principles he established was the conservation of charge, one of the most important laws of physics. In a paper published in 1750, he announced the discovery of the induced charge and broadly outlined the existence of the electron. His experiments led him to coin many of the terms currently used in the science of electricity, including "battery," "conductor," "condenser," "charge," "discharge," "uncharged," "negative," "minus," "plus," "electric shock," and "electrician."

As Franklin came to understand the nature of electricity, he began to theorize about the electrical nature of lightning. In 1751, he outlined in a British scientific journal his idea for an experiment that involved placing a long metal rod on a high tower or steeple to draw an electric charge from passing thunder clouds, which would throw off visible electric sparks. A year later, French scientist Georges-Louis Leclerc successfully conducted such an experiment.

The Kite Runner

Franklin had not heard of Leclerc's success when he undertook his own experiment in June 1752. Instead of a church spire, he affixed his kite to a sharp, pointed wire. To the end of his kite string he tied a key, and to the key a ribbon made of silk (for insulation). While flying his kite on a cloudy day as a thunderstorm approached, Franklin noticed that loose threads on the kite string stood erect, as if they had been suspended from a common conductor. The key sparked when he touched it, showing it was charged with electricity. But had the kite actually been struck by lightning, Franklin would likely have been killed, as was Professor Georg Wilhelm Richmann of St. Petersburg, Russia, when he attempted the same experiment a few months later.

The Lightning Rod

Although Franklin did not discover electricity, he did uncover many of its fundamental principles and proved that lightning is, in fact, electricity. He used his knowledge to create the lightning rod, an invention that today protects land structures and ships at sea. He never patented the lightning rod but instead generously promoted it as a boon to humankind. In 21st-century classrooms, the lightning rod is still cited as a classic example of the way fundamental science can produce practical inventions.

Cybernetic Stars

Robotlike machines date back nearly 2,000 years to the ancient Greeks, who designed impressive automatons—mechanical human and animal figures. But true robots—machines that can sense and respond to their environment independently—weren't a reality until the mid-20th century. Since then, engineers have created robots with a wide range of abilities. Here are some of the more notable robots.

❋　❋　❋　❋

The First Robots

THE FIRST TRUE robots were Elmer and Elsie, two machines created in the 1940s by neurophysiologist William Grey Walter. Each of Grey's bulky robots, which he called *tortoises*, had three wheels, a light-detecting photoelectric cell, electric sensors that detected contact with other objects, a rechargeable telephone battery, and an electronic circuit comprising two vacuum tubes enclosed in a clear plastic shell. The robots would move toward light sources and retreat when the light got very bright and when they encountered obstacles. When Walter attached lights to each of them, they would even dance with each other.

The Smallest Robot

In the future, we may think nothing of microscopic nanobots fixing up our bodies and cleaning our houses. But today, it's very difficult to shrink robotic technology. There are a few wee 'bots, however—depending on how loosely you define "robot."

The smallest contender, developed at Dartmouth, measures 250 micrometers by 60 micrometers—about the width of a human hair. It's a tiny silicon strip that moves along like an inchworm by alternately extending and scrunching itself. However, it only works when placed on a grid of electrodes, which provides power and guides the robot's motion. So, it's not a truly autonomous robot.

In 2007, roboticists at the Technion–Israel Institute of Technology announced that they had designed a robot with similar constraints: a millimeter-long machine designed to crawl through blood vessels. In this case, an external magnetic field powers and guides the robot.

The smallest fully autonomous robot with a built-in power supply is a tracked vehicle developed at Sandia National Laboratories. The microbot is one centimeter tall and a quarter of a cubic inch at the base—small enough to literally turn on a dime. It boasts eight kilobytes of brain power, runs on three watch batteries, and can zip along at 20 inches per minute.

The Deadliest Robots

As of 2009, the U.S. military had 12,000 robots on the ground and 7,000 in the air. The deadliest of the bunch are the Predator and the Reaper uncrewed aircrafts. The military initially used the $4.5 million Predator as an unarmed reconnaissance drone, loaded with cameras and sensors But after 9/11, the military reconfigured it to carry two laser-guided Hellfire missiles. The Predator's newer, bigger cousin, the Reaper, can carry 14 Hellfire missiles or four missiles and two 500-pound bombs. Most of the 200 Predators and 30 Reapers in the U.S. fleet are controlled via satellite by crews at a base outside Las Vegas. The drones handle some tasks autonomously, but human controllers always decide whether to attack possible targets. The total Predator and Reaper body count isn't clear, but the Air Force says that in 2007 and 2008, the drones fired missiles in 244 missions in Afghanistan and Iraq. Drones have taken out at least 11 al-Qaeda leaders.

The Top Android

Honda bills its 43 ASIMO as "the world's most advanced humanoid robot," and most people would agree. The culmination of more than 20 years of research and development, ASIMO can walk, dance, climb stairs, and respond to commands. With a top speed of 3.7 miles per hour, the current version also holds the record as fastest robotic runner.

Chapter Twelve

Flora and Fauna

Strange Plants

When the first Western explorers returned from the Congo, they told tall tales of plants that demanded human flesh. Although we now know that no such plants exist, there are plenty of weird and scary plants in the world—enough for a little shop of horrors.

✳ ✳ ✳ ✳

Kudzu—Native to China and Japan, when this vine was brought to the United States in 1876, its ability to grow a foot per day quickly made it a nuisance. With 400-pound roots, 4-inch-diameter stems, and a resistance to herbicides, it is nearly impossible to eliminate. Kudzu currently covers more than two million acres of land in the southern United States.

Cow's Udder—This shrub is known alternately as Nipple Fruit, Titty Fruit, and Apple of Sodom. (Did a group of 4th graders name it?) A relative of the tomato, it sports poisonous orange fruit that look like inflated udders.

King Monkey Cup—The largest of carnivorous pitcher plants traps its prey in pitchers up to 14 inches long and 6 inches wide. It then digests them in a half gallon of enzymatic fluid. The plant has been known to catch scorpions, mice, rats, and birds.

Titan Arum—Known in Indonesia as a "corpse flower," this plant blooms in captivity only once every three years. The six-foot-tall flower weighs more than 140 pounds and looks, as its

Latin name says, like a "giant shapeless penis." Even less appealingly, it secretes cadaverene and putrescine, odor compounds that are responsible for its smell of rotting flesh.

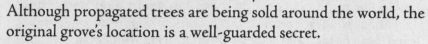

Wollemi pine—Previously known only through 90-million-year-old fossils, the Wollemi pine tree was rediscovered in Australia in 1994. Fewer than 100 adult trees exist today. Although propagated trees are being sold around the world, the original grove's location is a well-guarded secret.

Rafflesia arnoldii—Also known as a "meat flower," this parasitic plant has the largest single bloom of any plant, measuring three feet across. It can hold several gallons of nectar, and its smell has been compared to "buffalo carcass in an advanced stage of decomposition."

Hydnora africana—This parasitic plant is found in Namibia and South Africa growing on the roots of the Euphorbia succulent. Most of the plant is underground, but the upper part of the flower looks like a gaping, fang-filled mouth. And, because smelling like rotting flesh is de rigueur in the weird-plant world, it emits a putrid scent to attract dung or carrion beetles.

Aquatic duckweed—Also known as watermeal because it resembles cornmeal floating on the surface of water, this is the smallest flowering plant on earth. The plant is only .61 millimeter long, and the edible fruit, similar to a (very tiny) fig, is about the size of a grain of salt.

Baobab tree—The baobab is the world's largest succulent, reaching heights of 75 feet. It can also live for several thousand years. Its strange, root-like branches gave rise to the legend that the baobab grows upside down. The enormous trunks are often hollowed out and used as shelters.

Freaky Facts: Frogs

Kermit, Jeremiah the Bullfrog, Prince Charming—frogs are clearly special creatures with many talents. They're also sort of gross. Check out these freaky frog facts that are sure to delight and disgust.

※ At about four weeks old, tadpoles get a bunch of very tiny teeth, which help them turn their food into mushy, oxygenated particles.

※ Horned lizards are often called horny toads, though they're not actually amphibians. Horny toads can squirt blood from their eyeballs to attack predators. This only happens in extreme cases, but they can shoot it up to three feet, so watch out.

※ The Goliath frog of West Africa is the largest frog in the world. When fully stretched out, this sucker is often more than two and a half feet long!

※ When frogs aren't near water, they will often secrete mucus to keep their skin moist.

※ Frogs typically eat their old skin once it's been shed.

※ One European common toad lived to be 40 years old, making it the oldest known toad on record.

※ While swallowing, a frog's eyeballs retreat into its head, applying pressure that helps push food down its throat.

※ A frog's ear is connected to its lungs. When a frog's eardrum vibrates, its lungs do, too. This special pressure system keeps frogs from hurting themselves when they blast their seriously loud mating calls.

※ The earliest known frog fossils were found in Arizona and are thought to be about 190 million years old.

Well, Blow Me Down!

Will a house survive a tornado if its windows are opened?
Explosive evidence reveals the crushing answer.

✳ ✳ ✳ ✳

WITH ROARING WINDS that can exceed 300 miles per hour, anything in a tornado's path is in peril. Accordingly, people have devised ways to protect themselves and their homes should one of these whirlwinds come visiting. The idea that opening windows will save one's home represents humankind's hubris against a clearly overwhelming force.

Breezy Logic

This popular idea, aimed at saving a dwelling, instructs occupants to open windows to equalize pressure differentials between their structure and the storm. This, it is said, will keep the home from exploding should the funnel cloud pass overhead. This may sound plausible, but it stems from logic that's severely flawed. In fact, insurance adjusters reserve a name for homes "protected" in such a manner. They are labeled "destroyed." Here's why.

Before a tornado's low-pressure effect is encountered (at the very center of the vortex), winds ranging from 100 to 200 mph will be felt. These gusts usually contain flying debris from devastated structures and other objects. Such projectiles will create vent holes in a building that would theoretically protect it from a drop in pressure. Yet such homes are routinely smashed.

Don't Bother

A study by Texas Tech's Institute for Disaster Research found that the pressure drop experienced in a 260-mph tornado is about 10 percent less than that of surrounding pressures. Most dwellings can vent this difference through existing openings. But the point is moot, anyway. A violent tornado will blow a house apart quicker than you can read this sentence. Open windows have little effect against such devastating fury.

The Cat Toss Conundrum

Cats are curious creatures: Many people believe that a dropped kitty will right itself and land safely on its feet, only to step away aloof and unaffected.

❋ ❋ ❋ ❋

A BELGIAN LEGEND HAS it that in A.D. 962, Baldwin III, Count of Ypres, threw several cats from a tower. It must have been a slow news year, because the residents of Ypres named the last day of their annual town fair "Cat Wednesday" and commemorated it by having the village jester throw live cats from a belfry tower—a height of almost 230 feet. But there's no need to call PETA: The last time live cats were used for this ceremony was in 1817, and since then stuffed animals have been thrown in their place.

As cruel as this custom was, it is unclear whether the cat toss was meant to kill cats or to demonstrate their resilience. After that last live toss in 1817, the village record keeper wrote the following: "In spite of the height of the fall, the animal ran off quickly so that it might never be caught again in a similar ceremony." How could the cat have survived such a tumble?

Twist and Meow

Cats have an uncanny knack for righting themselves in midair. Even if a cat starts falling headfirst, it almost always hits the ground on its paws. The people of Ypres weren't the only ones amazed and amused by this feline feat. In 1894, French physiologist Etienne-Jules Marey decided to get to the bottom of the mechanics of cat-righting by taking a series of rapid photographs of a cat in midfall. Marey held a cat upside down by its paws and then dropped it several feet onto a cushion.

The resulting 60 sequential photos demonstrated that as the cat fell, it initiated a complex maneuver, rotating the front of its body clockwise and then the rear part counterclockwise. This motion conserved energy and prevented the cat from spinning in the air. It then pulled in its legs, reversed the twist again, and extended its legs slightly to land with minimal impact.

High-Rise Syndrome

The story gets even more interesting. In 1987, two New York City veterinarians examined 132 cases involving cats that had fallen out of the windows of high-rise buildings (the average fall was five and a half stories). Ninety percent of the cats survived, though some sustained serious injuries. When the vets analyzed the data, they found that, predictably, the cats suffered progressively greater injuries as the height from which they fell increased. But this pattern continued only up to seven stories; above that, the farther the cat fell, the greater chance it had of surviving relatively unharmed.

The researchers named this peculiar phenomenon High-Rise Syndrome and explained it this way: A cat that fell about five stories reached its terminal velocity—that is, maximum downward speed—of 60 miles per hour. If it fell any distance beyond that, it had the time not only to right itself in midair but also to relax and spread itself out to slow down its fall, much like a flying squirrel or a parachute.

✳ **The large cats of the world are divided into two groups—those that roar, such as tigers and African lions, and those that purr. Mountain lions purr, hiss, scream, and snarl, but they cannot roar.**

✳ **Ancient Egyptian families mourned the death of a pet cat by shaving off their eyebrows.**

All Creatures Great and Obscure

The animal kingdom is vast and varied, full of exotic specimens. Yet, there are quite a few inhabitants of the animal kingdom that you've probably never heard of. Here are a few that might fascinate and amaze you ... or just give you the creeps.

✳ ✳ ✳ ✳

Raccoon Dog: Named for its similarity in appearance to a raccoon, this solitary creature is actually an omnivorous member of the canine family. Found in China, Korea, and Japan, the raccoon dog has the least-sharp teeth of the canine family. It also plays dead to avoid predators and other natural enemies.

Cookiecutter Shark: This small shark, infrequently seen by human eyes, has big lips and a belly that glows a pale blue-green color to help camouflage it from prey. Its name comes from the small, cookie-shaped bite marks it leaves.

Vampire Squid: This fast-moving, gelatinous little squid has the largest eyes relative to its body of any animal in the world. Though it has no ink sac, with the aid of photophores it is able to light up its entire body. It is also able to invert itself, making it appear as if it's covered in suckers and sharp spikes.

Blobfish: Found lurking in the depths off the coasts of Australia and Tasmania, this strange-looking creature has been called the "most disgusting fish in the world." The blobfish does not have (nor need) muscles because its jellylike flesh is lighter than water, allowing it to simply float in the high-pressure areas of the ocean.

Pistol Shrimp: These striped crustaceans differ from other shrimp in that they have claws of differing sizes, one larger than the other. The pistol shrimp pulls back the larger claw and snaps it shut, producing a loud sound that stuns its prey. It has been said that the noise produced by a colony of these shrimp snapping their claws in unison is so loud it can block the sonar tracking of nearby submarines.

Shoebill: Discovered in the 19th century, this large bird is named for its beak, which is indeed shaped like a shoe. A long-legged, broad-winged relative of the stork, the shoebill stands four feet tall and has a seven-foot-wide wingspan. It also has a sharp hook on the end of its hefty beak, which is used for catching prey such as catfish.

Suckerfooted Bat: A rare, diminutive bat, the suckerfoot is found in the western forests of Madagascar. It has small suction cups on its hands allowing it to cling to smooth surfaces as it glides through the forests in search of its next meal.

The Yeti Crab: The pincers of this recently discovered crustacean from the depths of the South Pacific Ocean are covered in yellowish, bacteria-filled hair. Scientists hypothesize that the crabs possibly eat the bacteria, or perhaps use it to detoxify poisonous minerals.

Chinese Giant Salamander: This particular salamander, found in the lakes and streams of China, is the world's largest living amphibian. Though its wrinkled appearance is similar to that of other salamanders, this variety can grow to over five feet in length, making it the undisputed king of salamanders.

Shrike: At first glance, this little bird seems gentle and charming; however, the shrike is infamous for catching and impaling its prey (usually insects, lizards, or small mammals) on thorns. This ultimately helps the bird tear its victims apart, for smaller, more manageable meals. The torn carcasses are then left on the thorns, so the shrike can return for snacks.

Star-Nosed Mole: This lowland-living critter resembles a common mole, but with a nose that resembles a pink, many-armed starfish. Still, those weird nasal tentacles have nearly 100,000 minute touch receptors. Scientists have recently found that the star-nosed mole is also able to sniff underwater, by quickly inhaling the air bubbles that are blown out through its nostrils.

Oregon's Ghost Forests

The gnarled, twisted shapes rising up from Oregon's coastline are memorials to the magnificent forests that stood ages ago. These "ghost forests" are shrouded in mystery: What caused the mighty trees to fall? Why are they still here? And where are they going?

* * * *

THESE GROVES OF ancient tree stumps—called "ghost forests" because of their age (approximately 1,000 to 4,000 years old) and bleak appearance—emerge along the 46-mile stretch between Lincoln City and Tillamook. For years, tourists and scientists alike have been perplexed by the forests' strange beauty. Some trees extend out of the sand like angular sculptures; others are just visible as tiny tips poking through the water.

All are remnants of the giant Sitka spruce forests, which towered 200 feet above Oregon's coastline for years. That is, until something knocked them down.

A Cataclysmic Collapse

No one knows for sure just what that "something" was, but experts agree that for such forests to be preserved, the trees must have been very suddenly submerged in sand, clay, or mud. This submersion would not only kill the trees but also keep them frozen in time by shutting off their oxygen.

The original (and still widely held) belief is that there was a giant earthquake, which suddenly dropped the ground 25 feet below sea level and immersed the trees in sand and water. Another theory is that it wasn't an earthquake but a tsunami that struck, drowning the trees under a massive tidal wave. A third theory suggests that it was a combination of the two—an earthquake buried the trees and then caused a tsunami that lopped off the tree tops, leaving only stumps behind. A newer theory is that the trees died as a result of sudden landscape changes, with sand levels rising over the course of a few decades (that's "sudden" when you're speaking in geologic terms) to eventually overwhelm the forest.

Seasonal Specters

For decades, ghost forests were seen only occasionally during the harsh winter months, when violent waves strip away layers of sand, exposing the tree stumps just briefly before the calmer waves of spring and summer carry sand back to the shores and bury them once again.

But lately, the ghost forests have become less of a rarity. Since 1998, more and more trees have been popping up—the result of a decade of rough winters, washing away as much as 17 feet of sand in some areas, combined with less sand recovery in the spring and summer. In 2007, Arch Cape saw stumps for the first time in 40 years, along with the mud-cliff remains of a forest floor, and in the winter of 2008, an unprecedented ten-foot drop in sand level revealed a new forest at Cape Kiwanda.

Just a few miles away at Hug Point, the waves uncovered stumps that could date back 80,000 years to the Pleistocene era, when woolly mammoths and saber-toothed tigers roamed the earth. And the remains of roots marred by saws at Moolack Beach show that early European settlers harvested the trees for fire and shelter. Oregon's most impressive and most famous ghost forest is found at Neskowin, where 100 twisted shapes can be seen poking through the water year-round.

But the erosion that has newly exposed these phantom forests may also be destroying them. The stumps at Neskowin and Cape Lookout are reportedly showing so much that waves are ripping them out by the roots.

Some experts believe this increased erosion means the coastline is gradually disappearing—and taking the ghost forests with it. Perhaps soon, the ghost forests of Oregon will haunt only our memories.

The Tunguska Event

What created an explosion 1,000 times greater than the atomic bomb at Hiroshima and destroyed 80 million trees, but left no hole in the ground?

✳ ✳ ✳ ✳

The Event

ON JUNE 30, 1908, a powerful explosion ripped through the remote Siberian wilderness near the Tunguska River. Witnesses, from nomadic herdsmen and passengers on a train to a group of people at the nearest trading post, reported seeing an object streak through the sky and explode into an enormous fireball. The resulting shockwave flattened approximately 830 square miles of forest. Seismographs in England recorded the event twice, once as the initial shockwave passed and then again after it had circled the planet. A huge cloud of ash reflected sunlight from over the horizon across Asia and Europe. People reported there being enough light in the night sky to facilitate reading.

Incredibly, nearly 20 years passed before anyone visited the site. Everyone had a theory of what happened, and none of it good. Outside Russia, however, the event itself was largely unknown. The English scientists who recorded the tremor, for instance, thought that it was simply an earthquake. Inside Russia, the unstable political climate of the time was not conducive to mounting an expedition. Subsequently, the economic and social upheaval created by World War I and the Russian Revolution made scientific expeditions impossible.

Looking for a Hole in the Ground

In 1921, mineralogist Leonid A. Kulik was charged by the Mineralogical Museum of St. Petersburg with locating meteorites that had fallen inside the Soviet Union. Having read old newspapers and eyewitness testimony from the Tunguska region, Kulik convinced the Academy of Sciences in 1927 to fund an expedition to locate the crater and meteorite he was certain existed.

The expedition was not going to be easy, as spring thaws turned the region into a morass. And when the team finally reached the area of destruction, their superstitious guides refused to go any further. Kulik, however, was encouraged by the sight of millions of trees splayed to the ground in a radial pattern pointing outward from an apparent impact point. Returning again, the team finally reached the epicenter where, to their surprise, they found neither a meteor nor a crater. Instead, they found a forest of what looked like telephone poles—trees stripped of their branches and reduced to vertical shafts. Scientists would not witness a similar sight until 1945 in the area below the Hiroshima blast.

So, What Happened?

Here are some of the many theories regarding what happened.

Stony Asteroid: Traveling at a speed of about 33,500 miles per hour, a large space rock heated the air around it to 44,500 degrees Fahrenheit and exploded at an altitude of about 28,000 feet. This produced a fireball that utterly annihilated the asteroid.

Kimberlite Eruption: Formed nearly 2,000 miles below the Earth's surface, a shaft of heavy kimberlite rock carried a huge quantity of methane gas to the Earth's surface where it exploded with great force.

Black Holes & Antimatter: As early as 1941, some scientists believed that a small antimatter asteroid exploded when it encountered the upper atmosphere. In 1973, several theorists proposed that the Tunguska event was the result of a tiny black hole passing through the Earth's surface.

In June 2008, scientists from around the world marked the 100-year anniversary of the Tunguska event with conferences in Moscow. Yet scientists still cannot reach a consensus as to what caused the event. In fact, the anniversary gathering was split into two opposing factions—extraterrestrial versus terrestrial—that met at different sites in the city.

The Narwhal: Mother Nature's 35-Million-Year-Old Joke

Perhaps if Herman Melville had made Moby Dick a narwhal instead of a boring old white whale, we'd all have a little more love for this bizarre-looking (but lovable) aquatic animal.

✳ ✳ ✳ ✳

✳ A typical narwhal averages somewhere between 11.5 and 16.4 feet, and weighs in at around 3,500 pounds.

✳ Narwhals swim upside down! Researchers are still trying to figure out exactly why narwhals spend 80 percent of their time inverted, but they think it's because the animals send sonar signals underwater to detect prey. Swimming upside down may direct the sonar beam downwards, where lunch is likely to be most abundant.

✳ The most distinguishing characteristic of a narwhal is its long, unicornlike tusk. The tusk points slightly downward, which is another reason narwhals may swim on their backs—while looking for food on the sea floor, they don't want to bust their horns on a rock.

✳ Over 10 million tiny nerve endings are found on the surface of a narwhal tusk, making it an essential tool for sensory perception.

✳ Narwhals lack a dorsal fin, which is unusual in underwater creatures of their kind. Scientists believe the narwhal evolved without a dorsal fin as an adaptation to navigate beneath ice-covered waters.

✳ If you see a group of narwhals above water, rubbing their tusks together, they're "tusking." This activity helps the narwhals clean their tusks—kind of like when humans brush their teeth.

Fast Facts

❋ A typical American dog owner spends more than $14,000 on his or her pet by the end of its life.

❋ In 1869, visionary inventor Thomas Edison patented the first electronic vote recorder. The recorder registered voters' choices as they were made and provided total vote counts, as well as a paper trail. His invention was such a radical departure from voting tradition that it was a commercial failure.

❋ Ten percent of Dalmatians are considered deaf.

❋ Flies taste with their feet.

❋ The idea of a "tip" for a waiter or waitress comes from 17th-century boxes in restaurants labeled "To Insure Promptness." Diners would put some cash in the box before eating to get better service.

❋ Lyndon B. Johnson was the first U.S. commander-in-chief to wear contact lenses.

❋ That early morning jolt of caffeine can be costly in Moscow. The price of an average cup of coffee is $10.19 U.S., the highest in the world.

❋ Barbed wire played a large part in the formation of the American West. In 1873, an Illinois farmer named Joseph Glidden was credited with designing the most popular barbed wire, winning out in court battles and in the marketplace, beating over 570 other patented designs.

❋ The human body contains approximately four ounces of salt.

❋ Louisa May Alcott, author of the best-selling classics *Little Men* and *Little Women,* actually disliked children. What's more, Alcott was a schoolteacher.

❋ Sea turtles absorb a lot of salt from the seawater in which they live. They excrete excess salt from their eyes, so it often looks as though they are crying.

An Underground Mystery: The Hollow Earth Theory

For centuries, people have believed that Earth is hollow. They claim that civilizations may live inside Earth's core or that it might be a landing base for alien spaceships. This sounds like fantasy, but believers point to startling evidence, including explorers' reports and modern photos taken from space.

✳ ✳ ✳ ✳

A Prize Inside?

HOLLOW EARTH BELIEVERS agree that our planet is a shell between 500 and 800 miles thick, and inside that shell is another world. It may be a gaseous realm, an alien outpost, or home to a utopian society.

Some believers add a spiritual spin. Calling the interior world Agartha or Shambhala, they use concepts from Eastern religions and point to ancient legends supporting these ideas.

Many Hollow Earth enthusiasts are certain that people from the outer and inner worlds can visit each other by traveling through openings in the outer shell. One such entrance is a hole in the ocean near the North Pole. A November 1968 photo by the ESSA-7 satellite showed a dark, circular area at the North Pole that was surrounded by ice fields.

Another hole supposedly exists in Antarctica. Some Hollow Earth enthusiasts say Hitler believed that Antarctica held the true opening to Earth's core. Leading Hollow Earth researchers such as Dennis Crenshaw suggest that President Roosevelt ordered the 1939 South Pole expedition to find the entrance before the Germans did.

The poles may not hold the only entrances to a world hidden deep beneath our feet. Jules Verne's famous novel *Journey to the Center of the Earth* supported yet another theory about passage between the worlds. In his story, there were many access points, including waterfalls and inactive volcanoes. Edgar Allan Poe and Edgar Rice Burroughs also wrote about worlds inside Earth. Their ideas were based on science as well as fantasy.

Scientists Take Note

Many scientists have taken the Hollow Earth theory seriously. One of the most noted was English astronomer Edmund Halley, of Halley's Comet fame. In 1692, he declared that our planet is hollow, and as evidence, he pointed to global shifts in Earth's magnetic fields, which frequently cause compass anomalies. According to Halley, those shifts could be explained by the movement of rotating worlds inside Earth. In addition, he claimed that the source of gravity—still debated in the 21st century—could be an interior world.

In Halley's opinion, Earth is made of three separate layers or shells, each rotating independently around a solid core. We live on the outer shell, but the inner worlds might be inhabited, too.

Halley also suggested that Earth's interior atmospheres are luminous. We supposedly see them as gas leaking out of Earth's fissures. At the poles, that gas creates the *aurora borealis*.

Scientists Look Deeper

Hollow Earth researchers claim that the groundwork for their theories was laid by some of the most notable scientific minds of the 17th and 18th centuries. Although their beliefs remain controversial and largely unsubstantiated, they are still widely discussed and have a network of enthusiasts.

Some researchers claim that Leonhard Euler (1707–1783), one of the greatest mathematicians of all time, believed that Earth's interior includes a glowing core that illuminates life for a well-developed civilization, much like the sun lights our world. Another mathematician, Sir John Leslie (1766–1832), suggested that Earth has a thin crust and also believed the interior cavity was filled with light.

In 1818, a popular lecturer named John Cleves Symmes Jr. proposed an expedition to prove the Hollow Earth theory. He believed that he could sail to the North Pole, and upon reaching the opening to Earth's core, he could steer his ship over the lip of the entrance, which he believed resembled a waterfall. Then he would continue sailing on waters inside the planet. In 1822 and 1823, Symmes petitioned Congress to fund the expedition, but he was turned down. He died in 1829, and his gravestone in Hamilton, Ohio, is decorated with his model of the Hollow Earth.

Proof Gets Woolly and Weird

In 1846, a remarkably well-preserved—and long extinct—woolly mammoth was found frozen in Siberia. Most woolly mammoths died out about 12,000 years ago, so researchers were baffled by its pristine condition.

Hollow Earth enthusiasts say there is only one explanation: The mammoth lived inside Earth, where mammoths are not extinct. The beast had probably become lost, emerged into our world, and froze to death shortly before the 1846 discovery.

Eyewitnesses at the North Pole

Several respected scientists and explorers have visited the poles and returned with stories that suggest a hollow Earth.

At the start of the 20th century, Arctic explorers Dr. Frederick A. Cook and Rear Admiral Robert E. Peary sighted land—not just an icy wasteland—at the North Pole. Peary first described it as "the white summits of a distant land." A 1913 Arctic expedition also reported seeing "hills, valleys, and snow-capped peaks." All of these claims were dismissed as mirages but would later be echoed by the research of Admiral Richard E. Byrd, the first man to fly over the North Pole. Hollow Earth believers suggest that Byrd actually flew into the interior world and then out again, without realizing it. They cite Byrd's notes as evidence, as he describes his navigational instruments and compasses spinning out of control.

Unidentified Submerged Objects

Support for the Hollow Earth theory has also come from UFO enthusiasts. People who study UFOs have also documented USOs, or unidentified submerged objects. These mysterious vehicles have been spotted—mostly at sea—since the 19th century.

USOs look like "flying saucers," but instead of vanishing into the skies, they plunge beneath the surface of the ocean. Some are luminous and fly upward from the sea at a fantastic speed . . . and without making a sound.

UFO enthusiasts believe that these spaceships are visiting worlds beneath the sea. Some are certain that these are actually underwater alien bases. Other UFO researchers think that the ocean conceals entries to a hollow Earth, where the aliens maintain outposts.

The Search Continues

Scientists have determined that the most likely location for a northern opening to Earth's interior is at 84.4° N Latitude, 141° E Longitude. It's a spot near Siberia, about 600 miles from the North Pole. Photos taken by *Apollo 8* in 1968 and *Apollo 16* in 1972 show dark, circular areas confirming the location.

Some scientists are studying seismic tomography, which uses natural and human-made explosions as well as earthquakes and other seismic waves to chart Earth's interior masses. So far, scientists confirm that Earth is comprised of three separate layers. And late 20th-century images may suggest a mountain range at Earth's core.

What may seem like fantasy from a Jules Verne novel could turn out to be an astonishing reality. Hollow Earth societies around the world continue to look for proof of this centuries-old legend . . . and who knows what they might find?

A Trek of No Return

Many people attempt to climb Mount Everest—and many never return.

✳ ✳ ✳ ✳

I T'S NO SECRET that ascending Everest, the tallest mountain in the world, is a risky feat. It's also no secret that some climbers die trying: In fact, more than 200 people have perished in their attempt to summit the 29,035-foot-tall peak. But did you know that many of these dead bodies remain on the mountain, never to receive a proper burial? There are many explanations as to why climbers die on Everest and why their bodies are left behind, yet the issue remains steeped in ethical debate.

The Death Zone

Among the dangers of climbing Mount Everest are avalanches, falling ice, fierce winds, the possibility of falling into a crevasse, severe cold, inadequate equipment, and lack of physical preparation. The majority of deaths, however, are caused by high-altitude sickness. This occurs where the technical climbing begins, far above the final base camp at 26,000 feet. The area is known as the "Death Zone," because the conditions here—specifically the amount of oxygen—cannot sustain human life.

A 2008 study conducted by a group of researchers from Massachusetts General Hospital found that most deaths on Everest were associated with "excessive fatigue, a tendency to fall behind other climbers, and arriving at the summit later in the day." The limited oxygen in the Death Zone contributes to confusion, disorientation, and a loss of physical coordination. Most of the climbers who die do so after reaching the summit, on their way down the mountain.

Frozen in Time

Because of the severe conditions in the Death Zone, most of the dead bodies are left behind. It would be extremely dangerous to attempt to take them off Everest, and there's really nowhere to bury them on the icy upper slopes. In other words, as climbers ascend, along the way they pass the frozen forms of those who have made the trek before them—sometimes decades prior.

Among those frozen in time is George Mallory, who attempted to summit Everest in 1924 but never returned from his climb. When asked why he wanted to climb the tallest mountain on the planet, he famously responded, "Because it's there." In May 1999, Mallory's body was found below the summit at 27,200 feet, a climbing rope still cinched around his waist. To this day, no one knows if Mallory and his climbing partner Andrew Irvine arrived at the summit before they died. If they had, they would have been the first to do so, preceding Sir Edmund Hillary and Tenzig Norgay's ascent in 1953.

In May 1996, eight climbers lost their lives in a sudden storm on their return from the summit. Two bodies from the expedition were never found. In 1998, Francys Arsentiev collapsed and died on her descent from the summit. For years her body lay close to the trail, in full view of climbers on their way up the mountain. A mountaineer named Ian Woodall, who was unable to help her as she neared her death, returned to Everest in 2007 to bury her in an American flag. Alas, he and his climbing partner were met with harsh weather conditions and only had time for a brief ceremony before dropping her body over the edge of the North Face. Some climbers criticized Woodall for initially abandoning Arsentiev, so perhaps this burial was a gesture of putting the controversy to rest.

Some of the most skilled climbers, the local sherpas, make it a point to avoid corpses. Teams from China have planned a cleanup of the mountain, which has been called "the world's highest garbage dump." In addition to picking up oxygen canisters, camping gear, and other materials discarded on the northern side of Everest, the crew intends to bring back any bodies that can be safely transported.

Inside the Belly of the Beast

Some sharks will take a bite out of pretty much anything, as evidenced by the fact that the Navy has discovered shark bite marks on their submarines. Check out some wild things that have been discovered inside the bellies of these beasts.

✳   ✳   ✳   ✳

✳ An entire roll of roof paper was discovered inside one shark's stomach. We can't help wondering whether it stuck to the roof of the shark's mouth on the way down!

✳ Although the acid in the critter's stomach will burn human skin, it didn't destroy the five-gallon steel bucket found in one shark.

✳ Shark digestion is slow, but humans are slower. That might explain the bits of surfboard and rubber flipper munchies found in many a shark belly.

✳ More than one shark, when caught, has regurgitated bits of human. In some cases, shark stomach contents have even been used as forensic evidence to help solve murders.

✳ Though sharks can't drive, they apparently find cars irresistible: license plates, tires, and other car parts have been discovered in their stomachs.

✳ While it's normal for a shark to eat fish and seals, other odd things have been discovered on their menu, including entire carcasses of dogs, horses, sheep, and polar bears. One shark was found with a whole side of beef (presumably from a cruise ship) in his innards.

✳ In the early 1820s, a shark was reportedly found in the West Indies with a cannonball in his belly.

✳ Nearly 900 kilos of cocaine were discovered inside frozen shark carcasses in the summer of 2009.

15 Waterfalls that Will Blow Your Mind

Majestic beyond compare, the world's greatest waterfalls are frothy-white wonders of nature. Featuring wispy cascades, gushing troughs, and dizzying drops, each "chute" is a variation on a theme with its own unique charm and character.

✳ ✳ ✳ ✳

1. **Niagara Falls, New York/Canada:** When it comes to waterfalls, none gush more famous than Niagara Falls. From the look of abject terror on the face of 63-year-old Annie Edson Taylor—the first daredevil to ride over the falls in a barrel (1901)—to Marilyn Monroe's suggestive sway as she walked beside the spray in *Niagara* (1953), the Niagara cataract has captivated like no other. Comprised of two separate falls (American and Horseshoe) Niagara's notoriety comes not only from its height (176 feet and 167 feet, respectively) but from its combined width of nearly three-quarters  of a mile. Today, a thriving tourist industry replete with casinos and amusements lures visitors in droves, and the azure-blue water of the falls never fails to mesmerize.

2. **Angel Falls, Venezuela:** When aviator Jimmie Angel flew over this 3,212-foot wonder in 1933, he probably didn't know that he was gazing at the world's tallest waterfall or that someday the falls would be named for his "discovery." A narrow ribbon by Niagara's standard, Angel Falls drops

so far that its waters actually atomize into mist before reaching the ground.

3. **Yosemite Falls, California:** Located in Yosemite National Park, this lofty spigot is the United States' answer to Angel Falls. At 2,425 feet, the waterfall is America's tallest and the sixth tallest in the world.

4. **Victoria Falls, Zambia/Zimbabwe:** Africa's giant, this 360-foot waterfall doubles Niagara in height and easily surpasses it in width (Victoria Falls is one mile wide). Victoria's flow is generally about one-half that of Niagara, but during the annual rainy season, the waterfall can flow twice as hard as its North American rival.

5. **Multnomah Falls, Oregon:** With a total drop of 620 feet, this waterfall runs mid-pack in the height wars, but its true claim to fame lies in its approachability and stunning beauty. It ranks as Oregon's tallest.

6. **Iguacú Falls, Argentina/Brazil:** Comprised of some 275 separate channels, this famous waterfall's signature element is its massive volume. Reaching 269 feet at its tallest point, Iguacú Falls currently flaunts the greatest average annual flow worldwide.

7. **Lower Yellowstone Falls, Wyoming:** At 308 feet in height and 70 feet in width, this majestic waterfall caps off any visit to Yellowstone National Park. It's considered the largest volume major waterfall in the U.S. Rocky Mountains.

8. **Cumberland Falls, Kentucky:** To the uninitiated, this waterfall seems somewhat ordinary. At 68 feet tall and 125 feet wide, the curtain of water, while undeniably scenic, is almost minuscule by world standards. But during a full moon, a lunar rainbow or *moonbow* appears before the falling sheet. This prompts sighting parties to visit the falls well *after* sundown, a strange occurrence indeed.

9. **Gavarnie Falls, France:** France's tallest at 1,384 feet, the *grande cascade* spills into a huge natural amphitheater of uncommon beauty.

10. **Gocta Catarata, Peru:** This well-hidden 2,531-foot (estimated) sliver was only recently "discovered" by Peruvian officials in 2002. If the fall's true height comes near this estimate, it will easily knock Yosemite Falls out of its sixth-tallest berth.

11. **Kaieteur Falls, Guyana:** At 741 feet tall and 370 feet wide, this waterfall features great height and great width. Its resultant hydro power ranks it among the most forceful on Earth.

12. **Langfoss, Norway:** A cascading waterfall of incomparable grandeur, Langfoss slides down 2,008 feet of bare rock before splashing into Akra fjord.

13. **Sutherland Falls, New Zealand:** This 1,904-foot waterfall is powered by Lake Quill, a glacial-fed body of water that produces many of its own waterfalls. It is one of New Zealand's most celebrated spillways.

14. **Depot Creek Falls, Washington:** Water appears to rush down this frenetic waterfall. That's because the 967-foot waterfall veils down a smooth granite headwall at a comparatively shallow angle. This promotes a gushing torrent that kicks up an impressive cloud of spray.

15. **Montmorency Falls, Quebec, Canada:** A natural waterfall seemingly created for tourists, 272-foot *Chute Montmorency* is a sight to behold. A suspension bridge above and decks below bring people frightfully close to the action, while a tramline spanning the gorge fills in the remaining visual gaps.

Freaky Facts: Deer

✳ In Blacksburg, Virginia, in 2003, a six-point buck ran into a supermarket. The deer leapt over soup cans and knocked over displays before escaping out a back door, where it was hit, but not killed, by a passing vehicle.

✳ The legend of a ghost deer echoes through the canyons of Mt. Eddy in northern California. Hunters describe a giant buck with 12 points on one antler and 10 on the other. Those who have shot at it say bullets pass right through, and its tracks are said to disappear at natural barriers such as great ridges or bodies of water.

✳ On August 1, 2003, Joshua Laprise spotted a pure white albino deer eating in a field in Rhode Island. The chances of seeing an adult albino white-tailed deer in the wild are about one in a million. Most albinos do not live more than a few years due to lack of protective coloration but are protected by law in Illinois, Iowa, Tennessee, and Wisconsin.

✳ In the late 1940s, white-colored deer began populating what is now known as the Conservation Area (CA) in Seneca, New York. It seems that some of the white-tailed deer in the CA carried a gene for white coloration. Today, there are more than 200 white deer living in the CA, making it the only place in the world with such a large population of white deer.

✳ The antlers of white-tailed deer can become self-defeating traps—if two battling males lock horns, they may be unable to separate and consequently starve to death or be killed by a predator.

New Straitsville's Underground Fire

A labor strike started a fire underground, where it had enough fuel to burn unabated—for more than 125 years.

✳   ✳   ✳   ✳

IN 1884, MINERS striking against the Plummer Hill Mine in the town of New Straitsville, Ohio, crammed oil-soaked timbers into bank cars, set them on fire, and rolled them deep into the mine. By the time company executives discovered the fire, it had grown too large to extinguish. As the months passed, owners estimated that Hocking Valley mines had lost $50 million in damages due to the fire that refused to go out. This fire continues to burn like a massive coal stove more than 100 years later, and it still has plenty of fuel. In Perry County village, locals have literally fried eggs over hot cracks in the ground.

The state doesn't consider the fire dangerous so long as it is monitored, but area residents say they can feel the heat and sometimes see parts of fields and yards collapse from it. They claim the fire goes dormant, only to inexplicably reignite itself again and again.

In the early to mid-1900s, entrepreneurs started hot-spot tours and brewed coffee over the hot cracks. Signs identified the spots as "Devil's Garden," "Inferno Land," and "Hell's Half Acre." Famed journalist Ernie Pyle, a roving reporter in the 1930s, came to New Straitsville to feel the fire. "Just to look around over these rolling green hills of southern Ohio," he wrote, "you wouldn't believe that hell is only a few feet underneath."

Before World War II, federal employees tried to contain the fire by constructing rock barriers and trenches, but the blaze outwitted them. By 1940, the fire had calmed down. These days, few tourists stop to ask to fry an egg over a crack in the ground, although local residents insist it can still be done, with help from the fire that refuses to burn out.

Animals Behaving Badly

They're brave, beautiful, and often loving ... that is, until you cross them. Sometimes it's unprovoked, but other times it's hard to tell who is the bigger animal—man or beast.

✳   ✳   ✳   ✳

Now Who's King of the Jungle?

MOSES LEKALAU, a 35-year-old Kenyan herdsman, was walking home from a neighboring village in 2007 when he was attacked by a lion. He fought the beast for a half hour with just a spear and a club, eventually killing it. Turning from his ordeal, however, Lekalau was set upon by a pack of hyenas. The animals bit off his hands and toes, and he died from his injuries.

Leave Me Alone!

In South Africa in 2005, 49-year-old animal-lover Elsie Van Tonder was only trying to help a cute young seal return to the ocean when the animal informed her in no uncertain terms to leave it alone—by biting off her nose! Volunteers located the nose, but doctors were unable to reattach it. After Van Tonder underwent reconstructive surgery, a coastal management official said the seal was using its own way of telling the woman it didn't want to go back into the water.

Don't Play with Your Food

In 2005, after robbing a couple at knifepoint, a thief in Bloemfontein, South Africa, found himself cornered by security guards. With nowhere to go, he took the only route open to him: over a fence and into a Bengal tiger cage at the city zoo, where the animals made short work of him. When the crook's body was removed, officials noted that because the tigers had already been fed, they merely killed the intruder instead of making a meal out of him.

What Goes Around, Comes Around

Carl Hulsey, a retired poultry worker from Canton, Georgia, wanted to turn his goat Snowball into a watchdog, so he beat the animal with a stick to make it more aggressive. His wife warned him: "This goat's going to kill you if you keep that up." In 1991, Hulsey approached the goat with his stick, but this time Snowball was ready. The 110-pound animal repeatedly butted Hulsey in the stomach until it knocked him off the porch and five feet to the ground. The goat had ruptured the man's stomach, and Hulsey died where he fell. As officials were debating whether or not to put Snowball down, they were besieged by hundreds of calls to spare the goat, insisting it was only defending itself against a cruel owner. Snowball was turned over to a private shelter for abused animals, neutered, and renamed "Snow."

Well . . . *Duh*

In 1995, someone brought a gopher to three custodians at the Carroll Fowler Elementary School in Ceres, California, and asked them to deal with the rodent. The men decided to kill the animal and took it into a small supply room where they sprayed it with solvent. The gopher hung on, even after being subjected to three cans of the chemical. As the custodians took a break to discuss their next move, one of the men lit a cigarette and the shed exploded, injuring all three men as well as 16 nearby students. After the explosion, the frightened gopher was found clinging to a wall. It was released into the wild, while all three custodians were sent to the hospital.

Attack of the Killer Monkeys

While reading the newspaper on his terrace in 2007, Delhi Deputy Mayor Surinder Singh Bajwa was attacked by monkeys. He tried to scare away the Rhesus macaques with a stick but fell from the balcony and suffered fatal injuries. This sort of attack is becoming more common as Indian officials struggle to deal with the brash simians, which are seen as manifestations of the Hindu monkey god, Hanuman. Locals give the animals food and allow them to roam as they please due to their holy status.

Caught in a Web of Deceit

Thirty-year-old Mark Voegel wanted nothing more than to have his own botanical garden in his apartment in Dortmund, Germany. He filled it with more than 200 spiders, including a black widow named Bettina, as well as poisonous frogs, a boa constrictor, and other snakes and lizards. In 2004, neighbors finally complained about the smell and alerted police. When authorities entered the apartment, they found the odor was not from the animals but from Voegel himself. He had died from a black widow bite, and his animal friends had turned on him, using his corpse as their food source. Police said the scene resembled a horror movie: Voegel's body was covered in webs, spiders, and insects—inside and out.

Minks Gone Wild

In 1998, the Animal Liberation Front invaded the Crow Hill Farm in England and released 6,500 minks with the belief they would disappear into the countryside, mate with the wild mink population, and live happily ever after. Instead, the minks used the surrounding area as a buffet. They attacked a local wild bird sanctuary and went after a local dog. Some minks were found holed up at a pub, while others were shot by locals worried about the safety of their livestock. Ironically, the animal rights activists stood by their actions: "Had they stayed where they were, they would have been killed in a barbarous manner," activist Robin Webb said.

It Was Self-Defense

In 2004, Jerry Bradford of Florida decided to shoot a litter of three-month-old puppies because he couldn't find them a home. However, one of the dogs had other ideas. After killing three of them, Bradford prepared to shoot another when the puppy he was holding slipped its paw into the trigger of the man's .38-caliber revolver and shot him in the wrist. Bradford was hospitalized before being charged with felony animal cruelty, and the surviving puppies were placed in loving homes.

Playing with Fire

In 2006, 81-year-old Luciano Mares had a mouse problem in his house. After finally catching one of the little rascals in a glue trap, he threw it into a leaf fire outside his New Mexico home. The fire melted the glue and the mouse was able to escape, but its fur had caught fire. It ran into Mares's house, and within minutes the home was ablaze, leaving Mares homeless.

Turkey Takes a Stand

When Nancy Arena arrived at her video store near Buffalo, New York, in 2002, she was astonished to find the front window smashed and feathers littering the floor. She called police thinking the store had been vandalized. When authorities arrived they found the mischievous individual still lurking about—a 12-pound turkey. As they grabbed the bird, officers noticed something odd about the section where it had decided to do its damage: The turkey had destroyed several hunting videos and defecated on them.

Fallacies & Facts: Redwoods

Fallacy: A redwood is the same as a sequoia.

Fact: In North America, there are just two native species of cone-bearing redwoods: the coast redwood and the giant sequoia. Thus, sequoias are redwoods, but not all redwoods are sequoias. Other parts of the world have leaf-bearing redwoods, but none so mighty as California's.

Fallacy: Redwoods are the oldest trees.

Fact: Not even close. Compared to Methuselah, a spry little California bristlecone pine more than 4,700 years old, the oldest living redwood is a relative youngster. Seven other tree types in the United States can outlive redwoods. General Sherman, in California's Sequoia National Park, is the biggest—and thus probably the oldest—sequoia. The National Park Service estimates that the General is between 1,800 and 2,700 years old (sprouted between 700 B.C. and A.D. 200). Put another way: When Methuselah was a sapling, Egyptians were just getting the bright idea to pile up stones into big pointy tombs. By the time General Sherman began to grow, Egypt's days of might and grandeur were long over.

Fallacy: Redwoods require dense fog to thrive.

Fact: If that were the case, they wouldn't survive in such fog-poor places as Rotorua, New Zealand, where the tallest redwoods reach 200 feet. Nor would they grow well in areas where summer heat can hit triple digits. Excessive wind will stunt their growth, and they drink literally tons of groundwater, but irrigation can supply this when nature will not. It's just a question of how badly one wants a redwood tree.

Fallacy: Redwoods grow at a snail's pace.

Fact: In fact, the things grow like weeds in the right conditions (moist, well-drained soil; moderate cold). Timber companies love them, of course, because redwoods can gain an inch of diameter and a yard of height per year in ideal conditions. Redwoods aren't an endangered species; they're just immense evergreens.

Fallacy: Redwoods won't grow tall in the eastern United States.

Fact: It's true that eastern climates are rough on redwoods. The trees do not like high winds, so it stands to reason that they like twisters and hurricanes even less. Their height makes them targets for Dixie's vicious lightning storms. But those are outside factors. If nature doesn't batter or stunt a redwood, it'll have no trouble growing 100 feet tall in eastern soils.

Fallacy: Redwoods aren't found above altitudes of 3,000 feet.

Fact: A redwood grove on Maui extends to 6,000 feet above sea level. The myth persists because California redwoods can't thrive above 3,000 feet, but that's because California winters can be punishingly inhospitable at those altitudes.

Fallacy: "Bonsai giant sequoia" is a contradictory term.

Fact: People actually grow these, but remember that "giant sequoia" is a species name, and every tree begins as a tiny sprout.

Fallacy: There is one redwood tree so big, someone has carved an opening so you can drive your car through it.

Fact: There are actually three such trees, all in northern California. If you think the privilege is worth three bucks, drive carefully.

Animal Acts

Rarely do animals and baseball go hand-in-hand, but some key moments on the field have made animals the stars of the show.

✳   ✳   ✳   ✳

BALLPLAYERS KNOW TO expect the unexpected, to try to be prepared for whatever pitches, hits, or plays they might encounter. But sometimes the unexpected arrives in a different package—a furry or feathered one—when an animal makes a surprise appearance on the field.

Fowl Balls

Even the best batters admit that hitting Randy Johnson's fastball isn't easy, but a dove flying a bit too close to the action at a 2001 spring-training game certainly made solid, if not tragic, contact. Johnson's seventh-inning delivery, intended for Giants outfielder Calvin Murray, hit the bird instead. Feathers erupted, and the ball—and what was left of the bird—ricocheted into foul territory behind the first base line. The delivery was ruled a non-pitch.

On August 4, 1983, Dave Winfield of the Yankees had a similar "fowl" incident, but with more dramatic consequences. Between innings of a game against the Blue Jays in Exhibition Stadium, Winfield struck and killed a seagull while throwing in the outfield. He was arrested after the game on a charge of cruelty to animals. He posted $500 bail and was scheduled for a court date the next time the Yankees visited Toronto, but the charges were later dropped. If convicted, Winfield could have faced up to six months in jail. "They say he hit the gull on purpose," remarked Yankees manager Billy Martin. "They wouldn't say that if they'd seen the throws he'd been making all year."

The Curse of the Cat?

Occasionally in player-animal matchups, it's the players who fall victim. A stray black cat made an eerie appearance in a critical

Mets-Cubs game on September 9, 1969. Just as Billy Williams dug into the batter's box in the first inning, the cat darted out from beneath the Shea Stadium stands, stopped briefly to consider Williams, slinked past Ron Santo in the on-deck circle, then headed for the visiting dugout, where Mets fans believe he hissed at Cubs manager Leo Durocher.

Was it an omen? It marked the last night of the season that the Cubs went to bed in first place. Despite holding a lead as large as ten games over the Mets on August 13, the Cubs' 7–1 loss the night the cat appeared reduced their lead to a half-game, which the surging Mets erased the next night. Like the cat, the Cubs weren't heard from again.

Her Dogs Called the Schotts

Marge Schott, the brash one-time owner of the Cincinnati Reds, was known for her inappropriate behavior and comments and also for her love of animals. Her beloved St. Bernards, Schottzie and Schottzie 02, like several of her struggling Reds teams, were known to leave a mess on the Riverfront Stadium field. However, it was the dogs, not the players, who graced the cover of the team's media guides.

In September 1998, Mark McGwire arrived in Cincinnati fresh from breaking Roger Maris's home run record, only to be humiliated when Schott forced him to pet Schottzie and rub the dog's hair on his Cardinals jersey for good luck. Unfortunately, McGwire was not so lucky. He's allergic to dogs.

Fleeing the Bees

In March 2005, a spring-training game between the Rockies and the Diamondbacks was called after a swarm of bees invaded the field. Colorado Rockies pitcher Darren Oliver was literally chased off the mound by the swarm. He suspected coconut-scented gel in his hair was to blame. However, after he fled, the bees chased shortstop Sergio Santos out to deep center field before umpires stepped in. "I guess we've got to call that a 'bee' game," said Arizona manager Bob Melvin.

Fast Facts

❋ The sport of badminton was once called "poona."

❋ The world's largest bowling alley is the 156-lane Nagoya Grand Bowl in Japan.

❋ Legend has it that Thomas Edison—inventor of the light bulb—was quite scared of the dark.

❋ Astronaut Buzz Aldrin, the second man to walk on the moon, has a second connection to the giant circle in the sky: His mother's maiden name was, fittingly, Moon.

❋ Bamboo is the world's tallest grass, growing as much as 90 centimeters in a single day.

❋ Australian toilets are designed to flush counterclockwise.

❋ Barbie has a full name that many people don't know: Barbara Millicent Roberts. Not quite as catchy.

❋ An airplane mechanic came up with the idea for the Slinky toy while working with engine springs.

❋ Mr. Potato Head holds the honor of being the first toy featured in a television commercial.

❋ In Tennessee, it's apparently all right to shoot whales from a moving car, but in land-locked Oklahoma, hunting whales is forbidden.

❋ Pac-Man was originally going to be called Puck Man. The name was changed because of a fear that troublemaking teens would change the "P" to another, less-appropriate letter on arcade machines.

❋ Most women work through six pounds of lipstick in their lives.

❋ There are 318,979,564,000 different ways to play the first four moves per side in a game of chess.

❋ Toys for Tots began its yearly donation drive during the 1947 Christmas season.

Caligula and Incitatus

Caligula (A.D. 12–41) is the poster child for depraved Roman emperors, and not without reason. An oft-repeated story about his life says that he appointed his horse a consul of Rome. It makes a great tale, but there's no evidence that it's true.

✳   ✳   ✳   ✳

BOTH SURVIVING ANCIENT accounts, Suetonius's *Lives of the Twelve Caesars* and the papers of historian Cassius Dio, were written long after Caligula's death. These chroniclers agreed that "Little Boot" (in Latin, "Caligula"; his proper name was Gaius) was touchy, boorish, unpredictable, dangerous—and particularly fond of his horse Incitatus. It's said that Caligula went so far as to handpick and purchase a "wife" for Incitatus, a mare named Penelope.

According to Dio, Caligula had Incitatus over for dinner, toasted his health, fed him gold-flecked grain, appointed him a priest, and promised to make him a consul. Dio believed it was a serious vow. Suetonius wrote that Caligula gave Incitatus a luxurious stable with an ivory feed trough, lavish purple blankets, jeweled collars, and many attendants. On evenings before races, the emperor forbade any noisemaking that might agitate Incitatus. Suetonius also mentioned the plans of consular promotion.

No ancient source says the horse was ever actually consul. Priest, maybe, if you believe Dio. We have the consular list from during Caligula's reign (37–41), and Incitatus isn't on it. Both Dio and Suetonius convincingly describe him as a pampered pet; only one feels Rome might have had a neigh-saying consul had Caligula lived longer. Both describe Caligula as someone descending into lunacy, capable of any number of mad deeds. Had he lived, we might today gaze upon Roman coins bearing Incitatus's horsey countenance. Perhaps, near the end of the sordid Caligula reign, Incitatus was the only creature his master truly liked and trusted.

Meet the Bug Men

About one in three movies features at least one scene containing an insect, whether it's a single fly landing on a windowsill or a swarm of 3,000 locusts terrorizing an entire town. Stay seated for the end credits and you'll likely spot a credit for an "insect wrangler." Alternately known as a "bug wrangler" or simply "bug man," an insect wrangler is a trained entomologist responsible for not only providing various creepy-crawlies used in a movie or TV show but also for manipulating them onscreen so they swarm, run, or fly on cue.

✳   ✳   ✳   ✳

So, how do you train an insect?

You DON'T. INSECTS can't be trained—they can only be manipulated. Wranglers have to understand why insects do things and then work out how you can manipulate that behavior to fit the needs of the script. Spiders, for example, refuse to walk on Lemon Pledge furniture wax. If you spray the area you don't want them in, they will unfailingly avoid it. Similarly, cockroaches will always run from a light source.

To make an insect fly toward a window, wranglers will place a bright light out of shot behind the window. To make an insect fly away and then return to the window, they attach a tiny harness made of very fine silk and control the bug like a puppet.

Is there a casting process for bugs?

It may sound strange, but casting is very important. You need to choose the right insect according to the demands of the shot. In the 1990 movie *Arachnophobia*, in which deadly tropical spiders terrorize a small California town, the insect wranglers deliberately chose to use the New Zealand Avendale spider for the swarm scenes. After testing a variety of other species, they found it was the only spider that would run when it was crowded rather than just attack the other spiders.

What about makeup for insects?

Absolutely! When the insect wrangler on *The Silence of the Lambs* set couldn't obtain specimens of the rare moth needed for the movie, he had to use common moths instead. He anesthetized each moth and painted on the distinctive markings (resembling a human skull) of the death's-head hawk moth onto its body. In *Spider-Man,* the insect wrangler had to paint the tiny blue-and-white Steatoda spider that bites the Peter Parker character. The wrangler used water-based, nontoxic paint, of course, so that it would easily wash off without harming the spider.

Are insects ever harmed during filming?

No. The U.S. Humane Society monitors most movie and television sets. If moviemakers want the "No Animals Were Harmed" end-credit disclaimer, they have to meet the Humane Society's strict guidelines. Wranglers work closely with the actors on how to handle bugs so as not to mistreat them. In the 2005 movie *The Three Burials of Melquiades Estrada,* for example, Tommy Lee Jones's character comes across a dead body covered in ants. In the first shot, the insect wrangler used real ants on a dummy body. But for the shot when Jones sets fire to the corpse, the real ants were replaced with rubber ones so that no ants would be harmed.

Tricks of the Trade

* To create a cockroach death scene, a bug wrangler will administer just the right dose of carbon dioxide. This will make the cockroach run a few feet before flipping onto its back and lying unconscious for several minutes. It will regain consciousness just in time for a second take.

* To get spiders to run up a wall, an insect wrangler will hide out of shot and blow a hair dryer up the wall toward the spider.

* Parts of a floor can be heated or cooled to control the direction of swarming spiders. Electric fields or shivering wires will stop the spiders from swarming too far.

The Astonishing Elephant

Compassionate, astonishingly strong, intelligent, and resourceful, the elephant is one of Mother Nature's coolest characters. Check out these pachyderm pointers!

✳   ✳   ✳   ✳

1. For the past 32 years and counting, the Asian elephant has been on the endangered species list.

2. A female elephant is pregnant for 22 months—almost two years. Yikes.

3. Depending on the weather, an Asian elephant can guzzle 30 to 50 gallons of water every day.

4. The largest known specimen of the African savanna elephant is on display at the Smithsonian's National Museum of Natural History in Washington, D.C. When it was alive it stood 13 feet tall and weighed 22,000 pounds.

5. An elephant's trunk comprises 150,000 different muscle fibers.

6. Having a "fat day"? Forget it. The average male Asian elephant weighs between 10,000 and 12,000 pounds.

7. The closest relatives to the elephant are the hyraxes (small chunky mammals that resemble fat gophers), dugongs and manatees, and aardvarks.

8. Although Asian and African elephants look alike, several physical characteristics distinguish them from one another. Asian elephants are generally smaller, with shorter tusks. They also have two domed bulges on their foreheads, rounded backs, less wrinkly skin, and their trunks have a fingerlike projection at the tip.

9. Elephants supplement the sodium in their food by visiting nearby mineral licks.

10. African elephants speak their own special language. Communication takes place using rumbles, moans, and growls. These low-frequency sounds can travel a mile or more.

11. Ever wonder why an elephant has a trunk in the first place? It's because an elephant's neck is so short that it wouldn't be able to reach the ground. The trunk allows the elephant to eat from the ground as well as the treetops.

12. An elephant's trunk weighs about 400 pounds.

13. Just as humans are either right- or left-handed, elephants are either right- or left-tusked.

14. Between 1979 and 1989, Africa's elephant population plummeted from 1.3 million to 750,000, as a result of ivory poaching.

15. The first time elephants were seen in Europe was in 280 B.C., when an army of 25,000 men and 20 elephants crossed from North Africa to Italy.

16. Adult elephants can't jump.

17. Under the right conditions, an elephant can smell water from approximately three miles away.

18. Elephants are noted for their social behavior. They sometimes "hug" by wrapping their trunks together as a way of greeting one another. Baby elephants may suck their trunk for comfort—sort of the equivalent of a human sucking his or her thumb.

Unwanted Visitors!

You don't have to go globe hopping to see the world's wildest flora and fauna. Just visit South Florida.

✳   ✳   ✳   ✳

SINCE THE 1950S, nonindigenous mammals, birds, fish, reptiles, amphibians, and foreign plants have invaded the Sunshine State. And thanks to Florida's subtropical climate, wildlife biologists report that these newcomers have become so well established that it's practically impossible to get rid of them.

It's an eclectic mix of critters, too. Flocks of colorful parrots from South America, Asia, and Africa cause a ruckus on South Florida's golf courses. Fire ants from Brazil build mounds in homeowners' backyards. Walking catfish from Thailand meander in search of a new pond to call home.

Coming to (North) America

These unwanted visitors came to Florida in a variety of ways. Some, such as pythons and boa constrictors, were discarded pets that grew too large or ornery to keep at home. With plentiful food and South Florida's warm temperatures very much like that of their native South America, the giant snakes quickly became a dominant species in an ecosystem that had never seen anything like them before.

Others, such as the various types of parrots, escaped from local zoos following a hurricane. And a handful of species simply fled into the wild when no one was looking, such as the nine-banded armadillo, a native of South and Central America. Though common to the southwestern states since the 1880s, armadillos were unknown to Florida until 1922, when a man named Gus Edwards added a few of the armored animals to his 15-cent zoo in Cocoa Beach. The crafty critters escaped within days and skedaddled into the Florida wilderness, where they continued to breed until the state was practically knee-deep in 'dillos.

The Bad, the Ugly, and the Bitey

Other nonindigenous species were intentionally introduced into the state, with unforeseen consequences. The water-sucking melaleuca tree, for example, was imported from Australia as a windbreak and swamp drainer. But there was just one problem: Melaleuca trees are practically impossible to kill. They spread with alarming speed, and now the trees threaten to overrun the Everglades. Worse, the tree's bark is like paper, which makes forest fires especially nasty.

The warty, irascible muscovy duck, a native of South America, is another example of do-goodery gone wrong. Introduced as colorful additions to municipal ponds, the ducks began breeding like crazy and now pose a serious risk to indigenous waterfowl.

Indeed, the dangers posed by the growing number of nonnative species in South Florida are many. Some, like the fire ant, can give a painful bite or sting, or, like the *Bufo marinus* toad, emit a dangerous toxin when touched. Others can have a devastating effect on native species and/or ecosystems, sometimes years or decades after their initial introduction.

Luckily for Floridians, truly dangerous species have, so far, been unable to get a foothold. Piranhas, the meat-eating scourge of the Amazon River, have been caught a handful of times by local fishermen. Biologists investigated the area each time a piranha was hooked and determined that they were individual releases, meaning there were no breeding schools. Spiny catfish and other unusual fish have also been caught on occasion, and wildlife officials in Miami have stopped more than one electric eel from entering the country and, quite possibly, local waters.

These days, most Floridians have come to accept the invaders that have taken over their yards. After all, there's little that can be done now to eradicate them. So the next time you're vacationing in Miami, you may just run into an international visitor who decided to stay.

Sponge Party

Deep-sea sponges + fiber optics = undersea rave?

✳   ✳   ✳   ✳

No one likes to be left in the dark—including giant sea sponges. Yet the bottom of the ocean, where these sponges are found, is a very dark place indeed. To deal with this problem, some massive deep-sea sponges have evolved fiber optic exoskeletons by which they illuminate their surroundings. These aren't sponges of the squishy, ideal-for-washing-dishes variety; they're sturdy sponges that produce reinforced glass tubes known as *spicules*. Although sponges are some of the world's most primitive creatures, these spicules are astoundingly intricate, growing up to about three feet in length and rivaling some of humanity's spiffier architectural designs.

How does a sponge grow such an intricate exoskeleton? First, it spins silica from the ocean into microscopic bits of glass. It then adheres together these thin pieces of glass to form little fibers. The sponge arranges these fibers into a complex lattice, which it reinforces with a kind of glass cement. According to a report on NPR's *All Things Considered*, this lattice design resembles techniques used for building skyscrapers, such as the Swiss Tower in London or the Eiffel Tower in Paris. And just like these manufactured structures, the sponges light up.

The undersea light show occurs because the spicules behave like fiber-optic rods, enabling the sponge to transport light throughout its tissue. Many tiny life-forms live inside the sponge—such as green algae and glass shrimp—because these organisms need its light to survive. According to scientists, the spicules conduct light in such a way that they're more sophisticated than many human-made fiber-optic cables. Plus, they don't require the high temperatures needed for manufactured fibers. So if you ever find yourself on the ocean floor and in need of a light source, look for the sponges with spicules. It's where the little shrimp like to party!

Freaky Facts: Insects

✳ Caddisfly larvae construct little houses in ponds to live in until they reach their winged stage. Some species build little structures from bits of leaves to achieve dome or turret shapes, some stack up small pebbles and shells, and one is able to exactly reproduce the shape of a snail shell by binding sand with a silky extrusion.

✳ Earwigs, once widely (and wrongly) reputed to crawl inside human ears to lay their eggs, actually feed mostly on caterpillars, slugs, and already dead flesh. They still look creepy due to the large, pincerlike claws protruding from their rear ends that are used to grab prey.

✳ The crafty ant lion digs a sand pit by scooting itself backward and using its head as a shovel. It then hides itself in the pit with only its giant mouth sticking out and waits for an ant to tumble down into the pit.

✳ Whirligig beetles, which live in ponds and streams, have eyes that are divided into two sections: one part suited for underwater viewing and the other for ogling the atmosphere.

✳ Froghoppers are small insects that look a bit like frogs. Young froghoppers clamp onto plant stems and drain them of juice while excreting a whitish foam from their abdomens until they are completely covered in a bubble bath of their own making, resembling blobs of spittle.

✳ Tree crickets sing in exact mathematic ratio to the temperature of the air. No need for a thermometer on a summer night—just count the number of chirps a cricket makes in 15 seconds, add 40, and the result will be the current temperature in degrees Fahrenheit.

✳ The female praying mantis is a pitiless lover. Her mate is also her dinner, and she often eats his head as an appetizer while he is still in the act of fertilizing her eggs.

Chapter Thirteen

Something to Believe In

Tax-Exempt Religions (No, Really!)

The Pastafarians who worship the Flying Spaghetti Monster may inspire a few chuckles, but it's not a tax-exempt religion in the eyes of the U.S. government. Here are some that are.

✳   ✳   ✳   ✳

THE ORDO TEMPLI Orientis (OTO), aka Order of Oriental Templars, was founded in 1904 by British mystic Aleister Crowley. The group currently has 44 lodges in 26 states, including the Leaping Laughter Lodge of Minneapolis and the Subtlety of Force Encampment of Albuquerque. Based on a system of beliefs called Thelema, the OTO claims to promote the acquisition of "light, wisdom, understanding, knowledge, and power through beauty, courage, and wit."

Eckankar teaches that people can connect with other realities through out-of-body experiences. This faith was founded in 1965 by spiritualist Paul Twitchel. Followers call themselves Eckists, and their leaders are referred to as Living Eck Masters.

The **Raelians,** by contrast, focus their attention on the future. Founded by race-car enthusiast Claude Vorilhon in 1974, the movement believes humans were created by extraterrestrials called Elohim who will one day return to Earth as foretold in Vorilhon's book *Let's Welcome Our Fathers from Outer Space.*

9 Little-Known Patron Saints

Here are nine lesser-known saints and the people—and things—they watch over.

❊　❊　❊　❊

1. Geneviève—Patron Saint of Disasters and Paris

When her hometown of Paris was under siege by Childeric, King of the Franks, Geneviève risked her own safety to go into the city to find food and supplies for the suffering. Years later, she faced another dangerous conqueror: Attila the Hun. As Parisians prepared to leave their homes rather than face the wrath of the barbarians, Geneviève convinced them to stay in their homes and pray instead. It is still unknown why Attila didn't attack Paris. Geneviève died in A.D. 500.

2. Blaise—Patron Saint of Throat Ailments, Veterinarians, and Wild Animals

As a bishop, Blaise was arrested for praying and went into hiding to avoid martyrdom. He shared a cave with wild animals that he cared for. He was eventually found and ordered to stand trial, but on his way to the trial, he convinced a wolf to return a woman's stolen pig. When he was sentenced to a slow, painful death by starvation, the grateful owner of the pig secretly slipped him food so that he wouldn't die. During this time, a woman came to Blaise in need of help. Her son was choking on a fish bone, but Blaise was able to save his life. When the governor learned that Blaise hadn't yet starved to death, he ordered him skinned alive and then beheaded. He died in A.D. 316.

3. Casimir of Poland—Patron Saint of Bachelors

Born a prince in Poland, this exceptional young man rose through the ranks of the Catholic church and was ultimately put in charge of his native country. His father tried to arrange a marriage with the daughter of the emperor of Germany, but Casimir wanted to stay single. He died soon afterward in 1484. Stories of his great charm, sense of justice, and belief in chastity abound.

4. Denis—Patron Saint of Headaches

In A.D. 258, during the persecution of Emperor Decius, Denis, the first bishop of Paris, was imprisoned, tortured, and beheaded. His headless body is said to have carried his severed head away from his own execution. His body was dumped into the River Seine, but his followers pulled it out.

5. Edward the Confessor—Patron Saint of Difficult Marriages

Edward became the King of England in 1042. He was a very peaceful leader, only going into battle when necessary to defend his allies. He was concerned with the fair treatment of all people and wanted to do away with unjust taxation. He built churches, the most famous being Westminster Abbey. He took a vow of chastity early in life, but he eventually took a wife, Editha, to please the people of his kingdom. He remained celibate throughout his life and died in 1066.

6. Felicity—Patron Saint of Barren Women and Parents Who Have Had a Child Die

Felicity rose from slave to sainthood, but the road wasn't easy. The legend of Felicity varies: One version says that her seven sons were killed in front of her for choosing Christianity, then she was beheaded. Another version says that Felicity was eight months pregnant when she and five others were sentenced to die a martyr's death. They were baptized and led away to suffer greatly in prison. Felicity was upset because she didn't think she would be able to suffer martyrdom at the same time as the others—the law forbade the execution of pregnant women. In A.D. 203 she delivered a baby girl just days before the "games" and was able to die in the amphitheater along with the others. Their killers? A wild boar, a bear, and a leopard ripped the men apart; a wild cow slaughtered the women.

7. Lydwina—Patron Saint of Ice Skaters

Lydwina was from a poor family in Holland. She was a very religious girl and prayed often. In 1395, she broke several ribs in an ice-skating accident and gangrene spread throughout her body, causing her severe pain for the rest of her life. Lydwina experienced visions, including one of a rosebush with the inscription, "When this shall be in bloom, your suffering will be at an end." In 1433, she saw the rosebush and died soon after.

8. Columba—Patron Saint of Bookbinders, Poets, and Ireland

Legend has it that around 560, Columba became involved in a battle with St. Finnian, which resulted in the deaths of many people. As penance, Columba went to Scotland to work as a missionary to convert as many people as had been killed in the battle. Columba reputedly wrote several hymns and more than 300 books in his lifetime. Columba died in 597, and although he spent much of his life in Scotland, he is one of the patron saints of Ireland, along with St. Patrick and St. Brigid.

9. Alexis of Rome—Patron Saint of Beggars

Alexis, the son of a distinguished Roman, fled his father's house on his wedding night and sustained a frugal and religious existence. As his fame as a holy man grew, he returned to Rome and lived as a beggar beneath the stairs of his father's palace for the remaining 17 years of his life. When he died in A.D. 417, he was found with a document on his body that declared his identity.

Philosophers and Their Beliefs

To make more sense of the cosmos and human relationships (among other curiosities), people often turn to philosophers. But what did these guys know, anyway?

❋　❋　❋　❋

Q: Was Machiavelli the author of new levels of conniving evil?

A: Most would say no. Born in 1469, Niccolò Machiavelli was a patriot during the Renaissance, when his beloved city-state of Florence was caught between Venice, Milan, France, Spain, the Papal States, and several other greedy enemies. He believed in using all practical methods to further the lot of one's own people and nation, being humane when possible and rough when necessary. His bad reputation largely comes from the Catholic Church, which banned his writings—an act of hypocrisy, given the political climate of the time, and the insurgence of the Inquisition.

Q: How did Socrates view the world?

A: He didn't leave us any writings, so we only know from the words of others. Socratic thought questioned everything: religion, politics, dogmas, and "things everybody knows." He questioned not merely conclusions but the underlying assumptions, annoying the power structure of ancient Athens.

Q: Nietzsche: proto-Nazi?

A: That would be a bold assertion, but Nietzsche certainly believed in the morality of power; he glorified strength and despised weakness. Primarily, he advocated the development of superior beings. But in his last years, he started to suggest outlandish things that even Nazis wouldn't have liked, including the idea that European powers should all invade Germany.

Q: What's Neo-Platonism?

A: Neo-Platonism arose in the third century. Since then, it has evolved from the version advanced by the philosophers Plotinus and Porphyry, who interpreted Plato their own way. Neo-Platonism has a religious bent, advocating Monism— the belief that there is a transcendent one divinity immensely superior to all lesser divinities, angels, and so on. Thomas Taylor, to better distinguish Plotinus's thought from Plato's original, came up with the term "Neo-Platonism" in the 19th century.

Q: Aleister Crowley proclaimed himself the biblical "Great Beast." What did he believe?

A: Crowley, born 1875, liked to shock people. He founded a philosophy called Thelema (Greek for "will"), which has adherents today. Its founding and core statement: "Do what thou wilt shall be the whole of the law." That sounds anarchic, but Crowley was advocating that each person should define and seek his or her own highest purpose in life. He was only a beast to those who believed we should live strictly regimented and carefully pious lives.

"Even philosophers will praise war as ennobling mankind, forgetting the Greek who said: 'War is bad in that it begets more evil than it kills.'"

—IMMANUEL KANT

"I attribute the little I know to my not having been ashamed to ask for information, and to my rule of conversing with all descriptions of men on those topics that form their own peculiar professions and pursuits."

—JOHN LOCKE

The Origin of Christian Science

Mary Baker Eddy believed that she was learning to evoke Christlike healing powers in the modern day, regaining humanity's gift from the divine.

✳   ✳   ✳   ✳

Something About Mary

MARY BAKER WAS born into a Congregational (Calvinist) New Hampshire family in 1821. Growing up, she was often ill, which was particularly unfortunate in an era when doctors did as much harm as good. They found little in the way of modern medicine to heal her.

Young Mary had an independent religious streak. She was devoted to Christianity, but she questioned core Calvinist tenets such as original sin and predestination.

Mary's young adulthood was full of pain and calamity. Her first husband died in 1844 when she was pregnant with their son. She moved back home to live with her parents, but her mother died five years later. Mary was never in robust health, and at times her chronic illness required her to foster her son with family acquaintances. Her second husband abandoned her in 1866.

Mary started taking matters into her own hands. Since doctors had never provided Mary much medical relief, she experimented at developing her own therapies. She tried diets, homeopathy, mentalism, placebo, therapeutic touch, and other nontraditional healing methods, with mixed results.

In 1866, Mary slipped on a patch of ice and injured her back. Bedridden, she asked to be brought her Bible. As she studied passages about Jesus' healing episodes, she noticed her back pain fading. She considered it a manifest miracle of divine healing— like those the New Testament attributed to Jesus of Nazareth.

Mary was convinced that humanity could rediscover this art. For the next nine years, she researched the art and science of spiritual healing. In 1875, she published her findings in a guide, *Science and Health with Key to the Scriptures.*

Church of Christ, Scientist

She hoped, perhaps a bit naively, that Christian churches would welcome her healing methods. It wasn't happening, so in 1879 she started the Church of Christ, Scientist (CS). Its mission: "reinstate primitive Christianity and its lost element of healing." (The Church still bases its procedures upon Mary's manual.)

Like most new Christian sects, CS sought to rediscover the Christian knowledge from which modern churches had wandered. While tens of thousands of people were drawn to her message, many others opposed it—some quite vociferously—on moral, ethical, or spiritual grounds.

Nonetheless, the message spread, and more and more Christians were attracted to it. Church of Christ, Scientist, got its first actual church building in Boston in 1894. Today, about 2,000 churches exist worldwide.

Spreading the Word

Since Mary was doing a lot of writing, it made sense for CS to start a publishing house. The Christian Science Publishing Society is still around. You're probably familiar with one of its publications: *The Christian Science Monitor,* an internationally respected (and mostly secular) newspaper founded in 1908. This too was Mary's idea. The 20th century opened in an atmosphere of "yellow journalism." Sensationalized stories were used by newspaper bigwigs to manipulate the opinions of their readers. Yellow journalism disgusted Mary, especially when it took swipes at CS. The *Monitor's* goal was, and is, "to injure no man, but to bless all mankind" (in short, to present news as news, free of bias and sensationalism).

Fast Facts

✳ In 1865, Mary Walker, a Civil War surgeon, became the first (and so far, only) woman to receive the Congressional Medal of Honor.

✳ In 1916, Jeanette Rankin became the first woman elected to the U.S. Congress. She is also the only person who voted against both World Wars I and II.

✳ The phrase "mad as a hatter" referred to 19th-century hatmakers who were poisoned by the mercury they used to treat the felt in their hats. Mercury poisoning often causes neurological problems such as excitable or irrational behavior, trembling, and the jumbling of words when speaking.

✳ Three of the first five presidents died on Independence Day. John Adams and Thomas Jefferson died on the same day—July 4, 1826. James Monroe died on July 4, 1831.

✳ Each king in a deck of playing cards is meant to represent a king from history: the king of spades is for King David, the king of clubs represents Alexander the Great, the king of hearts depicts Charlemagne, and the king of diamonds is reserved for Julius Caesar.

✳ Napoleon Bonaparte suffered from ailurophobia—the fear of cats.

✳ You didn't want to be naked on deck in the U.S. Navy in the 1840s; it would get you nine lashes. More severe was filthiness (twelve lashes), but less severe was throwing a spittoon lid overboard (six lashes).

✳ In 1969, Native American activists took over Alcatraz. They claimed that since the island was inhospitable, lacking in any facilities or means of support, and a former prison, it fit the past reservation traditions perfectly.

✳ Pepsi-Cola was the first foreign consumer product sold in the former Soviet Union.

Fallacies & Facts: St. Patrick

Fallacy: St. Patrick drove the snakes out of Ireland.

Fact: There weren't any snakes in Ireland at that time. Snakes first appeared in the Southern Hemisphere on the supercontinent known as Gondwanaland before it separated into South America, Africa, India, Australia, and Antarctica. From there, snakes migrated north and eventually covered most of the globe. But they never made it to Ireland, which is surrounded by water.

Fallacy: St. Patrick was Irish.

Fact: Actually, he was born in Britannia, a Roman province that later became what we know as England. From Patrick's own writings, we know that he was captured by Irish raiders when he was 16 and carried off to Ireland, where he was a slave for six years. He escaped and returned to his family but was later inspired by a vision to return to Ireland to spread the Christian gospel.

Fallacy: St. Patrick used a shamrock to promote Christianity.

Fact: Although many believe St. Patrick used the three-leaf shamrock as a teaching symbol of the Christian trinity, there is no record of this in any of his writings or those of his contemporaries.

Fallacy: His name was Patrick.

Fact: Some historians say his birth name was Maewyn Succat. He took the name Patrick when he began his missionary work for the Catholic Church.

Fallacy: St. Patrick introduced Christianity to Ireland.

Fact: Ireland had strong trade relations with the Roman Empire, so it's likely that Christianity existed in the country before Patrick arrived.

White Buffalo Miracle

When Dave and Valerie Heider decided to raise buffalo on their hobby farm in the late 1990s, they had no idea what fate had in store for them.

✳ ✳ ✳ ✳

Follow the Star

Hoping to earn a little extra money for their retirement years, the Heiders raised buffalo in their spare time and kept their day jobs in Janesville, Wisconsin. Then in August 1994, one of the buffalo cows prepared to give birth and her white calf was not just a surprise—she was a miracle. And that's how she got her name.

The Heider family considered Miracle's appearance to be a bit unusual, but they were totally unprepared for the attention that soon descended on their little farm. It turns out that white buffalo are very significant in Native American mythology. The Associated Press picked up the story, and soon people from all over the country wanted to see the baby calf that was causing such a stir.

In fact, the day after the story hit the presses, the first Native Americans had arrived in Janesville. To the Native American tribes of the Midwest, a white buffalo is akin to the second coming of Christ, according to a Lakota medicine man who saw the calf. They wanted merely to see her, pray, and leave an offering.

What's It All About?

Buffalo, of course, were very important to certain Native American peoples. They relied on the beasts for food, clothing, and shelter, as well as tools and utensils. But even more important for this story, in light of everything buffalo added to their lives, Native Americans forged a spiritual relationship with the buffalo that did not exist with other animals.

The Legend of the White Buffalo varies a little depending on who tells it, but the most important points remain the same. Long ago, when the Sioux inhabited the Great Plains, a group of hunters went out in search of game. Some say the hunters saw a beautiful woman, while others say they saw a white buffalo that then turned into a woman.

The woman instructed the hunters to return to their village and tell people that she would be coming. They did and she came, bringing a sacred pipe. Before leaving, the White Buffalo Calf Woman promised she would return as a white female buffalo calf. This event would symbolize a new harmony among people of all colors.

Along Came a Miracle

So imagine the excitement among Native Americans when a white calf was born. While some said she should have been born to one of the Native American nations, others thought the fact that she was born on a farm owned by a "white man" was significant—possibly a necessity for restoring peace among nations.

Whatever the reason that Miracle was born on the Heider farm, it seemed to be a stroke of luck. The Heiders had never heard the white buffalo tale before her birth, and Dave Heider himself admits he saw dollar signs when she first appeared. But once the family saw the religious and cultural significance that Miracle held, they changed their minds. They considered Miracle a special gift and went so far as to open their farm to visitors. Onlookers were not allowed within the gates—and in fact, the Heiders eventually needed to install a sturdy fence to protect the buffalo and to hold the numerous gifts and offerings that visitors brought with them and draped over the fence to honor her.

And people did come—thousands of them. They came from all over to pay their respects, satisfy their curiosity, and to meditate. One man even came all the way from Ireland.

The family had opportunities to sell the calf but turned down each offer. Ted Turner, who owns a large private buffalo herd, made an offer. So did Ted Nugent, who wrote a song about a white buffalo. Circuses and carnivals came calling, as well, but in each case, the answer was no.

Miracle was never about money to the Heiders. They didn't sell posters or mugs. They didn't even charge admission. They finally sold photos of the calf for a dollar, if only to discourage visitors from taking their own pictures and selling them for profit.

One in a Million . . . or So

The reason for all the uproar is that a white buffalo, as you may have guessed, doesn't come along every day. In fact, the last documented white buffalo died in 1959. And just for the record, Miracle was not an albino, a genetic oddity; she had brown eyes. One source says the odds of the birth of a true white female buffalo are as low as one in a million. Other sources maintain that the chance is considerably less than that. In any case, your odds of winning the lottery are quite possibly higher.

Miracle lived a relatively short life (she died of natural causes at age ten), considering many buffalo live as long as 40 years. During her short life, she didn't remain white but changed color four times. This too was part of the ancient prophecy, to unify the four peoples of red, white, black, and yellow.

Native Americans believe Miracle lived up to her name as the return of the White Buffalo Calf Woman. No matter what, she was surely a symbol of hope. Today, you'll find a statue of the White Buffalo Calf Woman erected in her honor on the Heider's farm in Janesville.

From the Vaults of History

Our Thoughts *Eggs*-actly

As foods go, eggs fill a rather mundane but important part of diets around the world. But they have also been at the center of many cultural beliefs. Long thought of as a symbol of life and rebirth, the Greeks and Romans revered eggs and buried them in tombs along with the dead. The Maoris also held eggs in high esteem and would place them in the hands of the dead before burial. Many other egg customs still exist: Eggs that are laid on Good Friday and eaten on Easter Sunday are believed to protect their consumer throughout the entire year. In Germany, eggs that are hung in evergreen trees represent powerful symbols of rebirth and renewal.

Fabulous Fabergé

In the 19th century, Carl Fabergé, the court jeweler to the Czar of Russia, took the plain old egg to dizzyingly  new heights by creating beautiful, hand-decorated eggs out of porcelain, gold, and crystal. The incredibly intricate Fabergé eggs are still coveted and sold as priceless works of art around the world. In fact, Soviet dictator Joseph Stalin paid at least one special agent with the fab eggs, who in turn sold them for a profit.

Egg Fight!

In one wild story from the so-called "Easter Wars" circa A.D. 975, a light-hearted battle broke out, pitting the Bishop and Dean of Chester, England, against the cathedral choir. As legend has it, an egg fight began during the Easter service and lasted for more than an hour until all combatants ran out of "ammunition."

The Intergalactic Journey of Scientology

There are few who don't know about the aura of mystery and scandal that surrounds the Church of Scientology, which boasts a small membership and a seismic pocketbook. Scientology frequently graces the headlines, with stories ranging from accounts of Tom Cruise tomfoolery to an endless stream of lawsuits and accusations of bribery and abuse.

✳   ✳   ✳   ✳

THE FANTASTICAL ELEMENTS of the saga of Scientology were perhaps written into the religion from its beginning, given that Scientology sprang from the fertile mind of its late creator, pulp fiction writer turned religious messiah, L. Ron Hubbard. Hubbard, born in 1911, began his writing career in the 1930s after flunking out of college. Hubbard had always preferred imagination to reality: Accounts of his past reveal hallucinogenic drug abuse and an obsession with black magic and Satanism. In between prolific bouts of writing, Hubbard served in the Navy during World War II, became involved in various start-up ventures, and, of course, dabbled in black magic ceremonies. Allegation has it that Hubbard and wealthy scientist friend John Parsons performed a ritual in which they attempted to impregnate a woman with the antichrist. The woman was Parsons's girlfriend, but she soon became Hubbard's second wife—though he was still married to his first wife.

Down to a Science

In 1949, Hubbard developed a self-help process that he called Dianetics. All of humanity's problems, according to Dianetics, stem from the traumas of past lives. These traumas are called *engrams*, and Hubbard's own e-meter (a machine using simple lie detector technology) purportedly can identify and help eliminate these engrams, which in turn may increase intelligence and cure blindness. The first Dianetics article appeared in a sci-fi publication called *Astounding Science Fiction*. In 1950, Hubbard opened the Hubbard Dianetic Research Foundation in New Jersey, and in that same year *Dianetics: The Modern Science of Mental Health* was published and sold well.

Hubbard and his followers attempted to establish Dianetics as an official science. But the medical profession didn't appreciate Dianetics masquerading as science. The Dianetic Research Foundation came under investigation by the IRS and the American Medical Association. Hubbard soon fled New Jersey.

Actually, It's a Religion...

Dianetics wasn't making the cut as a scientific theory, so Hubbard played another card. Years before, Hubbard is reputed to have told a friend "writing for a penny a word is ridiculous. If a man really wants to make a million dollars, the best way would be to start his own religion." After fleeing Jersey, Hubbard moved to Phoenix, Arizona, declared Dianetics an "applied religious philosophy," and, in 1954, Hubbard's organization was recognized as a religion by the IRS and granted tax-exempt status.

Thus the Church of Scientology was born. Hubbard added new stories to the original Dianetics creation, and by the 1960s, he said humans were spiritual descendants of the alien Thetans, who were banished to live on Earth by the intergalactic terrorist dictator Xenu 75 million years ago. Scientologist disciples must not only expel the traumas of past lives but of past lives on different planets. Discovering these traumas is an expensive process, so the Church actively recruits wealthy devotees. As for Hubbard, he died in 1986, soon after the IRS accused him of stealing $200 million from the Church. Today, Scientology and its various offshoot nonprofit groups and private business ventures hold a vast fortune, and Scientology's ongoing litigation with the IRS, the press, and ex-devotees (hundreds of lawsuits are pending) are so bizarre, they seem almost out of this world.

Biblical Measurements

Noah's Ark is said to be 300 cubits long, 50 cubits wide, and 30 cubits high—but what on earth does that mean? Here are some biblical measurements and their conversions.

✳   ✳   ✳   ✳

Handbreadth—on an adult hand, three to four fingers held together, or three to four inches

A Day's Journey—roughly 20 to 30 miles, half that when traveling in a large company (with women and children)

Sabbath's Day Journey—just over a half mile, in reference to restricted travel on the day of rest

Span—the width from the end of the thumb to the tip of the little finger, fully extended, which measured about nine inches

Cubit—about 18 inches, represented by the length of an adult arm from the point of the elbow to the tip of the middle finger

Bath—between six and eight gallons, which was the largest liquid measure used by the Jews in the Old Testament

Homer—less than eight bushels; originally signified "an ass load," or the amount a donkey could carry

Talent—75 pounds, the Bible's largest unit of measurement

Mite—the smallest Jewish coin in use, which represented only half a farthing

Shekel—approximately 58 cents; 3,000 shekels equal a talent

Marx's Word Choice

Karl Marx said many things, but he didn't say, "Religion is the opiate of the people." It's odd that the man who penned The Communist Manifesto *and* Das Kapital *may be best known for writing a single word—even if people seldom get that word right.*

✳   ✳   ✳   ✳

Opium or opiate? With religious zealots addressing the masses with overblown rhetoric, it's not surprising that secular sensationalists often reference the renowned religious diatribe that Karl Marx authored in February 1843. In the introduction to his paragraph-by-paragraph critique of Hegel's 1820 book *Elements of the Philosophy of Right*, Marx remarked: "Religious suffering is, at one and the same time, the expression of real suffering and a protest against real suffering. Religion is the sigh of the oppressed creature, the heart of a heartless world, and the soul of the soulless conditions. It is the opium of the people."

To some analysts, Marx was saying that religion is a drug that dulls people's pain but leaves them incapable of or unwilling to affect change. To others, the erudite economist was of the opinion that religion provides solace to people in distress and eases whatever pain they may be feeling, much like a drug such as opium. At the time, opium was a legal pain-reducing product, though attempts were beginning to prohibit its production.

Marx's most famous statement is continually misquoted and misprinted to read, "Religion is the opiate of the people." What's more, "masses" is often substituted for "people," and that misquote is further spread by followers of the Arizona industrial-metal band Opiate for the Masses.

Looking for an Afterlife

For many researchers, inventors, and weekend mad scientists, the potential payoff of proving there's life after death is well worth any skeptical taunting. Here are some highlights from a century of prodding into the great hereafter.

✳   ✳   ✳   ✳

✳ In 1901, surgeon Duncan Macdougall attempted to weigh the human soul. He laid dying tuberculosis patients on massive scales and noted any changes at the moment of death. Based on six weigh-ins, he determined that body weight drops about ¾ ounce (21 grams) when a person dies—presumably because the immortal soul exits the premises.

✳ In 2000, an Oregon rancher named Lewis Hollander Jr. tried his hand at soul-weighing, enlisting eight sheep, three lambs, and a goat as his subjects (the animals were already at death's door). No animals lost weight as they passed on, but all of the sheep gained weight for one to six seconds after death. One sheep put on almost two pounds.

✳ In the 1920s, two Dutch physicists claimed a disembodied spirit had explained to them, via séance, how to build a soul-detecting machine. The spirit said the human soul lives on as a gaseous body, which could interact with the physical world by expanding and contracting. The physicists built an elaborate pressure detector and reported that the spirit did indeed alter gas pressure on demand.

✳ At the time of his death in 1931, Thomas Edison was reportedly working on a type of megaphone to allow, in his words, "personalities which have left this earth to communicate with us." No one has ever turned up any "Spirit Phone" prototypes or technical specs, however.

✳ In order to stop fake mediums from capitalizing on his fame when he died, escape artist and enthusiastic spiritualist debunker Harry Houdini vowed that if he could communicate from beyond the grave, he would relay a ten-word code, known only to his wife. For ten years, Houdini's wife held séances on the anniversary of his death (Halloween), but the code never came through.

* Beginning in the 1960s, Latvian writer Konstantin Raudive made 70,000 recordings of electronic voice phenomena (EVP), the supposed voices of ghosts captured on audio tape.

* In the 1970s, two Icelandic scientists spent four years examining accounts from 1,000 doctors and nurses of what American and Indian patients experienced as they approached death. With the help of computer analysis, they noted persistent common details in the accounts, including a bright light, an overpowering feeling of peace, and a sense of an otherworldly realm.

* Michael Persinger, a professor of neuroscience at Laurentian University, has found that when subjects place their heads in strong electromagnetic fields, most sense a ghostly presence. His theory is that intense electromagnetic fields either cause hallucinations or enable people to sense ghosts that are there all the time.

* In order to test the validity of near-death, out-of-body experience reports, psychiatry professor Bruce Greyson displays distinctive images while patients who undergo implanted defibrillator testing are briefly brain dead. So far, no one has recalled seeing the pictures.

* In 2008, the English physician Sam Parnia launched a similar experiment designed to gauge the validity of out-of-body experiences in heart attack survivors. He outfitted an operating room with shelves showing pictures that are only visible from the top of the room. His hope is to analyze the near-death recollections of 1,500 patients.

Fast Facts

✳ Both poison oak and poison ivy are considered members of the cashew family.

✳ Adults have weaker taste buds compared to kids.

✳ You can increase the life of a rubber band by storing it in the fridge.

✳ Tooth enamel is the hardest substance in a human body.

✳ Kermit the Frog got his name from a friend of Jim Henson. Kermit Scott grew up with Henson and went on to become a philosophy professor at Purdue University.

✳ Up to 33 percent of all Americans are chronically underhydrated.

✳ More than half of all turns on roads are right turns.

✳ The 200 buffalo that roam California's Catalina Island are descendants of a few that were taken there for a movie shoot in the 1920s and left behind.

✳ Fire ants first entered the United States in 1920 at Mobile, Alabama, on a cargo ship from South America.

✳ The average person breathes 25,000 times on a normal day.

✳ There are almost 12,000 species of grasshoppers worldwide.

✳ Lake Michigan was once known as "Lake of the Stinking Water."

✳ The inability to remember a word is called lethologica. Try to remember that one.

✳ In 1791, Vermont became the first state to be added to the United States since the original 13.

✳ Herman Melville's *Moby-Dick* was inspired by a real event perhaps more spellbinding than the book. In 1820, the Nantucket whale ship *Essex* was repeatedly rammed by a large sperm whale and sank in the Pacific Ocean, leaving the 20 crewmembers adrift in three small whaleboats for 95 days. Only eight men survived.

Do Unto Others: the Golden Rule

The Golden Rule is one of the world's most widespread moral philosophies. It's also the basis of a series of quotes so often misquoted as to make misquotes irrelevant.

✳   ✳   ✳   ✳

Socrates may never have said, "Do unto others as you would like done to you," but he did say something to the effect of "Do not do unto others what angers you if done to you by others." This translation wins few points for eloquence, but the bottom line is that Socrates, Confucius, or Jesus could all be attributed with stating the Golden Rule in one version or another, and it serves as the moral basis for religion and philosophy the world over.

The Golden Rule is so pervasive that many modern ethicists think it represents some fundamental truth of human morality. Adherence to the rule necessitates empathy and imagination, as it requires one person to imagine how another person would feel in a given situation. So whoever said which version, the essence remains the same: Treat people how you want to be treated.

Variations on the Golden Rule

Here are some examples of variations of the Golden Rule: "He sought for others the good he desired for himself. Let him pass," from the Egyptian Book of the Dead; "Do to others what you would have them do to you," from the Bible; "What is hateful to you, do not to your fellow. That is the whole Torah; the rest is but commentary," from the Talmud; "This is the sum of duty: Do naught unto others which would cause you pain if done to you," from the Mahabharata; and, finally, to mix it up with some imagery, a proverb of Nigeria's Yoruba tribe: "One going to take a pointed stick to pinch a baby bird should first try it on himself to feel how it hurts."

The Vatican Ratline

One of the most shocking stories in the aftermath of the Holocaust was the participation of the Roman Catholic Church, at its highest levels, in helping tens of thousands of Nazis escape prosecution. Appropriately called "the Vatican ratline," it had the support of high-ranking clergymen and alleged American intelligence conspirators—and some say even the tacit approval of the pope himself.

✳   ✳   ✳   ✳

TANGLED AS THE truth has become in the mists of time and purposeful confusion, we know that the ratlines (for there were several) organized escapes for a number of marquee names of the Third Reich. These included Adolf Eichmann (eventually captured by the Israelis, tried, and hanged for war crimes); the infamous "Angel of Death," Dr. Josef Mengele, whose cruel medical experiments still revolt even the most jaded; Klaus Barbie, nicknamed the "Butcher" (what did you have to do in those circles to earn such a nickname?); and many others who slithered to freedom. They are estimated to number around 30,000, although this figure has been disputed.

The Church Gets into the Act

While one ratline, made famous by Frederick Forsyth's 1972 thriller novel *The Odessa File* (which was also made into a film), was run by former SS members, most others were organized and administered by the prominent Roman Catholic lay group Intermarium, which not only smuggled war criminals to safety but later reportedly became the single most important source of Nazi recruits for the U.S. Central Intelligence Agency. One of Intermarium's most active members was a proudly anti-Semitic bishop, Dr. Alois (aka Luigi) Hudal. An Austrian, he was concerned about what he thought were attempts by "the Semitic race . . . to set itself apart and dominate." He also fantasized about a Jewish conspiracy to seize Rome's financial assets. As early as 1937, Hudal was publicly praising Hitler in his book *The Foundations of National Socialism*.

In 1943, Hudal met SS intelligence chief Josef Rauff, the developer of mobile extermination-gas vans, then stationed in Milan. The two began setting up a network to be used as a later escape route for major Nazis (including Rauff himself, who was personally protected by Hudal until he could flee to Syria, then Chile). Two years later, Hudal mentored Otto Wachter, who had organized the Warsaw Ghetto and was a key member of Operation Reinhard, which led to the slaughter of more than two million Polish Jews. Wachter lived disguised as a monk in a Roman monastery under Hudal's personal protection until his 1949 death.

Smuggled to Safety

In 1944, Hudal attained control of the Austrian section of the Pontifical Commission of Assistance (PCA). This position allowed him and other priests to organize the escape of more big-time Nazis, including Franz Stangl, commanding officer of the Treblinka death camp—who was given cash, a Red Cross passport, and a visa to Syria. Then there was SS captain Edward Roschmann, known as the "Butcher of Riga"; Gustav Wagner, commanding officer of the Sobibor death camp; and many more who made their way to freedom. Other major clergy involved in helping the Nazis included Monsignor Karlo Petranovic; Father Edoardo Domoter, a Franciscan who personally forged Eichmann's Red Cross passport; and Croatian Franciscan Father Krunoslav Draganovic, who was later retained by the United States during the Cold War (he received a paycheck from the Pentagon).

Draganovic's highly sophisticated operation made Hudal's look positively makeshift. He had an Austrian-based priest make contact with Nazis hiding there and then get them across the border to Italy, where other priests (including Draganovic himself) would provide shelter in monasteries as false papers were processed. Once those were in place, Draganovic procured passage on ships sailing to South America.

His ratline was so professional that many war criminals reached safe havens in such civilized destinations as Britain, Canada, Australia, and the United States. This was reportedly an open secret in Rome's intelligence and diplomatic circles as early as August 1945.

Coming into the Open

Who actually "discovered" the Vatican ratline is still open to debate: It might have been U.S. Army Counter Intelligence Corps agent William Gowen, serving in Rome after the war as a Nazi hunter and investigator. Or it could have been Vincent La Vista, another American counterintelligence agent, who in May 1947 forwarded a report to his superiors detailing all the Vatican-linked branches of this underground railroad.

That year, an Italian newspaper revealed Hudal's wartime activities, which resulted in a scandal. He hung onto his post until 1952, however, when the Holy See pressured him into resigning. Up until his death 11 years later, Hudal still maintained that he had done "a just thing...expected of a true Christian," snidely adding: "We do not believe in the eye for an eye of the Jew."

What About the Pope?

The question is no longer whether certain priests aided and abetted the Nazis, it's whether they did so on their own or with the knowledge, consent, and/or aid of the Vatican. Monsignor Karl Bayer, director of Caritas in Rome, admitted: "The Pope [Pius XII] did provide money for this [Nazi smuggling]; in driblets sometimes, but it did come." More financing arrived courtesy of the United States, specifically the American National Catholic Welfare Conference, which gave Hudal "substantial funds for his 'humanitarian' aid."

As for Pius XII, he was possibly neither as bad as is sometimes claimed, nor as good as he might have been. Terrified of a godless Communism, he considered the Nazis the lesser of two evils. Hitler had been pressuring him since 1942 to either embrace the Nazis or face destruction of the Church. The Vatican then became "neutral," in favor of Germany. Pius allegedly managed to get Mussolini's forces to purposely screw up shipments of Italian Jews to concentration camps, and he might have saved thousands when he said that the Church would protect any Jew who married a Catholic. His supporters claim that while Churchill and Roosevelt spoke up, they did nothing; but Pius, although remaining silent, did something.

The Vatican's 1998 statement on the Holocaust, entitled "We Remember," claims that Pius saved "hundreds of thousands of Jewish lives," which would be difficult to prove—or disprove, for that matter.

In the Cathedral and on the Court

In 2000, the world-famous Harlem Globetrotters exhibition basketball team visited the Vatican. After a parade in Rome celebrating their 75th anniversary, the team met with Pope John Paul II and named the pontiff an honorary Globetrotter. However, no photos were released of the Pope spinning a basketball on his finger.

Roots of the Kabbalistic Tree

Judaism's mystic tradition extends so far back it's hard to see its exact origins, but we can identify some transformational teachers and phases.

✳ ✳ ✳ ✳

Scattered Seeds

KABBALAH (PRONOUNCED "ka-ba-LAH" in Hebrew) may predate the rise of Christianity, with influence from various pre-Christian Near Eastern spiritual systems. Jewish tradition dates it as far back as Judaism itself. Only scattered writings from this era hint at the subject; perhaps there were as many Kabbalot (plural) as there were mystics. You couldn't sign up for Kabbalah night classes at your synagogue; an adept would have to train you, likely through oral tradition and Torah study. In any case, no written text survives from this era. Most adepts had probably heard of a few others and had actually met fewer still. That's vague, but so is Kabbalah's early history.

Sapling

The oldest surviving manuscripts with clear reference to Kabbalah date to about A.D. 100–200. Kabbalah has never been a monolith, but by the end of the first millennium A.D., it acquired a sort of broad consensus orthodoxy. Jews call this era the *Diaspora*, or dispersion: a time when their ancestors did a lot of migrating to avoid persecution, mostly away from Palestine but in some cases back to it. This phase paid a dividend for Kabbalah. With diverse subgroups of Jews meeting up here and there, scholars shared Kabbalistic views—and, for the first enduring time, wrote them down. A difficult period, but one of intellectual ferment born in adversity.

Bearing Leaves

The Kabbalah known to modern scholars came together in the high to late Middle Ages (A.D. 1100–1400). Several Kabbalistic texts from this phase formed the basis for the *Zohar*, compiled in the late 1200s by Spanish rabbi Moshe ben Shem-Tov. The *Zohar* was the first widely read mystical Torah commentary, taken by modern Kabbalistic scholars as its fundamental text. In this phase, too, came the first known use of the actual term *Kabbalah* (a transliteration, though often spelled "Qabalah").

Kabbalah's next major influence was Rabbi Yitzhak Luria (1534–72). In Tsfat, Palestine, Luria taught (what we now call) the Lurianic Kabbalah as a structured system of Jewish mysticism. Luria clearly defined the ten *s'firot* ("spheres"), which compose the Tree of Life, Kabbalah's central mandala and depiction. Much of today's written material is based on Lurianic teaching.

Branching

As early as the 1600s, non-Jews were adapting Kabbalistic notions to their own views of the cosmos. Come the 1800s, a group of Masonic mystics in England formed a society called the Golden Dawn, a magical/religious stew of tarot, Egyptian, Masonic, Kabbalistic, Hermetic, and astrological thought. Aleister Crowley was one influential member.

Some modern Kabbalists orient themselves toward the Golden Dawn's descendant beliefs; others follow the Jewish tradition. Thanks to a recent fad among celebrities, many modern Americans have heard of Kabbalah. The fad will one day fade, but Kabbalah won't; after all, it hasn't faded in two millennia.

A Little More About Kabbalah

❋ Famed *Golden Dawn* author Dion Fortune calls Kabbalah "the Yoga of the West." It's hard to improve upon her concise summary.

❋ *Kabbalah*, or *Qabalah*, comes from the Hebrew letters *quph*, *bet*, and *lamed*, representing the concept of receiving something (in this case, teachings). Modern shorthand for Qabalah is "QBL," representing these root letters.

❋ The goal of traditional Kabbalah is to perfect one's understanding of the Torah, and by extension Hashem (Elohim, or God).

The Oneida Community

Perhaps the most successful "utopian community" was the
Oneida Community of upstate New York.

✳ ✳ ✳ ✳

JOHN HUMPHREY NOYES was born in 1811. In the 1830s, while studying divinity at Yale, he decided a Christian could transcend sin. He called this philosophy *Perfectionism*. When Noyes pronounced himself without sin, Yale cast the first stone by revoking his ministry license and kicking him out in 1837.

Putney and Perfectionism

Noyes yearned to build a Perfectionist community. After a spiritual crisis (or perhaps a bout of psychological self-torment), which he considered a desperate Satanic assault, he moved back to Putney, Vermont, where his family lived. Converting his siblings and some locals, he insisted Christ's Second Coming had already occurred in A.D. 70. According to Noyes, marriage and monogamy were nonexistent in heaven—but sex wasn't. (Noyes himself got married anyway.)

For the next nine years, he gathered and taught his flock. Members spent their time farming, studying scripture, and publishing a Perfectionist magazine. Women shared ownership and benefits with relative equality. As for sex, Noyes taught a doctrine called "complex marriage" (all males are married to all females). Men, he taught, should practice "male continence"—refraining from ejaculation unless children were desired. It was the best sexual deal American women would see until the 1960s.

Here began Noyes's concept of "Bible Communism": communally held property, focused on biblical teachings (as interpreted by Noyes). Group criticism sessions were a social norm. But remember: Sino-Soviet Communism hadn't been invented, nor had Lenin, gulags, Mao, etc. Marx only wrote the *Communist Manifesto* in 1848, just as Noyes's community was moving to New

York. Noyes would have considered Marx proof of Satan's ability to pervert scripture.

The Putney situation imploded in 1847, when the local sheriff arrested Noyes for adultery. Compelled to flee Vermont, in 1848 Noyes found his people's Zion: 40 acres and a sawmill owned by some Perfectionists near Oneida, New York. By year-end, the Oneida Community was 87 strong and busy as beavers: buying and clearing land, planting, and building.

Many new arrivals brought useful skills. Noyes believed people should change jobs often to ward off drudgery. Complex marriage meant that postmenopausal women initiated boys into sex after puberty, until the males learned control. Older men (often Noyes himself) initiated girls into sex shortly after menarche. In practice, Noyes decided who should have sex, prioritizing his own very healthy appetites in this regard. Since God advised Noyes, disagreeing with Noyes equaled disagreement with God. Those who disagreed with God/Noyes were welcome to hit the bricks.

The community built, invested, and thrived, growing to about 300 members. Oneida women invented bloomeresque pantaloons two years before Amelia Bloomer. Diverse industries arose: canning, silk, animal traps, furniture, and eventually silverware. Oneida hired outside employees, treating them well.

Downfall

By 1879, the Oneida experiment was a great commercial success but socially beleaguered. Noyes's attempt to install his son as his successor failed. Dissidents wanted to abandon complex marriage. When Noyes learned of his impending arrest for statutory rape, he bailed to Canada, where he advised his members from afar.

The remaining members reorganized Oneida as a joint stock company and kept up the business. The firm sold off all but the silverware business by 1916. The last member of the community died in 1950. In 2005, Oneida Limited finally outsourced silverware manufacture overseas.

7 Things the Pope Wears in Public

He's got a sweet ride, he lives in a gold-plated mansion, and he performs to billions around the globe. Here are seven essential items of papal regalia.

1. **The Ring of the Fisherman:** The solid gold Ring of the Fisherman is named after St. Peter, who was a fisherman by trade; it is decorated with a representation of Peter angling from a boat, with the name of the current pope inscribed above it. The pope uses the ring to seal official papal documents.

2. **The Papal Cross:** The pope once carried a shepherd's crook to symbolize that he was the head of Christ's flock. Now, he wields a cross topped by a figure of the crucified Jesus.

3. **Papal Shoes:** Blazing carmine is the color of choice for papal footwear, whether that be the papal slippers worn indoors or the shoes worn outside.

4. **Cope:** That sweeping, flowing, heavily embroidered cape the pope wears is called a cope. It's so heavy it requires two assistants (usually deacons) to carry it.

5. **Fanon:** The fanon is another capelike garment, made of white silk lined with gold.

6. **Pallium:** The pope also sometimes dons a pallium, a scarf-type band worn around the neck and shoulders and weighed down by lead pendants.

7. **Mitre:** That pointy hat adorning the papal crown is actually known as a mitre. Pope Benedict XVI is known to be fond of his headgear, often breaking out new mitres for big events.

In Mushrooms We Trust

Meet John Allegro: linguist, showman, and certifiable eccentric.

✳ ✳ ✳ ✳

IT'S NOT OFTEN that the world of academia produces a character like John Marco Allegro. Born in 1923, Allegro first studied for the Methodist ministry but later became a brilliant scholar of Hebrew dialects. This latter course of study made him a perfect fit for the international team assembled to decipher the Dead Sea Scrolls, the earliest surviving manuscripts of the Bible.

Because Allegro was part scholar and part showman, he became a star in the otherwise sober world of biblical scholarship. At the time, the historical importance of the scrolls was a cause for controversy, and Allegro gleefully submerged himself into the debate.

Suddenly, however, Allegro took the debate in an absurd direction with his infamous book: *The Sacred Mushroom and the Cross*. In it, he argued that biblical figures like Moses and Jesus were actually literary inventions. In fact, he contended that the Jewish and Christian scriptures were allegories, written to promote an ancient fertility cult. To Allegro, Jesus represented a hallucinogenic mushroom, which followers ingested to enhance their perception of God.

Allegro tried to prove that the Bible was actually a coded text written to preserve the secrets of this drug-worshipping cult. When the writers of these "folktales" died, he argued, their original meaning was forever lost. Subsequent followers—early Christians—began taking scripture literally and interpreted as factual what Allegro maintained had always been meant as fable.

This peculiar thesis was roundly panned by the academic community. Allegro's reputation was destroyed. Though he died in disrepute, Allegro did inspire a group of supporters who, even to this day, still try to defend the man and his zany thesis.

Scandalous Cults

Groups like these give cults a bad name.

✳ ✳ ✳ ✳

Aum Shinrikyo: The Japanese religious movement earned two strikes against it—as both a cult and a terrorist group—after members carried out a sarin gas attack on the Tokyo subway system in 1995. Japanese police began raiding Aum Shinrikyo locations days later.

Branch Davidians: Followers of David Koresh looked upon him as one of God's messengers. Koresh thought of himself the same way. The U.S. government, however, had a different point of view (including allegations of polygamy, child abuse, and rape). Koresh and many followers of his religious sect were killed in 1993 when federal agents attempted to raid the group's compound near Waco, Texas. The ensuing 51-day standoff ended on April 19 when the Branch Davidian compound burned to the ground. The fallout wasn't limited to Koresh and company—the federal government was highly criticized for its handling of the situation.

Heaven's Gate: UFOs and Comet Hale-Bopp were the basis of this cult, which was led by Marshall Applewhite. Members believed that Earth was about to be "recycled" and instead opted to commit mass suicide. Thirty-nine members of the cult (including Applewhite as well as the brother of *Star Trek* actress Nichelle Nichols) were found dead in a San Diego mansion in 1997.

Manson Family: More than 40 years after his followers murdered Leno and Rosemary LaBianca and actress Sharon Tate, the name "Charles Manson" still sends a chill down the spines of many people. Manson was charged with murder and conspiracy and has been serving a life sentence. Among the members of the Manson family was Lynette "Squeaky" Fromme, who attempted to assassinate President Gerald R. Ford in 1975.

Order of the Solar Temple: Cultists do like their space-aged names...even secret societies headquartered in Europe. Started in 1984 and based on the ideals of the Knights Templar, leaders sought to unify many different beliefs before the end of the world. Things went bad for the members in 1994 after one of its founders, Joseph Di Mambro, ordered the murder of the three-month-old child of another member. The reason? The child was the antichrist (at least according to Di Mambro). A few days later, members in Canada and Switzerland are believed to have killed other followers before committing suicide.

The People's Temple: About 900 followers of a quasi-religious group led by Reverend Jim Jones drank cyanide as part of a mass suicide in Jonestown, Guyana, in 1978. Many experts view the event as one of the largest mass suicides in recorded history. For the record, Jones chose not to imbibe the poisonous drink he offered the others. He shot himself in the head instead. Oh, but the story isn't over. Before things fell apart at his headquarters, Jones ordered a group of his followers to a nearby Georgetown airstrip to stop the departure of some People's Temple followers who had lost the faith. The armed men opened fire on the group as they were departing. Among those killed was U.S. Representative Leo Ryan of California, who had traveled to Guyana to investigate the cult on the behalf of concerned family members.

Unification Church: Led by the Reverend Sun Myung Moon, the controversial church has faced allegations of fraud by some elderly members as well as highly publicized allegations of brainwashing, though these claims have never been proven.

"The only difference between a cult and a religion is the amount of real estate they own."

—FRANK ZAPPA

9 Facts About Jehovah's Witnesses

Study up for your next porch encounter with our handy primer.

✳ ✳ ✳ ✳

1. Jehovah's Witnesses date back to a Pennsylvania Bible study group established in 1872.

2. There are more than 7.1 million Jehovah's Witnesses worldwide, spanning 236 countries and 95,000 congregations.

3. Witnesses believe Jesus Christ is the son of Jehovah (God) but is an inferior spiritual being, not Jehovah incarnate.

4. Witnesses believe the world will soon end in a battle between good and evil. After Satan is defeated, 144,000 resurrected true believers will rule with Christ in heaven. Other believers will enjoy eternal life in an earthly paradise.

5. The church estimates Witnesses dedicate about one billion hours per year to "Bible education"—largely conducted door-to-door.

6. The church has published *The Watchtower Announcing Jehovah's Kingdom* under various names since 1879. It distributes approximately 37 million copies of each issue in 174 languages.

8. Witnesses believe only God is worthy of allegiance and so won't serve in the military, vote, or salute any flag.

9. Witnesses have been involved in 72 Supreme Court cases—more than any other group aside from the government. Among other things, they've won the right for adults to refuse blood transfusions, which Witnesses believe are forbidden in the Bible.

Least Religious of the United States

They say God is everywhere ... but residents in New England and the Pacific Northwest aren't so sure.

✳ ✳ ✳ ✳

ACCORDING TO A 2008 Gallup poll, 65 percent of 350,000 U.S. citizens age 18 and older said that religion is an important part of their lives. Not surprisingly, the highest concentrations were found in the "Bible Belt" of the southern states. New Englanders weren't quite so certain.

In Vermont, only 42 percent of those questioned responded that religion was an important part of their daily lives. The trend continued from respondents in neighboring New Hampshire (46 percent), Maine, and Massachusetts (48 percent). This lack of faith then took a turn to the Pacific Northwest, with the number-five spot held by, of all places, Alaska (51 percent), followed closely by Washington (52 percent) and Oregon, tied with itty bitty Rhode Island, with 53 percent. Rounding out the list was Nevada (54 percent—perhaps those praying to hit it big in Las Vegas were too busy to reply) and another East Coast favorite, Connecticut (55 percent).

A similar study conducted by the Pew Forum on Religion and Public Life, a Washington, D.C., organization, revealed that 16.1 percent of Americans surveyed said that they were not affiliated with any religion, with a scant 1.6 percent of that number maintaining that they were atheists.

Of course, all this begs the question of whether Canadian secularism is seeping into American culture. A 2008 study showed that approximately one in four Canadians (23 percent of those surveyed) said that they do not believe in any god.

Chapter Fourteen

Crime and Death

Last Meal Requests

U.S. prisoners on death row traditionally have the chance to order a special last meal on the night before they are to be executed. Here are some of the more memorable last meals ordered by prisoners.

✳ ✳ ✳ ✳

Velma Barfield, who killed five people, made history when she was executed by lethal injection at Central Prison in Raleigh, North Carolina, in 1984. She was the first woman in the United States to be executed after capital punishment was reinstated in 1977. Barfield, who became a devoted Christian while in prison, had simple tastes: She ordered a bag of Cheez Doodles and a can of Coca-Cola for her last meal.

Timothy McVeigh, a veteran of the U.S. Army, was responsible for 168 deaths when he bombed the Alfred P. Murrah Federal Building in Oklahoma City. Prior to September 11, 2001, the Oklahoma City bombing ranked as the deadliest terrorist attack in the United States. McVeigh was executed on June 11, 2001. He ordered two pints of mint chocolate chip ice cream as his last meal.

No one knows exactly how many victims serial killer **Ted Bundy** claimed, but the estimates range from 26 to 100. Bundy did not request a last meal before he was executed on January

24, 1989, in Florida. Instead, he was given the traditional last meal of steak, eggs over easy, hash browns, toast, milk, coffee, juice, butter, and jelly.

The crimes of **John Wayne Gacy** shocked the nation. Gacy was arrested in 1978 and was ultimately convicted of murdering 33 boys and young men in Illinois. He was executed on May 10, 1994, at Stateville Correctional Center in Crest Hill, Illinois. Before the execution, Gacy ate a last meal of a dozen deep-fried shrimp, a bucket of Kentucky Fried Chicken, French fries, and a pound of strawberries.

Serial killer **William Bonin** was known as the Freeway Killer and is thought to have killed as many as 36 young men and boys. He was convicted for 14 of those murders. Bonin, who was put to death on February 23, 1996, in San Quentin State Prison, was the first person executed by lethal injection in California. For his last meal, he ordered two sausage-and-pepperoni pizzas, three servings of chocolate ice cream, and 15 cans of Coca-Cola.

Victor Feguer killed a doctor in 1960 in Illinois, after picking him at random from the phone book. On March 15, 1963, Feguer was hanged at the Fort Madison Penitentiary in Iowa. Feguer requested one of the more unusual last meals—a solitary olive with a pit in it. Feguer was buried with the olive pit in his suit pocket.

Philip Workman was convicted in 1982 of murdering a police officer during a failed robbery of a fast-food restaurant in Memphis. Workman's conviction was controversial, with many doubting that he was the man who fired the shot that killed the officer. Before he was executed on May 9, 2007, Workman made an unusual request for a last meal: He asked that a large vegetarian pizza be donated to a homeless person in Nashville. Prison officials denied this request, and Workman subsequently ate nothing for his last meal. However, other people across the country donated vegetarian pizzas to homeless shelters in the state on the day Workman was executed, honoring his final request.

Fumbling Felons

Hold Up 101

Two would-be robbers from Palm Beach, Florida, needed a lesson in whom *not* to rob. They walked into a local police station and demanded cash from the receptionist. To complete their tough-guy illusion, they held their hands in their pockets to indicate that they were holding guns. The crooks—finger guns and all—were quickly apprehended.

A Matter of Perspective

An obviously drunk man was driving a van that had already sustained considerable damage. The Georgia police officer that stopped the van discovered several outstanding warrants on the driver. When the drunkard was brought in to the police station, he told the cops he didn't even have change for a phone call. Incredibly, the man had won $3 million in a lottery just five months prior!

As the man told it, he had so far received an initial payment of $94,000. First he dropped $30,000 in the Atlantic City casinos. Next he spent another $30,000 on the van, which he later rolled because he had drunk copious amounts of expensive French wine (approximately $10,000 worth). Curious, the cop asked what had happened to the other $24,000. "Oh," the guy replied. "I spent the other $24,000 foolishly."

The Not-So-Great Escape

Some criminals need a really big wall calendar. This was certainly the case with the Rhode Island man who was sentenced to 90 days in jail. Determined to show that no Big House could hold him, he labored on an elaborate escape scheme. He finally put his plan into action—on the 89th day of his sentence. Initially, everything went according to plan; he actually escaped for all of five minutes. After his recapture, he was sentenced to 18 months in prison, which gave him more than enough time to learn how to keep an accurate tally of the passing days.

Spending Eternity on the Rock

Alcatraz, nicknamed "The Rock," was the ultimate American prison—a place that hardened criminals and assorted public enemies called home. Surrounded by the heavy mist and rolling fog of San Francisco Bay, the damp prison on Alcatraz Island kept more than a thousand dangerous men cloistered from the rest of the world.

✳ ✳ ✳ ✳

The Island of Pelicans

WHEN THE SPANISH first explored the area in 1775, they dubbed the island *La Isla de los Alcatraces*, or "the Island of the Pelicans." What they found was a rocky piece of land that was completely uninhabited, sparsely vegetated, and surrounded by churning water and swift currents.

The U.S. military took over Alcatraz Island in 1850. For several decades, it was the army's first long-term prison, and it quickly gained a reputation for being a tough facility. The military used the island until 1934, when high operating costs coupled with the financial constraints of the Great Depression forced their exit.

From 1934 to 1963, during its reign as a federal prison, Alcatraz was not a facility for rehabilitating hardened criminals; it was a place of harsh punishment and limited privilege. Those who endured their stay were fortunate to leave with their sanity or—as many believe—their souls.

America's Devil's Island

The rise of criminal activity in the 1920s and early '30s put a new focus on Alcatraz. Federal authorities decided to construct an imposing, escape-proof prison that would strike fear into even the hardest criminals, and Alcatraz was the chosen site. In 1934, the Federal Bureau of Prisons took control of the facility and implemented a strict set of rules and regulations. The top guards and officers of the federal penal system were transferred to the island, and soon Alcatraz was transformed into an impregnable fortress.

Across the country, prison wardens were asked to send their worst inmates to Alcatraz. This included inmates with behavioral issues, those who had previously attempted to escape, and the most notorious criminals of the day, including Al Capone, George "Machine Gun" Kelly, Doc Barker (of the Ma Barker Gang), and Alvin "Creepy" Karpis.

Life on the Rock was anything but luxurious. Each cell measured five feet by nine feet and featured a fold-up bunk, desk, chair, toilet, and sink. Each day was exactly the same, from chow times to work assignments. The routine never varied and was completely methodical. Compliance was expected, and the tough guards sometimes meted out severe punishment if rules were not followed.

If prisoners broke the rules, they could be sent to a punishment cell known as "the hole." There were several of these cells, which were dreaded by the convicts. Here, men were stripped of all but their basic right to food. During the daytime, mattresses were taken away and steel doors blocked out any natural light. Prisoners might spend as long as 19 days in the hole in complete isolation from other inmates. Time spent there usually meant psychological and physical abuse from the

guards as well. Screams from hardened criminals could be heard echoing throughout the entire building in a stark warning to the other prisoners.

After time spent in the hole, men often came out with pneumonia or arthritis after spending days or weeks on the cold cement floor with no clothing. Others came out devoid of their sanity. Some men never came out of the hole alive.

Alcatraz and "Scarface" Al Capone

Al Capone arrived at Alcatraz in August 1934 after being convicted on charges of tax evasion. He was fairly well behaved, but life on the Rock was not easy for the ex-crime boss. He was involved in a number of fights during his incarceration, was once stabbed with a pair of scissors, and spent some time in isolation while at Alcatraz.

Attempts on his life, beatings, and the prison routine itself took their toll on Capone. Seeking a diversion, he played the banjo in a prison band. Some legends say that Scarface spent most of his time strumming his banjo alone, hoping to avoid other prisoners. In reality, after more than three years in Alcatraz, Capone was on the edge of total insanity. He spent the last year of his federal sentence in the hospital ward, undergoing treatment for an advanced case of syphilis.

When Capone left Alcatraz, he definitely seemed worse for the wear. It appeared that the Rock (and his nasty case of syphilis) had completely broken him. In January 1939, he was transferred to another prison to serve out a separate sentence. Capone was released to his family and doctors in November 1939 and became a recluse at his Florida estate. He died, broken and insane, in 1947.

Al Capone was not the only inmate to lose his grip on reality at Alcatraz. While working in the prison garage, convicted bank robber Rufe Persful picked up an ax and chopped the fingers off his left hand. Laughing maniacally, he asked another prisoner to cut off his right hand as well. An inmate named Joe Bowers sustained a superficial wound when he tried to slash his own throat with a pair of broken eyeglasses. Ed Wutke, who was at Alcatraz for murder, managed to use a pencil sharpener blade to fatally cut through his jugular vein.

These were not the only suicide attempts, and many other men suffered mental breakdowns at Alcatraz.

Escapes from Alcatraz

During Alcatraz's 29 years as a federal prison, 34 different men tried to escape the island in 14 separate attempts. In almost every case, the escapees were killed or recaptured. Two escape attempts are particularly infamous.

In May 1946, six inmates captured a gun cage, obtained prison keys, and took over a cell house in less than an hour. Unfortunately for them, the only key they did not get was the one that would let them out of the cell building, which effectively grounded the escape plot. The prison break turned into a heated gunfight that led to the deaths of three of the escapees, as well as several guards. When it was over, two of the surviving escapees were sentenced to death and the third received a life sentence.

Though the 1946 incident may have been the most violent escape attempt at Alcatraz, it is not the most famous. That distinction belongs to a 1962 attempt by Frank Morris and brothers Clarence and John Anglin. Over several months, the men chipped away at the vent shafts in their cells using tools they had stolen from work sites. They also created makeshift rafts and inflatable life vests using raincoats. They even collected hair from the barbershop and made lifelike dummies to fool the guards on duty during the escape. Then, on the night of June 11, 1962, after making their way out of the prison, the trio boarded their rafts and set out into the cold waters of the bay, never to be seen again.

More than four decades later, it is still unclear whether or not the escapees survived. According to the Bureau of Prisons, the men are either missing or presumed drowned. The story of the escape was brought to the silver screen in the 1979 film *Escape from Alcatraz*, starring Clint Eastwood.

The Haunted Prison

On March 23, 1963, less than a year after this last escape attempt, Alcatraz ended its run as a federal prison, and the island remained largely abandoned until the early 1970s. Congress placed the island under the purview of the National Park Service in 1972, and Alcatraz opened to the public in 1973. It is now one of the most popular historic sites in America.

In the daytime, the former prison bustles with the activity of tour guides and visitors, but at night, the buildings play host to some unexplainable phenomena. Many believe that some of those who served time on the Rock linger for all eternity.

Accounts of hauntings have been widely reported since Alcatraz first shut its doors. Park service employees and visitors to Alcatraz report weird, ghostly encounters in the crumbling, old buildings. Unexplained clanging sounds, footsteps, and disembodied voices and screams are commonly heard coming from the empty corridors and long-abandoned cells. Some guides have reportedly witnessed strange events in certain areas of the prison, such as the infamous "holes," where prisoners suffered greatly.

But perhaps the most eerie sound is the faint banjo music sometimes heard in the shower room. Legend has it that Al Capone would often sit and strum his banjo in that spot rather than risk going out into the yard. Is it the broken spirit of Al Capone that creates this mournful melody on his phantom instrument? Or is it another ghostly inmate, unable to escape, even after death?

Odd Ordinances

✳ In the 1930s, it was a crime to serve apple pie without a cheese topping in Wisconsin.

✳ Throwing pickle juice on a trolley is illegal in Rhode Island.

✳ Firemen aren't allowed to rescue women wearing nightgowns in St. Louis, Missouri.

✳ The city of Pasadena, California, made it illegal for secretaries to be alone with their bosses.

✳ Bathing without clothes is not allowed in the state of Florida.

✳ Women are not allowed to bathe in business offices in Carmel, California.

✳ It's illegal to fall asleep in a bathtub in Detroit.

✳ In Brooklyn, people can sleep in tubs—but donkeys cannot.

✳ Not taking a bath on a Saturday night is against the law in Barre, Vermont.

✳ Driving a car while asleep is a crime anywhere in Tennessee.

✳ It's illegal to drive a car if you're blind in New York.

✳ In Cleveland, the law prohibits you from driving if you are sitting in someone else's lap.

✳ Husbands, listen up: It's illegal for a mother-in-law to visit her kids more than 30 days out of any given year at California's Paiute Indian Reservation.

✳ Throwing banana peels on the streets will get you in trouble in Waco, Texas. The reason? They could cause a horse to slip.

✳ Riding an ugly horse on a public street in Wilbur, Washington, is a crime.

✳ Horses in Fort Lauderdale, Florida, are required to wear horns and headlights.

✳ Drunken men and women cannot be married in Pennsylvania. Good thing that's not the case in Las Vegas.

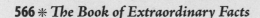

You Big Fakers!

Celebrities are known to do weird things—bark crazy demands, shave their heads (hello, Britney!), throw objects at their employees, or—in extreme cases—fake their own deaths. Granted, sometimes it's not the celeb's fault—enduring fans often simply refuse to let their heroes die. Here are some stories of celebrities whose obituaries may or may not be false.

✻ ✻ ✻ ✻

Elvis Presley

ELVIS MIGHT HAVE left the building, but many of his devoted fans believe he is still among the living. Despite reports of his death at Graceland on August 16, 1977, some believe Presley had grown weary of the star lifestyle and just wanted out.

However, death doesn't mean The King hasn't been making the rounds. Presley is one of the most impersonated singers in the world, which makes it hard to determine whether sightings of the singer are indeed real. The first sighting reportedly occurred just hours after Presley's death was announced, when a man by the name of John Burrows paid cash for a one-way ticket to Buenos Aires—and the name John Burrows was one of the aliases that Presley often used. Today, more than 30 years after his death, there are still regularly reported Presley sightings.

Jim Morrison

As early as 1967, The Doors' snakelike singer, Jim Morrison, was talking about possibly faking his own death and starting anew in Africa. He even invented an alter ego, Mr. Mojo Risin' (an anagram of his name). So when he was found dead in a bathtub in Paris, France, on July 3, 1971, some people had their doubts. Rumors were fueled by the fact that in the time it took his parents, family, and friends to get to Paris, Morrison's body was already sealed inside a coffin. Upon seeing Morrison's gravesite, Doors drummer John Densmore is said to have remarked that the grave was too short.

The first two years after Morrison's death were when he was most often spotted. In 1973, he was even reportedly spotted inside the Bank of America in San Francisco conducting business. But as time went on, the sightings eventually stopped, leaving all of us to scratch our heads and wonder if and when Morrison finally decided to break on through to the other side.

Weldon Kees

Few tourists snapping photographs of the iconic Golden Gate Bridge in San Francisco are aware of its dark side. Since 1937, more than 1,280 individuals are known to have committed suicide by jumping from the bridge—a number that more than likely is a low estimate because some bodies are never recovered. So on July 19, 1955, when the car belonging to author Weldon Kees was found on the north end of the Golden Gate Bridge, keys still in the ignition, most believed he had become another sad statistic. Friends reported that Kees had been depressed; he had even telephoned his friend Janet Richards to tell her, "things are pretty bad here."

Yet there seemed to be something staged about the whole scene at the Golden Gate Bridge. It seemed too perfect. After friends searched his apartment and discovered that items such as his wallet, savings account book, and sleeping bag were missing, it was thought that Kees might have faked his own death. Perhaps he was depressed with the way his life had turned out and was looking to reinvent himself. A possible clue lies in one of the things Kees said to Richards the day before he disappeared: "I may go to Mexico. To stay."

Alan Abel

On January 2, 1980, both *The New York Times* and *The New York Daily News* published an obituary for author and satirist Alan Abel, stating that he had died of a heart attack while skiing at a Utah resort.

There was only one problem—Abel was still alive. The following day, Abel held a press conference to declare the whole thing an elaborate hoax. Abel said he had spent more than six months plotting out the specifics of the clever ruse, including having an actor stop by the ski resort claiming to be a funeral director who needed to collect Abel's belongings. Abel also had a woman pretend to be his widow and contact the newspapers to verify his death. Years later, a mutual friend introduced Abel to an aspiring actor and comedian that was fascinated with Abel's death hoax: Andy Kaufman.

Andy Kaufman

Whether it was proclaiming himself the holder of a nonexistent wrestling title or staging fistfights on live national television, Kaufman loved nothing better than to pull a fast one. So when it was announced on May 16, 1984, that Kaufman, a nonsmoker, had passed away at age 35, a mere five months after being diagnosed with a rare form of lung cancer, people couldn't help but think it was his latest stunt. Even Kaufman's close friend and sometime co-conspirator Bob Zmuda had his doubts, especially since Kaufman had previously said that he was considering faking his own death. In the years following his death, there were several reports of Kaufman making appearances in nightclubs disguised as one of his alter egos, Tony Clifton.

On May 16, 2004, the 20th anniversary of Kaufman's death, Zmuda and some of Andy's closest friends threw a "Welcome Home" party and patiently waited for Andy to crash it. Unfortunately, he never showed.

What a Way to Go!

Some people are choosing to buck the bummer burial tradition by creating customized coffins that are to die for.

✳   ✳   ✳   ✳

THE GA PEOPLE of Ghana fashion coffins into shapes that reflect the lifestyles or livelihoods of the deceased. For instance, a leopard-shape coffin signifies the person was powerful; a chicken represents a maternal figure. Carpenters have respectfully carved caskets into various symbolic animals, including cows, elephants, crocodiles, lobsters, sharks, and objects such as shoes, cell phones, Coca-Cola bottles, cigarettes, and cars.

However, as unusual as some of these coffins are, the one designed for a gynecologist out-weirds the rest: a giant uterus complete with ovaries. Apparently, what was good enough to carry him into this world was good enough to carry him out.

In England, one can find picture-box coffins that use the entire outer surface of the casket as a colorful canvas. Giving new meaning to the term "still" art, these coffins are painted with landscapes, floral arrangements, sports motifs, etc. Buyers even have the option of predesigning their own coffins.

However, even the stiff-upper-lip set can get loose with their burial boxes, commissioning specialty shaped coffins such as a giant satin ballet shoe, a replica of a beloved guitar, and a large Dumpster. One Brit even ordered a sleek wooden egg and requested to be buried upright in the fetal position.

Americans take a much more pragmatic approach to their dualistic coffin creations, which can also serve as entertainment centers, coffee tables, or beer-can-shaped coolers. With just a little know-how, an oak coffin becomes a wooden shelving unit. Fill the cooler coffin with beer and it becomes a fitting centerpiece for a living wake—albeit a potentially sobering experience for the guest of honor.

Cold Case: The Cadaver Synod

The Cadaver Synod—or Cadaver Trial—is considered the lowest point in papal history. How low? Try six feet under.

✳   ✳   ✳   ✳

V as in Vengeance (and Stephen VII)

The mastermind behind what became known as the Cadaver Synod was Italy's King Lambert, who sought revenge for Pope Formosus's actions against his father, Guido, the Duke of Spoleto. Previously, Formosus's predecessor Pope Stephen VI had crowned Guido and Lambert co-Holy Roman Emperors in A.D. 892. But Formosus favored the German king Arnulf, and he convinced Arnulf to invade Italy and usurp the crown. Guido died before he was forcibly removed from office, and in February 896, Arnulf was crowned emperor.

Physical paralysis ultimately cut short Arnulf's reign; he returned to Germany, leaving Lambert to take over and exact his revenge on Formosus. The pope died before Lambert got a chance to strike, but that didn't stop Lambert: He ordered Formosus's successor Pope Stephen VII—himself a Spoletian sympathizer—to dig up the pope's body and put it on trial for perjury, violating church canons, and coveting the papacy.

A Trial of the Grotesque

No transcript of the Cadaver Synod exists, but historians agree as to how it probably went down: In January 897, the rotting corpse (it was only nine months after Formosus's death) was exhumed, carried into the courtroom, dressed in elaborate papal vestments, and propped in a chair, behind which cowered a teenage deacon, who was in charge of speaking for the dead pope. Stephen ranted and screamed at Formosus's body, which, of course, was found guilty of all charges.

As punishment, Stephen ordered that all of Formosus's papal ordinances be overturned, that the three fingers on his right hand used to give papal blessings be hacked off, and that his body be stripped of its papal vestments, dressed in peasant's clothes, and reburied in a common grave. After the sentence was carried out, the pope's body was dug up yet again and tossed in the Tiber River, from which a monk retrieved and buried it. Again.

The Cadaver Synod caused a public rebellion, and within a few months, Stephen was deposed, stripped of his vestments, and sent to prison where he was strangled to death in 897.

Return of the Synod

In 897, Pope Theodore II held a synod to annul the Cadaver Synod—one his few actions as pope, since his pontificate lasted only 20 days. Formosus's body was dug up once more and carried back to St. Peter's Basilica, where it was redressed in papal vestments and returned to its tomb. The next pope, John IX, held another synod to confirm Theodore II's decision. He also declared it illegal to put a dead body on trial.

But John's successor, Pope Sergio III, who participated in the Cadaver Synod and was a "violent hater of Formosus," held his own synod to reverse the decisions made by the previous two popes. Maybe because it was finally illegal to dig up and put dead bodies on trial, he simply had an epitaph made for Stephen's tomb that heaped insults on Formosus. Sergio's ruling was never overturned, however; it was just ignored.

✳ Formosus means "good-looking" in Latin.

✳ From A.D. 896 to 904, there were nine popes—the same number of popes throughout the entire 20th century.

✳ Pope Sergio III was quite the controversial figure. His papacy has been called "The Rule of the Harlots."

✳ Though Formosus has been unanimously vindicated and cleared of all charges, there has never been a Pope Formosus II. Cardinal Pietro Barbo apparently thought about taking the name in 1464 but was talked out of it. He took Paul II instead.

The Franklin Syndicate

What does it take to fleece the public? Confidence, a believable lie, and something everybody wants: money. Take a closer look at the first big American pyramid scheme.

✳   ✳   ✳   ✳

IN 1898, A low-wage clerk named William F. Miller was working at a New York brokerage firm, desperately trying to support his family on meager earnings. At only 19 years old, Miller was tantalizingly close to the world of financial success but lacked the funds to participate. One evening while leading his Bible study class, Miller hit upon the idea of inviting the men in his group to invest $10 each in return for a 10 percent return every week. Though skeptical at first but knowing that their friend had some sort of job on Wall Street, the men eventually agreed.

Although Miller originally conceived his scheme as a means to raise quick money to speculate in the stock market, he quickly realized that it was far easier to simply find new investors and pocket the profits. These investors, convinced by the returns being paid to the current investors, gladly contributed money and most often chose to reinvest their dividends. Miller named his new enterprise "The Franklin Syndicate" and set up a Brooklyn office. Because he promised a 10 percent return every week (520 percent per year), he quickly became known as "520% Miller."

144 Floyd Street

All of the syndicate's advertising featured the visage of Benjamin Franklin and his quotation: "The way to wealth is as plain as the road to the market." Indeed, many were beguiled into believing that the road to wealth lay in Miller's office, located in a house at 144 Floyd Street. Miller soon began hiring clerks to accommodate the crush of eager investors.

At the peak of the syndicate's popularity, the house was a beehive of financial activity with 50 clerks working into the night. Miller, sitting at the top of the front porch stoop, received the cash, distributed receipts, and seemed to hardly notice as the money piled up behind him. His clerks opened correspondence, distributed dividends, and mailed advertisements. It was reputed that investors could receive or drop off money in any of the rooms, including the kitchen, parlor, or laundry.

People from as far away as Louisiana and Manitoba, Canada, sent money. The activity and evidence of so much money easily enticed even the delivery men and postal carriers to deposit their cash as well. The press of people eager to hand over their hard-earned wages was so great on one particular Friday that the stoop collapsed. At the end of each day, Miller and his clerks literally waded through knee-high mounds of cash.

Overwhelmed, Miller added Edward Schlessinger as a partner. Schlessinger helped open the Franklin Syndicate's second office in Boston. In return, he took a third of the profits away in a money-filled bag every evening.

Enter the Colonel

When the newspapers, particularly the *Boston Post* and a New York financial paper edited by E. L. Blake, began to cast doubts about the syndicate's legitimacy, Miller's advertising agent introduced him to an attorney named Colonel Robert A. Ammon. Charismatic, compelling, and utterly corrupt, Ammon incorporated the company, did battle with the press, and increasingly became the syndicate's chief behind-the-scenes operator.

When the *Post* alleged that the Franklin Syndicate was a swindle, Ammon and Miller took $50,000 in a bag to the paper's office to prove their liquidity. When a police chief referred to the Franklin Syndicate as a "green goods business" the two men repeated the display, whereupon the police chief apologized.

The Swindler Is Swindled

Miller, Ammon, and Schlessinger knew that the end was near, but only Ammon knew just how close it really was. Having fully duped Miller into believing he was acting in his best interest, Ammon prodded the young man to squeeze every last dollar from the enterprise before it collapsed.

On November 21, 1899, Miller placed $30,500 in a satchel and went to Ammon's office. Ammon advised his client to give him the money to protect it from the investors. Ammon also convinced Miller to surrender securities, bonds, and a certificate of deposit, all of which totaled more than $250,000. On Ammon's advice, Miller opened the Floyd Street office the following day, a Friday and the last best chance to gather additional funds. After work, Miller was pursued by a detective but eluded his pursuer by ducking through a Chinese laundry and fleeing to Ammon's office. Upon learning that Miller had been indicted in Kings County for conspiracy to defraud, the lawyer convinced his client to flee to Canada.

Die in Prison or Let Your Family Suffer?

It's unclear whether Miller returned two weeks later because he missed his wife and baby or because Ammon, nervous about scrutiny being cast on his own role in the syndicate, convinced him to come back. What is certain is that, with Ammon acting as his counsel, Miller was sentenced to the maximum ten years in Sing Sing prison. Knowing that Miller was the only man capable of implicating him, Ammon gave his client's family $5 a week and reminded Miller that without the allowance his family would starve. After three years, the District Attorney finally convinced Miller, sick from his years in prison and tempted by the possibility of a pardon, to turn evidence against Ammon.

Just Desserts?

Ammon served five years—the maximum penalty for receiving stolen goods. Schlessinger fled with $175,000 in cash to Europe where he gambled and lived well until his premature death in 1903. Miller was released after five years in prison. He moved his family to Long Island where he operated a grocery until his death.

Fast Facts

✳ Fingerprints are unique to each individual, of course. But the same goes for tongue prints and lip prints.

✳ Until 1862, currency from the U.S. Mint took the form of coins. During the Civil War, the Union Congress authorized the Treasury to print the first paper money, which became known as "legal tenders" or "greenbacks" because of the green ink used.

✳ While working as a cook in New York during the early 1900s, Mary Mallon, who became known as "Typhoid Mary," infected at least 53 people, 3 of whom died. She was quarantined for three years, released for a short time when she promised she would no longer work as a cook, then was quarantined again after she broke her promise. She was never released from her second quarantine, which lasted until her death 23 years later.

✳ Beginning with Super Bowl XXXIV in 2000, game footballs have been marked with synthetic DNA to prevent sports-memorabilia fraud. Souvenirs from the 2000 Summer Olympics were marked with human DNA in the ink.

✳ A raisin dropped into a glass of a carbonated drink will float up and down continually from the bottom of the glass to the top.

✳ Comanche code-talkers, used in World War II by the Army Signal Corps to send encrypted messages that German troops could not break, referred to Adolf Hitler as *posah-tai-vo*, which means "crazy white man."

✳ An official balance beam in women's gymnastics is just four inches wide, less than the length of a ballpoint pen.

✳ In 1956, Johnny Mathis decided to record an album instead of answering an invitation to try out for the U.S. Olympic team as a high jumper. He became one of the top-selling artists of all time.

Murderess

It was the trial of the century—for what may well have been the most poorly executed murder of the time.

✻   ✻   ✻   ✻

IT WAS A terrible thing to wake up to on that March morning in 1927. Nine-year-old Lorraine Snyder found her mother Ruth, her hands and feet bound, begging for help in the hall outside her bedroom. The girl rushed to her neighbors in the New York City suburb, and they called the police.

What the police found was more terrible still. Ruth Snyder's husband Albert lay dead in the bedroom—his skull smashed, wire strung around his neck, and a chloroform-soaked cloth shoved up his nose. His 32-year-old widow told the police that a large Italian man had knocked her out, stolen her jewelry, and assaulted her husband.

But the police found her jewels under a mattress; they also discovered a bloody pillowcase and a bloody, five-pound sash weight in a closet. As if this evidence wasn't damning enough, police located a check Ruth had written to Henry Judd Gray in the amount of $200. Gray's name was found in her little black book—along with the names of 26 other men. Little Lorraine told the cops that "Uncle Judd" had been in the home the previous night. A tie clip with the initials HJG was found on the floor.

A Marriage on the Rocks

Ruth Brown met Albert Snyder—14 years her senior—in 1915. He was an editor of *Motor Boating* magazine, and Ruth was a secretary. She and Albert married and had Lorraine, but their union was flawed from the start. Albert was still enthralled with his former fiancée of ten years ago, who had died; he named his boat after her and displayed her photograph in his and Ruth's home.

In the meantime, Ruth haunted the jazz clubs of Roaring Twenties Manhattan, drinking and dancing 'til the wee hours of the morning without her retiring spouse, whom she had dubbed "the old crab."

In 1925, the unhappy wife went on a blind date and met Judd Gray, a low-key corset salesperson. Soon the duo was meeting for afternoon trysts at the Waldorf=Astoria—leaving Lorraine to play in the hotel lobby. Eventually, Ruth arranged for her unsuspecting husband to sign a life insurance policy worth more than $70,000.

The Jig Is Up

At the murder scene, the police questioned Ruth about Gray. "Has he confessed?," she blurted. It wasn't long before she had spilled her guts, though she claimed it was Gray who'd actually strangled Albert.

Meanwhile, 33-year-old Gray—not exactly the sharpest knife in the drawer—was found at a hotel in Syracuse, New York. It didn't take police long to locate him; after leaving Ruth's house, he had actually stopped to ask a police officer when he could catch the next bus to New York City. Gray quickly confessed but claimed it was Ruth who'd strangled Albert. Ruth had mesmerized him, he stated, through alcohol, sex, and threats.

A month after the arrest of the murderous duo, a brief trial ensued. For three weeks, the courtroom was jammed with 1,500 spectators. In attendance were such luminaries as songwriter Irving Berlin and the producers of the Broadway play *Chicago*. Also on hand was novelist James M. Cain, who drew on the case for his novel *Double Indemnity*, later turned into a film noir classic by director Billy Wilder and writer Raymond Chandler.

The media frenzy over the courtroom drama even exceeded coverage of the execution of anarchist-bombers Sacco and Vanzetti. Miming the fevered reporting of city tabloids such as

The Daily News, the stodgy *New York Times* carried page-one stories on the crime for months.

Guilty!

Ruth and Gray were pronounced guilty after a 100-minute deliberation by an all-male jury. When their appeal failed and their plea for clemency to Governor Al Smith was denied, the deadly pair was driven 30 miles "up the river" to Sing Sing Prison's death row. En route, excited onlookers hung from rooftops to catch a glimpse of the doomed couple.

Robert Elliott, the man slated to execute the pair, professed angst over putting a woman to death; Ruth would be the first female executed since 1899. "It will be something new for me to throw the switch on a woman," he told reporters, "and I don't like the job." The former electrical contractor received threats because of his role as executioner. He asked the warden for a raise to help salve the stress. Yet, Elliott would long continue his grim work, sending a total of 387 convicts to the next world.

The End

On January 12, 1928, at 11 P.M., 20 witnesses—chosen from the 1,500 who'd applied—watched Ruth enter the execution chamber. The Blonde Butcher, as she had been dubbed, was strapped weeping into a wooden chair, a leather cap clamped on her head. "Jesus, have mercy on me," she moaned, "for I have sinned."

In a room close by, Elliott threw a switch, and 2,000 volts surged through Ruth's body. At that instant, a reporter for *The Daily News* triggered a camera hidden in his pants. A garish photo of the murderess's last moment would appear on the paper's front page the next day. The headline read, "DEAD."

Minutes later, it was Gray's turn. Although his feet caught fire during the execution, for most witnesses it was Ruth's final moments that were stamped indelibly in their minds.

Call of the Wild

In Japan's Aokigahara Forest, the desperate take their lives in the dark shadow of Mt. Fuji.

✳ ✳ ✳ ✳

JAPAN'S SUICIDE RATE is one of the highest in the world, and, within the country, Aokigahara Forest (nicknamed the Sea of Trees) is home to the most self-inflicted deaths. Every year, scores of people, many distraught over a wrecked economy, travel to the forest and take their own lives, often by hanging themselves or exposing themselves to the elements in the dead of winter.

So what attracts people to this dense forest? It could be the fact that the forest sits at the foot of Mt. Fuji, a naturally compelling and spiritual place. Or maybe people find comfort in the idea that the forest is full of the spirits of those who've gone before, or lore that features the forest as a safe haven for suicide. In the 1960s, a book called *The Pagoda of Waves* described a woman who kills herself in the forest; later, Seicho Matsumoto wrote a book called *Kuroi Jukai (Black Sea of Trees)* that perhaps further romanticized the notion.

In 1994, a Japanese book called *The Complete Manual of Suicide* named the Sea of Trees as "the perfect place to die." Police and volunteers go into the forest once or more a year to collect the dead bodies, but because of its dense nature, many bodies are never found or are found only after many years.

The communities that surround the forest do their best to prevent unnecessary deaths. Cameras look for suspicious hikers (such as men in suits), and police regularly patrol the area. Words of encouragement, such as, "Your life is a precious gift from your parents," are scattered throughout the forest. There are also counselors who work in the forest, looking for lost souls, and credit consolidation companies post their phone numbers on trees as a lifeline for the financially fallen.

You. It's What's for Dinner.

Anthropologists debate whether cannibalism is actually a common practice in tribal cultures, or whether it happens only occasionally and under duress, as it does in so-called "civilized" society. Over the years, many people have had a taste for—and tasted—human flesh. Ready for some grisly tales? Here are nine folks who have (or are rumored to have) taken a bite.

✳ ✳ ✳ ✳

1. **Sawney Bean**—Sawney Bean lived circa the 1400s in a cave near Ballantrae, in Aynshire, Scotland with his wife and their numerous children and grandchildren. According to lore, from their hideout, they robbed, killed, pickled, dried, and devoured hundreds of passersby for more than 20 years. However, some scholars argue that Bean was merely a figment of English propaganda, designed to emphasize Scottish barbarism.

2. **Diego Rivera**—For a period in 1904, it is said that legendary Mexican painter Diego Rivera and his friends purchased female corpses from a morgue, preferring their flavor and texture to male flesh. He believed that cannibalism would become acceptable in the future, when "man will have thrown off all of his superstitions and irrational taboos." According to one biography, he made no bones about favoring "women's brains in vinaigrette."

3. **Karl Denke**—"Papa Denke," as his neighbors and fellow churchgoers in Munsterberg, Germany, knew him, was the organist at his church and ran a popular boarding house. Upon his arrest in 1924, police found the remains of at least 30 former lodgers pickled in barrels in his basement. According to reports, he told police that he had eaten only human flesh for the past three years.

4. Albert Fish—Dubbed the "Gray Man" by witnesses, Albert Fish appeared to be a harmless old man, but in truth he tortured hundreds of children and reportedly killed more than a dozen throughout the East Coast. He was caught, convicted, and executed for the 1928 murder of ten-year-old Grace Budd after he wrote to her mother and described how he killed, roasted, and ate her daughter.

5. Edward Gein—When police entered Edward Gein's Plainfield, Wisconsin, farmhouse in November 1957, they found a scene right out of a horror movie—a scene that was in fact the inspiration for the films *Psycho* and *Silence of the Lambs*. A woman's body was strung up and splayed, her heart was in a pot on the stove, and her head was in a paper bag. Human skulls were used as bowls and decorated the bed frame, and there was a chair, a lampshade, and a wastebasket made of human skin. Despite the number of corpses that must have gone into such endeavors, Gein was only prosecuted for the murders of two local women.

6. Joachim Kroll—This German killer lost count of how many people he had killed during a grisly career that spanned two decades, though he was sure that there had been at least 14. Kroll's activities were finally discovered in 1976 when a plumber was called to unblock the communal toilet in his apartment building, which Kroll said was clogged "with guts." The plumber pulled out a child's lungs and entrails; police found several bags full of human meat and a pot on the stove simmering with carrots, potatoes, and the hand of a four-year-old girl.

7. Nathaniel Bar-Jonah—Born David Paul Brown in 1957 in Massachusetts, Bar-Jonah was a convicted child molester and kidnapper with a history of sadistic violence toward young boys. In 1991, he was released from the Bridgewater State Hospital and moved to Great Falls, Montana, during which time he also changed his name. After he was arrested in 1999 for lurking near an elementary school, carrying a stun gun, he became a suspect in the death of a local ten-year-old boy. A police search of his apartment yielded encrypted recipes for dishes such as "Little Boy Pot Pie." Bar-Jonah's neighbors testified that he would frequently bring them casseroles or invite them to cookouts featuring funny-tasting meat he claimed to have hunted and dressed himself.

8. **Katherine Mary Knight**—On February 29, 2000, an Australian woman named Katherine Mary Knight stabbed her common-law husband 37 times, and, using the skills she learned while working in a slaughterhouse, skinned and decapitated him. She then boiled his head, roasted pieces of his corpse, and served them with vegetables to his adult children. Knight was sentenced to life in prison without parole.

9. **Armin Meiwes**—In 2001, a German computer technician named Armin Meiwes went online for an odd purpose. No, he didn't scan the Web in search of a paramour; instead, he posted an advertisement for a well-built fellow who would be willing to be slaughtered and eaten. While it's hard to imagine anyone agreeing to this, a man named Bernd-Jürgen Brandes answered the ad. Brandes willingly came to Meiwes' house, where Meiwes sliced off Brandes' penis. The pair attempted to eat it but found it inedible. After Brandes passed out from alcohol, sleeping pills, and loss of blood, Meiwes stabbed and dissected him. He ate Brandes's body over a ten-month period, garnished with potatoes and pepper sauce. Shockingly, Meiwes also filmed the event. In jail, an unrepentant Meiwes became a vegetarian.

Old Sparky

For the 104 electrifying years that it remained in service, "Old Sparky" shocked Ohioans—literally and figuratively. But most of them never knew that the invention of the electric chair had direct connections to their state.

✳ ✳ ✳ ✳

FROM 1897 TO 1963, 315 men and women died in Ohio's electric chair, nicknamed "Old Sparky," which would remain on call for three decades after its final use. The chair was moved into the Ohio Penitentiary's new Death House in Columbus in 1913. Seventeen-year-old Willie Haas, who was convicted of raping and murdering a farmer's wife near Cincinnati, was the first and youngest criminal to die in it.

An Impressive Résumé

Nationally, electric chairs killed many famous 20th-century criminals, including Bruno Hauptmann, killer of the Lindbergh baby; Julius and Ethel Rosenberg, the atom bomb spies; and serial killer Ted Bundy. Chillingly effective, the chairs sent 2,000 volts surging through their victims via an electrode on the head. The current was typically applied for one minute, but when used correctly, the charge would stop the heart in a fraction of a second.

Although the chair seems ghastly today, consider that one era's antiquated technology is another's high-tech. In the 1880s, when most states still used the gallows, a dentist named Alfred Southwick conceived of an electric chair for execution. A few years later, Harold Brown, who worked for native Ohioan Thomas Edison, built the first such device. (Some historians credit Dr. David Rockwell, who lived in Edison's hometown of Milan, with building Ohio's chair, as he believed it was faster and more humane than the rope.)

Old Methods Die Hard

In Ohio, the demise of "Old Sparky" came slowly. After the mid-1960s, the state allowed death row prisoners a choice—strap on the electrodes or take a lethal injection. Every one of them chose the needle. Then came John W. Byrd, convicted of killing a convenience store clerk near Cincinnati in 1983. Appeals delayed his execution, which was slated for 1994. That year, prison officials tuned up their aging death chair by hiring an electrician to design, build, and install a modern control panel, a high-voltage transformer, new cables, and body electrodes. When Byrd's appeals ran out in 2001, he requested the chair, which prompted lawsuits by death-penalty opponents and raised awareness of punishment by electrocution. Ohio's legislature banned the chair before Byrd could sit on it. He died by lethal injection the next year.

By then, Old Sparky was gathering dust in a Lucasville prison, which relieved Reginald Wilkinson, director of the Department of Corrections. None of his employees had ever executed anyone in the chair. "In modern society," Wilkinson told a reporter, "we shouldn't have to depend on technology that's over 100 years old."

The chair went to the Ohio Historical Society in Columbus in 2002, while a replica of it was donated to the Mansfield Reformatory Preservation Society (Ohio's death row was moved to the Mansfield Correctional Institution in 1995). These days, museum visitors need not worry if they stand too close to Old Sparky. Unplugged and unrepentant, the dreaded chair now has a more quiet and efficient role—illustrating death-penalty history.

Odd Ordinances

✳ Kissing a woman while she's asleep is a crime in Logan County, Colorado.

✳ Any man with a mustache is not allowed to kiss women in Eureka, Nevada.

✳ Flirting in public is against the law in Little Rock, Arkansas.

✳ Michigan law states that a woman's hair is technically owned by her husband.

✳ It's illegal for kids under the age of seven to attend college in Winston–Salem, North Carolina (sorry, Doogie).

✳ A child talking on the phone without a parent on the line is a crime in Blue Earth, Minnesota.

✳ You can't buy a lollipop without a doctor's note while church services are in session if you live in Kalispell, Montana.

✳ Any man who comes face-to-face with a cow has to remove his hat in Fruithill, Kentucky.

✳ It's illegal to eat chicken with a fork in Gainesville, Georgia.

✳ You could go to jail for making an ugly face at a dog in the state of Oklahoma.

✳ A frog—yes, a frog—can be arrested for keeping a person awake with its "ribbit" noises in Memphis, Tennessee.

✳ Eating nuts on a city bus in Charleston, South Carolina, could cost you a $500 fine or even 60 days in jail.

✳ Don't get too friendly at happy hour in Nyala, Nevada—buying drinks for more than three people in a single round is against the law there.

✳ North Dakota has outlawed the serving of beer with pretzels at public restaurants and bars.

You *Can* Take It with You

No one is sure what happens to us after we die, so many people like to leave this world prepared for anything by having odd or unusual objects buried with them.

✳ ✳ ✳ ✳

1. **Tutankhamen (King Tut):** Tutankhamen, better known as King Tut, was an Egyptian pharaoh who ruled from 1333 B.C. to 1324 B.C. When his tomb was discovered by Howard Carter in 1923, thousands of items were found buried with Tut, including a solid gold mask that covered the head of the mummified king, hundreds of gold figurines, jewelry, weapons, a small chair made of ebony inlaid with ivory, and enough seeds to plant a large garden.

2. **Reuben John Smith:** In 1899, Reuben John Smith of Buffalo, New York, was buried in a leather recliner chair with a checkerboard sitting on his lap. Smith also requested that he be dressed in a hat and warm coat with the key to the tomb inside his coat pocket.

3. **Humphrey Bogart:** Legendary actor Humphrey Bogart appeared in 75 movies, many of them classics like *The Maltese Falcon*, *Casablanca*, and *The African Queen*. In 1944, he starred in *To Have and Have Not* with Lauren Bacall, who became his fourth wife. A famous line from the movie, delivered by Bacall to Bogart, was, "If you need anything, just whistle." So when Bogart died in 1957, Bacall placed a whistle inscribed with the line inside the silver urn with his ashes.

4. **Sandra Ilene West:** When California socialite Sandra Ilene West died in 1977, she was buried in San Antonio, Texas, in her 1964 Ferrari 330 America. She asked to be clad in her favorite lace nightgown with the driver's seat positioned at a comfortable angle. West and her car were placed in a large box, which was covered with cement to discourage vandals.

Shoot-out at Little Bohemia

Infamous gangster John Dillinger was something of a media darling during his criminal career. He was also the force behind one of the most embarrassing federal mishaps of all time. Here's the story behind this mobster's fatal end.

✳ ✳ ✳ ✳

IN AN ERA known for its long list of public enemies, John Dillinger and his crew looked more like endeared celebrities than the convicted killers and robbers they were known to be. Historians attribute this strange awe to the gang's Robin Hood—like appeal during a stressful time for the public.

Robbing the Rich

The public, demoralized by the ongoing Depression, lacked financial and bureaucratic faith after suffering devastating losses at what they saw to be the hands of irresponsible government and financial institutions. When the dashing, physically graceful Dillinger and his equally charismatic crew began tearing through banks, they not only provided an exciting and dramatic media distraction, they also destroyed banks' potentially devastating mortgage paperwork in their wake. The masses seemed eager to clasp onto the real-life drama and connect it to their own plights. The public was more than willing to forgive the sins of outlaws such as Dillinger's crew in favor of the payback the robbers provided to financial institutions that had ruined so many families already.

Law officials, however, weren't so keen on the criminals. J. Edgar Hoover and his newly formed Federal Bureau of Investigation were weary of gangsters' soft public perception and crafted a series of hard-hitting laws meant to immobilize them. Those found guilty of crimes such as robbing banks would now face stiffer penalties. Dillinger, one of the most prominent, popular, and evasive of the lot, was at the top of Hoover's hit list. However, keeping the gangster in jail and strapped with a sufficient sentence seemed like more work than Hoover could handle.

Hiding Out

Dillinger, always hard to contain, had fled the supposedly escape-proof county jail in Crown Point, Indiana, in March 1934. A month and a few bank robberies later, Dillinger and company ended up hiding out in a woodsy Wisconsin lodge called Little Bohemia, so named because of the owner's Bohemian ethnic roots. Tipped off by the lodge owner's wife, Hoover and a team of federal investigators from Chicago responded with an ill-fated ambush that would go down in history as one of the greatest federal fiascoes of all time.

The Dillinger gang, including well-known characters as Harry Pierpont and "Baby Face" Nelson, plus gang members' wives and girlfriends, had planned only a short layover at the wilderness retreat. Although owner Emil Wanatka and wife Nan had befriended an outlaw or two during the days of Prohibition, the Dillinger crew was a notch or two above the types they had known. The couple didn't share the public's glorified view of these men. So, upon discovering that their new slew of guests were members of the notorious gang, Wanatka made a bold move and confronted them. Dillinger assured him that they would be of no inconvenience and would not stay long. Apparently bank robbers are not the most trustworthy folks, because in the several days of their stay the bunch proved to be much more than an inconvenience.

Wanatka and his wife were basically held hostage at their humble hostel for the entire length of the Dillinger gang's stay. Telephone calls were monitored, lodge visitors were subject to scrutiny at both arrival and departure, and anyone, including Emil and Nan, who went into town for supplies was forced to travel with a Dillinger escort. In addition, the sheer fear of housing sought-after sociopaths was too much for the

Wanatka couple and their young son to handle. A plan for relief was soon hatched.

Knowing that any lodge departure would be surveyed closely, the Wanatkas decided to plant a note on Nan to pass to police. They would convince the gangsters that she and their ten-year-old son were merely departing for a nephew's birthday party and then would find a way to transmit their cry for help. Although Dillinger gave permission for the pair's trip, the frightened mother soon discovered "Baby Face" Nelson hot on their trail and ready to jump at the first sight of suspicious activity. Still, Nan managed to pass word to her family, who then contacted the authorities. At the birthday party for her nephew, Nan provided details that were ultimately shared with law enforcement. Officials planned a siege.

The Heat Is On

Seizing the opportunity to make an example of Dillinger and his exploits, FBI agents Hugh Clegg and Melvin Purvis plotted an ambush at the lodge under Hoover's guidance. Unfortunately for the agents and innocent bystanders, Dillinger and company were not so easily taken.

As the agents approached, the lodge's watchdogs barked at the strangers, but only after a series of miscalculated gunshots did the Dillinger gang stir. Clegg and Purvis had mistakenly fired at three patrons leaving the lodge's bar. This was the first tragedy of Little Bohemia that day: One of the patrons was killed instantly, and the other two were brutally wounded. The Dillinger gang had long grown weary of the watchdogs' random yelps, but when they heard these unfortunate shots, they knew their hideout had been discovered.

The ever-elusive bunch had plotted an escape plan upon their arrival at the lodge. The agents didn't have the same knowledge of the land's lay and fell victim to a nearby ditch and a wall of barbed wire. Wounded and entangled, the agents were sitting ducks. Their suspects were free to flee and take return fire now that they had the upper hand.

Unhappy Ending

A premature and somewhat pompous notion had Hoover pledging a significant story to the press in anticipation of the planned attack. Unluckily for him, with the unintentional victims and their families involved, the story would be a hellish one. The ambush resulted in not a single loss for the Dillinger gang. On the other side were two injured law officers, two wounded bystanders, and the death of a complete innocent.

Although Purvis didn't find success on that infamous day, he would eventually have another chance. On July 22, 1934, Dillinger was shot dead by Purvis's agents outside a Chicago cinema in which the criminal "darling" had just enjoyed his last gangster flick.

Details, Details

In the 1957 flick *Guns Don't Argue* (which was a composite of three episodes of a 1952 TV series called *Gangbusters*), 1930s gangsters John Dillinger, "Ma" Barker, "Baby Face" Nelson, Bonnie and Clyde, and others outmaneuver the feds in zippy cars. But the production company got a couple of details very wrong: These '30s-era hoodlums drive 1950s cars and sport 1950s wardrobes.

---

5 Reasons You Won't Survive a Fall from a Cruise Ship

1. Force of Impact: Unless you're an experienced diver, the sheer impact of plunging 70 feet from a cruise ship deck into the ocean is dangerous. Even if the impact isn't enough to kill you or knock you unconscious, the many other dangers of falling into the water unexpectedly—such as slamming into a part of the ship—mean you'll drown before anybody even knows you're gone.

2. Inebriation : An enormous percentage of "overboard incidents" occur due to drunken stupidity. And there is no shortage of drunken stupidity on your average cruise. According to analysts, alcohol sales make up a healthy percentage of the cruise industry's $24.9 billion in gross revenue. It's difficult enough to survive a fully clothed plunge into choppy, cold seawater—but doing it while heavily inebriated is almost impossible.

3. Hypothermia: Hypothermia, a potentially deadly condition in which the body loses heat faster than it can produce it, is the most likely reason why you won't last long even if you do survive a trip over the railing. Experts state that the average person can only survive for about 20 minutes in chilly water (about 40°F). And while you'll last longer in the balmy waters of the Caribbean than, say, if you tumbled off a ship during an Antarctic cruise, being submerged for extended periods of time in even warm water can lead to hypothermia.

4. Sharks: Sharks are drawn to human bodily fluids, so even if you manage to stave off drowning and hypothermia, odds are you're going to attract a shark eventually. The Florida Museum of Natural History states that there have been more than 1,000 instances of sharks attacking humans world-wide since 1990. Before leaping into  the drink, consider your geography: You'll probably want to avoid diving into the waters off South Africa, which boasts three of the world's ten most shark-infested beaches. However, in the Mediterranean, you won't have to be quite as worried: According to a 2008 study, the once plentiful Mediterranean sharks are now "functionally extinct."

5. Dehydration: The human body can only survive for three to five days without water. Sadly, seawater won't help—the high levels of salt and other minerals in seawater will only serve to increase dehydration and hasten your demise.

✳ The cruise liner *Queen Elizabeth II* moves only six inches for each gallon of diesel fuel that it burns.

✳ Unless the captain of a vessel happens to also be an ordained minister, judge, or recognized official (such as a notary public), he or she generally doesn't have the authority to perform a legally binding marriage at sea. In fact, a suitably licensed captain is no more qualified to perform marriages than a similarly licensed head chef, deck hand, or galley worker. There are a few specific exceptions: Captains of Japanese vessels can perform marriages at sea, as long as both the bride and groom hold valid Japanese passports. And thanks to a quirk in Bermudian law, captains with Bermuda licenses are also legally authorized to officiate weddings aboard ships.

The Real Bonnie and Clyde

Bonnie and Clyde, Texas's most notorious outlaws, rose to fame during the Great Depression of the 1930s. But the real Bonnie and Clyde were very different from the figures portrayed by the popular media.

✳ ✳ ✳ ✳

THE EARLY 1930S was a time when businesses folded at an unprecedented rate and plummeting crop prices forced farmers from their lands in record numbers. Men desperate for work trawled city streets looking for jobs, soup kitchens were swamped, and the value of a dollar plunged. When Bonnie and Clyde began their crime spree, the public viewed them as outsiders fighting back against an uncaring system that had failed the working man.

Where They Started

Bonnie Parker was born on October 1, 1910, in Rowena, Texas. When she met Clyde Barrow in 1930, she was already married to a man who was used to being on the wrong side of the law. However, Bonnie was not a typical gangster's moll—she was an honor-roll student in high school who excelled in creative writing and even won a spelling championship. After her husband was sentenced to the penitentiary, Bonnie scraped together a living by working as a waitress in West Dallas. Then Clyde Barrow entered her life.

Clyde was born on March 24, 1909, in Telico just south of Dallas, and spent more of his poverty-stricken youth in trouble with the law than he did in school. He was arrested for stealing turkeys, auto theft, and safecracking. Soon after his romance with Bonnie began, he was sentenced to two years for a number of burglaries and car thefts. Bonnie managed to smuggle a Colt revolver to him, and Clyde was able to escape with his cell mate, William Turner.

A Life on the Run

Clyde and Turner were soon recaptured and sentenced to 14 years at the Texas State Penitentiary. But Clyde was pardoned in February 1932 after his mother intervened and he had had a fellow inmate chop off two of his toes in order to garner sympathy.

After two months of attempting to go straight, Clyde started a crime spree with Bonnie that stretched from Texas to Oklahoma, Missouri, Iowa, New Mexico, and Louisiana. They robbed gas stations, liquor stores, banks, and jewelry stores. They also captured the public imagination by frequently taking hostages as they made their daring escapes and then releasing them unharmed when they were out of danger. Other outlaws came and went from the Barrow Gang, but it was only after several of the robberies culminated in murder that public opinion turned against Bonnie and Clyde.

In total, the Barrow Gang is believed to have murdered at least nine police officers and several civilians during their robberies. While Bonnie posed clutching a machine gun for photos, many argue that at no time did she ever fire a weapon, let alone kill or injure anyone. Another popular misconception had her dubbed as the cigar-smoking moll of the Barrow Gang. Again, Bonnie was known to smoke only cigarettes, but she once posed with a cigar in what became a famous photograph.

Bonnie and Clyde Are Finished

The end came on May 23, 1934, along a desolate road in Bienville Parish, Louisiana. The gang had murdered two Texas police officers, so they were on the run again. A posse of four Texas Rangers and two Louisiana officers waited patiently for hours near the gang's hideout. When Bonnie and Clyde pulled up, the lawmen opened fire, pumping 167 rounds into the outlaws' car. So many gunshots hit the pair that the fingers on Bonnie's right hand were blown away. At the time of their deaths, Bonnie was 23 years old; Clyde, 24.

Death by Stupidity

Death is a fact of life. But you might be surprised to learn that throughout history, a surprising number of people have actually invited death through what can only be described as sheer stupidity. Here are some of the more bizarre examples.

✳ ✳ ✳ ✳

Death by Frozen Chicken: A true renaissance man, Francis Bacon was a respected statesman, scientist, philosopher, and author whose works include *Novum Organum* and *The New Atlantis*. In March 1626, Bacon came up with the bright idea that meat could be preserved by freezing it. To test his theory, he went to town, bought a gutted chicken, and then stood in inclement weather and stuffed the bird with snow. He promptly developed pneumonia and died a few months later.

Death by Martini: In 1941, during a party aboard an ocean liner bound for Brazil, author Sherwood Anderson accidentally swallowed a martini olive, toothpick and all. The tiny sliver of wood embedded in Anderson's intestines, leading to peritonitis, which ultimately killed him.

Death by Scarf: A groundbreaking and influential dancer in her day, Isadora Duncan was strangled by her own scarf on September 14, 1927, when the long, flowing garment became tangled in the rear wheel of the car in which she was riding.

Death by Light Bulb: On March 11, 1978, Claude Francois, a popular French pop singer, was standing in a filled bathtub in his Paris apartment when he noticed a broken light bulb. Obsessed with orderliness, Francois immediately tried to change the bulb, electrocuting himself in the process.

Death by Bottle Cap: According to friends and family, Tennessee Williams—the award-winning author of *The Glass Menagerie*, *A Streetcar Named Desire*, and *Cat on a Hot Tin Roof*—had a habit of opening the cap of his eye-drop bottles with his teeth, then tilting his head backward to moisten his eyes. The system worked until February 25, 1983, when Williams accidentally inhaled the cap and choked to death.

Death by Full Bladder: Tycho Brahe, a Danish nobleman and an influential astronomer, suffered from recurring bladder problems. In 1601, he attended a formal banquet and was unable to visit the bathroom to relieve himself before the festivities started. Supposedly, he drank heavily over the course of the evening and managed to hold his urine for the duration. This proved to be a fatal mistake—the strain on his bladder resulted in a serious infection, which killed him 11 days later. A more scientific theory, formulated after his body was exhumed in 1996, suggests death by mercury poisoning.

Death by Overcoat: A tailor by trade, Franz Reichelt created a garment that was both an overcoat and a parachute. On February 4, 1912, he decided to test his invention by jumping off the Eiffel Tower. He told authorities that he was going to use a mannequin first, but he decided at the last minute to try it himself. Confident that his invention would work, Reichelt calmly stepped off a platform and plunged to his death.

Death by Helicopter: Vic Morrow was a well-known actor with scores of screen credits when he signed on to costar as a bigot who learns his lesson the hard way in a segment of *Twilight Zone: The Movie* (1983). However, things went horribly wrong during the night filming of a combat scene set in Vietnam, and Morrow was decapitated by the blades of a crashing helicopter. Two child actors also perished in the accident.

Come into My Parlor

H. H. Holmes secured a place in history as one of the most horrifyingly prolific killers the world has ever seen.

❋ ❋ ❋ ❋

BORN IN MAY 1860 in New Hampshire, Herman Webster Mudgett was a highly intelligent child, but he was constantly in trouble. Charming, handsome, and charismatic, he nevertheless displayed traits of detachment and dispassion from an early age. As a teen, he became abusive to animals—a classic sign of a sociopath.

Fascinated with skeletons and the human body, Mudgett decided to pursue a career as a doctor. After marrying Clara Lovering, he enrolled in medical school. There, he had access to skeletons and cadavers. He came up with a scheme to fleece insurance companies by taking out policies for family members and friends, using stolen cadavers to fake their deaths, and then collecting the insurance money.

When authorities became suspicious, he abandoned Clara and their newborn baby, moved from city to city and took on various jobs, most likely scheming and manipulating everyone he crossed. In 1886, the charming liar and thief surfaced in Chicago with a new name: H. H. Holmes. The city would become the site of his deadliest swindle of all.

A "Castle" with a Most Intriguing Floor Plan

If you lived in Chicago in the late 1800s, you were likely consumed with thoughts of the World's Columbian Exposition. Planners hoped it would make America a superstar country and put Chicago on the map as an A-list city. The Great Fire of 1871 had demolished the town, but the fair would bring the city back—and in a big way.

With new people flooding into the city every day looking to nab one of the world's fair jobs, Chicago was experiencing a population boom that made it very easy for people to simply vanish. The handsome and charismatic Holmes recognized this as an opportunity to lure women into his clutches while most others had their focus elsewhere.

He married his second wife, Myrta, in 1887, without ever securing a divorce from Lovering. Holmes quickly shipped Myrta off to live in suburban Wilmette, while he took up residence in Chicago, free to do as he pleased. He secured a position as a pharmacist at a drugstore in Englewood, working for the elderly Mrs. Holden, who was happy to have a handsome young doctor to help out at her store. When Mrs. Holden suddenly disappeared, Holmes told people that she had moved to California, and that he had purchased the store.

Next, Holmes bought a vacant lot across the street from the drugstore and began constructing a house with a floor plan he designed himself. The three-story building at 63rd and Wallace would have more than 60 rooms, secret passageways, gas pipes with nozzles that piped noxious fumes into windowless rooms, chutes that led down to the basement, and an airtight vault. Holmes hired and fired construction crews on a regular basis; it was said that his swindler's streak got him out of paying for most of the materials and labor used to create this "Murder Castle."

Up & Running

Advertised as a lodging for world's fair tourists, the building opened in 1892. Holmes placed ads in newspapers to rent rooms, but also listed classified ads calling for females interested in working for a start-up company. Of course, there was no start-up company, and Holmes hired the prettiest women or those who could offer him some sort of financial gain. One by one, they inevitably succumbed to his charm. He made false promises to woman after woman, luring them deeper into his confidence. He took advantage of their naïveté to gain their trust and steal their money.

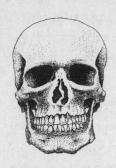 When he was done with a woman, either because she became suspicious of him or because he had simply gotten what he wanted from her, Holmes got rid of her—without remorse or emotion. Sometimes he piped gas into a victim's room to kill her in her sleep; other times he locked her in his airtight vault and listened as she slowly suffocated. Evidence shows he tortured some of them before killing them. After he brutalized the unfortunate soul, he destroyed the evidence in a vat of acid or a kiln he had built expressly for that purpose, often selling his victims' bones and organs to contacts in the medical field.

The End of "Doctor Death"

After the world's fair ended, creditors put pressure on Holmes, and he knew it was time to flee. Strange as it seems, when Holmes was finally brought to justice, it initially wasn't for homicide—it was for one of his many financial swindles. But as clues about missing women emerged, investigators became suspicious of him for other reasons.

Detective Frank Geyer began to follow the trail of this mysterious man whose identity changed with the weather. Geyer had traced many missing world's fair women back to Holmes's lodging house. He was particularly interested in the whereabouts of three children—Howard, Nellie, and Alice Pietzel. Geyer followed their tracks across the Midwest and into Canada. In Toronto he finally found a house where Holmes had allegedly stayed with several children in tow. Buried in a shallow grave in the backyard, stuffed in a single traveling trunk, he discovered the bodies of the two Pietzel girls. Geyer found the boy's remains several months later in an oven in an Indianapolis home.

When the evidence was brought back to court, Geyer got full clearance to investigate every inch of Holmes's Chicago dwelling. The investigation turned up a lot more than detectives anticipated, and one of America's most chilling stories of murder and crime officially broke.

Inside his heavily guarded cell, Herman Webster Mudgett admitted his crimes. He officially confessed to 27 murders, six attempted murders, and a whole lot of fraud. What he didn't confess to, however, were any feelings of remorse.

Holmes was executed by hanging in 1896. He was buried in Holy Cross Cemetery near Philadelphia in a coffin lined with cement, topped with more cement, and buried in a double grave—per his own request. Was he ready to rest eternally after a life of such monstrosity? Or was he afraid that someone would conduct experiments on him as he had done to so many hapless victims?

So They Said

"I was born with the devil in me. I could not help the fact that I was a murderer, no more than the poet can help the inspiration to sing."

—H. H. HOLMES

"My religious belief teaches me to feel as safe in battle as in bed. God has fixed the time for my death. I do not concern myself about that, but to always be ready, no matter when it may overtake me."

—THOMAS JONATHAN "STONEWALL" JACKSON

"Hearing nuns' confessions is like being stoned to death with popcorn."

—ARCHBISHOP FULTON J. SHEEN

"They couldn't hit an elephant at this distance."

—UNION GENERAL JOHN SEDGWICK, JUST MOMENTS BEFORE BEING SHOT DEAD BY A CONFEDERATE SNIPER AT SPOTSYLVANIA

Three-Ring Tragedies

For more than 200 years, circuses have brought smiles to the faces of American children of all ages. They're popular attractions, but they've also been the sites of horrendous disasters.

✳   ✳   ✳   ✳

The Wallace Brothers Circus Train Disaster

ON AUGUST 6, 1903, two trains owned by the Wallace Brothers Shows were involved in a rear-end collision at the Grand Trunk Railroad Yard in Durand, Michigan. Twenty-three people were killed instantly, and several others died shortly after; nearly 100 individuals were injured. Numerous animals also perished in the crash.

The *Owosso Argus Press* described the aftermath this way: "The scene that followed is indescribable, the cries and groans from the injured persons and frightened passengers, the roars from the terrified animals and the escaping steam aroused the whole city, and hundreds rushed to the scene to assist in every way in the sad task of caring for the dead and wounded."

The Hagenbeck-Wallace Circus Train Disaster

In the early morning hours of June 22, 1918, the Hagenbeck-Wallace Circus train was struck by an empty troop train just outside Hammond, Indiana. Of the 300 passengers asleep in the circus train, 86 were killed and more than 127 were injured. As a result of the ensuing fire, fed by the wood-constructed Pullman cars, many of the dead were burned beyond recognition.

Thanks to assistance from its competitors, including Ringling Bros. and Barnum & Bailey, which loaned equipment and performers, the Hagenbeck–Wallace Circus had to cancel only two performances.

The Hartford Circus Fire

Perhaps the nation's best-known circus disaster is the devastating fire that broke out during an afternoon performance of the

Ringling Bros. and Barnum & Bailey Circus on July 6, 1944, in Hartford, Connecticut. An estimated 167 people—most of them children—died in the blaze and the ensuing mayhem, and several hundred were injured (exact totals vary depending on the source). The cause of the fire remains a mystery, but investigators blamed the speed with which the fire spread on the fact that the massive circus tent had been waterproofed by coating it with gasoline and paraffin.

The Death of Jumbo the Elephant

Standing 11 feet tall, Jumbo was one of the star attractions of the Barnum & Bailey Circus when the celebrated pachyderm was struck and killed by a train at a marshaling yard in St. Thomas, Ontario, Canada, on September 15, 1885. Ever the showman, P. T. Barnum told the press Jumbo had managed to toss a younger elephant to safety right before the train struck, though eyewitness accounts suggest the story isn't true.

Barnum had acquired Jumbo from the London Zoological Gardens for $10,000 in 1882. After Jumbo's death, his skeleton was donated to the American Museum of Natural History in New York City; his heart was sold to Cornell University; and his hide was stuffed and mounted. Barnum continued to exhibit Jumbo's remains until 1889, at which time he donated the stuffed behemoth to Tufts University, where it was displayed until it was destroyed by a fire in 1975.

The Death of Karl Wallenda

The "Flying Wallendas" were one of the most publicized tightrope acts in modern circus history, dazzling audiences with amazing stunts such as the seven-person chair pyramid. But on March 22, 1978, Karl Wallenda, the family's 73-year-old patriarch, fell to his death during a promotional tightrope walk in San Juan, Puerto Rico. His was not the first family tragedy—Karl's sister-in-law Rietta Wallenda fell to her death in 1963, and his son-in-law, Richard Guzman, was killed in 1972 when he accidentally touched a live wire while holding part of the metal rigging.

Chapter Fifteen

Weird!

Creepy Coincidences

From a prophetic book written decades before a tragic event took place to a man struck repeatedly by lightning, life's great coincidences are often truly mind-boggling.

✳   ✳   ✳   ✳

Think of Laura

On a whim, ten-year-old Laura Buxton of Burton, Staffordshire, England, jotted her name and address on a luggage label in 2001. She then attached it to a helium balloon and released it into the sky. Supported by air currents for 140 miles, the balloon eventually touched down in Pewsey, Wiltshire, England. Bizarrely, another ten-year-old girl named Laura Buxton read the note, got in touch with its sender, and the girls became fast friends. In addition to their identical names and ages, each child had fair hair and owned a black Labrador retriever, a guinea pig, and a rabbit.

He's Awl That

Most people recognize the name Louis Braille, the world-renowned inventor of the Braille system of reading and writing for the blind. But what many people don't know is how Braille himself became blind and how it led to his invention.

When he was only three years old, Braille accidentally poked himself in the eye with a stitching awl owned by his father, a saddle maker. At first his injury didn't seem serious, but when an autoimmune disease known as sympathetic ophthalmia set in, he went blind in both eyes.

In 1824, at age 15, he invented a system of raised dots that enabled the blind to read and write through use of their fingertips. To form each dot on a page, Braille employed a stitching awl—the same tool that had injured him as a child.

Attractive Gent

Do some people attract lightning the way a movie star attracts fans? In the case of Major Walter Summerford, an officer in the British Army, the evidence nods toward the affirmative. In 1918, Summerford received his first jolt when he was knocked from his horse by a flash of lightning. Injuries to his lower body forced him to retire from the military, so he moved to Vancouver, British Columbia.

In 1924, Summerford was fishing beside a river when a bolt of lightning struck the tree he was sitting beneath, and he was zapped again. But by 1926, Summerford had recovered from his injuries to the degree that he was able to take walks. He continued with this therapy until one tragic summer's day in 1930 when, unbelievably, lightning found him yet again. This time it paralyzed him for good. He died two years after the incident.

Finally, in 1936, a lightning bolt took aim at a cemetery. The bolt passed its energy harmlessly into the ground—but not before striking Summerford's headstone.

Four's a Crowd

In 1838, Edgar Allan Poe penned a novel entitled *The Narrative of Arthur Gordon Pym of Nantucket*. His fictitious account centers around four survivors of a shipwreck who find themselves adrift in an open lifeboat. After many days of hunger and torment, they decide the only way for any of them to survive is for one to be sacrificed for food. They draw straws, and cabin boy Richard Parker comes up short. He is subsequently killed, and the three remaining seamen partake of his flesh.

In 1884, some 46 years after the tale was first told, the yacht *Mignonette* broke apart during a hurricane in the South Atlantic. Its four survivors drifted in a lifeboat for 19 days before turning desperate from hunger and thirst. One sailor, a cabin boy, became delirious after guzzling copious quantities of seawater. Upon seeing this, the other three determined that the man was at death's door and decided to kill him. They then devoured his remains. His name: Richard Parker.

Downed Damsels

Mary Ashford was born in 1797, and Barbara Forrest in 1954, yet circumstances surrounding their eventual murders are eerily similar. On May 27, 1817, Ashford was raped and killed in Erdington, England. On May 27, 1974, Forrest was also raped and murdered in Erdington, just 400 yards away from the site of Ashford's murder. The day preceding each murder was Whit Monday, a floating religious holiday on the Christian calendar celebrated mostly in Europe. The murders occurred at approximately the same time of day, and attempts were made to conceal both bodies.

That's not all. Each woman had visited a friend on the night before Whit Monday, changed into a new dress during the evening, and attended a dance. Curiously, suspects in both cases shared the surname "Thornton." Both were subsequently tried and acquitted of murder. Paintings and photos show that the two women also shared very similar facial features.

The Wacked-Out World of Sir George Sitwell

Fancy a breakfast of meat eggs? Does the history of the fork fascinate you? Do you like being ignored? If so, you'd get along famously with Sir George Sitwell.

✳ ✳ ✳ ✳

THE SITWELLS, A gentrified English clan, were one of the most celebrated literary families of the 20th century. Dame Edith Sitwell (1887–1964) was an acclaimed author, poet, and literary critic. Her brothers, Sir Osbert Sitwell (1892–1969) and Sir Sacheverell Sitwell (1897–1988), made their marks in the literary world as an author and art critic, respectively. All three were noted for the frivolity, intelligence, and sophistication of their written works.

The literary accomplishments of the Sitwell siblings may seem remarkable when you consider that they were the offspring of Sir George Reresby Sitwell (1860–1943), an "out there" member of the English gentry of his day.

Sir George, like his progeny, made a name for himself, but not through literary greatness. Instead, he earned a more dubious reputation by penning scholarly tomes on inane topics, inventing thoroughly useless things, and exhibiting eccentric behavior that often left acquaintances wondering from what planet he originated.

Idle Hands, Busy Mind

Sir George, it should be noted, never worked a day in his life. He became master of Renishaw Hall and Lord Manor of Eckington at a young age, allowing him to live off the income from his family estates as an English gentleman. He enjoyed the lifestyle of the idly rich, perhaps fostering the disconnection with the real world that he blithely displayed his whole life.

Sir George's idle hands were offset by a highly active mind—though he was certainly strange, he was definitely no dummy. He was a renowned antiquarian and genealogist and was highly knowledgeable about medieval society. His research filled seven studies within Renishaw Hall and spawned numerous manuscripts, including such gripping treatises as "Wool-Gathering in Medieval Times and Since," "Domestic Manners in Sheffield in the Year 1250," and "Acorns as an Article of Medieval Diet." Sir George was also keenly interested in garden design, and in 1909 published a successful book entitled *On the Making of Gardens*.

Sir George fancied himself a Renaissance man who possessed wisdom that extended well beyond medieval history and gardening. His extracurricular intellectual endeavors, however, revealed his true inner wackiness, suggesting something entirely different.

Books Nobody Read, Inventions Nobody Wanted

Sir George wrote a number of erudite works that demonstrated his skewed perspective as to what made for compelling reading. Included in these were densely worded dissertations such as "The History of the Fork" and "The History of the Cold." To Sir George's dismay, none of his writings made it to the printing press. He also provided parenting expertise in a volume entitled "The Errors of Modern Parents," though his own parenting skills were questionable. During a short spell as a gentleman farmer, Sir George once tried to pay Sacheverell's Eton College fees in produce, and gave Osbert an allowance of the same amount that a previous Lord Manor of Eckington had given his eldest son 500 years earlier.

Sir George also tried his hand at inventing. One of his creations was an "egg" that featured a yolk of smoked meat, a white of compressed rice, and an ersatz lime shell. Sir George viewed his egg as a handy, nutritious snack for travelers. He was so convinced of its potential that he presented it to a prestigious London publicity firm, announcing, "I am Sir George Sitwell and I have brought my egg with me." It didn't go over well, and Sir George never spoke of his egg again.

Undaunted, he later invented a tiny pistol designed specifically for shooting wasps, as well as an oversize toothbrush that played music.

A Sociable Antisocial

It was while in the company of others that Sir George's detachment from reality was most vividly displayed. Guests invited to Renishaw Hall were greeted with a notice that read: "I must ask anyone entering the house never to contradict me in any way, as it interferes with the functioning of the gastric juices and prevents my sleeping at night." Usually he would eat alone, well before his guests sat down to dine, and would mingle only when approached. In typical Sir George illogic, he once lamented, "I never know anybody in this house."

His indifference to new acquaintances sometimes got him into sticky situations. On one occasion, he offered up a long and harsh critique of the writings of Rupert Brooke, completely unaware that amongst those listening to him was the young poet's mother. When delicately apprised of this, Sir George gave her a puzzled look and simply stopped talking.

Usually though, Sir George just didn't understand other people. He once went into a prolonged snit over the "bad behavior" of an acquaintance who had failed to deliver him a piece of jewelry as promised. The person, hoping to arrange another meeting with Sir George, had told him in passing that he would give him a "ring" next Thursday.

Yes, Sir George was an odd duck. Daughter Edith would later publish a book entitled *English Eccentrics*, but, perhaps out of respect for her father, she made only a passing reference to him in it.

Make no mistake, however. Edith could easily have dedicated a whole chapter to Sir George.

P. T. Barnum's Giant Sucker

P. T. Barnum, the consummate huckster, supposedly laughed at the audiences he tricked, saying, "There's a sucker born every minute." But have we misjudged America's Greatest Showman?

✳ ✳ ✳ ✳

THE PHRASE—WHICH SUGGESTS that every scam, no matter how obvious, will find a gullible mark—has been attributed to several late-19th-century sources, including con man Joseph "Paper Collar Joe" Bessimer and humorist Mark Twain. Most often, it is attributed to P. T. Barnum.

What a Circus!

Phineas Taylor Barnum (1810–91) both amused and appalled audiences with his collections of freaks, oddities, and wonders. Writer Herman Melville boldly declared him "sole heir to all . . . lean men, fat women, dwarfs, two-headed cows, amphibious sea-maidens, large-eyed owls, small-eyed mice, rabbit-eating anacondas, bugs, monkies and mummies." In the name of entertainment, he promoted "humbugs"—obvious hoaxes designed to delight and entertain, such as the "Feejee Mermaid" and a woman he claimed was George Washington's 161-year-old nanny.

Barnum insisted that people enjoyed being fooled so long as they got their money's worth. Though it seems likely that such a showman would utter this dismissive phrase, Barnum's acquaintances denied it upon inquiry from his biographer, saying that Barnum treasured and respected his patrons.

Start of the Punchline

The true story behind the phrase can be traced to George Hull, a businessman from Binghamton, New York. In 1868,

Hull (a fervent atheist) argued with a fundamentalist preacher who insisted the Bible be taken literally, including Genesis 6:4 ("There were giants in the earth in those days"). Hull purchased an enormous slab of gypsum and hired a stonecutter to carve it into a ten-foot-tall statue of a giant with lifelike details such as toenails, fingernails, and pores. The statue was stained with sulfuric acid and ink and shipped to a farm near Cardiff, New York, where it was then buried.

A year later, Hull hired workers to dig a well near the spot where the statue was buried. As he intended, the workers discovered the statue and were excited by their find. (Six months earlier, fossils had been unearthed—with much publicity—at a nearby farm.) Hull had the workers excavate the statue, and then he charged people to see the Cardiff Giant, as it had become known.

Hull sold his statue for nearly $40,000 to a group of exhibitors headed by David Hannum. Barnum became interested in the find and offered to rent it for $50,000, but Hannum refused. Rather than make a higher offer, Barnum built his own Cardiff Giant, which he put on display, declaring that Hannum had sold him the giant after all and that Hannum's was the forgery. Newspapers widely publicized Barnum's story, causing audiences to flock to Barnum while Hannum bitterly declared, "There's a sucker born every minute," in reference to the duped crowds.

Careful What You Sue For

Hannum sued Barnum for calling his giant a sham. At trial, Hull admitted that the original giant was a hoax. The judge ruled in Barnum's favor, saying that it is not a crime to call a fake a fake.

Afterward, one of Barnum's competitors, Adam Forepaugh, mistakenly attributed (or intentionally misattributed) Hannum's phrase to Barnum. The consummate showman didn't deny saying it; in fact, he thanked Forepaugh for the publicity.

A Haunting on Chicago's Magnificent Mile

Chicago's Water Tower stands more than 150 feet tall along the world-famous Magnificent Mile—one of the city's most popular tourist attractions. However, many visitors don't realize that the site is haunted by a hero who died during the Great Chicago Fire of 1871.

✳ ✳ ✳ ✳

Mrs. O'Leary Lit a Lantern in the Shed

ON THE EVENING of October 8, 1871, the Great Chicago Fire began behind the home of Patrick O'Leary. Contrary to popular belief, the fire was not started by a cow kicking over a lantern. Nevertheless, the flames spread quickly from O'Leary's barn.

When the smoke cleared a couple of days later, charred buildings and ashes littered the city. The fire had cut a path nearly a mile wide and four miles long, leaving more than 100,000 people homeless. Approximately 300 people died in the fire, but the heat was so intense that only 125 bodies were recovered. One of those bodies was a suicide victim found inside the Chicago Water Tower.

A Hero's Last Resort?

According to legend, a lone fireman remained steadfast at the water-pumping station in Chicago's Streeterville neighborhood trying to save as many homes as possible. But as the flames closed in around him, he realized it was a losing battle. With his back to the Chicago Water Tower, there was no place to run.

As the fire edged closer, the brave fireman considered his options. Apparently, a slow death by fire seemed more frightening than a quicker end by his own hand. So the story goes that the fireman climbed the stairs inside the water tower, strung a rope from a beam near the top of the structure, and, in a moment of desperation, looped the rope around his neck and jumped to his death.

The Solitary Ghost

The heat of the fire did not destroy the Chicago Water Tower, but it scorched everything inside. The heroic fireman's identity was never ascertained, but his spirit lingers. Hundreds of people have seen the sad figure of the hanging man and smelled a suggestion of smoke inside the tower, especially on October nights around the anniversary of the tragedy.

From outside the historic structure, some people see a pale man staring down at them from a window near the top of the tower. His expression is sad and resigned, and he seems to look right through those on the ground.

Other visitors have reported an eerie, sorrowful whistling that seems to come from inside the structure. It echoes through the tower, and then it stops abruptly.

However, most people who've seen the Water Tower ghost describe him with a rope around his neck, swinging and turning slowly. His face is twisted, grotesque, and highlighted as if there are flames just beneath him. The ghost appears so real that many witnesses have called police to report a suicide. But responding officers, who have often seen the apparition themselves, know that he's a ghost . . . and a reminder of valor during a tragic fire more than a century ago.

Entertainment or Exploitation?

Nobody would choose to be born with a disability or disfigurement. But if you were born that way before 1940 or so, chances were good that you'd be labeled a "freak" and go straight into a sideshow. During the vaudeville and circus sideshow era, many of these famous "freaks" were put on display for the masses. For better or worse, the following individuals made such an impression on the public that their names are hard to forget.

✳   ✳   ✳   ✳

Eng and Chang—Siamese Twins

The term "Siamese twins" started with Eng and Chang Bunker, conjoined twins born in Siam (modern day Thailand) in 1811. A sideshow act discovered the twins when they were about 18 and took them all over the world, which later led them to tour with P. T. Barnum. Eventually, the twins settled down, became farmers, married sisters, and fathered 21 children between them. In January 1874, Chang died, possibly from a cerebral clot following a severe case of bronchitis. Eng followed just a couple of hours later.

Grace McDaniels—The Mule-Faced Woman

A degenerative genetic condition known as Sturge-Weber syndrome was likely to blame for Grace McDaniels's lot in life. Born in 1888, Grace's face grew and twisted into an alarming balloonlike mass of tissue and discolored skin as she got older. She joined F. W. Miller's freak show in 1935 after winning an "ugly woman" contest, though she much preferred to be known as "The Mule-Faced Woman."

General Tom Thumb

Charles S. Stratton was born in Connecticut in 1838 weighing a hearty 9.2 pounds. But by age six, he had stopped growing at only about two feet tall. P. T. Barnum discovered Stratton in 1843 when he was just five years old, nicknamed him General Tom Thumb, and took him on the road. General Tom Thumb became one of the biggest celebrities of the 19th century. He met queens, kings, and politicians, and when he married his wife Lavinia (she was slightly taller at around 33 inches), congressmen and millionaires were in attendance.

Grady Stiles Jr.—Lobster Boy

For several generations, the Stiles family suffered from a disfiguring condition known as ectrodactyly, which shapes hands and feet into claws or pincerlike stumps. This is why Grady Stiles Jr. came to be known as "Lobster Boy." Born in 1937, he did his share of exhibition shows and interviews because of his disfigurement, but his name would make the news many years later for a more sinister reason. An abusive, aggressive man, Stiles shot and killed his daughter's boyfriend. He was convicted, but because the prison system wasn't equipped to deal with his physical challenges, he got off with 15 years of probation. In November 1992, in a tragic twist of fate, Stiles was murdered by a hitman hired by his wife, Maria.

Simon Metz—aka Schlitzie the Pinhead

Microcephalus is a condition that causes a person's cranium to be abnormally small and pointed. People born with this condition used to be called "pinheads," and Simon Metz was the most famous of them all. Born in the Bronx in 1901 and sold by his parents to a show a few years later, Simon was billed as a female because he often wore a dress due to his incontinence. His condition affected his mental capacity and speech, but that didn't keep Metz—known for his childlike attitude and ever-present smile—from working with some of the biggest names in the business, including circuses in America and abroad. Metz was steadily employed until he retired in the 1960s. He passed away at a nursing home in 1971.

Prince Randian—The Human Caterpillar

In 1871, a deformed baby was born in British Guyana to servant parents. The baby, whose real name is lost to history, arrived with no arms or legs, although he possessed a fully developed head that sat atop a healthy torso. Named "Prince Randian" by P. T. Barnum's scouts, the boy was put on the sideshow circuit in 1889 when he was around 18, where he performed incredible feats such as writing, painting, and rolling and lighting a cigarette using the dexterity of his lips and tongue. Randian and his wife, Sarah, had several children and retired to New Jersey, where he lived until his death in 1934.

Robert Wadlow—The World's Tallest Man

Born in Alton, Illinois, in 1918, Robert Wadlow appeared to be a normal, healthy boy. Then he started growing—and he didn't stop. Wadlow's excessive growth stemmed from a hormone abnormality, which resulted in gigantism. At age eight, he was over six feet tall. By the time he was in his early twenties, Wadlow weighed almost 450 pounds and was nearly nine feet tall. His size garnered him publicity and a tour with the Ringling Brothers Circus. Unfortunately, the abnormality that made him a celebrity came at a price. In 1940, Wadlow needed braces to walk, which caused blisters. When one of the blisters became infected, the world's tallest man required a blood transfusion, which failed. More than 40,000 people attended Wadlow's funeral—12 pallbearers were needed to carry the casket.

Captain Fred Walters

Born in England in 1855, Captain Fred Walters wasn't always sad, but he was definitely blue. The Captain suffered from a neural condition known as locomotor ataxia, but that's not what gave his skin its distinct blue-gray hue. The Captain was given silver compounds as a treatment for his disease. The silver turned his skin blue, so Walters decided to profit from it. He took as much silver as he could to remain as blue as can be, receiving much attention and publicity for it. Unfortunately, the silver poisoned him, and his heart gave out when he was 68.

Saartjee Baartman—The Hottentot Venus

Saartjee, or "Sara," Baartman, a young woman from South Africa, was taken from her homeland and exhibited as a freak in sideshows across Britain. Her voluptuous body earned her the title of the "Hottentot Venus" and laid the foundation for the disparaging attitudes toward the sexuality of women of African descent.

But Baartman's body wasn't actually "disfigured." For 19th-century Europeans, her dark skin, full figure, and native dress were enough for them to label her a sideshow spectacle. Later studied by French anatomists, Baartman's private parts and skeleton were exhibited in Paris until 1985.

Jo-Jo the Dog-Faced Boy

Like his father, Fedor Jefticheiv was born with a medical condition called generalized hypertrichosis—excessive, full-body hair growth. By the time Fedor hit puberty, hair covered his entire face and much of his body. Spotted by a P. T. Barnum talent scout in 1884, Fedor was dubbed "Jo-Jo the Dog-Faced Boy" and was one of the most astonishing attractions of the show. Audience members would pull "Jo-Jo's" beard, stroke his head, and basically taunt him mercilessly, which caused Jo-Jo to snarl occasionally, reinforcing the dog moniker. In 1904, Fedor died of pneumonia at age 35.

Joseph Merrick—The Elephant Man

Perhaps the most famous of the "freaks," Joseph Merrick was the subject of many books, films, and medical studies during his lifetime and since his death in 1890. Today, doctors believe that Merrick suffered from Proteus syndrome, an incredibly rare disease characterized by abnormal, excessive, debilitating, and often disfiguring overgrowth of both tissues and bones. Victorian Britain was fascinated by the hideously disfigured Merrick, who in the face of such extremely trying circumstances was still the picture of decorum. Merrick died at age 27 in the care of doctors who rescued him from abusive sideshow producers and often cruel public treatment.

Tooth Be Told

In the United States, the Tooth Fairy usually trades cash for baby teeth. But how do other cultures handle this rite of passage?

✳   ✳   ✳   ✳

Molar Mice

A S IT TURNS out, the Tooth Fairy isn't universal. In fact, she only visits kids in the United States, Canada, Australia, England, and Denmark (where she's called Tandfeen). But before you start feeling bad that the Tooth Fairy doesn't get around more often, know that in most parts of the world, it's a tooth *mouse* who reigns supreme.

Known as El Ratón in Mexico, El Ratoncito in Argentina, El Ratón Perez in Spain, and Le Petite Souris in France, this magical mouse has the same M.O. as the Tooth Fairy, taking baby teeth from under a pillow, or sometimes from a glass of water, in exchange for money or candy. But that's not the only place children put their baby teeth. In South Africa, mice swipe the tooth from a slipper, but in Uganda, the tooth is hidden behind a pot.

And not every culture trades teeth for trinkets. In Russia and Afghanistan, children drop their teeth down mouse holes in hopes that their teeth will grow in like mice's teeth: strong, sharp, and white. In Kazakhstan, teeth are dropped under bathtubs with similar wishes.

Fangs of Fire

Ancient Egyptians believed the sun strengthened teeth, which may explain why in many North African and Middle Eastern countries, such as Egypt and Libya, teeth are tossed toward the sun.

Dental Diners

Some cultures prefer to feed a child's tooth to a specific animal in hopes that the animal will replace the tooth with one like its own. The native Yupik of Alaska feed lost teeth to dogs. However, in the 19th century, children from Cornwall, England, had their first teeth burnt so as to avoid having "dog's teeth" grow in (that is, crooked teeth).

Tooth Tossers

Strange as it sounds, tossing a tooth on the roof is common in many cultures, although it's not always a mouse who makes the trade but another sharp-toothed rodent. In Sri Lanka, it's a squirrel; among the Cherokee, a beaver. In the Dominican Republic and Haiti, the tooth is simply tossed on the roof. In China, Japan, and other Asian countries, only a lower tooth is tossed on the roof; an upper one is thrown straight to the ground, buried, or placed at the foot of the bed. The belief is that the new tooth will grow in the direction of the old one.

Bicuspid Burial

But why toss teeth when you can bury them? In Turkey, a tooth is buried at a site that symbolizes the parents' hope for their child's success. For instance, if they wish their child to become a doctor, the tooth is buried on the grounds of a hospital; a scholar, on the grounds of a university. Malaysian tradition holds that, as part of the body, teeth must be returned to the earth, and in Tajikistan, teeth are planted in a field so they can grow into warriors.

The Navajo traditionally take a lost tooth to the southeast, away from the family home, and bury it on the east side of a young bush or tree. Other native cultures, such as the aboriginal Australians and the Yellowknife Dene of Canada's Northwest Territories, plant a tooth inside a tree in hopes that as the tree grows straight, so will the child's new tooth.

Ivory Accessories

Still, there are cultures that are loath to part with their children's pearly whites. Lithuanians hang on to them as keepsakes, and in certain Central American countries, such as Chile and Costa Rica, a baby tooth is dipped in gold or silver and made into jewelry for the child to wear—a custom that resembles the Viking tradition of wearing baby teeth as good luck charms.

Fast Facts

✳ Soviet gymnast Larissa Latynina won a record 18 Olympic medals. She competed in three Olympic Games, in 1956, 1960, and 1964.

✳ In 1674, King Louis XIV of France learned that a nine-year-old Irish boy had made fun of his bald head. He had the youth imprisoned in the Bastille, where he remained for 69 years.

✳ Although no one will ever know for sure, the surface of the sun is thought to be about 10,000°F.

✳ Marie Maynard Daily became the first African American woman to earn a PhD in chemistry when she earned a doctorate from Columbia University in 1947.

✳ Portuguese explorer Pedro Álvares Cabral set out for the Americas with 13 ships in March 1500. He discovered Brazil a month and a half later, claiming it for Portugal.

✳ Tears kill bacteria that get into your eye.

✳ The Vermont Teddy Bear Company created and sold a product called the Crazy for You Bear in 2005. It came in a straitjacket with commitment papers.

✳ Nero's wife, Poppaea, regularly took a bath filled with the milk from 500 female asses to make her skin softer and whiter. When she was exiled from Rome, she was permitted only 50 asses.

✳ Chinese dialects are the second-most widely spoken language in Australia.

✳ The highest temperature ever recorded in the United States was 134°F at Greenland Ranch in Death Valley, California.

✳ The @ sign is believed to be at least six centuries old.

✳ A hippopotamus can open its mouth wide enough to accommodate a four-foot-tall child.

✳ Bees have five eyes: three small eyes on the top of its head and two larger eyes in front.

Lifestyles of the Eccentric

William Lyon Mackenzie King (1874–1950)

Canada's longest-serving prime minister, William Lyon Mackenzie King kept unusual political advisors—particularly, the spirits he summoned through his Ouija board and crystal ball. Canadian voters considered King to be rather dull, but postmortem details from his journals revealed frequent chats with his deceased mother, Leonardo da Vinci, and several generations of dead pet terriers (all named Pat).

Benjamin O'Neill-Stratford (1808–c. 1870)

This Irish eccentric worked for more than 20 years designing and building the world's largest hot air balloon. He kept only one servant, had his meals delivered so he didn't have to employ a cook, and even bought a landing strip by the Seine River in preparation for his maiden voyage. Unfortunately, a fire destroyed both the balloon and O'Neill-Stratford's dreams. He ended up a broken man, hoarding dirty dishes in hotel rooms in Spain, only moving out after the dishes filled the room.

Richard Feynman (1918–1988)

A true genius who won the Nobel Prize for physics and participated in the development of the atomic bomb, Feynman found time to pursue a variety of hobbies: juggling, lock picking, and samba bongo drumming. Feynman once proclaimed strip clubs to be a "public need," and indeed, much of his research was done in adult entertainment joints. The title of one of his popular books says it all: *What Do You Care What Other People Think?*

The Real Hound of the Baskervilles

Spent from writing his famous Sherlock Holmes series of detective stories, Sir Arthur Conan Doyle set off on what he believed was a relaxing golf holiday. But he was wrong. His experiences at England's Royal Links Hotel in the town of Cromer led to the most famous Holmes adventure ever, and it all began with the story of a shaggy dog.

✳ ✳ ✳ ✳

SOON AFTER DOYLE arrived at the Royal Links Hotel in March 1901, the famous author heard an amazing tale. A huge, sinister, ghostly dog was said to haunt the nearby coast, and the animal could be seen from the hotel on stormy nights. Supposedly, the black dog was the size of a calf and had glowing red eyes and an odor like brimstone. In Conan Doyle's words, it was "a spectral hound, black, silent, and monstrous." The author immediately began searching for this extraordinary beast.

England's Black Shuck

Throughout most of England, this type of terrifying hound is called a "black shuck." Some people describe it as an unusually large black wolfhound; others say it is a hound from hell. Shucks have been reported for hundreds of years, including some late 20th-century encounters with the police.

Most shuck sightings occur along England's picturesque southeastern coast. The town of Cromer, where Conan Doyle vacationed, is at the heart of this area. During the daytime, Cromer is a deceptively quaint and peaceful town, but on stormy nights, the town has a much darker reputation. In his 1901 book, *Highways and Byways of East Anglia*, author William Dutt described Cromer's black shuck. "He takes the form of a huge black dog, and prowls along dark lanes and lonesome field footpaths, where, although his howling makes the hearer's blood run cold, his footfalls make no sound."

Neither an Officer nor a Gentleman

Squire Richard Cabell—the basis of Arthur Conan Doyle's villain, Hugo Baskerville—may have been the first person killed by a black shuck. Cabell was born around 1620 and grew up in Brook Manor near what is now England's eerie Dartmoor National Park. Like his father, Cabell supported the Royalists, who taxed peasants rather than landowners. This made the Cabell family unpopular with their neighbors, and some people claimed that Richard Cabell had sold his soul to the devil.

The Black Shuck's Revenge

When the Royalists were defeated in the English Civil War, Cabell hastily married Elizabeth Fowell, the daughter of the local tax collector. According to local lore, Cabell resented his wife and was also insanely jealous and abusive toward her. One night, Elizabeth and her dog attempted to flee across the moor as Squire Cabell chased after them.

When Cabell caught up with his wife and began to beat her, the dog increased in size and its skin stretched over its expanding frame, giving the hound a skeletal appearance. Then, his eyes began to glow with rage, or perhaps the fires of hell. The dog ripped Cabell's throat out and then disappeared across the moor, leaving the corpse at Elizabeth's feet. From that moment on, similar hounds have been sighted around Dartmoor as well as along Norfolk's coastline.

The Devil Claims His Own

Soon after Richard Cabell was interred in the Holy Trinity Church graveyard, people began reporting strange occurrences at the cemetery. Some claimed they'd seen Cabell on stormy nights, rising from his grave and leading a pack of phantom hounds on a hunt across the moor, possibly searching for Elizabeth. According to legend, the squire's eyes glowed red with rage, and he would attack anyone who crossed his path.

Allegedly for protection, the town placed a heavy stone slab over Cabell's grave. Still, the reports of his ghost continued, along with sightings of the black shuck. Later, a huge stone building—referred to as "the sepulchre"—was constructed around the grave. A heavy wooden door was added, along with metal bars on the windows, to keep Cabell's spirit inside.

To this day, people report an ominous red glow emanating from inside the building. According to local lore, if you run around the crypt seven times and reach through the window, either Cabell or the devil will lick or bite your fingertips.

Cabell's Revenge

Whether these stories of Cabell's afterlife prison are true or not, the graveyard and the church next to it have been the victims of extraordinarily bad luck since the 1800s.

First, the cemetery became a target for body snatchers in the 1820s. Then the church caught fire several times, including a blaze in 1849 that was attributed to arson. Later, around 1885, the church was struck by lightning. Some years after that, the stained-glass windows shattered and had to be replaced. The church was plagued by problems like these until 1992, when a fire started under the altar. The flames were so intense that the church's ancient Norman font exploded from the heat. Area residents, weary of such calamities, decided not to repair the church. Today, Holy Trinity Church is an empty shell and perhaps a monument to the Cabell curse.

The Real Baskerville

Sir Arthur Conan Doyle's novel *The Hound of the Baskervilles* matches many of the chilling details of the Richard Cabell legend. He describes the fictional Hugo Baskerville as "a most wild, profane, and godless man" with "a certain wanton and cruel humour." In the novel, Baskerville kidnaps the lovely daughter of a nearby landowner and holds her captive until she marries him. After mistreating his wife, Baskerville is attacked and killed by a vicious, phantom hound.

Conan Doyle intended *The Hound of the Baskervilles* to be fiction, so he did not choose to call his villain Richard Cabell. Instead, the author whimsically used the surname of William Henry "Harry" Baskerville, the coachman who drove him around Devon during his research. Interestingly, Harry was a distant relative of Elizabeth Fowell, whose storied flight from Richard Cabell was the inspiration for the legend of Dartmoor's black shucks.

The Shucks Still Roam

On stormy days and damp nights, many believe that black shucks can still be seen throughout England. Some also think that a black shuck left scratches and burn marks on the door at Blythburgh's Holy Trinity Church, also called the Cathedral of the Marshes. Throughout the 20th century, shuck sightings continued to be reported. Shuck Lane in the coastal Norfolk town of Overstrand was given that name because the beast is said to frequently appear there.

According to paranormal researchers, the best place to find a black shuck is at Coltishall Bridge just north of Norwich. If you walk that bridge at night, you may sense or hear the beast. If you are especially unlucky, you may actually see it. But close your eyes if you think a black shuck is nearby, for—as William Dutt reported in his book—"to meet him is to be warned that your death will occur by the end of the year."

Winchester Mystery House

Thanks to the dubious advisement of psychics and spirits, this baffling house grew and grew.

✳   ✳   ✳   ✳

Pretty and talented 22-year-old Sarah Pardee was exceedingly popular. Nicknamed the "Belle of New Haven," she had her pick of suitors. In the end, she chose a young man named William W. Winchester, the only son of Oliver Winchester, a stockholder with the successful New Haven Arms Company. When Sarah and William married in 1862, William planned to expand the business by buying out some of his competition and introducing the repeating rifle, so named because its lever action allowed a gunman to fire many shots in succession. The gun became known as "The Gun that Won the West," and the now fabulously wealthy Winchester name was woven into the fabric of American history.

Can't Buy Me Love

In the summer of 1866, Sarah gave birth to a daughter, but the joy of a new baby was brief. The child was born sickly, diagnosed with marasmus, a protein deficiency that typically afflicts infants in third-world countries. The baby was unable to gain weight and succumbed to the disease in just a few weeks. Sarah and William were both bereft, but Sarah took it the hardest. She sank into a serious depression from which she would never totally recover.

Fifteen years later, when Oliver Winchester passed away, William stepped into his dad's shoes at the family business. However, he had only held the job for a few months when he lost a battle with tuberculosis and died in 1881.

Sarah was now 41 years old and alone. She was also extremely wealthy. In the late 1880s, the average family income hovered around $500 per year. Sarah was pulling in about $1,000 per day! Because her husband had left her everything, she had more than 700 shares of stock in addition to income from current sales. When William's mother died in 1898, Sarah inherited 2,000 more shares, which meant that she owned about 50 percent of the business. Sarah Winchester was all dressed up and had absolutely nowhere to go—although even if she did have someplace, there was no one with whom she could share it.

Today, most people regard psychics with more than a little suspicion and skepticism, but in the late 19th century, psychics had grabbed much of the public's attention and trust. The period after the Civil War and the onslaught of new industry had left so much destruction and created so much change for people that many were looking for answers in a confusing world. With claims that they could commune with the "Great Beyond," psychics were consulted by those hoping for some insight.

Sarah was not doing well after the death of her husband. Losing her child had been a debilitating blow, but after her husband's passing, she was barely able to function. Fearing for her life, one of Sarah's friends suggested she visit a psychic to see if she could contact her husband or daughter or both. Sarah agreed to visit a Boston medium named Adam Coons, who wasted no time in telling her that William was trying to communicate with her, and the message wasn't good.

Apparently, William was desperate to tell Sarah that the family was cursed as a result of the invention of the repeating rifle. Native Americans, settlers, and soldiers all over the world were dead because of the gun, and the spirits of these people were out for Sarah next. The only way for her to prolong her life was to move to California. Once there, she would have to build a huge house where all those spirits could live happily together. Sarah was told that construction on the house could never cease, or the spirits would claim her and she would die. So Sarah packed up and left New Haven for California in 1884.

Now That's a House!

Sarah bought an eight-room farmhouse on the outskirts of the burgeoning town of San Jose, on the southern end of San

Francisco Bay. Legend has it that she hired more than 20 workmen and a foreman and kept them working 24 hours a day, 365 days a year. To ensure that they would keep quiet about what they were doing, she paid them a whopping $3 per day—more than twice the going rate of the time.

The workmen built as their client wished, though it made no sense whatsoever. Sarah was not an architect, but she gave the orders for the house's design, which resulted in a rather unusual abode—stairs lead to ceilings, windows open into brick walls, and some rooms have no doors. There are also Tiffany windows all over the place, many containing the number 13, with which Sarah was obsessed. There are spiderweb-paned windows, which, although lovely, didn't do much to dispel rumors that Sarah was preoccupied with death and the occult.

The house kept on growing, all because the spirits were supposedly "advising" Sarah. Chimneys were built and never used. There were so many rooms that counting them was pointless. Reportedly, one stairway in the house went up seven steps and down eleven, and one of the linen closets is bigger than most three-bedroom apartments.

Very few people ever saw the lady of the house. When she shopped in town, merchants came to her car, as she rarely stepped out. Rumors were rampant in San Jose: Who was this crazy lady? Was the house haunted by spirits or just the energy of the aggrieved widow who lived there? Would the hammers ever stop banging? The workers knew how weird the house was, but no one knew for sure what went on inside Sarah's head.

Still, Sarah was generous in the community. She donated to the poor, occasionally socialized, and, in the early days, even threw a party every once in a while. She had a maid she was quite fond of and was exceedingly kind to any children she encountered. But as the house grew and the years passed, the rumors became more prevalent and the increasingly private Sarah retreated further into her bizarre hermitage.

The End

In 1922, Sarah Winchester died in her sleep, and the construction finally ceased after 38 years. In her will, Sarah left huge chunks of her estate to nieces, nephews, and loyal employees. The will was divided into exactly 13 parts and was signed 13 times. Her belongings, everything from ornate furniture to chandeliers to silver dinner services, were auctioned off. It took six weeks to remove everything.

And as for the house itself, it wasn't going to find a buyer any time soon: The structure at the time of Sarah's passing covered several acres and had more than 10,000 window panes, 160 rooms, 467 doorways, 47 fireplaces, 40 stairways, and 6 kitchens. A group of investors bought the house in hopes of turning it into a tourist attraction, which they did. What they didn't do was employ guides or security, however, so for a small fee, thousands of curious people came from all over the country to traipse through the house, scribbling graffiti on the walls and stealing bits of wallpaper. It wasn't until the house was purchased in the 1970s and renamed the Winchester Mystery House that it was restored to its original state. Millions of people have visited the house, which continues to be one of the top tourist attractions in California.

The Footnote

With so many people going in and out of the house over the years, it's not surprising that there are tales of "strange happenings" in the Winchester mansion. People have claimed that they've heard and seen banging doors, mysterious voices, cold spots, moving lights, doorknobs that turn by themselves, and more than a few say that Sarah herself still roams the many rooms. Psychics who have visited the house solemnly swear that it is indeed haunted.

This can't be proven, of course, but it doesn't stop the claims, and it didn't stop the lady of the house from undertaking one of the world's most incredible construction projects.

That's a Crime Too: Monster Laws

Planning to bag Bigfoot? Want to capture yourself a Yeti? Or net yourself a sea monster? Better think again. Because believe it or not, there are laws on the books protecting these creatures from harm—even though they may not even exist (the creatures, not the laws). Check it out:

✳ In 1969, the board of commissioners in Washington state's Skamania County passed an ordinance making it illegal to kill a Bigfoot. The punishments for violating this law are quite severe: a $10,000 fine and a prison sentence of five years.

The law's text cites the high number of purported Bigfoot sightings in the county as justification. The law also covers its bases by mandating protection not only for creatures called "Bigfoot," but also for those called "Yeti," "Sasquatch," and "Giant Hairy Ape." Of course, it's hard to tell how serious commissioners were about this law: It was originally passed on April 1.

✳ Some monsters are more beloved than others. Champ, a twisty sea monster rumored to live beneath the surface of Lake Champlain, is protected by law in not just one state but two.

In the 1980s, both Vermont and New York passed resolutions that made it illegal to harm Champ in any way. The sea serpent is held in such high esteem in the region that the community of Port Henry, New York, celebrates Champ Day each summer. During this festival, vendors flock to the streets of Port Henry to hawk elephant ears, folk art, and lots of T-shirts with Champ appliqués.

* Champ isn't the only sea monster who's earned protection from hunters and poachers. In 1973, the Arkansas state senate passed a resolution sponsored by Senator Robert Harvey naming certain sections of the White River a safe refuge for a sea monster called Whitey. Whitey is a household name for many Arkansans. Sightings of the creature, described by one witness as a gray-skinned beast as wide as a car and three car lengths long, began in 1915. The creature has been a part of Arkansas folklore ever since.

  In the summer of 1937, inventive monster hunters began building a giant rope net to capture Whitey after a sighting. Whitey escaped capture, though, when hunters ran out of money and materials to build their net.

* U.S. residents aren't the only ones obsessed with protecting undiscovered creatures. In Bhutan (a small Buddhist country bordered by India and China) the government set up the Sakteng Wildlife Sanctuary in 2001 to protect the mythical migoi, a Himalayan creature similar to the Yeti. The ape-like beasts are rumored to tower eight feet tall and boast reddish-brown fur. Legends say that the migoi are clever enough to walk backward to mislead trackers. Apparently, if hunters get too close, the creatures can even render themselves invisible.

  The Sakteng Wildlife Sanctuary encompasses 253 square miles of land set aside as protected land for the migoi. Again, though, it's difficult to tell just how serious the Bhutan government was when creating the sanctuary. The Sakteng Wildlife Sanctuary also provides a home for snow leopards, tigers, and other wildlife that actually do exist. The "migoi habitat" angle may be a way to attract additional tourists to the region.

The Dyatlov Pass Incident

Nine experienced hikers and skiers trekked into the Russian wilderness and promptly disappeared. Read on for a closer look at one of the greatest (and creepiest) unsolved mysteries of modern times.

✳ ✳ ✳ ✳

Off to the Otorten Mountain

IN EARLY 1959, a group of outdoor enthusiasts formed a skiing and hiking expedition to Otorten Mountain, which is part of the northern Ural Mountain range in Russia. The group, led by Igor Dyatlov, consisted of seven other men and two women: Yury Doroshenko, Georgy Krivonischenko, Alexander Kolevatov, Rustem Slobodin, Nicolas Thibeaux-Brignolle, Yuri Yudin, Alexander Zolotaryov, Lyudmila Dubinina, and Zinaida Kolmogorova.

The group's journey began on January 27. The following day, Yudin became ill and had to return home. It would be the last time he would see his friends alive. Using personal photographs and journals belonging to the members of the ski trip to piece together the chain of events, it appeared as though on February 1, the group got disoriented making their way to Otorten Mountain and ended up heading too far to the west. Once they realized they were heading in the wrong direction, the decision was made to simply set up camp for the night. What happened next is a mystery to this day.

Mountain of the Dead

When no one had heard from the group by February 20, eight days after their planned return, a group of volunteers organized a search. On February 26, they found the group's abandoned campsite on the east side of the mountain Kholat Syakhl. (As if the story were written by a horror novelist, *Kholat Syakhl* happens to mean "Mountain of the Dead" in the Mansi language.) The search team found a badly damaged tent that appeared to have been ripped open from the inside. They also found several sets of footprints. Following the trail of footprints, searchers discovered the bodies of Krivonischenko and Doroshenko, shoeless and dressed only in their underwear. Three more bodies—those belonging to Dyatlov, Kolmogorova and Slobodin—were found nearby. It was later determined that all five had died from hypothermia.

On May 4, the bodies of the four other hikers were recovered in the woods near where the bodies of Krivonischenko and Doroshenko had been found. The discovery of these four raised even more questions. To begin with, Thibeaux-Brignolle's skull had been crushed and both Dubunina and Zolotaryov had major chest fractures. The force needed to cause these wounds was compared to that of a high-speed car crash. Oddly, Dubinina's tongue appeared to have been ripped out.

Looking at the evidence, it appeared as though all nine members had bedded down for the night, only to be woken up by something so frightening that they all quickly left the tent and ran into the freezing cold night. One by one, they either froze to death or else succumbed to their injuries, the cause of which was never determined.

Remains a Mystery

Things got even stranger at the funerals for the nine individuals. Family members would later remark that some of the deceased's skin had become orange and their hair had turned gray. Medical tests and a Geiger counter brought to the site showed some of the bodies had high levels of radiation.

So what happened to the hikers? Authorities eventually concluded that "an unknown compelling force" caused the deaths. The case would be officially closed in the spring of 1959 due to the "absence of a guilty party." Stories and theories still abound, pointing to everything from the Russian government covering up secret military exercises in the area to violent UFO encounters. Today, the area where the nine hikers met their untimely demise is known as Dyatlov Pass, after the leader of the ill-fated group.

Time to Pay the Piper

It's an intriguing story about a mysterious piper and more than 100 missing children. Made famous by the eponymous Brothers Grimm, this popular fairy tale has captivated generations of boys and girls. But is it actually more fact than fiction?

✳ ✳ ✳ ✳

THE LEGEND OF The Pied Piper of Hamelin documents the story of a mysterious musician who rid a town of rats by enchanting the rodents with music from his flute. The musician led the mesmerized rats to a nearby river, where they drowned. When the townsfolk refused to pay him, the rat catcher returned several weeks later, charmed a group of 130 children with the same flute, and led them out of town. They disappeared—never to be seen again.

It's a story that dates back to approximately 1300 and has its roots in a small German town called Hamelin. Several accounts written between the 14th and 17th centuries tell of a stained-glass window in the town's main church. The window pictured the Pied Piper with hands clasped, standing over a group of youngsters. Encircling the window was the following verse (this is a rough translation): "In the year 1284, on John's and Paul's day was the 26th of June. By a piper, dressed in all kinds of colors, 130 children born in Hamelin were seduced and lost at the calvarie near the koppen."

The verse is quite specific: precise month and year, exact number of children involved in the incident, and detailed place names. Because of this, some scholars believe this window, which was removed in 1660 and either accidentally destroyed or lost, was created in memory of an actual event. Yet, the verse makes no mention of the circumstances regarding the departure of the children or their specific fate. What exactly happened in Hamelin, Germany, in 1284? The truth is, no one actually knows—at least not for certain.

Theories Abound

Gernot Hüsam, the current chairman of the Coppenbrügge Castle Museum, believes the word *koppen* in the inscription may reference a rocky outcrop on a hill in nearby Coppenbrügge, a small town previously known as Koppanberg. Hüsam also believes the word *calvarie* is in reference to either the medieval connotation of the gates of hell—or since the Crusades—a place of execution.

One theory put forward is that Coppenbrügge resident Nikolaus von Spiegelberg recruited Hamelin youth to emigrate to areas in Pomerania near the Baltic Sea. This theory suggests the youngsters were either murdered because they took part in summertime pagan rituals, or drowned in a tragic accident while in transit to the new colonies.

But this is not the only theory. Here are some ideas about what really happened:

* They suffered from the Black Plague or a similar disease and were led from the town to spare the rest of the population.

* They were part of a crusade to the Holy Land.

* They were lost in the 1260 Battle of Sedemünder.

* They died in a bridge collapse over the Weser River or a landslide on Ith Mountain.

* They emigrated to settle in other parts of Europe, including Maehren, Oelmutz, Transylvania, or Uckermark.

* They were actually young adults who were led away and murdered for performing pagan rituals on a local mountain.

Historians believe that emigration, bridge collapse/natural disaster, disease, or murder are the most plausible explanations.

Tracing the Piper's Path

Regardless of what actually happened in Hamelin hundreds of years ago, the legend of the Pied Piper has endured. The earliest accounts of the Piper had roots to the actual incident, but as time passed, the story took on a life of its own.

According to early versions of the story, a Hamelin church leader, Deacon von Lude, was said to be in possession of a chorus book with a Latin verse related to the legend written on the front cover by his grandmother. The book was misplaced in the late 17th century and has never been found.

The oldest surviving account—according to amateur Pied Piper historian Jonas Kuhn—appears as an addition to a 14th-century manuscript from Luneburg. Written in Latin, the note is almost identical to the verse on the stained-glass window and translates roughly to:

"In the year of 1284, on the day of Saints John and Paul on the 26th of June 130 children born in Hamelin were seduced by a piper, dressed in all kinds of colors, and lost at the place of execution near the koppen."

Sixteenth-century physician and philosopher Jobus Fincelius believed the Pied Piper was the devil. In his 1556 book, *Concerning the Wonders of His Times*, Fincelius wrote: "It came about in Hamelin in Saxony on the River Weser...the Devil visibly in human form walked the lanes of Hamelin and by playing a pipe lured after him many children...to a mountain. Once there, he with the children...could no longer be found."

In 1557, Count Froben Christoph von Zimmern wrote a chronicle detailing his family's lineage. Sprinkled throughout the book were several folklore tales including one that refer-enced the Pied Piper. For some unknown reason, the count introduced rats into his version of the story: "He passed through the streets of the town with his small pipe... immediately all the rats...collected outside the houses and followed his footsteps." This first insertion of rodents into the legend led other writers to follow suit.

In 1802, Johann Wolfgang von Goethe wrote "Der Rattenfanger," a poem based on the legend. The monologue was told in the first person through the eyes of the rat catcher. Goethe's poem made no direct reference to the town of Hamelin, and in Goethe's version the Piper played a stringed instrument instead of a pipe. The Piper also made an appearance in Goethe's literary work *Faust*.

Jacob and Wilhelm Grimm began collecting European folktales in the early 1800s. Best known for a series of books that documented 211 fairy tales, the brothers also published two volumes between 1816 and 1818 detailing almost 600 German folklore legends. One of the volumes contained the story of "Der Rattenfanger von Hameln."

The Grimm brothers' research for "The Pied Piper" drew on 11 different sources, from which they deduced two children were left behind (a blind child and a mute child); the piper led the children through a cave to Transylvania; and a street in Hamelin was named after the event.

No End in Sight

While the details of the historical event surrounding the legend of the Pied Piper have been lost to time, the mystique of the story endures. Different versions of the legend have even appeared in literature outside of Germany: A rat catcher from Vienna helped rid the nearby town of Korneuburg of rats. When he wasn't paid, he stole off with the town's children and sold them as slaves in Constantinople. A vagabond rid the English town of Newton on the Isle of Wight of their rats, and when he wasn't paid, led the town's children into an ancient oak forest where they were never seen again. A Chinese version had a Hangchow district official use magic to convince the rats to leave his city.

The legend's plot has been adapted over time to fit whichever media is currently popular and has been used as a story line in children's books, ballet, theater, and even a radio drama. The intriguing story of the mysterious piper will continue to interest people as long as there is mystery surrounding the original event.

Fast Facts

✳ A mother kangaroo can have two babies of different ages in her pouch at the same time. She produces different milk for each of them, depending on their age and nutritional needs.

✳ The original Hollywood Production Code of the 1930s stated that excessive kissing, illegal drugs, and indecent exposure were completely forbidden in any movie.

✳ George Welch, a flying ace and Medal of Honor recipient, claimed to have broken the sound barrier on October 1, 1947, two weeks before Chuck Yeager.

✳ Only one person has played both Major League baseball and NHL hockey. Born in 1895, Jim Riley played baseball for St. Louis and Washington and hockey with Chicago and Detroit.

✳ The Nike swoosh was designed by Carolyn Davidson, a graphic design student at Portland State University, in 1971. She was paid $35 for the famous trademark.

✳ In 1960, the USS *Triton*, a nuclear submarine, was the first vessel to circumnavigate the planet submerged. It only surfaced once during its journey, to remove a sick crew member.

✳ The Great Fire of London started in a bakery in 1666 and lasted three days. It consumed the older section of the city and destroyed 13,200 homes. Some reports state that only 16 people died.

✳ Dame Judi Dench had just eight minutes of screen time in the movie *Shakespeare in Love,* but that less-than-15-minutes-of-fame won her the Best Supporting Actress Oscar for 1998.

✳ Originally marketed as "zero proof moonshine," Mountain Dew once featured bottles with the image of a hillbilly on them. They are now collector's items worth five to ten dollars each.

✳ Half of the world's present calorie consumption comes from a small variety of wheat and barley grains first cultivated in the Middle East around 8000 B.C.

Ghosts of the Gold Rush

The California Gold Rush of 1848—and its frenzy of ambition and greed—is what made the Wild West truly wild. So it's little wonder that some folks would find it difficult to leave, even after they've supposedly passed on to the great gold mine in the sky. Check out these haunted locales next time you wander through California's Gold Rush territory.

✳   ✳   ✳   ✳

Jamestown Hotel

SINCE OPENING IN 1858, the Jamestown Hotel in Jamestown has served as a boarding house, bordello, bus depot, and hospital. The resident ghost story is every bit as dramatic as the building's history. In 1938, Mary Rose, the granddaughter of a wealthy and influential prospector, fell in love with a handsome British soldier. Her grandfather was not pleased. The soldier was promptly shipped off to India, where he met a violent death. Mary Rose, desolate, pregnant, and unmarried, checked into what was then the Mother Lode Hospital to await the birth of her child. Unfortunately, neither mother nor child survived childbirth, but guests at the hotel say they've seen misty apparitions of the spirits of Mary Rose and her soldier.

1859 Historic National Hotel

With doors slamming, lights flickering on and off, clothes being tossed from suitcases by unseen hands, and an invisible woman sobbing in the hallway in the middle of the night, how does anyone get any sleep in this place? Also located in Jamestown, the 1859 Historic National Hotel's resident ghost, affectionately named Flo, usually remains upstairs, favoring the rooms toward the front of the building. She has occasionally been spotted floating through the downstairs dining room, but only in the early morning. Current hotel owner Stephen Willey says that, although he's never personally encountered Flo, he has come across many a hotel guest who arrived a skeptic and left a believer.

Willow Steakhouse & Saloon

A mine once ran underneath what is now the Willow Steakhouse (located in, you guessed it, Jamestown), and it plays a part in the restaurant's violent history. There, a mine collapse killed 23 miners; there were violent deaths at the Willow's bar; and a man was lynched in his own room. From the time the building was first built in 1862, a series of mysterious fires have plagued the property, the most recent in 1985. Some blame restless spirits, saying that the place is crowded with ghosts, including a short man who roams the upstairs halls, a dapper gambler who favors the bar, and a redheaded woman who was shot by her husband in the bar during the Gold Rush years.

City Hotel

Located within the Columbia State Historic Park, this Gold Rush—era hotel still welcomes guests, although visitors may share their lodgings with an unexpected roommate. When the hotel was restored for its current use, authentic period antiques reflecting Columbia's heyday (1850–1870) were brought in from nearby San Francisco. Among them was an especially ornate and finely carved wooden bed, originally imported from Europe more than a century before it found its way to the City Hotel. With the bed came the hotel's resident ghost, Elizabeth, a woman who reportedly died in it during childbirth. Since the arrival of the bed (and Elizabeth), doors now open and close at random in Room 1; a sweet perfume often wafts through the air; and guests, especially children, have reported seeing a woman in a white dress standing at the foot of the bed.

The Groveland Hotel

This historic hotel in Groveland is actually two buildings: One was built in 1849 and served as lodging for miners and prospectors working at the now defunct gold mine behind the building. The other was built in 1919 for workers doing construction on the Hetch Hetchy Dam. According to lore, a prospector named Lyle remains. A recluse, Lyle was dead for several days before anyone thought to check his room to see if he was all right. As a ghost, Lyle is quirky. He can't stand to see women's cosmetics on the dresser, and he's not shy about moving them. When people talk about him, Lyle tends to respond by flickering the lights or rushing by as a cold breeze. Once Lyle even helped current owner Peggy Mosley with her baking by flinging open the oven door at the precise moment the bread was finished. Sometimes Lyle disappears for weeks—perhaps to go prospecting—but he always returns to The Groveland Hotel.

Vineyard House

Modern visitors to this beautiful bed-and-breakfast in Coloma would never guess its troubled and violent past. Construction on the house finished in 1878, and a year later, its first owner reportedly went insane and had to be chained in the home's cellar "for his own protection." He went on a hunger strike, starving himself to death and leaving his wife in dire financial straits. The family's grapevines dried up and its wine business went under. The widow was forced to take in boarders to make ends meet and for a time even resorted to renting the house as a jail, a period when two hangings took place in the front yard. Misty apparitions roam the hotel, accompanied by the sound of rattling chains.

Bodie, California

Sure, it's not a hotel, but in its heyday, Bodie personified the Wild West. A Gold Rush town that seemingly sprang up overnight, more than 10,000 people called Bodie home in the late 1870s. No fewer than 70 saloons served up suds to the men who worked the area's 30 mines. Numerous bordellos, gambling halls, and opium dens provided further "amusement," and gunfights were common. During this period, at least one man was killed every day in Bodie. When the gold veins depleted, the town withered; by the time the last mine closed during World War II, only six people remained. Today about 160 buildings still stand, left just as they were when their inhabitants departed. However, some Bodie residents remain eternally. The sound of a nonexistent piano often floats through the streets, and a spectral white mule haunts the Standard Mine on the outskirts of town.

Old Hickory's Big Cheese

How America's first populist president traded 12 bottles of wine for the largest wheel of cheese he had ever seen.

✳ ✳ ✳ ✳

IN THE EARLY 19th century, Sandy Creek, New York, was a small farming community renowned for its dairy products, particularly its cheese. In 1835, one of the town's more colorful citizens, Colonel Thomas S. Meacham, conceived of a plan to deliver an enormous wheel of cheddar cheese to President Andrew Jackson in the name of the governor and the people of the State of New York. For five days, the colonel collected milk from 150 cows and piled the curd into an enormous cheese hoop and press he had constructed for the project. The resulting wheel of cheddar weighed in at half a ton, but this did not satisfy Meacham's lofty ambition. He enlarged the hoop and added more curds until the cheese reached a gargantuan 1,400 pounds. Judging his creation fit for a president, Meacham used a team of 48 horses to transport the cheese to Port Ontario, New York, and—amid firing cannons and cheering crowds—the cheese embarked on a water journey to Washington, D.C. Meacham accompanied his creation and delivered passionate orations to throngs of well-wishers at every stop. When the mammoth cheese was presented to President Jackson, the appreciative president, whose love of cheese was well known, gave Meacham a dozen bottles of wine and his hearty thanks.

At the order of the president, the cheese was allowed to age for two years in the White House lobby. Finally, on the occasion of Washington's birthday in 1837, Jackson determined that the cheese was ready for consumption and threw open the doors of the White House so the public could dine upon the cheddar.

It was common practice at the time for citizens to freely enter the White House during parties. In fact, the throng of revelers had grown so large during Jackson's first inauguration party that the new president escaped through a window and spent the night at the tavern where he had lodged before his election. The rumor of a giant, free wheel of cheese had a similar effect upon the populace, and scores of people pressed into the hall. Some even entered on walkways built to the windows to accommodate the large crowd. Among the notable people present at the cheese party were Vice President Martin Van Buren, Daniel Webster, Colonel Benton, and Colonel Trowbridge. The people carved huge chunks from the cheddar wheel and passed balls of cheese back to waiting guests. In the ensuing feeding frenzy, Meacham's entire creation was consumed in a scant two hours. All that remained of the mighty wheel were some curds, which had been trampled into the carpet during the rush. For years afterward, the lobby of the White House reeked of cheddar.

Van Buren, who succeeded Jackson as president soon afterward, also received cheese from Meacham (though it weighed in at a mere 700 pounds) and attempted to continue the cheese reception tradition. However, it soon ended when it became obvious that the White House finery could not bear the wear and tear of repeated cheese exposure.

Over the years, other U.S. presidents have received gifts of cheese as well:

* Thomas Jefferson enjoyed the 1,235-pound cheddar given to him by the citizens of Cheshire, Massachusetts. Jefferson first ordered that the cheese be served at the White House's New Year's Eve party, but the wheel lasted for several such occasions.

* Calvin Coolidge received a 147-pound Swiss cheese from the grateful citizens of Wisconsin, who approved of his heavy tariff on imports (including cheese) from Switzerland.

* George W. Bush, while campaigning in Wisconsin in 2004, stopped into a cheese factory in the town of Wilson. The surprised staff presented him with a platter of cheese curds. The resulting photos of the president, holding the curds and surrounded by hair-netted employees, made national news.

The End of the World

Since before Roman times, prophets and doomsday cults have been predicting the end of the world, and fearmongers and television preachers continue the tradition today. Fortunately, all of them have been incredibly wrong—so far.

✳ ✳ ✳ ✳

Pre-Christian Doomsday Cults: Most people associate doomsday cults with the Rapture or the Second Coming of Jesus, but doomsday prophets were spreading dread even before Christ's birth. In fact, archaeologists discovered an Assyrian tablet dating back to 2800 B.C., lamenting the corruption and degeneracy of the age and stating quite authoritatively that "the world is speedily coming to an end." Care to narrow that down for us?

Millennial Cults Lotharingian: Scholars in present-day northwest Europe determined that the world would end on March 25, A.D. 970. The prophets' evidence? Their belief that the date represented the anniversary of Jesus' conception and crucifixion, the parting of the Red Sea, and the creation of Adam. That the date was preposterous didn't stop a frenzy of terror from sweeping across Europe as the end of the first millennium approached.

The Millerites: One of the first American doomsday cults, the Millerites were a group of Adventists who followed the teachings of William Miller, who prophesied that the Second Coming of Jesus Christ would be some time around 1843. Miller demonstrated little evidence for his predictions, but Millerism spread like wildfire throughout much of the eastern half of the United States nevertheless. Alas, 1843 came and went (throughout the year, Millerites constantly revised the precise end date) with no sign of Jesus. In 1844, the sect definitively established that the end would come on October 22. On that date, a large group of Miller's followers gathered upon hilltops and roofs to wait for Jesus' arrival. They were sorely disappointed.

Heaven's Gate: Heaven's Gate, the most famous doomsday cult of the modern era, was founded in the 1970s by Marshall Applewhite. Applewhite and his followers believed that Earth would soon be "recycled" and "spaded under," and that human civilization would be wiped away with it. The harbinger of this end-time came in the form of the Hale-Bopp comet, which blazed across the night sky throughout much of 1997. But as luck would have it, a spaceship traveling along with the comet would whisk cult members away from our doomed planet. In preparation, on March 26, 1997, 39 members of the Heaven's Gate cult dressed in identical black shirts, sweatpants, and running shoes and committed mass suicide in a rented mansion located in a wealthy San Diego suburb. Each was covered by a purple cloth. Nobody has come up with a viable explanation for why they were dressed in such a way, nor is there any explanation for the items cult members were carrying at the time of their deaths—five dollars and a stack of quarters.

Y2K Cults: As the year 2000 approached, panic over what would happen when a computer bug went haywire led to countless groups of hysterical survivalists bunkering down with weaponry and canned goods. How common was this irrational and, in retrospect, unfounded fear? According to a *TIME* magazine survey taken in 1999, a whopping 9 percent of Americans believed the world was going to end on January 1, 2000.

December 21, 2012: Today there is no shortage of doomsayers proclaiming that the world is going to end in 2012. Their proof for this little prediction? The ancient Mayans said so. Supposedly. According to the Mayan calendar, December 21, 2012, will mark the end of a 5,126-year cycle, and the calendar will reset to zero. Although there's no evidence that the Mayans believed this meant the world was going to end, fear-peddling prophets continue to churn out books about the end-time by the truckload.

The Champion of American Lake Monsters

In 1609, French explorer Samuel de Champlain was astonished to see a thick, eight- to ten-foot-tall creature in the waters between present-day Vermont and New York. His subsequent report set in motion the legend of Champ, the "monster" in Lake Champlain.

✳ ✳ ✳ ✳

Eerie Encounters

EVEN BEFORE CHAMPLAIN's visit, Champ was known to Native Americans as Chaousarou. Over time, Champ has become one of North America's most famous lake monsters. News stories of its existence were frequent enough that in 1873, showman P. T. Barnum offered $50,000 for the creature, dead or alive. That same year, Champ almost sank a steamboat, and in the 1880s, a number of people, including a sheriff, glimpsed it splashing playfully offshore. It is generally described as dark in color (olive green, gray, or brown) with a serpentlike body.

Sightings have continued into modern times, and witnesses have compiled some film evidence that is difficult to ignore. In 1977, a woman named Sandra Mansi photographed a long-necked creature poking its head out of the water near St. Albans, Vermont, close to the Canadian border. She estimated the animal was 10 to 15 feet long and told an investigator that its skin looked "slimy" and similar to that of an eel. Mansi presented her photo and story at a 1981 conference held at Lake Champlain. Although she had misplaced the negative by then, subsequent analyses of the photo have generally failed to find any evidence that it was manipulated.

In September 2002, a researcher named Dennis Hall, who headed a lake monster investigation group known as Champ Quest, videotaped what looked like three creatures undulating through the water near Ferrisburgh, Vermont. Hall claimed that he saw unidentifiable animals in Lake Champlain on 19 separate occasions.

In 2006, two fishermen captured video footage of what appeared to be parts of a very large animal swimming in the lake. The images were thoroughly examined under the direction of ABC News technicians, and though the creature on the video could not be proved to be Champ, the team could find nothing to disprove it, either.

Champ or Chump?

As the sixth-largest freshwater lake in the United States (and stretching about six miles into Quebec, Canada), Lake Champlain provides ample habitat and nourishment for a good-size water cryptic, or unknown animal. The lake plunges as deep as 400 feet in spots and covers 490 square miles.

Skeptics offer the usual explanations for Champ sightings: large sturgeons, floating logs or water plants, otters, or an optical illusion caused by sunlight and shadow. Others think Champ could be a remnant of a species of primitive whale called a zeuglodon or an ancient marine reptile known as a plesiosaur, both believed by biologists to be long extinct. But until uncontestable images of the creature's entire body are produced, this argument will undoubtedly continue.

Champ does claim one rare, official nod to the probability of its existence: Legislation by both the states of New York and Vermont proclaim that Champ is a protected—though unknown—species and make it illegal to harm the creature in any way.

Chapter Sixteen

Odds and Ends

Red-Hot Redheads

Fiery-tempered. Mischievous. Sensual. Stereotypes aside, redheads demand attention. The following carrot-tops parlayed their locks of flame into positions of fame.

✳   ✳   ✳   ✳

Ruling Reds

Pharaoh Ramses II, aka Ramses the Great: During his prolific 67-year reign, this ruler constructed countless temples, monuments, and statues—and sired up to 100 offspring.

King David: Goliath should have known better than to mess with a redhead! This feisty fireball eventually became king of Judah and Israel and established Jerusalem as its capital city.

Elizabeth I: The red-crowned daughter of Henry VIII and Anne Boleyn reigned as queen for 45 years and is considered by many to be England's greatest monarch.

U.S. presidents: George Washington, Thomas Jefferson, and Martin Van Buren were all undisputed redheads.

Creative Carrot-tops

William Shakespeare: Proud redheads the world over claim Shakespeare as one of their own. Unfortunately, since no descriptions or portraits of the Bard's appearance were recorded during his lifetime, it's a little hard to prove.

Samuel Clemens: Generally known as Mark Twain, this celebrated writer also wrote under the pen name Thomas Jefferson Snodgrass. Defiantly proud of his red hair, Clemens alleged that Adam and Eve were redheads and admonished that "deteriorated black headed descendants" who disdained red hair showed a tasteless "departure from original beauty."

Vincent van Gogh: Ridiculed by the townspeople of Arles, who wanted the mayor to lock up the artist, van Gogh was called *"fou-rou"* (crazy redhead).

Redheaded Rebels

Judas Iscariot: Whether Jesus' betrayer was truly a redhead is unknown, but early artists are thought to have painted Judas's hair red to exploit traditional prejudices against redheads.

Jesse James: Rumor has it this preacher's-kid-turned-bank-robber outsmarted the law by faking his own death. Could be, since the corpse laid to rest in James's grave is reported to have had dark hair, while the outlaw's hair was fiery red.

Rumors of Redness

Lucille Ball: Arguably the world's most beloved redhead, Lucy's trademark locks were contrived to capitalize on television's Technicolor revolution. Lucy joked that she kept Egypt's economy afloat with the henna used to maintain her carrot-top mop.

Lizzie Borden: Despite the fact that this infamous alleged murderess sported a mousy, light-brown mane, a more sensational image persists of Borden as a hot-tempered, axe-wielding redhead.

Jesus Christ: Some assert that Jesus inherited red hair from his ancestor King David. Original paintings uncovered in circa A.D. 586 Rabula Gospels depict Jesus with curly red hair.

11 People Who Fell from a Great Height and Survived

1. In 1960, a boating accident sent seven-year-old Roger Woodward over Niagara Falls (Horseshoe Falls, specifically). Wearing only a bathing suit and a life preserver, he plummeted 161 feet, missed the rocks at the foot of the falls, and emerged unscathed. For 43 years, he was the only person to survive the drop without protective gear.

2. (and 3.) In 1979, newlyweds Kenneth and Donna Burke fell from a sixth-story balcony while posing for pictures during their wedding reception. They landed on grass 72 feet below, narrowly missing a concrete patio and brick wall.

4. In 2004, a 102-year-old Italian woman toppled over the railing of her fourth-story balcony. A plastic playhouse broke her fall, and apart from an arm fracture, she was fine.

5. In 1999, Joan Murray from Charlotte, North Carolina, couldn't get her parachute to open after jumping from a plane at 14,500 feet (2.7 miles). At 700 feet, her reserve chute opened but then quickly deflated. She hit the ground at 80 miles per hour, landing directly on a mound of fire ants. Doctors believed the shock of more than 200 ant bites actually kept her heart beating. Less than two years later, she went on her 37th skydive.

6. (and 7.) When a man in Kuala Lumpur, Malaysia, returned home and caught two burglars in his apartment, they jumped out the window—16 stories up—and landed in a Dumpster. The trash cushioned their fall.

8. John Kevin Hines is one of about two dozen people to survive leaping off the Golden Gate Bridge in San Francisco. He jumped in 2000, when he was 19 and suffering from

severe depression. He immediately regretted his decision and turned himself around during the 25-story drop so he could hit feet first, like a diver. He hit the water at about 75 miles per hour, breaking his back. After he recovered, he launched a speaking campaign calling for the addition of protective barriers on the bridge.

9. In 2007, brothers Alcides and Edgar Moreno were washing the windows on a New York high-rise when the cables holding their support swing failed. Edgar hit a fence below and died instantly. Alcides survived the 47-story fall by holding onto the 16-foot swing. Physicists believe the aluminum platform acted like a giant surfboard, slowed by air currents rising between the buildings.

10. In 1985, mountain climber Joe Simpson broke his leg while he and Simon Yates were descending Siula Grande in Peru. Yates and Simpson tied their ropes together, and Yates steadily lowered Simpson down the mountain. But when Simpson slipped off a cliff, Yates cut the rope to keep from falling himself. Yates assumed Simpson was dead and made his way back to camp. After falling 100 feet into a crevasse, Simpson dragged himself back to base camp. He made the six-mile trek in three days, with no food or water.

11. Serbian flight attendant Vesna Vulovic was the only survivor when Yugoslav Airlines Flight 367 broke up over Czechoslovakia in 1972. An explosion, apparently from a bomb, ripped the DC-9 plane apart when it was 33,333 feet (6.3 miles) in the air. When the wreckage fell to the ground, a villager found Vulovic lying in a piece of fuselage. She made a full recovery, and in 1985 was inducted into *Guinness World Records* for surviving the highest fall without a parachute.

The Ultimate Cat Lady

Barely five feet tall, Mabel Stark didn't look fierce enough to train tigers. But some girls won't back down from a catfight.

✳ ✳ ✳ ✳

TALK ABOUT A CAVEAT: The young woman who'd previously held Mabel Stark's position as an assistant to the tiger trainer for the Barnes Circus met a grizzly fate: attacked and eaten by a tiger in the ring. Even so, Stark couldn't sign up for the gig fast enough. Training tigers is what she'd wanted to do her whole life.

Mabel was born Mary Haynie sometime between 1889 and 1904 (she was cagey about her real age, and dubious about many facts of her life) to Kentucky tobacco farmers who died when she was in her early teens. Orphaned, she was shipped off to Louisville to live with an aunt and uncle. Stark took to spending her afternoons at the zoo, dreaming about becoming a wild animal trainer. But societal conventions held sway, and the petite blonde headed to nursing school when she was (supposedly) 18 years old.

The Lady or the Tiger?

By her own account, Stark headed to Los Angeles in 1911 on a post-graduation trip, where she ran into Barnes Circus owner Al G. Barnes. She was hired on the spot—but she was disappointed to find that she'd been assigned to train a horse. When her contract came up for another year, Stark demanded she work with tiger trainer Louis Roth to learn his trade.

In another version, historians say Mabel left nursing school in 1911 to become a stripper in the Great Parker Carnival, working under the name Mabel Aganosticus. (This was possibly the last name of her first ex-husband; she would go on to collect four or five more.) A year later, she left to marry a "rich Texan," but the relationship quickly went kaput.

In keeping with the second story, now using the surname "Stark," Mabel returned to the carnival, where she hung around the animals and befriended their trainer, Al Barnes. A year later, Barnes left to start his own circus and took Mabel with him as an animal trainer—but she was disappointed to find that she'd been assigned to train goats. To convince tiger trainer Roth to hire her as a replacement for his assistant who'd been devoured, she married him.

In the early 1900s, no one knew for sure how to train an animal to do something. But Roth had a hunch. While most animal trainers at the time beat their subjects into submission, Roth used a method called "gentling," rewarding tigers for good behavior with fresh horse meat.

Roth devolved into alcoholism, and the two divorced. Stark took the gentling method into the ring, though she also packed a whip and a pistol that fired blanks, noisy enough to frighten the tigers.

Maim Attraction

Over the decades, Stark made a name for herself, performing her "cat act" with Barnes, Ringling Bros. and Barnum & Bailey, and several small circuses before landing with the JungleLand theme park in Thousand Oaks, California.

Stark firmly believed that tigers could never be tamed, only subdued, and only when they felt like it. Eighteen times Stark was mauled, yet she never blamed the cats for acting out—only herself for not paying attention. And though nearly every inch of her body was eventually covered with scars, she continued working well into old age.

Stark once said she couldn't live without her tigers, and that would prove true. Stark's demise was shrouded in rumor, much like her beginnings. In 1968, JungleLand closed its doors. Also, some say Stark's favorite tiger, Rajah, whom Barnes had given to her as a cub and whom she'd brought home and walked like a dog around her neighborhood, had died. Three months after the park closed, Stark was found dead in her home of an apparent barbiturate overdose—an unfortunate end to an exciting life.

How It All Began

The Little Black Dress

The "little black dress," aka LBD, is an essential part of any woman's wardrobe. The original LBD was made by famed Parisian couturier Coco Chanel. It was given its particularly functional name in a 1926 issue of *Vogue* magazine, which also referred to it as a "Ford"—recognizing that here was an item that could, and would, be reproduced endlessly through mechanical means, making it affordable to the masses. While expensive couture frocks were considerably different from cars coming off an assembly line, the association the *Vogue* writer was making came from a famous line in Henry Ford's autobiography: "Any customer can have a car painted any color that he wants so long as it is black."

The World's First Movie Premiere

In 1894, French chemists (and brothers) Louis Jean and August Marie Lumière saw Thomas Edison's miraculous Kinetoscope at a Parisian arcade. Unfortunately, because viewers peered into the device through small holes, watching movies through a Kinetoscope was limited to one person at a time. So the siblings had the idea to adapt a mechanism that was commonly used in sewing machines to invent a device that could both project and expose film, allowing a number of people to watch it at the same time.

The Lumières got their patent in February 1895, and on December 28 of that year, they held the world's first public screening of a motion picture in the Grand Café in Paris on their Cinematographe. The cost of admission was one franc, for which the audience was entitled to see, among other films, *Workers Leaving the Lumière Factory*, *The Blacksmith at Work*, and *The Sprinkler Sprinkled*. As far as we know, there was no red carpet, preening starlets, or exchange of empty compliments involved.

Fast Facts

✳ Towns in ancient Japan held contests to see which person could break wind the loudest.

✳ In medieval Japan, any woman found alone in a room with a man other than her husband was immediately put to death, no questions asked.

✳ At one time, natives of the Solomon Islands used dog teeth as money.

✳ When inflation was running rampant in Germany's Weimar Republic in the early 1920s, one American dollar was equal to one trillion German marks.

✳ Flounders are one flatfish that's learned to adapt. They spend much of their lives lying on their side on sea beds, which should mean that one eye is always in the sand, right? Well, not quite. The eye in the sand moves to the topside of the flounder's head so that both eyes are facing up.

✳ BVD stands for Bradley, Voorhees, and Day—the New York City company that initially made the brand of underwear.

✳ When the volcano Krakatau erupted in 1883, people in Bangkok, China—3,000 miles away—heard the sound.

✳ Famed adventurer and lover Casanova ended his life as a librarian.

✳ Lord Byron kept four geese as pets and brought them everywhere.

✳ Your hair doesn't all grow at the same time; each hair is on a separate and slightly staggered schedule.

✳ During World War II, British pilot and double amputee Douglas Bader was forced to bail out of his aircraft, leaving one of his artificial legs behind. Under a special temporary truce agreed to by his German captors, the RAF delivered a replacement leg by parachute.

Penny for Your Thoughts?

We handle thousands of them every year, but how much do we really know about the familiar penny?

✳   ✳   ✳   ✳

✳ Since they were introduced in 1787, more than 300 billion pennies have been produced. Today, there are about 150 billion pennies in circulation—enough to circle Earth 137 times.

✳ Since 1909, Abraham Lincoln has been the star of the penny, but it wasn't always that way. There have been 11 different designs, including the popular Indian Head penny, which was introduced in 1859.

✳ The princess on the Indian Head penny was neither a Native American nor a princess. She was, in fact, Sarah Longacre—the sculptor's daughter.

✳ On the 200th anniversary of Lincoln's birth, the U.S. Mint introduced pennies that depicted four different representations of Lincoln's life. These replaced the Lincoln Memorial on the penny.

✳ Examine the faces on a penny, an original Jefferson nickel, a dime, and a quarter. All the presidents except Lincoln are facing left. People have long imagined a secret meaning behind this, but Victor David Brenner, the sculptor of the Lincoln penny, explained that he had worked from an image of Lincoln facing to the right.

✳ If you have a strong magnifying glass, you can see the initials of the sculptors who designed the pennies. Since 1959, the initials of Frank Gasparro have been near the shrubbery to the right of the Lincoln Memorial. Pennies dated 1918 to 1958 have the initials VDB (Victor David Brenner) under Lincoln's shoulder.

✳ Pennies haven't been made of pure copper since 1864. During World War II, the U.S. Mint helped the war effort by recycling: It melted shell casings to make pennies. To conserve further, it considered creating plastic pennies but settled on zinc-covered steel. After the war, the Mint returned to a zinc-and-copper combination.

✳ Pennies have become popular souvenirs thanks to the penny-press machines at museums, amusement parks, and family vacation spots. These machines, introduced at Chicago's World Fair in 1893, flatten and elongate a penny between two rollers and imprint a new image—anything from an octopus to the Liberty Bell to Mickey Mouse. Each year, these machines roll out more than 12 million pennies into fun oval shapes.

✳ Money is shrinking—and not just in value. When the penny was introduced in 1787, it was about twice the size of today's version. The penny didn't shrink to its current size until 1857.

✳ See a penny, pick it up. There are about forty 1943 copper pennies in existence. One sold in 1999 for $112,500.

✳ You can't use pennies to pay your fare at a tollbooth—unless you're in Illinois. Lincoln's home state has a soft spot for pennies.

✳ A coin toss isn't a game of luck if you use a penny and call heads. The penny is the only coin with the face of the same person on both sides. A magnifying glass will reveal Lincoln sitting inside the Lincoln Memorial.

✳ Pennies got their reputation as being lucky from the Victorian wedding saying "Something old, something new, something borrowed, something blue, and a silver sixpence in your shoe." In the United States, the penny replaced the sixpence as a guard against want for the newlywed couple.

✳ In 1839, the nickname for a U.S. cent was "Silly Head" because people thought the image of Miss Liberty on the front looked strange.

17 Unusual Book Titles

We dare you to read some of these far-out titles in public!

✳   ✳   ✳   ✳

1. *How to Avoid Huge Ships* by John W. Trimmer

2. *Scouts in Bondage* by Michael Bell

3. *Be Bold with Bananas* by Crescent Books

4. *Fancy Coffins to Make Yourself* by Dale L. Power

5. *The Flat-Footed Flies of Europe* by Peter J. Chandler

6. *101 Uses for an Old Farm Tractor* by Michael Dregni

7. *Across Europe by Kangaroo* by Joseph R. Barry

8. *101 Super Uses for Tampon Applicators* by Lori Katz and Barbara Meyer

9. *Suture Self* by Mary Daheim

10. *The Making of a Moron* by Niall Brennan

11. *How to Make Love While Conscious* by Guy Kettelhack

12. *Underwater Acoustics Handbook* by Vernon Martin Albers

13. *Superfluous Hair and Its Removal* by A. F. Niemoeller

14. *Lightweight Sandwich Construction* by J. M. Davies

15. *The Devil's Cloth: A History of Stripes* by Michel Pastoureaut

16. *How to Be a Pope: What to Do and Where to Go Once You're in the Vatican* by Piers Marchant

17. *How to Read a Book* by Mortimer J. Adler and Charles Van Doren

12 Signs of the Zodiac

The stargazing Greeks used the zodiac symbols to make sense of the connection between time, space, and humans. Astrologers swear we can all find insight into our personalities by studying the zodiac sign that corresponds to our birthday.

✳ ✳ ✳ ✳

1. **Aries: The Ram (March 21–April 19)** Aries personalities are Minotaur-like, meaning that they are headstrong folks who seek excitement. They are often innovative, assertive, quick-tempered, and self-assured. If you find yourself playing golf with Aries Russell Crowe, watch out: He'll either bop you on the head or leave you hanging, since Aries are notoriously bad at finishing what they start.

2. **Taurus: The Bull (April 20–May 20)** These folks are stubborn, cautious, persistent, conservative, materialistic, and dependable. But Tauruses are most noted for their determination. Case in point: Cher, who is on comeback number 4,628.

3. **Gemini: The Twins (May 21–June 21)** Named after the twin brothers of Helen of Troy, Geminis can like something and its opposite at the same time. They are known to be flexible, lively, quick-witted conversationalists that embody the yin and the yang. Watch out for duplicity in a Gemini (a trait some would say business tycoon Donald Trump possesses), and enjoy the fruits of a Gemini's boundless curiosity (as with award-winning journalist Bill Moyers).

4. **Cancer: The Crab (June 22–July 22)** Cancers are emotional, sensitive, security-conscious, moody, maternal, and can be quite traditional. The word cancer literally means "the crab," and modern slang has produced the misconception that Cancers are grouchy.

5. **Leo: The Lion (July 23–August 22)** The lion symbol has origins in Hebrew culture but is also connected to the Greek god Apollo. Apollo represented order and intellectual pursuits and served as the leader of the Muses, the spirits that bring inspiration to artists. Leos are notoriously egocentric and love the limelight. They are also optimistic, dignified, confident, flamboyant, competitive, and have strong leadership skills. All this and a desperate need for approval? Just ask Leos Madonna and Martha Stewart.

6. **Virgo: The Virgin (August 23–September 22)** Modesty is one of the main traits of a Virgo, as exhibited in Virgo Mother Teresa. That doesn't mean Virgos are prudish, however—considering that Pee Wee Herman was also born under this sign. Other traits Virgos possess include practicality, responsibility, discriminating taste, and a critical eye. Virgos are loyal but can become obsessed with perfection.

7. **Libra: The Scale (September 23–October 23)** The judicial system adopted the Libra image of the scales to represent the balance of justice. This makes sense, considering Libras are idealistic peacemakers, diplomatic, poised, kind, courteous, and fair-minded. Unfortunately for the judicial system, the scales represent people who can be painfully indecisive. Famous level-headed Libras include Barbara Walters, Sting, and Jimmy Carter.

8. **Scorpio: The Scorpion (October 24–November 21)** These stingers are intense and powerful, courageous, resourceful, mysterious, and self-reliant. Aside from the scorpion, the phoenix is another symbol for this sign. Some believe that within one year before or after the death of a Scorpio, there will be a birth within the same family. Wonder if that was true when Scorpios Bill Gates or Hillary Clinton were born?

9. **Sagittarius: The Centaur (November 22–December 21)** The centaur is a character from Greek mythology that was half man, half horse. People born under this sign follow their

big hearts but can become bulls in china shops if they're not careful. Famous Sag Jon Stewart is a good example of someone using their strong Sagittarius opinions to their advantage. These generally friendly people are often idealistic, optimistic, freedom-loving, casual, gregarious, enthusiastic, and philosophical. Woody Allen and Britney Spears are well-known Sagittarians.

10. **Capricorn: The Goat (December 22–January 19)** According to Greek mythology, Zeus was weaned on goat's milk and that was enough to include the animal in the pantheon of astrological signs. Capricorns are ambitious, self-disciplined, conservative, practical, persistent, and methodical. Famous Capricorn Mel Gibson has lost his footing a few times, but he's good at dusting himself off and starting again, a classic Capricorn maneuver.

11. **Aquarius: The Water Bearer (January 20–February 18)** Symbolized by the water bearer—a young man or woman with water barrels hoisted over the shoulder, who brings together the community of humankind—these folks hold on to the concept of friendship stronger than anyone. Always individualistic, progressive, independent, and altruistic, they can sink into detachment. They seem to "march to the beat of a different drummer." Think of Oprah Winfrey, a textbook Aquarius, who is famous for her generous and independent nature.

12. **Pisces: The Fish (February 19–March 20)** The symbol of two fish pointing in different directions tends to throw people off, making them think Pisces people can't make up their minds. On the contrary, this group is focused and choosy, going for the big time or the quiet time with little in between. Think Liza Minnelli blazing her public career path or Bobby Fischer checkmating (no pun intended) cloistered monks in Madagascar. These fishy folks are compassionate, artistic, dedicated, and can be more than a little reclusive.

He Said, She Said

"Champions keep playing until they get it right."

—BILLIE JEAN KING

"Religion is what keeps the poor from murdering the rich."

—NAPOLEON BONAPARTE

"The best argument against democracy is a five-minute conversation with the average voter."

—WINSTON CHURCHILL

"When the missionaries first came to Africa, they had the Bible and we had the land. They said, 'Let us pray.' We closed our eyes. When we opened them, we had the Bible and they had the land."

—DESMOND TUTU

"A man in love is incomplete until he has married. Then he's finished."

—ZSA ZSA GABOR

"The buck stops with the guy who signs the checks."

—RUPERT MURDOCH

"A people that values its privileges above its principles soon loses both."

—DWIGHT D. EISENHOWER

"What is the use of a house if you haven't got a tolerable planet to put it on?"

—HENRY DAVID THOREAU

Broadmoor's Most Famous Residents

In Britain, the criminally insane wind up in Broadmoor mental hospital. Here one has a wide variety of neighbors, from artists to "rippers" and cannibals.

✳ ✳ ✳ ✳

Welcome to Broadmoor

COMPLETED IN 1863, this imposing collection of brick structures stands on the Berkshire moors about 30 miles from London. The Broadmoor "criminal lunatic asylum" was the first institution dedicated specifically to the detained treatment of those deemed too mentally ill to be guilty but too dangerous to be free. Conceived as a hospital (not a prison), Broadmoor opened with a farm, 57 staff cottages, and a school. Its first patients were women, many of whom most likely suffered from what would now be identified as postpartum depression. Within a year, however, a block for men opened.

Long the repository of some of England's most notorious individuals, over time Broadmoor has been identified with the violence committed by outwardly normal men whose minds compel them to perform horrific acts. Here are some of Broadmoor's more notable inmates.

Richard Dadd (painter): On August 28, 1843, a young aspiring painter named Richard Dadd became possessed with the notion that his father was the devil, and so Dadd killed him with a razor. Committed to the Bethlehem Hospital (aka "Bedlam") asylum, Dadd was allowed to continue his painting and spent nine of his years there completing his most well-known work, *The Fairy Feller's Master-Stroke*, which now hangs in the Tate Gallery. In 1864, he was among the first male patients transferred to Broadmoor; there he prepared the stage scenery for the hospital's theater and painted murals and portraits for Superintendent

Dr. William Orange. Dadd died in Broadmoor in 1886 of "an extensive disease of the lungs."

Thomas Hayne Cutbush (Jack the Ripper?): In 1888, young Thomas Cutbush began to act increasingly mentally unstable. His days were spent sleeping, and at night he could be found prowling the streets. Then Cutbush took to drawing anatomical portrayals of dissected women. They were curious habits, particularly in light of the Jack the Ripper killings occurring in London at the time. When Cutbush's name appeared on a list of possible suspects, his uncle, a superintendent at Scotland Yard, had the name removed. Detained as a wandering lunatic, Thomas escaped, purchased a knife, and tried to kill two women before being apprehended. Deemed unfit for trial, he was sent to Broadmoor, where he spent the rest of his life. But was Cutbush Jack the Ripper? Consider the following:

* The Jack the Ripper killings, which targeted prostitutes, lasted from April 3, 1888, to February 13, 1891. Cutbush reportedly contracted syphilis in 1888 (indicating his involvement with prostitutes, as well as a possible explanation for his madness) and was arrested on March 5, 1891.

* When Cutbush's name later appeared in the papers in connection with the attempted stabbings, his uncle was devastated and committed suicide two years later, some say of guilt.

* Recently released Broadmoor documents include a description of Cutbush's piercing blue eyes and limp, both physical characteristics noted by Jack the Ripper witnesses.

Robert Maudsley ("Hannibal the Cannibal"): Born in 1953, young Maudsley was subject to frequent and violent physical abuse at the hands of his parents. Cast out into the streets, he turned to prostitution to survive. After strangling a man who showed him pictures of abused boys in 1974, Robert was sent to Broadmoor, where in 1977 he and another psychopathic inmate barricaded themselves in a cell with a pedophile. After torturing the man for nine hours, they strangled him and then allowed the staff to enter. It was observed that part of the victim's skull had been cracked open and a spoon inserted into the brain material. Maudsley admitted to consuming the brain matter. He was sent to Wakefield Prison, known as "Monster Mansion," where in 1978 he killed two inmates. Afterward, Maudsley was imprisoned in a two-room specially made cell of hard plastic featuring cardboard furniture.

Graham Young ("The Teacup Murderer"): In 1961, Graham Young began a lifelong fascination with poisons, which the 14 year old tested in small doses on his family. A year later, his stepmother died from these "experiments." Young confessed his hobby to a psychiatrist, who had him arrested. He served nine years of a 15-year sentence at Broadmoor, where he researched poisons in the library and tested his concoctions on fellow inmates.

After his release in 1971, Young went to work at a photographic supply store in Bovingdon, where he prepared tea for clerks and customers. Over the course of several months, Young administered non-fatal doses of poison to more than 70 people. He kept a detailed journal of the poisons and their effects; he also noted which coworkers he ultimately planned to kill. When two employees at the shop died similarly agonizing deaths, the police launched an investigation into the so-called "Bovingdon Bug." Young helpfully suggested to the police that they should consider thallium poisoning as a possible cause. Not being stupid, the police searched Young's apartment and found his notebook and a small pharmacy of poisons. Young received a life sentence; he died of a heart attack in Parkhurst prison at age 42.

But Somebody's Got to Do It...

So Monday comes around too soon for you. You've got a lousy boss, a rotten job, and a terrible way to make a living. Before you give your two weeks' notice, you might want to consider how bad you really have it. After all, you could have one of these jobs.

❋　❋　❋　❋

❋ **Breath Odor Evaluator:** Next time you move in for a kiss, you can thank the people who sniff morning breath, garlic breath, smoker's breath, and bad denture breath to assess the effectiveness of mouthwash, mints, and toothpaste. Come to think of it, both the kisser and the kissee have a lot to be thankful for.

❋ **Porta-Potty Supplier:** They supply those smelly little shanties for county fairs, concerts, rallies, parades, and other events. Not so bad, huh? Don't forget that somebody's got to clean them when the fun is done.

❋ **Dog Food Tester and Dog Sniffer:** Most dogs will eat anything, right? Unfortunately, Fido can't tell you whether or not something tastes yummy. Enter the dog food tester, who checks for taste, consistency, and crumbliness (because dog owners hate a mess). On the other side of the kennel, someone gets paid to take a whiff of Rover's breath to be sure his fangs are in good shape after he's eaten the dog food.

❋ **Biohazard Clean-Up Crew:** These folks have strong arms and stronger stomachs. Their job is, among other things, to clean up bodies that have lain for days or weeks in one spot, homicides (after the police are through with the crime scene), and the aftermath of suicide.

❋ **Diener:** Dying for a new job? Check out a career as a diener. The diener prepares dead bodies (in any state of decomposition) for autopsies so the coroner can do his or her job more efficiently.

✳ **Jobs in Underwear:** Someone has to design the tighty whities and thongs of tomorrow. There are also jobs available for people who make undies with special charcoal filters so that the excessively flatulent don't offend. And somebody's got to test those undies, too.

✳ **Beer Tester and Ice Cream Tester:** Sounds like a great job until you understand that they don't get to swallow the samples. They only get to taste, then they have to spit it out. Drat.

✳ **Chewing Gum Remover:** Remember sticking your ABC (already been chewed) gum under the park bench, on the sidewalk, to a tree, beneath a desk? Well, somebody's got to remove it so you can do it again.

✳ **Bovine Artificial Inseminator and Semen Collector:** Moooove over if you think you might like these careers. Semen collectors collect bull ejaculate so that valuable cows can be impregnated with the right genes. To get that job done, AIs have to stick their hand, um, well, up inside . . . you know. Or maybe you don't want to know.

✳ **Magician's Assistant:** Not a bad way to make bucks, unless the boss decides he might want to try his hand (and your head) at being a knife thrower, too.

✳ **Mosquito Researcher:** It's not like you can call a mosquito and she'll come running, right? Nope, mosquito researchers generally offer themselves up as bait to get skeeters to bite. Not surprisingly, such researchers are slapped with mosquito-borne illnesses quite often.

✳ **Hazardous Materials Diver:** Love the water? Can't wait to take a quick, refreshing dip? Then grab your swimsuit and more: Haz-mat divers swim beneath sewage and toxic spills to find bodies, evidence, and other items that need to be recovered in the muck and murk. They also work to clean up toxic accidents in bodies of water.

Gang Nation

Over the past century there have been thousands of street gangs prowling city neighborhoods around the world. Here are some with surprisingly amusing names.

Classic Chicago Street Gangs
- ✳ The Almighty Bishops
- ✳ Casanova Stones
- ✳ Old Hatchet
- ✳ Little Loafers
- ✳ Party Masters

Global Gangs
- ✳ Mongrel Mob (New Zealand)
- ✳ The Yardies (Jamaica)
- ✳ The Numbers (South Africa)
- ✳ Cheetham Hill Hillbillies (England)
- ✳ Indian Posse (Canada)

Least Intimidating Gang Names
- ✳ Chaplains (Chicago)
- ✳ Young Asian Boys (Los Angeles)
- ✳ Happy Gentlemen (Chicago)
- ✳ Hawaiian Gardens (Los Angeles)
- ✳ The South Side Winos (Los Angeles)
- ✳ East Side Peckerwoods (Los Angeles)

10 Notable Beauty Pageant Moments

Beauty contests aren't all roses and tiaras. Here are a few highlights (and lowlights) in the history of beauty pageants.

✳   ✳   ✳   ✳

1. **Sideshow/Freak Show:** The first American beauty pageant was staged in 1854 by circus magnate P. T. Barnum. But even before women's suffrage changed the role of women in modern society, no one was terribly excited about their wives and sisters being part of a circus sideshow, and the competition didn't last long.

2. **You're Never Too Young for Drama:** Marian Bergeron won the Miss America crown in 1932. Trouble was, she was only 15 years old at the time. Pageant officials were duly upset, but another scandal kept them from setting things straight: Before they could reclaim the crown, someone stole it from Bergeron's dressing room.

3. **Like Beauty Queens to the Slaughter:** In 1935, beauty pageants needed a little boost. Enter Lenora Slaughter, a woman who would forever shape the world's concept of the beauty pageant. Slaughter was a savvy businesswoman who pandered to the nation's Hollywood fever, offering screen tests to Miss America winners—Dorothy Lamour was "discovered" this way. Slaughter was also the brain behind adding the talent competition in 1938 and offering college scholarships to winners beginning in 1945. She ruled the pageant for more than 30 years.

4. **Mazel Tov, Miss America!:** In 1945, America crowned its first Jewish Miss America when New York's Bess Myerson won the title, even after being told that unless she changed her name to something "less Jewish," she would never win the competition. Myerson refused and won anyway, though

her reign was not without controversy. Catalina swimsuits, the Miss America swimsuit supplier, did not ask Myerson to be a spokeswoman for their product, even though every queen before her had inked a deal. Myerson wasn't fazed and went on to serve in politics and won numerous awards for her philanthropic work.

5. **Miss Black America Fights Back:** Not until 1983 did an African American woman win the Miss America crown. However, African Americans didn't wait around to be recognized in the beauty pageant circuit; instead, they organized the first Miss Black America contest in 1968. The pageant started as a local contest in Philadelphia but went national a year later. In the 1969 contest, The Jackson 5 made their first television appearance, and an ambitious young woman named Oprah Winfrey competed as Miss Black Tennessee in 1971.

6. **So Long, Bert:** The opening line of the Miss America theme song—"There she is, Miss America"—sparked thousands of girlhood dreams. The man who sang it was Bert Parks, host of the pageant from 1954 to 1980. Pageant producers thought a host change would boost ratings, but many Parks loyalists emerged, including Johnny Carson, who launched a letter-writing campaign to reinstate Parks. Despite their efforts, the "Bring Back Bert" campaign failed and Parks was replaced by various hosts over the years, including Regis Philbin and Kathie Lee Gifford in the early 1990s.

7. **Say It Ain't So, Vanessa:** Statuesque and articulate with a voice like an angel, Vanessa Williams was the darling of the 1983 competition and won the crown with ease, becoming the first black Miss America. But by July 1984, controversy had erupted. *Penthouse* magazine planned to publish nude photos of the beloved beauty queen without her consent, so she resigned. Williams was then replaced by runner-up Suzette Charles, also an African American. The scandal didn't faze Williams for long; she went on to record several

R&B albums and had a number-one song in 1992 with "Save the Best for Last."

8. **Heather Makes History:** Although a childhood illness left Heather Whitestone profoundly deaf, the strikingly pretty girl excelled in a school for the hearing impaired and began competing in local beauty pageants during college. In 1995, she danced a ballet routine to music she couldn't hear and aced the interview with Regis Philbin by reading his lips. Whitestone was crowned the first Miss America with a disability.

9. **Platforms: Not Just Shoes Anymore:** In 1989, the Miss America organization officially required each contestant to choose a cause or charity to support. The idea was to not only give airtime to myriad issues affecting the nation, but to also have Miss America use her status to "address community service organizations, business and civic leaders, the media and others about [her] platform issues." Since then, the role of Miss America has been strictly philanthropic. The beauty queen travels, speaking to community leaders, politicians, and school organizations about her cause, which might be STD prevention, homelessness, domestic violence, voter registration, or literacy.

10. **Mike Tyson: Miss Black America Special Guest/ Defendant:** Heavyweight boxing champ Mike Tyson was asked to be a special guest at the Miss Black America pageant in 1991. As it turned out, this was not the best move on the part of pageant producers. Contestant Desiree Washington claimed that Tyson had raped her in the days before the contest, and numerous other contestants came forth to say that they too were groped and harassed by Tyson. The boxing star was convicted and sentenced to six years in prison.

How It All Began

The Meter Men

We can blame Carl Magee of Oklahoma City for one of the great curses of urban living. No, he didn't cause the first toxic smog, nor did he engineer the first axle-snapping pothole. Worse, in 1932 he invented the coin-operated parking meter.

As if that wasn't enough, in 1953, a Colorado violinist named Frank Marugg invented the Denver Boot, a device that immobilizes vehicles until the associated parking tickets are paid. Thanks a lot, fellas.

Tea Time

Tea and politics have never mixed well. Ever since the infamous Boston Tea Party, many Americans have been slow to hop on the tea bandwagon. Yet it was an American, Thomas Sullivan, who came up with the first tea bag in 1908, which was, one could say, a revolution in its own right. On the other hand, perhaps because it was an American invention, the British didn't accept it for many years.

Sullivan's original tea bags were decidedly upscale, featuring hand-sewn silk. In other words, the bag was more costly than the tea leaves it contained. Hemp bags were tried, but they were discontinued in favor of the tasteless paper bags used today.

Sweets for a Sweetie

Sugar was once marketed in large, rock-hard chunks, which was inconvenient and messy. It certainly didn't suit Juliana Rad, a housewife in Dačice, Czechoslovakia. Somewhat accident prone, Juliana cut herself one day while trying to whittle off enough sugar for her cup of tea. Mercifully, her husband Jakub took charge. Alas, he wasn't any great shakes at either first aid or patience, so, in 1843, he created the sugar cube.

How to Escape Quicksand

In countless adventure movies, people fall prey to quicksand. But most of quicksand's properties are pure hype. You don't have to be Houdini to escape this natural pitfall.

✳   ✳   ✳   ✳

QUICKSAND IS A unique substance made of fine sand, clay, and salt water. Stress causes the compound to become more fluid, which is why people struggling tend to sink lower down. But it's impossible for a human to be pulled all the way under; our bodies aren't dense enough for that to happen. Still, one errant step and you'll find yourself stuck—unless you know how to beat the trap.

Avoid Moving: Because of the sand's stress factor, struggling and writhing around will only hurt your chances of escape. Relax and remain as still as possible. In fact, the people who have drowned in quicksand only did so because they panicked and were flailing about.

Don't Get Pulled: Having friends pull on you will not do any good; in fact, it will make matters worse. That kind of pressure may actually injure you. The best way they can help is by spreading wooden boards across the ground until they can reach you and give you a solid surface to climb up on.

Use Leg Power: Scientists suggest gently pumping your legs as if you were riding a bicycle. This creates open space in the sand where water can flow in and help loosen the stuff.

Plan in Advance: The leg movements can work, but your best bet is to carry a thick wooden pole, or walking stick, with you while in an area known for having quicksand. Then, the second you start to sink, lay the pole flat on the ground, horizontally across the surface of the quicksand. Move your body so the pole is under your back. This will stop you from sinking. Then, one leg at a time, pull yourself out and slowly move to stable ground.

Being Jeeves

Think being a butler is all bowing and opening doors? Not so!

✳   ✳   ✳   ✳

Q: Do butlers do anything besides answer the door?

A: Butlers, also known as household managers, take care of everything that's happening in and around the house, including tending to guests, managing the budget, supervising other household personnel, organizing dinner parties, taking care of the silverware and other household items, and organizing the wine cellar. Some butlers may also serve as personal assistants, running errands, planning travel, and keeping the family's schedule.

Q: I graduated with a degree in psychology. Can I be a butler?

A: A good personality and manners are more important than a formal education, so while the degree may come in handy, it's not necessary. Most employers do look for previous experience, however, so it might behoove you to take a course at a school such as The International Butler Academy.

Q: Do butlers make any money?

A: As with any job, your salary as a butler will depend on your location, skills, and responsibilities. According to the Butlers Guild, a butler is likely to make anywhere from $40,000 to $150,000 a year. And, the job usually comes with a bevy of perks, including housing, food, and a car. Sure, the money sounds smashing, but don't forget, you're on call 24 hours a day.

Q: Are all butlers British?

A: No. Actually, the word derives from the Old French term *bouteillier*, who was the person who oversaw the wine cellars and poured the booze. Servants such as butlers have been used all over the world, but it was the British that turned this everyday job into an art form.

9 Euphemisms for Being Fired

Here are some new ways to hear bad news.

✳   ✳   ✳   ✳

1. **Reduction in Force:** In true corporate fashion, the annoying euphemism "reduction in force" has been further modified into an acronym: RIF. As in, "I've been RIFed."

2. **Synergy-Related Headcount Reduction:** This euphemism was used by Nokia Siemens when firing 3,000 employees in 2008.

3. **Rightsizing:** Apparently "downsizing" was too much of a downer for HR departments around the corporate globe.

4. **Work Force Reduction Notification:** RadioShack fired 400 employees in 2006 via mass e-mail stating that "the work force reduction notification had begun." Huh?

5. **Made Redundant:** Of all the euphemisms, this might be the most offensive: Not only is this an annoying euphemism, it's actually an insult!

6. **Special Forces Philosophy:** Believe it or not, this has nothing to do with the military. It was the euphemism employed by Tesla Motors when firing 10 percent of its staff in 2008.

7. **Simplification:** eBay called its round of 2008 mass firings "employee simplification." If they really wanted to simplify things they would have just said "firings."

8. **Reengineering Plan:** This euphemism has the unintended effect of making fired employees feel as if they are part of a dystopian science-fiction novel.

9. **Optimized:** It's hard to imagine somebody who has just been fired believing that there is anything optimal about it.

Poisoned Puddings and Puritanism: Harvard's Early Days

Today, Harvard is famed for a vast endowment, but its early days were marked by a struggle to get by with quarter-bushels of wheat donated by local farmers.

✳ ✳ ✳ ✳

The School's Scandalous First Leader

IN 1640, THE tiny college of Harvard was in crisis. Founded four years before by the Massachusetts Bay Colony, Harvard had a student body of nine, a "yard" liberated from cows, and a single, hated instructor.

Harvard's 30-year-old schoolmaster, Nathaniel Eaton, was known to beat wayward students. Other students charged Eaton's wife, Elizabeth, of putting goat dung into their cornmeal porridge, or "hasty pudding." (Harvard's theatrical society is named for the dish.) Finally, Master Eaton went too far and was hauled into court after clubbing a scholar with a walnut-tree cudgel. He was also accused of embezzling 100 pounds (then an ample sum).

In 1639, Eaton and his wife were sent packing. Master Eaton returned to England, was made a vicar, then died in debtor's prison. Following the Eaton affair, Harvard's reputation lay in tatters; its operations were suspended, and its students were scattered.

The Roots of Learning

The money and work Massachusetts had put into the school seemed for naught. The colony's General Court had allotted 400 pounds for a college in what became known as Cambridge, Massachusetts, across the Charles River from Boston. The school was named for John Harvard, a clergyman from England's Cambridge University, which at the time was known to be a hotbed of Puritanism.

John Harvard was a scholar whose family had known William Shakespeare. When the plague felled his brothers and his father, John inherited a considerable estate, including the Queen's Head Tavern. After immigrating to the Boston region, he became a preacher in Charleston, but his career was short. In 1638, at the age of 31, he died of consumption, having bequeathed money and his personal library to the planned college.

Comeback Under the First President

In 1640, the colony's founders were desperate for educational cachet. They offered the post of Harvard president to Henry Dunster, a new arrival from England and another graduate of Cambridge University.

The energetic Dunster tapped into the colony's inherent educational edge. Many of the new Puritan arrivals had studied at the Oxford and Cambridge academies: Some 130 alumni of the two schools were in New England by 1646. Dunster himself was a leading scholar in "Oriental" languages, that is, biblical tongues such as Hebrew.

Led primarily by a Protestant culture that stressed reading the Bible, Boston set up the first free grammar school in 1635; within 12 years, every town in Massachusetts was required by law to have one. Harvard's new president mandated a four-year graduation requirement and rode out angry students who protested over a commencement fee. Dunster obtained Harvard's charter and authored the school's "Rules and Precepts." He bankrolled the facilities through donations of livestock and, over the course of 13 years, some 250 pounds of wheat. He took a modest salary, being underpaid through 14 years of service, and piled up personal debts. Fortunately, his wife, Elizabeth Glover, kept a printing press in their home. It was the American colonies' first press, and its profits underwrote her husband's work. Dunster managed to turn the school around. Harvard's reputation soared, and students from throughout the colonies, the Caribbean, and the mother country flocked to newly built dorms.

Religious Schisms and a President's Heresies

Yet Dunster tripped up on one of the many religious disputes roiling the Puritan colony. In 1648, it was a criminal offense to engage in "Blasphemy, Heresie, open contempt of the Word preached, Profanation of the Lord's Day"; separation of church and state was unknown.

A source of controversy was infant baptism, which the Puritan fathers required by law. Drawing on his biblical knowledge, Dunster noted that John the Baptist had baptized the adult Jesus, but he could find no biblical examples of children being baptized.

In 1653, he refused to have his son Jonathan baptized. At Cambridge's Congregational Church, Dunster preached against "corruptions stealing into the Church, which every faithful Christian ought to [bear] witness against."

This put the Puritans of Boston and Cambridge in a quandary. Dunster's views made him a heretic, yet he was much liked for his work at the college. Early the next year, the colony's officers wrote that Dunster "hath by his practice and opinions rendered himself offensive to this government." They assembled a conference of 11 ministers and elders to interrogate him. Egged on by this assembly, in May 1654 the General Court forbade schools to employ those "that have manifested themselves unsound in the faith, or scandalous in their lives." Dunster resigned from Harvard.

The ex-president then petitioned the court to let him stay in the colony until he could repay the many debts he'd accumulated from his work. Court authorities coldly responded that "they did not know of [such] extraordinary labor or sacrifices. For the space of 14 years we know of none." Dunster, with Elizabeth and their youngest child ill, then beseeched the court to at least let his family stay the winter. The magistrates agreed grudgingly, but the following spring they banished the Dunster family to the backwater town of Scituate. Harvard's first president died there four years later, at the age of 47.

He Said, She Said

"My advice to you is get married: if you find a good wife you'll be happy; if not, you'll become a philosopher."

—SOCRATES

"I have never killed a man, but I have read many obituaries with great pleasure."

—CLARENCE DARROW

"I can accept failure, but I can't accept not trying."

—MICHAEL JORDAN

"Opportunity is missed by most people because it is dressed in overalls and looks like work."

—THOMAS A. EDISON

"Music should strike fire from the heart of man, and bring tears from the eyes of woman."

—LUDWIG VAN BEETHOVEN

"Middle age is when you've met so many people that every new person you meet reminds you of someone else."

—OGDEN NASH

"If slaughterhouses had glass walls, everyone would be a vegetarian. "

—PAUL MCCARTNEY

"I've done the calculation and your chances of winning the lottery are identical whether you play or not."

—FRAN LEBOWITZ

11 Stupid Legal Warnings

Our lawsuit-obsessed society has forced product manufacturers to cover their "you-know-whats" by writing warning labels to protect us from ourselves. Some are funny, some are absolutely ridiculous, but all are guaranteed to stand up in court.

✳   ✳   ✳   ✳

1. Child-size Superman and Batman costumes come with this warning: "Wearing of this garment does not enable you to fly."

2. A clothes iron comes with this caution: "Warning: Never iron clothes on the body." Ouch!

3. The instructions for a medical thermometer advise: "Do not use orally after using rectally."

4. The side of a Slush Puppy cup warns: "This ice may be cold." The only thing dumber would be a disclaimer stating: "No puppies were harmed in the making of this product."

5. The box of a 500-piece puzzle reads: "Some assembly required."

6. A Power Puff Girls costume discourages: "You cannot save the world!"

7. A box of PMS relief tablets has this advice: "Warning: Do not use if you have prostate problems."

8. Cans of Easy Cheese contain this instruction: "For best results, remove cap."

9. A warning label on a nighttime sleep-aid reads: "Warning: May cause drowsiness."

10. Cans of self-defense pepper spray caution: "May irritate eyes."

11. Both boys and girls should read the label on the Harry Potter toy broom: "This broom does not actually fly."

Familiar Numbers and the Logic Behind Them

ZIP Codes

* ZIP ("Zoning Improvement Plan") codes were introduced in 1963 as a way to help ease the massive burden on the post office.

* The first digit represents the geographic area of the country (the higher the number, the farther west).

* The next two digits represent the "sectional facility"—one of several hundred major distribution centers maintained by the post office.

* The last two digits represent the individual post office or zoning area.

Social Security Numbers

* The first three digits are called the "area number" and were originally supposed to represent the state in which the card was issued, though now they are based on the ZIP code of the applicant.

* The two digits that follow the area number are known as the "group number." These numbers are issued based on a convoluted odd/even numbering sequence. The logic of the group number defies explanation.

* The last four digits are known as a "serial number." These numbers are issued consecutively from 0000 to 9999 within each group.

666

Any fan of horror movies can tell you that there's nothing good about the number 666. But they might be less certain about the reason why the number is associated with the Devil. The number 666—also known as the Number of the Beast—gets its evil connotation from the Book of Revelation in the New

Testament, specifically in chapter 13, verse 18: "Wisdom is needed here; one who understands can calculate the number of the beast, for it is a number that stands for a person. His number is six hundred and sixty-six." Thus, the number of both the Devil and the Antichrist is revealed to be 666.

Many people have noted that this is unusually specific for a book that otherwise deals with what are presumably symbols, such as dragons coming out of the earth and fire shooting from the sky. As with the interpretation of the Book of Revelation in general, there has been a lot of debate about the precise meaning of this number.

On one side, there is the lunatic fringe, which ascribes the sign of the beast to whichever public figure has raised its ire. In the 1980s, for example, some malcontents pointed out that President Reagan's full name—Ronald Wilson Reagan— is composed of three six-letter groupings.

A more sane theory attributes the number 666 to the Roman emperor Nero. Nero blamed the Christians for the infamous burning of Rome in the first century A.D., and consequently started a brutal campaign of persecution against the fledgling religion. It is believed that the author of the Book of Revelation, John the Apostle, was attempting to send a coded message to his fellow Christians to give them hope that Nero's tyranny would soon come to an end.

To ensure that only other Christians would understand his message, John used Hebrew numerology. John chose Hebrew because it is the language of Judaism, the religion that Christianity grew out of after the arrival of Christ. In Hebrew, each letter corresponds with a number. The letters/numbers from Nero's full name in Hebrew, Neron Qeisar, add up to— you guessed it—666.

Index

✳ ✳ ✳ ✳

Hutchins, Levi, 473
Hydnora africana (plant), 479
Hyperthymesic syndrome, 117
Hypnotism, 126–27
Hysteria, 120–21

I
Iguacú Falls, 500
Incitatus, 513
Incredibles, The, 50, 51
Insanity (amusement park ride), 67
Insects, 514–15, 519, 521
Intermarium, 544
Internal Revenue Service
    (IRS), 537
Internment camps, 378–79
In the Bag, 51
Isabella (queen), 316
Iscariot, Judas, 649
"It's a Small World" (amusement
    park ride), 68

J
Jack in the Box, 163
Jackson, Andrew, 194, 346, 642–43
Jackson, Michael, 252
Jackson, Thomas Jonathan
    "Stonewall," 601
Jagger, Mick, 8, 241
James, Jesse, 649
Jamestown Hotel, 639
Japanese puffer fish (food), 140, 152
Jeep, 469–71
Jefferson, Thomas, 164, 346,
    643, 648
Jefticheiv, Fedor, 617
Jehovah's Witnesses, 556
Jellied eels, 179
Jesus Christ, 649
Joanna (queen), 317
Joan of Arc, 326
John, Elton, 229
John IX (pope), 572
John Paul II (pope), 547
Johnson, Lyndon Baines, 281, 347
Johnson, Randy, 510
Johnston, Albert Sidney, 412
John the Apostle, 682
Jones, Hettie, 279

Jones, Jim, 555
Jones Soda Co., 165
Joplin, Janis, 281
Jordan, Michael, 679
Journey to the Center of the Earth
    (Verne), 492–93
Jousting, 76–77
Joyce, William, 416
Judaism, 553
Judd, Ashley, 25
Judd, Donald, 284–85
Jumbo, 603

K
Kabbalah, 548–49
Kaieteur Falls, 501
Kannibal, 41
Kansas City Royals, 89
Kant, Immanuel, 527
Karpis, Alvin "Creepy," 562
Kaufman, Andy, 569
Kees, Weldon, 568
Keller, Helen, 332
Kellogg, John, 220
Kellogg, Will, 220
Kellogg's Corn Flakes, 220
Kelly, George "Machine Gun," 562
Kersey, Hannah, 131
Kevorkian, Jack, 331
Killebrew, Harmon, 63
Kilts, 377
Kimchee, 180
King, Billie Jean, 229, 662
King, William Lyon
    Mackenzie, 621
King Kong, 16
King Kong (character), 16–17
King Kong vs. Godzilla, 17
King monkey cup (plant), 478
Kirby, Jack, 413
Kissinger, Henry, 332
Kitchener, Horatio Herbert, 420
Knapp, Michelle, 463
Knight, Katherine Mary, 583
Knowles, Beyoncé, 124
Kobayashi, Takeru
    "The Tsunami," 156
Kohl's Frozen Custard, 163

W

Wachter, Otto, 545
Wadlow, Robert, 616
Wahlberg, Mark, 129
Wallace Brothers Circus, 602
Wallenda, Karl, 603
Walter, William Grey, 476
Walters, Fred, 616
Wanatka, Emil and Nan, 589–90
Warhol, Andy, 265–67
Warner, Jack, 34
War of 1812, 404
Washington, Desiree, 671
Washington, George, 350–51, 648
Watchtower Announcing Jehovah's Kingdom, The, 556
Waterfalls
  Angel Falls, 499
  Cumberland Falls, 500
  Depot Creek Falls, 501
  Gavarnie Falls, 501
  Gocta Catarata, 501
  Horseshoe Falls, 650
  Iguacú Falls, 500
  Kaieteur Falls, 501
  Langfoss, 501
  Lower Yellowstone Falls, 500
  Montmorency Falls, 501
  Multnomah Falls, 500
  Niagara Falls, 499, 650
  Sutherland Falls, 501
  Victoria Falls, 500
  Yosemite Falls, 500
Wayne, John, 37, 232–33
WD-40, 342
Weather forecasts, natural, 442–43
Weddings
  arranged, 204–5
  customs, 182–84
  dress, 202–3
  Mexican, 196–97
  South American, 196–97
Weeble, 248
West, Mae, 33, 214, 332
West, Sandra Illene, 587
What Do You Care What Other People Think? (Feynman), 621
When Harry Met Sally, 228

Where's Waldo? (Hanford), 298
Whiskey Rebellion, 412
White buffalo, 532–34
White Buffalo Calf Woman, 533–34
White Men Can't Jump, 64
Whitestone, Heather, 671
Whitey, 631
Who Framed Roger Rabbit, 50
Whooppee Soda, 137
Who Wants to Be a Millionaire, 22
Why We Fight, 36
Wickliffe, Conway, 18
Wilde, Oscar, 214
Wilder, Billy, 578
Wilkinson, Reginald, 585
Williams, Betty Lou, 131
Williams, Billy, 511
Williams, Dave "Tiger," 92–93
Williams, Tennessee, 596–97
Williams, Vanessa, 670–71
Willis, Bruce, 25, 33
Willow Steakhouse & Saloon, 640
Willys-Overland, 469–71
Wilson, Brian, 289
Wilson, Samuel, 404
Wilson, Woodrow, 318
Winchester, Sarah, 626–29
Winchester Mystery House, 626–29
Windham, Trav, 56–57
Winfield, Dave, 510
Winfrey, Oprah, 670
Wodehouse, P. G., 417
Wollemi pine, 479
Wolves, 191
Wonder Woman, 414
Wonder Years, The, 234–35
Wood, Francis Derwent, 435
Woodall, Ian, 497
Woodstock Music Festival, 241
Woodward, Roger, 650
Woolf, Virginia, 352
Woollcott, Alexander, 290
Workman, Philip, 559
World Hockey Association, 58
World War I
  Christmas truce, 428–29
  destruction, 434–36